Freemasonry
A Volume of Classical Works

Containing: The Principles of Masonic Law (1856)

Mysteries of Freemasonry (1800?)

The Symbolism of Freemasonry (1882)

Compiled by J.B. Lumpkin (M∴M∴)

Freemasonry
A Volume of Classical Works

Containing: The Principles of Masonic Law (1856)
Mysteries of Freemasonry (1800?)
The Symbolism of Freemasonry (1882)

Compiled by J.B. Lumpkin (M∴M∴)

ISBN: 9781936533862

Published 2020 by
Fifth Estate, Incorporated
Alabama USA

Table of Contents

The Principles of Masonic Law:

A Treatise on the Constitutional Laws, Usages And Landmarks of Freemasonry,

By

Albert G. Mackey, M.D.,

Author of
"The Lexicon of Freemasonry," "The Mystic Tie,"
"Legends and Traditions of Freemasonry,"
Etc., Etc.,

Grand Lecturer and Grand Secretary of The Grand Lodge of South Carolina; Secretary General of the Supreme Council of the Ancient and Accepted Rite for the Southern Jurisdiction of the United States, Etc., Etc., Etc.

"Est enim unum jus, quo devincta est hominum societas, quod lex constituit una; quæ lex est recta ratio imperandi atque prohibendi, quam qui ignorat is est injustus."

Cicero de Legibus. c. XV.

New York:
Jno. W. Leonard & Co., Masonic Publishers,
383 Broadway.

1856.

To

Brother J.J.J. Gourgas,

Sovereign Grand Inspector General in the Supreme Council for the Northern Jurisdiction of the United States,

I Dedicate This Work,

As a Slight Testimonial of My Friendship and Esteem for Him
As a Man,
And of My Profound Veneration for His Character
As a Mason;
Whose Long and Useful Life Has Been Well Spent in the
Laborious Prosecution of the Science,
And the Unremitting Conservation of the Principles of Our
Sublime Institution.

Table of Contents

Book Third.
The Law of Individuals.

Book Fourth.
Of Masonic Crimes and Punishments.

Preface.

In presenting to the fraternity a work on the Principles of Masonic Law, it is due to those for whom it is intended, that something should be said of the design with which it has been written, and of the plan on which it has been composed. It is not pretended to present to the craft an encyclopedia of jurisprudence, in which every question that can possibly arise, in the transactions of a Lodge, is decided with an especial reference to its particular circumstances. Were the accomplishment of such an herculean task possible, except after years of intense and unremitting labor, the unwieldy size of the book produced, and the heterogeneous nature of its contents, so far from inviting, would rather tend to distract attention, and the object of communicating a knowledge of the Principles of Masonic Law, would be lost in the tedious collation of precedents, arranged without scientific system, and enunciated without explanation.

When I first contemplated the composition of a work on this subject, a distinguished friend and Brother, whose opinion I much respect, and with whose advice I am always anxious to comply, unless for the most satisfactory reasons, suggested the expediency of collecting the decisions of all Grand Masters, Grand Lodges, and other masonic authorities upon every subject of Masonic Law, and of presenting them, without commentary, to the fraternity.

But a brief examination of this method, led me to perceive that I would be thus constructing simply a digest of decrees, many of which would probably be the results of inexperience, of prejudice, or of erroneous views of the masonic system, and from which the authors themselves have, in repeated instances, subsequently receded—for Grand Masters and Grand Lodges, although entitled to great respect, are not infallible—and I could not, conscientiously, have consented to assist, without any qualifying remark, in the extension and perpetuation of edicts and opinions, which, however high the authority from which they emanated, I did not believe to be in accordance with the principles of Masonic jurisprudence.

Another inconvenience which would have attended the adoption of such a method is, that the decisions of different Grand Lodges and Grand Masters are sometimes entirely contradictory on the same points of Masonic Law. The decree of one jurisdiction, on any particular question, will often be found at variance with that of another, while a third will differ from both. The consultor of a work, embracing within its pages such distracting judgments, unexplained by commentary, would be in doubt as to which decision he should adopt, so that coming to the inspection with the desire of solving a legal question, he would be constrained to close the volume, in utter despair of extracting truth or information from so confused a mass of contradictions.

This plan I therefore at once abandoned. But knowing that the jurisprudence of Masonry is founded, like all legal science, on abstract principles, which govern and control its entire system, I deemed it to be a better course to present these principles to my readers in an elementary and methodical treatise, and to develop from them those necessary deductions which reason and common sense would justify.

Hence it is that I have presumed to call this work "The Principles of Masonic Law." It is not a code of enactments, nor a collection of statutes, nor yet a digest of opinions; but simply an elementary treatise, intended to enable every one who consults it, with competent judgment, and ordinary intelligence, to trace for himself the bearings of the law upon any question which he seeks to investigate, and to form, for himself, a correct opinion upon the merits of any particular case.

Blackstone, whose method of teaching I have endeavored, although I confess "ab longo inter-vallo," to pursue, in speaking of what an academical expounder of the law should do, says:

"He should consider his course as a general map of the law, marking out the shape of the country, its connections, and boundaries, its greater divisions, and principal cities; it is not his business to describe minutely the subordinate limits, or to fix the longitude and latitude of every inconsiderable hamlet."

Such has been the rule that has governed me in the compilation of this work. But in delineating this "general map" of the Masonic Law, I have sought, if I may continue the metaphor, so to define boundaries, and to describe countries, as to give the inspector no difficulty in "locating" (to use an Americanism) any subordinate point. I have treated, it is true, of principles, but I have not altogether lost sight of cases.

There are certain fundamental laws of the Institution, concerning which there never has been any dispute, and which have come down to us with all the sanctions of antiquity, and universal acceptation. In announcing these, I have not always thought it necessary to defend their justice, or to assign a reason for their enactment.

The weight of unanimous authority has, in these instances, been deemed sufficient to entitle them to respect, and to obedience.

But on all other questions, where authority is divided, or where doubts of the correctness of my decision might arise, I have endeavored, by a course of argument as satisfactory as I could command, to assign a reason for my opinions, and to defend and enforce my views, by a reference to the general principles of jurisprudence, and the peculiar character of the masonic system. I ask, and should receive no deference to my own unsupported theories—as a man, I am, of course, fallible—and may often have decided erroneously. But I do claim for my arguments all the weight and influence of which they may be deemed worthy, after an attentive and unprejudiced examination. To those who may at first be ready—because I do not agree with all their preconceived opinions—to doubt or deny my conclusions, I would say, in the language of Themistocles, "Strike, but hear me."

Whatever may be the verdict passed upon my labors by my Brethren, I trust that some clemency will be extended to the errors into which I may have fallen, for the sake of the object which I have had in view: that, namely, of presenting to the Craft an elementary work, that might enable every Mason to know his rights, and to learn his duties.

The intention was, undoubtedly, a good one. How it has been executed, it is not for me, but for the masonic public to determine.

Albert G. Mackey.

Charleston, S.C., January 1st., 1856.

Introduction.

The Authorities for Masonic Law.

The laws which govern the institution of Freemasonry are of two kinds, *unwritten* and *written*, and may in a manner be compared with the "lex non scripta," or common law, and the "lex seripta," or statute law of English and American jurists.

The "lex non scripta," or *unwritten law* of Freemasonry is derived from the traditions, usages and customs of the fraternity as they have existed from the remotest antiquity, and as they are universally admitted by the general consent of the members of the Order. In fact, we may apply to these unwritten laws of Masonry the definition given by Blackstone of the "leges non scriptæ" of the English constitution—that "their original institution and authority are not set down in writing, as acts of parliament are, but they receive their binding power, and the force of laws, by long and immemorial usage and by their universal reception throughout the kingdom." When, in the course of this work, I refer to these unwritten laws as authority upon any point, I shall do so under the appropriate designation of "ancient usage."

The "lex scripta," or written law of Masonry, is derived from a variety of sources, and was framed at different periods. The following documents I deem of sufficient authority to substantiate any principle, or to determine any disputed question in masonic law.

1. The "Ancient Masonic charges, from a manuscript of the Lodge of Antiquity," and said to have been written in the reign of James II.[1]

2. The regulations adopted at the General Assembly held in 1663, of which the Earl of St. Albans was Grand Master.[2]

3. The interrogatories propounded to the Master of a lodge at the time of his installation, and which, from their universal adoption, without alteration, by the whole fraternity, are undoubtedly to be considered as a part of the fundamental law of Masonry.

4. "The Charges of a Freemason, extracted from the Ancient Records of Lodges beyond sea, and of those in England, Scotland, and Ireland, for the use of the Lodges in London," printed in the first edition of the Book of Constitutions, and to be found from p. 49 to p. 56 of that work.[3]

5. The thirty-nine "General Regulations," adopted "at the annual assembly and feast held at Stationers' hall on St. John the Baptist's day, 1721," and which were published in the first edition of the Book of Constitutions, p. 58 to p.

6. The subsequent regulations adopted at various annual communications by the Grand Lodge of England, up to the year 1769, and published in different editions of the Book of Constitutions. These, although not of such paramount importance and universal acceptation as the Old Charges and the Thirty-nine Regulations, are, nevertheless, of great value as the means of settling many disputed questions, by showing what was the law and usage of the fraternity at the times in which they were adopted.

Soon after the publication of the edition of 1769 of the Book of Constitutions, the Grand Lodges of America began to separate from their English parent and to organize independent jurisdictions. From that period, the regulations adopted by the Grand Lodge of England ceased to have any binding efficacy over the craft in this country, while the laws passed by the American Grand Lodges lost the character of general regulations, and were invested only with local authority in their several jurisdictions.

Before concluding this introductory section, it may be deemed necessary that something should be said of the "Ancient Landmarks of the Order," to which reference is so often made.

Various definitions have been given of the landmarks. Some suppose them to be constituted of all the rules and regulations which were in existence anterior to the revival of Masonry in 1717, and which were confirmed and adopted by the Grand Lodge of England at that time. Others, more stringent in their definition, restrict them to the modes of recognition in use among the fraternity. I am disposed to adopt a middle course, and to define the Landmarks of Masonry to be, all those usages and customs of the craft— whether ritual or legislative—whether they relate to forms and ceremonies, or to the organization of the society—which have existed from time immemorial, and the alteration or abolition of which would materially affect the distinctive character of the institution or destroy its identity. Thus, for example, among the legislative landmarks, I would enumerate the office of Grand Master as the presiding officer over the craft, and among the ritual landmarks, the legend of the third degree. But the laws, enacted from time to time by Grand Lodges for their local government, no matter how old they may be, do not constitute landmarks, and may, at any time, be altered or expunged, since the 39th regulation declares expressly that "every annual Grand Lodge has an inherent power and authority to make new regulations or to alter these (viz., the thirty-nine articles) for the real benefit of this ancient fraternity, provided always that the old landmarks be carefully preserved."

Book First

The Law of Grand Lodges.

It is proposed in this Book, first to present the reader with a brief historical sketch of the rise and progress of the system of Grand Lodges; and then to explain, in the subsequent sections, the mode in which such bodies are originally organized, who constitute their officers and members, and what are their acknowledged prerogatives.

Chapter I.

Historical Sketch.

Grand Lodges under their present organization, are, in respect to the antiquity of the Order, of a comparatively modern date. We hear of no such bodies in the earlier ages of the institution. Tradition informs us, that originally it was governed by the despotic authority of a few chiefs. At the building of the temple, we have reason to believe that King Solomon exercised an unlimited and irresponsible control over the craft, although a tradition (not, however, of undoubted authority) says that he was assisted in his government by the counsel of twelve superintendants, selected from the twelve tribes of Israel. But we know too little, from authentic materials, of the precise system adopted at that remote period, to enable us to make any historical deductions on the subject.

The first historical notice that we have of the formation of a supreme controlling body of the fraternity, is in the "Gothic Constitutions"[4] which assert that, in the year 287, St. Alban, the protomartyr of England, who was a zealous patron of the craft, obtained from Carausius, the British Emperor, "a charter for the Masons to hold a general council, and gave it the name of assembly." The record further states, that St. Alban attended the meeting and assisted in making Masons, giving them "good charges and regulations." We know not, however, whether this assembly ever met again; and if it did, for how many years it continued to exist. The subsequent history of Freemasonry is entirely silent on the subject.

The next general assemblage of the craft, of which the records of Freemasonry inform us, was that convened in 926, at the city of York, in England, by Prince Edwin, the brother of King Athelstane, and the grandson of Alfred the Great. This, we say, was the next general assemblage, because the Ashmole manuscript, which was destroyed at the revival of Freemasonry in 1717, is said to have stated that, at that time, the Prince obtained from his brother, the king, a permission for the craft "to hold a yearly communication and a general assembly." The fact that such a power of meeting was then granted, is conclusive that it did not before exist: and would seem to prove that the assemblies of the craft, authorised by the charter of Carausius, had long since ceased to be held. This yearly communication did not, however, constitute, at least in the sense we now understand it, a Grand Lodge. The name given to it was that of the "General Assembly of Masons." It was not restricted, as now, to the Masters and Wardens of the subordinate lodges, acting in the capacity of delegates or representatives, but was composed, as Preston has observed, of as many of the fraternity at large as, being within a convenient distance, could attend once or twice a year, under the auspices of one general head, who was elected and installed at one of these meetings, and who, for the time being, received homage as the governor of the whole body. Any Brethren who were competent to discharge the duty, were allowed, by the regulations of the Order, to open and hold lodges at their discretion, at such times and places as were most convenient to them, and without the necessity of what we now call a Warrant of Constitution, and then and there to initiate members into the Order.[5] To the General Assembly, however, all the craft, without distinction, were permitted to repair; each Mason present was entitled to take part in the deliberations, and the rules and regulations enacted were the result of the votes of the whole body. The General Assembly was, in fact, precisely similar to those political congregations which, in our modern phraseology, we term "mass meetings."

These annual mass meetings or General Assemblies continued to be held, for many centuries after their first establishment, at the city of York, and were, during all that period, the supreme judicatory of the fraternity. There are frequent references to the annual assemblies of Freemasons in public documents. The preamble to an act passed in 1425, during the reign of Henry VI., just five centuries after the meeting at York, states that, "by the *yearly congregations* and confederacies made by the Masons in their *general assemblies,* the good course and effect of the statute of laborers were openly violated and broken." This act which forbade such meetings, was, however, never put in force; for an old record, quoted in the Book of Constitutions, speaks of the Brotherhood having frequented this "mutual assembly," in 1434, in the reign of the same king. We have another record of the General Assembly, which was held in York on the 27th December, 1561, when Queen Elizabeth, who was suspicious of their secrecy, sent an armed force to dissolve the meeting. A copy is still preserved of the regulations which were adopted by a similar assembly held in 1663, on the festival of St. John the Evangelist; and in these regulations it is declared that the private lodges shall give an account of all their acceptations made during the year to the General Assembly. Another regulation, however, adopted at the same time, still more explicitly acknowledges the existence of a General Assembly as the governing body of the fraternity. It is there provided, "that for the future, the said fraternity of Freemasons shall be regulated and governed by one Grand Master and as many Wardens as the said society shall think fit to appoint at every Annual General Assembly."

And thus the interests of the institution continued, until the beginning of the eighteenth century, or for nearly eight hundred years, to be entrusted to those General Assemblies of the fraternity, who, without distinction of rank or office, annually met at York to legislate for the government of the craft.

But in 1717, a new organization of the governing head was adopted, which gave birth to the establishment of a Grand Lodge, in the form in which these bodies now exist. So important a period in the history of Masonry demands our special attention.

After the death, in 1702, of King William, who was himself a Mason, and a great patron of the craft, the institution began to languish, the lodges decreased in number, and the General Assembly was entirely neglected for many years. A few old lodges continued, it is true, to meet regularly, but they consisted of only a few members.

At length, on the accession of George I., the Masons of London and its vicinity determined to revive the annual communications of the society. There were at that time only four lodges in the south of England, and the members of these, with several old Brethren, met in February, 1717, at the Apple Tree Tavern, in Charles street, Covent Garden, and organized by putting the oldest Master Mason, who was the Master of a lodge, in the chair; they then constituted themselves into what Anderson calls, "a Grand Lodge *pro tempore;*" resolved to hold the annual assembly and feast, and then to choose a Grand Master.

Accordingly, on the 24th of June, 1717, the assembly and feast were held; and the oldest Master of a lodge being in the chair, a list of candidates was presented, out of which Mr. Anthony Sayer was elected Grand Master, and Capt. Joseph Elliott and Mr. Jacob Lamball, Grand Wardens.

The Grand Master then commanded the Masters and Wardens of lodges to meet the Grand Officers every quarter, in communication, at the place he should appoint in his summons sent by the Tiler.

This was, then, undoubtedly, the commencement of that organization of the Masters and Wardens of lodges into a Grand Lodge, which has ever since continued to exist.

The fraternity at large, however, still continued to claim the right of being present at the annual assembly; and, in fact, at that meeting, their punctual attendance at the next annual assembly and feast was recommended.

At the same meeting, it was resolved "that the privilege of assembling as Masons, which had been hitherto unlimited, should be vested in certain lodges or assemblies of Masons convened in certain places; and that every lodge to be hereafter convened, except the four old lodges at this time existing, should be legally authorized to act by a warrant from the Grand Master for the time being, granted to certain individuals by petition, with the consent and approbation of the Grand Lodge in communication; and that, without such warrant, no lodge should be hereafter deemed regular or constitutional."

In consequence of this regulation, several new lodges received Warrants of Constitution, and their Masters and Wardens were ordered to attend the communications of the Grand Lodge. The Brethren at large vested all their privileges in the four old lodges, in trust that they would never suffer the old charges and landmarks to be infringed; and the old lodges, in return, agreed that the Masters and Wardens of every new lodge that might be constituted, should be permitted to share with them all the privileges of the Grand Lodge, except precedence of rank. The Brethren, says Preston, considered their further attendance at the meetings of the society unnecessary after these regulations were adopted; and therefore trusted implicitly to their Masters and Wardens for the government of the craft; and thenceforward the Grand Lodge has been composed of all the Masters and Wardens of the subordinate lodges which constitute the jurisdiction.

The ancient right of the craft, however, to take a part in the proceedings of the Grand Lodge or Annual Assembly, was fully acknowledged by a new regulation, adopted about the same time, in which it is declared that all alterations of the Constitutions must be proposed and agreed to, at the third quarterly communication preceding the annual feast, and be offered also to the perusal of *all* the Brethren before dinner, *even of the youngest Entered Apprentice*[6]

This regulation has, however, (I know not by what right,) become obsolete, and the Annual Assembly of Masons has long ceased to be held; the Grand Lodges having, since the beginning of the eighteenth century, assumed the form and organization which they still preserve, as strictly representative bodies.

Chapter II.

Of the Mode of Organizing Grand Lodges.

The topic to be discussed in this section is, the answer to the question, How shall a Grand Lodge be established in any state or country where such a body has not previously existed, but where there are subordinate lodges working under Warrants derived from Grand Lodges in other states? In answering this question, it seems proper that I should advert to the course pursued by the original Grand Lodge of England, at its establishment in 1717, as from that body nearly all the Grand Lodges of the York rite now in existence derive their authority, either directly or indirectly, and the mode of its organization has, therefore, universally been admitted to have been regular and legitimate.

In the first place, it is essentially requisite that the active existence of subordinate lodges in a state should precede the formation of a Grand Lodge; for the former are the only legitimate sources of the latter. A mass meeting of Masons cannot assemble and organize a Grand Lodge. A certain number of lodges, holding legal warrants from a Grand Lodge or from different Grand Lodges, must meet by their representatives and proceed to the formation of a Grand Lodge. When that process has been accomplished, the subordinate lodges return the warrants, under which they had theretofore worked, to the Grand Lodges from which they had originally received them, and take new ones from the body which they have formed.

That a mass meeting of the fraternity of any state is incompetent to organize a Grand Lodge has been definitively settled—not only by general usage, but by the express action of the Grand Lodges of the United States which refused to recognize, in 1842, the Grand Lodge of Michigan which had been thus irregularly established in the preceding year. That unrecognized body was then dissolved by the Brethren of Michigan, who proceeded to establish four subordinate lodges under Warrants granted by the Grand Lodge of New York. These four lodges subsequently met in convention and organized the present Grand Lodge of Michigan in a regular manner.

It seems, however, to have been settled in the case of Vermont, that where a Grand Lodge has been dormant for many years, and all of its subordinates extinct, yet if any of the Grand Officers, last elected, survive and are present, they may revive the Grand Lodge and proceed constitutionally to the exercise of its prerogatives.

The next inquiry is, as to the number of lodges required to organize a new Grand Lodge. Dalcho says that *five* lodges are necessary; and in this opinion he is supported by the Ahiman Rezon of Pennsylvania, published in 1783 by William Smith, D.D., at that time the Grand Secretary of that jurisdiction, and also by some other authorities. But no such regulation is to be found in the Book of Constitutions, which is now admitted to contain the fundamental law of the institution. Indeed, its adoption would have been a condemnation of the legality of the Mother Grand Lodge of England, which was formed in 1717 by the union of only *four* lodges. The rule, however, is to be found in the Ahiman Rezon of Laurence Dermott, which was adopted by the "Grand Lodge of Ancient Freemasons," that seceded from the lawful Grand Lodge in 1738. But as that body was undoubtedly, under our present views of masonic law, schismatic and illegal, its regulations have never been considered by masonic writers as being possessed of any authority.

In the absence of any written law upon the subject, we are compelled to look to precedent for authority; and, although the Grand Lodges in the United States have seldom been established with a representation of less than four lodges, the fact that that of Texas was organized in 1837 by the representatives of only *three* lodges, and that the Grand Lodge thus instituted was at once recognized as legal and regular by all its sister Grand Lodges, seems to settle the question that three subordinates are sufficient to institute a Grand Lodge.

Three lodges, therefore, in any territory where a Grand Lodge does not already exist, may unite in convention and organize a Grand Lodge. It will then be necessary, that these lodges should surrender the warrants under which they had been previously working, and take out new warrants from the Grand Lodge which they have constituted; and, from that time forth, all masonic authority is vested in the Grand Lodge thus formed.

The Grand Lodge having been thus constituted, the next inquiries that suggest themselves are as to its members and its officers, each of which questions will occupy a distinct discussion.

Chapter III.

Of the Members of a Grand Lodge.

It is an indisputable fact that the "General Assembly" which met at York in 926 was composed of all the members of the fraternity who chose to repair to it; and it is equally certain that, at the first Grand Lodge, held in 1717, after the revival of Masonry, all the craft who were present exercised the right of membership in voting for Grand Officers,[7] and must, therefore, have been considered members of the Grand Lodge. The right does not, however, appear to have been afterwards claimed. At this very assembly, the Grand Master who had been elected, summoned only the Master and Wardens of the lodges to meet him in the quarterly communications; and Preston distinctly states, that soon after, the Brethren of the four old lodges, which had constituted the Grand Lodge, considered their attendance on the future communications of the society unnecessary, and therefore concurred with the lodges which had been subsequently warranted in delegating the power of representation to their Masters and Wardens, "resting satisfied that no measure of importance would be adopted without their approbation."

Any doubts upon the subject were, however, soon put at rest by the enactment of a positive law. In 1721, thirty-nine articles for the future government of the craft were approved and confirmed, the twelfth of which was in the following words:

"The Grand Lodge consists of, and is formed by, the Masters and Wardens of all the regular particular lodges upon record, with the Grand Master at their head, and his Deputy on his left hand, and the Grand Wardens in their proper places."

From time to time, the number of these constituents of a Grand Lodge were increased by the extension of the qualifications for membership. Thus, in 1724, Past Grand Masters, and in 1725, Past Deputy Grand Masters, were admitted as members of the Grand Lodge. Finally it was decreed that the Grand Lodge should consist of the four present and all past grand officers; the Grand Treasurer, Secretary, and Sword-Bearer; the Master, Wardens, and nine assistants of the Grand Stewards' lodge, and the Masters and Wardens of all the regular lodges.

Past Masters were not at first admitted as members of the Grand Lodge. There is no recognition of them in the old Constitutions. Walworth thinks it must have been after 1772 that they were introduced.[8] I have extended my researches to some years beyond that period, without any success in finding their recognition as members under the Constitution of England. It is true that, in 1772, Dermott prefixed a note to his edition of the Ahiman Rezon, in which he asserts that "Past Masters of warranted lodges on record are allowed this privilege (of membership) whilst they continue to be members of any regular lodge." And it is, doubtless, on this imperfect authority, that the Grand Lodges of America began at so early a period to admit their Past Masters to seats in the Grand Lodge. In the authorized Book of Constitutions, we find no such provision. Indeed, Preston records that in 1808, at the laying of the foundation-stone of the Covent Garden Theatre, by the Prince of Wales, as Grand Master, "the Grand Lodge was opened by Charles Marsh, Esq., attended by the *Masters and Wardens* of all the regular lodges;" and, throughout the description of the ceremonies, no notice is taken of Past Masters as forming any part of the Grand Lodge. The first notice that we have been enabled to obtain of Past Masters, as forming any part of the Grand Lodge of England, is in the "Articles of Union between the two Grand Lodges of England," adopted in 1813, which declare that the Grand Lodge shall consist of the Grand and Past Grand Officers, of the actual Masters and Wardens of all the warranted lodges, and of the "Past Masters of Lodges who have regularly served and passed the chair before the day of Union, and who continued, without secession, regular contributing members of a warranted lodge." But it is provided, that after the decease of all these ancient Past Masters, the representation of every lodge shall consist of its Master and Wardens, and one Past Master only. There is, I presume, no doubt that, from 1772, Past Masters had held a seat in the Athol Grand Lodge of Ancient Masons, and that they did not in the original Grand Lodge, is, I believe, a fact equally indisputable. By the present constitutions of the United Grand Lodge of England, Past Masters are members of the Grand Lodge, while they continue subscribing members of a private lodge. In some of the Grand Lodges of the

United States, Past Masters have been permitted to retain their membership, while in others, they have been disfranchised.

On the whole, the result of this inquiry seems to be, that Past Masters have no inherent right, derived from the ancient landmarks, to a seat in the Grand Lodge; but as every Grand Lodge has the power, within certain limits, to make regulations for its own government, it may or may not admit them to membership, according to its own notion of expediency.

Some of the Grand Lodges have not only disfranchised Past Masters but Wardens also, and restricted membership only to acting Masters. This innovation has arisen from the fact that the payment of mileage and expenses to three representative would entail a heavy burden on the revenue of the Grand Lodge. The reason may have been imperative; but in the practice, pecuniary expediency has been made to override an ancient usage.

In determining, then, who are the constitutional members of a Grand Lodge, deriving their membership from inherent right, I should say that they are the Masters and Wardens of all regular lodges in the jurisdiction, with the Grand Officers chosen by them. All others, who by local regulations are made members, are so only by courtesy, and not by prescription or ancient law.

Chapter IV.

Of the Officers of a Grand Lodge.

The officers of a Grand Lodge may be divided into two classes, *essential* and *accidental*, or, as they are more usually called, *Grand* and *Subordinate*. The former of these classes are, as the name imports, essential to the composition of a Grand Lodge, and are to be found in every jurisdiction, having existed from the earliest times. They are the Grand and Deputy Grand Masters, the Grand Wardens, Grand Treasurer, and Grand Secretary. The Grand Chaplain is also enumerated among the Grand Officers, but the office is of comparatively modern date.

The subordinate officers of a Grand Lodge consist of the Deacons, Marshal, Pursuivant, or Sword-Bearer, Stewards, and others, whose titles and duties vary in different jurisdictions. I shall devote a separate section to the consideration of the duties of each and prerogatives of these officers.

Section I.

Of the Grand Master.

The office of Grand Master of Masons has existed from the very origin of the institution; for it has always been necessary that the fraternity should have a presiding head. There have been periods in the history of the institution when neither Deputies nor Grand Wardens are mentioned, but there is no time in its existence when it was without a Grand Master; and hence Preston, while speaking of that remote era in which the fraternity was governed by a General Assembly, says that this General Assembly or Grand Lodge "was not then restricted, as it is now understood to be, to the Masters and Wardens of private lodges, with the Grand Master and his Wardens at their head; it consisted of as many of the Fraternity *at large* as, being within a convenient distance, could attend, once or twice in a year, under the auspices of one general head, who was elected and installed at one of these meetings; and who for the time being received homage as the sole governor of the whole body."[9] The office is one of great honour as well as power, and has generally been conferred upon some individual distinguished by an influential position in society; so that his rank and character might reflect credit upon the craft.[10]

The Grand Mastership is an elective office, the election being annual and accompanied with impressive ceremonies of proclamation and homage made to him by the whole craft. Uniform usage, as well as the explicit declaration of the General Regulations,[11] seems to require that he should be installed by the last Grand Master. But in his absence the Deputy or some Past Grand Master may exercise the functions of installation or investiture. In the organization of a new Grand Lodge, ancient precedent and the necessity of the thing will authorize the performance of the installation by the Master of the oldest lodge present, who, however, exercises, *pro hac vice*, the prerogatives and assumes the place of a Grand Master.

The Grand Master possesses a great variety of prerogatives, some of which are derived from the "lex non scripta," or ancient usage; and others from the written or statute law of Masonry.[12]

I. He has the right to convene the Grand Lodge whenever he pleases, and to preside over its deliberation. In the decision of all questions by the Grand Lodge he is entitled to two votes. This is a privilege secured to him by Article XII. of the General Regulations.

It seems now to be settled, by ancient usage as well as the expressed opinion of the generality of Grand Lodges and of masonic writers, that there is no appeal from his decision. In June, 1849, the Grand Master of New York, Bro. Williard, declared an appeal to be out of order and refused to submit it to the Grand Lodge. The proceedings on that eventful occasion have been freely discussed by the Grand Lodges of the United States, and none of them have condemned the act of the Grand Master, while several have sustained it in express terms. "An appeal," say the Committee of Correspondence of Maryland, "from the decision of the Grand Master is an anomaly at war with every principle of Freemasonry, and as such, not for a moment to be tolerated or countenanced."[13] This opinion is also sustained by the Committee of the Grand Lodge of Florida in the year 1851, and at various times by other Grand Lodges. On the other hand, several Grand Lodges have made decisions adverse to this prerogative, and the present regulations of the Grand Lodge of England seem, by a fair interpretation of their phraseology, to admit of an appeal from the Grand Master. Still the general opinion of the craft in this country appears to sustain the doctrine, that no appeal can be made from the decision of that officer. And this doctrine has derived much support in the way of analogy from the report adopted by the General Grand Chapter of the United States, declaring that no appeal could lie from the decision of the presiding officer of any Royal Arch body.

Since we have enunciated this doctrine as masonic law, the question next arises, in what manner shall the Grand Master be punished, should he abuse his great prerogative? The answer to this question admits of no doubt. It is to be found in a regulation, adopted in 1721, by the Grand Lodge of England, and is in these words:—"If the Grand Master should abuse his great power, and render himself unworthy of the obedience and submission of the Lodges, he shall be treated in a way and manner to be agreed upon in a new regulation." But the same series of regulations very explicitly prescribe, how this new regulation is to be made; namely, it is to be "proposed and agreed to at the third quarterly communication preceding the annual Grand Feast, and offered to the perusal of all the Brethren before dinner, in writing, even of the youngest entered apprentice; the approbation and consent of the majority of all the Brethren present being absolutely necessary, to make the same binding and obligatory."[14] This mode of making a new regulation is explicitly and positively prescribed—it can be done in no other way—and those who accept the old regulations as the law of Masonry, must accept this provision with them. This will, in the present organization of many Grand Lodges, render it almost impracticable to make such a new regulation, in which case the Grand Master must remain exempt from other punishment for his misdeeds, than that which arises from his own conscience, and the loss of his Brethren's regard and esteem.

II. The power of granting dispensations is one of the most important prerogatives of the Grand Master. A dispensation may be defined to be an exemption from the observance of some law or the performance of some duty. In Masonry, no one has the authority to grant this exemption, except the Grand Master; and, although the exercise of it is limited within the observance of the ancient landmarks, the operation of the prerogative is still very extensive. The dispensing power may be exercised under the following circumstances:

1. The fourth old Regulation prescribes that "no lodge shall make more than five new Brothers at one and the same time without an urgent necessity."[15] But of this necessity the Grand Master may judge, and, on good and sufficient reason being shown, he may grant a dispensation enabling any lodge to suspend this regulation and make more than five new Brothers.

2. The next regulation prescribes "that no one can be accepted a member of a particular lodge without previous notice, one month before given to the lodge, in order to make due inquiry into the reputation and capacity of the candidate." But here, also, it is held that, in a suitable case of emergency, the Grand Master may exercise his prerogative and dispense with this probation of one month, permitting the candidate to be made on the night of his application.

3. If a lodge should have omitted for any causes to elect its officers or any of them on the constitutional night of election, or if any officer so elected shall have died, been deposed or removed from the jurisdiction subsequent to his election, the Grand Master may issue a dispensation empowering the lodge to proceed to an election or to fill the vacancy at any other specified communication; but he cannot grant a dispensation to elect a new master in consequence of the death or removal of the old one, while the two Wardens or either of them remain—because the Wardens succeed by inherent right and in order of seniority to the vacant mastership. And, indeed, it is held that while one of the three officers remains, no election can be held, even by dispensation, to fill the other two places, though vacancies in them may have occurred by death or removal.

4. The Grand Master may grant a dispensation empowering a lodge to elect a Master from among the members on the floor; but this must be done only when every Past Master, Warden, and Past Warden of the lodge has refused to serve,[16] because ordinarily a requisite qualification for the Mastership is, that the candidate shall, previously, have served in the office of Warden.

5. In the year 1723 a regulation was adopted, prescribing "that no Brother should belong to more than one lodge within the bills of mortality." Interpreting the last expression to mean three miles—which is now supposed to be the geographical limit of a lodge's jurisdiction, this regulation may still be considered as a part of the law of Masonry; but in some Grand Lodges, as that of South Carolina, for instance, the Grand Master will sometimes exercise his prerogative, and, dispensing with this regulation, permit a Brother to belong to two lodges, although they may be within three miles of each other.

6. But the most important power of the Grand Master connected with his dispensing prerogative is, that of constituting new lodges. It has already been remarked that, anciently, a warrant was not required for the formation of a lodge, but that a sufficient number of Masons, met together within a certain limit, were empowered, with the consent of the sheriff or chief magistrate of the place, to make Masons and practice the rites of Masonry, without such warrant of Constitution. But, in the year 1717, it was adopted as a regulation, that every lodge, to be thereafter convened, should be authorised to act by a warrant from the Grand Master for the time being, granted to certain persons by petition, with the consent and approbation of the Grand Lodge in communication. Ever since that time, no lodge has been considered as legally established, unless it has been constituted by the authority of the Grand Master. In the English Constitutions, the instrument thus empowering a lodge to meet, is called, when granted by the Grand Master, a Warrant of Constitution. It is granted by the Grand Master and not by the Grand Lodge. It appears to be a final instrument, notwithstanding the provision enacted in 1717, requiring the consent and approbation of the Grand Lodge; for in the Constitution of the United Grand Lodge of England, there is no allusion whatever to this consent and approbation.

But in this country, the process is somewhat different, and the Grand Master is deprived of a portion of his prerogative. Here, the instrument granted by the Grand Master is called a Dispensation. The lodge receiving it is not admitted into the register of lodges, nor is it considered as possessing any of the rights and privileges of a lodge, except that of making Masons, until a Warrant of Constitution is granted by the Grand Lodge. The ancient prerogative of the Grand Master is, however, preserved in the fact, that after a lodge has been thus warranted by the Grand Lodge, the ceremony of constituting it, which embraces its consecration and the installation of its officers, can only be performed by the Grand Master in person, or by his special Deputy appointed for that purpose.[17]

III. The third prerogative of the Grand Master is that of visitation. He has a right to visit any lodge within his jurisdiction at such times as he pleases, and when there to preside; and it is the duty of the Master to offer him the chair and his gavel, which the Grand Master may decline or accept at his pleasure. This prerogative admits of no question, as it is distinctly declared in the first of the Thirty-nine Regulations, adopted in 1721, in the following words: —

"The Grand Master or Deputy has full authority and right, not only to be present, but to preside in every lodge, with the Master of the lodge on his left hand, and to order his Grand Wardens to attend him, who are not to act as Wardens of particular lodges, but in his presence and at his command; for the Grand Master, while in a particular lodge, may command the Wardens of that lodge, or any other Master Masons, to act as his Wardens, *pro tempore*."

But in a subsequent regulation it was provided, that as the Grand Master cannot deprive the Grand Wardens of that office without the consent of the Grand Lodge, he should appoint no other persons to act as Wardens in his visitation to a private lodge, unless the Grand Wardens were absent. This whole regulation is still in existence.

The question has been lately mooted, whether, if the Grand Master declines to preside, he does not thereby place himself in the position of a private Brother, and become subject, as all the others present, to the control of the Worshipful Master. I answer, that of course he becomes subject to and must of necessity respect those rules of order and decorum which are obligatory on all good men and Masons; but that he cannot, by the exercise of an act of courtesy in declining to preside, divest himself of his prerogative, which, moreover, he may at any time during the evening assume, and demand the gavel. The Grand Master of Masons can, under no circumstances, become subject to the decrees and orders of the Master of a particular lodge.

IV. Another prerogative of the Grand Master is that of appointment; which, however, in this country, has been much diminished. According to the old regulations, and the custom is still continued in the Constitutions of the Grand Lodge of England, the Grand Master has the right of appointing his Deputy and Wardens. In the United States, the office has been shorn of this high prerogative, and these Officers are elected by the Grand Lodge. The Deputy, however, is still appointed by the Grand Master, in some of the States, as Massachusetts, North Carolina, Wisconsin, and Texas. The appointment of the principal subordinate officers, is also given to the Grand Master by the American Grand Lodges.

V. The last and most extraordinary power of the Grand Master, is that of *making Masons at sight*.

The power to "make Masons at sight" is a technical term, which may be defined to be the power to initiate, pass, and raise candidates by the Grand Master, in a lodge of emergency, or as it is called in the Book of Constitutions, "an occasional lodge," especially convened by him, and consisting of such Master Masons as he may call together for that purpose only—the lodge ceasing to exist as soon as the initiation, passing, or raising, has been accomplished and the Brethren have been dismissed by the Grand Master.

Whether such a power is vested in the Grand Master, is a question that, within the last few years, has been agitated with much warmth, by some of the Grand Lodges of this country; but I am not aware that, until very lately, the prerogative was ever disputed.[18]

In the Book of Constitutions, however, several instances are furnished of the exercise of this right by various Grand Masters.

In 1731, Lord Lovel being Grand Master, he "formed an occasional lodge at Houghton Hall, Sir Robert Walpole's House in Norfolk," and there made the Duke of Lorraine, afterwards Emperor of Germany, and the Duke of Newcastle, Master Masons.[19]

I do not quote the case of the initiation, passing, and raising of Frederick, Prince of Wales, in 1737, which was done in "an occasional lodge," over which Dr. Desaguliers presided,[20] because as Desaguliers was not the Grand Master, nor even, as has been incorrectly stated by the New York Committee of Correspondence, Deputy Grand Master, but only a Past Grand Master, it cannot be called *a making at sight*. He most probably acted under the dispensation of the Grand Master, who at that time was the Earl of Darnley.

But in 1766, Lord Blaney, who was then Grand Master, convened "an occasional lodge" and initiated, passed, and raised the Duke of Gloucester.[21]

Again in 1767, John Salter, the Deputy, then acting as Grand Master, convened "an occasional lodge," and conferred the three degrees on the Duke of Cumberland.[22]

In 1787, the Prince of Wales was made a Mason "at an occasional lodge, convened," says Preston, "for the purpose, at the Star and Garter, Pall Mall, over which the Duke of Cumberland, (Grand Master) presided in person."[23]

But it is unnecessary to multiply instances of the right, exercised by former Grand Masters, of congregating occasional lodges, and making Masons at sight. It has been said, however, by the oppugners of this prerogative, that these "occasional lodges" were only special communications of the Grand Lodge, and the "makings" are thus supposed to have taken place under the authority of that body, and not of the Grand Master. The facts, however, do not sustain this position. Throughout the Book of Constitutions, other meetings, whether regular or special, are distinctly recorded as meetings of the Grand Lodge, while these "occasional lodges" appear only to have been convened by the Grand Master, for the purpose of making Masons. Besides, in many instances, the lodge was held at a different place from that of the Grand Lodge, and the officers were not, with the exception of the Grand Master, the officers of the Grand Lodge. Thus the occasional lodge, which initiated the Duke of Lorraine, was held at the residence of Sir Robert Walpole, in Norfolk, while the Grand Lodge always met in London. In 1766, the Grand Lodge held its communications at the Crown and Anchor; but the occasional lodge, which, in the same year, conferred the degrees on the Duke of Gloucester, was convened at the Horn Tavern. In the following year, the lodge which initiated the Duke of Cumberland was convened at the Thatched House Tavern, the Grand Lodge continuing to meet at the Crown and Anchor.

This may be considered very conclusive evidence of the existence of the prerogative of the Grand Master, which we are now discussing, but the argument *à fortiori*, drawn from his dispensing power, will tend to confirm the doctrine.

No one doubts or denies the power of the Grand Master to constitute new lodges by dispensation. In 1741, the Grand Lodge of England forgot it for a moment, and adopted a new regulation, that no new lodge should be constituted until the consent of the Grand Lodge had been first obtained, "But this order, afterwards appearing," says the Book of Constitutions,[24] "to be an infringement on the prerogative of the Grand Master, and to be attended with many inconveniences and with damage to the craft, was repealed."

It is, then, an undoubted prerogative of the Grand Master to constitute lodges by dispensation, and in these lodges, so constituted, Masons may be legally entered, passed, and raised. This is done every day. Seven Master Masons, applying to the Grand Master, he grants them a dispensation, under authority of which they proceed to open and hold a lodge, and to make Masons. This lodge is, however, admitted to be the mere creature of the Grand Master, for it is in his power, at any time, to revoke the dispensation he had granted, and thus to dissolve the lodge.

But, if the Grand Master has the power thus to enable others to confer the degrees and make Masons by his individual authority out of his presence, are we not permitted to argue *à fortiori* that he has also the right of congregating seven Brethren and causing a Mason, to be made in his sight? Can he delegate a power to others which he does not himself possess? And is his calling together "an occasional lodge," and making, with the assistance of the Brethren thus assembled, a Mason "at sight," that is to say, in his presence, anything more or less than the exercise of his dispensing power, for the establishment of a lodge under dispensation, for a temporary period, and for a special purpose. The purpose having been effected, and the Mason having been made, he revokes his dispensation, and the lodge is dismissed. If we assumed any other ground than this, we should be compelled to say, that though the Grand Master might authorise others to make Masons, when he was absent, as in the usual case of lodges under dispensation yet the instant that he attempted to convey the same powers to be exercised in his presence, and under his personal supervision, his authority would cease. This course of reasoning would necessarily lead to a contradiction in terms, if not to an actual absurdity.

It is proper to state, in conclusion, that the views here set forth are not entertained by the very able Committee of Foreign Correspondence of the Grand Lodge of Florida, who only admit the power of the Grand Master to make Masons in the Grand Lodge. On the other hand, the Grand Lodge of Wisconsin, at its last communication, adopted a report, asserting "that the Grand Master has the right to make Masons at sight, in cases which he may deem proper"—and the Committee of Correspondence of New York declares, that "since the time when the memory of man runneth not to the contrary, Grand Masters have enjoyed the privilege of making Masons at sight, without any preliminaries, and at any suitable time or place."

The opinions of the two last quoted Grand Lodges embody the general sentiment of the Craft on this subject.[25] But although the prerogative is thus almost universally ceded to Grand Masters, there are many very reasonable doubts as to the expediency of its exercise, except under extraordinary circumstances of emergency.

In England, the practice has generally been confined to the making of Princes of the Royal Family, who, for reasons of state, were unwilling to reduce themselves to the level of ordinary candidates and receive their initiation publicly in a subordinate lodge.

But in the exercise of this prerogative, the Grand Master cannot dispense with any of the requisite forms of initiation, prescribed by the oral laws of the Order. He cannot communicate the degrees, but must adhere to all the established ceremonies—the conferring of degrees by "communication" being a form unknown to the York rite. He must be assisted by the number of Brethren necessary to open and hold a lodge. Due inquiry must be made into the candidate's character, (though the Grand Master may, as in a case of emergency, dispense with the usual probation of a month). He cannot interfere with the business of a regular lodge, by making one whom it had rejected, nor finishing one which it had commenced. Nor can he confer the three degrees, at one and the same communication. In short, he must, in making Masons at sight, conform to the ancient usages and landmarks of the Order.

Section II.

The Deputy Grand Master.

The office of Deputy Grand Master is one of great dignity, but not of much practical importance, except in case of the absence of the Grand Master, when he assumes all the prerogatives of that officer. Neither is the office, comparatively speaking, of a very ancient date. At the first reorganization of the Grand Lodge in 1717, and for two or three years afterwards, no Deputy was appointed, and it was not until 1721 that the Duke of Montagu conferred the dignity on Dr. Beal. Originally the Deputy was intended to relieve the Grand Master of all the burden and pressure of business, and the 36th of the Regulations, adopted in 1721, states that "a Deputy is said to have been always needful when the Grand Master was nobly born," because it was considered as a derogation from the dignity of a nobleman to enter upon the ordinary business of the craft. Hence we find, among the General Regulations, one which sets forth this principle in the following words:

"The Grand Master should not receive any private intimations of business, concerning Masons and Masonry, but from his Deputy first, except in such cases as his worship can easily judge of; and if the application to the Grand Master be irregular, his worship can order the Grand Wardens, or any other so applying, to wait upon the Deputy, who is immediately to prepare the business, and to lay it orderly before his worship."

The Deputy Grand Master exercises, in the absence of the Grand Master, all the prerogatives and performs all the duties of that officer. But he does so, not by virtue of any new office that he has acquired by such absence, but simply in the name of and as the representative of the Grand Master, from whom alone he derives all his authority. Such is the doctrine sustained in all the precedents recorded in the Book of Constitutions.

In the presence of the Grand Master, the office of Deputy is merely one of honour, without the necessity of performing any duties, and without the power of exercising any prerogatives.

There cannot be more than one Deputy Grand Master in a jurisdiction; so that the appointment of a greater number, as is the case in some of the States, is a manifest innovation on the ancient usages. District Deputy Grand Masters, which officers are also a modern invention of this country, seem to take the place in some degree of the Provincial Grand Masters of England, but they are not invested with the same prerogatives. The office is one of local origin, and its powers and duties are prescribed by the local regulations of the Grand Lodge which may have established it.

Section III.

Of the Grand Wardens.

The Senior and Junior Grand Wardens were originally appointed, like the Deputy, by the Grand Master, and are still so appointed in England; but in this country they are universally elected by the Grand Lodge. Their duties do not materially differ from those performed by the corresponding officers in a subordinate lodge. They accompany the Grand Master in his visitations, and assume the stations of the Wardens of the lodge visited.

According to the regulations of 1721, the Master of the oldest lodge present was directed to take the chair of the Grand Lodge in the absence of both the Grand Master and Deputy; but this was found to be an interference with the rights of the Grand Wardens, and it was therefore subsequently declared that, in the absence of the Grand Master and Deputy, the last former Grand Master or Deputy should preside. But if no Past Grand or Past Deputy Grand Master should be present, then the Senior Grand Warden was to fill the chair, and, in his absence, the Junior Grand Warden, and lastly, in absence of both these, then the oldest Freemason[26] who is the present Master of a lodge. In this country, however, most of the Grand Lodges have altered this regulation, and the Wardens succeed according to seniority to the chair of the absent Grand Master and Deputy, in preference to any Past Grand Officer.

Section IV.

Of the Grand Treasurer.

The office of Grand Treasurer was first established in 1724, in consequence of a report of the Committee of Charity of the Grand Lodge of England. But no one was found to hold the trust until the 24th of June, 1727, when, at the request of the Grand Master, the appointment was accepted by Nathaniel Blackerby, Deputy Grand Master. The duties of the office do not at all differ from those of a corresponding one in every other society; but as the trust is an important one in a pecuniary view, it has generally been deemed prudent that it should only be committed to "a brother of good worldly substance," whose ample means would place him beyond the chances of temptation.

The office of Grand Treasurer has this peculiarity, that while all the other officers below the Grand Master were originally, and still are in England, appointed, that alone was always elective.

Section V.

Of the Grand Secretary.

This is one of the most important offices in the Grand Lodge, and should always be occupied by a Brother of intelligence and education, whose abilities may reflect honor on the institution of which he is the accredited public organ. The office was established in the year 1723, during the Grand Mastership of the Duke of Wharton, previous to which time the duties appear to have been discharged by the Grand Wardens.

The Grand Secretary not only records the proceedings of the Grand Lodge, but conducts its correspondence, and is the medium through whom all applications on masonic subjects are to be made to the Grand Master, or the Grand Lodge.

According to the regulations of the Grand Lodges of England, New York and South Carolina, the Grand Secretary may appoint an assistant, who is not, however, by virtue of such appointment, a member of the Grand Lodge. The same privilege is also extended in South Carolina to the Grand Treasurer.

Section VI.

Of the Grand Chaplain.

This is the last of the Grand Offices that was established, having been instituted on the 1st of May, in the year 1775. The duties are confined to the reading of prayers, and other sacred portions of the ritual, in consecrations, dedications, funeral services, etc. The office confers no masonic authority at all, except that of a seat and a vote in the Grand Lodge.

Section VII.

Of the Grand Deacons.

But little need be said of the Grand Deacons. Their duties correspond to those of the same officers in subordinate lodges. The office of the Deacons, even in a subordinate lodge, is of comparatively modern institution. Dr. Oliver remarks that they are not mentioned in any of the early Constitutions of Masonry, nor even so late as 1797, when Stephen Jones wrote his "Masonic Miscellanies," and he thinks it "satisfactorily proved that Deacons were not considered necessary, in working the business of a lodge, before the very latter end of the eighteenth century."[27]

But although the Deacons are not mentioned in the various works published previous to that period, which are quoted by Dr. Oliver, it is nevertheless certain that the office existed at a time much earlier than that which he supposes. In a work in my possession, and which is now lying before me, entitled "Every Young Man's Companion, etc., by W. Gordon, Teacher of the Mathematics," sixth edition printed at London, in 1777, there is a section, extending from page 413 to page 426, which is dedicated to the subject of Freemasonry and to a description of the working of a subordinate lodge. Here the Senior and Junior Deacons are enumerated among the officers, their exact positions described and their duties detailed, differing in no respect from the explanations of our own ritual at the present day. The positive testimony of this book must of course outweigh the negative testimony of the authorities quoted by Oliver, and shows the existence in England of Deacons in the year 1777 at least.

It is also certain that the office of Deacon claims an earlier origin in America than the "very latter end of the eighteenth century;" and, as an evidence of this, it may be stated that, in the "Ahiman Rezon" of Pennsylvania, published in 1783, the Grand Deacons are named among the officers of the Grand Lodge, "as particular assistants to the Grand Master and Senior Warden, in conducting the business of the Lodge." They are to be found in all Grand Lodges of the York Rite, and are usually appointed, the Senior by the Grand Master, and the Junior by the Senior Grand Warden.

Section VIII.

Of the Grand Marshal.

The *Grand Marshal*, as an officer of convenience, existed from an early period. We find him mentioned in the procession of the Grand Lodge, made in 1731, where he is described as carrying "a truncheon, blue, tipped with gold," insignia which he still retains. He takes no part in the usual work of the Lodge; but his duties are confined to the proclamation of the Grand Officers at their installation, and to the arrangement and superintendence of public processions.

The Grand Marshal is usually appointed by the Grand Master.

Section IX.

Of the Grand Stewards.

The first mention that is made of Stewards is in the Old Regulations, adopted in 1721. Previous to that time, the arrangements of the Grand Feast were placed in the hands of the Grand Wardens; and it was to relieve them of this labor that the regulation was adopted, authorizing the Grand Master, or his Deputy, to appoint a certain number of Stewards, who were to act in concert with the Grand Wardens. In 1728, it was ordered that the number of Stewards to be appointed should be twelve. In 1731, a regulation was adopted, permitting the Grand Stewards to appoint their successors. And, in 1735, the Grand Lodge ordered, that, "in consideration of their past service and future usefulness," they should be constituted a Lodge of Masters, to be called the Stewards' Lodge, which should have a registry in the Grand Lodge list, and exercise the privilege of sending twelve representatives. This was the origin of that body now known in the Constitutions of the Grand Lodges of England and New York,[28] as the Grand Stewards' Lodge, although it has been very extensively modified in its organization. In New York, it is now no more than a Standing Committee of the Grand Lodge; and in England, although it is regularly constituted, as a Lodge of Master Masons, it is by a special regulation deprived of all power of entering, passing, or raising Masons. In other jurisdictions, the office of Grand Stewards is still preserved, but their functions are confined to their original purpose of preparing and superintending the Grand Feast.

The appointment of the Grand Stewards should be most appropriately vested in the Junior Grand Warden.

Section X.

Of the Grand Sword-Bearer.

Grand Sword-Bearer.— It was an ancient feudal custom, that all great dignitaries should have a sword of state borne before them, as the insignia of their dignity. This usage has to this day been preserved in the Masonic Institution, and the Grand Master's sword of state is still borne in all public processions by an officer specially appointed for that purpose. Some years after the reorganization of the Grand Lodge of

England, the sword was borne by the Master of the Lodge to which it belonged; but, in 1730, the Duke of Norfolk, being then Grand Master, presented to the Grand Lodge the sword of Gustavus Adolphus, King of Sweden, which had afterwards been used in war by Bernard, Duke of Saxe Weimar, and which the Grand Master directed should thereafter be adopted as his sword of state. In consequence of this donation, the office of Grand Sword-Bearer was instituted in the following year. The office is still retained; but some Grand Lodges have changed the name to that of *Grand Pursuivant*.

Section XI.

Of the Grand Tiler.

It is evident from the Constitutions of Masonry, as well as from the peculiar character of the institution, that the office of Grand Tiler must have existed from the very first organization of a Grand Lodge. As, from the nature of the duties that he has to perform, the Grand Tiler is necessarily excluded from partaking of the discussions, or witnessing the proceedings of the Grand Lodge, it has very generally been determined, from a principle of expediency, that he shall not be a member of the Grand Lodge during the term of his office.

The Grand Tiler is sometimes elected by the Grand Lodge, and sometimes appointed by the Grand Master.

Chapter V.

Of the Powers and Prerogatives of a Grand Lodge.

Section I.

General View.

The necessary and usual officers of a Grand Lodge having been described, the rights, powers, and prerogatives of such a body is the next subject of our inquiry.

The foundation-stone, upon which the whole superstructure of masonic authority in the Grand Lodge is built, is to be found in that conditional clause annexed to the thirty-eight articles, adopted in 1721 by the Masons of England, and which is in these words:

"Every annual Grand Lodge has an inherent power and authority to make new regulations, or to alter these for the real benefit of this ancient fraternity; PROVIDED ALWAYS THAT THE OLD LANDMARKS BE CAREFULLY PRESERVED; and that such alterations and new regulations be proposed and agreed to at the third quarterly communication preceding the annual Grand Feast; and that they be offered also to the perusal of all the Brethren before dinner, in writing, even of the youngest Entered Apprentice: the approbation and consent of the majority of all the Brethren present being absolutely necessary, to make the same binding and obligatory."

The expression which is put in capitals—"provided always that the old landmarks be carefully preserved"—is the limiting clause which must be steadily borne in mind, whenever we attempt to enumerate the powers of a Grand Lodge. It must never be forgotten (in the words of another regulation, adopted in 1723, and incorporated in the ritual of installation), that "it is not in the power of any man, or body of men, to make any alteration or innovation in the body of Masonry."

"With these views to limit us, the powers of a Grand Lodge may be enumerated in the language which has been adopted in the modern constitutions of England, and which seem to us, after a careful comparison, to be as comprehensive and correct as any that we have been able to examine. This enumeration is in the following language:

"In the Grand Lodge, alone, resides the power of enacting laws and regulations for the permanent government of the craft, and of altering, repealing, and abrogating them, always taking care that the ancient landmarks of the order are preserved. The Grand Lodge has also the inherent power of investigating, regulating, and deciding all matters relative to the craft, or to particular lodges, or to individual Brothers, which it may exercise either of itself, or by such delegated authority, as in its wisdom and discretion it may appoint; but in the Grand Lodge alone resides the power of erasing lodges, and expelling Brethren from the craft, a power which it ought not to delegate to any subordinate authority in England."

In this enumeration we discover the existence of three distinct classes of powers: — 1, a legislative power; 2, a judicial power; and 3, an executive power. Each of these will occupy a separate section.

Section II.

Of the Legislative Power of a Grand Lodge.

In the passage already quoted from the Constitutions of the Grand Lodge of England it is said, "in the Grand Lodge, alone, resides the power of enacting laws and regulations for the government of the craft, and of altering, repealing, and abrogating them." General regulations for the government of the whole craft throughout the world can no longer be enacted by a Grand Lodge. The multiplication of these bodies, since the year 1717, has so divided the supremacy that no regulation now enacted can have the force and authority of those adopted by the Grand Lodge of England in 1721, and which now constitute a part of the fundamental law of Masonry, and as such are unchangeable by any modern Grand Lodge.

Any Grand Lodge may, however, enact local laws for the direction of its own special affairs, and has also the prerogative of enacting the regulations which are to govern all its subordinates and the craft generally in its own jurisdiction. From this legislative power, which belongs exclusively to the Grand Lodge, it follows that no subordinate lodge can make any new bye-laws, nor alter its old ones, without the approval and confirmation of the Grand Lodge. Hence, the rules and regulations of every lodge are inoperative until they are submitted to and approved by the Grand Lodge. The confirmation of that body is the enacting clause; and, therefore, strictly speaking, it may be said that the subordinates only propose the bye-laws, and the Grand Lodge enacts them.

Section III.

Of the Judicial Power of a Grand Lodge.

The passage already quoted from the English Constitutions continues to say, that "the Grand Lodge has the inherent power of investigating, regulating and deciding all matters relative to the craft, or to particular lodges, or to individual Brothers, which it may exercise, either of itself, or by such delegated authority as in its wisdom and discretion it may appoint." Under the first clause of this section, the Grand Lodge is constituted as the Supreme Masonic Tribunal of its jurisdiction. But as it would be impossible for that body to investigate every masonic offense that occurs within its territorial limits, with that full and considerate attention that the principles of justice require, it has, under the latter clause of the section, delegated this duty, in general, to the subordinate lodges, who are to act as its committees, and to report the results of their inquiry for its final disposition. From this course of action has risen the erroneous opinion of some persons, that the jurisdiction of the Grand Lodge is only appellate in its character. Such is not the case. The Grand Lodge possesses an original jurisdiction over all causes occurring within its limits. It is only for expediency that it remits the examination of the merits of any case to a subordinate lodge as a *quasi* committee. It may, if it thinks proper, commence the investigation of any matter concerning either a lodge, or an individual brother within its own bosom, and whenever an appeal from the decision of a lodge is made, which, in reality, is only a dissent from the report of the lodge, the Grand Lodge does actually recommence the investigation *de novo*, and, taking the matter out of the lodge, to whom by its general usage it had been primarily referred, it places it in the hands of another committee of its own body for a new report. The course of action is, it is true, similar to that in law, of an appeal from an inferior to a superior tribunal. But the principle is different. The Grand Lodge simply confirms or rejects the report that has been made to it, and it may do that without any appeal having been entered. It may, in fact, dispense with the necessity of an investigation by and report from a subordinate lodge altogether, and undertake the trial itself from the very inception. But this, though a constitutional, is an unusual course. The subordinate lodge is the instrument which the Grand Lodge employs in considering the investigation. It may or it may not make use of the instrument, as it pleases.

Section IV.

Of the Executive Power of a Grand Lodge.

The English Constitutions conclude, in the passage that has formed the basis of our previous remarks, by asserting that "in the Grand Lodge, alone, resides the power of erasing lodges and expelling Brethren from the craft, a power which it ought not to delegate to any subordinate authority." The power of the Grand Lodge to erase lodges is accompanied with a coincident power of constituting new lodges. This power it originally shared with the Grand Master, and still does in England; but in this country the power of the Grand Lodge is paramount to that of the Grand Master. The latter can only constitute lodges temporarily, by dispensation, and his act must be confirmed, or may be annulled by the Grand Lodge. It is not until a lodge has received its Warrant of Constitution from the Grand Lodge, that it can assume the rank and exercise the prerogatives of a regular and legal lodge.

The expelling power is one that is very properly intrusted to the Grand Lodge, which is the only tribunal that should impose a penalty affecting the relations of the punished party with the whole fraternity. Some of the lodges in this country have claimed the right to expel independently of the action of the Grand Lodge. But the claim is founded on an erroneous assumption of powers that have never existed, and which are not recognized by the ancient constitutions, nor the general usages of the fraternity. A subordinate lodge tries its delinquent member, under the provisions which have already been stated, and, according to the general usage of lodges in the United States, declares him expelled. But the sentence is of no force nor effect until it has been confirmed by the Grand Lodge, which may, or may not, give the required confirmation, and which, indeed, often refuses to do so, but actually reverses the sentence. It is apparent, from the views already expressed on the judicial powers of the Grand Lodge, that the sentence of expulsion uttered by the subordinate is to be taken in the sense of a recommendatory report, and that it is the confirmation and adoption of that report by the Grand Lodge that alone gives it vitality and effect.

The expelling power presumes, of course, coincidently, the reinstating power. As the Grand Lodge alone can expel, it also alone can reinstate.

These constitute the general powers and prerogatives of a Grand Lodge. Of course there are other local powers, assumed by various Grand Lodges, and differing in the several jurisdictions, but they are all derived from some one of the three classes that we have enumerated. From these views, it will appear that a Grand Lodge is the supreme legislative, judicial, and executive authority of the Masonic jurisdiction in which it is situated. It is, to use a feudal term, "the lord paramount" in Masonry. It is a representative body, in which, however, it constituents have delegated everything and reserved no rights to themselves. Its authority is almost unlimited, for it is restrained by but a single check:—*It cannot alter or remove the ancient landmarks.*

Book Second

Laws of Subordinate Lodges.

Having thus succinctly treated of the law in relation to Grand Lodges, I come next in order to consider the law as it respects the organization, rights, powers, and privileges of subordinate Lodges; and the first question that will engage our attention will be, as to the proper method of organizing a Lodge.

Chapter I.

Of the Nature and Organization of Subordinate Lodges.

The old charges define a Lodge to be "a place where Masons assemble and work;" and also "that assembly, or duly organized society of Masons." The lecture on the first degree gives a still more precise definition. It says that "a lodge is an assemblage of Masons, duly congregated, having the Holy Bible, square, and compasses, and a charter, or warrant of constitution, empowering them to work."

Every lodge of Masons requires for its proper organization, that it should have been congregated by the permission of some superior authority, which may be either a Grand Master or a Grand Lodge. When a lodge is organized by the authority of a Grand Master, it is said to work under a Dispensation, and when by the authority of a Grand Lodge, it is said to work under a warrant of constitution. In the history of a lodge, the former authority generally precedes the latter, the lodge usually working for some time under the dispensation of the Grand Master, before it is regularly warranted by the Grand Lodge. But this is not necessarily the case. A Grand Lodge will sometimes grant a warrant of constitution at once, without the previous exercise, on the part of the Grand Master, of his dispensing power. As it is, however, more usually the practice for the dispensation to precede the warrant of constitution, I shall explain the formation of a lodge according to that method.

Any number of Master Masons, not under seven, being desirous of uniting themselves into a lodge, apply by petition to the Grand Master for the necessary authority. This petition must set forth that they now are, or have been, members of a regularly constituted lodge, and must assign, as a reason for their application, that they desire to form the lodge "for the conveniency of their respective dwellings," or some other sufficient reason. The petition must also name the brethren whom they desire to act as their Master and Wardens, and the place where they intend to meet; and it must be recommended by the nearest lodge.

Dalcho says that not less than three Master Masons should sign the petition; but in this he differs from all the other authorities, which require not less than seven. This rule, too, seems to be founded in reason; for, as it requires seven Masons to constitute a quorum for opening and holding a lodge of Entered Apprentices, it would be absurd to authorize a smaller number to organize a lodge which, after its organization, could not be opened, nor make Masons in that degree.

Preston says that the petition must be recommended "by the Masters of three regular lodges adjacent to the place where the new lodge is to be held." Dalcho says it must be recommended "by three other known and approved Master Masons," but does not make any allusion to any adjacent lodge. The laws and regulations of the Grand Lodge of Scotland require the recommendation to be signed "by the Masters and officers of two of the nearest lodges." The Constitutions of the Grand Lodge of England require that it must be recommended "by the officers of some regular lodge." The recommendation of a neighboring lodge is the general usage of the craft, and is intended to certify to the superior authority, on the very best evidence that can be obtained, that, namely, of an adjacent lodge, that the new lodge will be productive of no injury to the Order.

If this petition be granted, the Grand Secretary prepares a document called a *dispensation*, which authorizes the officers named in the petition to open and hold a lodge, and to "enter, pass, and raise Freemasons." The duration of this dispensasation is generally expressed on its face to be, "until it shall be revoked by the Grand Master or the Grand Lodge, or until a warrant of constitution is granted by the Grand Lodge." Preston says, that the Brethren named in it are authorized "to assemble as Masons for forty days, and until such time as a warrant of constitution can be obtained by command of the Grand Lodge, or that authority be recalled." But generally, usage continues the dispensation only until the next meeting of the Grand Lodge, when it is either revoked, or a warrant of constitution granted.

If the dispensation be revoked by either the Grand Master or the Grand Lodge (for either has the power to do so), the lodge of course at once ceases to exist. Whatever funds or property it has accumulated revert, as in the case of all extinct lodges, to the Grand Lodge, which may be called the natural heir of its subordinates; but all the work done in the lodge, under the dispensation, is regular and legal, and all the Masons made by it are, in every sense of the term, "true and lawful Brethren."

Let it be supposed, however, that the dispensation is confirmed or approved by the Grand Lodge, and we thus arrive at another step in the history of the new lodge. At the next sitting of the Grand Lodge, after the dispensation has been issued by the Grand Master, he states that fact to the Grand Lodge, when, either at his request, or on motion of some Brother, the vote is taken on the question of constituting the new lodge, and, if a majority are in favor of it, the Grand Secretary is ordered to grant a warrant of constitution.

This instrument differs from a dispensation in many important particulars. It is signed by all the Grand Officers, and emanates from the Grand Lodge, while the dispensation emanates from the office of the Grand Master, and is signed by him alone. The authority of the dispensation is temporary, that of the warrant permanent; the one can be revoked at pleasure by the Grand Master, who granted it; the other only for cause shown, and by the Grand Lodge; the one bestows only a name, the other both a name and a number; the one confers only the power of holding a lodge and making Masons, the other not only confers these powers, but also those of installation and of succession in office. From these differences in the characters of the two documents, arise important differences in the powers and privileges of a lodge under dispensation and of one that has been regularly constituted. These differences shall hereafter be considered.

The warrant having been granted, there still remain certain forms and ceremonies to be observed, before the lodge can take its place among the legal and registered lodges of the jurisdiction in which it is situated. These are its consecration, its dedication, its constitution, and the installation of its officers. We shall not fully enter into a description of these various ceremonies, because they are laid down at length in all the Monitors, and are readily accessible to our readers. It will be sufficient if we barely allude to their character.

The ceremony of constitution is so called, because by it the lodge becomes constituted or established. Orthoepists define the verb to constitute, as signifying "to give a formal existence to anything." Hence, to constitute a lodge is to give it existence, character, and standing as such; and the instrument that warrants the person so constituting or establishing it, in this act, is very properly called the "warrant of constitution."

The consecration, dedication, and constitution of a lodge must be performed by the Grand Master in person; or, if he cannot conveniently attend, by some Past Master appointed by him as his special proxy or representative for that purpose. On the appointed evening, the Grand Master, accompanied by his Grand Officers, repairs to the place where the new lodge is to hold its meetings, the lodge[29] having been placed in the centre of the room and decently covered with a piece of white linen or satin. Having taken the chair, he examines the records of the lodge and the warrant of constitution; the officers who have been chosen are presented before him, when he inquires of the Brethren if they continue satisfied with the choice they have made. The ceremony of consecration is then performed. The Lodge is uncovered; and corn, wine, and oil—

the masonic elements of consecration—are poured upon it, accompanied by appropriate prayers and invocations, and the lodge is finally declared to be consecrated to the honor and glory of God.

This ceremony of consecration has been handed down from the remotest antiquity. A consecrating—a separating from profane things, and making holy or devoting to sacred purposes—was practiced by both the Jews and the Pagans in relation to their temples, their altars, and all their sacred utensils. The tabernacle, as soon as it was completed, was consecrated to God by the unction of oil. Among the Pagan nations, the consecration of their temples was often performed with the most sumptuous offerings and ceremonies; but oil was, on all occasions, made use of as an element of the consecration. The lodge is, therefore, consecrated to denote that henceforth it is to be set apart as an asylum sacred to the cultivation of the great masonic principles of Friendship, Morality, and Brotherly Love. Thenceforth it becomes to the conscientious Mason a place worthy of his reverence; and he is tempted, as he passes over its threshold, to repeat the command given to Moses: "Put off thy shoes from off thy feet, for the place whereon thou standest is holy ground."

The corn, wine, and oil are appropriately adopted as the Masonic elements of consecration, because of the symbolic signification which they present to the mind of the Mason. They are enumerated by David as among the greatest blessings which we receive from the bounty of Divine Providence. They were annually offered by the ancients as the first fruits, in a thank-offering for the gifts of the earth; and as representatives of "the corn of nourishment, the wine of refreshment, and the oil of joy," they symbolically instruct the Mason that to the Grand Master of the Universe he is indebted for the "health, peace, and plenty" that he enjoys.

After the consecration of the lodge, follows its dedication. This is a simple ceremony, and principally consists in the pronunciation of a formula of words by which the lodge is declared to be dedicated to the holy Saints John, followed by an invocation that "every Brother may revere their character and imitate their virtues."

Masonic tradition tells us that our ancient Brethren dedicated their lodges to King Solomon, because he was their first Most Excellent Grand Master; but that modern Masons dedicate theirs to St. John the Baptist and St. John the Evangelist, because they were two eminent patrons of Masonry. A more appropriate selection of patrons to whom to dedicate the lodge, could not easily have been made; since St. John the Baptist, by announcing the approach of Christ, and by the mystical ablution to which he subjected his proselytes, and which was afterwards adopted in the ceremony of initiation into Christianity, might well be considered as the Grand Hierophant of the Church; while the mysterious and emblematic nature of the Apocalypse assimilated the mode of teaching adopted by St. John the Evangelist to that practiced by the fraternity. Our Jewish Brethren usually dedicate their lodges to King Solomon, thus retaining their ancient patron, although they thereby lose the benefit of that portion of the Lectures which refers to the "lines parallel." The Grand Lodge of England, at the union in 1813, agreed to dedicate to Solomon and Moses, applying the parallels to the framer of the tabernacle and the builder of the temple; but they have no warranty for this in ancient usage, and it is unfortunately not the only innovation on the ancient landmarks that that Grand Lodge has lately permitted.

The ceremony of dedication, like that of consecration, finds its archetype in the remotest antiquity. The Hebrews made no use of any new thing until they had first solemnly dedicated it. This ceremony was performed in relation even to private houses, as we may learn from the book of Deuteronomy.[30] The 30th Psalm is a song said to have been made by David on the dedication of the altar which he erected on the threshing-floor of Ornan the Jebusite, after the grievous plague which had nearly devastated the kingdom. Solomon, it will be recollected, dedicated the temple with solemn ceremonies, prayers, and thank-offerings. The ceremony of dedication is, indeed, alluded to in various portions of the Scriptures.

Selden[31] says that among the Jews sacred things were both dedicated and consecrated; but that profane things, such as private houses, etc., were simply dedicated, without consecration. The same writer informs us that the Pagans borrowed the custom of consecrating and dedicating their sacred edifices, altars, and images, from the Hebrews.

The Lodge having been thus consecrated to the solemn objects of Freemasonry, and dedicated to the patrons of the institution, it is at length prepared to be constituted. The ceremony of constitution is then performed by the Grand Master, who, rising from his seat, pronounces the following formulary of constitution:

"In the name of the most Worshipful Grand Lodge, I now constitute and form you, my beloved Brethren, into a regular lodge of Free and Accepted Masons. From this time forth, I empower you to meet as a regular lodge, constituted in conformity to the rites of our Order, and the charges of our ancient and honorable fraternity;—and may the Supreme Architect of the Universe prosper, direct, and counsel you, in all your doings."

This ceremony places the lodge among the registered lodges of the jurisdiction in which it is situated, and gives it a rank and standing and permanent existence that it did not have before. In one word, it has, by the consecration, dedication, and constitution, become what we technically term "a just and legally constituted lodge," and, as such, is entitled to certain rights and privileges, of which we shall hereafter speak. Still, however, although the lodge has been thus fully and completely organized, its officers have as yet no legal existence. To give them this, it is necessary that they be inducted into their respective offices, and each officer solemnly bound to the faithful performance of the duties he has undertaken to discharge. This constitutes the ceremony of installation. The Worshipful Master of the new lodge is required publicly to submit to the ancient charges; and then all, except Past Masters, having retired, he is invested with the Past Master's degree, and inducted into the oriental chair of King Solomon. The Brethren are then introduced, and due homage is paid to their new Master, after which the other officers are obligated to the faithful discharge of their respective trusts, invested with their insignia of office, and receive the appropriate charge. This ceremony must be repeated at every annual election and change of officers.

The ancient rule was, that when the Grand Master and his officers attended to constitute a new lodge, the Deputy Grand Master invested the new Master, the Grand Wardens invested the new Wardens, and the Grand Treasurer and Grand Secretary invested the Treasurer and Secretary. But this regulation has become obsolete, and the whole installation and investiture are now performed by the Grand Master. On the occasion of subsequent installations, the retiring Master installs his successor; and the latter installs his subordinate officers.

The ceremony of installation is derived from the ancient custom of inauguration, of which we find repeated instances in the sacred as well as profane writings. Aaron was inaugurated, or installed, by the unction of oil, and placing on him the vestments of the High Priest; and every succeeding High Priest was in like manner installed, before he was considered competent to discharge the duties of his office. Among the Romans, augurs, priests, kings, and, in the times of the republic, consuls were always inaugurated or installed. And hence, Cicero, who was an augur, speaking of Hortensius, says, "it was he who installed me as a member of the college of augurs, so that I was bound by the constitution of the order to respect and honour him as a parent."[32] The object and intention of the ancient inauguration and the Masonic installation are precisely the same, namely, that of setting apart and consecrating a person to the duties of a certain office.

The ceremonies, thus briefly described, were not always necessary to legalize a congregation of Masons. Until the year 1717, the custom of confining the privileges of Masonry, by a warrant of constitution, to certain individuals, was wholly unknown. Previous to that time, a requisite number of Master Masons were authorized by the ancient charges to congregate together, temporarily, at their own discretion, and as best suited their convenience, and then and there to open and hold lodges and make Masons; making, however, their return, and paying their tribute to the General Assembly, to which all the fraternity annually repaired, and by whose awards the craft were governed.

Preston, speaking of this ancient privilege, says: "A sufficient number of Masons met together within a certain district, with the consent of the sheriff or chief magistrate of the place, were empowered at this time to make Masons and practice the rights of Masonry, without a warrant of constitution." This privilege, Preston says, was inherent in them as individuals, and continued to be enjoyed by the old lodges, which formed the Grand Lodge in 1717, as long as they were in existence.

But on the 24th June, 1717, the Grand Lodge of England adopted the following regulation: "That the privilege of assembling as Masons, which had hitherto been unlimited, should be vested in certain lodges or assemblies of Masons, convened in certain places; and that every lodge to be hereafter convened, except the four old lodges at this time existing, should be legally authorized to act by a warrant from the Grand Master for the time being, granted to certain individuals by petition, with the consent and approbation of the Grand Lodge in communication; and that, without such warrant, no lodge should be hereafter deemed regular or constitutional."

This regulation has ever since continued in force, and it is the original law under which warrants of constitution are now granted by Grand Lodges for the organization of their subordinates.

Chapter II.

Of Lodges under Dispensation.

It is evident, from what has already been said, that there are two kinds of lodges, each regular in itself, but each peculiar and distinct in its character. There are lodges working under a dispensation, and lodges working under a warrant of constitution. Each of these will require a separate consideration. The former will be the subject of the present chapter.

A lodge working under a dispensation is a merely temporary body, originated for a special purpose, and is therefore possessed of very circumscribed powers. The dispensation, or authority under which it acts, expressly specifies that the persons to whom it is given are allowed to congregate that they may "admit, enter, pass, and raise Freemasons;" no other powers are conferred either by words or implication, and, indeed, sometimes the dispensation states, that that congregation is to be "with the sole intent and view, that the Brethren so congregated, admitted, entered, and made, when they become a sufficient number, may be duly warranted and constituted for being and holding a regular lodge."[33]

A lodge under dispensation is simply the creature of the Grand Master. To him it is indebted for its existence, and on his will depends the duration of that existence. He may at any time revoke the dispensation, and the dissolution of the lodge would be the instant result. Hence a lodge working under a dispensation can scarcely, with strict technical propriety, be called a lodge; it is, more properly speaking, a congregation of Masons, acting as the proxy of the Grand Master.

With these views of the origin and character of lodges under dispensation, we will be better prepared to understand the nature and extent of the powers which they possess.

A lodge under dispensation can make no bye-laws. It is governed, during its temporary existence, by the general Constitutions of the Order and the rules and regulations of the Grand Lodge in whose jurisdiction it is situated. In fact, as the bye-laws of no lodge are operative until they are confirmed by the Grand Lodge, and as a lodge working under a dispensation ceases to exist as such as soon as the Grand Lodge meets, it is evident that it would be absurd to frame a code of laws which would have no efficacy, for want of proper confirmation, and which, when the time and opportunity for confirmation had arrived, would be needless, as the society for which they were framed would then have no legal existence—a new body (the warranted lodge) having taken its place.

A lodge under dispensation cannot elect officers. The Master and Wardens are nominated by the Brethren, and, if this nomination is approved, they are appointed by the Grand Master. In giving them permission to meet and make Masons, he gave them no power to do anything else. A dispensation is itself a setting aside of the law, and an exception to a general principle; it must, therefore, be construed literally. What is not granted in express terms, is not granted at all. And, therefore, as nothing is said of the election of officers, no such election can be held. The Master may, however, and always does for convenience, appoint a competent Brother to keep a record of the proceedings; but this is a temporary appointment, at the pleasure of the Master, whose deputy or assistant he is; for the Grand Lodge looks only to the Master for the records, and the office is not legally recognized. In like manner, he may depute a trusty Brother to take charge of the funds, and must, of course, from time to time, appoint the deacons and tiler for the necessary working of the lodge.

As there can be no election, neither can there be any installation, which, of course, always presumes a previous election for a determinate period. Besides, the installation of officers is a part of the ceremony of constitution, and therefore not even the Master and Wardens of a lodge under dispensation are entitled to be thus solemnly inducted into office.

A lodge under dispensation can elect no members. The Master and Wardens, who are named in the dispensation, are, in point of fact, the only persons recognized as constituting the lodge. To them is granted the privilege, as proxies of the Grand Master, of making Masons; and for this purpose they are authorized to congregate a sufficient number of Brethren to assist them in the ceremonies. But neither the Master and Wardens, nor the Brethren, thus congregated have received any power of electing members. Nor are the persons made in a lodge under dispensation, to be considered as members of the lodge; for, as has already been shown, they have none of the rights and privileges which attach to membership—they can neither make bye-laws nor elect officers. They, however, become members of the lodge as soon as it receives its warrant of constitution.

Chapter III.

Of Lodges Working under a Warrant of Constitution.

Section I.

Of the Powers and Rights of a Lodge.

In respect to the powers and privileges possessed by a lodge working under a warrant of constitution, we may say, as a general principle, that whatever it does possess is inherent in it—nothing has been delegated by either the Grand Master or the Grand Lodge—but that all its rights and powers are derived originally from the ancient regulations, made before the existence of Grand Lodges, and that what it does not possess, are the powers which were conceded by its predecessors to the Grand Lodge. This is evident from the history of warrants of constitution, the authority under which subordinate lodges act. The practice of applying by petition to the Grand Master or the Grand Lodge, for a warrant to meet as a regular lodge, commenced in the year 1718. Previous to that time, Freemasons were empowered by inherent privileges, vested, from time immemorial, in the whole fraternity, to meet as occasion might require, under the direction of some able architect; and the proceedings of these meetings, being approved by a majority of the Brethren convened at another lodge in the same district, were deemed constitutional.[34] But in 1718, a year after the formation of the Grand Lodge of England, this power of meeting *ad libitum* was resigned into the hands of that body, and it was then agreed that no lodges should thereafter meet, unless authorized so to do by a warrant from the Grand Master, and with the consent of the Grand Lodge. But as a memorial that this abandonment of the ancient right was entirely voluntary, it was at the same time resolved that this inherent privilege should continue to be enjoyed by the four old lodges who formed the Grand Lodge. And, still more effectually to secure the reserved rights of the lodges, it was also solemnly determined, that while the Grand Lodge possesses the inherent right of making new regulations for the good of the fraternity, provided that the *old landmarks be carefully preserved*, yet that these regulations, to be of force, must be proposed and agreed to at the third quarterly communication preceding the annual grand feast, and submitted to the perusal of all the Brethren, in writing, even of the youngest entered apprentice; "*the approbation and consent of the majority of all the Brethren present being absolutely necessary, to make the same binding and obligatory.*"[35]

The corollary from all this is clear. All the rights, powers, and privileges, not conceded, by express enactment of the fraternity, to the Grand Lodge, have been reserved to themselves. Subordinate lodges are the assemblies of the craft in their primary capacity, and the Grand Lodge is the Supreme Masonic Tribunal, only because it consists of and is constituted by a representation of these primary assemblies. And, therefore, as every act of the Grand Lodge is an act of the whole fraternity thus represented, each new regulation that may be made is not an assumption of authority on the part of the Grand Lodge, but a new concession on the part of the subordinate lodges.

This doctrine of the reserved rights of the lodges is very important, and should never be forgotten, because it affords much aid in the decision of many obscure points of masonic jurisprudence. The rule is, that any doubtful power exists and is inherent in the subordinate lodges, unless there is an express regulation conferring it on the Grand Lodge. With this preliminary view, we may proceed to investigate the nature and extent of these reserved powers of the subordinate lodges.

A lodge has the right of selecting its own members, with which the Grand Lodge cannot interfere. This is a right that the lodges have expressly reserved to themselves, and the stipulation is inserted in the "general regulations" in the following words:

"No man can be entered a Brother in any particular lodge, or admitted a member thereof, without the unanimous consent of all the members of that lodge then present, when the candidate is proposed, and when their consent is formally asked by the Master. They are to give their consent in their own prudent way, either virtually or in form, but with unanimity. Nor is this inherent privilege subject to a dispensation, because the members of a particular lodge are the best judges of it; and because, if a turbulent member should be imposed upon them, it might spoil their harmony, or hinder the freedom of their communication; or even break and disperse the lodge, which ought to be avoided by all true and faithful."[36]

But although a lodge has the inherent right to require unanimity in the election of a candidate, it is not necessarily restricted to such a degree of rigor.

A lodge has the right to elect its own officers. This right is guaranteed to it by the words of the Warrant of Constitution. Still the right is subject to certain restraining regulations. The election must be held at the proper time, which, according to the usage of Masonry, in most parts of the world, is on or immediately before the festival of St. John the Evangelist. The proper qualifications must be regarded. A member cannot be elected as Master, unless he has previously served as a Warden, except in the instance of a new lodge, or other case of emergency. Where both of the Wardens refuse promotion, where the presiding Master will not permit himself to be reelected, and where there is no Past Master who will consent to take the office, then, and then only, can a member be elected from the floor to preside over the lodge.

By the Constitutions of England, only the Master and Treasurer are elected officers.[37] The Wardens and all the other officers are appointed by the Master, who has not, however, the power of removal after appointment, except by consent of the lodge;[38] but American usage gives the election of all the officers, except the deacons, stewards, and, in some instances, the tiler, to the lodge.

As a consequence of the right of election, every lodge has the power of installing its officers, subject to the same regulations, in relation to time and qualifications, as given in the case of elections.

The Master must be installed by a Past Master,[39] but after his own installation he has the power to install the rest of the officers. The ceremony of installation is not a mere vain and idle one, but is productive of important results. Until the Master and Wardens of a lodge are installed, they cannot represent the lodge in the Grand Lodge, nor, if it be a new lodge, can it be recorded and recognized on the register of the Grand Lodge. No officer can permanently take possession of the office to which he has been elected, until he has been duly installed.[40] The rule of the craft is, that the old officer holds on until his successor is installed, and this rule is of universal application to officers of every grade, from the Tiler of a subordinate lodge, to the Grand Master of Masons.

Every lodge that has been duly constituted, and its officers installed, is entitled to be represented in the Grand Lodge, and to form, indeed, a constituent part of that body.[41] The representatives of a lodge are its Master and two Wardens.[42] This character of representation was established in 1718, when the four old lodges, which organized the Grand Lodge of England, agreed "to extend their patronage to every lodge which should hereafter be constituted by the Grand Lodge, according to the new regulations of the society; and while such lodges acted in conformity to the ancient constitutions of the Order, to admit their Masters and Wardens to share with them all the privileges of the Grand Lodge, excepting precedence of rank."[43] Formerly all Master Masons were permitted to sit in the Grand Lodge, or, as it was then called, the General Assembly, and represent their lodge; and therefore this restricting the representation to the three superior officers was, in fact, a concession of the craft. This regulation is still generally observed; but I regret to see a few Grand Lodges in this country innovating on the usage, and still further confining the representation to the Masters alone.

The Master and Wardens are not merely in name the representatives of the lodge, but are bound, on all questions that come before the Grand Lodge, truly to represent their lodge, and vote according to its instructions. This doctrine is expressly laid down in the General Regulations, in the following words: "The majority of every particular lodge, when congregated, not else, shall have the privilege of giving instructions to their Master and Wardens, before the meeting of the Grand Chapter, or Quarterly Communication; because the said officers are their representatives, and are supposed to speak the sentiments of their Brethren at the said Grand Lodge."[44]

Every lodge has the power to frame bye-laws for its own government, provided they are not contrary to, nor inconsistent with, the general regulations of the Grand Lodge; nor the landmarks of the order.[45] But these bye-laws will not be valid, until they are submitted to and approved by the Grand Lodge. And this is the case, also, with every subsequent alteration of them, which must in like manner be submitted to the Grand Lodge for its approval.

A lodge has the right of suspending or excluding a member from his membership in the lodge; but it has no power to expel him from the rights and privileges of Masonry, except with the consent of the Grand Lodge. A subordinate lodge tries its delinquent member, and, if guilty, declares him expelled; but the sentence is of no force until the Grand Lodge, under whose jurisdiction it is working, has confirmed it. And it is optional with the Grand Lodge to do so, or, as is frequently done, to reverse the decision and reinstate the Brother. Some of the lodges in this country claim the right to expel, independently of the action of the Grand Lodge; but the claim is not valid. The very fact that an expulsion is a penalty, affecting the general relations of the punished party with the whole fraternity, proves that its exercise never could, with propriety, be intrusted to a body so circumscribed in its authority as a subordinate lodge. Accordingly, the general practice of the fraternity is opposed to it; and therefore all expulsions are reported to the Grand Lodge, not merely as matters of information, but that they may be confirmed by that body. The English Constitutions are explicit on this subject. "In the Grand Lodge alone," they declare, "resides the power of erasing lodges and expelling Brethren from the craft, a power which it ought not to delegate to any subordinate authority in England." They allow, however, a subordinate lodge to *exclude* a member from the lodge; in which case he is furnished with a certificate of the circumstances of his exclusion, and then may join any other lodge that will accept him, after being made acquainted with the fact of his exclusion, and its cause. This usage has not been adopted in this country.

A lodge has a right to levy such annual contribution for membership as the majority of the Brethren see fit. This is entirely a matter of contract, with which the Grand Lodge, or the craft in general, have nothing to do. It is, indeed, a modern usage, unknown to the fraternity of former times, and was instituted for the convenience and support of the private lodges.

A lodge is entitled to select a name for itself, to be, however, approved by the Grand Lodge.[46] But the Grand Lodge alone has the power of designating the number by which the lodge shall be distinguished. By its number alone is every lodge recognized in the register of the Grand Lodge, and according to their numbers is the precedence of the lodges regulated.

Finally, a lodge has certain rights in relation to its Warrant of Constitution. This instrument having been granted by the Grand Lodge, can be revoked by no other authority. The Grand Master, therefore, has no power, as he has in the case of a lodge under dispensation, to withdraw its Warrant, except temporarily, until the next meeting of the Grand Lodge. Nor is it in the power of even the majority of the lodge, by any act of their own, to resign the Warrant. For it has been laid down as a law, that if the majority of the lodge should determine to quit the lodge, or to resign their warrant, such action would be of no efficacy, because the Warrant of Constitution, and the power of assembling, would remain with the rest of the members, who adhere to their allegiance.[47] But if all the members withdraw themselves, their Warrant ceases and becomes extinct. If the conduct of a lodge has been such as clearly to forfeit its charter, the Grand Lodge alone can decide that question and pronounce the forfeiture.

Section II.

Of the Duties of a Lodge.

So far in relation to the rights and privileges of subordinate lodges. But there are certain duties and obligations equally binding upon these bodies, and certain powers, in the exercise of which they are restricted. These will next engage our attention.

The first great duty, not only of every lodge, but of every Mason, is to see that the landmarks of the Order shall never be impaired. The General Regulations of Masonry—to which every Master, at his installation, is bound to acknowledge his submission—declare that "it is not in the power of any man, or body of men, to make innovations in the body of Masonry." And, hence, no lodge, without violating all the implied and express obligations into which it has entered, can, in any manner, alter or amend the work, lectures, and ceremonies of the institution. As its members have received the ritual from their predecessors, so are they bound to transmit it, unchanged, in the slightest degree, to their successors. In the Grand Lodge, alone, resides the power of enacting new regulations; but, even *it* must be careful that, in every such regulation, the landmarks are preserved. When, therefore, we hear young and inexperienced Masters speak of making improvements (as they arrogantly call them) upon the old lectures or ceremonies, we may be sure that such Masters either know nothing of the duties they owe to the craft, or are willfully forgetful of the solemn obligation which they have contracted. Some may suppose that the ancient ritual of the Order is imperfect, and requires amendment. One may think that the ceremonies are too simple, and wish to increase them; another, that they are too complicated, and desire to simplify them; one may be displeased with the antiquated language; another, with the character of the traditions; a third, with something else. But, the rule is imperative and absolute, that no change can or must be made to gratify individual taste. As the Barons of England, once, with unanimous voice, exclaimed, "Nolumus leges Angliæ mutare!" so do all good Masons respond to every attempt at innovation, "We are unwilling to alter the customs of Freemasonry."

In relation to the election of officers, a subordinate lodge is allowed to exercise no discretion. The names and duties of these officers are prescribed, partly by the landmarks or the ancient constitutions, and partly by the regulations of various Grand Lodges. While the landmarks are preserved, a Grand Lodge may add to the list of officers as it pleases; and whatever may be its regulation, the subordinate lodges are bound to obey it; nor can any such lodge create new offices nor abolish old ones without the consent of the Grand Lodge.

Lodges are also bound to elect their officers at a time which is always determined; not by the subordinate, but by the Grand Lodge. Nor can a lodge anticipate or postpone it unless by a dispensation from the Grand Master.

No lodge can, at an extra meeting, alter or amend the proceedings of a regular meeting. If such were not the rule, an unworthy Master might, by stealth, convoke an extra meeting of a part of his lodge, and, by expunging or altering the proceedings of the previous regular meeting, or any particular part of them, annul any measures or resolutions that were not consonant with his peculiar views.

No lodge can interfere with the work or business of any other lodge, without its permission. This is an old regulation, founded on those principles of comity and brotherly love that should exist among all Masons. It is declared in the manuscript charges, written in the reign of James II., and in the possession of the Lodge of Antiquity, at London, that "no Master or Fellow shall supplant others of their work; that is to say, that, if he hath taken a work, or else stand Master of any work, that he shall not put him out, unless he be unable of cunning to make an end of his work." And, hence, no lodge can pass or raise a candidate who was initiated, or initiate one who was rejected, in another lodge. "It would be highly improper," says the Ahiman Rezon, "in any lodge, to confer a degree on a Brother who is not of their house-hold; for, every lodge ought to be competent to manage their own business, and are the best judges of the qualifications of their own members."

I do not intend, at the present time, to investigate the qualifications of candidates—as that subject will, in itself, afford ample materials for a future investigation; but, it is necessary that I should say something of the restrictions under which every lodge labors in respect to the admission of persons applying for degrees.

In the first place, no lodge can initiate a candidate, "without previous notice, and due examination into his character; and not unless his petition has been read at one regular meeting and acted on at another." This is in accordance with the ancient regulations; but, an exception to it is allowed in the case of an emergency, when the lodge may read the petition for admission, and, if the applicant is well recommended, may proceed at once to elect and initiate him. In some jurisdictions, the nature of the emergency must be stated to the Grand Master, who, if he approves, will grant a dispensation; but, in others, the Master, or Master and Wardens, are permitted to be competent judges, and may proceed to elect and initiate, without such dispensation. The Grand Lodge of South Carolina adheres to the former custom, and that of England to the latter.

Another regulation is, that no lodge can confer more than two degrees, at one communication, on the same candidate. The Grand Lodge of England is still more stringent on this subject, and declares that "no candidate shall be permitted to receive more than one degree, on the same day; nor shall a higher degree in Masonry be conferred on any Brother at a less interval than four weeks from his receiving a previous degree, nor until he has passed an examination, in open lodge, in that degree." This rule is also in force in South Carolina and several other of the American jurisdictions. But, the law which forbids the whole three degrees of Ancient Craft Masonry to be conferred, at the same communication, on one candidate, is universal in its application, and, as such, may be deemed one of the ancient landmarks of the Order.

There is another rule, which seems to be of universal extent, and is, indeed, contained in the General Regulations of 1767, to the following effect: "No lodge shall make more than five new Brothers at one and the same time, without an urgent necessity."

All lodges are bound to hold their meetings at least once in every calendar month; and every lodge neglecting so to do for one year, thereby forfeits its warrant of constitution.

The subject of the removal of lodges is the last thing that shall engage our attention. Here the ancient regulations of the craft have adopted many guards to prevent the capricious or improper removal of a lodge from its regular place of meeting. In the first place, no lodge can be removed from the town in which it is situated, to any other place, without the consent of the Grand Lodge. But, a lodge may remove from one part of the town to another, with the consent of the members, under the following restrictions: The removal cannot be made without the Master's knowledge; nor can any motion, for that purpose, be presented in his absence. When such a motion is made, and properly seconded, the Master will order summonses to every member, specifying the business, and appointing a day for considering and determining the affair. And if then a majority of the lodge, with the Master, or two-thirds, without him, consent to the removal, it shall take place; but notice thereof must be sent, at once, to the Grand Lodge. The General Regulations of 1767 further declare, that such removal must be approved by the Grand Master. I suppose that where the removal of the lodge was only a matter of convenience to the members, the Grand Lodge would hardly interfere, but leave the whole subject to their discretion; but, where the removal would be calculated to affect the interests of the lodge, or of the fraternity—as in the case of a removal to a house of bad reputation, or to a place of evident insecurity—I have no doubt that the Grand Lodge, as the conservator of the character and safety of the institution, would have a right to interpose its authority, and prevent the improper removal.

I have thus treated, as concisely as the important nature of the subjects would permit, of the powers, privileges, duties, and obligations of lodges, and have endeavored to embrace, within the limits of the discussion, all those prominent principles of the Order, which, as they affect the character and operations of the craft in their primary assemblies, may properly be referred to the Law of Subordinate Lodges.

Chapter IV.

Of the Officers of a Subordinate Lodge.

Section I.

Of the Officers in General.

Four officers, at least, the ancient customs of the craft require in every lodge; and they are consequently found throughout the globe. These are the Master, the two Wardens, and the Tiler. Almost equally universal are the offices of Treasurer, Secretary, and two Deacons. But, besides these, there may be additional officers appointed by different Grand Lodges. The Grand Lodge of England, for instance, requires the appointment of an officer, called the "Inner Guard." The Grand Orient of France has prescribed a variety of officers, which are unknown to English and American Masonry. The Grand Lodges of England and South Carolina direct that two Stewards shall be appointed, while some other Grand Lodges make no such requisition. Ancient usage seems to have recognized the following officers of a subordinate lodge: the Master, two Wardens, Treasurer, Secretary, two Deacons, two Stewards, and Tiler; and I shall therefore treat of the duties and powers of these officers only, in the course of the present chapter.

The officers of a lodge are elected annually. In this country, the election takes place on the festival of St. John the Evangelist, or at the meeting immediately previous; but, in this latter case, the duties of the offices do not commence until St. John's day, which may, therefore, be considered as the beginning of the masonic year.

Dalcho lays down the rule, that "no Freemason chosen into any office can refuse to serve (unless he has before filled the same office), without incurring the penalties established by the bye-laws." Undoubtedly a lodge may enact such a regulation, and affix any reasonable penalty; but I am not aware of any ancient regulation which makes it incumbent on subordinate lodges to do so.

If any of the subordinate officers, except the Master and Wardens, die, or be removed from office, during the year, the lodge may, under the authority of a dispensation from the Grand Master, enter into an election to supply the vacancy. But in the case of the death or removal of the Master or either of the Wardens, no election can be held to supply the vacancy, even by dispensation, for reasons which will appear when I come to treat of those offices.

No officer can resign his office after he has been installed. Every officer is elected for twelve months, and at his installation solemnly promises to perform the duties of that office until the next regular day of election; and hence the lodge cannot permit him, by a resignation, to violate his obligation of office.

Another rule is, that every officer holds on to his office until his successor has been installed. It is the installation, and not the election, which puts an officer into possession; and the faithful management of the affairs of Masonry requires, that between the election and installation of his successor, the predecessor shall not vacate the office, but continue to discharge its duties.

An office can be vacated only by death, permanent removal from the jurisdiction, or expulsion. Suspension does not vacate, but only suspends the performance of the duties of the office, which must then be temporarily discharged by some other person, to be appointed from time to time; for, as soon as the suspended officer is restored, he resumes the dignities and duties of his office.

Section II.

Of the Worshipful Master.

This is probably the most important office in the whole system of Masonry, as, upon the intelligence, skill, and fidelity of the Masters of our lodges, the entire institution is dependent for its prosperity. It is an office which is charged with heavy responsibilities, and, as a just consequence, is accompanied by the investiture of many important powers.

A necessary qualification of the Master of a lodge is, that he must have previously served in the office of a Warden.[48] This qualification is sometimes dispensed with in the case of new lodges, or where no member of an old lodge, who has served as a Warden, will accept the office of Master. But it is not necessary that he should have served as a Warden in the lodge of which he is proposed to be elected Master. The discharge of the duties of a Warden, by regular election and installation in any other lodge, and at any former period, will be a sufficient qualification.

One of the most important duties of the Master of a lodge is, to see that the edicts and regulations of the Grand Lodge are obeyed by his Brethren, and that his officers faithfully discharge their duties.

The Master has particularly in charge the warrant of Constitution, which must always be present in his lodge, when opened.

The Master has a right to call a special meeting of his lodge whenever he pleases, and is the sole judge of any emergency which may require such special communication.

He has, also, the right of closing his lodge at any hour that he may deem expedient, notwithstanding the whole business of the evening may not have been transacted. This regulation arises from the unwritten law of Masonry. As the Master is responsible to the Grand Lodge for the fidelity of the work done in his lodge, and as the whole of the labor is, therefore, performed under his superintendence, it follows that, to enable him to discharge this responsibility, he must be invested with the power of commencing, of continuing, or of suspending labor at such time as he may, in his wisdom, deem to be the most advantageous to the edifice of Masonry.

It follows from this rule that a question of adjournment cannot be entertained in a lodge. The adoption of a resolution to adjourn, would involve the necessity of the Master to obey it. The power, therefore, of controlling the work, would be taken out of his hands and placed in those of the members, which would be in direct conflict with the duties imposed upon him by the ritual. The doctrine that a lodge cannot adjourn, but must be closed or called off at the pleasure of the Master, appears now to me to be very generally admitted.

The Master and his two Wardens constitute the representatives of the lodge in the Grand Lodge, and it is his duty to attend the communications of that body "on all convenient occasions."[49] When there, he is faithfully to represent his lodge, and on all questions discussed, to obey its instructions, voting in every case rather against his own convictions than against the expressed wish of his lodge.

The Master presides not only over the symbolic work of the lodge, but also over its business deliberations, and in either case his decisions are reversible only by the Grand Lodge. There can be no appeal from his decision, on any question, to the lodge. He is supreme in his lodge, so far as the lodge is concerned, being amenable for his conduct in the government of it, not to its members, but to the Grrand Lodge alone. If an appeal were proposed, it would be his duty, for the preservation of discipline, to refuse to put the question. If a member is aggrieved by the conduct or decisions of the Master, he has his redress by an appeal to the Grrand Lodge, which will, of course, see that the Master does not rule his lodge "in an unjust or arbitrary manner." But such a thing as an appeal from the Master of the lodge to its members is unknown in Masonry.

This may, at first sight, appear to be giving too despotic power to the Master. But a slight reflection will convince any one that there can be but little danger of oppression from one so guarded and controlled as a Master is, by the sacred obligations of his office, and the supervision of the Grand Lodge, while the placing in the hands of the craft so powerful, and at times, and with bad spirits, so annoying a privilege as that of immediate appeal, would necessarily tend to impair the energies and lessen the dignity of the Master, while it would be subversive of that spirit of discipline which pervades every part of the institution, and to which it is mainly indebted for its prosperity and perpetuity.

The ancient charges rehearsed at the installation of a Master, prescribe the various moral qualifications which are required in the aspirant for that elevated and responsible office. He is to be a good man, and peaceable citizen or subject, a respecter of the laws, and a lover of his Brethren—cultivating the social virtues and promoting the general good of society as well as of his own Order.

Within the last few years, the standard of intellectual qualifications has been greatly elevated. And it is now admitted that the Master of a lodge, to do justice to the exalted office which he holds, to the craft over whom he presides, and to the candidates whom he is to instruct, should be not only a man of irreproachable moral character, but also of expanded intellect and liberal education. Still, as there is no express law upon this subject, the selection of a Master and the determination of his qualifications must be left to the judgment and good sense of the members.

Section III.

Of the Wardens.

The Senior and Junior Warden are the assistants of the Master in the government of the lodge. They are selected from among the members on the floor, the possession of a previous office not being, as in the case of the Master, a necessary qualification for election. In England they are appointed by the Master, but in this country they are universally elected by the lodge.

During the temporary absence of the Master the Senior Warden has the right of presiding, though he may, and often does by courtesy, invite a Past Master to assume the chair. In like manner, in the absence of both Master and Senior Warden, the Junior Warden will preside, and competent Brethren will by him be appointed to fill the vacant seats of the Wardens. But if the Master and Junior Warden be present, and the Senior Warden be absent, the Junior Warden does not occupy the West, but retains his own station, the Master appointing some Brother to occupy the station of the Senior Warden. For the Junior Warden succeeds by law only to the office of Master, and, unless that office be vacant, he is bound to fulfill the duties of the office to which he has been obligated.

In case of the death, removal from the jurisdiction, or expulsion of the Master, by the Grand Lodge, no election can be held until the constitutional period. The Senior Warden will take the Master's place and preside over the lodge, while his seat will be temporarily filled from time to time by appointment. The Senior Warden being in fact still in existence, and only discharging one of the highest duties of his office, that of presiding in the absence of the Master, his office cannot be declared vacant and there can be no election for it. In such case, the Junior Warden, for the reason already assigned, will continue at his own station in the South.

In case of the death, removal, or expulsion of both Master and Senior Warden, the Junior Warden will discharge the duties of the Mastership and make temporary appointments of both Wardens. It must always be remembered that the Wardens succeed according to seniority to the office of Master when vacant, but that neither can legally discharge the duties of the other. It must also be remembered that when a Warden succeeds to the government of the lodge, he does not become the Master; he is still only a Warden discharging the functions of a higher vacated station, as one of the expressed duties of his own office. A recollection of these distinctions will enable us to avoid much embarrassment in the consideration of all the questions incident to this subject. If the Master be present, the Wardens assist him in the government of the lodge. The Senior Warden presides over the craft while at labor, and the Junior when they are in refreshment. Formerly the examination of visitors was intrusted to the Junior Warden, but this duty is now more appropriately performed by the Stewards or a special committee appointed for that purpose.

The Senior Warden has the appointment of the Senior Deacon, and the Junior Warden that of the Stewards.

Section IV.

Of the Treasurer.

Of so much importance is this office deemed, that in English Lodges, while all the other officers are appointed by the Master, the Treasurer alone is elected by the lodge. It is, however, singular, that in the ritual of installation, Preston furnishes no address to the Treasurer on his investiture. Webb, however, has supplied the omission, and the charge given in his work to this officer, on the night of his installation, having been universally acknowledged and adopted by the craft in this country, will furnish us with the most important points of the law in relation to his duties.

It is, then, in the first place, the duty of the Treasurer "to receive all moneys from the hands of the Secretary." The Treasurer is only the banker of the lodge. All fees for initiation, arrearages of members, and all other dues to the lodge, should be first received by the Secretary, and paid immediately over to the Treasurer for safe keeping.

The keeping of just and regular accounts is another duty presented to the Treasurer. As soon as he has received an amount of money from the Secretary, he should transfer the account of it to his books. By this means, the Secretary and Treasurer become mutual checks upon each other, and the safety of the funds of the lodge is secured.

The Treasurer is not only the banker, but also the disbursing officer of the lodge; but he is directed to pay no money except with the consent of the lodge and on the order of the Worshipful Master. It seems to me, therefore, that every warrant drawn on him should be signed by the Master, and the action of the lodge attested by the counter-signature of the Secretary.

It is usual, in consequence of the great responsibility of the Treasurer, to select some Brother of worldly substance for the office; and still further to insure the safety of the funds, by exacting from him a bond, with sufficient security. He sometimes receives a per centage, or a fixed salary, for his services.

Section V.

Of the Secretary.

It is the duty of the Secretary to record all the proceedings of the lodge, "which may be committed to paper;" to conduct the correspondence of the lodge, and to receive all moneys due the lodge from any source whatsoever. He is, therefore, the recording, corresponding, and receiving officer of the lodge. By receiving the moneys due to the lodge in the first place, and then paying them over to the Treasurer, he becomes, as I have already observed, a check upon that officer.

In view of the many laborious duties which devolve upon him, the Secretary, in many lodges, receives a compensation for his services.

Should the Treasurer or Secretary die or be expelled, there is no doubt that an election for a successor, to fill the unexpired term, may be held by dispensation from the Grand Master. But the incompetency of either of these officers to perform his duties, by reason of the infirmity of sickness or removal from the seat of the lodge, will not, I think, authorize such an election. Because the original officer may recover from his infirmity, or return to his residence, and, in either case, having been elected and installed for one year, he must remain the Secretary or Treasurer until the expiration of the period for which he had been so elected and installed, and, therefore, on his recovery or his return, is entitled to resume all the prerogatives and functions of his office. The case of death, or of expulsion, which is, in fact, masonic death, is different, because all the rights possessed during life cease *ex necessitate rei*, and forever lapse at the time of the said physical or masonic death; and in the latter case, a restoration to all the rights and privileges of Masonry would not restore the party to any office which he had held at the time of his expulsion.

Section VI.

Of the Deacons.

In every lodge there are two of these officers—a Senior and a Junior Deacon. They are not elected, but appointed; the former by the Master, and the latter by the Senior Warden.

The duties of these officers are many and important; but they are so well defined in the ritual as to require no further consideration in this place.

The only question that here invites our examination is, whether the Deacons, as appointed officers, are removable at the pleasure of the officers who appointed them; or, whether they retain their offices, like the Master and Wardens, until the expiration of the year. Masonic authorities are silent on this subject; but, basing my judgment upon analogy, I am inclined to think that they are not removable: all the officers of a lodge are chosen to serve for one year, or, from one festival of St. John the Evangelist to the succeeding one. This has been the invariable usage in all lodges, and neither in the monitorial ceremonies of installation, nor in any rules or regulations which I have seen, is any exception to this usage made in respect to Deacons. The written as well as the oral law of Masonry being silent on this subject, we are bound to give them the benefit of this silence, and place them in the same favorable position as that occupied by the superior officers, who, we know, by express law are entitled to occupy their stations for one year. Moreover, the power of removal is too important to be exercised except under the sanction of an expressed law, and is contrary to the whole spirit of Masonry, which, while it invests a presiding officer with the largest extent of prerogative, is equally careful of the rights of the youngest member of the fraternity.

From these reasons I am compelled to believe that the Deacons, although originally appointed by the Master and Senior Warden, are not removable by either, but retain their offices until the expiration of the year.

Section VII.

Of the Stewards.

The Stewards, who are two in number, are appointed by the Junior Warden, and sit on the right and left of him in the lodge. Their original duties were, "to assist in the collection of dues and subscriptions; to keep an account of the lodge expenses; to see that the tables are properly furnished at refreshment, and that every Brother is suitably provided for." They are also considered as the assistants of the Deacons in the discharge of their duties, and, lately, some lodges are beginning to confide to them the important trusts of a standing committee for the examination of visitors and the preparation of candidates.

What has been said in relation to the removal of the Deacons in the preceding section, is equally applicable to the Stewards.

Section VIII.

Of the Tiler.

This is an office of great importance, and must, from the peculiar nature of our institution, have existed from its very beginning. No lodge could ever have been opened until a Tiler was appointed, and stationed to guard its portals from the approach of "cowans and eavesdroppers." The qualifications requisite for the office of a Tiler are, that he must be "a worthy Master Mason." An Entered Apprentice, or a Fellow Craft, cannot tile a lodge, even though it be opened in his own degree. To none but Master Masons can this important duty of guardianship be intrusted. The Tiler is not necessarily a member of the lodge which he tiles. There is no regulation requiring this qualification. In fact, in large cities, one Brother often acts as the Tiler of several lodges. If, however, he is a member of the lodge, his office does not deprive him of the rights of membership, and in ballotings for candidates, election of officers, or other important questions, he is entitled to exercise his privilege of voting, in which case the Junior Deacon will temporarily occupy his station, while he enters the lodge to deposit his ballot. This appears to be the general usage of the craft in this country.

The Tiler is sometimes elected by the lodge, and sometimes appointed by the Master. It seems generally to be admitted that he may be removed from office for misconduct or neglect of duty, by the lodge, if he has been elected, and by the Master, if he has been appointed.

Chapter V.

Of Rules of Order.

The safety of the minority, the preservation of harmony, and the dispatch of business, all require that there should be, in every well-regulated society, some rules and forms for the government of their proceedings, and, as has been justly observed by an able writer on parliamentary law, "whether these forms be in all cases the most rational or not, is really not of so great importance; for it is much more material that there should be a rule to go by, than what that rule is."[50] By common consent, the rules established for the government of Parliament in England, and of Congress in the United States, and which are known collectively under the name of "Parliamentary Law," have been adopted for the regulation of all deliberative bodies, whether of a public or private nature. But lodges of Freemasons differ so much in their organization and character from other societies, that this law will, in very few cases, be found applicable; and, indeed, in many positively inapplicable to them. The rules, therefore, for the government of masonic lodges are in general to be deduced from the usages of the Order, from traditional or written authority, and where both of them are silent, from analogy to the character of the institution. To each of these sources, therefore, I shall apply, in the course of the present chapter, and in some few instances, where the parliamentary law coincides with our own, reference will be made to the authority of the best writers on that science.

Section I.

Of the Order of Business.

When the Brethren have been "congregated," or called together by the presiding officer, the first thing to be attended to is the ceremony of opening the lodge. The consideration of this subject, as it is sufficiently detailed in our ritual, will form no part of the present work.

The lodge having been opened, the next thing to be attended to is the reading of the minutes of the last communication. The minutes having been read, the presiding officer will put the question on their confirmation, having first inquired of the Senior and Junior Wardens, and lastly of the Brethren "around the lodge," whether they have any alterations to propose. It must be borne in mind, that the question of confirmation is simply a question whether the Secretary has faithfully and correctly recorded the transactions of the lodge. If, therefore, it can be satisfactorily shown by any one that there is a mis-entry, or the omission of an entry, this is the time to correct it; and where the matter is of sufficient importance, and the recording officer, or any member disputes the charge of error, the vote of the lodge will be taken on the subject, and the journal will be amended or remain as written, according to the opinion so expressed by the majority of the members. As this is, however, a mere question of memory, it must be apparent that those members only who were present at the previous communication, the records of which are under examination, are qualified to express a fair opinion. All others should ask and be permitted to be excused from voting.

As no special communication can alter or amend the proceedings of a regular one, it is not deemed necessary to present the records of the latter to the inspection of the former. This preliminary reading of the minutes is, therefore, always omitted at special communications.

After the reading of the minutes, unfinished business, such as motions previously submitted and reports of committees previously appointed, will take the preference of all other matters. Special communications being called for the consideration of some special subject, that subject must of course claim the priority of consideration over all others.

In like manner, where any business has been specially and specifically postponed to another communication, it constitutes at that communication what is called, in parliamentary law, "the order of the day," and may at any time in the course of the evening be called up, to the exclusion of all other business.

The lodge may, however, at its discretion, refuse to take up the consideration of such order; for the same body which determined at one time to consider a question, may at another time refuse to do so. This is one of those instances in which parliamentary usage is applicable to the government of a lodge. Jefferson says: "Where an order is made, that any particular matter be taken up on any particular day, there a question is to be put, when it is called for, Whether the house will now proceed to that matter?" In a lodge, however, it is not the usage to propose such a question, but the matter being called up, is discussed and acted on, unless some Brother moves its postponement, when the question of postponement is put.

But with these exceptions, the unfinished business must first be disposed of, to avoid its accumulation and its possible subsequent neglect.[51]

New business will then be taken up in such order as the local bye-laws prescribe, or the wisdom of the Worshipful Master may suggest.

In a discussion, when any member wishes to speak, he must stand up in his place, and address himself not to the lodge, nor to any particular Brother, but to the presiding officer, styling him "Worshipful."

When two or more members rise nearly together, the presiding officer determines who is entitled to speak, and calls him by his name, whereupon he proceeds, unless he voluntarily sits down, and gives way to the other. The ordinary rules of courtesy, which should govern a masonic body above all other societies, as well as the general usage of deliberative bodies, require that the one first up should be entitled to the floor. But the decision of this fact is left entirely to the Master, or presiding officer.

Whether a member be entitled to speak once or twice to the same question, is left to the regulation of the local bye-laws of every lodge. But, under all circumstances, it seems to be conceded, that a member may rise at any time with the permission of the presiding officer, or for the purpose of explanation.

A member may be called to order by any other while speaking, for the use of any indecorous remark, personal allusion, or irrelevant matter; but this must be done in a courteous and conciliatory manner, and the question of order will at once be decided by the presiding officer.

No Brother is to be interrupted while speaking, except for the purpose of calling him to order, or to make a necessary explanation; nor are any separate conversations, or, as they are called in our ancient charges, "private committees," to be allowed.

Every member of the Order is, in the course of the debate as well as at all other times in the lodge, to be addressed by the title of "Brother," and no secular or worldly titles are ever to be used.

In accordance with the principles of justice, the parliamentary usage is adopted, which permits the mover of a resolution to make the concluding speech, that he may reply to all those who have spoken against it, and sum up the arguments in its favor. And it would be a breach of order as well as of courtesy for any of his opponents to respond to this final argument of the mover.

It is within the discretion of the Master, at any time in the course of the evening, to suspend the business of the lodge for the purpose of proceeding to the ceremony of initiation, for the "work" of Masonry, as it is technically called, takes precedence of all other business.

When all business, both old and new, and the initiation of candidates, if there be any, has been disposed of, the presiding officer inquires of the officers and members if there be anything more to be proposed before closing. Custom has prescribed a formulary for making this inquiry, which is in the following words.

The Worshipful Master, addressing the Senior and Junior Wardens and then the Brethren, successively, says: "Brother Senior, have you anything to offer in the West for the good of Masonry in general or of this lodge in particular? Anything in the South, Brother Junior? Around the lodge, Brethren?" The answers to these inquiries being in the negative on the part of the Wardens, and silence on that of the craft, the Master proceeds to close the lodge in the manner prescribed in the ritual.

The reading of the minutes of the evening, not for confirmation, but for suggestion, lest anything may have been omitted, should always precede the closing ceremonies, unless, from the lateness of the hour, it be dispensed with by the members.

Section II.

Of Appeals from the Decision of the Chair.

Freemasonry differs from all other institutions, in permitting no appeal to the lodge from the decision of the presiding officer. The Master is supreme in his lodge, so far as the lodge is concerned. He is amenable for his conduct, in the government of the lodge, not to its members, but to the Grand Lodge alone. In deciding points of order as well as graver matters, no appeal can be taken from that decision to the lodge. If an appeal were proposed, it would be his duty, for the preservation of discipline, to refuse to put the question.

It is, in fact, wrong that the Master should even by courtesy permit such an appeal to be taken; because, as the Committee of Correspondence of the Grand Lodge of Tennessee have wisely remarked, by the admission of such appeals by *courtesy*, "is established ultimately a precedent from which will be claimed *the right to take* appeals."[52] If a member is aggrieved with the conduct or the decisions of the Master, he has his redress by an appeal to the Grand Lodge, which will of course see that the Master does not rule his lodge "in an unjust or arbitrary manner." But such a thing as an appeal from the Master to the lodge is unknown in Masonry.

This, at first view, may appear to be giving too despotic a power to the Master. But a little reflection will convince any one that there can be but slight danger of oppression from one so guarded and controlled as the Master is by the obligations of his office and the superintendence of the Grand Lodge, while the placing in the hands of the craft so powerful, and, with bad spirits, so annoying a privilege as that of immediate appeal, would necessarily tend to impair the energies and lessen the dignity of the Master, at the same time that it would be totally subversive of that spirit of strict discipline which pervades every part of the institution, and to which it is mainly indebted for its prosperity and perpetuity.

In every case where a member supposes himself to be aggrieved by the decision of the Master, he should make his appeal to the Grand Lodge.

It is scarcely necessary to add, that a Warden or Past Master, presiding in the absence of the Master, assumes for the time all the rights and prerogatives of the Master.

Section III.

Of the Mode of Taking the Question.

The question in Masonry is not taken *viva voce* or by "aye" and "nay." This should always be done by "a show of hands." The regulation on this subject was adopted not later than the year 1754, at which time the Book of Constitutions was revised, "and the necessary alterations and additions made, consistent with the laws and rules of Masonry," and accordingly, in the edition published in the following year, the regulation is laid down in these words—"The opinions or votes of the members are always to be signified by each holding up one of his hands: which uplifted hands the Grand Wardens are to count; unless the number of hands be so unequal as to render the counting useless. Nor should any other kind of division be ever admitted among Masons."[53]

Calling for the yeas and nays has been almost universally condemned as an unmasonic practice, nor should any Master allow it to be resorted to in his lodge.

Moving the "previous question," a parliamentary invention for stopping all discussion, is still more at variance with the liberal and harmonious spirit which should distinguish masonic debates, and is, therefore, never to be permitted in a lodge.

Section IV.

Of Adjournments.

Adjournment is a term not recognized in Masonry. There are but two ways in which the communication of a lodge can be terminated; and these are either by *closing* the lodge, or by *calling from labor to refreshment*. In the former case the business of the communication is finally disposed of until the next communication; in the latter the lodge is still supposed to be open and may resume its labors at any time indicated by the Master.

But both the time of closing the lodge and of calling it from labor to refreshment is to be determined by the absolute will and the free judgment of the Worshipful Master, to whom alone is intrusted the care of "setting the craft to work, and giving them wholesome instruction for labor." He alone is responsible to the Grand Master and the Grand Lodge, that his lodge shall be opened, continued, and closed in harmony; and as it is by his "will and pleasure" only that it is opened, so is it by his "will and pleasure" only that it can be closed. Any attempt, therefore, on the part of the lodge to entertain a motion for adjournment would be an infringement of this prerogative of the Master. Such a motion is, therefore, always out of order, and cannot be; and cannot be acted on.

The rule that a lodge cannot adjourn, but remain in session until closed by the Master, derives an authoritative sanction also from the following clause in the fifth of the Old Charges.

"All Masons employed shall meekly receive their wages without murmuring or mutiny, *and not desert the Master till the work is finished*."

Section V.

Of the Appointment of Committees.

It is the prerogative of the Master to appoint all Committees, unless by a special resolution provision has been made that a committee shall otherwise be appointed.

The Master is also, *ex officio*, chairman of every committee which he chooses to attend, although he may not originally have been named a member of such committee. But he may, if he chooses, waive this privilege; yet he may, at any time during the session of the committee, reassume his inherent prerogative of governing the craft at all times when in his presence, and therefore take the chair.

Section VI.

Of the Mode of Keeping the Minutes.

Masonry is preeminently an institution of forms, and hence, as was to be expected, there is a particular form provided for recording the proceedings of a lodge. Perhaps the best method of communicating this form to the reader will be, to record the proceedings of a supposititious meeting or communication.

The following form, therefore, embraces the most important transactions that usually occur during the session of a lodge, and it may serve as an exemplar, for the use of secretaries.

"A regular communication of — — Lodge, NO. — —, was holden at — —; on ----, the — — day of — —A∴ L∴ 58—.

```
Present.       Bro∴ A. B—, W∴ Master.       "      B. C—, S∴ Warden.
"      C. D—, J∴ Warden.      "      D. E—, Treasurer.      "      E. F—
, Secretary.      "      F. G—, S∴ Deacon.      "      G. H—, J∴:
Deacon.      "      H. I—, } Stewards.      "      I. K—, }      "      K.
L—, Tiler.      Members.      Bro∴ L. M—      M. N—
N. O—         O. P—      Visitors.      P. Q—      Q. R—
—         R. S—      S. T—
```

The Lodge was opened in due form on the third degree of Masonry.

"The minutes of the regular communication of — — were read and confirmed.[54]

"The committee on the petition of Mr. C. B., a candidate for initiation, reported favorably, whereupon he was balloted for and duly elected.

"The committee on the application of Mr. D. C., a candidate for initiation, reported favorably, whereupon he was balloted for, and the box appearing foul he was rejected.

"The committee on the application of Mr. E. D., a candidate for initiation, having reported unfavorably, he was declared rejected without a ballot.

"The petition of Mr. F. E., a candidate for initiation, having been withdrawn by his friends, he was declared rejected without a ballot.

"A petition for initiation from Mr. G.F., inclosing the usual amount and recommended by Bros. C. D.— — and H. I.— —, was referred to a committee of investigation consisting of Bros. G. H.— —, L. M.— —, and O. P.— —.

"Bro. S.R., an Entered Apprentice, having applied for advancement, was duly elected to take the second degree; and Bro. W.Y., a Fellow Craft, was, on his application for advancement, duly elected to take the third degree.

"A letter was read from Mrs. T. V.— —, the widow of a Master Mason, when the sum of twenty dollars was voted for her relief.

"The amendment to article 10, section 5 of the bye-laws, proposed by Bro. M. N. — — at the communication of — —, was read a third time, adopted by a constitutional majority and ordered to be sent to the Grand Lodge for approval and confirmation.

"The Lodge of Master Masons was then closed, and a lodge of Entered Apprentices opened in due form.

"Mr. C. B., a candidate for initiation, being in waiting, was duly prepared, brought forward and initiated as an Entered Apprentice, he paying the usual fee.

"The Lodge of Entered Apprentices was then closed, and a Lodge of Fellow Crafts opened in due form.

"Bro. S. R., an Entered Apprentice, being in waiting, was duly prepared, brought forward and passed to the degree of a Fellow Craft, he paying the usual fee.

"The Lodge of Fellow Crafts was then closed, and a lodge of Master Masons opened in due form.

"Bro. W. Y., a Fellow Craft, being in waiting, was duly prepared, brought forward and raised to the sublime degree of a Master Mason, he paying the usual fee.

Amount received this evening, as follows:

Petition of Mr. G. F., $5
Fee   of Bro. C. B.,   5
do.   of Bro. S. R.,   5
do.   of Bro. W. Y., 5 — Total, $20

all of which was paid over to the Treasurer.

There being no further business, the lodge was closed in due form and harmony.

E. F——,

Secretary.

Such is the form which has been adopted as the most convenient mode of recording the transactions of a lodge. These minutes must be read, at the close of the meeting, that the Brethren may suggest any necessary alterations or additions, and then at the beginning of the next regular meeting, that they may be confirmed, after which they should be transcribed from the rough Minute Book in which they were first entered into the permanent Record Book of the lodge.

Book Third.

The Law of Individuals.

Passing from the consideration of the law, which refers to Masons in their congregated masses, as the constituents of Grand and Subordinate Lodges, I next approach the discussion of the law which governs, them in their individual capacity, whether in the inception of their masonic life, as candidates for initiation, or in their gradual progress through each of the three degrees, for it will be found that a Mason, as he assumes new and additional obligations, and is presented with increased light, contracts new duties, and is invested with new prerogatives and privileges.

Chapter I.

Of the Qualifications of Candidates.

The qualifications of a candidate for initiation into the mysteries of Freemasonry, are four-fold in their character—moral, physical, intellectual and political.

The moral character is intended to secure the respectability of the Order, because, by the worthiness of its candidates, their virtuous deportment, and good reputation, will the character of the institution be judged, while the admission of irreligious libertines and contemners of the moral law would necessarily impair its dignity and honor.

The physical qualifications of a candidate contribute to the utility of the Order, because he who is deficient in any of his limbs or members, and who is not in the possession of all his natural senses and endowments, is unable to perform, with pleasure to himself or credit to the fraternity, those peculiar labors in which all should take an equal part. He thus becomes a drone in the hive, and so far impairs the usefulness of the lodge, as "a place where Freemasons assemble to work, and to instruct and improve themselves in the mysteries of their ancient science."

The intellectual qualifications refer to the security of the Order; because they require that its mysteries shall be confided only to those whose mental developments are such as to enable them properly to appreciate, and faithfully to preserve from imposition, the secrets thus entrusted to them. It is evident, for instance, that an idiot could neither understand the hidden doctrines that might be communicated to him, nor could he so secure such portions as he might remember, in the "depositary of his heart," as to prevent the designing knave from worming them out of him; for, as the wise Solomon has said, "a fool's mouth is his destruction, and his lips are the snare of his soul."

The political qualifications are intended to maintain the independence of the Order; because its obligations and privileges are thus confided only to those who, from their position in society, are capable of obeying the one, and of exercising the other without the danger of let or hindrance from superior authority.

Of the moral, physical and political qualifications of a candidate there can be no doubt, as they are distinctly laid down in the ancient charges and constitutions. The intellectual are not so readily decided.

These four-fold qualifications may be briefly summed up in the following axioms.

Morally, the candidate must be a man of irreproachable conduct, a believer in the existence of God, and living "under the tongue of good report."

Physically, he must be a man of at least twenty-one years of age, upright in body, with the senses of a man, not deformed or dismembered, but with hale and entire limbs as a *man* ought to be.

Intellectually, he must be a man in the full possession of his intellects, not so young that his mind shall not have been formed, nor so old that it shall have fallen into dotage; neither a fool, an idiot, nor a madman; and with so much education as to enable him to avail himself of the teachings of Masonry, and to cultivate at his leisure a knowledge of the principles and doctrines of our royal art.

Politically, he must be in the unrestrained enjoyment of his civil and personal liberty, and this, too, by the birthright of inheritance, and not by its subsequent acquisition, in consequence of his release from hereditary bondage.

The lodge which strictly demands these qualifications of its candidates may have fewer members than one less strict, but it will undoubtedly have better ones.

But the importance of the subject demands for each class of the qualifications a separate section, and a more extended consideration.

Section I.

Of the Moral Qualifications of Candidates.

The old charges state, that "a Mason is obliged by his tenure to obey the moral law." It is scarcely necessary to say, that the phrase, "moral law," is a technical expression of theology, and refers to the Ten Commandments, which are so called, because they define the regulations necessary for the government of the morals and manners of men. The habitual violation of any one of these commands would seem, according to the spirit of the Ancient Constitutions, to disqualify a candidate for Masonry.

The same charges go on to say, in relation to the religious character of a Mason, that he should not be "a stupid atheist, nor an irreligious libertine." A denier of the existence of a Supreme Architect of the Universe cannot, of course, be obligated as a Mason, and, accordingly, there is no landmark more certain than that which excludes every atheist from the Order.

The word "libertine" has, at this day, a meaning very different from what it bore when the old charges were compiled. It then signified what we now call a "free-thinker," or disbeliever in the divine revelation of the Scriptures. This rule would therefore greatly abridge the universality and tolerance of the Institution, were it not for the following qualifying clause in the same instrument:—

"Though in ancient times Masons were charged in every country to be of the religion of that country or nation, whatever it was, yet it is now thought more expedient only to oblige them to that religion in which all men agree, leaving their particular opinions to themselves; that is, to be good men and true, or men of honor and honesty, by whatever denominations or persuasions they may be distinguished."

The construction now given universally to the religious qualification of a candidate, is simply that he shall have a belief in the existence and superintending control of a Supreme Being.

These old charges from which we derive the whole of our doctrine as to the moral qualifications of a candidate, further prescribe as to the political relations of a Mason, that he is to be "a peaceable subject to the civil powers, wherever he resides or works, and is never to be concerned in plots and conspiracies against the peace and welfare of the nation, nor to behave himself undutifully to inferior magistrates. He is cheerfully to conform to every lawful authority; to uphold on every occasion the interest of the community, and zealously promote the prosperity of his own country."

Such being the characteristics of a true Mason, the candidate who desires to obtain that title, must show his claim to the possession of these virtues; and hence the same charges declare, in reference to these moral qualifications, that "The persons made Masons, or admitted members of a lodge, must be good and true men—no immoral or scandalous men, but of good report."

Section II.

Of the Physical Qualifications of Candidates.

The physical qualifications of a candidate refer to his sex, his age, and the condition of his limbs.

The first and most important requisite of a candidate is, that he shall be "*a man*." No woman can be made a Mason. This landmark is so indisputable, that it would be wholly superfluous to adduce any arguments or authority in its support.

As to age, the old charges prescribe the rule, that the candidate must be "of mature and discreet age." But what is the precise period when one is supposed to have arrived at this maturity and discretion, cannot be inferred from any uniform practice of the craft in different countries. The provisions of the civil law, which make twenty-one the age of maturity, have, however, been generally followed. In this country the regulation is general, that the candidate must be twenty-one years of age. Such, too, was the regulation adopted by the General Assembly, which met on the 27th Dec., 1663, and which prescribed that "no person shall be accepted unless he be twenty-one years old or more."[55] In Prussia, the candidate is required to be twenty-five; in England, twenty-one,[56] "unless by dispensation from the Grand Master, or Provincial Grand Master;" in Ireland, twenty-one, except "by dispensation from the Grand Master, or the Grand Lodge;" in France, twenty-one, unless the candidate be the son of a Mason who has rendered important service to the craft, with the consent of his parent or guardian, or a young man who has served six months with his corps in the army—such persons may be initiated at eighteen; in Switzerland, the age of qualification is fixed at twenty-one, and in Frankfort-on-Mayn, at twenty. In this country, as I have already observed, the regulation of 1663 is rigidly enforced, and no candidate, who has not arrived at the age of twenty-one, can be initiated.

Our ritual excludes "an old man in his dotage" equally with a "young man under age." But as dotage signifies imbecility of mind, this subject will be more properly considered under the head of intellectual qualifications.

The physical qualifications, which refer to the condition of the candidate's body and limbs, have given rise, within a few years past, to a great amount of discussion and much variety of opinion. The regulation contained in the old charges of 1721, which requires the candidate to be "a perfect youth," has in some jurisdictions been rigidly enforced to the very letter of the law, while in others it has been so completely explained away as to mean anything or nothing. Thus, in South Carolina, where the rule is rigid, the candidate is required to be neither deformed nor dismembered, but of hale and entire limbs, as a man ought

51

to be, while in Maine, a deformed person may be admitted, provided "the deformity is not such as to prevent him from being instructed in the arts and mysteries of Freemasonry."

The first written law which we find on this subject is that which was enacted by the General Assembly held in 1663, under the Grand Mastership of the Earl of St. Albans, and which declares "that no person shall hereafter be accepted a Freemason but such as are of *able* body."[57]

Twenty years after, in the reign of James II., or about the year 1683, it seems to have been found necessary, more exactly to define the meaning of this expression, "of able body," and accordingly we find, among the charges ordered to be read to a Master on his installation, the following regulation:

"Thirdly, that he that be made be able in all degrees; that is, free-born, of a good kindred, true, and no bondsman, and that *he have his right limbs as a man ought to have.*"[58]

The old charges, published in the original Book of Constitutions in 1723, contain the following regulation:

"No Master should take an Apprentice, unless he be a perfect youth having no maim or defect that may render him uncapable of learning the art."

Notwithstanding the positive demand for *perfection*, and the positive and explicit declaration that he must have *no maim or defect*, the remainder of the sentence has, within a few years past, by some Grand Lodges, been considered as a qualifying clause, which would permit the admission of candidates whose physical defects did not exceed a particular point. But, in perfection, there can be no degrees of comparison, and he who is required to be perfect, is required to be so without modification or diminution. That which is *perfect* is complete in all its parts, and, by a deficiency in any portion of its constituent materials, it becomes not less perfect, (which expression would be a solecism in grammar,) but at once by the deficiency ceases to be perfect at all—it then becomes imperfect. In the interpretation of a law, "words," says Blackstone, "are generally to be understood in their usual and most known signification," and then "perfect" would mean, "complete, entire, neither defective nor redundant." But another source of interpretation is, the "comparison of a law with other laws, that are made by the same legislator, that have some affinity with the subject, or that expressly relate to the same point."[59] Applying this law of the jurists, we shall have no difficulty in arriving at the true signification of the word "perfect," if we refer to the regulation of 1683, of which the clause in question appears to have been an exposition. Now, the regulation of 1683 says, in explicit terms, that the candidate must "*have his right limbs as a man ought to have.*" Comparing the one law with the other, there can be no doubt that the requisition of Masonry is and always has been, that admission could only be granted to him who was neither deformed nor dismembered, but of hale and entire limbs as a man should be.

But another, and, as Blackstone terms it, "the most universal and effectual way of discovering the true meaning of a law" is, to consider "the reason and spirit of it, or the cause which moved the legislator to enact it." Now, we must look for the origin of the law requiring physical perfection, not to the formerly operative character of the institution, (for there never was a time when it was not speculative as well as operative,) but to its symbolic nature. In the ancient temple, every stone was required to be *perfect*, for a perfect stone was the symbol of truth. In our mystic association, every Mason represents a stone in that spiritual temple, "that house not made with hands, eternal in the heavens," of which the temple of Solomon was the type. Hence it is required that he should present himself, like the perfect stone in the material temple, a perfect man in the spiritual building. "The symbolic relation of each member of the Order to its mystic temple, forbids the idea," says Bro. W.S. Rockwell, of Georgia,[60] "that its constituent portions, its living stones, should be less perfect or less a type of their great original, than the immaculate material which formed the earthly dwelling place of the God of their adoration." If, then, as I presume it will be readily conceded, by all except those who erroneously suppose the institution to have been once wholly operative and afterwards wholly speculative, perfection is required in a candidate, not for the physical reason that he may be enabled to give the necessary signs of recognition, but because the defect would destroy the symbolism of that perfect stone which every Mason is supposed to represent in the spiritual temple, we thus arrive at a knowledge of the causes which moved the legislators of Masonry to enact the law, and we see at once, and without doubt, that the words *perfect youth* are to be taken in an unqualified sense, as signifying one who has "his right limbs as a man ought to have."[61]

It is, however, but fair to state that the remaining clause of the old charge, which asserts that the candidate must have no maim or defect that may render him incapable of learning the art, has been supposed to intend a modification of the word "perfect," and to permit the admission of one whose maim or defect was not of such a nature as to prevent his learning the art of Masonry. But I would respectfully suggest that a criticism of this kind is based upon a mistaken view of the import of the words. The sentence is not that the candidate must have no such maim or defect as might, by possibility, prevent him from learning the art; though this is the interpretation given by those who are in favor of admitting slightly maimed candidates. It is, on the contrary, so worded as to give a consequential meaning to the word "*that*." He must have no maim or defect *that* may render him incapable; that is, *because*, by having such maim or defect, he would be rendered incapable of acquiring our art.

In the Ahiman Rezon published by Laurence Dermott in 1764, and adopted for the government of the Grand Lodge of Ancient York Masons in England, and many of the Provincial Grand and subordinate lodges of America, the regulation is laid down that candidates must be "men of good report, free-born, of mature age, not deformed nor dismembered at the time of their making, and no woman or eunuch." It is true that at the present day this book possesses no legal authority among the craft; but I quote it, to show what was the interpretation given to the ancient law by a large portion, perhaps a majority, of the English and American Masons in the middle of the eighteenth century.

A similar interpretation seems at all times to have been given by the Grand Lodges of the United States, with the exception of some, who, within a few years past, have begun to adopt a more latitudinarian construction.

In Pennsylvania it was declared, in 1783, that candidates are not to be "deformed or dismembered at the time of their making."

In South Carolina the book of Constitutions, first published in 1807, requires that "every person desiring admission must be upright in body, not deformed or dismembered at the time of making, but of hale and entire limbs, as a man ought to be."

In the "Ahiman Rezon and Masonic Ritual," published by order of the Grand Lodge of North Carolina and Tennessee, in the year 1805, candidates are required to be "hale and sound, not deformed or dismembered at the time of their making."[62]

Maryland, in 1826, sanctioned the Ahiman Rezon of Cole, which declares the law in precisely the words of South Carolina, already quoted.

In 1823, the Grand Lodge of Missouri unanimously adopted a report, which declared that all were to be refused admission who were not "sound in mind and *all their members*," and she adopted a resolution asserting that "the Grand Lodge cannot grant a letter or dispensation to a subordinate lodge working under its jurisdiction, to initiate any person maimed, disabled, or wanting the qualifications establishing by ancient usage."[63]

But it is unnecessary to multiply instances. There never seems to have been any deviation from the principle that required absolute physical perfection, until, within a few years, the spirit of expediency[64] has induced some Grand Lodges to propose a modified construction of the law, and to admit those whose maims or deformities were not such as to prevent them from complying with the ceremonial of initiation. Still, a large number of the Grand Lodges have stood fast by the ancient landmark, and it is yet to be hoped that all will return to their first allegiance. The subject is an important one, and, therefore, a few of the more recent authorities, in behalf of the old law may with advantage be cited.

"We have examined carefully the arguments 'pro and con,' that have accompanied the proceedings of the several Grand Lodges, submitted to us, and the conviction has been forced upon our minds, even against our wills, that we depart from the ancient landmarks and usages of Masonry, whenever we admit an individual wanting in one of the human senses, or who is in any particular maimed or deformed." — *Committee of Correspondence G. Lodge of Georgia*, 1848, *page* 36.

"The rationale of the law, excluding persons physically imperfect and deformed, lies deeper and is more ancient than the source ascribed to it.[65] It is grounded on a principle recognized in the earliest ages of the world; and will be found identical with that which obtained among the ancient Jews. In this respect the Levitical law was the same as the masonic, which would not allow any 'to go in unto the vail' who had a blemish—a blind man, or a lame, or a man that was broken-footed, or broken-handed, or a dwarf, &c....

"The learned and studious Freemasonic antiquary can satisfactorily explain the metaphysics of this requisition in our Book of Constitutions. For the true and faithful Brother it sufficeth to know that such a requisition exists. He will prize it the more because of its antiquity.... No man can in perfection be 'made a Brother,' no man can truly 'learn our mysteries,' and practice them, or 'do the work of a Freemason,' if he is not a *man* with body free from maim, defect and deformity." — *Report of a Special Committee of the Grand Lodge of New York, in* 1848.[66]

"The records of this Grand Lodge may be confidently appealed to, for proofs of her repeated refusal to permit maimed persons to be initiated, and not simply on the ground that ancient usage forbids it, but because the fundamental constitution of the Order—the ancient charges—forbid it." — *Committee of Correspondence of New York, for 1848, p. 70.*

"The lodges subordinate to this Grand Lodge are hereby required, in the initiation of applicants for Masonry, to adhere to the ancient law (as laid down in our printed books), which says he shall be of *entire limbs"* — *Resolution of the G.L. of Maryland, November, 1848.*

"I received from the lodge at Ashley a petition to initiate into our Order a gentleman of high respectability, who, unfortunately, has been maimed. I refused my assent.... I have also refused a similar request from the lodge of which I am a member. The fact that the most distinguished masonic body on earth has recently removed one of the landmarks, should teach *us* to be careful how we touch those ancient boundaries." — *Address of the Grand Master of New Jersey in 1849.*

"The Grand Lodge of Florida adopted such a provision in her constitution, [the qualifying clause permitting the initiation of a maimed person, if his deformity was not such as to prevent his instruction], but more mature reflection, and more light reflected from our sister Grand Lodges, caused it to be stricken from our constitution." — *Address of Gov. Tho. Brown, Grand Master of Florida in* 1849.

"As to the physical qualifications, the Ahiman Rezon leaves no doubt on the subject, but expressly declares, that every applicant for initiation must be a man, free-born, of lawful age, in the perfect enjoyment of his senses, hale, and sound, and not deformed or dismembered; this is one of the ancient landmarks of the Order, which it is in the power of no body of men to change. A man having but one arm, or one leg, or who is in anyway deprived of his due proportion of limbs and members, is as incapable of initiation as a woman." — *Encyclical Letter of the Grand Lodge of South Carolina to its subordinates in* 1849.

Impressed, then, by the weight of these authorities, which it would be easy, but is unnecessary, to multiply—guided by a reference to the symbolic and speculative (not operative) reason of the law—and governed by the express words of the regulation of 1683—I am constrained to believe that the spirit as well as the letter of our ancient landmarks require that a candidate for admission should be perfect in all his parts, that is, neither redundant nor deficient, neither deformed nor dismembered, but of hale and entire limbs, as a man ought to be.

Section III.

Of the Intellectual Qualifications of Candidates.

The Old Charges and Ancient Constitutions are not as explicit in relation to the intellectual as to the moral and physical qualifications of candidates, and, therefore, in coming to a decision on this subject, we are compelled to draw our conclusions from analogy, from common sense, and from the peculiar character of the institution. The question that here suggests itself on this subject is, what particular amount of human learning is required as a constitutional qualification for initiation?

During a careful examination of every ancient document to which I have had access, I have met with no positive enactment forbidding the admission of uneducated persons, even of those who can neither read nor write. The unwritten, as well as the written laws of the Order, require that the candidate shall be neither a *fool* nor an *idiot*, but that he shall possess a discreet judgment, and be in the enjoyment of all the senses of a man. But one who is unable to subscribe his name, or to read it when written, might still very easily prove himself to be within the requirements of this regulation. The Constitutions of England, formed since the union of the two Grand Lodges in 1813, are certainly explicit enough on this subject. They require even more than a bare knowledge of reading and writing, for, in describing the qualifications of a candidate, they say:

"He should be a lover of the liberal arts and sciences, and have made some progress in one or other of them; and he must, previous to his initiation, subscribe his name at full length, to a declaration of the following import," etc. And in a note to this regulation, it is said, "Any individual who cannot write is, consequently, ineligible to be admitted into the Order." If this authority were universal in its character, there would be no necessity for a further discussion of the subject. But the modern constitutions of the Grand Lodge of England are only of force within its own jurisdiction, and we are therefore again compelled to resort to a mode of reasoning for the proper deduction of our conclusions on this subject.

It is undoubtedly true that in the early period of the world, when Freemasonry took its origin, the arts of reading and writing were not so generally disseminated among all classes of the community as they now are, when the blessings of a common education can be readily and cheaply obtained. And it may, therefore, be supposed that among our ancient Brethren there were many who could neither read nor write. But after all, this is a mere assumption, which, although it may be based on probability, has no direct evidence for its support. And, on the other hand, we see throughout all our ancient regulations, that a marked distinction was made by our rulers between the Freemason and the Mason who was not free; as, for instance, in the conclusion of the fifth chapter of the Ancient Charges, where it is said: "No laborer shall be employed in the common work of Masonry, nor shall Freemasons work with those who are not free, without an urgent necessity." And this would seem to indicate a higher estimation by the fraternity of their own character, which might be derived from their greater attainments in knowledge. That in those days the ordinary operative masons could neither read nor write, is a fact established by history. But it does not follow that the Freemasons, who were a separate society of craftsmen, were in the same unhappy category; it is even probable, that the fact that they were not so, but that they were, in comparison with the unaccepted masons, educated men, may have been the reason of the distinction made between these two classes of workmen.

But further, all the teachings of Freemasonry are delivered on the assumption that the recipients are men of some education, with the means of improving their minds and increasing their knowledge. Even the Entered Apprentice is reminded, by the rough and perfect ashlars, of the importance and necessity of a virtuous education, in fitting him for the discharge of his duties. To the Fellow Craft, the study of the liberal arts and sciences is earnestly recommended; and indeed, that sacred hieroglyphic, the knowledge of whose occult signification constitutes the most solemn part of his instruction, presupposes an acquaintance at least with the art of reading. And the Master Mason is expressly told in the explanation of the forty-seventh problem of Euclid, as one of the symbols of the third degree, that it was introduced into Masonry to teach the Brethren the value of the arts and sciences, and that the Mason, like the discoverer of the problem, our ancient Brother Pythagoras, should be a diligent cultivator of learning. Our lectures, too, abound in allusions which none but a person of some cultivation of mind could understand or appreciate, and to address them, or any portion of our charges which refer to the improvement of the intellect and the augmentation of knowledge, to persons who can neither read nor write, would be, it seems to us, a mockery unworthy of the sacred character of our institution.

From these facts and this method of reasoning, I deduce the conclusion that the framers of Masonry, in its present organization as a speculative institution, must have intended to admit none into its fraternity whose minds had not received some preliminary cultivation, and I am, therefore, clearly of opinion, that a person who cannot read and write is not legally qualified for admission.

As to the inexpediency of receiving such candidates, there can be no question or doubt. If Masonry be, as its disciples claim for it, a scientific institution, whose great object is to improve the understanding and to enlarge and adorn the mind, whose character cannot be appreciated, and whose lessons of symbolic wisdom cannot be acquired, without much studious application, how preposterous would it be to place, among its disciples, one who had lived to adult years, without having known the necessity or felt the ambition for a knowledge of the alphabet of his mother tongue? Such a man could make no advancement in the art of Masonry; and while he would confer no substantial advantage on the institution, he would, by his manifest incapacity and ignorance, detract, in the eyes of strangers, from its honor and dignity as an intellectual society.

Idiots and madmen are excluded from admission into the Order, for the evident reason that the former from an absence, and the latter from a perversion of the intellectual faculties, are incapable of comprehending the objects, or of assuming the responsibilities and obligations of the institution.

A question here suggests itself whether a person of present sound mind, but who had formerly been deranged, can legally be initiated. The answer to this question turns on the fact of his having perfectly recovered. If the present sanity of the applicant is merely a lucid interval, which physicians know to be sometimes vouched to lunatics, with the absolute certainty, or at best, the strong probability, of an eventual return to a state of mental derangement, he is not, of course, qualified for initiation. But if there has been a real and durable recovery (of which a physician will be a competent judge), then there can be no possible objection to his admission, if otherwise eligible. We are not to look to what the candidate once was, but to what he now is.

Dotage, or the mental imbecility produced by excessive old age, is also a disqualification for admission. Distinguished as it is by puerile desires and pursuits, by a failure of the memory, a deficiency of the judgment, and a general obliteration of the mental powers, its external signs are easily appreciated, and furnish at once abundant reason why, like idiots and madmen, the superannuated dotard is unfit to be the recipient of our mystic instructions.

Section IV.

Of the Political Qualifications of Candidates.

The Constitutions of Masonry require, as the only qualification referring to the political condition of the candidate, or his position in society, that he shall be *free-born*. The slave, or even the man born in servitude—though he may, subsequently, have obtained his liberty—is excluded by the ancient regulations from initiation. The non-admission of a slave seems to have been founded upon the best of reasons; because, as Freemasonry involves a solemn contract, no one can legally bind himself to its performance who is not a free agent and the master of his own actions. That the restriction is extended to those who were originally in a servile condition, but who may have since acquired their liberty, seems to depend on the principle that birth, in a servile condition, is accompanied by a degradation of mind and abasement of spirit, which no subsequent disenthralment can so completely efface as to render the party qualified to perform his duties, as a Mason, with that "freedom, fervency, and zeal," which are said to have distinguished our ancient Brethren. "Children," says Oliver, "cannot inherit a free and noble spirit except they be born of a free woman."

The same usage existed in the spurious Freemasonry or the Mysteries of the ancient world. There, no slave, or men born in slavery, could be initiated; because, the prerequisites imperatively demanded that the candidate should not only be a man of irreproachable manners, but also a free-born denizen of the country in which the mysteries were celebrated.

Some masonic writers have thought that, in this regulation in relation to free birth, some allusion is intended, both in the Mysteries and in Freemasonry, to the relative conditions and characters of Isaac and Ishmael. The former—the accepted one, to whom the promise was given—was the son of a free woman, and the latter, who was cast forth to have "his hand against every man, and every man's hand against him," was the child of a slave. Wherefore, we read that Sarah demanded of Abraham, "Cast out this bondwoman and her son; for the son of the bondwoman shall not be heir with my son." Dr. Oliver, in speaking of the grand festival with which Abraham celebrated the weaning of Isaac, says, that he "had not paid the same compliment at the weaning of Ishmael, because he was the son of a bondwoman, and, consequently, could not be admitted to participate in the Freemasonry of his father, which could only be conferred on free men born of free women." The ancient Greeks were of the same opinion; for they used the word δουλοπρεπεια or, "slave manners," to designate any very great impropriety of manners.

The Grand Lodge of England extends this doctrine, that Masons should be free in all their thoughts and actions, so far, that it will not permit the initiation of a candidate who is only temporarily deprived of his liberty, or even in a place of confinement. In the year 1782, the Master of the Royal Military Lodge, at Woolwich, being confined, most probably for debt, in the King's Bench prison, at London, the lodge, which was itinerant in its character, and allowed to move from place to place with its regiment, adjourned, with its warrant of constitution, to the Master in prison, where several Masons were made. The Grand Lodge, being informed of the circumstances, immediately summoned the Master and Wardens of the lodge "to answer for their conduct in making Masons in the King's Bench prison," and, at the same time, adopted a resolution, affirming that "it is inconsistent with the principles of Freemasonry for any Freemason's lodge to be held, for the purposes of making, passing, or raising Masons, in any prison or place of confinement."

Section V.

Of the Petition of Candidates for Admission, and the Action Thereon.

The application of a candidate to a lodge, for initiation, is called a "petition." This petition should always be in writing, and generally contains a statement of the petitioner's age, occupation, and place of residence, and a declaration of the motives which have prompted the application, which ought to be "a favorable opinion conceived of the institution and a desire of knowledge."[67] This petition must be recommended by at least two members of the lodge.

The petition must be read at a stated or regular communication of the lodge, and referred to a committee of three members for an investigation of the qualifications and character of the candidate. The committee having made the necessary inquiries, will report the result at the next regular communication and not sooner.

The authority for this deliberate mode of proceeding is to be found in the fifth of the 39 General Regulations, which is in these words:

"No man can be made or admitted a member of a particular lodge, without previous notice one month before given to the said lodge, in order to make due inquiry into the reputation and capacity of the candidate; unless by dispensation aforesaid."

The last clause in this article provides for the only way in which this probation of a month can be avoided, and that is when the Grand Master, for reasons satisfactory to himself, being such as will constitute what is called (sometimes improperly) a case of emergency, shall issue a dispensation permitting the lodge to proceed forthwith to the election.

But where this dispensation has not been issued, the committee should proceed diligently and faithfully to the discharge of their responsible duty. They must inquire into the moral, physical, intellectual and political qualifications of the candidate, and make their report in accordance with the result of their investigations.

The report cannot be made at a special communication, but must always be presented at a regular one. The necessity of such a rule is obvious. As the Master can at any time within his discretion convene a special meeting of his lodge, it is evident that a presiding officer, if actuated by an improper desire to intrude an unworthy and unpopular applicant upon the craft, might easily avail himself for that purpose of an occasion when the lodge being called for some other purpose, the attendance of the members was small, and causing a ballot to be taken, succeed in electing a candidate, who would, at a regular meeting, have been blackballed by some of those who were absent from the special communication.

This regulation is promulgated by the Grand Lodge of England, in the following words: "No person shall be made a Mason without a regular proposition at one lodge and a ballot at the next regular stated lodge;" it appears to have been almost universally adopted in similar language by the Grand Lodges of this country; and, if the exact words of the law are wanting in any of the Constitutions, the general usage of the craft has furnished an equivalent authority for the regulation.

If the report of the committee is unfavorable, the candidate should be considered as rejected, without any reference to a ballot. This rule is also founded in reason. If the committee, after a due inquiry into the character of the applicant, find the result so disadvantageous to him as to induce them to make an unfavorable report on his application, it is to be presumed that on a ballot they would vote against his admission, and as their votes alone would be sufficient to reject him, it is held unnecessary to resort in such a case to the supererogatory ordeal of the ballot. It would, indeed, be an anomalous proceeding, and one which would reflect great discredit on the motives and conduct of a committee of inquiry, were its members first to report against the reception of a candidate, and then, immediately afterwards, to vote in favor of his petition. The lodges will not suppose, for the honor of their committees, that such a proceeding will take place, and accordingly the unfavorable report of the committee is always to be considered as a rejection.

Another reason for this regulation seems to be this. The fifth General Regulation declares that no Lodge should ever make a Mason without "due inquiry" into his character, and as the duty of making this inquiry is entrusted to a competent committee, when that committee has reported that the applicant is unworthy to be made a Mason, it would certainly appear to militate against the spirit, if not the letter, of the regulation, for the lodge, notwithstanding this report, to enter into a ballot on the petition.

But should the committee of investigation report favorably, the lodge will then proceed to a ballot for the candidate; but, as this forms a separate and important step in the process of "making Masons," I shall make it the subject of a distinct section.

Section VI.

Of Balloting for Candidates.

The Thirty-nine Regulations do not explicitly prescribe the ballot-box as the proper mode of testing the opinion of the lodge on the merits of a petition for initiation. The sixth regulation simply says that the consent of the members is to be "formally asked by the Master; and they are to signify their assent or dissent *in their own prudent way* either virtually or in form, but with unanimity." Almost universal usage has, however, sanctioned the ballot box and the use of black and white balls as the proper mode of obtaining the opinion of the members.

From the responsibility of expressing this opinion, and of admitting a candidate into the fraternity or of repulsing him from it, no Mason is permitted to shrink. In balloting on a petition, therefore, every member of the Lodge is expected to vote; nor can he be excused from the discharge of this important duty, except by the unanimous consent of his Brethren. All the members must, therefore, come up to the performance of this trust with firmness, candor, and a full determination to do what is right—to allow no personal timidity to forbid the deposit of a black ball, if the applicant is unworthy, and no illiberal prejudices to prevent the deposition of a white one, if the character and qualifications of the candidate are unobjectionable. And in all cases where a member himself has no personal or acquired knowledge of these qualifications, he should rely upon and be governed by the recommendation of his Brethren of the Committee of Investigation, who he has no right to suppose would make a favorable report on the petition of an unworthy applicant.[68]

The great object of the ballot is, to secure the independence of the voter; and, for this purpose, its secrecy should be inviolate. And this secrecy of the ballot gives rise to a particular rule which necessarily flows out of it.

No Mason can be called to an account for the vote which he has deposited. The very secrecy of the ballot is intended to secure the independence and irresponsibility to the lodge of the voter. And, although it is undoubtedly a crime for a member to vote against the petition of an applicant on account of private pique or personal prejudice, still the lodge has no right to judge that such motives alone actuated him. The motives of men, unless divulged by themselves, can be known only to God; "and if," as Wayland says, "from any circumstances we are led to entertain any doubts of the motives of men, we are bound to retain these doubts within our own bosoms." Hence, no judicial notice can be or ought to be taken by a lodge of a vote cast by a member, on the ground of his having been influenced by improper motives, because it is impossible for the lodge legally to arrive at the knowledge; in the first place, of the vote that he has given, and secondly, of the motives by which he has been controlled.

And even if a member voluntarily should divulge the nature of his vote and of his motives, it is still exceedingly questionable whether the lodge should take any notice of the act, because by so doing the independence of the ballot might be impaired. It is through a similar mode of reasoning that the Constitution of the United States provides, that the members of Congress shall not be questioned, in any other place, for any speech or debate in either House. As in this way the freedom of debate is preserved in legislative bodies, so in like manner should the freedom of the ballot be insured in lodges.

The sixth General Regulation requires unanimity in the ballot. Its language is: "but no man can be entered a Brother in any particular lodge, or admitted to be a member thereof, without the *unanimous consent of all the members of that lodge* then present when the candidate is proposed." This regulation, it will be remembered, was adopted in 1721. But in the "New Regulations," adopted in 1754, and which are declared to have been enacted "only for amending or explaining the Old Regulations for the good of Masonry, without breaking in upon the ancient rules of the fraternity, still preserving the old landmarks," it is said: "but it was found inconvenient to insist upon unanimity in several cases; and, therefore, the Grand Masters have allowed the lodges to admit a member, if not above three black balls are against him; though some lodges desire no such allowance."[69]

The Grand Lodge of England still acts under this new regulation, and extends the number of black balls which will reject to three, though it permits its subordinates, if they desire it, to require unanimity. But nearly all the Grand Lodges of this country have adhered to the old regulation, which is undoubtedly the better one, and by special enactment have made the unanimous consent of all the Brethren present necessary to the election of a candidate.

Another question here suggests itself. Can a member, who by the bye-laws of his lodge is disqualified from the exercise of his other franchises as a member, in consequence of being in arrears beyond a certain amount, be prevented from depositing his ballot on the application of a candidate? That by such a bye-law he may be disfranchised of his vote in electing officers, or of the right to hold office, will be freely admitted. But the words of the old regulation seem expressly, and without equivocation, to require that *every member present* shall vote. The candidate shall only be admitted "by the unanimous consent of all the members of that lodge then present when the candidate is proposed." This right of the members to elect or reject their candidates is subsequently called "an inherent privilege," which is not subject to a dispensation. The words are explicit, and the right appears to be one guaranteed to every member so long as he continues a member, and of which no bye-law can divest him as long as the paramount authority of the Thirty-nine General Regulations is admitted. I should say, then, that every member of a lodge present at balloting for a candidate has a right to deposit his vote; and not only a right, but a duty which he is to be compelled to perform; since, without the unanimous consent of all present, there can be no election.

Our written laws are altogether silent as to the peculiar ceremonies which are to accompany the act of balloting, which has therefore been generally directed by the local usage of different jurisdictions. Uniformity, however, in this, as in all other ritual observances, is to be commended, and I shall accordingly here describe the method which I have myself preferred and practised in balloting for candidates, and which is the custom adopted in the jurisdiction of South Carolina.[70]

The committee of investigation having reported favorably, the Master of the lodge directs the Senior Deacon to prepare the ballot box. The mode in which this is accomplished is as follows:—The Senior Deacon takes the ballot box, and, opening it, places all the white and black balls indiscriminately in one compartment, leaving the other entirely empty. He then proceeds with the box to the Junior and Senior Wardens, who satisfy themselves by an inspection that no ball has been left in the compartment in which the votes are to be deposited. I remark here, in passing, that the box, in this and the other instance to be referred to hereafter, is presented to the inferior officer first, and then to his superior, that the examination and decision of the former may be substantiated and confirmed by the higher authority of the latter. Let it, indeed, be remembered, that in all such cases the usage of masonic *circumambulation* is to be observed, and that, therefore, we must first pass the Junior's station before we can get to that of the Senior Warden.

These officers having thus satisfied themselves that the box is in a proper condition for the reception of the ballots, it is then placed upon the altar by the Senior Deacon, who retires to his seat. The Master then directs the Secretary to call the roll, which is done by commencing with the Worshipful Master, and proceeding through all the officers down to the youngest member. As a matter of convenience, the Secretary generally votes the last of those in the room, and then, if the Tiler is a member of the lodge, he is called in, while the Junior Deacon tiles for him, and the name of the applicant having been told him, he is directed to deposit his ballot, which he does, and then retires.

As the name of each officer and member is called he approaches the altar, and having made the proper masonic salutation to the Chair, he deposits his ballot and retires to his seat. The roll should be called slowly, so that at no time should there be more than one person present at the box; for, the great object of the ballot being secrecy, no Brother should be permitted so near the member voting as to distinguish the color of the ball he deposits.

The box is placed on the altar, and the ballot is deposited with the solemnity of a masonic salutation, that the voters may be duly impressed with the sacred and responsible nature of the duty they are called on to discharge. The system of voting thus described, is, therefore, far better on this account than the one sometimes adopted in lodges, of handing round the box for the members to deposit their ballots from their seats

The Master having inquired of the Wardens if all have voted, then orders the Senior Deacon to "take charge of the ballot box." That officer accordingly repairs to the altar, and taking possession of the box, carries it, as before, to the Junior Warden, who examines the ballot, and reports, if all the balls are white, that "the box is clear in the South," or, if there is one or more black balls, that "the box is foul in the South." The

Deacon then carries it to the Senior Warden, and afterwards to the Master, who, of course, make the same report, according to the circumstances, with the necessary verbal variation of "West" and "East."

If the box is *clear*—that is, if all the ballots are white—the Master then announces that the applicant has been duly elected, and the Secretary makes a record of the fact.

But if the box is declared to be *foul*, the Master inspects the number of black balls; if he finds two, he declares the candidate to be rejected; if only one, he so states the fact to the lodge, and orders the Senior Deacon again to prepare the ballot box, and a second ballot is taken in the same way. This is done lest a black ball might have been inadvertently voted on the first ballot. If, on the second scrutiny, one black ball is again found, the fact is announced by the Master, who orders the election to lie over until the next stated meeting, and requests the Brother who deposited the black ball to call upon him and state his reasons. At the next stated meeting the Master announces these reasons to the lodge, if any have been made known to him, concealing, of course, the name of the objecting Brother. At this time the validity or truth of the objections may be discussed, and the friends of the applicant will have an opportunity of offering any defense or explanation. The ballot is then taken a third time, and the result, whatever it may be, is final. As I have already observed, in most of the lodges of this country, a reappearance of the one black ball will amount to a rejection. In those lodges which do not require unanimity, it will, of course, be necessary that the requisite number of black balls must be deposited on this third ballot to insure a rejection. But if, on inspection, the box is found to be "clear," or without a black ball, the candidate is, of course, declared to be elected. In any case, the result of the third ballot is final, nor can it be set aside or reversed by the action of the Grand Master or Grand Lodge; because, by the sixth General Regulation, already so frequently cited, the members of every particular lodge are the best judges of the qualifications of their candidates; and, to use the language of the Regulation, "if a fractious member should be imposed on them, it might spoil their harmony, or hinder their freedom, or even break and disperse the lodge."

Section VII.

Of the Reconsideration of the Ballot.

There are, unfortunately, some men in our Order, governed, not by essentially bad motives, but by frail judgments and by total ignorance of the true object and design of Freemasonry, who never, under any circumstances, have recourse to the black ball, that great bulwark of Masonry, and are always more or less incensed when any more judicious Brother exercises his privilege of excluding those whom he thinks unworthy of participation in our mysteries.

I have said, that these men are not governed by motives essentially bad. This is the fact. They honestly desire the prosperity of the institution, and they would not willfully do one act which would impede that prosperity. But their judgments are weak, and their zeal is without knowledge. They do not at all understand in what the true prosperity of the Order consists, but really and conscientiously believing that its actual strength will be promoted by the increase of the number of its disciples; they look rather to the *quantity* than to the *quality* of the applicants who knock at the doors of our lodges.

Now a great difference in respect to the mode in which the ballot is conducted, will be found in those lodges which are free from the presence of such injudicious brethren, and others into which they have gained admittance.

In a lodge in which every member has a correct notion of the proper moral qualifications of the candidates for Masonry, and where there is a general disposition to work well with a few, rather than to work badly with many, when a ballot is ordered, each Brother, having deposited his vote, quietly and calmly waits to hear the decision of the ballot box announced by the Chair. If it is "clear," all are pleased that another citizen has been found worthy to receive a portion of the illuminating rays of Masonry. If it is "foul," each one is satisfied with the adjudication, and rejoices that, although knowing nothing himself against the candidate, some one has been present whom a more intimate acquaintance with the character of the applicant has enabled to interpose his veto, and prevent the purity of the Order from being sullied by the admission of an unworthy candidate. Here the matter ends, and the lodge proceeds to other business.

But in a lodge where one of these injudicious and over-zealous Brethren is present, how different is the scene. If the candidate is elected, he, too, rejoices; but his joy is, that the lodge has gained one more member whose annual dues and whose initiation fee will augment the amount of its revenues. If he is rejected, he is indignant that the lodge has been deprived of this pecuniary accession, and forthwith he sets to work to reverse, if possible, the decision of the ballot box, and by a volunteer defense of the rejected candidate, and violent denunciations of those who opposed him, he seeks to alarm the timid and disgust the intelligent, so that, on a *reconsideration*, they may be induced to withdraw their opposition.

The *motion for reconsideration* is, then, the means generally adopted, by such seekers after quantity, to insure the success of their efforts to bring all into our fold who seek admission, irrespective of worth or qualification. In other words, we may say, that *the motion for reconsideration is the great antagonist of the purity and security of the ballot box*. The importance, then, of the position which it thus assumes, demands a brief discussion of the time and mode in which a ballot may be reconsidered.

In the beginning of the discussion, it may be asserted, that it is competent for any brother to move a reconsideration of a ballot, or for a lodge to vote on such a motion. The ballot is a part of the work of initiating a candidate. It is the preparatory step, and is just as necessary to his legal making as the obligation or the investiture. As such, then, it is clearly entirely under the control of the Master. The Constitutions of Masonry and the Rules and Regulations of every Grand and Subordinate lodge prescribe the mode in which the ballot shall be conducted, so that the sense of the members may be taken. The Grand Lodge also requires that the Master of the lodge shall see that that exact mode of ballot shall be pursued and no other, and it will hold him responsible that there shall be no violation of the rule. If, then, the Master is satisfied that the ballot has been regularly and correctly conducted, and that no possible good, but some probable evil, would arise from its reconsideration, it is not only competent for him, but it is his solemn duty to refuse to permit any such reconsideration. A motion to that effect, it may be observed, will always be out of order, although any Brother may respectfully request the Worshipful Master to order such a reconsideration, or suggest to him its propriety or expediency.

If, however, the Master is not satisfied that the ballot is a true indication of the sense of the lodge, he may, in his own discretion, order a reconsideration. Thus there may be but one black ball;—now a single black ball may sometimes be inadvertently cast—the member voting it may have been favorably disposed towards the candidate, and yet, from the hurry and confusion of voting, or from the dimness of the light or the infirmity of his own eyes, or from some other equally natural cause, he may have selected a black ball, when he intended to have taken a white one. It is, therefore, a matter of prudence and necessary caution, that, when only one black ball appears, the Master should order a new ballot. On this second ballot, it is to be presumed that more care and vigilance will be used, and the reappearance of the black ball will then show that it was deposited designedly.

But where two or three or more black balls appear on the first ballot, such a course of reasoning is not authorized, and the Master will then be right to refuse a reconsideration. The ballot has then been regularly taken—the lodge has emphatically decided for a rejection, and any order to renew the ballot would only be an insult to those who opposed the admission of the applicant, and an indirect attempt to thrust an unwelcome intruder upon the lodge.

But although it is in the power of the Master, under the circumstances which we have described, to order a reconsideration, yet this prerogative is accompanied with certain restrictions, which it may be well to notice.

In the first place, the Master cannot order a reconsideration on any other night than that on which the original ballot was taken.[71] After the lodge is closed, the decision of the ballot is final, and there is no human authority that can reverse it. The reason of this rule is evident. If it were otherwise, an unworthy

Master (for, unfortunately, all Masters are not worthy) might on any subsequent evening avail himself of the absence of those who had voted black balls, to order a reconsideration, and thus succeed in introducing an unfit and rejected candidate into the lodge, contrary to the wishes of a portion of its members.

Neither can he order a reconsideration on the same night, if any of the Brethren who voted have retired. All who expressed their opinion on the first ballot, must be present to express it on the second. The reasons for this restriction are as evident as for the former, and are of the same character.

It must be understood, that I do not here refer to those reconsiderations of the ballot which are necessary to a full understanding of the opinion of the lodge, and which have been detailed in the ceremonial of the mode of balloting, as it was described in the preceding Section.

It may be asked whether the Grand Master cannot, by his dispensations, permit a reconsideration. I answer emphatically, NO. The Grand Master possesses no such prerogative. There is no law in the whole jurisprudence of the institution clearer than this—that neither the Grand Lodge nor the Grand Master can interfere with the decision of the ballot box. In Anderson's Constitutions, the law is laid down, under the head of "Duty of Members" (edition of 1755, p. 312), that in the election of candidates the Brethren "are to give their consent in their own prudent way, either virtually or in form, but with unanimity." And the regulation goes on to say: "Nor is this inherent privilege *subject to a dispensation*, because the members of a lodge are the best judges of it; and because, if a turbulent member should be imposed upon them, it might spoil their harmony, or hinder the freedom of their communications, or even break and disperse the lodge." This settles the question. A dispensation to reconsider a ballot would be an interference with the right of the members "to give their consent in their own prudent way;" it would be an infringement of an "inherent privilege," and neither the Grand Lodge nor the Grand Master can issue a dispensation for such a purpose. Every lodge must be left to manage its own elections of candidates in its own prudent way.

I conclude this section by a summary of the principles which have been discussed, and which I have endeavored to enforce by a process of reasoning which I trust may be deemed sufficiently convincing. They are briefly these:

1. It is never in order for a member to move for the reconsideration of a ballot on the petition of a candidate for initiation, nor for a lodge to entertain such a motion.

2. The Master alone can, for reasons satisfactory to himself, order such a reconsideration.

3. The Master cannot order a reconsideration on any subsequent night, nor on the same night, after any member, who was present and voted, has departed.

4. The Grand Master cannot grant a dispensation for a reconsideration, nor in any other way interfere with the ballot. The same restriction applies to the Grand Lodge.

Section VIII.

Of the Renewal of Applications by Rejected Candidates.

As it is apparent from the last section that there can be no reconsideration by a lodge of a rejected petition, the question will naturally arise, how an error committed by a lodge, in the rejection of a worthy applicant, is to be corrected, or how such a candidate, when once rejected, is ever to make a second trial, for it is, of course, admitted, that circumstances may occur in which a candidate who had been once blackballed might, on a renewal of his petition, be found worthy of admission. He may have since reformed and abandoned the vicious habits which caused his first rejection, or it may have been since discovered that that rejection was unjust. How, then, is such a candidate to make a new application?

It is a rule of universal application in Masonry, that no candidate, having been once rejected, can apply to any other lodge for admission, except to the one which rejected him. Under this regulation the course of a second application is as follows:

Some Grand Lodges have prescribed that, when a candidate has been rejected, it shall not be competent for him to apply within a year, six months, or some other definite period. This is altogether a local regulation—there is no such law in the Ancient Constitutions—and therefore, where the regulations of the Grand Lodge of the jurisdiction are silent upon the subject, general principles direct the following as the proper course for a rejected candidate to pursue on a second application. He must send in a new letter, recommended and vouched for as before, either by the same or other Brethren—it must be again referred to a committee—lie over for a month—and the ballot be then taken as is usual in other cases. It must be treated in all respects as an entirely new petition, altogether irrespective of the fact that the same person had ever before made an application. In this way due notice will be given to the Brethren, and all possibility of an unfair election will be avoided.

If the local regulations are silent upon the subject, the second application may be made at any time after the rejection of the first, all that is necessary being, that the second application should pass through the same ordeal and be governed by the same rules that prevail in relation to an original application.

Section IX.

Of the Necessary Probation and Due Proficiency of Candidates before Advancement.

There is, perhaps, no part of the jurisprudence of Masonry which it is more necessary strictly to observe than that which relates to the advancement of candidates through the several degrees. The method which is adopted in passing Apprentices and raising Fellow Crafts—the probation which they are required to serve in each degree before advancing to a higher—and the instructions which they receive in their progress, often materially affect the estimation which is entertained of the institution by its initiates. The candidate who long remains at the porch of the temple, and lingers in the middle chamber, noting everything worthy of observation in his passage to the holy of holies, while he better understands the nature of the profession upon which he has entered, will have a more exalted opinion of its beauties and excellencies than he who has advanced, with all the rapidity that dispensations can furnish, from the lowest to the highest grades of the Order. In the former case, the design, the symbolism, the history, and the moral and philosophical bearing of each degree will be indelibly impressed upon the mind, and the appositeness of what has gone before to what is to succeed will be readily appreciated; but, in the latter, the lessons of one hour will be obliterated by those of the succeeding one; that which has been learned in one degree, will be forgotten in the next; and when all is completed, and the last instructions have been imparted, the dissatisfied neophyte will find his mind, in all that relates to Masonry, in a state of chaotic confusion. Like Cassio, he will remember "a mass of things, but nothing distinctly."

An hundred years ago it was said that "Masonry was a progressive science, and not to be attained in any degree of perfection, but by time, patience, and a considerable degree of application and industry."[72] And it is because that due proportion of time, patience and application, has not been observed, that we so often see Masons indifferent to the claims of the institution, and totally unable to discern its true character. The arcana of the craft, as Dr. Harris remarks, should be gradually imparted to its members, according to their improvement.

There is no regulation of our Order more frequently repeated in our constitutions, nor one which should be more rigidly observed, than that which requires of every candidate a "suitable proficiency" in one degree, before he is permitted to pass to another. But as this regulation is too often neglected, to the manifest injury of the whole Order, as well as of the particular lodge which violates it, by the introduction of ignorant and unskillful workmen into the temple, it may be worth the labor we shall spend upon the subject, to investigate some of the authorities which support us in the declaration, that no candidate should be promoted, until, by a due probation, he has made "suitable proficiency in the preceding degree."

In one of the earliest series of regulations that have been preserved—made in the reign of Edward III., it was ordained, "that such as were to be admitted Master Masons, or Masters of work, should be examined whether they be able of cunning to serve their respective Lords, as well the lowest as the highest, to the honor and worship of the aforesaid art, and to the profit of their Lords."

Here, then, we may see the origin of that usage, which is still practiced in every well governed lodge, not only of demanding a proper degree of proficiency in the candidate, but also of testing that proficiency by an examination.

This cautious and honest fear of the fraternity, lest any Brother should assume the duties of a position which he could not faithfully discharge, and which is, in our time, tantamount to a candidate's advancing to a degree for which he is not prepared, is again exhibited in the charges enacted in the reign of James II., the manuscript of which was preserved in the archives of the Lodge of Antiquity in London. In these charges it is required, "that no Mason take on no lord's worke, nor any other man's, unless he know himselfe well able to perform the worke, so that the craft have no slander." In the same charges, it is prescribed that "no master, or fellow, shall take no apprentice for less than seven years."

In another series of charges, whose exact date is not ascertained, but whose language and orthography indicate their antiquity, it is said: "Ye shall ordain the wisest to be Master of the work; and neither for love nor lineage, riches nor favor, set one over the work[73] who hath but little knowledge, whereby the Master would be evil served, and ye ashamed."

These charges clearly show the great stress that was placed by our ancient Brethren upon the necessity of skill and proficiency, and they have furnished the precedents upon which are based all the similar regulations that have been subsequently applied to Speculative Masonry.

In the year 1722, the Grand Lodge of England ordered the "Old Charges of the Free and Accepted Masons" to be collected from the ancient records, and, having approved of them, they became a part of the Constitutions of Speculative Freemasonry. In these Charges, it is ordained that "a younger Brother shall be instructed in working, to prevent spoiling the materials for want of judgment, and for increasing and continuing of brotherly love."

Subsequently, in 1767, it was declared by the Grand Lodge, that "no lodge shall be permitted to make and raise the same Brother, at one and the same meeting, without a dispensation from the Grand Master, or his Deputy;" and, lest too frequent advantage should be taken of this power of dispensation, to hurry candidates through the degrees, it is added that the dispensation, "*on very particular occasions only*, may be requested."

The Grand Lodge of England afterwards found it necessary to be more explicit on this subject, and the regulation of that body is now contained in the following language:

"No candidate shall be permitted to receive more than one degree on the same day, nor shall a higher degree in Masonry be conferred on any Brother at a less interval than four weeks from his receiving a previous degree, nor until he has passed an examination in open lodge in that degree."[74]

This seems to be the recognized principle on which the fraternity are, at this day, acting in this country. The rule is, perhaps, sometimes, and in some places, in abeyance. A few lodges, from an impolitic desire to increase their numerical strength, or rapidly to advance men of worldly wealth or influence to high stations in the Order, may infringe it, and neglect to demand of their candidates that suitable proficiency which ought to be, in Masonry, an essential recommendation to promotion; but the great doctrine that each degree should be well studied, and the candidate prove his proficiency in it by an examination, has been uniformly set forth by the Grand Lodge of the United States, whenever they have expressed an opinion on the subject.

Thus, for instance, in 1845, the late Bro. A.A. Robertson, Grand Master of New York, gave utterance to the following opinion, in his annual address to the intelligent body over which he presided:

"The practice of examining candidates in the prior degrees, before admission to the higher, in order to ascertain their proficiency, is gaining the favorable notice of Masters of lodges, and cannot be too highly valued, nor too strongly recommended to all lodges in this jurisdiction. It necessarily requires the novitiate to reflect upon the bearing of all that has been so far taught him, and consequently to impress upon his mind the beauty and utility of those sublime truths, which have been illustrated in the course of the ceremonies he has witnessed in his progress in the mystic art. In a word, it will be the means of making competent overseers of the work—and no candidate should be advanced, until he has satisfied the lodge, by such examination, that he has made the necessary proficiency in the lower degrees."[75]

In 1845, the Grand Lodge of Iowa issued a circular to her subordinates, in which she gave the following admonition:

"To guard against hasty and improper work, she prohibits a candidate from being advanced till he has made satisfactory proficiency in the preceding degrees, by informing himself of the lectures pertaining thereto; and to suffer a candidate to proceed who is ignorant in this essential particular, is calculated in a high degree to injure the institution and retard its usefulness."

The Grand Lodge of Illinois has practically declared its adhesion to the ancient regulation; for, in the year 1843, the dispensation of Nauvoo Lodge, one of its subordinates, was revoked principally on the ground that she was guilty "of pushing the candidate through the second and third degrees, before he could possibly be skilled in the preceding degree." And the committee who recommended the revocation, very justly remarked that they were not sure that any length of probation would in all cases insure skill, but they were certain that the ancient landmarks of the Order required that the lodge should know that the candidate is well skilled in one degree before being admitted to another.

The Grand Lodges of Massachusetts and South Carolina have adopted, almost in the precise words, the regulation of the Grand Lodge of England, already cited, which requires an interval of one month to elapse between the conferring of degrees. The Grand Lodge of New Hampshire requires a greater probation for its candidates; its constitution prescribes the following regulation: "All Entered Apprentices must work five months as such, before they can be admitted to the degree of Fellow Craft. All Fellow Crafts must work in a lodge of Fellow Crafts three months, before they can be raised to the sublime degree of Master Mason. Provided, nevertheless, that if any Entered Apprentice, or Fellow Craft, shall make himself thoroughly acquainted with all the information belonging to his degree, he may be advanced at an earlier period, at the discretion of the lodge."

But, perhaps, the most stringent rule upon this subject, is that which exists in the Constitution of the Grand Lodge of Hanover, which is in the following words:

"No Brother can be elected an officer of a lodge until he has been three years a Master Mason. A Fellow Craft must work at least one year in that degree, before he can be admitted to the third degree. An Entered Apprentice must remain at least two years in that degree."

It seems unnecessary to extend these citations. The existence of the regulation, which requires a necessary probation in candidates, until due proficiency is obtained, is universally admitted. The ancient constitutions repeatedly assert it, and it has received the subsequent sanction of innumerable Masonic authorities. But, unfortunately, the practice is not always in accordance with the rule. And, hence, the object of this article is not so much to demonstrate the existence of the law, as to urge upon our readers the necessity of a strict adherence to it. There is no greater injury which can be inflicted on the Masonic Order (the admission of immoral persons excepted), than that of hurrying candidates through the several degrees. Injustice is done to the institution, whose peculiar principles and excellencies are never properly presented—and irreparable injury to the candidate, who, acquiring no fair appreciation of the ceremonies through which he rapidly passes, or of the instructions which he scarcely hears, is filled either with an indifference that never afterwards can be warmed into zeal, or with a disgust that can never be changed into esteem. Masonry is betrayed in such an instance by its friends, and often loses the influence of an intelligent member, who, if he had been properly instructed, might have become one of its warmest and most steadfast advocates.

This subject is so important, that I will not hesitate to add to the influence of these opinions the great sanction of Preston's authority.

"Many persons," says that able philosopher of Masonry, "are deluded by the vague supposition that our mysteries are merely nominal; that the practices established among us are frivolous, and that our ceremonies may be adopted, or waived at pleasure. On this false foundation, we find them hurrying through all the degrees of the Order, without adverting to the propriety of one step they pursue, or possessing a single qualification requisite for advancement. Passing through the usual formalities, they consider themselves entitled to rank as masters of the art, solicit and accept offices, and assume the government of the lodge, equally unacquainted with the rules of the institution they pretend to support, or the nature of the trust they engage to perform. The consequence is obvious; anarchy and confusion ensue, and the substance is lost in the shadow. Hence men eminent for ability, rank, and fortune, are often led to view the honors of Masonry with such indifference, that when their patronage is solicited, they either accept offices with reluctance, or reject them with disdain."[76]

Let, then, no lodge which values its own usefulness, or the character of our institution, admit any candidate to a higher degree, until he has made suitable proficiency in the preceding one, to be always tested by a strict examination in open lodge. Nor can it do so, without a palpable violation of the laws of Masonry.

Section X.

Of Balloting for Candidates in each Degree.

Although there is no law, in the Ancient Constitutions, which in express words requires a ballot for candidates in each degree, yet the whole tenor and spirit of these constitutions seem to indicate that there should be recourse to such a ballot. The constant reference, in the numerous passages which were cited in the preceding Section, to the necessity of an examination into the proficiency of those who sought advancement, would necessarily appear to imply that a vote of the lodge must be taken on the question of this proficiency. Accordingly, modern Grand Lodges have generally, by special enactment, required a ballot to be taken on the application of an Apprentice or Fellow Craft for advancement, and where no such regulation has been explicitly laid down, the almost constant usage of the craft has been in favor of such ballot.

The Ancient Constitutions having been silent on the subject of the letter of the law, local usage or regulations must necessarily supply the specific rule.

Where not otherwise provided by the Constitutions of a Grand Lodge or the bye-laws of a subordinate lodge, analogy would instruct us that the ballot, on the application of Apprentices or Fellow Crafts for advancement, should be governed by the same principles that regulate the ballot on petitions for initiation.

Of course, then, the vote should be unanimous: for I see no reason why a lodge of Fellow Crafts should be less guarded in its admission of Apprentices, than a lodge of Apprentices is in its admission of profanes.

Again, the ballot should take place at a stated meeting, so that every member may have "due and timely notice," and be prepared to exercise his "inherent privilege" of granting or withholding his consent; for it must be remembered that the man who was worthy or supposed to be so, when initiated as an Entered Apprentice, may prove to be unworthy when he applies to pass as a Fellow Graft, and every member should, therefore, have the means and opportunity of passing his judgment on that worthiness or unworthiness.

If the candidate for advancement has been rejected once, he may again apply, if there is no local regulation to the contrary. But, in such a case, due notice should be given to all the members, which is best done by making the application at one regular meeting, and voting for it on the next. This, however, I suppose to be only necessary in the case of a renewed application after a rejection. An Entered Apprentice or a Fellow Craft is entitled after due probation to make his application for advancement; and his first application may be balloted for on the same evening, provided it be a regular meeting of the lodge. The members are supposed to know what work is before them to do, and should be there to do it.

But the case is otherwise whenever a candidate for advancement has been rejected. He has now been set aside by the lodge, and no time is laid down in the regulations or usages of the craft for his making a second application. He may never do so, or he may in three months, in a year, or in five years. The members are, therefore, no more prepared to expect this renewed application at any particular meeting of the lodge, than they are to anticipate any entirely new petition of a profane. If, therefore, the second application is not made at one regular meeting and laid over to the next, the possibility is that the lodge may be taken by surprise, and in the words of the old Regulation, "a turbulent member may be imposed on it."

The inexpediency of any other course may be readily seen, from a suppositions case. We will assume that in a certain lodge, A, who is a Fellow Craft, applies regularly for advancement to the third degree. On this occasion, for good and sufficient reasons, two of the members, B and C, express their dissent by depositing black balls. His application to be raised is consequently rejected, and he remains a Fellow Graft. Two or three meetings of the lodge pass over, and at each, B and C are present; but, at the fourth meeting, circumstances compel their absence, and the friends of A, taking advantage of that occurrence, again propose him for advancement; the ballot is forthwith taken, and he is elected and raised on the same evening. The injustice of this course to B and C, and the evil to the lodge and the whole fraternity, in this imposition of one who is probably an unworthy person, will be apparent to every intelligent and right-minded Mason.

I do not, however, believe that a candidate should be rejected, on his application for advancement, in consequence of objections to his moral worth and character. In such a case, the proper course would be to prefer charges, to try him as an Apprentice or Fellow Craft; and, if found guilty, to suspend, expel, or otherwise appropriately punish him. The applicant as well as the Order is, in such a case, entitled to a fair trial. Want of proficiency, or a mental or physical disqualification acquired since the reception of the preceding degree, is alone a legitimate cause for an estoppal of advancement by the ballot. But this subject will be treated of further in the chapter on the rights of Entered Apprentices.

Section XI.

Of the Number to be Initiated at one Communication.

The fourth General Regulation decrees that "no Lodge shall make more than five new Brothers at one time." This regulation has been universally interpreted (and with great propriety) to mean that not more than five degrees can be conferred at the same communication.

This regulation is, however, subject to dispensation by the Grand Master, or Presiding Grand Officer, in which case the number to be initiated, passed, or raised, will be restricted only by the words of the dispensation.

The following, or fifth General Regulation, says that "no man can be made or admitted a member of a particular lodge, without previous notice, one month before, given to the same lodge."

Now, as a profane cannot be admitted an Entered Apprentice, or in other words, a member of an Entered Apprentices' lodge, unless after one month's notice, so it follows that an Apprentice cannot be admitted a member of a Fellow Crafts' lodge, nor a Fellow Craft of a Masters', without the like probation. For the words of the regulation which apply to one, will equally apply to the others. And hence we derive the law, that a month at least must always intervene between the reception of one degree and the advancement to another. But this rule is also subject to a dispensation.

Section XII.

Of Finishing the Candidates of one Lodge in another.

It is an ancient and universal regulation, that no lodge shall interfere with the work of another by initiating its candidates, or passing or raising its Apprentices and Fellow Crafts. Every lodge is supposed to be competent to manage its own business, and ought to be the best judge of the qualifications of its own members, and hence it would be highly improper in any lodge to confer a degree on a Brother who is not of its household.

This regulation is derived from a provision in the Ancient Charges, which have very properly been supposed to contain the fundamental law of Masonry, and which prescribes the principle of the rule in the following symbolical language:

"None shall discover envy at the prosperity of a Brother, nor supplant him or put him out of his work, if he be capable to finish the same; for no man can finish another's work, so much to the Lord's profit, unless he be thoroughly acquainted with the designs and draughts of him that began it."

There is, however, a case in which one lodge may, by consent, legally finish the work of another. Let us suppose that a candidate has been initiated in a lodge at A— —, and, before he receives his second degree, removes to B— —, and that being, by the urgency of his business, unable either to postpone his departure from A— —, until he has been passed and raised, or to return for the purpose of his receiving his second and third degrees, then it is competent for the lodge at A— — to grant permission to the lodge at B— — to confer them on the candidate.

But how shall this permission be given—by a unanimous vote, or merely by a vote of the majority of the members at A— —? Here it seems to me that, so far as regards the lodge at A— —, the reasons for unanimity no longer exist. There is here no danger that a "fractious member will be imposed on them," as the candidate, when finished, will become a member of the lodge at B— —. The question of consent is simply in the nature of a resolution, and may be determined by the assenting votes of a majority of the members at A—-. It is, however, to be understood, that if any Brother believes that the candidate is unworthy, from character, of further advancement, he may suspend the question of consent, by preferring charges against him. If this is not done, and the consent of the lodge is obtained, that the candidate may apply to the lodge at B—-, then when his petition is read in that lodge, it must, of course, pass through the usual ordeal of a month's probation, and a unanimous vote; for here the old reasons for unanimity once more prevail.

I know of no ancient written law upon this subject, but it seems to me that the course I have described is the only one that could be suggested by analogy and common sense.

Section XIII.

Of the Initiation of Non-residents.

The subject of this section is naturally divided into two branches:—First, as to the initiation by a lodge of a candidate, who, residing in the same State or Grand Lodge jurisdiction, is still not an inhabitant of the town in which the lodge to which he applies is situated, but resides nearer to some other lodge; and, secondly, as to the initiation of a stranger, whose residence is in another State, or under the jurisdiction of another Grand Lodge.

1. The first of these divisions presents a question which is easily answered. Although I can find no ancient regulation on this subject, still, by the concurrent authority of all Grand Lodges in this country, at least, (for the Grand Lodge of England has no such provision in its Constitution,) every lodge is forbidden to initiate any person whose residence is nearer to any other lodge. If, however, such an initiation should take place, although the lodge would be censurable for its violation of the regulations of its superior, yet there has never been any doubt that the initiation would be good and the candidate so admitted regularly made. The punishment must fall upon the lodge and not upon the newly-made Brother.

2. The second division presents a more embarrassing inquiry, on account of the diversity of opinions which have been entertained on the subject. Can a lodge in one State, or Grand Lodge jurisdiction, initiate the resident of another State, and would such initiation be lawful, and the person so initiated a regular Mason, or, to use the technical language of the Order, a Mason made "in due form," and entitled to all the rights and privileges of the Order?

The question is one of considerable difficulty; it has given occasion to much controversy, and has been warmly discussed within the last few years by several of the Grand Lodges of the United States.

In 1847, the Grand Lodge of Alabama adopted the following regulation, which had been previously enacted by the Grand Lodge of Tennessee:

"Any person residing within the jurisdiction of this Grand Lodge, who has already, or shall hereafter, travel into any foreign jurisdiction, and there receive the degrees of Masonry, such person shall not be entitled to the rights, benefits, and privileges of Masonry within this jurisdiction, until he shall have been regularly admitted a member of the subordinate lodge under this Grand Lodge, nearest which he at the time resides, in the manner provided by the Constitution of this Grand Lodge for the admission of members."

The rule adopted by the Grand Lodge of Maryland is still more stringent. It declares, "that if any individual, from selfish motives, from distrust of his acceptance, or other causes originating in himself, knowingly and willfully travel into another jurisdiction, and there receive the masonic degrees, he shall be considered and held as a clandestine made Mason."

The Grand Lodge of New York, especially, has opposed these regulations, inflicting a penalty on the initiate, and assigns its reasons for the opposition in the following language:

"Before a man becomes a Mason, he is subject to no law which any Grand Lodge can enact. No Grand Lodge has a right to make a law to compel any citizen, who desires, to be initiated in a particular lodge, or in the town or State of his residence; neither can any Grand Lodge forbid a citizen to go where he pleases to seek acceptance into fellowship with the craft; and where there is no right to compel or to forbid, there can be no right to punish; but it will be observed, that the laws referred to were enacted to punish the citizens of Maryland and Alabama, as Masons and Brethren, for doing something before they were Masons and Brethren, which they had a perfect right to do as citizens and freemen; and it must certainly be regarded as an act of deception and treachery by a young Mason, on returning home, to be told, that he is 'a clandestine Mason,' that he 'ought to be expelled,' or, that he cannot be recognized as a Brother till he 'joins a lodge where his residence is,' because he was initiated in New York, in England, or in France, after having heard all his life of the universality and oneness of the institution."[77]

It seems to us that the Grand Lodge of New York has taken the proper view of the subject; although we confess that we are not satisfied with the whole course of reasoning by which it has arrived at the conclusion. Whatever we may be inclined to think of the inexpediency of making transient persons (and we certainly do believe that it would be better that the character and qualifications of every candidate should be submitted to the inspection of his neighbors rather than to that of strangers), however much we may condemn the carelessness and facility of a lodge which is thus willing to initiate a stranger, without that due examination of his character, which, of course, in the case of non-residents, can seldom be obtained, we are obliged to admit that such makings are legal—the person thus made cannot be called a clandestine Mason, because he has been made in a legally constituted lodge—and as he is a regular Mason, we know of no principle by which he can be refused admission as a visitor into any lodge to which he applies.

Masonry is universal in its character, and knows no distinction of nation or of religion. Although each state or kingdom has its distinct Grand Lodge, this is simply for purposes of convenience in carrying out the principles of uniformity and subordination, which should prevail throughout the masonic system. The jurisdiction of these bodies is entirely of a masonic character, and is exercised only over the members of the Order who have voluntarily contracted their allegiance. It cannot affect the profane, who are, of course, beyond its pale. It is true, that as soon as a candidate applies to a lodge for initiation, he begins to come within the scope of masonic law. He has to submit to a prescribed formula of application and entrance, long before he becomes a member of the Order. But as this formula is universal in its operation, affecting candidates who are to receive it and lodges which are to enforce it in all places, it must have been derived from some universal authority. The manner, therefore, in which a candidate is to be admitted, and the preliminary qualifications which are requisite, are prescribed by the landmarks, the general usage, and the ancient constitutions of the Order. And as they have directed the *mode how*, they might also have prescribed the *place where*, a man should be made a Mason. But they have done no such thing. We cannot, after the most diligent search, find any constitutional regulation of the craft, which refers to the initiation of non-residents. The subject has been left untouched; and as the ancient and universally acknowledged authorities of Masonry have neglected to legislate on the subject, it is now too late for any modern and local authority, like that of a Grand Lodge, to do so.

A Grand Lodge may, it is true, forbid—as Missouri, South Carolina, Georgia, and several other Grand Lodges have done—the initiation of non-residents, within its own jurisdiction, because this is a local law enacted by a local authority; but it cannot travel beyond its own territory, and prescribe the same rule to another Grand Lodge, which may not, in fact, be willing to adopt it.

The conclusions, then, at which we arrive no this subject are these: The ancient constitutions have prescribed no regulation on the subject of the initiation of non-residents; it is, therefore, optional with every Grand Lodge, whether it will or will not suffer such candidates to be made within its own jurisdiction; the making, where it is permitted, is legal, and the candidate so made becomes a regular Mason, and is entitled to the right of visitation.

What, then, is the remedy, where a person of bad character, and having, in the language of the Grand Lodge of Maryland, "a distrust of his acceptance" at home, goes abroad and receives the degrees of Masonry? No one will deny that such a state of things is productive of great evil to the craft. Fortunately, the remedy is simple and easily applied. Let the lodge, into whose jurisdiction he has returned, exercise its power of discipline, and if his character and conduct deserve the punishment, let him be expelled from the Order. If he is unworthy of remaining in the Order, he should be removed from it at once; but if he is worthy of continuing in it, there certainly can be no objection to his making use of his right to visit.

Chapter II.

Of the Rights of Entered Apprentices.

In an inquiry into the rights of Entered Apprentices, we shall not be much assisted by the Ancient Constitutions, which, leaving the subject in the position in which usage had established it, are silent in relation to what is the rule. In all such cases, we must, as I have frequently remarked before, in settling the law, have recourse to analogy, to the general principles of equity, and the dictates of common sense, and, with these three as our guides, we shall find but little difficulty in coming to a right conclusion.

At present, an Entered Apprentice is not considered a member of the Lodge, which privilege is only extended to Master Masons. This was not formerly the case. Then the Master's degree was not as indiscriminately conferred as it is now. A longer probation and greater mental or moral qualifications were required to entitle a candidate to this sublime dignity. None were called Master Masons but such as had presided over their Lodges, and the office of Wardens was filled by Fellow Crafts. Entered Apprentices, as well as Fellow Crafts, were permitted to attend the communications of the Grand Lodge, and express their opinions; and, in 1718, it was enacted that every new regulation, proposed in the Grand Lodge, should be submitted to the consideration of even the youngest Entered Apprentice. Brethren of this degree composed, in fact, at that time, the great body of the craft. But, all these things have, since, by the gradual improvement of our organization, undergone many alterations; and Entered Apprentices seem now, by universal consent, to be restricted to a very few rights. They have the right of sitting in all lodges of their degree, of receiving all the instructions which appertain to it, but not of speaking or voting, and, lastly, of offering themselves as candidates for advancement, without the preparatory necessity of a formal written petition.

These being admitted to be the rights of an Entered Apprentice, few and unimportant as they may be, they are as dear to him as those of a Master Mason are to one who has been advanced to that degree; and he is, and ought to be, as firmly secured in their possession. Therefore, as no Mason can be deprived of his rights and privileges, except after a fair and impartial trial, and the verdict of his peers, it is clear that the Entered Apprentice cannot be divested of these rights without just such a trial and verdict.

But, in the next place, we are to inquire whether the privilege of being passed as a Fellow Craft is to be enumerated among these rights? And, we clearly answer, No. The Entered Apprentice has the right of making the application. Herein he differs from a profane, who has no such right of application until he has qualified himself for making it, by becoming an Entered Apprentice. But, if the application is granted, it is *ex gratia*, or, by the favour of the lodge, which may withhold it, if it pleases. If such were not the case, the lodge would possess no free will on the subject of advancing candidates; and the rule requiring a probation and an examination, before passing, would be useless and absurd—because, the neglect of improvement or the want of competency would be attended with no penalty.

It seems to me, then, that, when an Apprentice applies for his second degree, the lodge may, if it thinks proper, refuse to grant it; and that it may express that refusal by a ballot. No trial is necessary, because no rights of the candidate are affected. He is, by a rejection of his request, left in the same position that he formerly occupied. He is still an Entered Apprentice, in good standing; and the lodge may, at any time it thinks proper, reverse its decision and proceed to pass him.

If, however, he is specifically charged with any offense against the laws of Masonry, it would then be necessary to give him a trial. Witnesses should be heard, both for and against him, and he should be permitted to make his defense. The opinion of the lodge should be taken, as in all other cases of trial, and, according to the verdict, he should be suspended, expelled, or otherwise punished.

The effect of these two methods of proceeding is very different. When, by a ballot, the lodge refuses to advance an Entered Apprentice, there is not, necessarily, any stigma on his moral character. It may be, that the refusal is based on the ground that he has not made sufficient proficiency to entitle him to pass. Consequently, his standing as an Entered Apprentice is not at all affected. His rights remain the same. He may still sit in the lodge when it is opened in his degree; he may still receive instructions in that degree; converse with Masons on masonic subjects which are not beyond his standing; and again apply to the lodge for permission to pass as a Fellow Craft.

But, if he be tried on a specific charge, and be suspended or expelled, his moral character is affected. His masonic rights are forfeited; and he can no longer be considered as an Entered Apprentice in good standing. He will not be permitted to sit in his lodge, to receive masonic instruction, or to converse with Masons on masonic subjects; nor can he again apply for advancement until the suspension or expulsion is removed by the spontaneous action of the lodge.

These two proceedings work differently in another respect. The Grand Lodge will not interfere with a subordinate lodge in compelling it to pass an Entered Apprentice; because every lodge is supposed to be competent to finish, in its own time, and its own way, the work that it has begun. But, as the old regulations, as well as the general consent of the craft, admit that the Grand Lodge alone can expel from the rights and privileges of Masonry, and that an expulsion by a subordinate lodge is inoperative until it is confirmed by the Grand Lodge, it follows that the expulsion of the Apprentice must be confirmed by that body; and that, therefore, he has a right to appeal to it for a reversal of the sentence, if it was unjustly pronounced.

Let it not be said that this would be placing an Apprentice on too great an equality with Master Masons. His rights are dear to him; he has paid for them. No man would become an Apprentice unless he expected, in time, to be made a Fellow Craft, and then a Master. He is, therefore, morally and legally wronged when he is deprived, without sufficient cause, of the capacity of fulfilling that expectation. It is the duty of the Grand Lodge to see that not even the humblest member of the craft shall have his rights unjustly invaded; and it is therefore bound, as the conservator of the rights of all, to inquire into the truth, and administer equity. Whenever, therefore, even an Entered Apprentice complains that he has met with injustice and oppression, his complaint should be investigated and justice administered.

The question next occurs—What number of black balls should prevent an Apprentice from passing to the second degree? I answer, the same number that would reject the application of a profane for initiation into the Order. And why should this not be so? Are the qualifications which would be required of one applying, for the first time, for admission to the degree of an Apprentice more than would subsequently be required of the same person on his applying for a greater favor and a higher honor—that of being advanced to the second degree? Or do the requisitions, which exist in the earlier stages of Masonry, become less and less with every step of the aspirant's progress? Viewing the question in this light—and, indeed, I know of no other in which to view it—it seems to me to be perfectly evident that the peculiar constitution and principles of our Order will require unanimity in the election of a profane for initiation, of an Apprentice for a Fellow Craft, and of a Fellow Craft for a Master Mason; and that, while no Entered Apprentice can be expelled from the Order, except by due course of trial, it is competent for the lodge, at any time, on a ballot, to refuse to advance him to the second degree. But, let it be remembered that the lodge which refuses to pass an Apprentice, on account of any objections to his moral character, or doubts of his worthiness, is bound to give him the advantage of a trial, and at once to expel him, if guilty, or, if innocent, to advance him when otherwise qualified.

Chapter III.

Of the Rights of Fellow Crafts.

In ancient times there were undoubtedly many rights attached to the second degree which have now become obsolete or been repealed; for formerly the great body of the fraternity were Fellow Crafts, and according to the old charges, even the Grand Master might be elected from among them. The Master and Wardens of Subordinate Lodges always were. Thus we are told that no Brother can be Grand Master, "unless he has been a Fellow Craft before his election," and in the ancient manner of constituting a lodge, contained in the Book of Constitutions,[78] it is said that "the candidates, or the new Master and Wardens, being yet among the Fellow Crafts, the Grand Master shall ask his Deputy if he has examined them," etc. But now that the great body of the Fraternity consists of Master Masons, the prerogatives of Fellow Crafts are circumscribed within limits nearly as narrow as those of Entered Apprentices. While, however, Apprentices are not permitted to speak or vote, in ancient times, and up, indeed, to a very late date. Fellow Crafts were entitled to take a part in any discussion in which the lodge, while open in the first or second degree, might engage, but not to vote. This privilege is expressly stated by Preston, as appertaining to a Fellow Craft, in his charge to a candidate, receiving that degree.

"As a Craftsman, in our private assemblies you may offer your sentiments and opinions on such subjects as are regularly introduced in the Lecture, under the superintendence of an experienced Master, who will guard the landmark against encroachment."[79]

This privilege is not now, however, granted in this country to Fellow Crafts. All, therefore, that has been said in the preceding chapter, of the rights of Entered Apprentices, will equally apply, *mutatis mutandis*, to the rights of Fellow Crafts.

Chapter IV.

Of the Rights of Master Masons.

When a Mason has reached the third degree, he becomes entitled to all the rights and privileges of Ancient Craft Masonry. These rights are extensive and complicated; and, like his duties, which are equally as extensive, require a careful examination, thoroughly to comprehend them. Four of them, at least, are of so much importance as to demand a distinct consideration. These are the rights of membership, of visitation, of relief, and of burial. To each I shall devote a separate section.

Section I.

Of the Right of Membership.

The whole spirit and tenor of the General Regulations, as well as the uniform usage of the craft, sustain the doctrine, that when a Mason is initiated in a lodge, he has the right, by signing the bye-laws, to become a member without the necessity of submitting to another ballot. In the Constitutions of the Grand Lodge of New York, this principle is asserted to be one of the ancient landmarks, and is announced in the following words: "Initiation makes a man a Mason; but he must receive the Master's degree, and sign the bye-laws before he becomes a member of the lodge."[80] If the doctrine be not exactly a landmark (which I confess I am not quite prepared to admit), it comes to us almost clothed with the authority of one, from the sanction of universal and uninterrupted usage.

How long before he loses this right by a *non-user*, or neglect to avail himself of it, is, I presume, a question to be settled by local authority. A lodge, or a Grand Lodge, may affix the period according to its discretion; but the general custom is, to require a signature of the bye-laws, and a consequent enrollment in the lodge, within three months after receiving the third degree. Should a Mason neglect to avail himself of his privilege, he forfeits it (unless, upon sufficient cause, he is excused by the lodge), and must submit to a ballot.

The reason for such a law is evident. If a Mason does not at once unite himself with the lodge in which he was raised, but permits an extended period of time to elapse, there is no certainty that his character or habits may not have changed, and that he may not have become, since his initiation, unworthy of affiliation. Under the general law, it is, therefore, necessary that he should in such case submit to the usual probation of one month, and an investigation of his qualifications by a committee, as well as a ballot by the members.

But there are other privileges also connected with this right of membership. A profane is required to apply for initiation to the lodge nearest his place of residence, and, if there rejected, can never in future apply to any other lodge. But the rule is different with respect to the application of a Master Mason for membership.

A Master Mason is not restricted in his privilege of application for membership within any geographical limits. All that is required of him is, that he should be an affiliated Mason; that is, that he should be a contributing member of a lodge, without any reference to its peculiar locality, whether near to or distant from his place of residence. The Old Charges simply prescribe, that every Mason ought to belong to a lodge. A Mason, therefore, strictly complies with this regulation, when he unites himself with any lodge, thus contributing to the support of the institution, and is then entitled to all the privileges of an affiliated Mason.

A rejection of the application of a Master Mason for membership by a lodge does not deprive him of the right of applying to another. A Mason is in "good standing" until deprived of that character by the action of some competent masonic authority; and that action can only be by suspension or expulsion. Rejection does not, therefore, affect the "good standing" of the applicant; for in a rejection there is no legal form of trial, and consequently the rejected Brother remains in the same position after as before his rejection. He possesses the same rights as before, unimpaired and undiminished; and among these rights is that of applying for membership to any lodge that he may select.

If, then, a Mason may be a member of a lodge distant from his place of residence, and, perhaps, even situated in a different jurisdiction, the question then arises whether the lodge within whose precincts he resides, but of which he is not a member, can exercise its discipline over him should he commit any offense requiring masonic punishment. On this subject there is, among masonic writers, a difference of opinion. I, however, agree with Brother Pike, the able Chairman of the Committee of Correspondence of Arkansas, that the lodge can exercise such discipline. I contend that a Mason is amenable for his conduct not only to the lodge of which he may be a member, but also to any one within whose jurisdiction he permanently resides. A lodge is the conservator of the purity and the protector of the integrity of the Order within its precincts. The unworthy conduct of a Mason, living as it were immediately under its government, is calculated most injuriously to affect that purity and integrity. A lodge, therefore, should not be deprived of the power of coercing such unworthy Mason, and, by salutary punishment, of vindicating the character of the institution. Let us suppose, by way of example, that a Mason living in San Francisco, California, but retaining his membership in New York, behaves in such an immoral and indecorous manner as to bring the greatest discredit upon the Order, and to materially injure it in the estimation of the uninitiated community. Will it be, for a moment, contended that a lodge in San Francisco cannot arrest the evil by bringing the unworthy Mason under discipline, and even ejecting him from the fraternity, if severity like that is necessary for the protection of the institution? Or will it be contended that redress can only be sought through the delay and uncertainty of an appeal to his lodge in New York? Even if the words of the ancient laws are silent on this subject, reason and justice would seem to maintain the propriety and expediency of the doctrine that the lodge at San Francisco is amply competent to extend its jurisdiction and exercise its discipline over the culprit.

In respect to the number of votes necessary to admit a Master Mason applying by petition for membership in a lodge, there can be no doubt that he must submit to precisely the same conditions as those prescribed to a profane on his petition for initiation. There is no room for argument here, for the General Regulations are express on this subject.

"No man can be made or *admitted a member* of a particular lodge," says the fifth regulation, "without previous notice one month before given to the said lodge."

And the sixth regulation adds, that "no man can be entered a Brother in any particular lodge, or *admitted to be a member* thereof, without the unanimous consent of all the members of that lodge then present."

So that it may be considered as settled law, so far as the General Regulations can settle a law of Masonry, that a Master Mason can only be admitted a member of a lodge when applying by petition, after a month's probation, after due inquiry into his character, and after a unanimous ballot in his favor.

But there are other rights of Master Masons consequent upon membership, which remain to be considered. In uniting with a lodge, a Master Mason becomes a participant of all its interests, and is entitled to speak and vote upon all subjects that come before the lodge for investigation. He is also entitled, if duly elected by his fellows, to hold any office in the lodge, except that of Master, for which he must be qualified by previously having occupied the post of a Warden.

A Master has the right in all cases of an appeal from the decision of the Master or of the lodge.

A Master Mason, in good standing, has a right at any time to demand from his lodge a certificate to that effect.

Whatever other rights may appertain to Master Masons will be the subjects of separate sections.

Section II.

Of the Right of Visit.

Every Master Mason, who is an affiliated member of a lodge, has the right to visit any other lodge as often as he may desire to do so. This right is secured to him by the ancient regulations, and is, therefore, irreversible. In the "Ancient Charges at the Constitution of a Lodge," formerly contained in a MS. of the Lodge of Antiquity in London, and whose date is not later than 1688,[81] it is directed "that every Mason receive and cherish strange fellows when they come over the country, and set them on work, if they will work as the manner is; that is to say, if the Mason have any mould stone in his place, he shall give him a mould stone, and set him on work; and if he have none, the Mason shall refresh him with money unto the next lodge."

This regulation is explicit. It not only infers the right of visit, but it declares that the strange Brother shall be welcomed, "received, and cherished," and "set on work," that is, permitted to participate in the work of your lodge. Its provisions are equally applicable to Brethren residing in the place where the lodge is situated as to transient Brethren, provided that they are affiliated Masons.

In the year 1819, the law was in England authoritatively settled by a decree of the Grand Lodge. A complaint had been preferred against a lodge in London, for having refused admission to some Brethren who were well known to them, alleging that as the lodge was about to initiate a candidate, no visitor could be admitted until that ceremony was concluded. It was then declared, "that it is the undoubted right of every Mason who is well known, or properly vouched, to visit any lodge during the time it is opened for general masonic business, observing the proper forms to be attended to on such occasions, and so that the Master may not be interrupted in the performance of his duty."[82]

A lodge, when not opened for "general masonic business," but when engaged in the consideration of matters which interest the lodge alone, and which it would be inexpedient or indelicate to make public, may refuse to admit a visitor. Lodges engaged in this way, in private business, from which visitors are excluded, are said by the French Masons to be opened "*en famille*."

To entitle him to this right of visit, a Mason must be affiliated, that is, he must be a contributing member of some lodge. This doctrine is thus laid down in the Constitutions of the Grand Lodge of England:

"A Brother who is not a subscribing member to some lodge, shall not be permitted to visit any one lodge in the town or place in which he resides, more than once during his secession from the craft."

A non-subscribing or unaffiliated Mason is permitted to visit each lodge once, and once only, because it is supposed that this visit is made for the purpose of enabling him to make a selection of the one with which he may prefer permanently to unite. But, afterwards, he loses this right of visit, to discountenance those Brethren who wish to continue members of the Order, and to partake of its pleasures and advantages, without contributing to its support.

A Master Mason is not entitled to visit a lodge, unless he previously submits to an examination, or is personally vouched for by a competent Brother present; but this is a subject of so much importance as to claim consideration in a distinct section.

Another regulation is, that a strange Brother shall furnish the lodge he intends to visit with a certificate of his good standing in the lodge from which he last hailed. This regulation has, in late years, given rise to much discussion. Many of the Grand Lodges of this country, and several masonic writers, strenuously contend for its antiquity and necessity, while others as positively assert that it is a modern innovation upon ancient usage.

There can, however, I think, be no doubt of the antiquity of certificates. That the system requiring them was in force nearly two hundred years ago, at least, will be evident from the third of the Regulations made in General Assembly, December 27, 1663, under the Grand Mastership of the Earl of St. Albans,[83] and which is in the following words:

"3. That no person hereafter who shall be accepted a Freemason, shall be admitted into any lodge or assembly, until he has brought a certificate of the time and place of his acceptation, from the lodge that accepted him, unto the Master of that limit or division where such a lodge is kept." This regulation has been reiterated on several occasions, by the Grand Lodge of England in 1772, and at subsequent periods by several Grand Lodges of this and other countries. It is not, however, in force in many of the American jurisdictions.

Another right connected with the right of visitation is, that of demanding a sight of the Warrant of Constitution. This instrument it is, indeed, not only the right but the duty of every strange visitor carefully to inspect, before he enters a lodge, that he may thus satisfy himself of the legality and regularity of its character and authority. On such a demand being made by a visitor for a sight of its Warrant, every lodge is bound to comply with the requisition, and produce the instrument. The same rule, of course, applies to lodges under dispensation, whose Warrant of Dispensation supplies the place of a Warrant of Constitution.

Section III.

Of the Examination of Visitors.

It has already been stated, in the preceding section, that a Master Mason is not permitted to visit a lodge unless he previously submits to an examination, or is personally vouched for by some competent Brother present. The prerogative of vouching for a Brother is an important one, and will constitute the subject of the succeeding section. At present let us confine ourselves to the consideration of the mode of examining a visitor.

Every visitor, who offers himself to the appointed committee of the lodge for examination, is expected, as a preliminary step, to submit to the Tiler's Obligation; so called, because it is administered in the Tiler's room. As this obligation forms no part of the secret ritual of the Order, but is administered to every person before any lawful knowledge of his being a Mason has been received, there can be nothing objectionable in inserting it here, and in fact, it will be advantageous to have the precise words of so important a declaration placed beyond the possibility of change or omission by inexperienced Brethren.

The oath, then, which is administered to the visitor, and which he may, if he chooses, require every one present to take with him, is in the following words

"I, A. B., do hereby and hereon solemnly and sincerely swear, that I have been regularly initiated, passed, and raised, to the sublime degree of a Master Mason, in a just and legally constituted lodge of such, that I do not now stand suspended or expelled, and know of no reason why I should not hold masonic communication with my Brethren.

This declaration having been given in the most solemn manner, the examination must then be conducted with the necessary forms. The good old rule of "commencing at the beginning" should be observed. Every question is to be asked and every answer demanded which is necessary to convince the examiner that the party examined is acquainted with what he ought to know, to entitle him to the appellation of a Brother. Nothing is to be taken for granted—categorical answers must be required to all that it is deemed important to be asked. No forgetfulness is to be excused, nor is the want of memory to be accepted as a valid excuse for the want of knowledge. The Mason, who is so unmindful of his duties as to have forgotten the instructions he has received, must pay the penalty of his carelessness, and be deprived of his contemplated visit to that society whose secret modes of recognition he has so little valued as not to have treasured them in his memory. While there are some things which may be safely passed over in the examination of one who confesses himself to be "rusty," or but recently initiated, because they are details which require much study to acquire, and constant practice to retain, there are still other things of great importance which must be rigidly demanded, and with the knowledge of which the examiner cannot, under any circumstances, dispense.

Should suspicions of imposture arise, let no expression of these suspicions be made until the final decree for rejection is pronounced. And let that decree be uttered in general terms, such as: "I am not satisfied," or, "I do not recognize you," and not in more specific terms, such as, "You did not answer this inquiry," or, "You are ignorant on that point." The visitor is only entitled to know, generally, that he has not complied with the requisitions of his examiner. To descend to particulars is always improper and often dangerous.

Above all, the examiner should never ask what are called "leading questions," or such as include in themselves an indication of what the answer is to be; nor should he in any manner aid the memory of the party examined by the slightest hint. If he has it in him, it will come out without assistance, and if he has it not, he is clearly entitled to no aid.

Lastly, never should an unjustifiable delicacy weaken the rigor of these rules. Let it be remembered, that for the wisest and most evident reasons, the merciful maxim of the law, which says, that it is better that ninety-nine guilty men should escape than that one innocent man should be punished, is with us reversed, and that in Masonry *it is better that ninety and nine true men should be turned away from the door of a lodge than that one cowan should be admitted.*

Section IV.

Of Vouching for a Brother.

An examination may sometimes be omitted when any competent Brother present will vouch for the visitor's masonic standing and qualifications. This prerogative of vouching is an important one which every Master Mason is entitled, under certain restrictions, to exercise; but it is also one which may so materially affect the well-being of the whole fraternity—since by its injudicious use impostors might be introduced among the faithful—that it should be controlled by the most stringent regulations.

To vouch for one, is to bear witness for him; and, in witnessing to truth, every caution should be observed, lest falsehood should cunningly assume its garb. The Brother who vouches should, therefore, know to a certainty that the one for whom he vouches is really what he claims to be. He should know this not from a casual conversation, nor a loose and careless inquiry, but, as the unwritten law of the Order expresses it, from "*strict trial, due examination, or lawful information.*"

Of strict trial and due examination I have already treated in the preceding section; and it only remains to say, that when the vouching is founded on the knowledge obtained in this way, it is absolutely necessary that the Brother so vouching shall be *competent* to conduct such an examination, and that his general intelligence and shrewdness and his knowledge of Masonry shall be such as to place him above the probability of being imposed upon. The important and indispensable qualification of a voucher is, therefore, that he shall be competent. The Master of a lodge has no right to accept, without further inquiry, the avouchment of a young and inexperienced, or even of an old, if ignorant, Mason.

Lawful information, which is the remaining ground for an avouchment, may be derived either from the declaration of another Brother, or from having met the party vouched for in a lodge on some previous occasion.

If the information is derived from another Brother, who states that he has examined the party, then all that has already been said of the competency of the one giving the information is equally applicable. The Brother, giving the original information, must be competent to make a rigid examination. Again, the person giving the information, the one receiving it, and the one of whom it is given, should be all present at the time; for otherwise there would be no certainty of identity. Information, therefore, given by letter or through a third party, is highly irregular. The information must also be positive, not founded on belief or opinion, but derived from a legitimate source. And, lastly, it must not have been received casually, but for the very purpose of being used for masonic purposes. For one to say to another in the course of a desultory conversation: "A.B. is a Mason," is not sufficient. He may not be speaking with due caution, under the expectation that his words will be considered of weight. He must say something to this effect: "I know this man to be a Master Mason," for such or such reasons, and you may safely recognize him as such. This alone will insure the necessary care and proper observance of prudence.

If the information given is on the ground that the person, vouched has been seen sitting in a lodge by the voucher, care must be taken to inquire if it was a "Lodge of Master Masons." A person may forget, from the lapse of time, and vouch for a stranger as a Master Mason, when the lodge in which he saw him was only opened in the first or second degree.

Section V.

Of the Right of Claiming Relief.

One of the great objects of our institution is, to afford relief to a worthy, distressed Brother. In his want and destitution, the claim of a Mason upon his Brethren is much greater than that of a profane. This is a Christian as well as a masonic doctrine. "As we have therefore opportunity," says St. Paul, "let us do good unto all men, especially unto them who are of the household of faith."

This claim for relief he may present either to a lodge or to a Brother Mason. The rule, as well as the principles by which it is to be regulated, is laid down in that fundamental law of Masonry, the Old Charges, in the following explicit words, under the head of "Behavior towards a strange Brother:"

"You are cautiously to examine him, in such a method as prudence shall direct you, that you may not be imposed upon by an ignorant, false pretender, whom you are to reject with contempt and derision, and beware of giving him any hints of knowledge.

"But if you discover him to be a true and genuine Brother, you are to respect him accordingly; and if he is in want, you must relieve him if you can, or else direct him how he may be relieved. You must employ him some days, or else recommend him to be employed. But you are not charged to do beyond your ability, only to prefer a poor Brother, that is a good man and true, before any other people in the same circumstances."

This law thus laid down, includes, it will be perceived, as two important prerequisites, on which to found a claim for relief, that the person applying shall be in distress, and that he shall be worthy of assistance.

He must be in distress. Ours is not an insurance company, a joint stock association, in which, for a certain premium paid, an equivalent may be demanded. No Mason, or no lodge, is bound to give pecuniary or other aid to a Brother, unless he really needs. The word " benefit," as usually used in the modern friendly societies, has no place in the vocabulary of Freemasonry. If a wealthy Brother is afflicted with sorrow or sickness, we are to strive to comfort him with our sympathy, our kindness, and our attention, but we are to bestow our eleemosynary aid only on the indigent or the destitute.

He must also be worthy. There is no obligation on a Mason to relieve the distresses, however real they may be, of an unworthy Brother. The claimant must be, in the language of the Charge, "true and genuine." True here is used in its good old Saxon meaning, of "faithful" or "trusty." A true Mason is one who is mindful of his obligations, and who faithfully observes and practices all his duties. Such a man, alone, can rightfully claim the assistance of his Brethren.

But a third provision is made in the fundamental law; namely, that the assistance is not to be beyond the ability of the giver. One of the most important landmarks, contained in our unwritten law, more definitely announces this provision, by the words, that the aid and assistance shall be without injury to oneself or his family. Masonry does not require that we shall sacrifice our own welfare to that of a Brother; but that with prudent liberality, and a just regard to our own worldly means, we shall give of the means with which Providence may have blessed us for the relief of our distressed Brethren.

It is hardly necessary to say, that the claim for relief of a worthy distressed Mason extends also to his immediate family.

Section VI.

Of the Right of Masonic Burial.

After a very careful examination, I can find nothing in the old charges or General Regulations, nor in any other part of the fundamental law, in relation to masonic burial of deceased Brethren. It is probable that, at an early period, when the great body of the craft consisted of Entered Apprentices, the usage permitted the burial of members, of the first or second degree, with the honors of Masonry. As far back as 1754, processions for the purpose of burying Masons seemed to have been conducted by some of the lodges with either too much frequency, or some other irregularity; for, in November of that year, the Grand Lodge adopted a regulation, forbidding them, under a heavy penalty, unless by permission of the Grand Master, or his Deputy.[84] As there were, comparatively speaking, few Master Masons at that period, it seems a natural inference that most of the funeral processions were for the burial of Apprentices, or, at least, of Fellow Crafts.

But the usage since then, has been greatly changed; and by universal consent, the law, as first committed to writing, by Preston, who was the author of our present funeral service, is now adopted.

The Regulation, as laid down by Preston, is so explicit, that I prefer giving it in his own words.[85]

"No Mason can be interred with the formalities of the Order, unless it be at his own special request, communicated to the Master of the Lodge of which he died a member—foreigners and sojourners excepted; nor unless he has been advanced to the third degree of Masonry, from which restriction there can be no exception. Fellow Crafts or Apprentices are not entitled to the funeral obsequies."

This rule has been embodied in the modern Constitutions of the Grand Lodge of England; and, as I have already observed, appears by universal consent to have been adopted as the general usage.

The necessity for a dispensation, which is also required by the modern English Constitutions, does not seem to have met with the same general approval, and in this country, dispensations for funeral processions are not usually, if at all, required. Indeed, Preston himself, in explaining the law, says that it was not intended to restrict the privileges of the regular lodges, but that, "by the universal practice of Masons, every regular lodge is authorized by the Constitution to act on such occasions when limited to its own members."[86] It is only when members of other lodges, not under the control of the Master, are convened, that a dispensation is required. But in America, Grand Lodges or Grand Masters have not generally interfered with the rights of the lodges to bury the dead; the Master being of course amenable to the constituted authorities for any indecorum or impropriety.

Chapter V.

Of the Rights of Past Masters.

I have already discussed the right of Past Masters to become members of a Grand Lodge, in a preceding part of this work,[87] and have there arrived at the conclusion that no such inherent right exists, and that a Grand Lodge may or may not admit them to membership, according to its own notion of expediency. Still the fact, that they are competent by their masonic rank of accepting such a courtesy when extended, in itself constitutes a prerogative; for none but Masters, Wardens, or Past Masters, can under any circumstances become members of a Grand Lodge.

Past Masters possess a few other positive rights.

In the first place they have a right to install their successors, and at all times subsequent to their installation to be present at the ceremony of installing Masters of lodges. I should scarcely have deemed it necessary to dwell upon so self-evident a proposition, were it not that it involves the discussion of a question which has of late years been warmly mooted in some jurisdictions, namely, whether this right of being present at an installation should, or should not, be extended to Past Masters, made in Royal Arch Chapters.

In view of the fact, that there are two very different kinds of possessors of the same degree, the Grand Lodge of England has long since distinguished them as "virtual" and as "actual" Past Masters. The terms are sufficiently explicit, and have the advantage of enabling us to avoid circumlocution, and I shall, therefore, adopt them.

An *actual Past Master* is one who has been regularly installed to preside over a symbolic lodge under the jurisdiction of a Grand Lodge. A *virtual Past Master* is one who has received the degree in a chapter, for the purpose of qualifying him for exaltation to the Royal Arch.

Now the question to be considered is this. Can a virtual Past Master be permitted to be present at the installation of an actual Past Master?

The Committee of Correspondence of New York, in 1851, announced the doctrine, that a Chapter, or virtual Past Master, cannot legally install the Master of a Symbolic Lodge; but that there is no rule forbidding his being present at the ceremony. This doctrine has been accepted by several Grand Lodges, while others again refuse to admit the presence of a virtual Past Master at the installation-service.

In South Carolina, for instance, by uninterrupted usage, virtual Past Masters are excluded from the ceremony of installation.

In Louisiana, under the high authority of the late Brother Gedge, it is asserted, that "it is the bounden duty of all Grand Lodges to prevent the possessors of the (chapter) degree from the exercise of any function appertaining to the office and attributes of an installed Master of a lodge of Symbolic Masonry, and refuse to recognize them as belonging to the order of Past Masters."[88]

Brother Albert Pike, whose opinion on masonic jurisprudence is entitled to the most respectful consideration, has announced a similar doctrine in one of his elaborate reports to the Grand Chapter of Arkansas. He does not consider "that the Past Master's degree, conferred in a chapter, invests the recipient with any rank or authority, except within the chapter itself; that it no ways qualifies or authorizes him to preside in the chair of a lodge: that a lodge has no legal means of knowing that he has received the degree in a chapter: for it is not supposed to know anything that takes place there any more than it knows what takes place in a Lodge of Perfection, or a Chapter of Knights of the Rose Croix;" and, of course, if the Past Masters of a lodge have no such "legal means" of recognition of Chapter Masters, they cannot permit them to be present at an installation.

This is, in fact, no new doctrine. Preston, in his description of the installation ceremony, says: "The new Master is then conducted to an adjacent room, where he is regularly installed, and bound to his trust in ancient form, in the presence of at least *three installed Masters*"[89] And Dr. Oliver, in commenting on this passage, says, "this part of the ceremony can only be orally communicated, nor can any but *installed Masters be present.*"[90]

And this rule appears to be founded on the principles of reason. There can be no doubt, if we carefully examine the history of Masonry in this country and in England, that the degree of Past Master was originally conferred by Symbolic Lodges as an honorarium or reward bestowed upon those Brethren who had been found worthy to occupy the Oriental Chair. In so far it was only a degree of office, and could be obtained only from the Lodge in which the office had been conferred. At a later period it was deemed an essential prerequisite to exaltation in the degree of Royal Arch, and was, for that purpose, conferred on candidates for that position, while the Royal Arch degree was under the control of the symbolic Lodges, but still only conferred by the Past Masters of the Lodge. But subsequently, when the system of Royal Arch Masonry was greatly enlarged and extended in this country, and chapters were organized independent of the Grand and symbolic Lodges, these Chapters took with them the Past Master's degree, and assumed the right of conferring it on their candidates. Hence arose the anomaly which now exists in American Masonry, of two degrees bearing the same name, and said to be almost identical in character, conferred by two different bodies under entirely different qualifications and for totally different purposes. As was to be expected, when time had in some degree obliterated the details of history, each party began to claim for itself the sovereign virtue of legitimacy. The Past Masters of the Chapters denied the right of the Symbolic Lodges to confer the degree, and the latter, in their turn, asserted that the degree, as conferred in the Chapter, was an innovation.

The prevalence of the former doctrine would, of course, tend to deprive the Symbolic Lodges of a vested right held by them from the most ancient times—that, namely, of conferring an honorarium on their Masters elect.

On the whole, then, from this view of the surreptitious character of the Chapter Degree, and supported by the high authority whom I have cited, as well as by the best usage, I am constrained to believe that the true rule is, to deny the Chapter, or Virtual Past Masters, the right to install, or to be present at the installation of the Master of a Symbolic Lodge. A Past Master may preside over a lodge in the absence of the Master, provided he is invited to do so by the Senior Warden present. The Second General Regulation gave the power of presiding, during the absence of the Master, to the last Past Master present, after the lodge had been congregated by the Senior Warden; but two years afterwards, the rule was repealed, and the power of presiding in such cases was vested in the Senior Warden. And accordingly, in this country, it has always been held, that in the absence of the Master, his authority descends to the Senior Warden, who may, however, by courtesy, offer the chair to a Past Master present, after the lodge has been congregated. Some jurisdictions have permitted a Past Master to preside in the absence of the Master and both Wardens, provided he was a member of that lodge. But I confess that I can find no warrant for this rule in any portion of our fundamental laws. The power of congregating the lodge in the absence of the Master has always been confined to the Wardens; and it therefore seems to me, that when both the Master and Wardens are absent, although a Past Master may be present, the lodge cannot be opened.

A Past Master is eligible for election to the chair, without again passing through the office of a Warden.

He is also entitled to a seat in the East, and to wear a jewel and collar peculiar to his dignity.

By an ancient regulation, contained in the Old Charges, Past Masters alone were eligible to the office of Grand Warden. The Deputy Grand Master was also to be selected from among the Masters, or Past Masters of Lodges. No such regulation was in existence as to the office of Grand Master, who might be selected from the mass of the fraternity. At the present time, in this country, it is usual to select the Grand officers from among the Past Masters of the jurisdiction, though I know of no ancient law making such a regulation obligatory, except in respect to the affairs of Grand Wardens and Deputy Grand Master.

Chapter VI.

Of Affiliation.

Affiliation is defined to be the act by which a lodge receives a Mason among its members. A profane is said to be "initiated," but a Mason is "affiliated."[91]

Now the mode in which a Mason becomes affiliated with a lodge, in some respects differs from, and in others resembles, the mode in which a profane is initiated.

A Mason, desiring to be affiliated with a lodge, must apply by petition; this petition must be referred to a committee for investigation of character, he must remain in a state of probation for one month, and must then submit to a ballot, in which unanimity will be required for his admission. In all these respects, there is no difference in the modes of regulating applications for initiation and affiliation. The Fifth and Sixth General Regulations, upon which these usages are founded, draw no distinction between the act of making a Mason and admitting a member. The two processes are disjunctively connected in the language of both regulations. "No man can be made, *or admitted a member* * * * * without previous notice one month before;" are the words of the Fifth Regulation. And in a similar spirit the Sixth adds: "But no man can be entered a Brother in any particular lodge, *or admitted to be a member* thereof, without the unanimous consent of all the members of that lodge."

None but Master Masons are permitted to apply for affiliation; and every Brother so applying must bring to the lodge to which he applies a certificate of his regular dismission from the lodge of which he was last a member. This document is now usually styled a "demit," and should specify the good standing of the bearer at the time of his resignation or demission.

Under the regulations of the various Grand Lodges of this country, a profane cannot, as has been already observed, apply for initiation in any other lodge than the one nearest to his residence. No such regulation, however, exists in relation to the application of a Mason for affiliation. Having once been admitted into the Order, he has a right to select the lodge with which he may desire to unite himself. He is not even bound to affiliate with the lodge in which he was initiated, but after being raised, may leave it, without signing the bye-laws, and attach himself to another.

A profane, having been rejected by a lodge, can never apply to any other for initiation. But a Mason, having been rejected, on his application for affiliation, by a lodge, is not thereby debarred from subsequently making a similar application to any other.

In some few jurisdictions a local regulation has of late years been enacted, that no Mason shall belong to more than one lodge. It is, I presume, competent for a Grand Lodge to enact such a regulation; but where such enactment has not taken place, we must be governed by the ancient and general principle.

The General Regulations, adopted in 1721, contain no reference to this case; but in a new regulation, adopted on the 19th February, 1723, it was declared that "no Brother shall belong to more than one lodge within the bills of mortality." This rule was, therefore, confined to the lodges in the city of London, and did not affect the country lodges. Still, restricted as it was in its operation, Anderson remarks, "this regulation is neglected for several reasons, and now obsolete."[92] Custom now in England and in other parts of Europe, as well as in some few portions of this country, is adverse to the regulation; and where no local law exists in a particular jurisdiction, I know of no principle of masonic jurisprudence which forbids a Mason to affiliate himself with more than one lodge.

The only objection to it is one which must be urged, not by the Order, but by the individual. It is, that his duties and his responsibilities are thus multiplied, as well as his expenses. If he is willing to incur all this additional weight in running his race of Masonry, it is not for others to resist this exuberance of zeal. The Mason, however, who is affiliated with more than one lodge, must remember that he is subject to the independent jurisdiction of each; may for the same offense be tried in each, and, although acquitted by all except one, that, if convicted by that one, his conviction will, if he be suspended or expelled, work his suspension or expulsion in all the others.

Chapter VII.

Of Demitting.

To demit from a lodge is to resign one's membership, on which occasion a certificate of good standing and a release from all dues is given to the applicant, which is technically called a *demit*.

The right to demit or resign never has, until within a few years, been denied. In 1853, the Grand Lodge of Connecticut adopted a regulation "that no lodge should grant a demit to any of its members, except for the purpose of joining some other lodge; and that no member shall be considered as having withdrawn from one lodge until he has actually become a member of another." Similar regulations have been either adopted or proposed by a few other Grand Lodges, but I much doubt both their expediency and their legality. This compulsory method of keeping Masons, after they have once been made, seems to me to be as repugnant to the voluntary character of our institution as would be a compulsory mode of making them in the beginning. The expediency of such a regulation is also highly questionable. Every candidate is required to come to our doors "of his own free will and accord," and surely we should desire to keep none among us after that free will is no longer felt. We are all familiar with the Hudibrastic adage, that

"A man convinced against his will,
Is of the same opinion still,"

and he who is no longer actuated by that ardent esteem for the institution which would generate a wish to continue his membership, could scarcely have his slumbering zeal awakened, or his coldness warmed by the bolts and bars of a regulation that should keep him a reluctant prisoner within the walls from which he would gladly escape. Masons with such dispositions we can gladly spare from our ranks.

The Ancient Charges, while they assert that every Mason should belong to a lodge, affix no penalty for disobedience. No man can be compelled to continue his union with a society, whether it be religious, political, or social, any longer than will suit his own inclinations or sense of duty. To interfere with this inalienable prerogative of a freeman would be an infringement on private rights. A Mason's initiation was voluntary, and his continuance in the Order must be equally so.

But no man is entitled to a demit, unless at the time of demanding it he be in good standing and free from all charges. If under charges for crime, he must remain and abide his trial, or if in arrears, must pay up his dues.

There is, however, one case of demission for which a special law has been enacted. That is, when several Brethren at the same time request demits from a lodge. As this action is sometimes the result of pique or anger, and as the withdrawal of several members at once might seriously impair the prosperity, or perhaps even endanger the very existence of the lodge, it has been expressly forbidden by the General Regulations, unless the lodge has become too numerous for convenient working; and not even then is permitted except by a Dispensation. The words of this law are to be found in the Eighth General Regulation, as follows:

"No set or number of Brethren shall withdraw or separate themselves from the lodge in which they were made Brethren, or were afterwards admitted members, unless the lodge becomes too numerous; nor even then, without a dispensation from the Grand Master or his Deputy; and when they are thus separated, they must either immediately join themselves to such other lodge as they shall like best, with the unanimous consent of that other lodge to which they go, or else they must obtain the Grand Master's warrant to join in forming a new lodge."

It seems, therefore, that, although a lodge cannot deny the right of a single member to demit, when a sort of conspiracy may be supposed to be formed, and several Brethren present their petitions for demits at one and the same time, the lodge may not only refuse, but is bound to do so, unless under a dispensation, which dispensation can only be given in the case of an over-populous lodge.

With these restrictions and qualifications, it cannot be doubted that every Master Mason has a right to demit from his lodge at his own pleasure. What will be the result upon himself, in his future relations to the Order, of such demission, will constitute the subject of the succeeding chapter.

Chapter VIII.

Of Unaffiliated Masons.

An unaffiliated Mason is one who is not connected by membership with any lodge. There can be no doubt that such a position is contrary to the spirit of our institution, and that affiliation is a duty obligatory on every Mason. The Old Charges, which have been so often cited as the fundamental law of Masonry, say on this subject: "every Brother ought to belong to a lodge and to be subject to its bye-laws and the General Regulations."

Explicitly as this doctrine has been announced, it has been too little observed, in consequence of no precise penalty having been annexed to its violation. In all times, unaffiliated Masons have existed—Masons who have withdrawn from all active participation in the duties and responsibilities of the Order, and who, when in the hour of danger or distress, have not hesitated to claim its protection or assistance, while they have refused in the day of their prosperity to add anything to its wealth, its power, or its influence. In this country, the anti-masonic persecutions of 1828, and a few years subsequently, by causing the cessation of many lodges, threw a vast number of Brethren out of all direct connection with the institution; on the restoration of peace, and the renewal of labor by the lodges, too many of these Brethren neglected to reunite themselves with the craft, and thus remained unaffiliated. The habit, thus introduced, was followed by others, until the sin of unaffiliation has at length arrived at such a point of excess, as to have become a serious evil, and to have attracted the attention and received the condemnation of almost every Grand Lodge.

A few Grand Lodges have denied the right of a Mason permanently to demit from the Order. Texas, for instance, has declared that "it does not recognize the right of a Mason to demit or separate himself from the lodge in which he was made, or may afterwards be admitted, except for the purpose of joining another lodge, or when he may be about to remove without the jurisdiction of the lodge of which he may be a member."[93] A few other Grand Lodges have adopted a similar regulation; but the prevailing opinion of the authorities appears to be, that it is competent to interfere with the right to demit, certain rights and prerogatives being, however, lost by such demission.

Arkansas, Missouri, Ohio, and one or two other Grand Lodges, while not positively denying the right of demission, have at various times levied a tax or contribution on the demitted or unaffiliated Masons within their respective jurisdictions. This principle, however, has also failed to obtain the general concurrence of other Grand Lodges, and some of them, as Maryland, have openly denounced it. After a careful examination of the authorities, I cannot deny to any man the *right* of withdrawing, whensoever he pleases, from a voluntary association—the laws of the land would not sustain us in the enforcement of such a regulation; and our own self-respect should prevent us from attempting it. If, then, he has a right to withdraw, it clearly follows that we have no right to tax him, which is only one mode of inflicting a fine or penalty for an act, the right to do which we have acceded. In the strong language of the Committee of Correspondence of Maryland:[94] "The object of Masonry never was to extort, *nolens volens*, money from its votaries. Such are not its principles or teaching. The advocating such doctrines cannot advance the interest or reputation of the institution; but will, as your committee fear, do much to destroy its usefulness. Compulsive membership deprives it of the title, *Free* and Accepted."

But as it is an undoubted precept of the Order that every Mason should belong to a lodge, and contribute, so far as his means will allow, to the support of the institution, and as, by his demission, for other than temporary purposes, he violates the principles and disobeys the precepts of the Order, it naturally follows that his withdrawal must place him in a different position from that which he would occupy as an affiliated Mason. It is now time for us to inquire what that new position is.

We may say, then, that, whenever a Mason permanently withdraws his membership, he at once, and while he continues unaffiliated, dissevers all connection between himself and the *Lodge organization* of the Order. He, by this act, divests himself of all the rights and privileges which belong to him as a member of that organization. Among these rights and privileges are those of visitation, of pecuniary aid, and of masonic burial. Whenever he approaches the door of a lodge, asking to enter or seeking for assistance, he is to be met in the light of a profane. He may knock, but the door must not be opened—he may ask, but he is not to receive. The work of the lodge is not to be shared by those who have thrown aside their aprons and their implements, and abandoned the labors of the Temple—the funds of the lodge are to be distributed only among these who are aiding, by their individual contributions, to the formation of similar funds in other lodges.

But from the well-known and universally-admitted maxim of "once a Mason, and always a Mason," it follows that a demitted Brother cannot by such demission divest himself of all his masonic responsibilities to his Brethren, nor be deprived of their correlative responsibility to him. An unaffiliated Mason is still bound by certain obligations, of which he cannot, under any circumstances, divest himself, and by similar obligations are the fraternity bound to him. These relate to the duties of secrecy and of aid in the imminent hour of peril. Of the first of these there can be no doubt; and as to the last, the words of the precept directing it leaves us no option; nor is it a time when the G.H.S. of D. is thrown out to inquire into the condition of the party.

Speaking on this subject, Brother Albert Pike, in his report to the Grand Lodge of Arkansas, says "if a person appeals to us as a Mason in imminent peril, or such pressing need that we have not time to inquire into his worthiness, then, lest we might refuse to relieve and aid a worthy Brother, we must not stop to inquire *as to anything*." But I do not think that the learned Brother has put the case in the strongest light. It is not alone "lest we might refuse to relieve and aid a worthy Brother," that we are in cases of "imminent peril" to make no pause for deliberation. But it is because we are bound by our highest obligations at all times, and to all Masons, to give that aid when *duly* called for.

I may, then, after this somewhat protracted discussion, briefly recapitulate the position, the rights and the responsibilities of an unaffiliated Mason as follows:

1. An unaffiliated Mason is still bound by all his masonic duties and obligations, excepting those connected with the organization of the lodge.

2. He has a right to aid in imminent peril when *he asks for that aid in the* proper *and conventional way.*

3. He loses the right to receive pecuniary relief.

4. He loses the general right to visit[95] lodges, or to walk in masonic processions.

5. He loses the right of masonic burial.

6. He still remains subject to the government of the Order, and may be tried and punished for any offense as an affiliated Mason would be, by the lodge within whose geographical jurisdiction he resides.

Book Fourth.

Of Masonic Crimes and Punishments.

Chapter I.

Of What Are Masonic Crimes.

The division of wrongs, by the writers on municipal law, into private and public, or civil injuries and crimes and misdemeanors, does not apply to the jurisprudence of Freemasonry. Here all wrongs are crimes, because they are a violation of the precepts of the institution; and an offense against an individual is punished, not so much because it is a breach of his private rights, as because it affects the well-being of the whole masonic community.

In replying to the question, "what are masonic crimes?" by which is meant what crimes are punishable by the constituted authorities, our safest guide will be that fundamental law which is contained in the Old Charges. These give a concise, but succinct summary of the duties of a Mason, and, of course, whatever is a violation of any one of these duties will constitute a masonic crime, and the perpetrator will be amenable to masonic punishment.

But before entering on the consideration of these penal offenses, it will be well that we should relieve the labor of the task, by inquiring what crimes or offenses are not supposed to come within the purview of masonic jurisprudence.

Religion and politics are subjects which it is well known are stringently forbidden to be introduced into Masonry. And hence arises the doctrine, that Masonry will not take congnizance of religious or political offenses.

Heresy, for instance, is not a masonic crime. Masons are obliged to use the words of the Old Charges, "to that religion in which all men agree, leaving their particular opinions to themselves;" and, therefore, as long as a Mason acknowledges his belief in the existence of one God, a lodge can take no action on his peculiar opinions, however heterodox they may be.

In like manner, although all the most ancient and universally-received precepts of the institution inculcate obedience to the civil powers, and strictly forbid any mingling in plots or conspiracies against the peace and welfare of the nation, yet no offense against the state, which is simply political in its character, can be noticed by a lodge. On this important subject, the Old Charges are remarkably explicit. They say, putting perhaps the strongest case by way of exemplifying the principle, "that if a Brother should be a rebel against the State, he is not to be countenanced in his rebellion, however he may be pitied as an unhappy man; and, if convicted of no other crime, though the loyal Brotherhood must and ought to disown his rebellion, and give no umbrage or ground of political jealousy to the government for the time being, *they cannot expel him from the lodge, and his relation to it remains indefeasible*"

The lodge can, therefore, take no cognizance of religious or political offenses.

The first charge says: "a Mason is obliged by his tenure to obey the moral law." Now, although, in a theological sense, the ten commandments are said to embrace and constitute the moral law, because they are its best exponent, yet jurists have given to the term a more general latitude, in defining the moral laws to be "the eternal, immutable laws of good and evil, to which the Creator himself, in all dispensations, conforms, and which he has enabled human reason to discover, so far as they are necessary for the conduct of human actions."[96] Perhaps the well known summary of Justinian will give the best idea of what this law is, namely, that we "should live honestly, (that is to say, without reproach,)[97] should injure nobody, and render to every one his just due."

If such, then, be the meaning of the moral law, and if every Mason is by his tenure obliged to obey it, it follows, that all such crimes as profane swearing or great impiety in any form, neglect of social and domestic duties, murder and its concomitant vices of cruelty and hatred, adultery, dishonesty in any shape, perjury or malevolence, and habitual falsehood, inordinate covetousness, and in short, all those ramifications of these leading vices which injuriously affect the relations of man to God, his neighbor, and himself, are proper subjects of lodge jurisdiction. Whatever moral defects constitute the bad man, make also the bad Mason, and consequently come under the category of masonic offenses. The principle is so plain and comprehensible as to need no further exemplification. It is sufficient to say that, whenever an act done by a Mason is contrary to or subsersive of the three great duties which he owes to God, his neighbor, and himself, it becomes at once a subject of masonic investigation, and of masonic punishment.

But besides these offenses against the universal moral law, there are many others arising from the peculiar nature of our institution. Among these we may mention, and in their order, those that are enumerated in the several sections of the Sixth Chapter of the Old Charges. These are, unseemly and irreverent conduct in the lodge, all excesses of every kind, private piques or quarrels brought into the lodge; imprudent conversation in relation to Masonry in the presence of uninitiated strangers; refusal to relieve a worthy distressed Brother, if in your power; and all "wrangling, quarreling, back-biting, and slander."

The lectures in the various degrees, and the Ancient Charges read on the installation of the Master of a lodge, furnish us with other criteria for deciding what are peculiarly masonic offenses. All of them need not be detailed; but among them may be particularly mentioned the following: All improper revelations, undue solicitations for candidates, angry and over-zealous arguments in favor of Masonry with its enemies, every act which tends to impair the unsullied purity of the Order, want of reverence for and obedience to masonic superiors, the expression of a contemptuous opinion of the original rulers and patrons of Masonry, or of the institution itself; all countenance of impostors; and lastly, holding masonic communion with clandestine Masons, or visiting irregular lodges.

From this list, which, extended as it is, might easily have been enlarged, it will be readily seen, that the sphere of masonic penal jurisdiction is by no means limited. It should, therefore, be the object of every Mason, to avoid the censure or reproach of his Brethren, by strictly confining himself as a point within that circle of duty which, at his first initiation, was presented to him as an object worthy of his consideration.

Chapter II.

Of Masonic Punishments.

Having occupied the last chapter in a consideration of what constitute masonic crimes, it is next in order to inquire how these offenses are to be punished; and accordingly I propose in the following sections to treat of the various modes in which masonic law is vindicated, commencing with the slightest mode of punishment, which is censure, and proceeding to the highest, or expulsion from all the rights and privileges of the Order.

Section I.

Of Censure.

A censure is the mildest form of punishment that can be inflicted by a lodge; and as it is simply the expression of an opinion by the members of the lodge, that they do not approve of the conduct of the person implicated, in a particular point of view, and as it does not in any degree affect the masonic standing of the one censured, nor for a moment suspend or abridge his rights and benefits, I have no doubt that it may be done on a mere motion, without previous notice, and adopted, as any other resolution, by a bare majority of the members present.

Masonic courtesy would, however, dictate that notice should be given to the Brother, if absent, that such a motion of censure is about to be proposed or considered, to enable him to show cause, if any he have, why he should not be censured. But such notice is not, as I have said, necessary to the legality of the vote of censure.

A vote of censure will sometimes, however, be the result of a trial, and in that case its adoption must be governed by the rules of masonic trials, which are hereafter to be laid down.

Section II.

Of Reprimand.

A reprimand is the next mildest form of masonic punishment. It should never be adopted on a mere motion, but should always be the result of a regular trial, in which the party may have the opportunity of defense.

A reprimand may be either private or public. If to be given in private, none should be present but the Master and the offender; or, if given by letter, no copy of that letter should be preserved.

If given in public, the lodge is the proper place, and the reprimand should be given by the Master from his appropriate station.

The Master is always the executive officer of the lodge, and in carrying out the sentence he must exercise his own prudent discretion as to the mode of delivery and form of words.

A reprimand, whether private or public, does not affect the masonic standing of the offender.

Section III.

Of Exclusion from the Lodge.

Exclusion from a lodge may be of various degrees.

1. A member may for indecorous or unmasonic conduct be excluded from a single meeting of the lodge. This may be done by the Master, under a provision of the bye-laws giving him the authority, or on his own responsibility, in which case he is amenable to the Grand Lodge for the correctness of his decision. Exclusion in this way does not affect the masonic standing of the person excluded, and does not require a previous trial.

I cannot entertain any doubt that the Master of a lodge has the right to exclude temporarily any member or Mason, when he thinks that either his admission, if outside, or his continuance within, if present, will impair the peace and harmony of the lodge. It is a prerogative necessary to the faithful performance of his duties, and inalienable from his great responsibility to the Grand Lodge for the proper government of the Craft intrusted to his care. If, as it is described in the ancient manner of constituting a lodge, the Master is charged "to preserve the cement of the Lodge," it would be folly to give him such a charge, unless he were invested with the power to exclude an unruly or disorderly member. But as Masters are enjoined not to rule their lodges in an unjust or arbitrary manner, and as every Mason is clearly entitled to redress for any wrong that has been done to him, it follows that the Master is responsible to the Grand Lodge for the manner in which he has executed the vast power intrusted to him, and he may be tried and punished by that body, for excluding a member, when the motives of the act and the other circumstances of the exclusion were not such as to warrant the exercise of his prerogative.

2. A member may be excluded from his lodge for a definite or indefinite period, on account of the non-payment of arrears. This punishment may be inflicted in different modes, and under different names. It is sometimes called, *suspension from the lodge*, and sometimes *erasure from the roll*. Both of these punishments, though differing in their effect, are pronounced, not after a trial, but by a provision of the bye-laws of the lodge. For this reason alone, if there were no other, I should contend, that they do not affect the standing of the member suspended, or erased, with relation to the craft in general. No Mason can be deprived of his masonic rights, except after a trial, with the opportunity of defense, and a verdict of his peers.

But before coming to a definite conclusion on this subject, it is necessary that we should view the subject in another point of view, in which it will be seen that a suspension from the rights and benefits of Masonry, for the non-payment of dues, is entirely at variance with the true principles of the Order.

The system of payment of lodge-dues does not by any means belong to the ancient usages of the fraternity. It is a modern custom, established for purposes of convenience, and arising out of other modifications, in the organization of the Order. It is not an obligation on the part of a Mason, to the institution at large, but is in reality a special contract, in which the only parties are a particular lodge and its members, of which the fraternity, as a mass, are to know nothing. It is not presented by any general masonic law, nor any universal masonic precept. No Grand Lodge has ever yet attempted to control or regulate it, and it is thus tacitly admitted to form no part of the general regulations of the Order. Even in that Old Charge in which a lodge is described, and the necessity of membership in is enforced, not a word is said of the payment of arrears to it, or of the duty of contributing to its support. Hence the non-payment of arrears is a violation of a special and voluntary contract with a lodge, and not of any general duty to the craft at large. The corollary from all this is, evidently, that the punishment inflicted in such a case should be one affecting the relations of the delinquent with the particular lodge whose bye-laws he has infringed, and not a general one, affecting his relations with the whole Order. After a consideration of all these circumstances, I am constrained to think that suspension from alodge, for non-payment of arrears, should only suspend the rights of the member as to his own lodge, but should not affect his right of visiting other lodges, nor any of the other privileges inherent in him as a Mason. Such is not, I confess, the general opinion, or usage of the craft in this country, but yet I cannot but believe that it is the doctrine most consonant with the true spirit of the institution. It is the practice pursued by the Grand Lodge of England, from which most of our Grand Lodges derive, directly or indirectly, their existence. It is also the regulation of the Grand Lodge of Massachusetts. The Grand Lodge of South Carolina expressly forbids suspension from the rights and benefits of Masonry for non-payment of dues, and the Grand Lodge of New York has a similar provision in its Constitution.

Of the two modes of exclusion from a lodge for non-payment of dues, namely, suspension and erasure, the effects are very different. Suspension does not abrogate the connection between the member and his lodge, and places his rights in abeyance only. Upon the payment of the debt, he is at once restored without other action of the lodge. But erasure from the roll terminates all connection between the delinquent and the lodge, and he ceases to be a member of it. Payment of the dues, simply, will not restore him; for it is necessary that he should again be elected by the Brethren, upon formal application.

The word exclusion has a meaning in England differing from that in which it has been used in the present section. There the prerogative of expulsion is, as I think very rightly, exercised only by the Grand Lodge. The term "expelled" is therefore used only when a Brother is removed from the raft, by the Grand Lodge. The removal by a District Grand Lodge, or a subordinate lodge, is called "exclusion." The effect, however, of the punishment of exclusion, is similar to that which has been here advocated.

90

Section IV.

Of Definite Suspension.

Suspension is a punishment by which a party is temporarily deprived of his rights and privileges as a Mason. It does not terminate his connection with the craft, but only places it in abeyance, and it may again be resumed in a mode hereafter to be indicated.

Suspension may be, in relation to time, either definite or indefinite. And as the effects produced upon the delinquent, especially in reference to the manner of his restoration, are different, it is proper that each should be separately considered.

In a case of definite suspension, the time for which the delinquent is to be suspended, whether for one month, for three, or six months, or for a longer or shorter period, is always mentioned in the sentence.

At its termination, the party suspended is at once restored without further action of the lodge. But as this is a point upon which there has been some difference of opinion, the argument will be fully discussed in the chapter on the subject of *Restoration*.

By a definite suspension, the delinquent is for a time placed beyond the pale of Masonry. He is deprived of all his rights as a Master Mason—is not permitted to visit any lodge, or hold masonic communication with his Brethren—is not entitled to masonic relief, and should he die during his suspension, is not entitled to masonic burial. In short, the amount of punishment differs from that of indefinite suspension or expulsion only in the period of time for which it is inflicted.

The punishment of definite suspension is the lightest that can be inflicted of those which affect the relations of a Mason with the fraternity at large. It must always be preceded by a trial, and the prevalent opinion is, that it may be inflicted by a two-thirds vote of the lodge.

Section V.

Of Indefinite Suspension.

Indefinite suspension is a punishment by which the person suspended is deprived of all his rights and privileges as a Mason, until such time as the lodge which has suspended him shall see fit, by a special action, to restore him.

All that has been said of definite suspension in the preceding section, will equally apply to indefinite suspension, except that in the former case the suspended person is at once restored by the termination of the period for which he was suspended; while in the latter, as no period of termination had been affixed, a special resolution of the lodge will be necessary to effect a restoration.

By suspension the connection of the party with his lodge and with the institution is not severed; he still remains a member of his lodge, although his rights as such are placed in abeyance. In this respect it materially differs from expulsion, and, as an inferior grade of punishment, is inflicted for offenses of a lighter character than those for which expulsion is prescribed.

The question here arises, whether the dues of a suspended member to his lodge continue to accrue during his suspension? I think they do not. Dues or arrears are payments made to a lodge for certain rights and benefits—the exercise and enjoyment of which are guaranteed to the member, in consideration of the dues thus paid. But as by suspension, whether definite or indefinite, he is for the time deprived of these rights and benefits, it would seem unjust to require from him a payment for that which he does not enjoy. I hold, therefore, that suspension from the rights and benefits of Masonry, includes also a suspension from the payment of arrears.

No one can be indefinitely suspended, unless after a due form of trial, and upon the vote of at least two-thirds of the members present.

Section VI.

Of Expulsion.[98]

Expulsion is the very highest penalty that can be inflicted upon a delinquent Mason. It deprives the party expelled of all the masonic rights and privileges that he ever enjoyed, not only as a member of the lodge from which he has been ejected, but also of all those which were inherent in him as a member of the fraternity at large. He is at once as completely divested of his masonic character as though he had never been admitted into the institution. He can no longer demand the aid of his Brethren, nor require from them the performance of any of the duties to which he was formerly entitled, nor visit any lodge, nor unite in any of the public or private ceremonies of the Order. No conversation on masonic subjects can be held with him, and he is to be considered as being completely without the pale of the institution, and to be looked upon in the same light as a profane, in relation to the communication of any masonic information.

It is a custom too generally adopted in this country, for subordinate lodges to inflict this punishment, and hence it is supposed by many, that the power of inflicting it is vested in the subordinate lodges. But the fact is, that the only proper tribunal to impose this heavy penalty is a Grand Lodge. A subordinate may, indeed, try its delinquent member, and if guilty declare him expelled. But the sentence is of no force until the Grand Lodge, under whose jurisdiction it is working, has confirmed it. And it is optional with the Grand Lodge to do so, or, as is frequently done, to reverse the decision and reinstate the Brother. Some of the lodges in this country claim the right to expel independently of the action of the Grand Lodge, but the claim is not valid. The very fact that an expulsion is a penalty, affecting the general relations of the punished party with the whole fraternity, proves that its exercise never could, with propriety, be intrusted to a body so circumscribed in its authority as a subordinate lodge. Besides, the general practice of the fraternity is against it. The English Constitutions vest the power to expel exclusively in the Grand Lodge.[99]

The severity of the punishment will at once indicate the propriety of inflicting it only for the most serious offenses, such, for instance, as immoral conduct, that would subject a candidate for initiation to rejection.

As the punishment is general, affecting the relation of the one expelled with the whole fraternity, it should not be lightly imposed, for the violation of any masonic act not general in its character. The commission of a grossly immoral act is a violation of the contract entered into between each Mason and his Order. If sanctioned by silence or impunity, it would bring discredit on the institution, and tend to impair its usefulness. A Mason who is a bad man, is to the fraternity what a mortified limb is to the body, and should be treated with the same mode of cure—he should be cut off, lest his example spread, and disease be propagated through the constitution.

The punishment of expulsion can only be inflicted after a due course of trial, and upon the votes of at least two-thirds of the members present, and should always be submitted for approval and confirmation to the Grand Lodge.

One question here arises, in respect not only to expulsion but to the other masonic punishments, of which I have treated in the preceding sections:—Does suspension or expulsion from a Chapter of Royal Arch Masons, an Encampment of Knights Templar, or any other of what are called the higher degrees of Masonry, affect the relations of the expelled party to Symbolic or Ancient Craft Masonry? I answer, unhesitatingly, that it does not, and for reasons which, years ago, I advanced, in the following language, and which appear to have met with the approval of the most of my contemporaries:—

"A chapter of Royal Arch Masons, for instance, is not, and cannot be, recognized as a masonic body, by a lodge of Master Masons. 'They hear them so to be, but they do not know them so to be,' by any of the modes of recognition known to Masonry. The acts, therefore, of a Chapter cannot be recognized by a Master Masons' lodge, any more than the acts of a literary or charitable society wholly unconnected with the Order. Again: By the present organization of Freemasonry, Grand Lodges are the supreme masonic tribunals. If, therefore, expulsion from a Chapter of Royal Arch Masons involved expulsion from a Blue Lodge, the right of the Grand Lodge to hear and determine causes, and to regulate the internal concerns of the institution, would be interfered with by another body beyond its control. But the converse of this proposition does not hold good. Expulsion from a Blue Lodge involves expulsion from all the higher degrees; because, as they are composed of Blue Masons, the members could not of right sit and hold communications on masonic subjects with one who was an expelled Mason."[100]

Chapter III.

Of Masonic Trials.

Having thus discussed the penalties which are affixed to masonic offenses, we are next to inquire into the process of trial by which a lodge determines on the guilt or innocence of the accused. This subject will be the most conveniently considered by a division into two sections; first, as to the form of trial; and secondly, as to the character of the evidence.

Section I.

Of the Form of Trial.

Although the authority for submitting masonic offenses to trials by lodges is derived from the Old Charges, none of the ancient regulations of the Order have prescribed the details by which these trials are to be governed. The form of trial must, therefore, be obtained from the customs and usages of the craft, and from the regulations which have been adopted by various Grand Lodges. The present section will, therefore, furnish a summary of these regulations as they are generally observed in this country.

A charge or statement of the offense imputed to the party is always a preliminary step to every trial.

This charge must be made in writing, signed by the accuser, and delivered to the Secretary, who reads it at the next regular communication of the lodge. A time and place are then appointed by the lodge for the trial.

The accused is entitled to a copy of the charge, and must be informed of the time and place that have been appointed for his trial.

Although it is necessary that the accusation should be preferred at a stated communication, so that no one may be taken at a disadvantage, the trial may take place at a special communication. But ample time and opportunity should always be given to the accused to prepare his defense.

It is not essential that the accuser should be a Mason. A charge of immoral conduct can be preferred by a profane; and if the offense is properly stated, and if it comes within the jurisdiction of the Order or the lodge, it must be investigated. It is not the accuser but the accused that Is to be put on trial, and the lodge is to look only to the nature of the accusation, and not to the individual who prefers it. The motives of the accuser, but not his character, may be examined.

If the accused is living beyond the jurisdiction of the lodge—that is to say, if he be a member and have removed to some other place without withdrawing his membership, not being a member, or if, after committing the offense, he has left the jurisdiction, the charge must be transmitted to his present place of residence, by mail or otherwise, and a reasonable time be allowed for his answer before the lodge proceeds to trial.

The lodge should be opened in the highest degree to which the accused has attained; and the examinations should take place in the presence of the accused and the accuser (if the latter be a Mason); but the final decision should always be made in the third degree.

The accused and the accuser have a right to be present at all examinations of witnesses, whether those examinations are taken in open lodge or in a committee, and to propose such relevant questions as they desire.

When the trial is concluded, the accused and accuser should retire, and the Master or presiding officer must then put the question of guilty or not guilty to the lodge. Of course, if there are several charges or specifications, the question must be taken on each separately. For the purposes of security and independence in the expression of opinion, it seems generally conceded, that this question should be decided by ballot; and the usage has also obtained, of requiring two-thirds of the votes given to be black, to secure a conviction. A white ball, of course, is equivalent to acquittal, and a black one to conviction.

Every member present is bound to vote, unless excused by unanimous consent.

If, on a scrutiny, it is found that the verdict is guilty, the Master or presiding officer must then put the question as to the amount and nature of the punishment to be inflicted.

He will commence with the highest penalty, or expulsion, and, if necessary, by that punishment being negatived, proceed to propose indefinite and then definite suspension, exclusion, public or private reprimand, and censure.

For expulsion or either kind of suspension, two-thirds of the votes present are necessary. For either of the other and lighter penalties, a bare majority will be sufficient.

The votes on the nature of the punishment should be taken by a show of hands.

If the residence of the accused is not known, or if, upon due summons, he refuses or neglects to attend, the lodge may, nevertheless, proceed to trial without his presence.

In trials conducted by Grand Lodges, it is usual to take the preliminary testimony in a committee; but the final decision must always be made in the Grand Lodge.

Section II.

Of the Evidence in Masonic Trials.

In the consideration of the nature of the evidence that is to be given in masonic trials, it is proper that we should first inquire what classes of persons are to be deemed incompetent as witnesses.

The law of the land, which, in this instance, is the same as the law of Masonry, has declared the following classes of person to be incompetent to give evidence.

1. Persons who have not the use of reason, are, from the infirmity of their nature, considered to be utterly incapable of giving evidence.[101] This class includes idiots, madmen, and children too young to be sensible of the obligations of an oath, and to distinguish between good and evil.

2. Persons who are entirely devoid of any such religious principle or belief as would bind their consciences to speak the truth, are incompetent as witnesses. Hence, the testimony of an atheist must be rejected; because, as it has been well said, such a person cannot be subject to that sanction which is deemed an indispensable test of truth. But as Masonry does not demand of its candidates any other religious declaration than that of a belief in God, it cannot require of the witnesses in its trials any profession of a more explicit faith. But even here it seems to concur with the law of the land; for it has been decided by Chief Baron Willes, that "an infidel who believes in a God, and that He will reward and punish him in this world, but does not believe in a future state, may be examined upon oath."

3. Persons who have been rendered infamous by their conviction of great crimes, are deemed incompetent to give evidence. This rule has been adopted, because the commission of an infamous crime implies, as Sir William Scott has observed, "such a dereliction of moral principle on the part of the witness, as carries with it the conclusion that he would entirely disregard the obligation of an oath." Of such a witness it has been said, by another eminent judge,[102] that "the credit of his oath is over-balanced by the stain of his iniquity."

4. Persons interested in the result of the trial are considered incompetent to give evidence. From the nature of human actions and passions, and from the fact that all persons, even the most virtuous, are unconsciously swayed by motives of interest, the testimony of such persons is rather to be distrusted than believed. This rule will, perhaps, be generally of difficult application in masonic trials, although in a civil suit at law it is easy to define what is the interest of a party sufficient to render his evidence incompetent. But whenever it is clearly apparent that the interests of a witness would be greatly benefited by either the acquittal or the conviction of the accused, his testimony must be entirely rejected, or, if admitted, its value must be weighed with the most scrupulous caution.

Such are the rules that the wisdom of successive generations of men, learned in the law, have adopted for the establishment of the competency or incompetency of witnesses. There is nothing in them which conflicts with the principles of justice, or with the Constitutions of Freemasonry; and hence they may, very properly, be considered as a part of our own code. In determining, therefore, the rule for the admission of witnesses in masonic trials, we are to be governed by the simple proposition that has been enunciated by Mr. Justice Lawrence in the following language:

"I find no rule less comprehensive than this, that all persons are admissible witnesses who have the use of their reason, and such religious belief as to feel the obligation of an oath, who have not been convicted of any infamous crime, and who are not influenced by interest."

The peculiar, isolated character of our institution, here suggests as an important question, whether it is admissible to take the testimony of a profane, or person who is not a Freemason, in the trial of a Mason before his lodge.

To this question I feel compelled to reply, that such testimony is generally admissible; but, as there are special cases in which it is not, it seems proper to qualify that reply by a brief inquiry into the grounds and reasons of this admissibility, and the mode and manner in which such testimony is to be taken.

The great object of every trial, in Masonry, as elsewhere, is to elicit truth; and, in the spirit of truth, to administer justice. From whatever source, therefore, this truth can be obtained, it is not only competent there to seek it, but it is obligatory on us so to do. This is the principle of law as well as of common sense. Mr. Phillips, in the beginning of his great "Treatise on the Law of Evidence," says: "In inquiries upon this subject, the great end and object ought always to be, the ascertaining of the most convenient and surest means for the attainment of truth; the rules laid down are the means used for the attainment of that end."

Now, if A, who is a Freemason, shall have committed an offense, of which B and C alone were cognizant as witnesses, shall it be said that A must be acquitted for want of proof, because B and C are not members of the Order? We apprehend that in this instance the ends of justice would be defeated, rather than subserved. If the veracity and honesty of B and C are unimpeached, their testimony as to the fact cannot lawfully be rejected on any ground, except that they may be interested in the result of the trial, and might be benefited by the conviction or the acquittal of the defendant. But this is an objection that would hold against the evidence of a Mason, as well as a profane.

Any other rule would be often attended with injurious consequences to our institution. We may readily suppose a case by way of illustration. A, who is a member of a lodge, is accused of habitual intemperance, a vice eminently unmasonic in its character, and one which will always reflect a great portion of the degradation of the offender upon the society which shall sustain and defend him in its perpetration. But it may happen—and this is a very conceivable case—that in consequence of the remoteness of his dwelling, or from some other supposable cause, his Brethren have no opportunity of seeing him, except at distant intervals. There is, therefore, no Mason, to testify to the truth of the charge, while his neighbors and associates, who are daily and hourly in his company, are all aware of his habit of intoxication.

If, then, a dozen or more men, all of reputation and veracity, should come, or be brought before the lodge, ready and willing to testify to this fact, by what process of reason or justice, or under what maxim of masonic jurisprudence, could their testimony be rejected, simply because they were not Masons? And if rejected—if the accused with this weight of evidence against him, with this infamy clearly and satisfactorily proved by these reputable witnesses, were to be acquitted, and sent forth purged of the charge, upon a mere technical ground, and thus triumphantly be sustained in the continuation of his vice, and that in the face of the very community which was cognizant of his degradation of life and manners, who could estimate the disastrous consequences to the lodge and the Order which should thus support and uphold him in his guilty course? The world would not, and could not appreciate the causes that led to the rejection of such clear and unimpeachable testimony, and it would visit with its just reprobation the institution which could thus extend its fraternal affections to the support of undoubted guilt.

But, moreover, this is not a question of mere theory; the principle of accepting the testimony of non-masonic witnesses has been repeatedly acted on. If a Mason has been tried by the courts of his country on an indictment for larceny, or any other infamous crime, and been convicted by the verdict of a jury, although neither the judge nor the jury, nor the witnesses were Masons, no lodge after such conviction would permit him to retain his membership, but, on the contrary, it would promptly and indignantly expel him from the Brotherhood. If, however, the lodge should refuse to expel him, on the ground that his conviction before the court was based on the testimony of non-masonic witnesses, and should grant him a lodge trial for the same offense, then, on the principle against which we are contending, the evidence of these witnesses as "profanes" would be rejected, and the party be acquitted for want of proof; and thus the anomalous and disgraceful spectacle would present itself—of a felon condemned and punished by the laws of his country for an infamous crime, acquitted and sustained by a lodge of Freemasons.

But we will be impressed with the inexpediency and injustice of this principle, when we look at its operation from another point of view. It is said to be a bad rule that will not work both ways; and, therefore, if the testimony of non-masonic witnesses against the accused is rejected on the ground of inadmissibility, it must also be rejected when given in his favor. Now, if we suppose a case, in which a Mason was accused before his lodge of having committed an offense, at a certain time and place, and, by the testimony of one or two disinterested persons, he could establish what the law calls an *alibi*, that is, that at that very time he was at a far-distant place, and could not, therefore, have committed the offense charged against him, we ask with what show of justice or reason could such testimony be rejected, simply because the parties giving it were not Masons? But if the evidence of a "profane" is admitted in favor of the accused, rebutting testimony of the same kind cannot with consistency be rejected; and hence the rule is determined that in the trial of Masons, it is competent to receive the evidence of persons who are not Masons, but whose competency, in other respects, is not denied.

It must, however, be noted, that the testimony of persons who are not Masons is not to be given as that of Masons is, within the precincts of the lodge. They are not to be present at the trial; and whatever testimony they have to adduce, must be taken by a committee, to be afterwards accurately reported to the lodge. But in all cases, the accused has a right to be present, and to interrogate the witnesses.

The only remaining topic to be discussed is the method of taking the testimony, and this can be easily disposed of.

The testimony of Masons is to be taken either in lodge or in committee, and under the sanction of their obligations.

The testimony of profanes is always to be taken by a committee, and on oath administered by a competent legal officer—the most convenient way of taking such testimony is by affidavit.

Chapter IV.

Of the Penal Jurisdiction of a Lodge.

The penal jurisdiction of a lodge is that jurisdiction which it is authorized to exercise for the trial of masonic offenses, and the infliction of masonic punishment. It may be considered as either geographical or personal.

The geographical jurisdiction of a lodge extends in every direction, half way to the nearest lodge. Thus, if two lodges be situated at the distance of sixteen miles from each other, then the penal jurisdiction of each will extend for the space of eight miles in the direction of the other.

The personal jurisdiction of a lodge is that jurisdiction which a lodge may exercise over certain individuals, respective or irrespective of geographical jurisdiction. This jurisdiction is more complicated than the other, and requires a more detailed enumeration of the classes over whom it is to be exercised.

1. A lodge exercises penal jurisdiction over all its members, no matter where they may reside. A removal from the geographical jurisdiction will not, in this case, release the individual from personal jurisdiction. The allegiance of a member to his lodge is indefeasible.

2. A lodge exercises penal jurisdiction over all unaffiliated Masons, living within its geographical jurisdiction. An unaffiliated Mason cannot release himself from his responsibilities to the Order. And if, by immoral or disgraceful conduct, he violates the regulations of the Order, or tends to injure its reputation in the estimation of the community, he is amenable to the lodge nearest to his place of residence, whether this residence be temporary or permanent, and may be reprimanded, suspended, or expelled.

This doctrine is founded on the wholesome reason, that as a lodge is the guardian of the purity and safety of the institution, within its own jurisdiction, it must, to exercise this guardianship with success, be invested with the power of correcting every evil that occurs within its precincts. And if unaffiliated Masons were exempted from this control, the institution might be seriously affected in the eyes of the community, by their bad conduct.

3. The personal jurisdiction of a lodge, for the same good reason, extends over all Masons living in its vicinity. A Master Mason belonging to a distant lodge, but residing within the geographical jurisdiction of another lodge, becomes amenable for his conduct to the latter, as well as to the former lodge. But if his own lodge is within a reasonable distance, courtesy requires that the lodge near which he resides should rather make a complaint to his lodge than itself institute proceedings against him. But the reputation of the Order must not be permitted to be endangered, and a case might occur, in which it would be inexpedient to extend this courtesy, and where the lodge would feel compelled to proceed to the trial and punishment of the offender, without appealing to his lodge. The geographical jurisdiction will, in all cases, legalize the proceedings.

4. But a lodge situated near the confines of a State cannot extend its jurisdiction over Masons residing in a neighboring State, and not being its members, however near they may reside to it: for no lodge can exercise

jurisdiction over the members of another Grand Lodge jurisdiction. Its geographical, as well as personal jurisdiction, can extend no further than that of its own Grand Lodge.

5. Lastly, no lodge can exercise penal jurisdiction over its own Master, for he is alone responsible for his conduct to the Grand Lodge. But it may act as his accuser before that body, and impeach him for any offense that he may have committed. Neither can a lodge exercise penal jurisdiction over the Grand Master, although under other circumstances it might have both geographical and personal jurisdiction over him, from his residence and membership.

Chapter V.

Of Appeals.

Every Mason, who has been tried and convicted by a lodge, has an inalienable right to appeal from that conviction, and from the sentence accompanying it, to the Grand Lodge.

As an appeal always supposes the necessity of a review of the whole case, the lodge is bound to furnish the Grand Lodge with an attested copy of its proceedings on the trial, and such other testimony in its possession as the appellant may deem necessary for his defense.

The Grand Lodge may, upon investigation, confirm the verdict of its subordinate. In this case, the appeal is dismissed, and the sentence goes into immediate operation without any further proceedings on the part of the lodge.

The Grand Lodge may, however, only approve in part, and may reduce the penalty inflicted, as for instance, from expulsion to suspension. In this case, the original sentence of the lodge becomes void, and the milder sentence of the Grand Lodge is to be put in force. The same process would take place, were the Grand Lodge to increase instead of diminishing the amount of punishment, as from suspension to expulsion. For it is competent for the Grand Lodge, on an appeal, to augment, reduce or wholly abrogate the penalty inflicted by its subordinate.

But the Grand Lodge may take no direct action on the penalty inflicted, but may simply refer the case back to the subordinate for a new trial. In this case, the proceedings on the trial will be commenced *de novo*, if the reference has been made on the ground of any informality or illegality in the previous trial. But if the case is referred back, not for a new trial, but for further consideration, on the ground that the punishment was inadequate—either too severe, or not sufficiently so—in this case, it is not necessary to repeat the trial. The discussion on the nature of the penalty to be inflicted should, however, be reviewed, and any new evidence calculated to throw light on the nature of the punishment which is most appropriate, may be received.

Lastly, the Grand Lodge may entirely reverse the decision of its subordinate, and decree a restoration of the appellant to all his rights and privileges, on the ground of his innocence of the charges which had been preferred against him. But, as this action is often highly important in its results, and places the appellant and the lodge in an entirely different relative position, I have deemed its consideration worthy of a distinct chapter.

During the pendency of an appeal, the sentence of the subordinate lodge is held in abeyance, and cannot; be enforced. The appellant in this case remains in the position of a Mason "under charges."

Chapter VI.

Of Restoration.

The penalties of suspension and expulsion are terminated by restoration, which may take place either by the action of the lodge which inflicted them, or by that of the Grand Lodge.

Restoration from definite suspension is terminated without any special action of the lodge, but simply by the termination of the period for which the party was suspended. He then at once reenters into the possession of all the rights, benefits, and functions, from which he had been temporarily suspended.

I have myself no doubt of the correctness of this principle; but, as it has been denied by some writers, although a very large majority of the authorities are in its favor, it may be well, briefly, to discuss its merits.

Let us suppose that on the 1st of January A.B. had been suspended for three months, that is, until the 1st day of April. At the end of the three months, that is to say, on the first of April, A.B. would no longer be a suspended member—for the punishment decreed will have been endured; and as the sentence of the lodge had expressly declared that his suspension was to last until the 1st of April, the said sentence, if it means anything, must mean that the suspension was, on the said 1st of April, to cease and determine. If he were, therefore, to wait until the 1st of May for the action of the lodge, declaring his restoration, he would suffer a punishment of four months' suspension, which was not decreed by his lodge upon his trial, and which would, therefore, be manifestly unjust and illegal.

Again: if the offense which he had committed was, upon his trial, found to be so slight as to demand only a dismissal for one night from the lodge, will it be contended that, on his leaving the lodge-room pursuant to his sentence, he leaves not to return to it on the succeeding communication, unless a vote should permit him? Certainly not. His punishment of dismissal for one night had been executed; and on the succeeding night he reentered into the possession of all his rights. But if he can do so after a dismissal or suspension of one night, why not after one or three, six or twelve months? The time is extended, but the principle remains the same.

But the doctrine, that after the expiration of the term of a definite suspension, an action by the lodge is still necessary to a complete restoration, is capable of producing much mischief and oppression. For, if the lodge not only has a right, but is under the necessity of taking up the case anew, and deciding whether the person who had been suspended for three months, and whose period of suspension has expired, shall now be restored, it follows, that the members of the lodge, in the course of their inquiry, are permitted to come to such conclusion as they may think just and fit; for to say that they, after all their deliberations, are, to vote only in one way, would be too absurd to require any consideration. They may, therefore, decide that A.B., having undergone the sentence of the lodge, shall be restored, and then of course all would be well, and no more is to be said. But suppose that they decide otherwise, and say that A.B., having undergone the sentence of suspension of three months, *shall not* be restored, but must remain suspended until further orders. Here, then, a party would have been punished a second time for the same offense, and that, too, after having suffered what, at the time of his conviction, was supposed to be a competent punishment—and without a trial, and without the necessary opportunities of defense, again found guilty, and his comparatively light punishment of suspension for three months changed into a severer one, and of an indefinite period. The annals of the most arbitrary government in the world—the history of the most despotic tyrant that ever lived—could not show an instance of more unprincipled violation of law and justice than this. And yet it may naturally be the result of the doctrine, that in a sentence of definite suspension, the party can be restored only by a vote of the lodge at the expiration of his term of suspension. If the lodge can restore him, it can as well refuse to restore him, and to refuse to restore him would be to inflict a new punishment upon him for an old and atoned-for offense.

On the 1st of January, for instance, A.B., having been put upon his trial, witnesses having been examined, his defense having been heard, was found guilty by his lodge of some offense, the enormity of which, whatever it might be, seemed to require a suspension from Masonry for just three months, neither more nor less. If the lodge had thought the crime still greater, it would, of course, we presume, have decreed a suspension of six, nine, or twelve months. But considering, after a fair, impartial, and competent investigation of the merits of the case (for all this is to be presumed), that the offended law would be satisfied with a suspension of three months, that punishment is decreed. The court is adjourned *sine die*; for it has done all that is required—the prisoner undergoes his sentence with becoming contrition, and the time having expired, the bond having been paid, and the debt satisfied, he is told that he must again undergo the ordeal of another trial, before another court, before he can reassume what was only taken from him for a definite period; and that it is still doubtful, whether the sentence of the former court may not even now, after its accomplishment, be reversed, and a new and more severe one be inflicted.

The analogy of a person who has been sentenced to imprisonment for a certain period, and who, on the expiration of that period, is at once released, has been referred to, as apposite to the case of a definite suspension. Still more appropriately may we refer to the case of a person transported for a term of years, and who cannot return until that term expires, but who is at liberty at once to do so when it has expired. "Another capital offense against public justice," says Blackstone, "is the returning from transportation, or being seen at large in Great Britain *before the expiration of the term for which the offender was sentenced to be transported.*" Mark these qualifying words: "before the expiration of the term:" they include, from the very force of language, the proposition that it is no offense to return *after* the expiration of the term. And so changing certain words to meet the change of circumstances, but leaving the principle unchanged, we may lay down the law in relation to restorations from definite suspensions, as follows:

It is an offense against the masonic code to claim the privileges of Masonry, or to attempt to visit a lodge after having been suspended, before the expiration of the term for which the offender was suspended.

Of course, it is no crime to resume these privileges after the term has expired; for surely he must have strange notions of the powers of language, who supposes that suspension for three months, and no more, does not mean, that when the three months are over the suspension ceases. And, if the suspension ceases, the person is no longer suspended; and, if no longer suspended he is in good standing, and requires no further action to restore him to good moral and masonic health.

But it is said that, although originally only suspended for three months, at the expiration of that period, his conduct might continue to be such as to render his restoration a cause of public reproach. What is to be done in such a case? It seems strange that the question should be asked. The remedy is only too apparent. Let new charges be preferred, and let a new trial take place for his derelictions of duty during the term of his suspension. Then, the lodge may again suspend him for a still longer period, or altogether expel him, if it finds him deserving such punishment. But in the name of justice, law, and common sense, do not insiduously and unmanfully continue a sentence for one and a former offense, as a punishment for another and a later one, and that, too, without the due forms of trial.

Let us, in this case, go again for an analogy to the laws of the land. Suppose an offender had been sentenced to an imprisonment of six months for a larceny, and that while in prison he had committed some new crime. When the six months of his sentence had expired, would the Sheriff feel justified, or even the Judge who had sentenced him, in saying: "I will not release you; you have guilty of another offense during your incarceration, and therefore, I shall keep you confined six months longer?" Certainly not. The Sheriff or the Judge who should do so high-handed a measure, would soon find himself made responsible for the violation of private rights. But the course to be pursued would be, to arrest him for the new offense, give him a fair trial, and, if convicted again, imprison or otherwise punish him, according to his new sentence, or, if acquitted, discharge him.

The same course should be pursued with a Mason whose conduct during the period of his suspension has been liable to reproach or suspicion. Masons have rights as well as citizens—every one is to be considered innocent until he is proved guilty—and no one should suffer punishment, even of the lightest kind, except after an impartial trial by his peers.

But the case of an indefinite suspension is different. Here no particular time has been appointed for the termination of the punishment. It may be continued during life, unless the court which has pronounced it think proper to give a determinate period to what was before indeterminate, and to declare that on such a day the suspension shall cease, and the offender be restored. In a case of this kind, action on the part of the lodge is necessary to effect a restoration.

Such a sentence being intended to last indefinitely—that is to say, during the pleasure of the lodge—may, I conceive, be reversed at any legal time, and the individual restored by a mere majority vote the of lodge. Some authorities think a vote of two-thirds necessary; but I see no reason why a lodge may not, in this as in other cases, reverse its decision by a vote of a simple majority. The Ancient Constitutions are completely silent on this and all its kindred points; and, therefore, where a Grand Lodge has made no local regulation on the subject, we must be guided by the principles of reason and analogy, both of which direct us to the conclusion that a lodge may express its will, in matters unregulated by the Constitutions, through the vote of a majority.

But the restoration of an expelled Mason requires a different action. By expulsion, as I have already said, all connection with the Order is completely severed. The individual expelled ceases to be a Mason, so far as respects the exercise of any masonic rights or privileges. His restoration to the Order is, therefore, equivalent to the admission of a profane. Having ceased on his expulsion to be a member of the lodge which had expelled him, his restoration would be the admission of a new member. The expelled Mason and the uninitiated candidate are to be placed on the same footing—both are equally unconnected with the institution—the one having never been in it, and the other having been completely discharged from it.

The rule for the admission of new members, as laid down in the Thirty-nine Regulations, seems to me, therefore, to be applicable in this case; and hence, I conceive that to reverse a sentence of expulsion and to restore an expelled Mason will require as unanimous a vote as that which is necessary on a ballot for initiation.

Every action taken by a lodge for restoration must be done at a stated communication and after due notice, that if any member should have good and sufficient reasons to urge against the restoration, he may have an opportunity to present them.

In conclusion, the Grand Lodge may restore a suspended or expelled Mason, contrary to the wishes of the lodge.

In such case, if the party has been suspended only, he, at once, resumes his place and functions in the lodge, from which, indeed, he had only been temporarily dissevered.

But in the case of the restoration of an expelled Mason to the rights and privileges of Masonry, by a Grand Lodge, does such restoration restore him to membership in his lodge? This question is an important one, and has very generally been decided in the negative by the Grand Lodges of this country. But as I unfortunately differ from these high authorities, I cannot refrain, as an apology for this difference of opinion, from presenting the considerations which have led me to the conclusion which I have adopted. I cannot, it is true, in the face of the mass of opposing authority, offer this conclusion as masonic law. But I would fain hope that the time is not far distant when it will become so, by the change on the part of Grand Lodges of the contrary decisions which they have made.

The general opinion in this country is, that when a Mason has been expelled by his lodge, the Grand Lodge may restore him to the rights and privileges, but cannot restore him to membership in his lodge. My own opinion, in contradiction to this, is, that when a Grand Lodge restores an expelled Mason, on the ground that the punishment of expulsion from the rights and privileges of Masonry was too severe and disproportioned to the offense, it may or may not restore him to membership in his lodge. It might, for instance, refuse to restore his membership on the ground that exclusion from his lodge is an appropriate punishment; but where the decision of the lodge as to the guilt of the individual is reversed, and the Grand Lodge declares him to be innocent, or that the charge against him has not been proved, then I hold, that it is compelled by a just regard to the rights of the expelled member to restore him not only to the rights and privileges of Masonry, but also to membership in his lodge.

I cannot conceive how a Brother, whose innocence has been declared by the verdict of his Grand Lodge, can be deprived of his vested rights as the member of a particular lodge, without a violation of the principles of justice. If guilty, let his expulsion stand; but, if innocent, let him be placed in the same position in which he was before the passage of the unjust sentence of the lodge which has been reversed.

The whole error, for such I conceive it to be, in relation to this question of restoration to membership, arises, I suppose, from a misapprehension of an ancient regulation, which says that "no man can be entered a Brother in any particular lodge, or admitted a member thereof, without the unanimous consent of all the members"—which inherent privilege is said not to be subject to dispensation, "lest a turbulent member should thus be imposed upon them, which might spoil their harmony, or hinder the freedom of their communication, or even break and disperse the Lodge." But it should be remembered that this regulation altogether refers to the admission of new members, and not to the restoration of old ones—to the granting of a favor which the candidate solicits, and which the lodge may or may not, in its own good pleasure, see fit to confer, and not to the resumption of a vested and already acquired right, which, if it be a right, no lodge can withhold. The practical working of this system of incomplete restoration, in a by no means extreme case, will readily show its absurdity and injustice. A member having appealed from expulsion by his lodge to the Grand Lodge, that body calmly and fairly investigates the case. It finds that the appellant has been falsely accused of an offense which he has never committed; that he has been unfairly tried, and unjustly convicted. It declares him innocent—clearly and undoubtedly innocent, and far freer from any sort of condemnation than the prejudiced jurors who convicted him. Under these circumstances, it becomes obligatory that the Grand Lodge should restore him to the place he formerly occupied, and reinvest him with the rights of which he has been unjustly despoiled. But that it cannot do. It may restore him to the privileges of Masonry in general; but, innocent though he be, the Grand Lodge, in deference to the prejudices of his Brethren, must perpetuate a wrong, and punish this innocent person by expulsion from his lodge. I cannot, I dare not, while I remember the eternal principles of justice, subscribe to so monstrous an exercise of wrong—so flagrant an outrage upon private rights.

Index.

A.

Expulsion, a masonic punishment
  should be inflicted by Grand Lodge or with its approval
  from higher degrees, its effect
  restoration from
Extinct lodges, funds of, revert to the Grand Lodge

F.

Family distressed, of a Mason, entitled to relief
Fellow Craft, rights of
  they formerly constituted the great body of the Fraternity
  formerly permitted to speak, but not vote
Finishing candidates of one lodge in another
Fool cannot be a Mason
Free, a candidate must be, at the time of making
Free-born, a Mason must be
  reason for the rule
Funds of extinct lodges revert to the Grand Lodge

G.

General Assembly. (*See Assembly, General.*)
God, belief in, a qualification of a candidate
Gothic constitutions adopted in 926
Grand Chaplain,
  office established in 1775
  duties of
Grand Deacons
  office more ancient than Oliver supposes
  duties of
  how appointed
Grand Lodge held in 1717
  mode of organizing one
  three lodges necessary to organize one
  dormant may be revived if a Grand Officer remains,
  all the Craft formerly members of
  Masters and Wardens of lodges are members
  Grand Officers are also members
  Past Masters are not members by inherent right
  its powers and prerogatives
  may make new regulations
  must observe the landmarks
Grand Lodges, historical sketch of
  are comparatively modern institutions
Grand Marshal
  appointed by the Grand Master
  duties of
Grand Master, duties and prerogatives of
  office of has existed since the origin of Masonry
  an elective officer
  by whom to be installed
  prerogatives of, derived from two sources
  no appeal from his decision
  may convene Grand Lodge when he chooses

H.

I.

Irreligious libertine cannot be a Mason
  " " definition of the term

J.

Judicial powers of a Grand Lodge,
Junior Grand Warden
Junior Warden,
  " " presides in absence of Master and Senior Warden,
  " " does not take the West in absence of Senior Warden,
  " " presides over the craft during refreshment
  " " appoints the stewards
Jurisdiction of a lodge
  " geographical or personal
  " is over all its members
  " " " unaffiliated Masons in its vicinity
  " cannot extend beyond State lines,
  " none over its Master

K.

Knowledge of reading and writing necessary to a Mason

L.

Labor, calling from, to refreshment
Landmarks, what they are,
  " ritual and legislative
  " must be observed by the Grand Lodge
Law of Grand Lodges
  " subordinate lodges
  " individuals
Lawful information, what it is
Laws, how to be interpreted
  " of Masonry are of two kinds—written and unwritten
  " written, whence derived
  " unwritten, whence derived
  " " same as ancient usage
Legislative powers of a Grand Lodge
Libertine, irreligious, cannot be a Mason
  meaning of the term
Lodge, subordinate
  definition of
  how organized
  must have been congregated by some superior authority
Lodge, under dispensation
  definition of
  generally precedes a warranted lodge
  how formed
  cannot make by-laws
  cannot elect officers
  cannot install officers
  cannot elect members

M.

Q.

R.

S.

T.

Footnotes

1. They will be found in Oliver's edition of Preston, p. 71, note, (U.M.L., vol. iii., p. 58), or in the American edition by Richards, Appendix i., note 5.

2. Found in Ol. Preston, n. 3 (p. 162. U.M.L., vol. iii., p. 134).

3. In all references to, or citations from, Anderson's Constitutions, I have used, unless otherwise stated, the first edition printed at London in 1723—a fac simile of which has recently been published by Bro. John W. Leonard, of New York. I have, however, in my possession the subsequent editions of 1738, 1755, and 1767, and have sometimes collated them together.

4. The Gothic Constitutions are that code of laws which was adopted by the General Assembly at York, in the year 926. They are no longer extant, but portions of them have been preserved by Anderson, Preston, and other writers.

5. Preston, book iv., sec, 2., p. 132, n. (U.M.L.,vol. iii., p. 109).

6. General Regulations, art. xxxix.

7. Chancellor Walworth, in his profound argument on the New York difficulties, asserted that this fact "does not distinctly appear, although it is, pretty evident that all voted."—p. 33. The language of Anderson does not, however, admit of a shadow of a doubt. "The Brethren," he says, "by a majority of hands, elected," &c.

8. Opinion of Chancellor Walworth upon the questions connected with the late masonic difficulties in the State of New York, p. 37. There is much historical learning displayed in this little pamphlet.

9. Preston, p. 131, n., Oliver's Edit. (U.M.L., vol. iii.,p. 109).

10. Of the thirty-six Grand Masters who have presided over the craft in England since the revival of Masonry in 1717, thirty have been noblemen, and three princes of the reigning family.

11. Article xxxiv.

12. His most important prerogatives are inherent or derived from ancient usage.

13. Proceedings G.L. Maryland, 1849, p. 25.

14. Art. xxxix.

15. The word "time" has been interpreted to mean *communication*.

16. And this is not because such past officer has an inherent right to the mastership, but because as long as such an one is present and willing to serve, there does not exist such an emergency as would authorize a dispensation of the law.

17. What further concerns a lodge under dispensation is referred to a special chapter in a subsequent part of the work.

18. It is well known, although it cannot be quoted as authority, that the Athol Constitutions expressly acknowledged the existence of this prerogative. See Dermott's Ahiman Rezon.

19. Book of Constitutions, edit. 1767, p. 222.

20. Book of Const., p. 233.

21. Book of Const., p. 313.

22. Book of Constitutions, p. 319.

23. Preston, p. 237, ed. 1802, (U.M.L., vol. iii., p. 223).

24. Book of Constitutions, p. 247

25. The existence of this prerogative is denied by the Grand Lodges of Missouri, Tennessee, Louisiana, and Massachusetts, while it is admitted by those of New York, Kentucky, North Carolina, South Carolina, Wisconsin, Vermont, Mississippi, Ohio, New Hampshire, Maryland, Indiana, Texas and Florida; in the last two, however, subject to limitation.

26. That is, the one who has longest been a Freemason.

27. Book of the Lodge, p. 115 (U.M.L., vol. i., book 2, p. 78).

28. It was abolished in New York in 1854.

29. This is a small chest or coffer, representing the ark of the covenant, and containing the three great lights of Masonry.

30. "What man is there that hath a new house and hath not dedicated it? Let him go and return to his house, lest he die in the battle and another man dedicate it." Deut. xx. 5.

31. De Syned. Vet. Ebræor., 1. iii., c. xiv., § 1.

32. Cicero, Brut. i.

33. See such a form of Dispensation in Cole's Masonic Library, p. 91.

34. Preston, Append., n. 4 (U.M.L., vol. iii., pp. 150, 151).

35. Book of Constitutions, orig. ed, p., 70 (U.M.L., vol. xv., book 1, p. 70).

36. General Regulations of 1722. A subsequent regulation permitted the election of a candidate, if there were not more than three black balls against him, provided the lodge desired such a relaxation of the rule. The lodges of this country, however, very generally, and, as I think, with propriety, require unanimity. The subject will be hereafter discussed.

37. Every lodge shall annually elect its Master and Treasurer by ballot. Such Master having been regularly appointed and having served as Warden of a warranted lodge for one year. *Constitutions of the Ancient Fraternity of Free and Accepted Masons, published by authority of the United Grand Lodge of England*, 1847, *p.* 58 (U.M.L., vol. ix., book 1).

38. The Wardens, or officers, of a lodge cannot be removed, unless for a cause which appears to the lodge to be sufficient; but the Master, if he be dissatisfied with the conduct of any of his officers, may lay the cause of complaint before the lodge; and, if it shall appear to the majority of the Brethren present that the complaint be well founded, he shall have power to displace such officer, and to nominate another. *English Constitutions, as above, p.* 80 (U.M.L., vol. ix., book 1).

39. It is not necessary that he should be a Past Master of the lodge.

40. No master shall assume the Master's chair, until he shall have been regularly installed, though he may in the interim rule the lodge. *English Constitutions* (U.M.L., vol. ix., book 1).

41. Every Warranted Lodge is a constituent part of the Grand Lodge, in which assembly all the power of the fraternity resides. *English Constitutions, p.* 70 (U.M.L., vol. ix., book 1).

42. We shall not here discuss the question whether Past Masters are members of the Grand Lodge, by inherent right, as that subject will be more appropriately investigated when we come to speak of the Law of Grand Lodges, in a future chapter. They are, however clearly, not the representatives of their lodge.

43. Preston, p. 167 (U.M.L., vol. iii., p. 151).

44. General Regulations. Of the duty of members, Art. X, (U.M.L., vol. xv., book 1, p. 61).

45. English Constitutions, p. 59 (U.M.L., vol. ix., book 1).

46. In selecting the name, the modern Constitutions of England make the approbation of the Grand Master or Provincial Grand Master necessary.

47. Such is the doctrine of the modern English Constitutions.

48. "No Brother can be a Warden until he has passed the part of a Fellow Craft; nor a Master until he has acted as a Warden." — *Old Charges*, IV. (U.M.L., vol. xv., book 1, p. 52).

49. Regulations on Installation of a Master, No. III. Preston, p. 74 (U.M.L., vol. iii., p. 61).

50. Hats. quoted in Jefferson, p. 14.

51. One of the ancient charges, which Preston tells us that it was the constant practice of our Ancient Brethren to rehearse at the opening and closing of the lodge, seems to refer to this rule, when it says, "the Master, Wardens, and Brethren are just and faithful, and *carefully finish the work they begin*." — Oliver's Preston, p. 27, *note* (U.M.L., vol. iii., p. 22).

52. Proceedings of G.L. of Tennessee, 1850. Appendix A, p. 8.

53. Book of Constitutions, edition of 1755, p. 282.

54. If it is an extra communication, this item of the transaction is, of course, omitted, for minutes are only to be confirmed at regular communications.

55. Oliver's Preston, p. 163, note (U.M.L., vol. iii., p. 135).

56. Such is the provision in the modern constitutions of England, but the 4th of the 39 Regulations required the candidate to be at least twenty-five.

57. See these regulations in Preston, p. 162, Oliver's ed. (U.M.L., vol. iii., p. 135).

58. Oliver's Preston, p. 72, (U.M.L., vol. iii., p. 59).

59. Blackstone, Com. I., Introd., § 2.

60. In an able report on this subject, in the proceedings of the Grand Lodge of Georgia for 1852. In accordance with the views there expressed, Bro. Rockwell decided officially, as District Deputy Grand Master, in 1851, that a man who had lost one eye was not admissible.

61. Potter, 184.

62. Page 18. In December, 1851, the Committee of Correspondence of North Carolina, unregardful of the rigid rule of their predecessors, decided that maimed candidates might be initiated, "provided their loss or infirmity will not prevent them from making full proficiency in Masonry."

63. Proceedings of the G.L. of Mo. for 1823, p. 5. The report and resolution were on the petitions of two candidates to be initiated, one with only one arm, and the other much deformed in his legs.

64. When the spirit of expediency once begins, we know not where it will stop. Thus a blind man has been initiated in Mississippi, and a one-armed one in Kentucky; and in France a few years since, the degrees were conferred by sign-language on a deaf mute!

65. Namely, the incorrectly presumed operative origin of the Order. The whole of this report, which is from the venerable Giles F. Yates, contains an able and unanswerable defense of the ancient law in opposition to any qualification.

66. See proceedings of New York, 1848, pp. 36, 37.

67. Such is the formula prescribed by the Constitutions of England as well as all the Monitors in this country.

68. See Mackey's Lexicon of Freemasonry, 3d Edit., art, *Ballot*.

69. Book of Constitutions. Edit. 1755, p. 312.

70. See Mackey's Lexicon of Freemasonry, 3d Edit., art. *Ballot*

71. Except when there is but one black ball, in which case the matter lies over until the next stated meeting. See preceding Section.

72. Masonry founded on Scripture, a Sermon preached in 1752, by the Rev. W. Williams.

73. That is, advance him, from the subordinate position of a serving man or Apprentice, to that of a Fellow Craft or journeyman.

74. This is also the regulation of the Grand Lodge of South Carolina.

75. Proceedings of Grand Lodge of New York, for 1845. He excepts, of course, from the operation of the rule, those made by dispensation; but this exception does not affect the strength of the principle.

76. Preston, edition of Oliver, p. 12 (U.M.L., vol. iii., p. 10).

77. Transactions of the G.L. of New York, anno 1848, p. 73.

78. Edition of 1723, page 71 (U.M.L., vol. xv., book 1, p. 71).

79. Preston, p. 48 (U.M.L., vol, iii., p. 40).

80. Const. New York, 1854, p. 13. The Constitutions of the Grand Lodge of England (p. 64) have a similar provision; but they require the Brother to express his wish for membership on the day of his initiation.

81. Preston, Oliver's Ed., p. 71, *note* (U.L.M., vol. iii., p. 60).

82. See Oliver, note in Preston, p. 75 (U.M.L., vol. iii, p. 61).

83. Oliver's Preston, p. 162 (U.M.L., vol. iii., p. 135.)

84. See Anderson's Const., 3d Edit., 1755, page 303.

85. Preston, Oliver's Edit., p. 89 (U.M.L., vol. iii., p. 72).

86. Preston, Oliver's Edit" p. 90 (U.M.L., vol. iii., p. 73).

87. Book I., chap. iii.

88. Proceedings of Louisiana, an. 1852.

89. Preston, Oliver's Edit., p. 76 (U.M.L., vol. iii, p. 62).

90. Ibid

91. See Mackey's Lexicon of Freemasonry, *in voce*.

92. Constitutions, Second Edition of 1738, p. 154.

93. Proceedings for 1853.

94. Proceedings for 1847.

95. The right to visit is restricted to once, by many Grand Lodges to enable him to become acquainted with the character of the lodge before he applies for membership.

96. Blackstone, Introd., § i.

97. For so we should interpret the word "honeste."

98. I have treated this subject of expulsion so fully in my "Lexicon of Freemasonry," and find so little more to say on the subject, that I have not at all varied from the course of argument, and very little from the phraseology of the article in that work.

99. In England, ejection from a membership by a subordinate lodge is called "exclusion," and it does not deprive the party of his general rights as a member of the fraternity.

100. Lexicon of Freemasonry.

101. Phillips, on Evidence, p. 3.

102. Chief Baron Gilbert.

THE

Mysteries of Freemasonry

CONTAINING

ALL THE DEGREES OF THE ORDER CONFERRED
IN A MASTER'S LODGE,

AS WRITTEN BY

CAPTAIN WILLIAM MORGAN.

**All the Degrees Conferred in the Royal Arch Chapter and
Grand Encampment of Knights Templars—Knights
of the Red Cross—of the Christian Mark—and
of the Holy Sepulchre.**

ALSO

**The Eleven Ineffable Degrees Conferred in the Lodge of Perfection—and the
still higher degrees of Prince of Jerusalem—Knights of the East and
West—Venerable Grand Masters of Symbolic Lodges—Knights
and Adepts of the Eagle or Sun—Princes of the Royal
Secret—Sovereign Inspector General, etc.**

**Revised and Corrected to Correspond with the Most Approved
Forms and Ceremonies in the Various Lodges of Free-Masons
Throughout the United States.**

By GEORGE R. CRAFTS,

Formerly Thrice Puissant Grand Master of Manitou Council, N.Y.

MORGAN'S EXPOSE OF FREEMASONRY.

Ceremonies of Opening a Lodge of Entered Apprentice Masons.

One rap calls the Lodge to order; one calls up the Junior and Senior Deacons; two raps call up the subordinate officers; and three, all the members of the Lodge.

The Master having called the Lodge to order, and the officers all seated, the Master says to the Junior Warden, "Brother Junior, are they all Entered Apprentice Masons in the South?" He answers, "They are, Worshipful." Master to the Senior Warden, "Brother Senior, are they all Entered Apprentice Masons in the West?" He answers, "They are, Worshipful." The Master then says, "They are in the East;" at the same time he gives a rap with the common gavel, or mallet, which calls up both Deacons. Master to Junior Deacon, "Attend to that part of your duty, and inform the Tyler that we are about to open a Lodge of Entered Apprentice Masons; and direct him to tyle accordingly." The Tyler then steps to the door and gives three raps, which are answered by three from without; the Junior Deacon then gives one, which is also answered by the Tyler with one; the door is then partly opened, and the Junior Deacon delivers his message and resumes his situation, and says, "The door is tyled, Worshipful" (at the same time giving the due-guard, which is never omitted when the Master is addressed). The Master to the Junior Deacon, "By whom?" He answers, "By a Master Mason without the door, armed with the proper implements of his office." Master to the Junior Deacon, "His duty there?" He answers, "To keep off all cowans and eave-droppers, see that none pass or repass without permission from the Master." [Some say without permission from the chair.] Master to Junior Deacon, "Brother Junior, your place in the Lodge?" He answers, "At the right hand of the Senior Warden in the West." Master to Junior Deacon, "Your business there, Brother Junior?" He answers, "To wait on the Worshipful Master and Wardens, act as their proxy in the active duties of the Lodge, and take charge of the door." Master to Junior Deacon, "The Senior Deacon's place in the Lodge?" He answers, "At the right hand of the Worshipful Master in the East." [The Master, while asking the last question, gives two raps, which call up all the subordinate officers.] Master to Senior Deacon, "Your duty there, Brother Senior?" He answers, "To wait on the Worshipful Master and Wardens, act as their proxy in the active duties of the Lodge, attend to the preparation and introduction of candidates—and welcome and clothe all visiting brethren." [i.e., furnish them with an apron.] Master to Senior Deacon, "The Secretary's place in the Lodge, Brother Senior?" He answers, "At the left hand of the Worshipful Master in the East." Master to the Secretary, "Your duty [Pg 4]there, Brother Secretary?" He answers, "The better to observe the Worshipful Master's will and pleasure, record the proceedings of the Lodge; transmit a copy of the same to the Grand Lodge, if required; receive all moneys and money-bills from the hands of the brethren, pay them over to the Treasurer, and take his receipt for the same." The Master to the Secretary, "The Treasurer's place in the Lodge?" He answers, "At the right hand of the Worshipful Master." Master to the Treasurer, "Your duty there, Brother Treasurer?" He answers, "Duly to observe the Worshipful Master's will and pleasure; receive all moneys and money-bills from the hands of the Secretary; keep a just and true account of the same; pay them out by order of the Worshipful Master and consent of the brethren." The Master to the Treasurer, "The Junior Warden's place in the Lodge, Brother Treasurer?" He answers, "In the South, Worshipful." Master to Junior Warden, "Your business there, Brother Junior?" He answers, "As the sun in the South at high meridian, is the beauty and glory of the day, so stands the Junior Warden in the South the better to observe the time; call the crafts from labor to refreshment; superintend them during the hours thereof; see that none convert the hours of refreshment into that of intemperance or excess; and call them on again in due season, that the Worshipful Master may have honor, and they pleasure and profit thereby." Master to the Junior Warden, "The Senior Warden's place in the Lodge?" He answers, "In the West, Worshipful." Master to the Senior Warden, "Your duty there, Brother Senior?" He answers, "As the sun sets in the West, to close the day, so stands the Senior Warden in the West, to assist the Worshipful Master in opening his Lodge; take care of the jewels and implements; see that none be lost; pay the craft their wages, if any be due; and see that none go away dissatisfied." Master to the Senior Warden, "The Master's place in the Lodge?" He answers, "In the East, Worshipful." Master to the Senior Warden, "His duty there?" He answers, "As the sun rises in the East to open and adorn the day, so presides the Worshipful Master in the East to open and adorn his Lodge; set his crafts to work with good and wholesome laws, or cause the same to be done." The Master now gives three raps, when all the brethren rise, and the Master, taking off his hat, proceeds as follows: "In like manner so do I, strictly forbidding all profane language, private committees, or any other disorderly conduct whereby the peace and harmony of this Lodge may be interrupted while engaged in its lawful pursuits, under no less penalty than the by-laws, or such penalty as a majority of the brethren present may see fit to inflict. Brethren, attend to giving the signs." [Here Lodges differ very much. In some they declare the Lodge open, as follows, before they give the sign.] The Master (all the brethren imitating him) extends his left arm from his body, so as to form an angle of about forty-five degrees, and holds his right hand traversely across his left, the palms thereof one inch apart. This is called the first sign of a Mason—is the sign of distress in this degree, and alludes to the position a candidate's hands are placed in when he takes the obligation of an Entered Apprentice Mason. The Master then draws his right hand across his throat, the hand open, with the thumb [Pg 5]next to the throat, and drops it down by his side. This is called the due-guard of an Entered Apprentice Mason (many call it the sign), and alludes to the penalty of an obligation. The Master then declares the Lodge opened in the following manner:—"I now declare the Lodge of Entered Apprentice Masons duly opened for the dispatch of business." The Senior Warden declares it to the Junior Warden, and he to the brethren. "Come, brethren, let us pray."

Prayer.—Most holy and glorious God! the great Architect of the Universe: the giver of all good gifts and graces. Thou hast promised that "Where two or three are gathered together in Thy name, Thou wilt be in the midst of them, and bless them." In Thy name we assemble, most humbly beseeching Thee to bless us in all our undertakings, that we may know and serve Thee aright, and that all our actions may tend to Thy glory, and our advancement in knowledge and virtue. And we beseech Thee, O Lord God, to bless our present assembling; and to illumine our minds through the influence of the Son of Righteousness, that we may walk in the Light of Thy countenance; and when the trials of our probationary state are over, be admitted into the temple not made with hands, eternal in the heavens. Amen. So mote it be.

Another Prayer.—Behold how good and how pleasant it is for brethren to dwell together in unity! It is like the precious ointment upon the head that ran down upon the beard, even Aaron's beard, that went down to the skirts of his garments; as the dew of Hermon, and as the dew that descended upon the mountain of Zion, for there the Lord commanded the blessing, evermore. Amen. So mote it be. [This prayer is likewise used on closing the Lodge.]

The Lodge being now open and ready to proceed to business, the Master directs the Secretary to read the minutes of the last meeting, which naturally brings to view the business of the present. If there are any candidates to be brought forward, that is the first business attended to.[1]

Ceremonies of the Admission and Initiation of a Candidate in the First Degree of Freemasonry.

At the first regular communication after the candidate has petitioned for admission, if no objection has been urged against him, the Lodge proceeds to a ballot. One black ball will reject a candidate. The boxes [Pg 6]may be passed three times. The Deacons are the proper persons to pass them; one of the boxes has black and white beans or balls in it, the other empty; the one with the balls in it goes before and furnishes each member with a black and white ball; the empty box follows and receives them. There are two holes in the top of this box, with a small tube in each, one of which is black, and the other white, with a partition in the box. The members put both their balls into this box as their feelings dictate; when the balls are received, the box is presented to the Master, Senior, and Junior Wardens, who pronounce clear or not clear, as the case may be. The ballot proving clear, the candidate (if present) is conducted into a small preparation room adjoining the Lodge; he is asked the following questions, and gives the following answers. Senior Deacon to candidate, "Do you sincerely declare, upon your honor before these gentlemen, that, unbiassed by friends, uninfluenced by unworthy motives, you freely and voluntarily offer yourself a candidate for the mysteries of Masonry?" Candidate answers, "I do." Senior Deacon to candidate, "Do you sincerely declare, upon your honor before these gentlemen, that you are prompt to solicit the privileges of Masonry, by a favorable opinion conceived of the institution, a desire of knowledge, and a sincere wish of being serviceable to your fellow-creatures?" Candidate answers, "I do." Senior Deacon to candidate, "Do you sincerely declare, upon your honor before these gentlemen, that you will cheerfully conform to all the ancient established usages and customs of the fraternity?" Candidate answers, "I do." After the above questions are proposed and answered, and the result reported to the Master, he says, "Brethren, at the request of Mr. A. B., he has been proposed and accepted in the regular form. I therefore recommend him as a proper candidate for the Mysteries of Masonry, and worthy to partake of the privileges of the fraternity; and in consequence of a declaration of his intentions, voluntarily made, I believe he will cheerfully conform to the rules of the Order." The candidate, during the time, is divested of all his apparel (shirt excepted), and furnished with a pair of drawers, kept in the Lodge for the use of candidates; he is then blindfolded, his left foot bare, his right in a slipper, his left breast and arm naked, and a rope, called a cable-tow, 'round his neck and left arm (the rope is not put 'round the arm in all Lodges) in which posture the candidate is conducted to the door, where he is caused to give, or the conductor gives, three distinct knocks, which are answered by three from within; the conductor gives one more, which is also answered by one from within. The door is then partly opened, and the Junior Deacon generally asks, "Who comes there? Who comes there? Who comes there?" The conductor *alias* the Senior Deacon, answers, "A poor, blind candidate, who has long been desirous of having and receiving a part of the rights and benefits of this worshipful Lodge, dedicated (some say erected) to God, and held forth to the holy order of St. John, as all true fellows and brothers have done, who have gone this way before him." The Junior Deacon then asks, "Is it of his own free will and accord he makes this request? Is he duly and truly prepared? Worthy and well qualified? And properly avouched for?" [Pg 7]All of which being answered in the affirmative, the Junior Deacon says to the Senior Deacon, "By what further right does he expect to obtain this benefit?" The Senior Deacon replies, "By being a man, free born, of lawful age, and under the tongue of good report." The Junior Deacon then says, "Since this is the case you will wait till the Worshipful Master in the East is made acquainted with his request, and his answer returned." The Junior Deacon repairs to the Master, when the same questions are asked, and answers returned as at the door; after which the Master says, "Since he comes endowed with all these necessary qualifications, let him enter this worshipful Lodge in the name of the Lord, and take heed on what he enters." The candidate then enters, the Junior Deacon at the same time pressing his naked left breast with the point of the compass, and asks the candidate, "Did you feel anything?" Ans.—"I did." Junior Deacon to the candidate, "What was it?" Ans.—"A torture." The Junior Deacon then says, "As this is a torture to your flesh, so may it ever be to your mind and conscience, if ever you should attempt to reveal the secrets of Masonry unlawfully." The candidate is then conducted to the centre of the Lodge, where he and the Senior Deacon kneel, and the Deacon says the following prayer:

"Vouchsafe Thine aid, Almighty Father of the Universe, to this, our present convention; and grant that this candidate for Masonry may dedicate and devote his life to Thy service, and become a true and faithful brother among us! Endue him with a competency of Thy divine wisdom, that by the secrets of our art, he may be the better enabled to display the beauties of holiness, to the honor of Thy holy name. So mote it be. Amen!"

The Master then asks the candidate, "In whom do you put your trust?" The candidate answers, "In God." The Master then takes him by the right hand, and says, "Since in God you put your trust, arise, follow your leader, and fear no danger." The Senior Deacon then conducts the candidate three times regularly around the Lodge and halts at the Junior Warden in the South, where the same questions are asked, and answers returned as at the door.

As the candidate and the conductor are going around the room, the Master reads the following passage of Scripture, and takes the same time to read it that they do to go around the Lodge three times.

"Behold how good and how pleasant it is for brethren to dwell together in unity! It is like the precious ointment upon the head, that ran down upon the beard, even Aaron's beard, that went down to the skirts of his garment; as the dew of Hermon, and as the dew that descended upon the mountains of Zion, for there the Lord commanded the blessing, even life forevermore."

The candidate is then conducted to the Senior Warden in the West, where the same Questions are asked, and answers returned as before; from thence he is conducted to the Worshipful Master in the East, where the same questions are asked, and answers returned as before. The Master likewise demands of him from whence he came, and whither he is traveling. The candidate answers, "From the West, and traveling to the East." Master inquires, "Why do you leave the West and travel [Pg 8]to the East?" He answers, "In search of light." Master then says "Since the candidate is traveling in search of light, you will please conduct him back to the West from whence he came, and put him in the care of the Senior Warden, who will teach him how to approach the East, the place of light, by advancing upon one upright regular step, to the first step, his feet forming the right angle of an oblong square, his body erect at the altar before the Master, and place him in a proper position to take upon himself the solemn oath or obligation of an Entered Apprentice Mason." The Senior Warden receives the candidate, and instructs him as directed. He first steps off with his left foot and brings up the heel of the right into the hollow thereof; the heel of the right foot against the ankle of the left, will, of course, form the right angle of an oblong square; the candidate then kneels on his left knee, and places his right foot so as to form a square with the left, he turns his foot around until the ankle bone is as much in front of him as the toes on the left; the candidate's left hand is then put under the Holy Bible, square and compass, and the right hand on them. This is the position in which a candidate is placed when he takes upon him the oath or obligation of an Entered Apprentice Mason. As soon as the candidate is placed in this position, the Worshipful Master approaches him, and says, "Mr. A. B., you are now placed in a proper position to take upon you the solemn oath or obligation of an Entered Apprentice Mason,[2] which I assure you is neither to affect your religion nor politics. If you are willing to take it, repeat your name, and say after me:

"I, A. B., of my own free will and accord, in presence of Almighty God, and this worshipful Lodge of Free and Accepted Masons, dedicated to God, and held forth to the holy order of St. John, do hereby and hereon most solemnly and sincerely promise and swear, that I will always hail, ever conceal, and never reveal any part or parts, art or arts, point or points of the secrets, arts and mysteries of ancient Free Masonry, which I have received, am about to receive, or may hereafter be instructed in, to any person or persons in the known world, except it be a true and lawful brother Mason, or within the body of a just and lawfully constituted Lodge of such, and not unto him, nor unto them whom I shall hear so to be, but unto them only after strict trial and due examination or lawful information. Furthermore, do I promise and swear that I will not write, print, stamp, stain, hew, cut, carve, indent, paint, or engrave it on anything moveable or immoveable, under the whole canopy of heaven, whereby, or whereon the least letter, figure, character, mark, stain, shadow, or resemblance of the same may become legible or intelligible to myself or any other person in the known world, whereby the secrets of Masonry may be unlawfully obtained through my unworthiness. To all which I do most solemnly and sincerely promise and swear, without the least equivocation, mental [Pg 9]reservation, or self-evasion of mind in me whatever; BINDING MYSELF UNDER NO LESS PENALTY THAN TO HAVE MY THROAT CUT ACROSS, MY TONGUE TORN OUT BY THE ROOTS, AND MY BODY BURIED IN THE ROUGH SANDS OF THE SEA AT LOW WATER MARK, WHERE THE TIDE EBBS AND FLOWS IN TWENTY-FOUR HOURS: so help me God, and keep me steadfast in the true performance of the same."

After the obligation, the Master addresses the candidate in the following manner: "Brother, to you the secrets of Masonry are about to be unveiled, and a brighter sun never shone lustre on your eyes; while prostrate before this sacred altar, do you not shudder at every crime? Have you not confidence in every virtue? May these thoughts ever inspire you with the most noble sentiments; may you ever feel that elevation of soul that shall scorn a dishonest act. Brother, what do you most desire?" The candidate answers, "Light." Master to brethren, "Brethren, stretch forth your hands and assist in bringing this new-made brother from darkness to light." The members having formed a circle round the candidate, the Master says, "And God said, Let there be light, and there was light." At the same time, all the brethren clap their hands and stamp on the floor with their right feet as heavy as possible, the bandage dropping from the candidate's eyes at the same instant, which, after having been so long blind, and full of fearful apprehensions all the time, this great and sudden transition from perfect darkness to a light brighter (if possible) than the meridian sun in a midsummer day, sometimes produces an alarming effect.

After the candidate is brought to light, the Master addresses him as follows: "Brother, on being brought to light, you first discover three great lights in Masonry by the assistance of three lesser; they are thus explained: The three great lights in Masonry are the Holy Bible, Square and Compass. The Holy Bible is given to us as a rule and guide for our faith and practice; the Square, to square our actions, and the Compass to keep us in due bounds with all mankind, but more especially with the brethren. Three lesser lights are three burning tapers, or candles placed on candlesticks (some say, or candles on pedestals), they represent the Sun, Moon, and Master of the Lodge, and are thus explained: As the sun rules the day, and the moon governs the night, so ought the Worshipful Master, with equal regularity, to rule and govern his Lodge, or cause the same to be done; you next discover me, as Master of this Lodge, approaching you from the East upon the first step of Masonry, under the sign and due-guard of an Entered Apprentice Mason, as already revealed to you. This is the manner of giving them; imitate me, as near as you can, keeping your position. First, step off with your left foot, and bring the heel of the right into the hollow thereof, so as to form a square." [This is the first step in Masonry.] The following is the sign of an Entered Apprentice Mason, and is the sign of distress in this degree; you are not to give it unless in distress. [It is given by holding your two hands traversely across each other, the right hand upwards, and one inch from the left.] The following is the due-guard of an Entered Apprentice Mason. [This is given by drawing your right hand across your throat, the thumb next to your throat, your arm as [Pg 10]high as the elbow, in a horizontal position.] "Brother, I now present you my right hand, in token of brotherly love and esteem, and with it the grip and name of the grip of an Entered Apprentice Mason." The right hands are joined together, as in shaking hands, and each sticks his thumb nail into the third joint or upper end of the forefinger; the name of the grip is Boaz, and is to be given in the following manner and no other: The Master gives the grip and word, and divides it for the instruction of the candidate; the questions are as follows: The Master and candidate holding each other by the grip as before described, the Master says, "What is this?" Candidate— "A grip." Master "A grip of what?" Candidate—"The grip of an Entered Apprentice Mason." Master—"Has it a name?" Candidate—"It has." Master—"Will you give it to me?" Candidate—"I did not so receive it, neither can I so impart it." Master—"What will you do with it?" Candidate—"Letter it, or halve it." Master—"Halve it and begin." Candidate—"You begin." Master—"Begin you." Candidate—"BO." Master—"AZ." Candidate—"BOAZ." Master says, "Right, Brother Boaz, I greet you. It is the name of the left hand pillar of the porch of King Solomon's Temple—arise, Brother Boaz, and salute the Junior and Senior Wardens as such, and convince them that you have been regularly initiated as an Entered Apprentice Mason, and have got the sign, grip, and word." The Master returns to his seat, while the Wardens are examining the candidate, and gets a lamb-skin or white apron, presents it to the candidate and observes, "Brother, I now present you with a lamb-skin, or white apron; it is an emblem of innocence, and the badge of a Mason; it has been worn by kings, princes, and potentates of the earth, who have never been ashamed to wear it; it is more honorable than the diamonds of kings, or pearls of princesses, when worthily worn; it is more ancient than the Golden Fleece or Roman Eagle; more honorable than the Star and Garter, or any other order that can be conferred upon you at this or any other time, except it be in the body of a just and fully constituted Lodge; you will carry it to the Senior Warden in the West, who will teach you how to wear it as an Entered Apprentice Mason." The Senior Warden ties the apron on, and turns up the flap, instead of letting it fall down in front of the apron. This is the way Entered Apprentice Masons wear, or ought to wear, their aprons until they are advanced. The candidate is now conducted to the Master in the East, who says, "Brother, as you are dressed, it is necessary you should have tools to work with; I will now present you with the working tools of an Entered Apprentice Mason, which are the twenty-four-inch gauge and common gavel; they are thus explained: The twenty-four-inch gauge is an instrument made use of by operative Masons to measure and lay out their work, but we, as Free and Accepted Masons, make use of it for the more noble and glorious purpose of dividing our time. The twenty-four inches on the gauge are emblematical of the twenty-four hours in the day, which we are taught to divide into three equal parts, whereby we find eight hours for the service of God and a worthy distressed brother; eight hours for our usual vocations; and eight for refreshment and sleep; the common gavel is an instrument made use of by operative Masons to break off the [Pg 11]corners of rough stones, the better to fit them for the builder's use; but we, as Free and Accepted Masons, use it for the more noble and glorious purpose of divesting our hearts and consciences of all the vices and superfluities of life, thereby fitting our minds as living and lively stones for that spiritual building, that house not made with hands, eternal in the Heavens. I also present you with a new name; it is CAUTION; it teaches you, as you are barely instructed in the rudiments of Masonry, that you should be cautious over all your words and actions, particularly when before the enemies of Masonry. I shall next present you with three precious jewels, which are a LISTENING EAR, a SILENT TONGUE, and a FAITHFUL HEART. A listening ear teaches you to listen to the instructions of the Worshipful Master, but more especially that you should listen to the cries of a worthy distressed brother. A silent tongue teaches you to be silent while in the Lodge, that the peace and harmony thereof may not be disturbed, but more especially that you should be silent before the enemies of Masonry, that the craft may not be brought into disrepute by your imprudence. A faithful heart teaches you to be faithful to the instructions of the Worshipful Master at all times, but more especially that you should be faithful, and keep and conceal the secrets of Masonry, and those of a brother when given to you in charge as such, that they may remain as secure and inviolable in your breast as his own, before communicated to you. I further present you with check-words two; their names are TRUTH and UNION, and are thus explained: Truth is a divine attribute, and the foundation of every virtue; to be good and true is the first lesson we are taught in Masonry; on this theme we contemplate, and by its dictates endeavor to regulate our conduct; hence, while influenced by this principle, hypocrisy and deceit are unknown among us, sincerity and plain dealing distinguish us, and the heart and tongue join in promoting each other's welfare, and rejoicing in each other's prosperity. Union is that kind of friendship which ought to appear conspicuous in every Mason's conduct. It is so closely allied to the divine attribute, truth, that he who enjoys the one is seldom destitute of the other. Should interest, honor, prejudice, or human depravity ever induce you to violate any part of the sacred trust we now repose in you, let these two important words, at the earliest insinuation, teach you to put on the check-line of truth, which will infallibly direct you to pursue that straight and narrow path which ends in the full enjoyment of the Grand Lodge above, where we shall all meet as Masons and members of the same family, in peace, harmony, and love; where all discord on account of politics, religion, or private opinion, shall be unknown, and banished from within our walls.

"Brother, it has been a custom from time immemorial to demand, or ask from a newly-made brother, something of a metallic kind, not so much on account of its intrinsic value, but that it may be deposited in the archives of the Lodge, as a memorial that you was herein made a Mason; a small trifle will be sufficient—anything of a metallic kind will do; if you have no money, anything of a metallic nature will be sufficient; even a button will do." [The candidate says he has nothing about him; it is known he has nothing.] "Search yourself," the Master [Pg 12]replies. He is assisted in searching—nothing is found. "Perhaps you can borrow a trifle," says the Master. [He tries to borrow, none will lend him; he proposes to go into the other room where his clothes are; he is not permitted: if a stranger, he is very much embarrassed.] Master to candidate, "Brother, let this ever be a striking lesson to you, and teach you, if you should ever see a friend, but more especially a brother, in a like penniless situation, to contribute as liberally to his relief as his situation may require, and your abilities will admit, without material injury to yourself or family." Master to Senior Deacon, "You will conduct the candidate back from whence he came, and invest him of what he has been divested, and let him return for further instruction. A zealous attachment to these principles will insure a public and private esteem. In the State, you are to be a quiet and peaceable subject, true to your government, and just to your country; you are not to countenance disloyalty, but faithfully submit to legal authority, and conform with cheerfulness to the government of the country in which you live. In your outward demeanor be particularly careful to avoid censure or reproach. Although your frequent appearance at our regular meetings is earnestly solicited, yet it is not meant that Masonry should interfere with your necessary vocations; for these are on no account to be neglected: neither are you to suffer your zeal for the institution to lead you into argument with those who, through ignorance, may ridicule it. At your leisure hours, that you may improve in Masonic knowledge, you are to converse with well-informed brethren, who will be always as ready to give, as you will be to receive information. Finally, keep sacred and inviolable the mysteries of the Order, as these are to distinguish you from the rest of the community, and mark your consequence among Masons. If, in the circle of your acquaintance, you find a person desirous of being initiated into Masonry, be particularly attentive not to commend him, unless you are convinced he will conform to our rules; that the honor, glory, and reputation of the institution may be firmly established, and the world at large convinced of its good effects." Here the initiation ends, and the candidate is congratulated by his Masonic friends.

After this, the business of the meeting proceeds according to the by-laws or regulations of the Lodge. Before adjourning, it is a very common practice to close a Lodge of Entered Apprentices, and open a Lodge of Fellow Crafts, and close that, and open a Master Mason's Lodge, all in the same evening.

Ceremony of Closing a Lodge of Entered Apprentices.

A brother having made a motion that the Lodge be closed, it being seconded and carried, the Master says to the Junior Deacon, "Brother Junior [giving one rap, which calls up both Deacons], the first as well as the last care of a Mason?" The Junior Deacon answers, "To see the Lodge tyled, Worshipful." Master to the Junior Deacon, "Attend to that part of your duty, and inform the Tyler that we are about to close this Lodge of Entered Apprentice Masons, and direct him to tyle accordingly." The Junior Deacon steps to the door and gives three [Pg 13]raps, which are answered by the Tyler with three more; the Junior Deacon then gives one, which is also answered by the Tyler by one. The Junior Deacon then opens the door, delivers his message, and resumes his place in the Lodge, and says, "The door is tyled, Worshipful." Master to Junior Deacon, "By whom?" Ans. "By a Master Mason without the door, armed with the proper implements of his office." Master to Junior Deacon, "His business there?" Ans. "To keep off all cowans and eavesdroppers, and see that none pass or repass without permission from the chair." Master to Junior Deacon, "Your duty there?" Ans. "To wait on the Worshipful Master and Wardens, act as their proxy in the active duties of the Lodge, and take care of the door." Master to Junior Deacon, "The Senior Deacon's place in the Lodge?" Ans. "At the right hand of the Worshipful Master in the East." Master to Senior Deacon, "Your duty there, Brother Senior?" Ans. "To wait on the Worshipful Master and Wardens, act as their proxy in the active duties of the Lodge, attend to the preparation and introduction of candidates; receive and clothe all visiting brethren." Master to the Senior Deacon, "The Secretary's place in the Lodge?" Ans. "At your left hand, Worshipful." Master to Secretary, "Your duty there, Brother Secretary?" The Secretary replies, "Duly to observe the Master's will and pleasure; record the proceedings of the Lodge; transmit a copy of the same to the Grand Lodge, if required; receive all moneys and money-bills from the hands of the brethren; pay them over to the Treasurer, and take his receipt for the same." Master to the Secretary, "The Treasurer's place in the Lodge?" Ans. "At the right hand of the Worshipful Master." Master to Treasurer, "Your business there, Brother Treasurer?" Treasurer answers, "Duly to observe the Worshipful Master's will and pleasure; receive all moneys and money-bills from the hands of the Secretary; keep a just and accurate account of the same; pay them out by order of the Worshipful Master and consent of the brethren." Master to the Treasurer, "The Junior Warden's place in the Lodge?" Ans. "In the South, Worshipful." Master to the Junior Warden, "Your business there, Brother Junior?" The Junior Warden says, "As the sun in the South, at high meridian, is the beauty and glory of the day, so stands the Junior Warden in the South at high twelve, the better to observe the time, call the crafts from labor to refreshment; superintend them during the hours thereof; see that none convert the purposes of refreshment into that of excess or intemperance; call them on again in due season; that the Worshipful Master may have honor, and they pleasure and profit thereby." The Master to the Junior Warden, "The Master's place in the Lodge?" Ans. "In the East, Worshipful." Master to Junior Warden, "His duty there?" Ans. "As the sun rises in the East to open and adorn the day, so presides the Worshipful Master in the East, to open and adorn his Lodge, set his crafts to work with good and wholesome laws, or cause the same to be done." Master to the Junior Warden, "The Senior Warden's place in the Lodge?" Ans. "In the West, Worshipful." Master to the Senior Warden, "Your business there, Brother Senior?" The Senior Warden replies, "As the sun sets in the West to close the day, so stands the Senior Warden in the West to assist the [Pg 14]Worshipful Master in opening and closing the Lodge; take care of the jewels and implements; see that none be lost; pay the craft their wages, if any be due; and see that none go away dissatisfied." The Master now gives three raps, when all the brethren rise, and the Master asks, "Are you all satisfied?" They answer in the affirmative by giving the due-guard. Should the Master discover that any declined giving it, inquiry is immediately made why it is so; and if any member is dissatisfied with any part of the proceedings, or with any brother, the subject is immediately investigated. Master to the brethren, "Attend to giving the signs; as I do, so do you give them downwards;" [which is by giving the last in opening, first in closing. In closing, on this degree, you first draw your right hand across your throat, as hereinbefore described, and then hold your two hands over each other as before described. This is the method pursued through all the degrees; and when opening on any of the upper degrees, all the signs of all the preceding degrees are given before you give the signs of the degree on which you are opening.] This being done, the Master proceeds, "I now declare this Lodge of Entered Apprentice Masons regularly closed in due and ancient form. Brother Junior Warden, please inform Brother Senior Warden, and request him to inform the brethren that it is my will and pleasure that this Lodge of Entered Apprentice Masons be now closed, and stand closed until our next regular communication, unless a case or cases of emergency shall require earlier convention, of which every member shall be notified; during which time it is seriously hoped and expected that every brother will demean himself as becomes a Free and Accepted Mason." Junior Warden to Senior Warden, "Brother Senior, it is the Worshipful Master's will and pleasure that this Lodge of Entered Apprentice Masons be closed, and stand closed until our next regular communication, unless a case or cases of emergency shall require earlier convention, of which every brother shall be notified; during which time it is seriously hoped and expected that every brother will demean himself as becomes a Free and Accepted Mason." Senior Warden to the brethren, "Brethren, you have heard the Worshipful Master's will and pleasure as communicated to me by Brother Junior; so let it be done." Master to the Junior Warden, "Brother Junior, how do Mason's meet?" Ans. "On the level." Master to Senior Warden, "How do Masons part?" Ans. "On the square." Master to the Junior and Senior Wardens, "Since we meet on the level, Brother Junior, and part on the square, Brother Senior, so let us ever meet and part in the name of the Lord." Master to the brethren, "Brethren, let us pray."

"Supreme Architect of the Universe! Accept our humble praises for the many mercies and blessings which Thy bounty has conferred upon us, and especially for this friendly and social intercourse. Pardon, we beseech Thee, whatever Thou hast seen amiss in us since we have been together; and continue to us Thy presence, protection and blessing. Make us sensible of the renewed obligations we are under to love Thee supremely, and to be friendly to each other. May all our irregular passions be subdued, and may we daily increase in faith, hope, and charity; but more especially in that charity which is the bond of peace, and [Pg 15]perfection of every virtue. May we so practice Thy precepts, that through the merits of the Redeemer we may finally obtain Thy promises, and find an acceptance through the gates and into the temple and city of our God. So mote it be. Amen."

It is often that the prayer is neglected and the following benediction substituted: May the blessing of heaven rest upon us, and all regular Masons! May brotherly love prevail, and every moral and social virtue cement us. So mote it be. Amen.

After the prayer the following charge ought to be delivered, but it is seldom attended to; in a majority of Lodges it is never attended to; Master to brethren, "Brethren, we are now about to quit this sacred retreat of friendship and virtue to mix again with the world. Amidst its concerns and employments, forget not the duties which you have heard so frequently inculcated, and so forcibly recommended in this Lodge. Remember that around this altar you have promised to befriend and relieve every brother who shall need your assistance. You have promised in the most friendly manner to remind him of his errors and aid a reformation. These generous principles are to extend further; every human being has a claim upon your kind offices. Do good unto all. Recommend it more 'especially to the household of the faithful.' Finally, brethren, be ye all of one mind, live in peace, and may the God of love and peace delight to dwell with and bless you."

In some Lodges, after the charge is delivered, the Master says, "Brethren, form on the square." Then all the brethren form a circle, and the Master, followed by every brother [except in using the words], says, "And God said, Let there be light, and there was light." At the same moment that the last of these words drops from the Master's lips, every member stamps with his right foot on the floor, and at the same instant brings his hands together with equal force, and in such perfect unison with each other, that persons situated so as to hear it would suppose it the precursor of some dreadful catastrophe. This is called "THE SHOCK." The members of the Lodge then separate.

The above comprises all the secret forms and ceremonies in a Lodge of Entered Apprentice Masons; but if the candidate would thoroughly understand the whole, he must commit to memory the following "Lecture." Very few do this except the officers of the Lodge. The "Lecture" is nothing more nor less than a recapitulation of the preceding ceremonies and forms by way of question and answer, in order fully to explain the same. In fact, the ceremonies and forms (masonically called the WORK) and Lecture are so much the same that he who possesses a knowledge of the Lecture cannot be destitute of a knowledge of what the ceremonies and forms are. The ceremonies used in opening and closing are the same in all the degrees.

FIRST SECTION.

Lecture on the First Degree of Masonry.

Question—From whence came you as an Entered Apprentice Mason? Answer—From the Holy Lodge of St. John at Jerusalem.

[Pg 16]Q. What recommendations do you bring? A. Recommendations from the Worshipful Master, Wardens, and brethren of that Right Worshipful Lodge, who greet you.

Q. What comest thou hither to do? A. To learn to subdue my passions, and improve myself in the secret arts and mysteries of Ancient Freemasonry.

Q. You are a Mason, then, I presume? A. I am.

Q. How do you know that you are a Mason? A. By being often tried, never denied, and willing to be tried again.

Q. How shall I know you to be a Mason? A. By certain signs, and a token.

Q. What are signs? A. All right angles, horizontals and perpendiculars.

Q. What is a token? A. A certain friendly and brotherly grip, whereby one Mason may know another in the dark as well as in the light.

Q. Where were you first prepared to be a Mason? A. In my heart.

Q. Where secondly? A. In a room adjacent to the body of a just and lawfully constituted Lodge of such.

Q. How were you prepared? A. By being divested of all metals, neither naked nor clothed, barefoot nor shod, hoodwinked, with a cable-tow about my neck, in which situation I was conducted to the door of the Lodge.

Q. You being hoodwinked, how did you know it to be a door? A. By first meeting with resistance, and afterwards gaining admission.

Q. How did you gain admission? A. By three distinct knocks from without, answered by the same from within.

Q. What was said to you from within? A. Who comes there? Who comes there? Who comes there?

Q. Your answer? A. A poor, blind candidate, who has long been desirous of having and receiving a part of the rights and benefits of this Worshipful Lodge, dedicated to God, and held forth to the Holy Order of St. John, as all true fellows and brothers have done, who have gone this way before me.

Q. What further was said to you from within? A. I was asked if it was of my own free will and accord I made this request; if I was duly and truly prepared, worthy and well qualified; all of which being answered in the affirmative, I was asked by what further rights I expected to obtain so great a favor or benefit.

Q. Your answer? A. By being a man, free-born, of lawful age, and well recommended.

Q. What was then said to you? A. I was bid to wait till the Worshipful Master in the East was made acquainted with my request and his answer returned.

Q. After his answer was returned, what followed? A. I was caused to enter the Lodge.

Q. How? A. On the point of some sharp instrument pressing my naked left breast, in the name of the Lord.

Q. How were you then disposed of? A. I was conducted to the centre of the Lodge, and there caused to kneel for the benefit of a prayer.

[Pg 17]Q. After prayer, what was said to you? A. I was asked in whom I put my trust.

Q. Your answer? A. God.

Q. What followed? A. The Worshipful Master took me by the right hand and said, Since in God you put your trust, arise, follow your leader, and fear no danger.

Q. How were you then disposed of? A. I was conducted three times regularly around the Lodge, and halted at the Junior Warden in the South, where the same questions were asked, and answers returned at the door.

Q. How did the Junior Warden dispose of you? A. He ordered me to be conducted to the Senior Warden in the West, where the same questions were asked, and answers returned as before.

Q. How did the Senior Warden dispose of you? A. He ordered me to be conducted to the Worshipful Master in the East, where the same questions were asked, and answers returned as before, who likewise demanded of me from whence I came, and whither I was traveling.

Q. Your answer? A. From the West, and traveling to the East.

Q. Why do you leave the West and travel to the East? A. In search of light.

Q. How did the Worshipful Master then dispose of you? A. He ordered me to be conducted back to the West, from whence I came, and put in care of the Senior Warden, who taught me how to approach the East, the place of light, by advancing upon one upright regular step to the first step, my feet forming the right angle of an oblong square, my body erect at the altar before the Worshipful Master.

Q. What did the Worshipful Master do with you? A. He made an Entered Apprentice Mason of me.

Q. How? A. In due form.

Q. What was that due form? A. My left knee bare and bent, my right forming a square, my left hand supporting the Holy Bible, Square and Compass; I took upon me the solemn oath or obligation of an Entered Apprentice Mason.

Q. After you had taken your obligation, what was said to you? A. I was asked what I most desired.

Q. Your answer? A. Light.

Q. Was you immediately brought to light? A. I was.

Q. How? A. By the direction of the Master, and assistance of the brethren.

Q. What did you first discover after being brought to light? A. Three great lights in Masonry, by the assistance of three lesser.

Q. What were those three great lights in Masonry? A. The Holy Bible, Square and Compass.

Q. How are they explained? A. The Holy Bible is given to us as a guide for our faith and practice; the Square, to square our actions; and the Compass to keep us in due bounds with all mankind, but more especially with the brethren.

Q. What were those three lesser lights? A. Three burning tapers, or candles on candlesticks.

[Pg 18]Q. What do they represent? A. The Sun, Moon, and Master of the Lodge.

Q. How are they explained? A. As the Sun rules the day, and the Moon governs the night, so ought the Worshipful Master to use his endeavors to rule and govern his Lodge with equal regularity, or cause the same to be done.

Q. What did you next discover? A. The Worshipful Master approaching me from the East, under the sign and due-guard of an Entered Apprentice Mason, who presented me with his right hand in token of brotherly love and esteem, and proceeded to give me the grip and word of an Entered Apprentice Mason, and bid me arise and salute the Junior and Senior Wardens, and convince them that I had been regularly initiated as an Entered Apprentice Mason, and was in possession of the sign, grip, and word.

Q. What did you next discover? A. The Worshipful Master a second time approaching me from the East, who presented me with a lamb-skin, or white apron, which he said was an emblem of innocence, and the badge of a Mason; that it had been worn by kings, princes, and potentates of the earth, who had never been ashamed to wear it; that it was more honorable than the diamonds of kings, or pearls of princesses, when worthily worn; and more ancient than the Golden Fleece or Roman Eagle; more honorable than the Star or Garter, or any other order that could be conferred on me at that time, or any time thereafter, except it be in the body of a just and lawfully constituted Lodge of Masons; and bid me carry it to the Senior Warden in the West, who taught me how to wear it as an Entered Apprentice Mason.

Q. What were you next presented with? A. The working tools of an Entered Apprentice Mason.

Q. What were they? A. The twenty-four-inch gauge and common gavel.

Q. How were they explained? A. The twenty-four-inch gauge is an instrument made use of by operative masons to measure and lay out their work; but we, as Free and Accepted Masons, are taught to make use of it for the more noble and glorious purpose of dividing our time; the twenty-four inches on the gauge are emblematical of the twenty-four hours in the day, which we are taught so divide into three equal parts, whereby we find eight hours for the service of God and a worthy distressed brother; eight hours for our usual vocation, and eight hours for refreshment and sleep. The common gavel is an instrument made use of by operative masons to break off the corners of rough stones, the better to fit them for the builder's use; but we, as Free and Accepted Masons, are taught to make use of it for the more noble and glorious purpose of divesting our hearts and consciences of all the vices and superfluities of life, thereby fitting our minds as lively and living stone for that spiritual building, that house not made with hands, eternal in the heavens.

Q. What was you next presented with? A. A new name.

Q. What was it? A. Caution.

[Pg 19]Q. What does it teach? A. It teaches me, as I was barely instructed in the rudiments of Masonry, that I should be cautious over all my words and actions, especially when before its enemies.

Q. What were you next presented with? A. Three precious jewels.

Q. What were they? A. A listening ear, a silent tongue, and a faithful heart.

Q. What do they teach? A. A listening ear teaches me to listen to the instructions of the Worshipful Master, but more especially that I should listen to the calls and cries of a worthy distressed brother. A silent tongue teaches me to be silent in the Lodge, that the peace and harmony thereof may not be disturbed; but more especially that I should be silent when before the enemies of Masonry. A faithful heart, that I should be faithful to the instructions of the Worshipful Master at all times; but more especially that I should be faithful and keep and conceal the secrets of Masonry, and those of a brother, when delivered to me in charge as such, that they may remain as secure and inviolable in my breast as in his own, before communicated to me.

Q. What was you next presented with? A. Check-words two.

Q. What were they? A. Truth and Union.

Q. How explained? A. Truth is a divine attribute, and the foundation of every virtue. To be good and true are the first lessons we are taught in Masonry. On this theme we contemplate, and by its dictates endeavor to regulate our conduct; hence, while influenced by this principle, hypocrisy and deceit are unknown amongst us; sincerity and plain dealing distinguish us; and the heart and tongue join in promoting each other's welfare, and rejoicing in each other's prosperity.

Union is that kind of friendship that ought to appear conspicuous in the conduct of every Mason. It is so closely allied to the divine attribute, truth, that he who enjoys the one, is seldom destitute of the other. Should interest, honor, prejudice, or human depravity ever influence you to violate any part of the sacred trust we now repose in you, let these two important words, at the earliest insinuation, teach you to put on the check-line of truth, which will infallibly direct you to pursue that straight and narrow path which ends in the full enjoyment of the Grand Lodge above, where we shall all meet as Masons and members of one family; where all discord on account of religion, politics, or private opinion, shall be unknown and banished from within our walls.

Q. What followed? A. The Worshipful Master in the East made a demand of me of something of a metallic kind, which, he said, was not so much on account of its intrinsic value, as that it might be deposited in the archives of the Lodge as a memorial that I had herein been made a Mason.

Q. How did the Worshipful Master then dispose of you? A. He ordered me to be conducted out of the Lodge and invested of what I had been divested, and return for further instruction.

Q. After you returned, how was you disposed of? A. I was conducted to the northeast corner of the Lodge, and there caused to stand upright like a man, my feet forming a square, and received a solemn injunction, ever to walk and act uprightly before God and man, and in addition thereto received too following charge. [For this charge see pages 10-12.]

[Pg 20]

SECOND SECTION.

Question—Why was you divested of all metals when you was made a Mason? Answer—Because Masonry regards no man on account of his worldly wealth or honors; it is therefore the internal, and not the external qualifications that recommend a man to Masons.

Q. A second reason? A. There was neither the sound of an axe, hammer, or any other metal tool heard at the building of King Solomon's Temple.

Q. How could so stupendous a fabric be erected without the sound of axe, hammer, or any other metal tool? A. All the stones were hewed, squared, and numbered in the quarries where they were raised, all the timbers felled and prepared in the forests of Lebanon, and carried down to Joppa on floats, and taken from thence up to Jerusalem and set up with wooden mauls, prepared for that purpose; which, when completed, every part thereof fitted with that exact nicety, that it had more the resemblance of the handy workmanship of the Supreme Architect of the Universe than of human hands.

Q. Why was you neither naked nor clothed? A. As I was an object of distress at that time, it was to remind me, if ever I saw a friend, more especially a brother, in a like distressed situation, that I should contribute as liberally to his relief as his situation required, and my abilities would admit, without material injury to myself or family.

Q. Why was you neither barefoot nor shod? A. It was an ancient Israelitish custom adopted among Masons; and we read in the Book of Ruth concerning their mode and manner of changing and redeeming, and to confirm all things, a brother plucked off his shoe and gave it to his neighbor, and that was testimony in Israel. This, then, therefore, we do in confirmation of a token, and as a pledge of our fidelity; therefore signifying that we will renounce our own will in all things, and become obedient to the laws of our ancient institutions.

Q. Why was you hoodwinked? A. That my heart might conceive before my eyes beheld the beauties of Masonry.

Q. A second reason? A. As I was in darkness at that time, it was to remind me that I should keep the whole world so respecting Masonry.

Q. Why had you a cable-tow about your neck? A. In case I had not submitted to the manner and mode of my initiation, that I might have been led out of the Lodge without seeing the form and beauties thereof.

Q. Why did you give three distinct knocks at the door? A. To alarm the Lodge, and let the Worshipful Master, Wardens and brethren know that a poor blind candidate prayed admission.

Q. What do those three distinct knocks allude to? A. A certain passage in Scripture wherein it says, "Ask and it shall be given, seek and ye shall find, knock and it shall be opened unto you."

132

Q. How did you apply this to your then case in Masonry? A. I asked the recommendation of a friend to become a Mason; I sought admission through his recommendations and knocked, and the door of Masonry opened unto me.

Q. Why was you caused to enter on the point of some sharp instrument pressing your naked left breast in the name of the Lord? A. As [Pg 21]this was a torture to my flesh, so might the recollection of it ever be to my flesh and conscience, if ever I attempted to reveal the secrets of Masonry unlawfully.

Q. Why was you conducted to the centre of the Lodge, and there caused to kneel for the benefit of a prayer? A. Before entering on this, or any other great and important undertaking, it is highly necessary to implore a blessing from Deity.

Q. Why was you asked in whom you put your trust? A. Agreeably to the laws of our ancient institution, no Atheist could be made a Mason; it was, therefore, necessary that I should believe in Deity; otherwise, no oath or obligation could bind me.

Q. Why did the Worshipful Master take you by the right hand and bid you rise, follow your leader, and fear no danger? A. As I was in darkness at that time, and could neither forsee nor avoid danger, it was to remind me that I was in the hands of an affectionate friend, in whose fidelity I might with safety confide.

Q. Why was you conducted three times regularly round the Lodge? A. That the Worshipful Master, Wardens and brethren might see that I was duly and truly prepared.

Q. Why did you meet with those several obstructions on the way? A. This, and every other Lodge is, or ought to be, a true representation of King Solomon's Temple, which, when completed, had guards stationed at the East, West, and South gates.

Q. Why had they guards stationed at those several gates? A. To prevent any one from passing or repassing that was not duly qualified.

Q. Why did you kneel on your left knee and not on your right, or both? A. The left side has ever been considered the weakest part of the body; it was, therefore, to remind me that that part I was then taking upon me was the weakest part of Masonry, it being that only of an Entered Apprentice.

Q. Why was your right hand placed on the Holy Bible, Square and Compass, and not your left, or both? A. The right hand has ever been considered the seat of fidelity, and our ancient brethren worshipped Deity under the name of Fides, which has sometimes been represented by two right hands joined together; at others, by two human figures holding each other by the right hand; the right hand, therefore, we use in this great and important undertaking, to signify, in the strongest manner possible, the sincerity of our intentions in the business we are engaged.

Q. Why did the Worshipful Master present you with a lamb-skin, or a white apron? A. The lamb-skin has, in all ages, been deemed an emblem of innocence; he, therefore, who wears the lamb-skin, as a badge of a Mason, is thereby continually reminded of that purity of life and rectitude of conduct, which is so essentially necessary to our gaining admission into the Celestial Lodge above, where the Supreme Architect of the Universe presides.

Q. Why did the Master make a demand of you of something of a metallic nature? A. As I was in a poor and penniless situation at the time, it was to remind me if ever I saw a friend, but more especially a brother, [Pg 22]in a like poor and penniless situation, that I should contribute as liberally to his relief as my abilities would admit and his situation required, without injuring myself or family.

Q. Why was you conducted to the northeast corner of the Lodge, and there caused to stand upright, like a man, your feet forming a square, receiving, at the same time, a solemn charge to walk and act uprightly before God and man? A. The first stone in every Masonic edifice is, or ought to be, placed at the northeast corner; that being the place where an Entered Apprentice Mason receives his first instructions to build his future Masonic edifice upon.

THIRD SECTION.

Question—We have been saying a good deal about a Lodge, I want to know what constitutes a Lodge? Answer—A certain number of Free and Accepted Masons, duly assembled in a room or place, with the Holy Bible, Square and Compass, and other Masonic Implements, with a charter from the Grand Lodge, empowering them to work.

Q. Where did our ancient brethren meet before Lodges were erected? A. On the highest hills, and in the lowest vales.

Q. Why on the highest hills and in the lowest vales? A. The better to guard against cowans and enemies either ascending or descending, that the brethren might have timely notice of their approach, to prevent being surprised.

Q. What is the form of your Lodge? A. An oblong square.

Q. How long? A. From East to West.

Q. How wide? A. Between North and South.

Q. How high? A. From the surface of the earth to the highest heavens.

Q. How deep? A. From the surface to the centre.

Q. What supports your Lodge? A. Three large columns or pillars.

Q. What are their names? A. Wisdom, Strength, and Beauty.

Q. Why so? A. It is necessary there should be wisdom to contrive, strength to support, and beauty to adorn, all great and important undertakings; but more especially this of ours.

Q. Has your Lodge any covering? A. It has; a clouded canopy, or starry-decked heaven, where all good Masons hope to arrive.

Q. How do you hope to arrive there? A. By the assistance of Jacob's ladder.

Q. How many principal rounds has it got? A. Three.

Q. What are their names? A. Faith, Hope, and Charity.

Q. What do they teach? A. Faith in God, hope in immortality, and charity to all mankind.

Q. Has your Lodge any furniture? A. It has; the Holy Bible, Square, and Compass.

Q. To whom do they belong? A. The Bible to God; the Square to the Master; and the Compass to the Craft.

Q. How explained? A. The Bible to God, it being the inestimable gift of God to man for his instruction, to guide him through the rugged paths of life; the Square to the Master, it being the proper emblem of [Pg 23]his office: the Compass to the Craft; by a due attention to which we are taught to limit our desires, curb our ambition, subdue our irregular appetites, and keep our passions and prejudices in due bounds with all mankind, but more especially with the brethren.

Q. Has your Lodge any ornaments? A. It has; the Mosaic, or checkered pavement; the indented tressel; that beautiful tesselated border which surrounds it, with the blazing star in the centre.

Q. What do they represent? A. The Mosaic, or checkered pavement, represents this world; which, though checkered over with good and evil, yet brethren may walk together thereon and not stumble; the indented tressel, with the blazing star in the centre, the manifold blessings and comforts with which we are surrounded in this life, but more especially those which we hope to enjoy hereafter; the blazing star, that prudence which ought to appear conspicuous in the conduct of every Mason, but more especially commemorative of the star which appeared in the East to guide the wise men to Bethlehem, to proclaim the birth and the presence of the Son of God.

Q. Has your Lodge any lights? A. It has; three.

Q. How are they situated? A. East, West, and South.

Q. Has it none in the North? A. It has not.

Q. Why so? A. Because this and every other Lodge is, or ought to be, a true representation of King Solomon's Temple, which was situated North of the ecliptic; the Sun and Moon, therefore, darting their rays from the South, no light was to be expected from the North; we, therefore, Masonically, term the North a place of darkness.

Q. Has your Lodge any jewels? A. It has; six; three movable and three immovable.

Q. What are the three movable jewels? A. The Square, Level, and Plumb.

Q. What do they teach? A. The Square, morality; the Level, equality; and the Plumb, rectitude of life and conduct.

Q. What are the three immovable jewels? A. The rough Ashlar, the perfect Ashlar, and the Tressel-Board.

Q. What are they? A. The rough Ashlar is a stone in its rough and natural state; the perfect Ashlar is also a stone, made ready by the working tools of the Fellow Craft to be adjusted in the building; and the Tressle-Board is for the master workman to draw his plans and designs upon.

Q. What do they represent? A. The rough Ashlar represents man in his rude and imperfect state by nature; the perfect Ashlar also represents man in that state of perfection to which we all hope to arrive, by means of a virtuous life and education, our own endeavors, and the blessing of God. In erecting our temporal building, we pursue the plans and designs laid down by the master workman on his Tressle-Board: but in erecting our spiritual building, we pursue the plans and designs laid down by the Supreme Geometrician of the Universe, in the Book of Life, which we, Masonically, term our spiritual Tressle-Board.

Q. Who did you serve? A. My Master.

Q. How long? A. Six days.

[Pg 24]Q. What did you serve him with? A. Freedom, Fervency, and Zeal.

Q. What do they represent? A. Chalk, Charcoal, and Earth.

Q. Why so? A. There is nothing freer than chalk, the slightest touch of which leaves a trace behind; nothing more fervent than heated charcoal; it will melt the most obdurate metals; nothing more zealous than the earth to bring forth.

Q. How is your Lodge situated? A. Due East and West.

Q. Why so? A. Because the Sun rises in the East and sets in the West.

Q. A second reason? A. The gospel was first preached in the East and is spreading to the West.

Q. A third reason? A. The liberal arts and sciences began in the East and are extending to the West.

Q. A fourth reason? A. Because all the churches and chapels are, or ought to be, so situated.

Q. Why are all churches and chapels so situated? A. Because King Solomon's Temple was so situated.

Q. Why was King Solomon's Temple so situated? A. Because Moses, after conducting the children of Israel through the Red Sea, by divine command, erected a tabernacle to God, and placed it due East and West, which was to commemorate, to the latest posterity, that miraculous East wind that wrought their mighty deliverance; and this was an exact model of Solomon's Temple; since which time, every well regulated and governed Lodge is, or ought to be, so situated.

Q. To whom did our ancient brethren dedicate their Lodges? A. To King Solomon.

Q. Why so? A. Because King Solomon was our most ancient Grand Master.

Q. To whom do modern Masons dedicate their Lodges? A. To St. John the Baptist and St. John the Evangelist.

Q. Why so? A. Because they were the two most ancient Christian patrons of Masonry; and, since their time, in every well-regulated and governed Lodge there has been a certain point within a circle, which circle is bounded on the East and the West by two perpendicular parallel lines, representing the anniversary of St. John the Baptist and St. John the Evangelist, who were two perfect parallels, as well in Masonry as Christianity, on the vertex of which rests the Book of the Holy Scriptures, supporting Jacob's Ladder, which is said to reach the watery clouds, and, in passing round this circle, we naturally touch on both these perpendicular parallel lines, as well as the Book of the Holy Scriptures; and while a Mason keeps himself thus circumscribed, he cannot materially err.

END OF THE LECTURE, AND OF THE FIRST DEGREE.

It is proper to add here that very few Masons ever learn the Lecture. Of course, it is necessary that the officers of the Lodge should understand their own particular part, and that is generally all they learn.

THE SECOND OR FELLOW CRAFT MASON'S DEGREE.

This degree is usually called "passing." The ceremonies of opening and closing the Lodge are precisely the same as in the first degree; except two [Pg 25]knocks are used in this degree, and the door is entered by the benefit of a pass-word. It is Shibboleth, and explained in the Lecture. The candidate, as before, is taken into the preparation room and prepared in the manner following: All his clothing taken off, except his shirt; furnished with a pair of drawers; his right breast bare; his left foot in a slipper; the right bare; a cable-tow twice 'round his neck; semi-hoodwinked; in which situation he is conducted to the door of the Lodge, where he gives two knocks, when the Senior Warden rises and says, "Worshipful, while we are peaceably at work on the second degree of Masonry, under the influence of faith, hope, and charity, the door of our Lodge is alarmed." Master to Junior Deacon, "Brother Junior, inquire the cause of that alarm." [In many Lodges they come to the door, knock, are answered by the Junior Deacon, and come in without being noticed by the Senior Warden or Master.] The Junior Deacon gives two raps on the inside of the door. The candidate gives one without. It is answered by the Junior Deacon with one; when the door is partly opened by the Junior Deacon, who inquires, "Who comes here? Who comes here?" The Senior Deacon, who is, or ought to be, the conductor, answers, "A worthy brother, who has been regularly initiated as an Entered Apprentice Mason, served a proper time as such, and now wishes for further light in Masonry, by being passed to the degree of Fellow Craft." Junior Deacon to Senior Deacon, "Is it of his own free will and accord he makes this request?" Senior Deacon replies, "It is." Junior Deacon to Senior Deacon, "Is he duly and truly prepared?" Ans. "He is." Junior Deacon to Senior Deacon, "Is he worthy and well qualified?" Ans. "He is." Junior Deacon to Senior Deacon, "Has he made suitable proficiency in the preceding degree?" Ans. "He has." Junior Deacon to Senior Deacon, "By what further rights does he expect to obtain this benefit?" Ans. "By the benefit of a pass-word." Junior Deacon to Senior Deacon, "Has he a pass-word?" Ans. "He has not, but I have it for him." Junior Deacon to Senior Deacon, "Give it to me." The Senior Deacon whispers in the Junior Deacon's ear, "Shibboleth." The Junior Deacon says, "The pass is right; since this is the case, you will wait until the Worshipful Master in the East is made acquainted with his request, and his answer returned." The Junior Deacon then repairs to the Master and gives two knocks, as at the door, which are answered by two by the Master; when the same questions are asked, and answers returned, as at the door. After which, the Master says, "Since he comes endued with all these necessary qualifications, let him enter this Worshipful Lodge in the name of the Lord, and take heed on what he enters." He enters; the angle of the Square is pressed hard against his naked right breast, at which time the Junior Deacon says, "Brother, when you entered this Lodge the first time, you entered on the point of the Compass pressing your naked left breast, which was then explained to you. You now enter it on the angle of the Square, pressing your naked right breast; which is to teach you to act upon the square with all mankind, but more especially with the brethren." The candidate is then conducted twice regularly 'round the Lodge and halted at the Junior Warden in the South, where he gives two raps, and is [Pg 26]answered by two, when the same questions are asked, and answers returned as at the door; from thence he is conducted to the Senior Warden, where the same questions are asked, and answers returned as before; he is then conducted to the Master in the East, where the same questions are asked, and answers returned as before; the Master likewise demands of him from whence he came, and whither he was traveling; he answers, "From the West, and traveling to the East." The Master says, "Why do you leave the West, and travel to the East?" The candidate answers, "In search of more light." The Master then says to the Senior Deacon, "Since this is the case, you will please conduct the candidate back to the West, from whence he came, and put him in the care of the Senior Warden, who will teach him how to approach the East, 'the place of light,' by advancing upon two upright regular steps to the second step (his heel is in the hollow of the right foot in this degree), his feet forming the right angle of an oblong square, and his body erect at the altar before the Worshipful Master, and place him in a proper position to take the solemn oath or obligation of a Fellow Craft Mason." The Master then leaves his seat and approaches the kneeling candidate (the candidate kneels on the right knee, the left forming a square; his left arm, as far as the elbow, in a horizontal position, and the rest of the arm in a vertical position, so as to form a square; his arm supported by the Square held under his elbow), and says, "Brother, you are now placed in a proper position to take on you the solemn oath or obligation of a Fellow Craft Mason, which, I assure you, as before, is neither to affect your religion nor politics; if you are willing to take it, repeat your name, and say after me:

"I, A. B., of my own free will and accord, in the presence of Almighty God, and this Worshipful Lodge of Fellow Craft Masons, dedicated to God, and held forth to the Holy Order of St. John, do hereby and hereon most solemnly and sincerely promise and swear, in addition to my former obligation, that I will not give the degree of a Fellow Craft Mason to any one of an inferior degree, nor to any one being in the known world, except it be to a true and lawful brother, or brethren Fellow Craft Masons, or within the body of a just and lawfully constituted Lodge of such; and not unto him nor unto them whom I shall hear so to be, but unto him and them only whom I shall find so to be, after strict trial and due examination, or lawful information. Furthermore, do I promise and swear, that I will not wrong this Lodge, nor a brother of this degree, to the value of two cents, knowingly, myself, nor suffer it to be done by others, if in my power to prevent it. Furthermore, do I promise and swear, that I will support the Constitution of the Grand Lodge of the United States, and of the Grand Lodge of this State, under which this Lodge is held, and conform to all the by-laws, rules, and regulations of this, or any other Lodge, of which I may at any time hereafter become a member, as far as in my power. Furthermore, do I promise and swear, that I will obey all regular signs and summons given, handed, sent, or thrown to me by the hand of a brother Fellow Craft Mason, or from the body of a just and lawfully constituted Lodge of such; provided it be within the length of my cable-tow, or a square and angle of my work. Furthermore, do I promise and swear, that I will be aiding and assisting all poor and penniless brethren Fellow Crafts, their widows and orphans, wheresoever disposed 'round the globe, they applying to me as such, as far as in my power, without injuring myself or family. To all which I do most solemnly and sincerely promise and swear, without the least hesitation, mental reservation, or self-evasion of mind in me whatever; binding myself under no [Pg 27]less penalty than to have my left breast torn open, and my heart and vitals taken from thence and thrown over my left shoulder, and carried into the valley of Jehosaphat, there to become a prey to the wild beasts of the fields, and vultures of the air, if ever I should prove wilfully guilty of violating any part of this my solemn oath or obligation of a Fellow Craft Mason; so keep me God, and keep me steadfast in the due performance of the same."

The Master then says, "Detach your hands and kiss the book, which is the Holy Bible, twice." The bandage is now (by one of the brethren) dropped over the other eye, and the Master says, "Brother (at the same time laying his hand on the top of the candidate's head), what do you most desire?" The candidate answers, after his prompter, "More light." The Master says, "Brethren, form on the square, and assist in bringing our new-made brother from darkness to light; 'And God said, Let there be light, and there was light.'" At this instant all the brethren clap their hands, and stamp on the floor, as in the preceding degree. The Master says to the candidate, "Brother, what do you discover different from before?" The Master says, after a short pause, "You now discover one point of the Compass elevated above the Square, which denotes light in this degree; but as one is yet in obscurity, it is to remind you that you are yet one material point in the dark respecting Masonry." The Master steps off from the candidate three or four steps, and says, "Brother, you now discover me as a Master of this Lodge, approaching you from the East, under the sign and due-guard of a Fellow Craft Mason; do as I do, as near as you can, keeping your position." The sign is given by drawing your right hand flat, with the palm of it next to your breast, across your breast, from the left to the right side, with some quickness, and dropping it down by your side; the due-guard is given by raising the left arm until that part of it between the elbow and shoulder is perfectly horizontal, and raising the rest of the arm in a vertical position, so that that part of the arm below the elbow, and that part above it, forms a square; this is called the due-guard of a Fellow Craft Mason. The two given together are called the sign and due-guard of a Fellow Craft Mason, and they are never given separate; they would not be recognized by a Mason if given separately. The Master, by the time he gives his steps, sign, and due-guard, arrives at the candidate, and says, "Brother, I now present you with my right hand, in token of brotherly love and confidence, and with it the pass-grip and word of a Fellow Craft Mason." The pass, or more properly the pass-grip, is given by taking each other by the right hand, as though going to shake hands, and each putting his thumb between the fore and second finger, where they join the hands, and pressing the thumb between the joints. This is the pass-grip of a Fellow Craft Mason; the name of it is Shibboleth. Its origin will be explained in the Lecture; the pass-grip some give without lettering or syllabling, and others give it in the same way they do the real grip. The real grip of a Fellow Craft Mason is given by putting the thumb on the joint of the second finger, where it joins the hand, and crooking your thumb so that each can stick the nail of his thumb into the joint of the other. This is the real grip of a Fellow Craft Mason; the name of it is Jachin; it is given in the following manner: If [Pg 28]you wish to examine a person, after having taken each other by the grip, ask him, "What is this?" A. "A grip." Q. "A grip of what?" A. "The grip of a Fellow Craft Mason." Q. "Has it a name?" A. "It has." Q. "Will you give it to me?" A. "I did not so receive it, neither can I so impart it." Q. "What will you do with it?" A. "I'll letter it or halve it." Q. "Halve it, and you begin." A. "No; begin you." Q. "You begin." A. "JA." Q. "CHIN." A. "JACHIN." Q. "Right, Brother Jachin, I greet you."

After the Master gives the candidate the pass-grip and grip, and their names, he says, "Brother, you will rise and salute the Junior and Senior Wardens as such, and convince them that you have been regularly passed to the degree of a Fellow Craft Mason, and have got the sign and pass-grip, real grip, and their names." [I do not here express it as expressed in Lodges generally; the Master usually says you will rise and salute the Wardens, &c., and convince them, &c., that you have got the sign, pass-grip, and word. It is obviously wrong, because the first thing he gives is the sign, then the due-guard, then the pass-grip, and their names.] While the Wardens are examining the candidate, the Master gets an apron, and returns to the candidate, and says, "Brother, I now have the honor of presenting you with a lamb-skin, or white apron, as before, which I hope you will continue to wear, with honor to yourself, and satisfaction to the brethren; you will please carry it to the Senior Warden in the West, who will teach you how to wear it as a Fellow Craft Mason." The Senior Warden ties on his apron, and turns up one corner of the lower end of the apron, and tucks it under the apron string. The Senior Deacon then conducts his pupil to the Master, who has by this time resumed his seat in the East, where he has, or ought to have, the floor carpet to assist him in his explanations. Master to the candidate, "Brother, as you are dressed, it is necessary you should have tools to work with; I will, therefore, present you with the tools of a Fellow Craft Mason. They are the Plumb, Square, and Level. The Plumb is an instrument made use of by operative masons to raise perpendiculars; the Square, to square their work; and the Level, to lay horizontals; but we, as Free and Accepted Masons, are taught to use them for more noble and glorious purposes; the Plumb teaches us to walk uprightly, in our several stations, before God and man; squaring our actions by the square of virtue; and remembering that we are traveling on the level of time to that 'undiscovered country, from whose bourne no traveler has returned.' I further present you with three precious jewels; their names are Faith, Hope, and Charity; they teach us to have faith in God, hope in immortality, and charity to all mankind." The Master to the Senior Deacon, "You will now conduct the candidate out of this Lodge, and invest him with what he has been divested." After he is clothed, and the necessary arrangements made for his reception, such as placing the columns and floor carpet, if they have any, and the candidate is reconducted back to the Lodge; as he enters the door, the Senior Deacon observes, "We are now about to return to the middle chamber of King Solomon's Temple." When within the door, the Senior Deacon proceeds, "Brother, we have worked [Pg 29]in speculative Masonry, but our forefathers wrought both in speculative and operative Masonry. They worked at the building of King Solomon's Temple, and many other Masonic edifices; they wrought six days; they did not work on the seventh, because in six days God created the heavens and the earth, and rested on the seventh day. The seventh, therefore, our ancient brethren consecrated as a day of rest; thereby enjoying more frequent opportunities to contemplate the glorious works of creation, and to adore their great Creator." Moving a step or two, the Senior Deacon proceeds, "Brother, the first thing that attracts our attention are two large columns, or pillars, one on the left hand, and the other on the right; the name of the one on the left hand is Boaz, and denotes strength; the name of the one on the right hand is Jachin, and denotes establishment; they collectively allude to a passage in Scripture, wherein God has declared in his word, 'In strength shall this house be established.' These columns are eighteen cubits high, twelve in circumference, and four in diameter; they are adorned with two large chapiters, one on each, and these chapiters are ornamented with net work, lily work, and pomegranates; they denote unity, peace, and plenty. The net work, from its connection, denotes union; the lily work, from its whiteness, purity and peace; and the pomegranate, from the exuberance of its seed, denotes plenty. They also have two large globes, or balls, one on each; these globes or balls contain, on their convex surfaces, all the maps and charts of the celestial and terrestrial bodies; they are said to be thus extensive to denote the universality of Masonry, and that a

Mason's charity ought to be equally extensive. Their composition is molten, or cast brass; they were cast on the banks of the river Jordan, in the clay-ground between Succoth and Zaradatha, where King Solomon ordered these and all other holy vessels to be cast; they were cast hollow; and were four inches, or a hand's breadth thick; they were cast hollow, the better to withstand inundations and conflagrations; they were the archives of Masonry, and contained the constitution, rolls, and records." The Senior Deacon having explained the columns, he passes between them, advances a step or two, observing as he advances, "Brother, we will pursue our travels; the next thing that we come to is a long, winding staircase, with three, five, seven steps, or more. The three first allude to the three principal supports in Masonry, viz., wisdom, strength, and beauty; the five steps allude to the five orders in architecture, and the five human senses; the five orders in architecture are the Tuscan, Doric, Ionic, Corinthian, and Composite; the five human senses are Hearing, Seeing, Feeling, Smelling, and Tasting; the three first of which have ever been highly essential among Masons: Hearing, to hear the word; Seeing, to see the sign; and Feeling, to feel the grip, whereby one Mason may know another in the dark as well as in the light. The seven steps allude to the seven sabbatical years; seven years of famine; seven years in building the temple; seven golden candlesticks; seven wonders of the world; seven planets; but more especially the seven liberal arts and sciences, which are Grammar, Rhetoric, Logic, Arithmetic, Geometry, Music, and Astronomy; for this, and many other reasons, the number seven has ever been held in high [Pg 30]estimation among Masons." Advancing a few steps, the Senior Deacon proceeds, "Brother, the next thing we come to is the outer door of the middle chamber of King Solomon's Temple, which is partly open, but closely tyled by the Junior Warden" [It is the Junior Warden in the South who represents the Tyler at the outer door of the middle chamber of King Solomon's Temple], who, on the approach of the Senior Deacon and candidate, inquires, "Who comes here? Who comes here?" The Senior Deacon answers, "A Fellow Craft Mason." Junior Warden to Senior Deacon, "How do you expect to gain admission?" A. "By a pass, and token of a pass." Junior Warden to Senior Deacon, "Will you give them to me?" [The Senior Deacon, or the candidate (prompted by him), gives them; this and many other tokens, or grips, are frequently given by strangers when first introduced to each other. If given to a Mason, he will immediately return it; they can be given in any company unobserved, even by Masons, when shaking hands. A pass, and token of a pass; the pass is the word Shibboleth; the token, alias the pass-grip, is given, as before described, by taking each other by the right hand, as if shaking hands, and placing the thumb between the forefinger and second finger, at the third joint, or where they join the hand, and pressing it hard enough to attract attention. In the Lecture it is called a token, but generally called the pass-grip. It is an undeniable fact that Masons express themselves so differently, when they mean the same thing, that they frequently wholly misunderstand each other.]

After the Junior Warden has received the pass Shibboleth, he inquires, "What does it denote?" A. "Plenty." Junior Warden to Senior Deacon, "Why so?" A. "From an ear of corn being placed at the water-ford." Junior Warden to Senior Deacon, "Why was this pass instituted?" A. "In consequence of a quarrel which had long existed between Jephthah, Judge of Israel, and the Ephraimites, the latter of whom had long been a stubborn, rebellious people, whom Jephthah had endeavored to subdue by lenient measures, but to no effect. The Ephraimites being highly incensed against Jephthah, for not being called to fight and share in the rich spoils of the Ammonitish war, assembled a mighty army, and passed over the river Jordan to give Jephthah battle; but he, being apprised of their approach, called together the men of Israel, and gave them battle, and put them to flight; and to make his victory more complete, he ordered guards to be placed at the different passes on the banks of the river Jordan, and commanded, if the Ephraimites passed that way, that they should pronounce the word Shibboleth; but they, being of a different tribe, pronounced it Sibboleth, which trifling defect proved them spies, and cost them their lives; and there fell that day, at the different passes on the banks of the river Jordan, forty and two thousand. This word was also used by our ancient brethren to distinguish a friend from a foe, and has since been adopted as a proper pass-word, to be given before entering any well-regulated and governed Lodge of Fellow Craft Masons." Since this is the case, you will pass on to the Senior Warden in the West for further examination. As they approach the Senior Warden in the West, the Senior Deacon says to the candidate, "Brother, the next thing we [Pg 31]come to is the inner door of the middle chamber of King Solomon's Temple, which we find partly open, but more closely tyled by the Senior Warden;" when the Senior Warden inquires, "Who comes here? Who comes here?" The Senior Deacon answers, "A Fellow Craft Mason." Senior Warden to Senior Deacon, "How do you expect to gain admission?" A. "By the grip and word." The Senior Warden to the Senior Deacon, "Will you give them to me?" They are then given as hereinbefore described. The word is Jachin. After they are given, the Senior Warden says, "They are right; you can pass on to the Worshipful Master in the East." As they approach the Master, he inquires, "Who comes here? Who comes here?" Senior Deacon answers, "A Fellow Craft Mason." The Master then says to the candidate, "Brother you have been admitted into the middle chamber of King Solomon's Temple for the sake of the letter G. It denotes Deity, before whom we all ought to bow with reverence, worship, and adoration. It also denotes Geometry, the fifth science: it being that on which this degree was principally founded. By Geometry we may curiously trace nature through her various windings to her most concealed recesses; by it we may discover the power, the wisdom, and the goodness of the Grand Artificer of the Universe, and view with delight the proportions which connect this vast machine; by it we may discover how the planets move in their different orbits, and demonstrate their various revolutions; by it we account for the return of a season, and the variety of scenes which each season displays to the discerning eye. Numberless worlds surround us, all formed by the same Divine Architect, which roll through this vast expanse, and all conducted by the same unerring law of nature. A survey of nature, and the observations of her beautiful proportions, first determined man to imitate the divine plan, and study symmetry and order. The architect began to design; and the plans which he laid down, being improved by experience and time, have produced works which are the admiration of every age. The lapse of time, the ruthless hand of ignorance, and the devastations of war, have laid waste and destroyed many valuable monuments of antiquity, on which the utmost exertions of human genius have been employed. Even the Temple of Solomon, so spacious and magnificent, and constructed by so many celebrated artists, escaped not the unsparing ravages of barbarous force. The ATTENTIVE EAR received the sound from the INSTRUCTIVE TONGUE; and the mysteries of Freemasonry are safely lodged in the repository of FAITHFUL BREASTS. Tools and implements of architecture, and symbolic emblems, most expressive, are selected by the fraternity to imprint on the mind wise and serious truths; and thus, through a succession of ages, are transmitted, unimpaired, the most excellent tenets of our institution."

Here the labor ends of the Fellow Craft's degree. It will be observed that the candidate has received, in this place, the second section of the Lecture on this degree. This course is not generally pursued, but it is much the most instructive method; and when it is omitted, I generally conclude that it is for want of a knowledge of the Lecture. Monitorial writers (who are by no means coeval with Masonry) all write, or copy, very much after each other, and they have all inserted in their books all [Pg 32]those clauses of the several Lectures which are not considered by the wise ones as tending to develop the secrets of Masonry. In some instances, they change the phraseology a little; in others, they are literal extracts from the Lectures. This, it is said, is done to facilitate the progress of learners, or young Masons; when, in fact, it has the contrary effect.

The following charge is, or ought to be, delivered to the candidate after he has got through the ceremonies; but he is generally told, "It is in the Monitor, and you can learn it at your leisure." "Brother, being advanced to the second degree of Masonry, we congratulate you on your preferment. The internal, and not the external, qualifications of a man are what Masonry regards. As you increase in knowledge, you will improve in social intercourse. It is unnecessary to recapitulate the duties which, as a Mason, you are bound to discharge; or enlarge on the necessity of a strict adherence to them, as your own experience must have established their value. Our laws and regulations you are strenuously to support; and be always ready to assist in seeing them duly executed. You are not to palliate or aggravate the offences of your brethren; but in the decision of every trespass against our rules, you are to judge with candor, admonish with friendship, and reprehend with justice. The study of the liberal arts, that valuable branch of education, which tends so effectually to polish and adorn the mind, is earnestly recommended to your consideration; especially the science of Geometry, which is established as the basis of our art. Geometry, or Masonry, originally synonymous terms, being of a divine moral nature, is enriched with the most useful knowledge; while it proves the wonderful properties of nature, it demonstrates the more important truths of morality. Your past behavior and regular deportment have merited the honor which we have now conferred, and, in your new character, it is expected that you will conform to the principles of the Order, by steadily persevering in the practice of every commendable virtue. Such is the nature of your engagements as a Fellow Craft, and to these duties you are bound by the most sacred ties."

I will now proceed with the Lecture on this degree; it is divided into two sections.

141

FIRST SECTION.

Question—Are you a Fellow Craft Mason? A. I am; try me.

Q. By what will you be tried? A. By the Square.

Q. Why by the Square? A. Because it is an emblem of virtue.

Q. What is a Square? A. An angle extending to ninety degrees, or the fourth part of a circle.

Q. Where was you prepared to be made a Fellow Craft Mason? A. In a room adjacent to the body of a just and lawfully constituted Lodge of such, duly assembled in a room or place, representing the middle chamber of King Solomon's Temple.

Q. How was you prepared? A. By being divested of all metals; neither naked nor clothed; barefooted nor shod; hoodwinked; with a [Pg 33]cable-tow twice 'round my neck; in which situation I was conducted to the door of the Lodge, where I gave two distinct knocks.

Q. What did those two distinct knocks allude to? A. To the second degree in Masonry, it being that on which I was about to enter.

Q. What was said to you from within? A. Who comes there? Who comes there?

Q. Your answer? A. A worthy brother, who has been regularly initiated as an Entered Apprentice Mason; served a proper time as such; and now wishes for further light in Masonry, by being passed to the degree of a Fellow Craft.

Q. What was then said to you from within? A. I was asked if it was of my own free will and accord I made this request; if I was duly and truly prepared, worthy and well qualified; and had made suitable proficiency in the preceding degree; all of which being answered in the affirmative, I was asked by what further rights I expected to obtain so great a benefit.

Q. Your answer? A. By the benefit of a pass-word.

Q. What is that pass-word? A. Shibboleth.

Q. What further was said to you from within? A. I was bid to wait till the Worshipful Master in the East was made acquainted with my request and his answer returned.

Q. After his answer was returned, what followed? A. I was caused to enter the Lodge.

Q. How did you enter? A. On the angle of the Square presented to my naked right breast, in the name of the Lord.

Q. How were you then disposed of? A. I was conducted twice regularly around the Lodge, and halted at the Junior Warden in the South, where the same questions were asked, and answers returned as at the door.

Q. How did the Junior Warden dispose of you? A. He ordered me to be conducted to the Senior Warden in the West, where the same questions were asked, and answers returned as before.

Q. How did the Senior Warden dispose of you? A. He ordered me to be conducted to the Worshipful Master in the East, where the same questions were asked, and answers returned as before, who likewise demanded of me from whence I came, and whither I was traveling.

Q. Your answer? A. From the West, and traveling to the East.

Q. Why do you leave the West and travel to the East? A. In search of more light.

Q. How did the Worshipful Master then dispose of you? A. He ordered me to be conducted back to the West, from whence I came, and put in care of the Senior Warden who taught me how to approach the East, by advancing upon two upright regular steps to the second step, my feet forming the right angle of an oblong square, and my body erect; at the altar before the Worshipful Master.

Q. What did the Worshipful Master do with you? A. He made a Fallow Craft Mason of me.

Q. How? A. In due form.

[Pg 34]Q. What was that due form? A. My right knee bare bent; my left knee forming a square; my right hand on the Holy Bible, Square, and Compass; my left arm forming an angle, supported by the Square, and my hand in a vertical position; in which posture I took upon me the solemn oath, or obligation, of a Fellow Craft Mason. [See pages 26 and 27 for obligation.]

Q. After your oath, or obligation, what was said to you? A. I was asked what I most desired.

Q. Your answer? A. More light.

Q. On being brought to light, what did you discover different from before? A. One point of the Compass elevated above the Square, which denoted light in this degree; but as one point was yet in obscurity, it was to remind me that I was yet one material point in the dark respecting Masonry.

Q. What did you next discover? A. The Worshipful Master approaching me from the East, under the sign and due-guard of a Fellow Craft Mason, who presented me with his right hand in token of brotherly love and confidence, and proceeded to give me the pass-grip and word of a Fellow Craft Mason, and bid me arise and salute the Junior and Senior Wardens, and convince them that I had been regularly passed to the degree of a Fellow Craft, and had the sign, grip, and word of a Fellow Craft Mason.

Q. What next did you discover? A. The Worshipful Master approaching me a second time from the East, who presented me a lamb-skin, or white apron, which, he said, he hoped I would continue to wear with honor to myself and satisfaction and advantage to my brethren.

Q. What was you next presented with? A. The working tools of a Fellow Craft Mason.

Q. What are they? A. The Plumb, Square, and Level.

Q. What do they teach? [I think this question ought to be, "How explained?"] A. The Plumb is an instrument made use of by operative Masons to raise perpendiculars; the Square, to square the work, and the Level, to lay horizontals; but we, as Free and Accepted Masons, are taught to make use of them for more noble and glorious purposes. The Plumb admonishes us to walk uprightly, in our several stations, before God and man; squaring our actions by the square of virtue; and remembering that we are all traveling upon the level of time, to that undiscovered country, from whose bourne no traveler returns.

Q. What was you next presented with? A. Three precious jewels.

Q. What were they? A. Faith, Hope, and Charity.

Q. What do they teach? A. Faith in God, hope in immortality, and charity to all mankind.

Q. How was you then disposed of? A. I was conducted out of the Lodge, and invested of what I had been divested.

SECOND SECTION.

Question—Have you ever worked as a Fellow Craft Mason? Answer—I have, in speculative; but our forefathers wrought both in speculative and operative Masonry.

[Pg 35]Q. Where did they work? A. At the building of King Solomon's Temple, and many other Masonic edifices.

Q. How long did they work? A. Six days.

Q. Did they not work on the Seventh? A. They did not.

Q. Why so? A. Because in six days God created the heavens and the earth, and rested on the seventh day; the seventh day, therefore, our ancient brethren consecrated as a day of rest from their labors; thereby enjoying more frequent opportunities to contemplate the glorious works of creation, and adore their great Creator.

Q. Did you ever return to the sanctum sanctorum, or holy of holies, of King Solomon's Temple? A. I did.

Q. By what way? A. Through a long porch, or alley.

Q. Did anything particular strike your attention on your return? A. There did; viz.: Two large columns, or pillars, one on the left hand, and the other on the right.

Q. What was the name of the one on the left hand? A. Boaz, to denote strength.

Q. What was the name of the one on the right hand? A. Jachin, denoting establishment.

Q. What do they collectively allude to? A. A passage in Scripture, wherein God has declared in his word, "In strength shall this house be established."

Q. What were their dimensions? A. Eighteen cubits in height, twelve in circumference, and four in diameter.

Q. Were they adorned with anything? A. They were; with two large chapiters, one on each.

Q. Were they ornamented with anything? A. They were; with wreaths of net work, lily work, and pomegranates.

Q. What do they denote? A. Unity, Peace, and Plenty.

Q. Why so? A. Net work, from its connection, denotes union; lily work, from its whiteness and purity, denotes peace; and pomegranates, from the exuberance of its seed, denotes plenty.

Q. Were those columns adorned with anything further? A. They were; viz.: Two large globes, or balls, one on each.

Q. Did they contain anything? A. They did; viz.; All the maps and charts of the celestial and terrestrial bodies.

Q. Why are they said to be so extensive? A. To denote the universality of Masonry, and that a Mason's charity ought to be equally extensive.

Q. What was their composition? A. Molten, or cast brass.

Q. Who cast them? A. Our Grand Master, Hiram Abiff.

Q. Where were they cast? A. On the banks of the river Jordan, in the clay ground between Succoth and Zaradatha, where King Solomon ordered these and all other holy vessels to be cast.

Q. Were they cast solid or hollow? A. Hollow.

Q. What was their thickness? A. Four inches, or a hand's breadth.

Q. Why were they cast hollow? A. The better to withstand inundations or conflagrations; were the archives of Masonry, and contained the constitution, rolls, and records.

[Pg 36]Q. What did you next come to? A. A long, winding staircase, with three, five, seven steps, or more.

Q. What does the three steps allude to? A. The three principal supports in Masonry, viz., Wisdom, Strength, and Beauty.

Q. What does the five steps allude to? A. The five orders in architecture, and the five human senses.

Q. What are the five orders in architecture? A. The Tuscan, Doric, Ionic, Corinthian, and Composite.

Q. What are the five human senses? A. Hearing, Seeing, Feeling, Smelling, and Tasting; the first three of which have ever been deemed highly essential among Masons: Hearing, to hear the word; Seeing, to see the sign; and Feeling, to feel the grip, whereby one Mason may know another in the dark as well as in the light.

Q. What does the seven steps allude to? A. The seven sabbatical years; seven years of famine; seven years In building the temple; seven golden candlesticks; seven wonders of the world; seven planets; but more especially the seven liberal arts and sciences, which are Grammar, Rhetoric, Logic, Arithmetic, Geometry, Music, and Astronomy; for these, and many other reasons, the number seven has ever been held in high estimation among Masons.

Q. What did you next come to? A. The outer door of the middle chamber of King Solomon's Temple, which I found partly open, but closely tyled by the Junior Warden.

145

Q. How did you gain admission? A. By a pass, and token of a pass.

Q. What was the name of the pass? A. Shibboleth.

Q. What does it denote? A. Plenty.

Q. Why so? A. From an ear of corn being placed at the water-ford.

Q. Why was this pass instituted? A. In consequence of a quarrel which had long existed between Jephthah, Judge of Israel, and the Ephraimites, the latter of whom had long been a stubborn, rebellious people, whom Jephthah had endeavored to subdue by lenient measures, but to no effect. The Ephraimites being highly incensed against Jephthah, for not being called to fight and share in the rich spoils of the Ammonitish war, assembled a mighty army, and passed over the river Jordan to give Jephthah battle; but he, being apprised of their approach, called together the men of Israel, and gave them battle, and put them to flight; and to make his victory more complete, he ordered guards to be placed at the different passes on the banks of the river Jordan, and commanded, if the Ephraimites passed that way, that they should pronounce the word Shibboleth; but they, being of a different tribe, pronounced it Sibboleth, which trifling defect proved them spies, and cost them their lives; and there fell that day, at the different passes on the banks of the river Jordan, forty and two thousand. This word was also used by our ancient brethren to distinguish a friend from a foe, and has since been adopted as a proper pass-word, to be given before entering any well-regulated and governed Lodge of Fellow Craft Masons.

Q. What did you next discover? A. The inner door of the middle chamber of King Solomon's Temple, which I found partly open, but closely tyled by the Senior Warden.

[Pg 37]Q. How did you gain admission? A. By the grip and word.

Q. How did the Senior Warden dispose of you? A. He ordered me to be conducted to the Worshipful Master in the East, who informed me that I had been admitted into the middle chamber of King Solomon's Temple for the sake of the letter G.

Q. Does it denote anything? A. It does; Deity—before whom we should all bow with reverence, worship, and adoration. It also denotes Geometry, the fifth science; it being that on which this degree was principally founded.

Thus ends the second degree of Masonry.

THE THIRD, OR MASTER MASON'S DEGREE.

The traditional account of the death, several burials, and resurrection of Hiram Abiff, the widow's son (as hereafter narrated), admitted as facts, this degree is certainly very interesting. The Bible informs us that there was a person of that name employed at the building of King Solomon's Temple; but neither the Bible, the writings of Josephus, nor any other writings, however ancient, of which I have any knowledge, furnish any information respecting his death. It is very singular that a man so celebrated as Hiram Abiff was, and arbiter between Solomon, King of Israel, and Hiram, King of Tyre, universally acknowledged as the third most distinguished man then living, and in many respects, the greatest man in the world, should pass off the stage of action, in the presence of King Solomon, three thousand, three hundred grand overseers, and one hundred and fifty thousand workmen, with whom he had spent a number of years, and neither King

Solomon, his bosom friend, nor any other among his numerous friends, even recorded his death, or anything about him.

A person who has received the two preceding degrees, and wishes to be raised to the sublime degree of a Master Mason, is (the Lodge being opened as in the preceding degrees) conducted from the preparation room to the door (the manner of preparing him is particularly explained in the Lecture), where he gives three distinct knocks, when the Senior Warden rises and says, "Worshipful, while we are peaceably at work on the third degree of Masonry, under the influence of humanity, brotherly love, and affection, the door of our Lodge appears to be alarmed." The Master to the Junior Deacon, "Brother Junior, inquire the cause of that alarm." The Junior Deacon then steps to the door and answers the three knocks that have been given by three more (the knocks are much louder than those given on any occasion, other than that of the admission of candidates in the several degrees); one knock is then given without, and answered by one from within, when the door is partly opened, and the Junior Deacon asks, "Who comes there? Who comes there? Who comes there?" The Senior Deacon answers, "A worthy brother, who has been regularly initiated as an Entered Apprentice Mason, passed to the degree of a Fellow Craft, and now wishes for further light in Masonry, by being raised to the sublime degree of a Master Mason." Junior Deacon to Senior Deacon, "Is it of his own free will and [Pg 38]accord he makes this request?" A. "It is." Junior Deacon to Senior Deacon, "Is he worthy and well qualified?" A. "He is." Junior Deacon to Senior Deacon, "Has he made suitable proficiency in the preceding degree?" A. "He has." Junior Deacon to Senior Deacon, "By what further rights does he expect to obtain this benefit?" A. "By the benefit of a pass-word." Junior Deacon to Senior Deacon, "Has he a pass-word?" A. "He has not, but I have it for him." Junior Deacon to Senior Deacon, "Will you give it to me?" The Senior Deacon then whispers in the ear of the Junior Deacon, "Tubal Cain." Junior Deacon says, "The pass is right; since this is the case, you will wait till the Worshipful Master be made acquainted with his request, and his answer returned." The Junior Deacon then repairs to the Master, and gives three knocks, as at the door; after answering which, the same questions are asked and answers returned, as at the door; when the Master says, "Since he comes endued with all these necessary qualifications, let him enter this Worshipful Lodge in the name of the Lord, and take heed on what he enters." The Junior Deacon returns to the door and says, "Let him enter this Worshipful Lodge in the name of the Lord, and take heed on what he enters." In entering, both points of the Compass are pressed against his naked right and left breasts, when the Junior Deacon stops the candidate and says, "Brother, when you first entered this Lodge, you was received on the point of the Compass pressing your naked left breast, which was then explained to you; when you entered it the second time, you were received on the angle of the Square, which was also explained to you; on entering it now, you are received on the two extreme points of the Compass pressing your naked right and left breasts, which are thus explained: As the most vital points of man are contained between the two breasts, so are the most valuable tenets of Masonry contained between the two extreme points of the Compass, which are 'Virtue, Morality, and Brotherly Love.'" The Senior Deacon then conducts the candidate three times regularly around the Lodge. [I wish the reader to observe, that on this, as well as every other degree, the Junior Warden is the first of the three principal officers that the candidate passes, traveling with the Sun, when he starts around the Lodge, and as he passes the Junior Warden, Senior Warden, and Master, the first time going around, they each give one rap; the second time, two raps; and the third time, three raps. The number of raps given on those occasions are the same as the number of the degree, except the first degree, on which three are given, I always thought improperly.] During the time the candidate is traveling around the room, the Master reads the following passage of Scripture, the conductor and candidate traveling, and the Master reading, so that the traveling and reading terminates at the same time:

"Remember now thy Creator in the days of thy youth, while the evil days come not, nor the years draw nigh, when thou shalt say, I have no pleasure in them: while the Sun, or the Moon, or the Stars be not darkened, nor the clouds return after the rain; in the day when the keepers of the house shall tremble, and the strong men shall bow themselves, and the grinders cease because they are few, and those that look out of the windows be darkened, and the doors shall be shut in the streets; [Pg 39]when the sound of the grinding is low, and he shall rise up at the voice of the bird, and all the daughters of music shall be brought low. Also, when they shall be afraid of that which is high, and fears shall be in the way, and the almond tree shall flourish, and the grasshopper shall be a burden, and desire shall fail, because man goeth to his long home, and the mourners go about the streets. Or ever the silver cord be loosed, or the golden bowl be broken, or the pitcher be broken at the fountain, or the wheel at the cistern. Then shall the dust return to the earth, as it was; and the spirit return unto God who gave it."

The conductor and candidate halt at the Junior Warden in the South, where the same questions are asked and answers returned, as at the door; he is then conducted to the Senior Warden, where the same questions are asked and answers returned as before; from thence he is conducted to the Worshipful Master in the East, who asks the same questions and receives the same answers as before; and who likewise asks the candidate from whence he came, and whither he is traveling? Ans. "From the West, and traveling to the East." Q. "Why do you leave the West and travel to the East?" A. "In search of more light." The Master then says to the Senior Deacon, "You will please conduct the candidate back to the West, from whence he came, and put him in the care of the Senior Warden, and request him to teach the candidate how to approach the East, by advancing upon three upright regular steps to the third step, his feet forming a square, his body erect at the altar before the Worshipful Master, and place him in a proper position to take upon him the solemn oath or obligation of a Master Mason." The Master then comes to the candidate and says, "Brother, you are now placed in a proper position (the Lecture explains it) to take upon you the solemn oath or obligation of a Master Mason, which I assure you, as before, is neither to affect your religion nor politics. If you are willing to take it, repeat your name, and say after me:

"I, A. B., of my own free will and accord, in the presence of Almighty God, and this Worshipful Lodge of Master Masons erected to God, and dedicated to the Holy Order of St. John, do hereby and hereon most solemnly and sincerely promise and swear, in addition to my former obligations, that I will not give the degree of a Master Mason to any one of an inferior degree, nor to any other being in the known world, except it be to a true and lawful brother, or brethren Master Masons, or within the body of a just and lawfully constituted Lodge of such; and not unto him, nor unto them, whom I shall hear so to be, but unto him and them only whom I shall find so to be, after strict trial and due examination, or lawful information received. Furthermore, do I promise and swear, that I will not give the Master's word, which I shall hereafter receive, neither in the Lodge, nor out of it, except it be on the five points of fellowship, and then not above my breath. Furthermore, do I promise and swear, that I will not give the grand hailing sign of distress, except I am in real distress, or for the benefit of the craft when at work; and should I ever see that sign given, or the word accompanying it, and the person who gave it appearing to be in distress, I will fly to his relief at the risk of my life, should there be a greater probability of saving his life than of losing my own. Furthermore, do I promise and swear, that I will not wrong this Lodge, nor a brother of this degree, to the value of one cent, knowingly, myself, nor suffer it to be done by others, if in my power to prevent it. Furthermore, do I promise and swear, that I will not be at the initiating, passing, and raising a candidate at one communication, without a regular dispensation from the Grand Lodge for the same. Furthermore, do I promise and swear, that I will not be at the initiating, passing, or raising a candidate in a clandestine Lodge, I knowing it to [Pg 40]be such. Furthermore, do I promise and swear, that I will not be at the initiating of an old man in dotage, a young man in nonage, an atheist, irreligious libertine, idiot, madman, hermaphrodite, nor woman. Furthermore, do I promise and swear, that I will not speak evil of a brother Master Mason, neither behind his back, nor before his face, but will apprise him of all approaching danger, if in my power. Furthermore, do I promise and swear, that I will not violate the chastity of a Master Mason's wife, mother, sister, or daughter, I knowing them to be such, nor suffer it to be done by others, if in my power to prevent it. Furthermore, do I promise and swear, that I will support the constitution of the Grand Lodge of the State of — —, under which this Lodge is held, and conform to all the by-laws, rules, and regulations of this, or any other Lodge, of which I may, at any time hereafter, become a member. Furthermore, do I promise and swear, that I will obey all regular signs, summons, or tokens given, handed, sent, or thrown to me from the hand of a brother Master Mason, or from the body of a just and lawfully constituted Lodge of such: provided it be within the length of my cable-tow. Furthermore, do I promise and swear, that a Master Mason's secrets, given to me in charge as such, and I knowing them to be such, shall remain as secure and inviolable in my breast as in his own, when communicated to me, murder and treason excepted; and they left to my own election. Furthermore, do I promise and swear, that I will go on a Master Mason's errand, whenever required, even should I have to go barefoot and bareheaded, if within the length of my cable-tow.[3] Furthermore, do I promise and swear, that I will always remember a brother Master Mason when on my knees, offering up my devotions to Almighty God. Furthermore, do I promise and swear, that I will be aiding and assisting all poor indigent Master Masons, their wives and orphans, wheresoever disposed 'round the globe, as far as in my power, without injuring myself or family materially. Furthermore, do I promise and swear, that if any part of this my solemn oath or obligation be omitted at this time, that I will hold myself amenable thereto, whenever informed. To all which I do most solemnly and sincerely promise and swear, with a fixed and steady purpose of mind in me, to keep and perform the same, binding myself under no less penalty than to have my body severed in two in the midst, and divided to the North and South, my bowels burnt to ashes in the centre, and the ashes scattered before the four winds of heaven, that there might not the least tract or trace of remembrance remain among men or Masons of so vile and perjured a wretch as I should be, were I ever to prove wilfully guilty of violating any part of this my solemn oath or obligation of a Master Mason; so help me God, and keep me steadfast in the due performance of the same."

The Master then asks the candidate, "What do you most desire?" The candidate answers after his prompter, "More light." The bandage which was tied 'round his head in the preparation room is, by one of the brethren who stands behind him for that purpose, loosened and put over both eyes, and he is immediately brought to light in the same manner as in the preceding degree, except three stamps on the floor, and three claps of the hands are given in this degree. On being brought to light, the Master says to the candidate, "You first discover, as before, three great lights in Masonry, by the assistance of three lesser, with this difference, both points of the Compass are elevated above the Square, which denotes to you that you are about to receive all the light that can be conferred on you in a Mason's Lodge." The Master steps back from the candidate and says, "Brother, you now discover me as Master of [Pg 41]this Lodge, approaching you from the East, under the sign and due-guard of a Master Mason." The sign is given by raising both hands and arms to the elbows perpendicularly, one on either side of the head, the elbows forming a square. The words accompanying this sign in case of distress are, "O Lord, my God, is there no help for the widow's son?" As the last words drop from your lips, you let your hands fall in that manner best calculated to indicate solemnity. King Solomon is said to have made this exclamation on the receipt of the information of the death of Hiram Abiff. Masons are all charged never to give the words except in the dark, when the sign cannot be seen. Here Masons differ very much; some contend that Solomon gave this sign, and made this exclamation when informed of Hiram's death, and work accordingly in their Lodges. Others say the sign was given, and the exclamation made at the grave when Solomon went there to raise Hiram, and, of course, they work accordingly; that is to say, the Master who governs a Lodge holding the latter opinion, gives the sign, &c., at the grave, when he goes to raise the body, and vice versa. The due-guard is given by putting the right hand to the left side of the bowels, the hand open, with the thumb next to the belly, and drawing it across the belly and let it fall; this is done tolerably quick. After the Master has given the sign and due-guard, which does not take more than a minute, he says, "Brother, I now present you with my right hand in token of brotherly love and affection, and with it the pass-grip and word." The pass-grip is given by pressing the thumb between the joints of the second and third fingers, where they join the hand, and the word or name is Tubal Cain. It is the pass-word to the Master's degree. The Master, after having given the candidate the pass-grip and word, bids him rise and salute the Junior and Senior Wardens, and convince them that he is an obligated Master Mason, and is in possession of the pass-grip and word. While the Wardens are examining the candidate, the Master returns to the East and gets an apron, and as he returns to the candidate, one of the Wardens (sometimes both) says to the Master, "Worshipful, we are satisfied that Brother —— is an obligated Master Mason." The Master then says to the candidate, "Brother, I now have the honor to present you with a lamb-skin, or white apron, as before, which, I hope, you will continue to wear with credit to yourself, and satisfaction and advantage to the brethren; you will please carry it to the Senior Warden in the West, who will teach you how to wear it as a Master Mason."

The Senior Warden ties on his apron, and lets the flap fall down before in its natural and common situation.

The Master returns to his seat, and the candidate is conducted to him. Master to candidate, "Brother, I perceive you are dressed; it is, of course, necessary you should have tools to work with; I will now present you with the working tools of a Master Mason, and explain their uses to you. The working tools of a Master Mason are all the implements of Masonry indiscriminately, but more especially the Trowel. The Trowel is an instrument made use of by operative Masons to spread the cement which unites a building into one common mass; but we, as Free and Accepted Masons, are taught to make use of it for the more noble [Pg 42]and glorious purpose of spreading the cement of brotherly love and affection; that cement which unites us into one sacred band or society of friends and brothers, among whom no contention should ever exist, but that noble contention, or rather emulation, of who can best work, or best agree. I also present you with three precious jewels; their names are Humanity, Friendship, and Brotherly Love. Brother, you are not yet invested with all the secrets of this degree, nor do I know whether you ever will, until I know how you withstand the amazing trials and dangers that await you. You are now about to travel to give us a specimen of your fortitude, perseverance, and fidelity, in the preservation of what you have already received; fare you well, and may the Lord be with you, and support you through your trials and difficulties." [In some Lodges they make him pray before he starts.] The candidate is then conducted out of the Lodge, clothed, and returns; as he enters the door, his conductor says to him, "Brother, we are now in a place representing the SANCTUM SANCTORUM, or HOLY OF HOLIES, of King Solomon's Temple. It was the custom of our Grand Master, Hiram Abiff, every day at high twelve, when the crafts were from labor to refreshment, to enter into the sanctum sanctorum and offer up his devotions to the ever living God. Let us, in imitation of him, kneel and pray." They then kneel, and the conductor says the following prayer:

"Thou, O God, knowest our downsitting and uprising, and understandest our thoughts afar off; shield and defend us from the evil intentions of our enemies, and support us under the trials and afflictions we are destined to endure while traveling through this vale of tears. Man that is born of a woman is of few days and full of trouble. He cometh forth as a flower, and is cut down; he fleeth also as a shadow, and continueth not. Seeing his days are determined, the number of his months are with Thee: Thou hast appointed his bounds that he cannot pass; turn from him, that he may rest till he shall accomplish his day. For there is hope of a tree, if it be cut down, that it will sprout again, and that the tender branch thereof will not cease. But man dieth and wasteth away; yea, man giveth up the ghost, and where is he? As the waters fail from the sea, and flood decayeth and drieth up, so man lieth down and riseth not up till the heavens shall be no more. Yet, O Lord! have compassion on the children of Thy creation; administer unto them comfort in time of trouble, and save them with an everlasting salvation. Amen. So mote it be."

They then rise, and the conductor says to the candidate, "Brother, in further imitation of our Grand Master, Hiram Abiff, let us retire at the South gate." They then advance to the Junior Warden (who represents Jubela, one of the ruffians), who exclaims, "Who comes here?" [The room is dark, or the candidate hoodwinked.] The conductor answers, "Our Grand Master, Hiram Abiff." "Our Grand Master, Hiram Abiff!" exclaims the ruffian, "he is the very man I wanted to see (seizing the candidate by the throat at the same time, and jerking him about with violence); give me the Master Mason's word, or I'll take your life." The conductor replies, "I cannot give it now, but if you will wait till the Grand Lodge assembles at Jerusalem, if you are worthy, you shall then receive it, otherwise you cannot." The ruffian then gives the candidate a blow with the twenty-four-inch gauge across the throat, on which he fled to the West gate, where he was accosted by the second ruffian, [Pg 43]Jubelo, with more violence, and on his refusing to comply with his request, he gave him a severe blow with the Square across his breast; on which he attempted to make his escape at the East gate, where he was accosted by the third ruffian, Jubelum, with still more violence, and refusing to comply with his request, the ruffian gave him a violent blow with the common gavel on the forehead, which brought him to the floor, on which one of them exclaimed, "What shall we do, we have killed our Grand Master, Hiram Abiff?" Another answers, "Let us carry him out at the East gate and bury him in the rubbish till low twelve, and then meet and carry him a westerly course and bury him." The candidate is then taken up in a blanket, on which he fell, and carried to the West end of the Lodge, and covered up and left; by this time the Master has resumed his seat (King Solomon is supposed to arrive at the Temple at this juncture), and calls to order, and asks the Senior Warden the cause of all that confusion; the Senior Warden answers, "Our Grand Master, Hiram Abiff, is missing, and there are no plans or designs laid down on the Tressle-Board for the crafts to pursue their labor." The Master, alias King Solomon, replies, "Our Grand Master missing; our Grand Master has always been very punctual in his attendance; I fear he is indisposed; assemble the crafts, and search in and about the Temple, and see if he can be found." They all shuffle about the floor a while, when the Master calls them to order, and asks the Senior Warden, "What success?" He answers, "We cannot find our Grand Master, my Lord." The Master then orders the Secretary to call the roll of workmen, and see whether any of them are missing. The Secretary calls the roll, and says, "I have called the roll, my Lord, and find that there are three missing, viz.: Jubela, Jubelo and Jubelum." His Lordship then observes, "This brings to my mind a circumstance that took place this morning—twelve Fellow Crafts, clothed in white gloves and aprons, in token of their innocence, came to me and confessed that they twelve, with three others, had conspired to extort the Master Mason's word from their Grand Master, Hiram Abiff, and in case of refusal to take his life; they twelve had recanted, but feared the other three had been base enough to carry their atrocious designs into execution." Solomon then ordered twelve Fellow Crafts to be drawn from the bands of the workmen, clothed in white aprons, in token of their Innocence, and sent three East, three West, three North, and three South, in search of the ruffians, and, if found, to bring them forward. Here the members all shuffle about the floor awhile, and fall in with a reputed traveler, and inquire of him if he had seen any traveling men that way; he tells them that he had seen three that morning near the coast of Joppa, who from their dress and appearance were Jews, and were workmen from the Temple, inquiring for a passage to Ethiopia, but were unable to obtain one, in consequence of an embargo which had recently been laid on all the shipping, and had turned back into the country. The Master now calls them to order again, and asks the Senior Warden, "What success?" He answers by relating what had taken place. Solomon observes, "I had this embargo laid to prevent the ruffians from making their escape;" and adds, "you will go and search [Pg 44]again, and search till you find them, if possible; and if they are not found, the twelve who confessed shall be considered as the reputed murderers, and suffer accordingly." The members all start again, and shuffle about awhile, until one of them, as if by accident, finds the body of Hiram Abiff, alias the candidate and hails his traveling companions, who join him, and while they are humming out something over the candidate, the three reputed ruffians, who are seated in a private corner near the candidate, are heard to exclaim in the following manner—first, Jubela, "O that my throat had been cut across, my tongue torn out, and my body buried in the rough sands of the sea at low-water mark, where the tide ebbs and flows twice in twenty-four hours, ere I had been accessory to the death of so good a man as our Grand Master, Hiram Abiff."

The second, Jubelo, "O that my left breast had been torn open, and my heart and vitals taken from thence, and thrown over my left shoulder, carried into the valley of Jehosaphat, and there to become a prey to the wild beasts of the field, and vultures of the air, ere I had conspired the death of so good a man as our Grand Master, Hiram Abiff."

The third, Jubelum, "O that my body had been severed in two in the midst, and divided to the North and South, my bowels burnt to ashes in the centre, and the ashes scattered by the four winds of heaven, that there might not the least track or trace of remembrance remain among men or Masons of so vile and perjured a wretch as I am. Ah, Jubela and Jubelo, it was I that struck him harder than you both—it was I that gave him the fatal blow—it was I that killed him outright."

The three Fellow Crafts who had stood by the candidate all this time listening to the ruffians, whose voices they recognized, says one to the other, "What shall we do, there are three of them, and only three of us?" "It is," said one in reply, "our cause is good, let us seize them;" on which they rush forward, and carry them to the Master, to whom they relate what had passed. The Master then addresses them in the following manner (they in many Lodges kneel, or lie down, in token of their guilt and penitence): "Well, Jubela, what have you got to say for yourself—guilty or not guilty?" A. "Guilty, my Lord." "Jubelo, guilty or not guilty?" A. "Guilty, my Lord." "Jubelum, guilty or not guilty?" A. "Guilty, my Lord." The Master to the three Fellow Crafts who took them, "Take them without the West gate of the Temple, and have them executed according to the several imprecations of their own mouths." They are then hurried off to the West end of the room. Here this part of the farce ends. The Master then orders fifteen Fellow Crafts to be elected from the bands of the workmen, and sent three East, three West, three North, three South; and three in and about the Temple, in search of their Grand Master, Hiram Abiff [In some Lodges they only send twelve, when their own Lectures say fifteen were sent], and charges them if they find the body, to examine carefully on and about it for the Master's word, or a key to it. The three that traveled a Westerly course come to the candidate and finger about him a little, and are called to order by the Master, when they report that they have [Pg 45]found the grave of their Grand Master, Hiram Abiff, and, on moving the earth till they came to the body, they involuntarily found their hands raised in this position [showing it at the same time; it is the due-guard of this degree], to guard their nostrils against the offensive affluvia which arose from the grave; and that they had searched carefully on and about the body for the Master's word, but had not discovered anything but a faint resemblance of the letter G on the left breast. The Master, on the receipt of this information (raising himself), raises his hand three several times above his head (as herein before described), and exclaims twice, "Nothing but a faint resemblance of the letter G! that is not the Master's word, nor a key to it, I fear the Master's word is forever lost!" [The third exclamation is different from the others—attend to it; it has been described in pages 40 and 41.] "Nothing but a faint resemblance of the letter G! that is not the Master's word, nor a key to it." "O Lord, my God, is there no help for the widow's son?" The Master then orders the Junior Warden to summon a Lodge of Entered Apprentice Masons, and repair to the grave to raise the body of their Grand Master, by the Entered Apprentice's grip. They go to the candidate and take hold of his forefinger and pull it, and return and tell the Master that they could not raise him by the Entered Apprentice's grip; that the skin cleaved from the bone. A Lodge of Fellow Crafts are then sent, who act as before, except that they pull the candidate's second finger. The Master then directs the Senior Warden [generally] to summon a Lodge of Master Masons, and says, "I will go with them myself in person, and try to raise the body by the Master's grip, or lion's paw." [Some say by the strong grip, or the lion's paw.] They then all assemble around the candidate, the Master having declared the first word spoken after the body was raised, should be adopted as a substitute for the Master's word, for the government of Master Mason's Lodges in all future generations; he proceeds to raise the candidate, alias the representative of the dead body of Hiram Abiff. He [the candidate] is raised on what is called the five points of fellowship, which are foot to foot, knee to knee, breast to breast, hand to back, and mouth to ear. This is done by putting the inside of your right foot to the inside of the right foot of the person to whom you are going to give the word, the inside of your knee to his, laying your right breast against his, your left hands on the back of each other, and your mouths to each other's right ear [in which position you are alone permitted to give the word], and whisper the word Mah-hah-bone. The Master's grip is given by taking hold of each other's right hand, as though you were going to shake hands, and sticking the nails of each of your fingers into the joint of the other's wrist, where it unites with the hand. In this position the candidate is raised, he keeping his whole body stiff, as though dead. The Master, in raising him, is assisted by some of the brethren, who take hold of the candidate by the arms and shoulders. As soon as he is raised to his feet they step back, and the Master whispers the word Mah-hah-bone in his ear, and causes the candidate to repeat it, telling him at the same time that he must never give it in any manner other than that in which he receives it. He is also told that Mah-hah-bone [Pg 46]signifies marrow in the bone. They then separate, and the Master makes the following explanation respecting the five points of fellowship. Master to candidate, "Brother, foot to foot teaches you that you should, whenever asked, go on a brother's errand, if within the length of your cable-tow, even if you should have to go barefoot and bareheaded. Knee to knee, that you should always remember a Master Mason in your devotion to Almighty God. Breast to breast, that you should keep the Master Mason's secrets, when given to you in charge as such, as secure and inviolable in your breast, as they were in his own, before communicated to you. Hand to back, that you should support a Master Mason behind his back, as well as before his face. Mouth to ear, that you should support his good name as well behind his back as before his face."

After the candidate is through with what is called the work part, the Master addresses him in the following manner: "Brother, you may suppose from the manner you have been dealt with to-night, that we have been fooling with you, or that we have treated you different from others, but I assure you that is not the case. You have, this night, represented one of the greatest men that ever lived, in the tragical catastrophe of his death, burial, and resurrection; I mean Hiram Abiff, the widow's son, who was slain by three ruffians at the building of King Solomon's Temple, and who, in his inflexibility, integrity, and fortitude, never was surpassed by man. The history of that momentous event is thus related. Masonic tradition informs us that at the building of King Solomon's Temple, fifteen Fellow Crafts discovering that the Temple was almost finished, and not having the Master Mason's word, became very impatient, and entered into a horrid conspiracy to extort the Master Mason's word from their Grand Master, Hiram Abiff, the first time they met him alone, or take his life, that they might pass as Masters in other countries, and receive wages as such; but before they could accomplish their designs, twelve of them recanted, but the other three were base enough to carry their atrocious designs into execution. Their names were Jubela, Jubelo, and Jubelum.

"It was the custom of our Grand Master, Hiram Abiff, every day at high twelve, when the crafts were from labor to refreshment, to enter into the sanctum sanctorum, and offer his devotions to the ever living God, and draw out his plans and designs on the Tressle-Board for the crafts to pursue their labor. On a certain day (not named in any of our traditional accounts), Jubela, Jubelo and Jubelum placed themselves at the South, West, and East gates of the Temple, and Hiram having finished his devotions and labor, attempted (as was his usual custom) to retire at the South gate, where he was met by Jubela, who demanded of him the Master Mason's word (some say the secrets of a Master Mason), and on his refusal to give it, Jubela gave him a violent blow with a twenty-four-inch gauge across the throat; on which Hiram fled to the West gate, where he was accosted in the same manner by Jubelo, but with more violence. Hiram told him that he could not give the word then, because Solomon, King of Israel, Hiram, King of Tyre, and himself had entered into a solemn league that the word never should be given, [Pg 47]unless they three were present; but if he would have patience till the Grand Lodge assembled at Jerusalem, if he was then found worthy he should then receive it, otherwise he could not; Jubelo replied in a very peremptory manner, "If you do not give me the Master's word, I'll take your life;" and on Hiram's refusing to give it, Jubelo gave him a severe blow with the Square across the left breast, on which he fled to the East gate, where he was accosted by Jubelum, in the same manner, but with still more violence. Here Hiram reasoned as before; Jubelum told him that he had heard his caviling with Jubela and Jubelo long enough, and that the Master's word had been promised to him from time to time for a long time; that he was still put off, and that the Temple was almost finished, and he was determined to have the word or take his life. "I want it so that I may be able to get wages as a Master Mason in any country to which I may go for employ, after the Temple is finished, and that I may be able to support my wife and children." Hiram persisting in his refusal, he gave Hiram a violent blow with the gavel on the forehead, which felled him to the floor and killed him; they took the body and carried it out of the West gate, and buried it in the rubbish till low twelve at night (which is twelve o'clock), when they three met agreeably to appointment, and carried the body a westerly course, and buried it at the brow of a hill, in a grave, dug due East and West, six feet perpendicular, and made their escape. King Solomon coming up to the Temple at low six in the morning (as was his usual custom), found the crafts all in confusion, and on inquiring the cause, was informed that their Grand Master, Hiram Abiff, was missing, and there was no plans or designs laid down on the Tressle-Board, for the crafts to pursue their labor. Solomon ordered search to be made inland about the Temple for him; no discovery being made, he then ordered the Secretary to call the roll of workmen to see if any were missing; it appearing that there were three, viz.: Jubela, Jubelo and Jubelum, Solomon observed, "This brings to my mind a circumstance that took place this morning. Twelve Fellow Crafts came to me, dressed in white gloves and aprons, in token of their innocence, and confessed that they twelve, with three others, had conspired to extort the Master Mason's word from their Grand Master, Hiram Abiff, and in case of his refusal to take his life; they twelve had recanted, but feared the three others had been base enough to carry their atrocious designs into execution." Solomon immediately ordered twelve Fellow Crafts to be selected from the bands of the workmen, clothed in white gloves and aprons, in token of their innocence, and sent three East, three West, three North, and three South, in search of the ruffians, and, if found, to bring them up before him. The three that traveled a westerly course, coming near the coast of Joppa, fell in with a wayfaring man, who informed them that he had seen three men pass that way that morning, who, from their appearance and dress, were workmen from the Temple, inquiring for a passage to Ethiopia, but were unable to obtain one, in consequence of an embargo which had recently been laid on all the shipping, and had turned back into the country. After making further and more diligent search, and making no further discovery, they returned to the Temple and reported [Pg 48]to Solomon the result of their pursuit and inquiries. On which Solomon directed them to go again, and search until they found their Grand Master, Hiram Abiff, if possible; and if he was not found, the twelve who had confessed should be considered as the murderers, and suffer accordingly.

They returned again in pursuit of the ruffians, and one of the three that traveled a westerly course, being more weary than the rest, sat down at the brow of a hill to rest and refresh himself; and, in attempting to rise, caught hold of a sprig of cassia, which easily gave, and excited his curiosity, and made him suspicious of a deception; on which he hailed his companions, who immediately assembled, and, on examination, found that the earth had been recently moved; and on moving the rubbish, discovered the appearance of the grave, and while they were confabulating about what measures to take, they heard voices issuing from a cavern in the clefts of the rocks, on which they immediately repaired to the place, where they heard the voice of Jubela exclaim: "O that my throat had been cut across, my tongue torn out, and my body buried in the rough sands of the sea at low-water mark, where the tide ebbs and flows twice in twenty-four hours, ere I had been accessory to the death of so good a man as our Grand Master, Hiram Abiff"—on which they distinctly heard the voice of Jubelo exclaim, "O that my left breast had been torn open, and my heart and vitals taken from thence, and thrown over my left shoulder, carried into the valley of Jehosaphat, there to become a prey to the wild beasts of the field, and vultures of the air, ere I had conspired to take the life of so good a man as our Grand Master, Hiram Abiff"—when they more distinctly heard the voice of Jubelum exclaim, "O that my body had been severed in two in the midst, and divided to the North and the South, my bowels burnt to ashes in the centre, and the ashes scattered by the four winds of heaven, that there might not remain the least trace of remembrance among men or Masons of so vile and perjured a wretch as I am, who wilfully took the life of so good a man as our Grand Master, Hiram Abiff. Ah, Jubela and Jubelo, it was I that struck him harder than you both—it was I that gave him the fatal blow—it was I that killed him outright!" on which they rushed forward, seized, bound, and carried them before King Solomon, who, after hearing the testimony of the three Fellow Crafts, and the three ruffians having pleaded guilty, order them to be taken out at the West gate of the Temple, and executed agreeably to the several imprecations of their own mouths. King Solomon then ordered fifteen Fellow Crafts to be elected from the bands of the workmen, clothed with white gloves and aprons, in token of their innocence, and sent three East, three West, three North, three South; and three in and about the Temple, in search of the body of our Grand Master, Hiram Abiff; and the three that traveled a westerly course found it under a sprig of cassia, where a worthy brother sat down to rest and refresh himself; and on removing the earth till they came to the coffin, they involuntarily found their hands raised, as hereinbefore described, to guard their nostrils against the offensive effluvia that 'rose from the [Pg 49]grave. It is also said that the body had lain there fourteen days; some say fifteen.

The body was raised in the manner herein before described, carried up to the Temple, and buried as explained in the closing clauses of the Lecture. Not one-third part of the preceding history of this degree is ever given to a candidate. A few general, desultory, unconnected remarks are made to him, and he is generally referred to the manner of raising, and to the Lecture, for information as to the particulars. Here follows a charge which ought to be, and sometimes is, delivered to the candidate after hearing the history of the degree.

An Address to be Delivered to the Candidate after the History Has Been Given.

"Brother, your zeal for the institution of Masonry, the progress you have made in the mystery, and your conformity to our regulations, have pointed you out as a proper object of our favor and esteem.

"You are bound by duty, honor, and gratitude to be faithful to your trust; to support the dignity of your character on every occasion; and to enforce, by precept and example, obedience to the tenets of the Order.

"In the character of a Master Mason you are authorized to correct the errors and irregularities of your uninformed brethren, and to guard them against a breach of fidelity.

"To preserve the reputation of the fraternity unsullied, must be your constant care, and for this purpose, it is your province to recommend to your inferiors, obedience and submission; to your equals, courtesy and affability; to your superiors, kindness and condescension. Universal benevolence you are always to inculcate; and, by the regularity of your own behavior, afford the best example for the conduct of others less informed. The ancient landmarks of the Order, entrusted to your care, you are carefully to preserve; and never suffer them to be infringed, or countenance a deviation from the established usages and customs of the fraternity.

"Your virtue, honor, and reputation are concerned in supporting, with dignity, the character you now bear. Let no motive, therefore, make you swerve from your duty, violate your vow, or betray your trust: but be true and faithful, and imitate the example of that celebrated artist whom you this evening represent: thus you will render yourself deserving the honor which we have conferred, and merit the confidence that we have reposed."

Here follows the Lecture on this degree, which is divided into three sections.

FIRST SECTION.

Question—Are you a Master Mason? Answer—I am; try me; disprove me if you can.

Q. Where were you prepared to be made a Master Mason? A. In a room adjacent to the body of a just and lawfully constituted Lodge of such, duly assembled in a room, representing the SANCTUM SANCTORUM, or HOLY OF HOLIES, of King Solomon's Temple.

Q. How were you prepared? A. By being divested of all metals; neither naked nor clothed; barefooted nor shod; with a cable-tow three times about my naked body; in which posture I was conducted to the door of the Lodge, where I gave three distinct knocks.

[Pg 50]Q. What did those three distinct knocks allude to? A. To the third degree in Masonry; it being that on which I was about to enter.

Q. What was said to you from within? A. Who comes there? Who comes there? Who comes there?

Q. Your answer? A. A worthy brother, who has been regularly initiated as an Entered Apprentice Mason, passed to the degree of a Fellow Craft, and now wishes for further light in Masonry, by being raised to the sublime degree of a Master Mason.

Q. What further was said to you from within? A. I was asked if it was of my own free will and accord I made this request; if I was duly and truly prepared; worthy and well qualified; and had made suitable proficiency in the preceding degree; all of which being answered in the affirmative, I was asked by what further rights I expected to obtain that benefit.

Q. Your answer? A. By the benefit of a pass-word.

Q. What was that pass-word? A. Tubal Cain.

Q. What was next said to you? A. I was bid to wait till the Worshipful Master in the East was made acquainted with my request, and his answer returned.

Q. After his answer was returned, what followed? A. I was caused to enter the Lodge on the two extreme points of the Compass pressing my right and left breasts, in the name of the Lord.

Q. How were you then disposed of? A. I was conducted three times regularly around the Lodge and halted at the Junior Warden in the South, where the same questions were asked and answers returned, as at the door.

Q. How did the Junior Warden dispose of you? A. He ordered me to be conducted to the Senior Warden in the West, where the same questions were asked and answers returned as before.

Q. How did the Senior Warden dispose of you? A. He ordered me to be conducted to the Worshipful Master in the East, where the same questions were asked, and answers returned as before; who likewise demanded of me from whence I came, and whither I was traveling.

Q. Your answer? A. From the West, and traveling to the East.

Q. Why do you leave the West and travel to the East? A. In search of light.

Q. How did the Worshipful Master dispose of you? A. He ordered me to be conducted back to the West, from whence I came, and put in care of the Senior Warden, who taught me how to approach the East, by advancing upon three upright regular steps to the third step, my feet forming a square, and my body erect at the altar before the Worshipful Master.

Q. What did the Worshipful Master do with you? A. He made an obligated Master Mason of me.

Q. How? A. In due form.

Q. What was that due form? A. Both my knees bare bent, they forming a square; both hands on the Holy Bible, Square, and Compass; in which posture I took upon me the solemn oath or obligation of a true Master Mason.

[Pg 51]Q. After your obligation, what was said to you? A. What do you most desire.

Q. Your answer? A. More light. [The bandage around the head is now dropped over the eyes.]

Q. Did you receive light? A. I did.

Q. On being brought to light on this degree, what did you first discover? A. Three great lights in Masonry, by the assistance of three less, and both points of the Compass elevated above the Square, which denoted to me that I had received, or was about to receive, all the light that could be conferred on me in a Master's Lodge.

Q. What did you next discover? A. The Worshipful Master approaching me from the East, under the sign and due-guard of a Master Mason, who presented me with his right hand in token of brotherly love and confidence, and proceeded to give me the pass-grip and word of a Master Mason [the word is the name of the pass-grip], and bid me rise and salute the Junior and Senior Wardens, and convince them that I was an obligated Master Mason, and had the sign, pass-grip, and word (Tubal Cain).

Q. What did you next discover? A. The Worshipful Master approaching me a second time from the East, who presented me with a lamb-skin, or white apron, which, he said, he hoped I would continue to wear with honor to myself, and satisfaction and advantage to the brethren.

Q. What were you next presented with? A. The working tools of a Master Mason.

Q. What are they? A. All the implements of Masonry indiscriminately, but more especially the Trowel.

Q. How explained? A. The Trowel is an instrument made use of by operative Masons to spread the cement which unites a building into one common mass; but we, as Free and Accepted Masons, are taught to make use of it for the more noble and glorious purposes of spreading the cement of brotherly love and affection; that cement which unites us into one sacred band, or society of brothers, among whom no contention should ever exist, but that noble emulation of who can best work, or best agree.

Q. What were you next presented with? A. Three precious jewels.

Q. What are they? A. Humanity, Friendship, and Brotherly Love.

Q. How were you then disposed of? A. I was conducted out of the Lodge, and invested of what I had been divested, and returned again in due season.

SECOND SECTION.

Question—Did you ever return to the SANCTUM SANCTORUM, or HOLY OF HOLIES, of King Solomon's Temple? Answer—I did.

Q. Was there anything in particular took place on your return? A. There was, viz., I was accosted by three ruffians, who demanded of me the Master Mason's word.

Q. Did you ever give it to them? A. I did not, but bid them wait, with time and patience, till the Grand Lodge assembled at Jerusalem, and [Pg 52]then, if they were found worthy, they should receive it, otherwise they could not.

Q. In what manner was you accosted? A. In attempting to retire at the South gate, I was accosted by one of them, who demanded of me the Master Mason's word, and, on my refusing to comply with his request, he gave me a blow with the twenty-four-inch gauge across my breast, on which I fled to the West gate, where I was accosted by the second with more violence, and, on my refusing to comply with his request, he gave me a severe blow with the Square across my breast; on which I attempted to make my escape at the East gate, where I was accosted by the third with still more violence, and, on my refusing to comply with his request, he gave me a violent blow with the common gavel on the forehead, and brought me to the floor.

Q. Whom did you represent at that time? A. Our Grand Master, Hiram Abiff, who was slain at the building of King Solomon's Temple.

Q. Was his death premeditated? A. It was—by fifteen Fellow Crafts, who conspired to extort from him the Master Mason's word; twelve of whom recanted, but the other three were base enough to carry their atrocious designs into execution.

Q. What did they do with the body? A. They carried it out at the West gate of the Temple, and buried it till low twelve at night, when they three met agreeably to appointment, and carried it a westerly course from the Temple, and buried it under the brow of a hill, in a grave six feet, due East and West, six feet perpendicular, and made their escape.

Q. What time was he slain? A. At high twelve at noon, when the crafts were from labor to refreshment.

Q. How came he to be alone at that time? A. Because it was the usual custom of our Grand Master, Hiram Abiff, every day at high twelve, when the crafts were from labor to refreshment, to enter into the SANCTUM SANCTORUM, or HOLY OF HOLIES, and offer up his adorations to the ever-living God, and draw out his plans and designs on his Tressle-Board, for the crafts to pursue their labor.

Q. At what time was he missing? A. At low six in the morning, when King Solomon came up to the Temple, as usual, to view the work, and found the crafts all in confusion; and, on inquiring the cause, he was informed that their Grand Master, Hiram Abiff, was missing, and no plans or designs were laid down on the Tressle-Board for the crafts to pursue their labor.

Q. What observations did King Solomon make at that time? A. He observed that our Grand Master, Hiram Abiff, had always been very punctual in attending, and feared that he was indisposed, and ordered search to be made in and about the Temple, to see if he could be found.

Q. Search being made, and he not found, what further remarks did King Solomon make? A. He observed he feared some fatal accident had befallen our Grand Master, Hiram Abiff; that morning twelve Fellow Crafts, clothed in white gloves and aprons, in token of their innocence, had confessed that they twelve with three others, had conspired to extort the Master Mason's word from their Grand Master, Hiram Abiff, [Pg 53]or take his life; that they twelve had recanted, but feared the other three had been base enough to carry their atrocious designs into execution.

Q. What followed? A. King Solomon ordered the roll of workmen to be called, to see if there were any missing.

Q. The roll being called, were there any missing? A. There were three, viz., Jubela, Jubelo, and Jubelum.

Q. Were the ruffians ever found? A. They were.

Q. How? A. By the wisdom of King Solomon, who ordered twelve Fellow Crafts to be selected from the bands of the workmen, clothed in white gloves and aprons, in token of their innocence, and sent three East, three West, three North, and three South, in search of the ruffians, and, if found, to bring them forward.

Q. What success? A. The three that traveled a westerly course from the Temple, coming near the coast of Joppa, were informed by a wayfaring man, that three men had been seen that way that morning, who, from their appearance and dress, were workmen from the Temple, inquiring for a passage to Ethiopia, but were unable to obtain one, in consequence of an embargo which had recently been laid on all the shipping, and had turned back into the country.

Q. What followed? A. King Solomon ordered them to go and search again, and search till they were found, if possible; and if they were not found, that the twelve who had confessed should be considered as the reputed murderers, and suffer accordingly.

Q. What success? A. One of the three that traveled a westerly course from the Temple, being more weary than the rest, sat down under the brow of a hill to rest and refresh himself; and, in attempting to rise, caught hold of a sprig of cassia, which easily gave way, and excited his curiosity, and made him suspicious of a deception; on which he hailed his companions, who immediately assembled, and, on examination, found that the earth had recently been moved; and on moving the rubbish, discovered the appearance of a grave, and while they were confabulating about what measures to take, they heard voices issuing from a cavern in the clefts of the rocks, on which they immediately repaired to the place, where they heard the voice of Jubela exclaim: "O that my throat had been cut across, my tongue torn out, and my body buried in the rough sands of the sea at low-water mark, where the tide ebbs and flows twice in twenty-four hours, ere I had been accessory to the death of so good a man as our Grand Master, Hiram Abiff"—on which they distinctly heard the voice of Jubelo exclaim, "O that my left breast had been torn open, and my heart and vitals taken from thence, and thrown over my left shoulder, carried into the valley of Jehosaphat, there to become a prey to the wild beasts of the field, and vultures of the air, ere I had conspired to take the life of so good a man as our Grand Master, Hiram Abiff"—when they more distinctly heard the voice of Jubelum exclaim, "O that my body had been severed in two in the midst, and divided to the North and the South, my bowels burnt to ashes in the centre, and the ashes scattered by the four winds of heaven, that there might not [Pg 54]remain the least track or trace of remembrance among men or Masons of so vile and perjured a wretch as I am, who wilfully took the life of so good a man as our Grand Master, Hiram Abiff. Ah, Jubela and Jubelo, it was I that struck him harder than you both—it was I that gave him the fatal blow—it was I that killed him outright!" on which they rushed forward, seized, bound, and carried them up before King Solomon.

Q. What did King Solomon do with them? A. He ordered them to be executed agreeably to the several imprecations of their own mouths.

Q. Was the body of our Grand Master, Hiram Abiff, ever found? A. It was.

Q. How? A. By the wisdom of King Solomon, who ordered fifteen (in some Lodges they say twelve) Fellow Crafts to be selected from the bands of the workmen, and sent three East, three West, three North, and three South; and three in and about the Temple, in search of the body.

Q. Where was it found? A. Under that sprig of cassia, where a worthy brother sat down to rest and refresh himself.

Q. Was there anything particular took place on the discovery of the body? A. There was, viz.: On removing the earth till they came to the coffin, they involuntarily found their hands raised in this position to guard their nostrils against the offensive effluvia that 'rose from the grave.

Q. How long had the body lain there? A. Fourteen days.

Q. What did they do with the body? A. Raised it in a Masonic form, and carried it up to the Temple for more decent interment.

Q. Where was it buried? A. Under the SANCTUM SANCTORUM, or HOLY OF HOLIES, of King Solomon's Temple, over which they erected a marble monument, with this inscription delineated thereon: A virgin weeping over a broken column, with a book open before her; in her right hand a sprig of cassia; in her left, an urn; Time standing behind her, with his hands infolded in the ringlets of her hair.

Q. What do they denote? A. The weeping virgin denotes the unfinished state of the Temple; the broken column, that one of the principal supporters of Masonry had fallen; the open book before her, that his memory was on perpetual record; the sprig of cassia, the timely discovery of his grave; the urn in her left hand, that his ashes were safely deposited under the SANCTUM SANCTORUM, or HOLY OF HOLIES, of King Solomon's Temple; and Time standing behind her, with his hands infolded in the ringlets of her hair, that time, patience, and perseverance will accomplish all things.

THIRD SECTION.

Question—What does a Master's Lodge represent? Answer—The SANCTUM SANCTORUM, or HOLY OF HOLIES, of King Solomon's Temple.

Q. How long was the Temple building? A. Seven years; during which it rained not in the daytime, that the workmen might not be obstructed in their labor.

[Pg 55]Q. What supported the Temple? A. Fourteen hundred and fifty-three columns, and two thousand, nine hundred and six pilasters, all hewn from the finest Parian marble.

Q. What further supported it? A. Three grand columns, or pillars.

159

Q. What were they called? A. Wisdom, Strength, and Beauty.

Q. What did they represent? A. The pillar of Wisdom represented Solomon, King of Israel, whose wisdom contrived the mighty fabric; the pillar of Strength, Hiram, King of Tyre, who strengthened Solomon in his glorious undertaking; the pillar of Beauty, Hiram Abiff, the widow's son, whose cunning craft and curious workmanship beautified and adorned the Temple.

Q. How many were there employed in the building of King Solomon's Temple? A. Three Grand Masters; three thousand, three hundred Masters, or overseers of the work; eighty thousand Fellow Crafts, and seventy thousand Entered Apprentices; all those were classed and arranged in such a manner, by the wisdom of Solomon, that neither envy, discord, nor confusion were suffered to interrupt that universal peace and tranquility that pervaded the work at that important period.

Q. How many constitutes an Entered Apprentice's Lodge? A. Seven; one Master and six Entered Apprentices.

Q. Where did they usually meet? A. On the ground floor of King Solomon's Temple.

Q. How many constitutes a Fellow Craft's Lodge? A. Five; two Masters and three Fellow Crafts.

Q. Where did they usually meet? A. In the middle chamber of King Solomon's Temple.

Q. How many constitutes a Master's Lodge? A. Three Master Masons.

Q. Where did they usually meet? A. In the SANCTUM SANCTORUM, or HOLY OF HOLIES, of King Solomon's Temple.

Q. Have you any emblems on this degree? A. We have several, which are divided into two classes.

Q. What are the first class? A. The pot of incense; the bee-hive; the book of constitutions, guarded by the Tyler's sword; the sword, pointing to a naked heart; the all-seeing eye; the anchor and ark; the forty-seventh problem of Euclid; the hour-glass; the scythe; and the three steps usually delineated on the Master's carpet, which are thus explained: The pot of INCENSE is an emblem of a pure heart, which is always an acceptable sacrifice to the Deity; and as this glows with fervent heat, so should our hearts continually glow with gratitude to the great and beneficent Author of our existence, for the manifold blessings and comforts we enjoy. The BEE-HIVE is an emblem of industry, and recommends the practice of that virtue to all created beings, from the highest seraph in heaven to the lowest reptile of the dust. It teaches us that as we came into the world rational and intelligent beings, so we should ever be industrious ones; never sitting down contented while our fellow-creatures around us are in want, when it is in our power to relieve them, without inconvenience to ourselves. When we take a survey of nature, we behold man, in his infancy, more helpless and indigent than the brute creation; he lies languishing for days, weeks, months, and [Pg 56]years, totally incapable of providing sustenance for himself; of guarding against the attacks of the field, or sheltering himself from the inclemencies of the weather. It might have pleased the great Creator of heaven and earth to have made man independent of all other beings, but as independence is one of the strongest bonds of society, mankind were made dependent on each other for protection and security, as they thereby enjoy better opportunities of fulfilling the duties of reciprocal love and friendship. Thus was man formed for social and active life, the noblest part of the work of God; and he, who will so demean himself as not to be endeavoring to add to the common stock of knowledge and understanding, may be deemed a DRONE in the HIVE of nature, a useless member of society, and unworthy of our protection as Masons. The BOOK OF CONSTITUTIONS, GUARDED BY THE TYLER'S SWORD, reminds us that we should be ever watchful and guarded, in our thoughts, words, and actions, and particularly when before the enemies of Masonry; ever bearing in remembrance those truly masonic virtues, SILENCE and CIRCUMSPECTION. The SWORD, POINTING TO A NAKED HEART, demonstrates that justice will sooner or later overtake us; and, although our thoughts, words, and actions may be hidden from the eyes of men, yet that ALL-SEEING EYE, whom the SUN, MOON, and STARS obey, and under whose watchful care even comets perform their stupendous revolutions, pervades the inmost recesses of the human heart, and will reward us according to our merits. The ANCHOR and ARK are emblems of a well-grounded hope and well-spent life. They are emblematical of that divine ARK which safely wafts us over this tempestuous sea of troubles, and that ANCHOR which shall safely moor us in a peaceful harbor, where the wicked cease from troubling, and the weary shall find rest. The forty-seventh problem of Euclid—this was an invention of our ancient friend and brother, the great Pythagoras, who, in his travels through Asia, Africa, and Europe, was initiated into several orders of priesthood, and raised to the sublime degree of a Master Mason.

This wise philosopher enriched his mind abundantly in a general knowledge of things, and more especially in Geometry or Masonry; on this subject he drew out many problems and theorems; and among the most distinguished, he erected this, which, in the joy of his heart, he called Eureka, in the Grecian language signifying, I have found it; and upon the discovery of which he is said to have sacrificed a hecatomb. It teaches Masons to be general lovers of the arts and sciences. The HOUR-GLASS is an emblem of human life. Behold! how swiftly the sands run, and how rapidly our lives are drawing to a close. We cannot, without astonishment behold the little particles which are contained in this machine; how they pass away almost imperceptibly, and yet, to our surprise, in the short space of an hour they are all exhausted.

Thus wastes man to-day; he puts forth the tender leaves of hope; to-morrow, blossoms, and bears his blushing honors thick upon him; the next day comes a frost, which nips the shoot, and when he thinks his greatness is still ripening, he falls, like autumn leaves, to enrich our mother earth. The SCYTHE is an emblem of time, which cuts the brittle thread of life, and launches us into eternity. Behold! what havoc the [Pg 57]scythe of time makes among the human race; if, by chance, we should escape the numerous evils incident to childhood and youth, and, with health and vigor, arrive to the years of manhood, yet withal, we must soon be cut down by the all-devouring scythe of time, and be gathered into the land where our fathers had gone before us. The THREE STEPS, usually delineated upon the Master's carpet, are emblematical of the three principal stages of human life, viz.: Youth, Manhood, and Age. In youth, as Entered Apprentices, we ought industriously to occupy our minds in the attainment of useful knowledge; in manhood, as Fellow Crafts, we should apply our knowledge to the discharge of our respective duties to God, our neighbors, and ourselves; so that in age, as Master Masons, we may enjoy the happy reflections consequent on a well-spent life, and die in the hope of a glorious immortality.

Q. What are the second class of emblems? A. The spade, coffin, death-head, marrow bones, and sprig of cassia, which are thus explained: The SPADE opens the vault to receive our bodies, where our active limbs will soon moulder to dust. The COFFIN, DEATH-HEAD, and MARROW BONES are emblematical of the death and burial of our Grand Master, Hiram Abiff, and are worthy our serious attention. The SPRIG OF CASSIA is emblematical of that immortal part of man which never dies; and when the cold winter of death shall have passed, and the bright summer's morn of the resurrection appears, the Son of Righteousness shall descend, and send forth his angels to collect our ransomed dust; then, if we are found worthy, by his pass-word we shall enter into the Celestial Lodge above, where the Supreme Architect of the Universe presides, where we shall see the King in the beauty of holiness, and with him enter into an endless fraternity.

Here ends the first three degrees of Masonry, which constitutes a Master Mason's Lodge. A Master Mason's Lodge and a Chapter of Royal Arch Masons are two distinct bodies, wholly independent of each other. The members of a Chapter are privileged to visit all Master Mason's Lodges when they please; and may be, and often are, members of both at the same time; and all the members of a Master Mason's Lodge who are Royal Arch Masons, though not members of any Chapter, may visit any Chapter. I wish the reader to understand that neither all Royal Arch Masons nor Master Masons are members of either Lodge or Chapter; there are tens of thousands who are not members, and scarcely ever attend, although privileged to do so.

A very small proportion of Masons, comparatively speaking, ever advance any further than the third degree, and consequently never get the great word which was lost by Hiram's untimely death. Solomon, King of Israel, Hiram, King of Tyre, and Hiram Abiff, the widow's son, having sworn that they, nor either of them, would ever give the word, except they three were present (and it is generally believed that there was not another person in the world, at that time, that had it), consequently the word was lost, and supposed to be forever; but the sequel will show it was found, after a lapse of four hundred and seventy years; notwithstanding, the word Mah-hah-bone, which was substituted by Solomon, still continues to be used by Master Masons, and no doubt will, [Pg 58]as long as Masonry attracts the attention of men; and the word which was lost is used in the Royal Arch Degree. What was the word of the Royal Arch Degree before they found the Master's word, which was lost at the death of Hiram Abiff, and was not found for four hundred and seventy years? Were there any Royal Arch Masons before the Master's word was found? I wish some masonic gentleman would solve these two questions.

The ceremonies, histories, and the Lecture, in the preceding degree are so similar that perhaps some one of the three might have been dispensed with, and the subject well understood by most readers, notwithstanding there is a small difference between the work and history, and between the history and the Lecture.

I shall now proceed with the Mark Master's degree, which is the first degree in the Chapter. The Mark Master's degree, the Past Master's, and the Most Excellent Master's, are Lodges of Mark Master Masons, Past Master, and Most Excellent Master; yet, although called Lodges, they are called component parts of the Chapter. Ask a Mark Master Mason if he belongs to the Chapter; he will tell you he does, but that he has only been marked. It is not an uncommon thing, by any means, for a Chapter to confer all four of the degrees in one night, viz:—the Mark Master, Past Master, Most Excellent Master, and Royal Arch degrees.

Test-Oath and Word.

The following "test-oath and word" were invented and adopted by the "Grand Lodge" of the State of New York, at their Session in June, 1827, for the purpose of guarding against Book Masons. They are given in a Master's Lodge. They were obtained from a gentleman in high standing in society, and among Masons, but a friend to Anti-Masonry. He was a member of the "Grand Lodge," and present when they were adopted.

A person wishing to be admitted into the Lodge, presents himself at the door; the Tyler (or some brother from within) demands or asks, "Do you wish to visit this Lodge?" The candidate for admission says, "If thought worthy." Tyler—"By what are you recommended?" Ans.—"By fidelity." Tyler says, "Prove that;" at the same time advances and throws out his hand or arm to an angle of about forty-five degrees obliquely forward, the hand open, and thumb upward. The candidate then advances, and places the back of his LEFT HAND against the PALM of the Tyler's RIGHT HAND—still extended puts his mouth to the Tyler's ear and whispers, L-O-S, and pronounces LOS.

Test-Oath.—"I, A. B., of my own free will and accord, in the presence of Almighty God, solemnly and sincerely promise and swear that I will not communicate the secret test-word, annexed to this obligation, to any but a true and lawful Master Mason, and that in the body of a lawful Lodge of such, in actual session, or at the door of a Lodge, for the purpose of gaining admission; under the penalty of being forever disgraced and dishonored as a man, and despised, degraded, and expelled as a Mason."

[Pg 59]

FOURTH, OR MARK MASTER'S DEGREE.

Ceremonies Used in Opening a Lodge of Mark Master Masons.

One rap calls the Lodge to order; one calls up the Junior and Senior Deacons; two raps call up the subordinate officers; and three, all the members of the Lodge. The Right Worshipful Master having called the Lodge to order, and all being seated, the Right Worshipful Master says to the Junior Warden, "Brother Junior, are they all Mark Master Masons in the South?" Junior Warden answers, "They are, Right Worshipful." R. W. M.—"I thank you, brother." R. W. M.—"Brother Senior, are they all Mark Master Masons in the West?" Senior Warden—"They are, Right Worshipful." R. W. M.—"They are in the East." At the same time gives a rap with the mallet which calls up both Deacons. R. W. M.—"Brother Junior, the first care of a Mason?" "To see the Lodge tyled, Right Worshipful." R. W. M.—"Attend to that part of the duty, and inform the Tyler that we are about to open a Lodge of Mark Master Masons, and direct him to tyle accordingly." Junior Deacon steps to the door and gives four raps, which are answered by four without by the Tyler; the Junior Deacon then gives one, which is answered by the Tyler with one; the door is then partly opened, and the Junior Deacon then delivers his message and resumes his station, gives the due-guard of a Mark Master Mason, and says, "The door is tyled, Right Worshipful." R. W. M.—"By whom?" J. D.—"By a Mark Master Mason without the door, armed with the proper implements of his office." R. W. M.—"His duty there?" J. D.—"To keep off all cowans and eavesdroppers, see that none pass or repass without permission from the Right Worshipful Master." R. W. M.—"Brother Junior, your place in the Lodge?" J. D.—"At the right hand of the Senior Warden in the West." R. W. M.—"Your business there, Brother Junior?" J. D.—"To wait on the Right Worshipful Master and Wardens, act as their proxy in the active duties of the Lodge, and take care of the door." R. W. M.—"The Senior Deacon's place in the Lodge?" J. D.—"At the right hand of the Worshipful Master in the East." R. W. M.—"I thank you, brother." He then gives two raps with the mallet, and the subordinate officers rise. R. W. M.—"Your duty there, Brother Senior?" S. D.—"To wait on the Right Worshipful Master and Wardens, act as their proxy in the active duties of the Lodge, attend to the preparation and introduction of candidates, and welcome and clothe all visiting brethren." R. W. M.—"The Secretary's place in the Lodge, Brother Junior?" J. D.—"At the right hand of the Worshipful Master in the East." R. W. M.—"I thank you, brother. Your duty there, Brother Secretary?" Sec.—"The better to observe the Right Worshipful Master's will and pleasure; record the proceedings of the Lodge; transmit the same to the Grand Lodge, if required; receive all monies and money-bills from the hands of the brethren, pay them over to the Treasurer, and take his receipt for the same." R. W. M.—"The Treasurer's place in the Lodge?" Sec.—"At the right hand of the Right Worshipful Master." R. W. M.—"I thank you, brother. Your duty there, Brother Treasurer?" Treasurer—"Duly to observe the Right Worshipful Master's will and pleasure; receive all [Pg 60]monies and money-bills from the hands of the Secretary; give a receipt for the same; keep a just and true account of the same; pay them out by order of the Right Worshipful Master and consent of the brethren." R. W. M.—"The Junior Overseer's place in the Lodge, Brother Treasurer?" Treas.—"At the right hand of the Junior Warden in the South, Right Worshipful." R. W. M.—"I thank you, brother. Your business there, Brother Junior Overseer?" J. O.—"To inspect all material brought up for the building of the Temple; approve or disapprove of the same; and, if approved, pass it on to the Senior Overseer for further inspection." R. W. M.—"The Senior Overseer's place in the Lodge?" J. O.—"At the right hand of the Senior Warden in the West, Right Worshipful." R. W. M.—"I thank you, brother. Your business there, Brother Senior Overseer?" S. O.—"To inspect all materials brought up for the building of the Temple; and, if approved, pass it on to the Master Overseer at the East gate for further inspection." R. W. M.—"The Master Overseer's place in the Lodge, Brother Senior Overseer?" S. O.—"At the right hand of the Right Worshipful Master in the East." R. W. M.—"I thank you, brother. Your business there, Brother Master Overseer?" M. O.—"To assist in the inspection of all materials brought up for the building of the Temple; and if disapproved, to call a council of my brother Overseers." R. W. M.—"The Junior Warden's place in the Lodge, Brother Master Overseer?" M. O.—"In the South, Right Worshipful." R. W. M.—"I thank you, brother. Your business there, Brother Junior?" J. W.—"As the sun in the South, at high meridian, is the beauty and glory of the day, so stands the Junior Warden in the South, the better to observe the time, call the crafts from labor to refreshment, superintend them during the hours thereof, see that none convert the hours of refreshment into that of intemperance or excess, and call them on again in due season, that the Right Worshipful Master may have honor, and they pleasure and profit thereby." R. W. M.—"The Senior Warden's place in the Lodge?" J.

163

W.—"In the West, Right Worshipful." R. W. M.—"I thank you, brother. Your duty there, Brother Senior?" S. W.—"As the sun sets in the West to close the day, so stands the Senior Warden in the West, to assist the Right Worshipful in opening and closing the Lodge; take care of the jewels and implements; see that none be lost; pay the craft their wages, if any be due; and see that none go away dissatisfied." R. W. M.—"The Master's place in the Lodge?" S. W.—"In the East, Right Worshipful." R. W. M.—"His duty there?" S. W.—"As the sun rises in the East to open and adorn the day, so presides the Right Worshipful Master in the East to open and adorn his Lodge, set his crafts to work, and govern them with good and wholesome laws, or cause the same to be done." R. W. M.—"I thank you, brother." Gives three raps with the mallet, which calls up all the brethren, takes off his hat and says, "In like manner, so do I, strictly prohibiting all profane language, private committees, or any other disorderly conduct, whereby the peace and harmony of this Lodge may be interrupted, while engaged in its lawful pursuits; under no less penalty than the by-laws enjoin, or a majority of the brethren present may see cause to inflict. Brethren, attend to giving the signs." [Pg 61]The Right Worshipful Master (all the brethren imitating him) extends his left arm from his body, so as to form an angle of about forty-five degrees, and holds his right hand transversely across his left, the palms thereof about an inch apart. This is called the first sign of a Mason—is the sign of distress in the first degree, and alludes to the position a candidate's hands are placed when he takes the obligation of an Entered Apprentice Mason; he then draws his right hand across his throat, the hand open, with his thumb next his throat, drops it down by his side. This is called the due-guard of an Entered Apprentice Mason, and alludes to the penal part of the obligation. Next he places the palm of his open right hand upon his left breast, and, at the same time, throws up his left hand, and so extends his left arm as to form a right angle; from the shoulder to the elbow it is horizontal, from the elbow to the tip of the finger it is perpendicular. This is the sign and due-guard of a Fellow Craft Mason, and also alludes to the penal part of the obligation, which is administered in this degree. After this, the Right Worshipful Master draws his right hand across his bowels, with his hand open, and thumb next his body, and drops it down by his side. This is the sign or due-guard of a Master Mason, and, like the others, alludes to the penalty of this degree. He then throws up the grand hailing sign of distress; this is given by raising both hands and arms to the elbow, perpendicularly, one on each side of the head, the elbows forming a square, his arms then drop by his side; he then clutches the third and little fingers of his right hand; with his thumb extended at the same time, his middle and forefingers, brings up his hand in such a manner as to have the side of the middle finger touch the rim of the right ear, then lets it drop, and, as it falls, brings the outward side of the little finger of the left hand across the wrist of the right, then lets them fall by his sides. This is the sign or due-guard of a Mark Master Mason, and also alludes to the penal part of the obligation in this degree. Here it is proper to remark that in the opening of any Lodge of Masons, they commence giving the signs of an Entered Apprentice, and go through all the signs of the different degrees, in regular gradation, until they arrive to the one which they are opening, and commence at the sign of the degree in which they are at work, and descend to the last when closing. After going through all the signs, as before described, the Right Worshipful Master declares the Lodge opened in the following manner: "I now declare this Lodge of Mark Master Masons duly opened for the dispatch of business." The Senior Warden declares it to the Junior Warden, and he to the brethren. The Right Worshipful Master then repeats a charge: "Wherefore, brethren, lay aside all malice and guile," &c., &c.

The Lodge being opened and ready for business, the Right Worshipful Master directs the Secretary to read the minutes of the last meeting, which generally brings to view the business of the present. If there are any candidates to be brought forward, that is generally the first business. A Master Mason, wishing for further light in Masonry, sends a petition to the Chapter, and requests to be advanced to the honorary degree of Mark Master Mason; if there is no serious objection to the petition, it is entered on the minutes, and a committee of several appointed [Pg 62]to inquire into his character, and report to the next regular communication: at that time, if the committee report in his favor, and no serious objection is made against him otherwise, a motion is made that the ballot pass; if carried, the Deacons pass the ballot boxes; these boxes are the same as in the preceding degrees. When the balls are received, the box is presented to the Right Worshipful Master, Senior and Junior Wardens. R. W. M.—"Clear in the West, Brother Senior?" S. W.—"Clear, Right Worshipful." R. W. M.—"Clear in the South, Brother Junior?" J. W.—"Clear, Right Worshipful." Right Worshipful Master says, "Clear in the East." This being the case, the candidate is accepted; but if there is one black ball in that end of the box which has the white tube, and the Senior Warden pronouncing "Not clear," all stop, and inquiry is made, and the ballot passes again; and, if blacked a third time, the candidate is rejected. It being otherwise, the Senior Deacon, who is the candidate's conductor, passes out of the Lodge into the adjoining room, where the candidate is in waiting, and there the conductor is furnished with a small oblong square, six inches long; the candidate is presented with a large white marble keystone, weighing, probably, twenty pounds, and is ordered, by his conductor, to take it by the little end, between his first and second fingers and thumb of his right hand. The door is then opened without ceremony, and they pass directly to the Junior Overseer's station at the South gate, which is nothing more than the Junior Warden's seat, and the conductor gives four raps, with his block of timber, on a pedestal in front of the Junior Overseer's station. J. O.—"Who comes here?" Cond.—"Two brother Fellow Crafts, with materials for the Temple." J. O.—"Have you a specimen of your labor?" Cond.—"I have." J. O.—"Present it." The conductor then presents the piece of timber before described; the Junior Overseer receives it, and applies a small trying square to its different angles, and they agreeing with the angles of the square, he says, "This is good work, square work, such work as we are authorized to receive." Returns the block of timber, and turning his eye upon the candidate, asks, "Who is this you have with you?" Cond.—"A brother Fellow Craft." J. O.—"Have you a specimen of your labor?" Cand.—"I have." J. O.—"Present it." The candidate then presents the keystone; the Junior Overseer receives it, and applies his square to all its angles, and they not agreeing with the angles of the square, he says, "What have you here, brother? this is neither an oblong nor a square, neither has it the regular mark of the craft upon it, but from its singular form and beauty, I am unwilling to reject it; pass on to the Senior Overseer at the West gate for further inspection." They then pass on to the Senior Overseer's station at the West gate, which is the Senior Warden's seat, and give four raps, as before, on the pedestal which stands in front of the Senior Overseer. S. O.—"Who comes here?" Cond.—"Two brother Fellow Crafts, with materials for the Temple." S. O.— "Have you a specimen of your labor?" Cond.—"I have." S. O.—"Present it." The conductor, as before, presents the block of timber; the Senior Overseer applies his square to it, and finding it agrees with the angles of his square, says, "This is good work, square work, such [Pg 63]work as we are authorized to receive; who is this you have with you?" Cond.—"A brother Fellow Craft." S. O.—"Have you a specimen of your labor?" Cand.—"I have." S. O.—"Present it." The candidate then presents the keystone, and he applies it, but not fitting, he says, "This is neither an oblong nor a square, neither has it the regular mark of the craft upon it; it is a curious wrought stone, and on account of its singular form and beauty, I am unwilling to reject it; pass on to the Master Overseer at the East gate for further inspection." They pass to to his station at the East gate, and give four raps. M. O.—"Who comes here?" Cond.—"Two brethren, Fellow Crafts, with their materials for the Temple." M. O.—"Have you a specimen of your labor?" Cond.—"I have." M. O.—"Present it." The conductor presents his billet of wood to him, applies his square to it, and, like the other Overseers, says, "This is good work, square work, such work as we are authorized to receive; who is this you have with you?" Cond.—"A brother Fellow Craft." M. O.—"Have you a specimen of your labor?" Cand.—"I have." M. O.—"Present it." [It ought here to be remarked that when the candidate is presented with the keystone, and takes it between his thumb and two fingers, it hangs suspended by his side, and he is requested to carry his work plumb, and the conductor taking good care to see that he does it, by the time he arrives at the Master Overseer's station at the East gate, and when the Master Overseer says "Present it," the candidate is extremely willing to hand over the keystone to him for inspection; for, by this time, it becomes very painful to hold any longer the stone which he has in charge.] The Master Overseer having received the keystone, he applies his square to the different angles of it, and, being found not to be square, he, like the other Overseers, says, "This is neither an oblong nor a square, neither has it the regular mark of the craft upon it." He then looks sternly upon the candidate and demands, "Is this your work?" Cand.—"It is not." M. O.—"Is this your mark?" Cand.—"It is not." M. O.—"Where did you get it?" Cond.—"I picked it up in the quarry." M. O.—"Picked it up in the quarry? this explains the matter; what! been loitering away your time this whole week, and now brought up another man's work to impose upon the Grand Overseers! this deserves the severest punishment. [Motions the candidate to stand.] Brother Junior and Senior Overseers, here is work brought up for inspection which demands a council." The Junior, Senior, and Master Overseers then assemble in council. M. O., presenting the stone—"Did a Fellow Craft present this to you for inspection, Brother Junior?" J. O.—"A Fellow Craft came to my office and presented this stone for inspection; I examined it, and found it was neither an oblong nor a square, neither, had it the regular mark of the craft upon it; but on account of its singular form and beauty, I was unwilling to reject it, and ordered it to the Senior Overseer at the West gate for further inspection." M. O.—"Brother Senior, was this stone presented to you for inspection?" S. O.—"It was; I know of no use for it in the Temple; I tried it with the square, and observed it was neither an oblong nor a square, neither had it the regular mark of the craft upon it; but on account of its singular form and beauty, I was unwilling to reject it, and, therefore, directed it [Pg 64]to the Master Overseer at the East gate for further inspection." M. O.—"It was also presented to me for inspection, but I do not know of any use which it can be in the building." S. O.—"I know of no use for it." J. O.—"I know of no use for it." M. O.—"Brother Senior, what shall we do with it?" S. O.—"Heave it over among the rubbish." The Master and Senior Overseers then take the stone between them, and after waving it backward and forward four times, they heave it over in such a manner that the one letting go while the stone is arriving at the highest point, it brings the stone in a quarterly direction over the other's left shoulder; the Junior Overseer, being stationed in a suitable position, at this moment receives the stone, and carries it away into the preparation room. R. W. M.—"Brother Senior Warden, assemble the crafts to receive wages." At this command the brethren all arise, and form a procession single file; the candidate is placed at the head of the procession, and when stationed, is told that "the last shall be first, and the first last." The procession being formed, they commence singing the following song: "Mark Masters all appear," &c., and, at the same time, commence a circular march (against the course of the sun) around the room, giving all the signs during their march, beginning with that of Entered Apprentice, and ending at that of Mark Master. They are given in the following manner: The first revolution each brother, when opposite the Right Worshipful Master, gives the first sign in Masonry. The second revolution, when opposite the Master, the second; and so on, until they give all the signs to that of Mark Master. While the ceremony is going on in the Lodge, the Senior Grand Warden procures a sufficient number of cents and passes into the preparation room, and opens a lattice window in the door which communicates to the Lodge room, and when the craftsmen arrive to the Mark Master Mason's sign, each of them, in their last revolution, puts his hand through the window in the door and gives a token (this is given by shutting the third and little fingers, extending the fore and middle fingers, and placing the thumb over them in a suitable manner to receive the penny or cent), and receives a penny or cent from the Senior Grand Warden. Matters are so timed in the march, that when they come to that part of the song which says, "Caution them to beware of the right hand," it comes the turn of the candidate to put his hand through the aperture of the door and receive his penny, but not being able to give the token, he is detected as an impostor, and the Senior Grand Warden, instead of giving him his penny, seizes him by the hand and draws his arm full length through the door and holds him securely, exclaiming at the same time, "An impostor! an impostor!" Others, who are in the room with the Senior Grand Warden, cry out, "Chop off his hand! chop off his hand!" At this moment the conductor steps to the candidate and intercedes warmly in his behalf. Cond.—"Spare him! spare him!" S. G. W.—"He is an impostor. He has attempted to receive wages without being able to give the token. The penalty must be inflicted." Cond.—"He is a brother Fellow Craft, and on condition that you will release him, I will be responsible that he shall be taken before the Right Worshipful Master, where all the circumstances shall be made known, and, if he condemns [Pg 65]him, I will see that the penalty is inflicted." S. G. W.—"On these conditions, I release him." The candidate is released, and taken before the Right Worshipful Master. Cond.—"This young Fellow Craft has brought up work for inspection, which was not his own, and has attempted to receive wages for it; he was detected at the Senior Grand Warden's apartment as an impostor, and I became responsible, on condition of his release, that he should appear before the Right Worshipful, and if, after a fair trial, you should pronounce him guilty, that I should see the penalty of an impostor inflicted upon him." R. W. M.—"Brother Junior Overseer, did this man bring up work to your station for inspection?" J. O.—"He did. I inspected it, and observed that it was neither an oblong nor a square, neither had it the regular mark of the craft upon it; but on account of its singular form and beauty, I was unwilling to reject it; therefore, I ordered it passed to the Senior Overseer's station at the West gate for further inspection." R. W. M.—"Brother Senior Overseer, did this young man bring up work to you for inspection?" S. O.—"He did; and I, for similar reasons offered by Brother Junior Overseer, was unwilling to reject it, and ordered it passed on to the Master Overseer at the East gate for further inspection." R. W. M.—"Brother Master Overseer, did this young man bring up work to you for inspection?" M. O.—"He did. I inspected the work, and observed that it was neither an oblong nor a square, neither had it the regular mark of the craft upon it; I then asked him if it was his work. He admitted that it was not. I asked him where he got it; he said he picked it up in the quarry. I rebuked him severely for his attempt to impose upon the Grand Overseers, and for loitering away his time, and then bringing up another man's work for inspection. I then called a council of my brother Overseers, and we, knowing no use for the work, hove it over among the rubbish." R. W. M.—"Senior Grand Warden, did the young man attempt to receive wages at your apartment?" S. G. W.—"He did, and I detected him as an impostor, and was about to inflict the penalty, but the conductor becoming responsible, that if I would release him, he would see the impostor taken before the Right Worshipful, and, if found guilty, that the penalty should be inflicted, I released him." R. W. M.—"Young man, it appears that you have been loitering away your time this whole week, and have now brought up another man's work for inspection, to impose upon the Grand Overseers, and what is more, you have attempted to receive wages for labor which you never performed; conduct like this deserves prompt punishment. The penalty of an impostor is that of having his right hand chopped off. This young man appears as though he deserved a better fate, and as though he might be serviceable in the building of the Temple. Are you a Fellow Craft?" Cand.—"I am." R. W. M.—"Can you give us any proof of it?" Candidate gives the sign of a Fellow Craft. R. W. M.—"He is a Fellow Craft. Have you ever been taught how to receive wages?" Cand.—"I have not." R. W. M.—"This serves, in a measure, to mitigate his crime. If you are instructed how to receive wages, will you do better in future, and never again attempt to impose on the Grand Overseers, and, above all, never attempt to receive wages for [Pg 66]labor which you never performed." Cand.—"I will." R. W. M.—"The penalty is remitted." The candidate is then taken into the preparation room and divested of his outward apparel, and all money and valuables, his breast bare, and a cable-tow four times around his body; in which condition he is conducted to the door, when the conductor gives four distinct knocks, upon the hearing of which the Senior Warden says to the Right Worshipful, "While we are peaceably at work on the fourth degree of Masonry, the door of our Lodge appears to be alarmed." R. W. M.—"Brother Junior, see the cause of that alarm." The Junior Warden then steps to the door and answers the alarm by four knocks, the conductor and himself each giving another; the door is then partly opened, and the Junior Warden then asks, "Who comes there?" Cond.—"A worthy brother, who has been regularly initiated as an Entered Apprentice, served a proper time as such; passed to the degree of Fellow Craft; raised to the sublime degree of a Master Mason; and now wishes further light in Masonry, by being advanced to the more honorable degree of a Mark Master Mason." J. W.—"Is it of his own free will and accord he makes this request?" Cond.—"It is." J. W.—"Is he duly and truly prepared?" Cond.—"He is." J. W.—"Has he wrought in the quarry, and exhibited specimens of his skill in the preceding degrees?" Cond.—"He has." J. W.—"By what further right or benefit does he expect to obtain this favor?" Cond.—"By the benefit of a pass-word." J. W.—"Has he a pass-word?" Cond.—"He has not, but I have it for him." J. W.—"Give it to me." Conductor whispers in his ear, "Joppa." J. W.—"The pass-word is right. You will let him wait until the Right Worshipful Master is made acquainted with his request and his answer returned." The Junior Warden returns him to the Right Worshipful Master, where the same questions are asked and answers returned, as at the door. The Right Worshipful Master then says, "Since he comes endowed with the necessary qualifications, let him enter in the name of the Lord, and take heed on what he enters. [Previous to the candidate's entering, one of the brethren, who is best qualified for the station, is selected and furnished with an engraving chisel and mallet, and placed near the door, so that when the candidate enters, it is on the edge of an engraving chisel, under the pressure of the mallet. As this is the business of no particular officer, we have, for convenience, styled him executioner.] Brother, it becomes my duty to put a mark on you, and such a one, too, as you will probably carry to your grave." Places the edge of the chisel near his left breast and makes several motions with the mallet, as though he was about to strike upon the head of the chisel. Executioner—"This is a painful undertaking; I do not feel able to perform it, Right Worshipful (turning to the Right Worshipful Master); this task is too painful; I feel that I cannot perform it; I wish the Right Worshipful would select some other brother to perform it in my stead." R. W. M.—"I know the task is unpleasant, and a painful one; but as you have undertaken to perform it, unless some other brother will volunteer his service and take your place, you must proceed." Exec—"Brother (calling the name), will you volunteer your service and take my place?" Brother—"I cannot consent to do it [Pg 67](after several solicitations and refusals)." Exec.—"Right Worshipful, no brother feels willing to volunteer his services, and I declare I feel unwilling and unable to perform it." R. W. M.—"As no brother feels disposed to take your station, it becomes your duty to perform it yourself." Exec. (taking his station) "Brethren, support the candidate (several take hold of the candidate); brother (naming some physician or surgeon), will you assist?" Doctor (stepping up)—"Brethren, it becomes necessary that we should have a bowl, or some other vessel, to receive the blood." A bowl is presented, having the appearance of blood upon it, and is held in a suitable position to receive the blood; the surgeon places his fingers on the left breast of the candidate, and gives counsel where it would be advisable to inflict the wound. The executioner then places the edge of the chisel near the spot and draws back the mallet, and while making several false motions, says, "Operative Masons make use of the engraving chisel and mallet to cut, hew, carve, and indent their work; but we, as Free and Accepted Masons, make use of them for a more noble and glorious purpose; we use them to cut, hew, carve, and indent the mind;" giving, at the instant the last word is pronounced, a severe blow with the mallet upon the head of the chisel, without the least injury to the candidate, which often terrifies him to an alarming degree. The candidate is then conducted four times around the Lodge, and each time, as he passes the station of the Master, Senior and

Junior Wardens, they each give one loud rap with their mallet; the Master, in the meantime, reads the following passages of Scripture: Psalms cxviii. 22. "The stone which the builders refused is become the headstone of the corner." Matt. xxi. 42. "Did ye never read in the Scriptures the stone which the builders rejected, the same is become the head of the corner?" Luke xx. 17. "What is this, then, that is written: The stone which the builders rejected, the same is become the head of the corner?" Acts iv. 11. "This is the stone which was set at nought of you builders which is become the head of the corner." The reading of them is so timed as to be completed just as the candidate arrives at the Junior Warden's post; here he stops, and the same questions are asked and answers returned, as at the door; the same passes at the Senior Warden and Master, who orders the candidate to be conducted back to the Senior Warden in the West, by him to be taught to approach the East by four upright regular steps, his feet forming a square, and body erect at the altar; the candidate then kneels and receives the obligation, as follows:

"I, A. B., of my own free will and accord, in presence of Almighty God, and this Right Worshipful Lodge of Mark Master Masons, do hereby and hereon, in addition to my former obligations, most solemnly and sincerely promise and swear, that I will not give the degree of a Mark Master Mason to anyone of an inferior degree, nor to any other person in the known world, except it be to a true and lawful brother or brethren of this degree, and not unto him nor unto them whom I shall hear so to be, but unto him and them only whom I shall find so to be, after strict trial and due examination, or lawful information given. Furthermore, do I promise and swear, that I will support the constitution of the General Grand Royal Arch Chapter of the United States of America, also the Grand Royal Arch Chapter of this State, under which this Lodge is held, and conform to all the by-laws, rules and regulations of this or any other Lodge of Mark Master Masons, of which I may at [Pg 68]any time hereafter become a member. Furthermore, do I promise and swear that I will obey all regular signs and summons given, handed, sent, or thrown to me from the hand of a brother Mark Master Mason, or from the body of a just and legally constituted Lodge of such, provided it be within the length of my cable tow. Furthermore do I promise and swear, that I will not wrong this Lodge, or a brother of this degree, to the value of his wages (or one penny), myself, knowingly, nor suffer it to be done by others, if in my power to prevent it. Furthermore, do I promise and swear, that I will not sell, swap, barter or exchange my mark, which I shall hereafter choose, nor send it a second time to pledge until it is lawfully redeemed from the first. Furthermore, do I promise and swear, that I will receive a brother's mark when offered to me requesting a favor, and grant him his request, if in my power and if it is not in my power to grant his request, I will return him his mark with the value thereof, which is half a shekel of silver, or quarter of a dollar. To all of which I do most solemnly and sincerely promise and swear, with a fixed and steady purpose of mind in me, to keep and perform the same, binding myself under no less penalty than to have my right ear smote off, that I may forever be unable to hear the word, and my right hand chopped off, as the penalty of an impostor, if I should ever prove wilfully guilty of violating any part of this my solemn oath or obligation of a Mark Master Mason. So help me God, and make me steadfast to keep and perform the same."

"Detach your hand and kiss the book"

The Master then produces the same keystone, concerning which so much has already been said, and says to the candidate, "We read in a passage of Scripture—Rev. II 17 'To him that overcometh will I give to each of the hidden manna, and will give him a white stone, and in the stone a new name written, which no man knoweth save him that receiveth it'" He then presents the stone to the candidate and says, 'I now present you with a white stone, on which is written a new name; we give the words that form this circle (the letters are so engraved on the stone as to form a circle), the initials are H T W S S T K S—Hiram Tyran, Widow's Son, sent to King Solomon. These, placed in this form were the mark of our Grand Master, Hiram Abiff. At present they are used as the general MARK of this degree, and in the centre of them each brother places his own individual MARK.' The stone is removed, and the candidate still remains on his knees at the altar, the Master then takes the jewel containing his mark from his neck and presents it to the candidate—requests of him some favor, such as the loan of five, ten, or twenty dollars. The candidate having left all his money and valuables in the preparation room, answers, "I cannot do it. I have no money about me," and offers to return the MARK to the Master, but he refuses to take it, and says to the candidate, "Have you not just sworn that you will receive a brother Mark Master's mark when offered to you, requesting a favor, and if not in your power to grant the favor, you would return him his mark with the value of it? Is this the way you mind your obligations? Here I presented my mark with a request for a small favor; you say you cannot grant it, and offer to return my MARK alone? Where is the quarter of a dollar you have sworn to return with it?" The candidate, much embarrassed, answers, "I cannot do even that. I have no money about me. It was all taken from me in the preparation room." The Master asks, "Are you quite sure you have none?" Candidate answers, "I am, it is all in the other room." [Pg 69]Master—"You have not examined; perhaps some friend has, in pity to your destitute situation, supplied you with that amount unknown to yourself; feel in all your pockets, and if you find, after a thorough search, that you have really none, we shall have less reason to think that you meant wilfully to violate your obligation." The candidate examines his pockets and finds a quarter of a dollar, which some brother had slyly placed there; this adds not a little to his embarrassment; he protests he had no intention of concealing it; really supposed he had none about him, and hands it to the Master, with his mark. The Master receives it and says to the candidate, "Brother, let this scene be a striking lesson to you: should you ever hereafter have a mark presented you by a worthy brother, asking a favor, before you deny him make diligent search, and be quite sure of your inability to serve him; perhaps you will then find, as in the present instance, that some unknown person has befriended you, and you are really in a better situation than you think yourself." The candidate then rises and is made acquainted with the grips, words, and signs of this degree. The pass-grip of this degree is made by extending the right arms and clasping the fingers of the right hands, as one would naturally do to assist another up a steep ascent; the pass-word is "Joppa;" the real grip is made by locking the little fingers of the right hand, bringing the knuckles together, placing the ends of the thumbs against each other; the word is "Mark well." The signs have been described. After the grips, words, and signs are given and explained (see Lectures), the Master says, "Brother, I now present you with the tools of a Mark Master (here he points them out in the carpet, or in the chart), which are the chisel and mallet; they are thus explained: The chisel morally demonstrates the advantages of discipline and education; the mind, like the diamond in its original state, is rude and unpolished, but as the effect of the chisel on the external coat soon presents to view the latent beauties of the diamond, so education discovers the latent beauties of the mind, and draws them forth to range the large field of matter and space, to display the summit of human knowledge, our duty to God and man. The mallet morally teaches to correct irregularities, and to reduce man to a proper level; so that by quiet deportment, he may, in the school of discipline, learn to be content. What the mallet is to the workmen, enlightened reason is to the passions; it curbs ambition, it depresses envy, it moderates anger, and it encourages good dispositions, whence arises among good Masons that comely order,

'Which nothing earthly gives, or can destroy,
The soul's calm sunshine, and the heartfelt joy.'"

The Worshipful Master then delivers a charge to the candidate, which completes the ceremony of advancement to this degree.

Ceremonies Generally Gone Through in Closing a Lodge of Mark Masons.

The Worshipful Master says, "Brother Junior Warden, assemble the brethren, and form a procession for the purpose of closing the Lodge." [Pg 70]The brethren then assemble and commence a circular march, singing the song, "Mark Masons all appear." After the song is completed, the brethren compare the wages they have received, and finding that all have received alike (one penny or cent), they begin to murmur among themselves, some pretending to think they ought to have more, as they have done all the labor. They finally throw down their wages upon the altar, declaring if they cannot be dealt justly with, they will have none. The Worshipful Master calls to order, and demands the cause of the confusion. Some brother answers, "Worshipful, we are not satisfied with the manner of paying the workmen, for we find those who have done nothing, and even the candidate just received, is paid just as much as we, who have borne the heat and burden of the day." Master says, "It is perfectly right." Brother—"It cannot be right—it is very unreasonable." Master—"Hear what the law says on the subject." He then reads the following parable—

169

Matt. XX. 1-16. "For the kingdom of heaven is like unto a man that is a householder, which went out early in the morning to hire laborers into his vineyard. And when he had agreed with the laborers for a penny a day, he sent them into his vineyard. And he went out about the third hour, and saw others standing idle in the market-place, and said unto them, 'Go ye also into the vineyard, and whatsoever is right, I will give you.' And they went their way. Again he went out about the sixth and ninth hour, and did likewise. And about the eleventh hour he went out and found others standing idle, and saith unto them, 'Why stand ye here all the day idle?' They say unto him, 'Because no man hath hired us.' He saith unto them, 'Go ye also into the vineyard, and whatsoever is right, that shall ye receive.' So when even was come, the lord of the vineyard said unto his steward, 'Call the laborers, and give them their hire, beginning from the last unto the first.' And when they came that were hired about the eleventh hour, they received every man a penny. But when the first came, they supposed that they should have received more, and they likewise received every man a penny. And when they had received it, they murmured against the good man of the house, saying, 'These last have wrought but one hour, and thou hast made them equal unto us, which have borne the burden and heat of the day.' But he answered one of them and said, 'Friend, I do thee no wrong; didst thou not agree with me for a penny? Take that thine is, and go thy way; I will give unto this last even as unto thee. Is it not lawful for me to do what I will with mine own? Is thine eye evil because I am good? So the last shall be first, and the first last; for many be called, but few chosen.'" The brethren then declare themselves satisfied; the signs are given from Mark Master down to the Entered Apprentice, and the Master declares the Lodge closed.

Lecture on the Fourth Degree of Masonry, or Mark Master's Degree.

FIRST SECTION.

Question—Are you a Mark Master Mason? Answer—I am; try me.

Q. By what will you be tried? A. By the engraving chisel and mallet.

[Pg 71]Q. Why by the engraving chisel and mallet? A. Because they are the proper masonic implements of this degree.

Q. On what was the degree founded? A. On a certain keystone which belonged to the principal arch of King Solomon's Temple.

Q. Who formed this keystone? A. Our worthy Grand Master, Hiram Abiff.

Q. What were the preparatory steps relative to your advancement to this degree? A. I was caused to represent one of the Fellow Craft at the building of King Solomon's Temple, whose custom it was, on the eve of every sixth day, to carry up their work for inspection.

Q. Why was you caused to represent these Fellow Crafts? A. Because our worthy Grand Master, Hiram Abiff, had completed this keystone agreeable to the original plan, and before he gave orders to have it carried up to the Temple, was slain by three ruffians, as already represented in the preceding degrees; and it so happened that on the eve of a certain sixth day, as the craft were carrying up work for inspection, a young Fellow Craft discovered this stone in the quarry, and from its singular form and beauty, supposing it to belong to some part of the Temple, carried it up for inspection.

Q. Who inspected it? A. The Grand Overseers, placed at the East, West, and South gates.

Q. How did they inspect it? A. On its being presented to the Junior Overseer at the South gate, he observed that it was neither an oblong or a square, neither had it the regular mark of the craft upon it; but from its singular form and beauty was unwilling to reject it, therefore ordered it to be passed to the Senior Overseer at the West gate for further inspection; who, for similar reasons, suffered it to pass to the Master Overseer at the East gate, who held a consultation with his brother Overseers, and they observed, as before, that it was neither an oblong or square, neither had it the regular mark of the craft upon it; and neither of them being Mark Master Masons, supposed it of no use in the building, and hove it over among the rubbish.

Q. How many Fellow Crafts were there engaged at the building of the Temple? A. Eighty thousand.

Q. Were not the Master Overseers liable to be imposed upon by receiving bad work from the hands of such a vast number of workmen? A. They were not.

Q. How was this imposition prevented? A. By the wisdom of King Solomon, who wisely ordered that the craftsman who worked should choose him a particular mark and place it upon all his work; by which it was known and distinguished when carried up to the building, and, if approved, to receive wages.

Q. What was the wages of a Fellow Craft? A. A penny a day.

Q. Who paid the craftsmen? A. The Senior Grand Warden.

Q. Was not the Senior Grand Warden liable to be imposed upon by impostors in paying off such a vast number of workmen? A. He was not.

Q. How was this imposition prevented? A. By the wisdom of King Solomon, who also ordered that every craftsman applying to receive wages, should present his right hand through a lattice window of the [Pg 72]door of the Junior Grand Warden's apartment, with a copy of his mark in the palm thereof, at the same time giving a token.

Q. What was that token? (This was before explained.)

Q. What did it allude to? A. To the manner of receiving wages; it was also to distinguish a true craftsman from an impostor.

Q. What is the penalty of an impostor? A. To have his right hand chopped off.

SECOND SECTION.

Question—Where was you prepared to be made a Mark Master Mason? A. In the room adjoining the body of a just and lawfully constituted Lodge of such, duly assembled in a room or place, representing a workshop that was erected near the ruins of King Solomon's Temple.

Q. How was you prepared? A. By being divested of all my outward apparel and all money; my breast bare, with a cable-tow four times about my body, in which situation I was conducted to the door of a Lodge, where I gave four distinct knocks.

Q. What do these four distinct knocks allude to? A. To the fourth degree of Masonry; it being that on which I was about to enter.

Q. What was said to you from within? A. Who comes there?

Q. Your answer? A. A worthy brother, who has been regularly initiated as an Entered Apprentice, served a proper time as such; passed to the Fellow Craft; raised to the sublime degree of a Master Mason; and now wishes further light in Masonry, by being advanced to the more honorable degree of a Mark Master Mason.

Q. What further was said to you from within? A. I was asked if it was of my own free will and accord I made this request; if I was duly and truly prepared; worthy and well qualified; had wrought in the quarries, and exhibited specimens of my skill and proficiency in the preceding degrees; all of which being answered in the affirmative, I was asked by what further right or benefit I expected to gain this favor.

Q. Your answer? A. By the benefit of a pass-word.

Q. What was that pass-word? A. Joppa.

Q. What did it allude to? A. The city of Joppa, the place where the materials were landed for building king Solomon's Temple, after being prepared in the forest of Lebanon, and carried there on floats (by sea). [Masonic tradition informs us that the banks of this place are so perpendicular that it was impossible to ascend them without assistance from above, which was effected by brethren stationed there, with this strong grip; this has been explained; which, together with the word Joppa, has since been adopted as a proper pass to be given before entering any well-regulated Lodge of Mark Master Masons.]

Q. What further was said to you from within? A. I was bid to wait till the Right Worshipful Master in the East was made acquainted with my request and his answer returned.

Q. When his answer was returned, what followed? A. I was caused to enter the Lodge.

Q. On what did you enter? A. On the edge of the engraving chisel, under the pressure of the mallet, which was to demonstrate the moral [Pg 73]precepts of this degree, and make a deep and lasting impression on my mind and conscience.

Q. How was you then disposed of? A. I was conducted four times regularly around the Lodge and halted at the Junior Warden's in the South, where the same questions were asked, and answers returned as at the door.

Q. How did the Junior Warden dispose of you? A. He ordered me to be conducted to the Senior Warden in the West, where the same questions were asked, and the same answers returned as before.

Q. How did the Senior Warden dispose of you? A. He ordered me to be conducted to the Right Worshipful Master in the East, where the same questions were asked, and answers returned as before; who likewise demanded of me from whence I came, and whither I was traveling.

Q. Your answer? A. From the West, and traveling to the East.

Q. Why do you leave the West and travel to the East? A. In search of light.

Q. How did the Right Worshipful Master dispose of you? A. He ordered me to be conducted back to the West, from whence I came, and put in the care of the Senior Warden, who taught me how to approach the East, the place of light, by advancing upon four upright regular steps to the fourth step, my feet forming a square, and my body erect at the altar before the Right Worshipful Master.

Q. What did the Right Worshipful Master do with you? A. He made a Mark Master Mason of me.

Q. How? A. In due form.

Q. What was that due form? A. Both knees bent, they forming a square, both my hands on the Holy Bible, Square, and Compass, my body being erect; in which posture I took upon me the solemn oath or obligation of a Mark Master Mason.

Q. Have you that oath or obligation? A. I have.

Q. Will you give it me? A. I will, with your assistance. [Here, as in the preceding degree, you repeat after the Right Worshipful Master, I, A. B., etc. See pages 67 and 68.]

Q. After your oath or obligation, what follows? A. Information was brought that the Temple was almost completed, but the craft was all in confusion for want of a certain keystone, which none of them had been instrumental to make.

Q. What followed? A. King Solomon believing in confidence, that our worthy Grand Master, Hiram Abiff, had completed this keystone agreeable to the original plan, ordered inquiry to be made among the Master Overseers, if a stone bearing a particular mark had been presented to them for inspection; and on inquiry being made, it was found that there had.

Q. What followed? A. King Solomon ordered search to be made for the stone, when it was found, and afterwards applied to its intended use.

Q. What color was the stone? A. White.

Q. What did it allude to? A. To a passage in Scripture, where it says, "To him that overcometh will I give to eat of the hidden manna, and I [Pg 74]will give him a white stone, and in the stone a new name written, which no man knoweth saving him that receiveth."

Q. What was that new name? A. The letters on the stone and the initials of the words for which they stand, viz.: H. T. W. S. S. T. K. S.

Q. Of what use is this new name to you in Masonry? A. It was the original mark of our worthy Grand Master, Hiram Abiff, and is the general mark of this degree, and the letters form the circle, in the centre of which every brother of this degree places his particular mark, to which his obligation alludes.

Q. What followed? A. I was more fully instructed with the secrets of this degree.

Q. Of what do they consist? A. Of signs and tokens.

Q. Have you a sign? A. I have.

Q. What is it called? A. Heave over.

Q. What does it allude to? A. To the manner of heaving over work that the Overseers said was unfit for the Temple; also the manner the keystone was hove over.

Q. Have you any other sign? A. I have (at the same time giving it).

Q. What is that? A. The due-guard of a Mark Master Mason.

Q. What does it allude to? A. To the penalty of my obligation; which is, that my right ear should be smote off, that I might forever be unable to hear the word, and my right hand be chopped off, as the penalty of an impostor, if I should ever prove wilfully guilty of revealing any part of my obligation.

Q. Have you any further sign? A. I have.

Q. What is that? A. The grand sign, or sign of distress.

Q. What does it allude to? A. To the manner the Fellow Crafts carry their work up to the Temple for inspection; also the manner I was taught to carry my work, on my advancement to this degree.

Q. Have you any other sign? A. I have not; but I have a token (gives it to him).

Q. What is this? A. The pass-grip of a Mark Master Mason.

Q. What is the name of it? A. "Joppa."

Q. What does it allude to? A. The city of Joppa.

Q. Have you any other token? A. I have.

Q. What is this? A. The real grip of a Mark Master Mason.

Q. What is the name of it? A. Mark well.

Q. What does it allude to? A. To a passage of Scripture, where it says, "Then he brought me back the way of the gate of the outward sanctuary, which looketh towards the East, and it was shut; and the Lord said unto me, son of man, mark well, and behold with thine eyes, and hear with thine ears, all that I say unto thee concerning all the ordinances of the house of the Lord, and the laws thereof, and mark well the entering in of the house, with the going forth of the sanctuary."

Q. Who founded this degree? A. Our three ancient Grand Masters, viz.: Solomon, King of Israel, Hiram, King of Tyre, and Hiram Abiff.

Q. Why was it founded? A. Not only as an honorary reward, to be conferred on all who have proved themselves meritorious in the preceding degrees, but to render it impossible for a brother to suffer for [Pg 75]the immediate necessities of life, when the price of his mark will procure them.

Q. A brother pledging his mark and asking a favor, who does he represent? A. Our worthy Grand Master, Hiram Abiff, who was a poor man, but on account of his great skill and mysterious conduct at the building of King Solomon's Temple, was most eminently distinguished.

Q. A brother receiving a pledge and granting a favor, whom does he represent? A. King Solomon, who was a rich man, but renowned for his benevolence.

THE PAST MASTER'S DEGREE.

This degree is very simple. It is necessary that a Master Mason should take this degree before he can, constitutionally, preside over a Lodge of Master Masons as Master of it; and when a Master Mason is elected Master of a Lodge, who has not previously received the Past Master's degree, it is then conferred upon him, often without any other ceremony than that of administering the obligation.

This Lodge is opened and closed in the same manner that the Lodges of the first three degrees are; the candidate petitions and is balloted for in the same manner, but he is received into the Lodge in a very different manner. He is conducted into the Lodge without any previous preparation, when the presiding officer rises and says, "Brethren, it is inconvenient for me to serve you any longer as Master of this Lodge. I wish you would select some other brother for that purpose." The candidate is nominated, the usual forms of balloting for officers are then dispensed with, and a vote of the Lodge is taken by yeas and nays. The candidate is elected, and generally refuses to serve, but he is eventually prevailed on to accept; whereupon the presiding officer addresses the Master-elect in the words following, viz.:

"Brother, previous to your investiture, it is necessary that you assent to those ancient charges and regulations, which point out the duty of a Master of a Lodge.

1. You agree to be a good man and true, and strictly to obey the moral law.

2. You agree to be a peaceable subject, and cheerfully to conform to the laws of the country in which you reside.

3. You promise not to be concerned in any plots or conspiracies against government; but patiently to submit to the decisions of the supreme legislature.

4. You agree to pay a proper respect to the civil magistrate, to work diligently, live creditably, and act honorably by all men.

5. You agree to hold in veneration the original rules and patrons of Masonry, and their regular successors, supreme and subordinate, according to their stations, and to submit to the awards and resolutions of your brethren when convened, in every case consistent with the constitution of the Order.

6. You agree to avoid private piques and quarrels, and to guard against intemperance and excess.

7. You agree to be cautious in carriage and behavior, cautious to your brethren, and faithful to your Lodge.

8. You promise to respect genuine brethren and discountenance impostors, and all dissenters from the original plan of Masonry.

9. You agree to promote the general good of society, to cultivate the social virtues, and to propagate a knowledge of the arts.

[Pg 76]10. You promise to pay homage to the Grand Master for the time being, and to his officer when duly installed, strictly to conform to every edict of the Grand Lodge or General Assembly of Masons that is not subversive of the principles and ground work of Masonry.

11. You admit that it is not in the power of any man, or body of men, to make innovations in the body of Masonry.

12. You promise a regular attendance on the committees and communications of the Grand Lodge, on receiving proper notice, and to pay attention to all the duties of Masonry on convenient occasions.

13. You admit that no new Lodge can be formed without permission of the Grand Lodge, and that no countenance be given to any irregular Lodge, or to any person clandestinely initiated therein, being contrary to the ancient charges of the Order.

14. You admit that no person can be regularly made a Mason in, or admitted a member of any regular Lodge, without previous notice, and due inquiry into his character.

15. You agree that no visitors shall be received into your Lodge without due examination, and producing proper vouchers of their having been initiated into a regular Lodge."

The presiding officer then asks the Master-elect (candidate), the following question, which he must answer in the affirmative: Q. "Do you submit to these charges and promise to support these regulations as Masters have done, in all ages, before you?" A. "I do." The presiding officer then addresses him: "Brother A. B., in consequence of your cheerful conformity to the charges and regulations of the Order, you are now to be installed Master of this degree, in full confidence of your care, skill, and capacity, to govern the same. But previous to your investiture, it is necessary you should take upon yourself the solemn oath or obligation appertaining to this degree; if you are willing to take it upon you, you will please to kneel before the altar, when you shall receive the same." [Here Lodges differ very materially, but this is the most prevalent mode of proceeding.] The candidate then kneels on both knees, lays both hands on the Holy Bible, Square and Compass, and takes the following oath or obligation:

"I, A. B., of my own free will and accord, in presence of Almighty God, and this Right Worshipful Lodge of Past Master Masons, do hereby and hereon, most solemnly and sincerely promise and swear, in addition to my former obligations, that I will not give the degree of Past Master Mason, or any of the secrets pertaining thereto, to anyone of an inferior degree, nor to any person in the known world, except it be to a true and lawful brother or brethren Past Master Masons, or within the body of a just and lawfully constituted Lodge of such, and not unto him or unto them whom I shall hear so to be, but unto him and them only whom I shall find so to be, after strict trial and examination, or lawful information. Furthermore, do I promise and swear, that I will obey all regular signs and summons sent, thrown, handed, or given from the hand of a brother of this degree, or from the body of a just and lawfully constituted Lodge of Past Masters, provided it be within the length of my cable-tow. Furthermore, do I promise and swear, that I will support the constitution of the General Grand Royal Arch Chapter of the United States of America, also that of the Grand Chapter of the State of — — , under which this Lodge is held, and conform to all the by-laws, rules and regulations of this or any other Lodge, of which I may at any time hereafter become a member, so far as in my power. Furthermore, do I promise and swear, that I will not assist, or be present at the conferring of this degree upon any person who has not, to the best of my knowledge and belief, regularly received the degrees of Entered Apprentice, Fellow Craft, Master Mason, and Mark Master, or been elected Master of a regular Lodge of Master [Pg 77]Masons. Furthermore, do I promise and swear, that I will aid and assist all poor and indigent Past Master Masons, their widows and orphans, wherever dispersed around the globe, they applying to me as such, and I finding them worthy, so far as in my power, without material injury to myself or family. Furthermore, do I promise and swear, that the secrets of a brother of this degree, delivered to me in charge as such, shall remain as secure and inviolable in my breast as they were in his own, before communicated to me, murder and treason excepted, and those left to my own election. Furthermore, do I promise and swear, that I will not wrong this Lodge, or a brother of this degree, to the value of one cent, knowingly, myself, nor suffer it to be done by others, if in my power to prevent it. Furthermore, do I promise and swear, that I will not govern this Lodge, nor any other over which I may be called to preside, in a haughty, arbitrary, or impious manner; but will at all times use my utmost endeavors to preserve peace and harmony among the brethren. Furthermore, do I promise and swear, that I will never open a Lodge of Master Masons, unless there be present three regular Master Masons, besides the Tyler, nor close the same without giving a Lecture, or some section or part of a Lecture, for the instruction of the Lodge. Furthermore, that I will not, knowingly, set in any Lodge where anyone presides who has not received the degree of Past Master. [This last point is, in many Lodges, entirely omitted. In some, the two last.] All which I do most solemnly and sincerely promise and swear, with a fixed and steady purpose of mind, to keep and perform the same, binding myself under no less penalty than to have my tongue split from tip to root, that I might forever thereafter be unable to pronounce the word, if ever I should prove wilfully guilty of violating any part of this my solemn oath or obligation of a Past Master Mason. So help me God, and make me steadfast to keep and perform the same."

The obligation being administered, the candidate rises,[4] and the Master proceeds to give the sign, word, and grip of this degree, as follows: The sign (sometimes called the due-guard) is given by laying the edge of the thumb of the right hand in a vertical position on the centre of the mouth, high enough to touch the upper lip. The word is given by taking each other by the Master's grip, and pulling the insides of their feet together, when the Master whispers the word, "Giblem,"[5] in the ear of the candidate. Then they clap their left hand on each other's right arm, between the wrist and elbow, disengaging (at the same moment) their right hand from the Master's grip; they each seize the left arm of the other with their right hands, between the wrist and elbow, and (almost at the same instant) yielding their left hand hold on each other's right arm, and moving their left hands with a brisk motion, they clasp each other's right arm with their left hands, above the elbow, pressing their finger nails hard against the arms, as they shift their hands from place to place; and the Master says (in union with these movements), "From grips to spans, and from spans to grips: a twofold cord is strong, but a threefold cord is not easily broken." The Master then conducts the candidate to the chair, and, as he ascends the steps, the Master says, "Brother, I now have the pleasure of conducting you into the oriental chair of King Solomon;" places a large cocked hat on his head, and comes down to the front of the newly-installed Master, and [Pg 78]addresses him as follows: "Worshipful brother, I now present you with the furniture and various implements of our profession; they are emblematical of our conduct in life, and will now be enumerated and explained as presented. The Holy Writings, that great light in Masonry, will guide you to all truth; it will direct your path to the temple of happiness, and point out to you the whole duty of man. The Square teaches to regulate our actions by rule and line, and to harmonize our conduct by the principles of morality and virtue. The Compass teaches to limit our desires in every station; thus rising to eminence by merit, we may live respected, and die regretted. The Rule directs that we should punctually observe our duty; press forward in the path of virtue, and neither inclining to the right or to the left, in all our actions have ETERNITY in view. The Line teaches the criterion of moral rectitude; to avoid dissimulation in conversation and action, and to direct our steps to the path that leads to IMMORTALITY. The Book of Constitutions you are to search at all times; cause it to be read in your Lodge, that none may pretend ignorance of the excellent precepts it enjoins. Lastly, you receive in charge the by-laws of your Lodge, which you are to see carefully and punctually executed. I will also present you with the mallet; it is an emblem of power. One stroke of the mallet calls to order, and calls up the Junior and Senior Deacons; two strokes call up all the subordinate officers; and three, the whole Lodge." The following charge is then delivered to the newly-installed Master (alias candidate) by the former Master:

"Worshipful Master, being appointed Master of this Lodge, you cannot be insensible of the obligations which devolve on you as their head; nor of your responsibility for the faithful discharge of the important duties annexed to your appointment. The honor, usefulness, and reputation of your Lodge will materially depend on the skill and assiduity with which you manage its concerns; while the happiness of its members will be generally promoted, in proportion to the zeal and ability with which you propagate the genuine principles of our institution. For a pattern of information, consider the luminary of nature, which, rising in the East, regularly diffuses light and lustre to all within its circle. In like manner, it is your province to spread and communicate light and instruction to the brethren of your Lodge. Forcibly impress upon them the dignity and high importance of Masonry, and seriously admonish them never to disgrace it. Charge them to practice out of the Lodge those duties which they have been taught in it; and by amiable, discreet, and virtuous conduct, to convince mankind of the goodness of the institution, so that, when anyone is said to be a member of it, the world may know that he is one to whom the burdened heart may pour out its sorrows—to whom distress may prefer its suit—whose hand is guided by justice, and his heart expanded by benevolence. In short, by a diligent observance of the by-laws of your Lodge, the constitution of Masonry, and, above all, the Holy Scriptures, which are given as a rule and guide of your faith, you will be enabled to acquit yourself with honor and reputation, and lay up a crown of rejoicing which shall continue when time shall be no more."[6]

The Master then says to the newly-installed Master, "I now leave you to the government of your Lodge." He then retires to a seat, and, after a moment or two, rises and addresses the candidate (now in the chair as [Pg 79]Master), "Worshipful Master, in consequence of my resignation, and the election of a new Master, the seats of the Wardens have become vacant. It is necessary you should have Wardens to assist you in the government of your Lodge. The constitution requires us to elect our officers by ballot, but it is common, on occasions of this kind, to dispense with those formalities, and elect by ayes and noes; I move we do so on the present occasion." The question is tried and carried in the affirmative. The Master has a right to nominate one candidate for office, and the brethren one. Here a scene of confusion takes place, which is not easily described. The newly-installed Worshipful is made the butt for every WORTHY brother to exercise his wit upon. Half a dozen are up at a time, soliciting the Master to nominate them for Wardens, urging their several claims, and decrying the merits of others with much zeal, others crying out, "Order, Worshipful, keep order!" Others propose to dance, and request the Master to sing for them; others whistle, or sing, or jump about the room; or scuffle, and knock down chairs or benches. One proposes to call from labor to refreshment; another compliments the Worshipful Master on his dignified appearance, and knocks off his hat, or pulls it down over his face; another informs him that a lady wishes to enter. If the Master calls to order, every one obeys the signal with the utmost promptness, and drops upon the nearest seat; the next instant, before the Master can utter a word, all are on their feet again and as noisy as ever. Finally, a nominal election is effected, and some prudent member, tired of such a ridiculous confusion, moves that the Lodge be closed; which, being done, the poor (and if a stranger) much embarrassed candidate, has his big hat taken from him, and is reduced to the ranks; but, for his consolation, the Worshipful Master informs him that the preceding scene, notwithstanding its apparent confusion, is designed to convey to him, in a striking manner, the important lesson, never to solicit or accept any office or station for which he does not know himself amply qualified.

The Lecture on the fifth, or Past Master's degree, is divided into five sections. The first section treats of the manner of constituting a Lodge of Master Masons. The second treats of the ceremony of installation, including the manner of receiving candidates to this degree, as given above. The third treats of the ceremonies observed at laying the foundation stones of public structures. The fourth section, of the ceremony observed at the dedications of Masonic halls. The fifth, of the ceremony observed at funerals, according to ancient custom, with the service used on the occasion.

The foregoing includes all the ceremonies ever used in conferring the degree of Past Master; but the ceremonies are more frequently shortened by the omission of some part of them; the presenting of the "various implements of the profession," and their explanations, are often dispensed with; and still more often, the charge.

[Pg 80]

MOST EXCELLENT MASTER'S DEGREE.

Ceremonies Used in Opening a Lodge of Most Excellent Masters.

The Lodge being called to order, the Most Excellent Master says, "Brother Junior, are they all Most Excellent Masters in the South?" The Junior Warden replies, "They are, Most Excellent." Most Excellent Master to Senior Warden, "Brother Senior, are they all Most Excellent Masters in the West?" The Senior Warden replies, "They are, Most Excellent." M. E. M.— "They are in the East (gives one rap, which calls up both Deacons); Brother Junior Deacon, the first care of a Mason?" J. D.— "To see the door tyled, Most Excellent." M. E. M.— "Attend to that part of your duty, and inform the Tyler that we are about to open this Lodge of Most Excellent Masters, and direct him to tyle accordingly." Junior Deacon steps to the door and gives six knocks, which the Tyler answers with six more; Junior Deacon gives one more, which the Tyler answers with one; the door is then partly opened, when the Junior Deacon informs the Tyler that a Lodge of Most Excellent Masters is about to be opened, and tells him to tyle accordingly; and then returns to his place in the Lodge and says, "Most Excellent Master, the Lodge is tyled." M. E. M. "By whom?" J. D.—

"By a Most Excellent Master Mason without the door, armed with the proper implements of his office." M. E. M.—"His duty there?" J. D.—"To keep off all cowans and eavedroppers, and see that none pass and repass without permission from the chair." M. E. M.—"Your place in the Lodge, Brother Junior?" J. D.—"At the right hand of the Senior Warden in the West, Most Excellent." M. E. M.—"Your duty there, Brother Junior?" J. D.—"To wait on the Most Excellent Master and Wardens, act as their proxy in the active duties of the Lodge, and take charge of the door." M. E. M.—"The Senior Deacon's place in the Lodge?" J. D.—"At the right hand of the Most Excellent Master in the East." M. E. M.—"I thank you, brother. Your duty in the East, Brother Senior?" S. D.—"To wait on the Most Excellent Master and Wardens, act as their proxy in the active duties of the Lodge; attend to the preparation and introduction of candidates; and receive and welcome all visiting brethren." M. E. M.—"The Secretary's place in the Lodge, Brother Senior?" S. D.—"At the left hand of the Most Excellent Master in the East." M. E. M.—"I thank you, brother. Your business there, Brother Secretary?" Sec.—"The better to observe the Most Excellent Master's will and pleasure; record the proceedings of the Lodge, and transmit a copy of the same to the Grand Chapter, if required; receive all monies and money-bills from the hands of the brethren; pay them over to the Treasurer, and take his receipt for the same." M. E. M.—"The Treasurer's place in the Lodge?" Sec.—"At your right hand, Most Excellent." M. E. M.—"I thank you, brother. Your duty there, Brother Treasurer?" Treas.—"The better to observe the Most Excellent Master's will and pleasure; receive all monies and money-bills from the hands of the Secretary; keep a just and true account of the same; pay them out by order of the Most Excellent Master, and consent of the brethren." M. E. M.—"The Junior Warden's place in the Lodge?" [Pg 81]Treas.—"In the South, Most Excellent." M. E. M.—"I thank you, brother. Your business in the South, Brother Junior?" J. W.—"As the sun in the South, at high meridian, is the beauty and glory of the day, so stands the Junior Warden in the South, the better to observe the time of high twelve; call the craft from labor to refreshment; superintend them during the hours thereof; see that none convert the hours of refreshment into that of intemperance or excess; call them again in due season; that the Most Excellent Master may have honor, and they profit thereby." M. E. M.—"The Senior Warden's place in the Lodge?" J. W.—"In the West, Most Excellent." M. E. M.—"I thank you, brother. Your duty in the West, Brother Senior?" S. W.—"As the sun sets in the West to close the day, so stands the Senior Warden in the West, to assist the Most Excellent Master in the opening of his Lodge; take care of the jewels and implements; see that none be lost; pay the craft their wages, if any be due, and see that none go away dissatisfied." M. E. M.—"The Most Excellent Master's place in the Lodge?" S. W.—"In the East, Most Excellent." M. E. M.—"His duty in the East, Brother Senior?" S. W.—"As the sun rises in the East to open and adorn the day, so presides the Most Excellent Master in the East to open and adorn his Lodge; to set his craft to work; govern them with good and wholesome laws, or cause the same to be done." [In some Lodges the forgoing ceremonies are omitted.] M. E. M.—"Brother Senior Warden, assemble the brethren around the altar for the purpose of opening this Lodge of Most Excellent Master Masons." S. W.—"Brethren, please to assemble around the altar for the purpose of opening this Lodge of Most Excellent Master Masons." In pursuance of this request, the brethren assemble around the altar and form a circle, and stand in such a position as to touch each other, leaving a space for the Most Excellent Master; they then all kneel on their left knee and join hands, each giving his right hand brother his left hand, and his left hand brother his right hand; their left arms uppermost, and their heads inclining downward; all being thus situated, the Most Excellent Master reads the following portion of Scripture: Psalm xxiv.—"The earth is the Lord's and the fulness thereof; the world and they that dwell therein. For he hath founded it upon the seas, and established it upon the floods. Who shall ascend into the hill of the Lord? and who shall stand in his holy place? He that hath clean hands and a pure heart; who hath not lifted up his soul unto vanity, nor sworn deceitfully. He shall receive the blessing from the Lord, and righteousness from the God of his salvation. This is the generation of them that seek him, that seek thy face, O Jacob. Selah. Lift up your heads, O ye gates; and be ye lifted up, ye everlasting doors; and the King of glory shall come in. Who is this King of glory? The Lord, strong and mighty; the Lord, mighty in battle. Lift up your heads, O ye gates; even lift them up, ye everlasting doors; and the King of glory shall come in. Who is this King of glory? The Lord of hosts; he is the King of glory. Selah." The reading being ended, the Most Excellent Master then kneels, joins hands with the others, which closes the circle; they all lift their hands, as joined together, up and down six times, keeping time with the words as the Most Excellent Master repeats [Pg 82]them—one, two, three; one, two, three. This is masonically called balancing. They then rise, disengage their hands, and lift them up above their heads with a moderate and somewhat graceful motion; cast up their eyes, turning, at the same time, to the right, they extend their arms and then suffer them to fall loose and nerveless against their sides. This sign is said by Masons to represent the sign of astonishment, made by the Queen of Sheba, on first viewing Solomon's Temple. The Most Excellent Master now resumes his seat and says, "Brethren, attend to giving the signs." The Most Excellent Master then gives all the signs from an Entered Apprentice Mason up to the degree of Most Excellent Master; in which they all join and imitate him. M. E. M.— "Brother Senior Warden, you will please to inform Brother Junior, and request him to inform the brethren that it is my will and pleasure that this Lodge of Most Excellent Master Masons be now opened for dispatch of business, strictly forbidding all private committees, or profane language, whereby the harmony of the same may be interrupted, while engaged in their lawful pursuits, under no less penalty than the by-laws enjoin, or a majority of the brethren may see cause to inflict." S. W.—"Brother Junior, it is the will and pleasure of the Most Excellent Master, that this Lodge of Most Excellent Master Masons be now opened for dispatch of business, strictly prohibiting all private committees, or profane language, whereby the harmony of the same may be interrupted, while engaged in their lawful pursuits, under no less penalty than the by-laws enjoin, or a majority of the brethren may see cause to inflict." J. W.—"Brethren, you have heard the Most Excellent Master's will and pleasure, as communicated to me by Brother Senior—so let it be done."

Ceremonies of Initiation.

The Lodge being now opened and ready for the reception of candidates, the Senior Deacon repairs to the preparation room, where the candidate is in waiting, takes off his coat, puts a cable-tow six times around his body, and in this situation conducts him to the door of the Lodge, against which he gives six distinct knocks, which are answered by the same number by the Junior Deacon from within; the Senior Deacon then gives one knock, and the Junior Deacon answers by giving one more; the door is then partly opened by the Junior Deacon, who says, "Who comes there?" Senior Deacon—"A worthy brother, who has been regularly initiated as an Entered Apprentice Mason; passed to the degree of Fellow Craft; raised to the sublime degree of Master Mason; advanced to the honorary degree of a Mark Master Mason; presided in the chair as Past Master; and now wishes for further light in Masonry by being received and acknowledged as a Most Excellent Master." Junior Deacon—"Is it of his own free will and accord he makes this request?" Senior Deacon—"It is." J. D.—"Is he duly and truly prepared?" S. D.—"He is." J. D.—"Is he worthy and well qualified?" S. D.—"He is." J. D.—"Has he made suitable proficiency in the preceding degrees?" S. D.—"He has." J. D.—"By what further right or benefit does he expect to obtain this favor?" S. D.—"By the benefit of a [Pg 83]pass-word." J. D.—"Has he a pass-word?" S. D.—"He has not, but I have it for him." J. D.—"Will you give it to me?" S. D. whispers in the ear of the Junior Deacon the word, "Rabboni." [In many Lodges the Past Master's word, "Giblem" is used as a pass-word for this degree, and the word, "Rabboni," as the real word.] J. D.—"The word is right; since this is the case, you will wait until the Most Excellent Master in the East is made acquainted with your request, and his answer returned." Junior Deacon repairs to the Most Excellent Master in the East and gives six raps, as at the door. M. E. M.—"Who comes here?" J. D.—"A worthy brother, who has been regularly initiated as an Entered Apprentice Mason; passed to the degree of a Fellow Craft; raised to the sublime degree of a Master Mason; advanced to the honorary degree of Mark Master Mason; presided in the chair as Past Master: and now wishes for further light in Masonry by being received and acknowledged as a Most Excellent Master." M. E. M.—"Is it of his own free will and choice he makes this request?" J. D.—"It is." M. E. M.—"Is he duly and truly prepared?" J. D.—"He is." M. E. M.—"Is he worthy and well qualified?" J. D.—"He is." M. E. M.—"Has he made suitable proficiency in the preceding degrees?" J. D.—"He has." M. E. M.—"By what further right or benefit does he expect to obtain this favor?" J. D.—"By the benefit of a pass-word." M. E. M.—"Has he a pass-word?" J. D.—"He has not, but I have it for him." M. E. M.—"Will you give it to me?" Junior Deacon whispers in the ear of the Most Excellent Master the word, "Rabboni." M. E. M.—"The pass is right; since he comes endowed with all these necessary qualifications, let him enter this Lodge of Most Excellent Masters in the name of the Lord." The candidate is then conducted six times around the Lodge by the Senior Deacon, moving with the sun. The first time they pass around the Lodge, when opposite the Junior Warden, he gives one blow with the gavel; when opposite the Senior Warden he does the same; and likewise when opposite the Most Excellent Master. The second time around, each gives two blows; the third, three; and so on, until they arrive to six. During this time, the Most Excellent Master reads the following passage of Scripture:

Psalm cxxii. "I was glad when they said unto me, Let us go into the house of the Lord. Our feet shall stand within Thy gates, O Jerusalem. Jerusalem is builded as a city that is compact together. Whither the tribes go up, the tribes of the Lord, unto the testimony of Israel, to give thanks unto the name of the Lord. For there are set thrones of judgment, the thrones of the house of David. Pray for the peace of Jerusalem; they shall prosper that love thee. Peace be within thy walls, and prosperity within thy palaces. For my brethren and companions' sakes I will now say, Peace be within thee. Because of the house of the Lord, our God, I will seek thy good."

The reading of the foregoing is so timed as not to be fully ended until the Senior Deacon and candidate have performed the sixth revolution. Immediately after this, the Senior Deacon and candidate arrive at the Junior Warden's station in the South, when the same questions are asked and answers returned, as at the door (Who comes here, etc.). The Junior Warden then directs the candidate to pass on to the Senior [Pg 84]Warden in the West for further examination; where the same questions are asked and answers returned, as before. The Senior Warden directs him to be conducted to the Right Worshipful Master in the East for further examination. The Right Worshipful Master asks the same questions, and receives the same answers as before. He then says, "Please to conduct the candidate back to the West from whence he came, and put him in the care of the Senior Warden, and request him to teach the candidate how to approach the East, by advancing upon six upright regular steps to the sixth step, and place him in a proper position to take upon him the solemn oath or obligation of a Most Excellent Master Mason." The candidate is conducted back to the West, and put in care of the Senior Warden, who informs him how to approach the East, as directed by the Most Excellent Master. The candidate kneels on both knees, and places both hands on the leaves of an opened Bible, Square and Compass. The Most Excellent Master now comes forward and says, "Brother, you are now placed in a proper position to take upon you the solemn oath or obligation of a Most Excellent Master Mason; which, I assure you, as before, is neither to affect your religion or politics. If you are willing to take it, repeat your name and say after me." The following obligation is then administered:

"I, A. B., of my own free will and accord, in presence of Almighty God, and this Lodge of Most Excellent Master Masons, do hereby and hereon, in addition to my former obligations, most solemnly and sincerely promise and swear, that I will not give the degree of a Most Excellent Master to any of an inferior degree, nor to any other person or persons in the known world, except it be to a true and lawful brother or brethren of this degree, and within the body of a just and lawfully constituted Lodge of such; and not unto him nor them whom I shall hear so to be, but unto him and them only whom I shall find so to be, after strict trial and due examination, or lawful information. Furthermore, do I promise and swear, that I will obey all regular signs and summons given, handed, sent, or thrown to me from a brother of this degree, or from the body of a just and lawfully constituted Lodge of such, provided it be within the length of my cable-tow, if in my power. Furthermore, do I promise and swear, that I will support the constitution of the General Grand Royal Arch Chapter of the United States of America, also the Grand Royal Arch Chapter of the State of — —, under which this Lodge is held, and conform to all the by-laws, rules and regulations of this or any other Lodge, of which I may at any time hereafter become a member, Furthermore, do I promise and swear, that I will aid and assist all poor and indigent brethren of this degree, their widows and orphans, wheresoever dispersed around the globe, as far as in my power, without injuring myself or family. Furthermore, do I promise and swear, that the secrets of a brother of this degree, given to me in charge as such, and I knowing them to be such, shall remain as secret and inviolable in my breast as in his own, murder and treason excepted, and the same left to my own free will and choice. Furthermore, do I promise and swear, that I will not wrong this Lodge of Most Excellent Master Masons, nor a brother of this degree, to the value of anything, knowingly, myself, nor suffer it to be done by others, if in my power to prevent it; but will give due and timely notice of all approaches of danger, if in my power. Furthermore, do I promise and swear, that I will dispense light and knowledge to all ignorant and uninformed brethren at all times, as far as in my power, without material injury to myself or family. To all which I do most solemnly swear, with a fixed and steady purpose of mind in me, to keep and perform the same binding myself under no less penalty than to have my breast torn [Pg 85]open, and my heart and vitals taken from thence and exposed to rot on the dunghill, if ever I violate any part of this my solemn oath or obligation of a Most Excellent Master Mason. So help me God, and keep me steadfast in the due performance of the same."

"Detach your hands and kiss the book."

The candidate is now requested to rise, and the Most Excellent Master gives him the sign, grip, and word appertaining to this degree. The sign is given by placing your hands, one on each breast, the fingers meeting in the centre of the body, and jerking them apart as though you were trying to tear open your breast; it alludes to the penalty of the obligation. The grip is given by taking each other by the right hand, and clasping them so that each compresses the third finger of the other with his thumb. [If one hand is large and the other small, they cannot both give the grip at the same time.] It is called the grip of all grips, because it is said to cover all the preceding grips. The Most Excellent holds the candidate by the hand, and puts the inside of his right foot to the inside of the candidate's right foot, and whispers in his ear, "Rabboni." In some Lodges the word is not given in a whisper, but in a low voice. After these ceremonies are over, and the members seated, some noise is intentionally made by shuffling the feet. M. E. M.— "Brother Senior, what is the cause of this confusion?" S. W.— "Is not this the day set apart for the celebration of the copestone, Most Excellent?" M. E. M.— "I will ask Brother Secretary. Brother Secretary, is this the day set apart for the celebration of the copestone?" Secretary (looking in his book)— "It is, Most Excellent." M. E. M.— "Brother Senior Warden, assemble the brethren, and form a procession, for the purpose of celebrating the copestone." The brethren then assemble (the candidate stands aside, not joining in the procession), form a procession double file, and march six times around the Lodge, against the course of the sun, singing the following song, and giving all the signs from an Entered Apprentice to that of Most Excellent Master. When opposite the Most Excellent Master, the first time they march around the Lodge, each member gives the first sign of an Entered Apprentice, and preserves it until he nearly arrives opposite the Most Excellent a second time, then gives the second sign, and continues it in the same manner, and so of all others, up to that of this degree, saying,

All hail to the morning that bids us rejoice, The Temple's completed, exalt high each voice. The copestone is finished—our labor is o'er, The sound of the gavel shall hail us no more.
To the power Almighty, who ever has guided The tribes of old Israel, exalting their fame; To Him who hath governed our hearts undivided, Let's send forth our vows to praise His great name.

> Companions, assemble on this joyful day
> (The occasion is glorious!) the keystone to lay;
> Fulfilled is the promise, by the Ancient of Days,
> To bring forth the copestone with shouting and praise.

The keystone is now produced and laid on the altar.

There is no more occasion for level or plumb-line,[Pg 86] For trowel or gavel, for compass or square;[7] Our works are completed, the ark safely seated,[8] And we shall be greeted as workmen most rare.
Names, those that are worthy our tribes, who have shared, And proved themselves faithful, shall meet their reward; Their virtue and knowledge, industry and skill, Have our approbation—have gained our good will.
We accept and receive them,[9] Most Excellent Masters, Trusted with honor, and power to preside Among worthy craftsmen where'er assembled, The knowledge of Masons to spread far and wide.

Almighty Jehovah,[10] descend now and fill This Lodge with Thy glory, our hearts with good-will; Preside at our meeting, assist us to find True pleasure in teaching good-will to mankind.

Thy wisdom inspired the great institution, Thy strength shall support it till nature expire; And when the creation shall fall into ruin, Its beauty shall rise through the midst of the fire.

[At the time the ark is placed on the altar, there is also placed on it a pot of incense, to which fire is communicated by the Most Excellent Master, just as the last line of the song is sung; this pot to contain incense is sometimes an elegant silver urn; but if the Lodge is too poor to afford that, a common teapot, with spout and handle broken off, answers every purpose; for incense some pieces of paper are dipped in spirits of turpentine.]

The members now all join hands, as in opening; and, while in this attitude, the Most Excellent reads the following passage of Scripture:

2 Chron. vii. 1-4. "Now when Solomon had made an end of praying, the fire came down from heaven and consumed the burnt-offering and the sacrifices; and the glory of the Lord filled the house. And the priests could not enter into the house of the Lord, because the glory of the Lord had filled the Lord's house. And when all the children of Israel saw how the fire came down, and the glory of the Lord upon the house, they bowed themselves with their faces to the ground upon the pavement, and worshipped, and praised the Lord, saying, For He is good;[11] for His mercy endureth forever."

The members now balance six times as before; in opening, rise and balance six times more, disengage themselves from each other and take their seats; the Most Excellent Master then delivers the following charge to the candidate:

"Brother, your admittance to this degree of Masonry, is a proof of the good opinion the brethren of this Lodge entertain of your Masonic [Pg 87]abilities. Let this consideration induce you to be careful of forfeiting by misconduct and inattention to our rules, that esteem which has raised you to the rank you now possess.

"It is one of your great duties, as a Most Excellent Master, to dispense light and truth to the uninformed Mason; and I need not remind you of the impossibility of complying with this obligation without possessing an accurate acquaintance with the Lectures of each degree.

"If you are not already completely conversant in all the degrees heretofore conferred on you, remember, that an indulgence, prompted by a belief that you will apply yourself with double diligence to make yourself so, has induced the brethren to accept you.

"Let it, therefore, be your unremitting study to acquire such a degree of knowledge and information as shall enable you to discharge with propriety the various duties incumbent on you, and to preserve unsullied the title now conferred upon you of a Most Excellent Master."

After this a motion is made by some of the members to close the Lodge. This motion being accepted and received, the Most Excellent says, "Brother Junior Warden, you will please assemble the brethren around the altar for the purpose of closing this Lodge of Most Excellent Masters." The brethren immediately assemble around the altar in a circle, and kneel on the right knee, put their left arms over and join hands, as before; while kneeling in this position, the Most Excellent reads the following Psalm: Psalm cxxxiv. "Behold, bless ye the Lord, all ye servants of the Lord, which by night stand in the house of the Lord. Lift up your hands in the sanctuary, and bless the Lord. The Lord that made heaven and earth bless thee out of Zion." The Most Excellent then closes the circle as in opening, when they balance six times, rise and balance six times more, disengaging their hands, and give all the signs downwards, and declares the Lodge closed.

ROYAL ARCH DEGREE.

All legally constituted bodies of Royal Arch Masons are called Chapters, as regular bodies of Masons of the preceding degrees are called Lodges. All the degrees from Mark Master to Royal Arch are given under the sanction of Royal Arch Chapters. A person making application to a Chapter for admission, is understood as applying for all the degrees, unless he states in his application the particular degree or degrees he wishes to receive. If you ask a Mark Master if he belongs to a Chapter, he will answer yes, but has only been marked. If a person make application for all the degrees, and wishes to receive them all at one time, he is frequently balloted for only on the Mark degree, it being understood that if accepted on that, he is to receive the whole. The members of Chapters who have received all the degrees, style each other companions; if they have not received the Royal Arch degree, brothers. It is a point of the Royal Arch degree "not to assist, or be present at the conferring of this degree upon more or less than three candidates at one time." If there are not three candidates present, one or two companions, as the case may be, volunteer to represent candidates, so as to make the requisite number, or a TEAM, as it is technically styled, and accompany the candidate or candidates through all the stages of exaltation. Every Chapter must consist of a High Priest, King, Scribe, [Pg 88]Captain of the Host, Principal Sojourner, Royal Arch Captain, three Grand Masters of the Veils, Treasurer, Secretary, and as many members as may be found convenient for working to advantage. In the Lodges for conferring the preparatory degrees, the High Priest presides as Master, the King as Senior Warden, the Scribe as Junior Warden, the Captain of the Host as Marshal, or Master of Ceremonies, the Principal Sojourner as Senior Deacon, the Royal Arch Captain as Junior Deacon, the Master of the First, Second, and Third Veils as Junior, Senior, and Master Overseers; the Treasurer, Secretary and Tyler as officers of corresponding rank. The Chapter is authorized to confer the degrees by a charter, or warrant from some Grand Chapter.

The members being assembled, the High Priest calls to order, and demands of the Royal Arch Captain if all present are Royal Arch Masons. The Royal Arch Captain ascertains and answers in the affirmative. The High Priest then directs him to cause the Tyler to be stationed, which, being done, the High Priest says, "Companions, Royal Arch Masons, you will please to clothe, and arrange yourselves for the purpose of opening the Chapter." The furniture of the Chapter is then arranged, the companions clothed with scarlet sashes and aprons, and the officers invested with the proper insignia of their respective offices, and repair to their proper stations. The High Priest then demands whether the Chapter is tyled, and is answered the same as in the Lodge. The stations and duties of the officers are then recited (see Lecture, First Section). After the duties of the officers are recited, the High Priest directs the Captain of the Host to assemble the companions of the altar. The companions form a circle about the altar, all kneeling on the right knee, with their arms crossed, right arm uppermost and hands joined, leaving a space for the High Priest, who reads the following passage of Scripture:

2 Thess. iii. 6-18. "Now, we command you, brethren, that you withdraw yourselves from every brother that walketh disorderly and not after the tradition that ye have received of us, for yourselves know how ye ought to follow us, for we behaved not ourselves disorderly among you, neither did we eat any man's bread for nought, but wrought with labor and travail night and day, that we might not be chargeable to any of you; not because we have not power, but to make ourselves an ensample unto you to follow us. For even when we were with you, this we commanded you, that if any man would not work, neither should he eat. For we hear that there are some, which walk among you disorderly, working not at all, but are busybodies. Now them that are such, we command and exhort, that with quietness they work and eat their own bread. But ye, brethren, be not weary in well doing. And if any man obey not our word, note that man and have no company with him, that he may be ashamed. Yet count him not as an enemy, but admonish him as a

brother. Now the Lord of peace Himself, give you peace always. The salutation of Paul, with mine own hand, which is the token, so I write."

[The reader is requested to compare this with Scripture—he will observe that the name of the Savior is intentionally left out.] The High Priest then takes his place in the circle. The whole circle then balance with their arms three times three, that is, they raise their arms and let them fall upon their knees three times in concert, after a short pause three times more, and after another pause three times more. Then all break into squads of three and raise the living arch. This is done by each [Pg 89]companion taking his left wrist in his right hand, and with their left hands the three grasp each other's right wrists, and raise them above their heads. This constitutes the living arch, under which the Grand Omnific Royal Arch word must be given, but it must also be given by three times three. In opening the Chapter, this is done in the following manner: After the three have joined hands they repeat these lines in concert, and at the close of each line raise them above their heads and say, "As we three did agree, the sacred word to keep, and as we three did agree, the sacred word to search, so we three do agree to raise this Royal Arch." At the close of the last line they keep their hands raised, while they incline their heads under them, and the first whispers in the ear of the second the syllable, J A H; the second to the third, B U H, and the third to the first, L U N. The second then commences, and it goes around again in the same manner, then the third, so that each companion pronounces each syllable of the word.[12] They then separate, each repairing to his station, and the High Priest declares the Chapter opened.

The Lecture of the Royal Arch degree is divided into two sections. The first section designates the appellation, number and station of the several officers, and points out the purpose and duties of their respective stations.

Question—Are you a Royal Arch Mason? Answer—I am That, I am.

Q. How shall I know you to be a Royal Arch Mason? A. By three times three.

Q. Where was you made a Royal Arch Mason? A. In a just and lawfully constituted Chapter of Royal Arch Masons, consisting of Most Excellent, High Priest, King and Scribe, Captain of the Host, Principal Sojourner, Royal Arch Captain, and the three Grand Masters of the Veils, assembled in a room or place representing the tabernacle erected by our ancient brethren near the ruins of King Solomon's Temple.

Q. Where is the High Priest stationed, and what are his duties? A. He is stationed in the sanctum sanctorum. His duty, with the King and Scribe, to sit in the Grand Council, to form plans and give directions to the workmen.

Q. The King's station and duty? A. At the right hand of the High Priest, to aid him by his advice and council, and in his absence to preside.

Q. The Scribe's station and duty? A. At the left hand of the High Priest, to assist him and the King in the discharge of their duties, and to preside in their absence.

Q. The Captain of the Host's station and duty? A. At the right hand of the Grand Council, and to receive their orders and see them duly executed.

Q. The Principal Sojourner's station and duty? A. At the left hand of the Grand Council, to bring the blind by a way that they know not, to [Pg 90]lead them in paths they have not known, to make darkness light before them, and crooked things straight.

Q. The Royal Arch Captain's station and duty? A. At the inner veil, or entrance of the sanctum sanctorium, to guard the same, and see that none pass but such as are duly qualified, and have the proper pass-words and signets of truth.

Q. What is the color of his banner? A. White, and is emblematical of that purity of heart and rectitude of conduct, which is essential to obtain admission into the divine sanctum sanctorum above.

Q. The stations and duties of the three Grand Masters of the Veils? A. At the entrance of their respective Veils: to guard the same, and see that none pass but such as are duly qualified and in possession of the proper pass-words and tokens.

Q. What are the colors of their banners? A. That of the third, scarlet, which is emblematical of fervency and zeal, and the appropriate color of the Royal Arch degree. It admonishes us to be fervent in the exercise of our devotions to God, and zealous in our endeavors to promote the happiness of men. Of the second, purple, which being produced by a due mixture of blue and scarlet, the former of which is the characteristic color of the symbolic, or three first degrees, and the latter, that of the Royal Arch degree, is an emblem of union, and is the characteristic color of the intermediate degrees. It teaches us to cultivate and improve that spirit of harmony between the brethren of the symbolic degrees and the companions of the sublime degrees, which should ever distinguish the members of a society founded upon the principles of everlasting truth and universal philanthropy. Of the first, blue, the peculiar color of the three ancient or symbolical degrees. It is an emblem of universal friendship and benevolence, and instructs us that in the mind of a Mason those virtues should be as expansive as the blue arch of heaven itself.

Q. The Treasurer's station and duty? A. At the right hand of the Captain of the Host; his duty to keep a just and regular account of all the property and funds of the Chapter placed in his hands, and exhibit them to the Chapter when called upon for that purpose.

Q. The Secretary's place in the Chapter? A. At the left of the Principal Sojourner; his duty to issue the orders and notifications of his superior officers, record the proceedings of the Chapter proper to be written, to receive all moneys due to the Chapter, and pay them over to the Treasurer.

Q. Tyler's place and duty? A. His station is at the outer avenue of the Chapter, his duty to guard against the approach of cowans and eavesdroppers, and suffer none to pass or repass but such as are duly qualified.

The second section describes the method of exaltation to this sublime degree as follows: "Companion, you informed me, at the commencement of this Lecture, that you was made a Royal Arch Mason in a just and legally constituted Chapter of Royal Arch Masons."

Q. Where was you prepared to be a Royal Arch Mason? A. In a room adjacent to the Chapter.

[Pg 91]Q. How was you prepared? A. In a company of three I was hoodwinked, with a cable-tow seven times around our bodies; in which condition we were conducted to the door of the Chapter and caused to give seven distinct knocks, which were answered by a like number from within, and we were asked "Who comes there?"

Q. Your answer? A. Three brethren, who have been regularly initiated as Entered Apprentices; passed to the degree of Fellow Craft; raised to the sublime degree of Master Mason; advanced to the more honorable degree of Mark Master; presided as Masters in the chair; accepted and received as Most Excellent Masters, and now wish for further light in Masonry by being exalted to the more sublime degree of Royal Arch Masons.

Q. What was then said to you? A. We were asked if we were duly and truly prepared, worthy and well qualified; had made suitable proficiency in the preceding degrees, and were properly avouched for. All of which being answered in the affirmative, we were asked by what further right or benefit we expected to obtain this favor.

Q. Your answer? A. By the benefit of a pass-word.

Q. Had you that pass-word? A. We had not, but our conductor gave it to us.

Q. What was then said to you? A. We were directed to wait with patience till the Grand Council could be informed of our request and their pleasure known.

Q. What answer was returned? A. Let them enter under a living arch, and remember to stoop low, for he that humbleth himself shall be exalted.

Q. Did you pass under a living arch? A. We did.

Q. How were you then disposed of? A. We were conducted to the altar, caused to kneel, and take upon ourselves the solemn oath or obligation of a Royal Arch Mason.

Q. Have you that obligation? A. I have.

Q. Will you give it me?

A. "I, A. B., of my own free will and accord, in the presence of Almighty God, and this Chapter of Royal Arch Masons, erected to God, and dedicated to the Holy Order of St. John, do hereby and hereon, most solemnly and sincerely promise and swear, in addition to my former obligations, that I will not give the degree of Royal Arch Mason to to anyone of an inferior degree, nor to any other being in the known world, except it be to a true and lawful companion Royal Arch Mason, or within the body of a just and legally constituted Chapter of such; and not unto him or unto them whom I shall hear so to be, but unto him or them only whom I shall find so to be, after strict trial, due examination, or legal information received. Furthermore, do I promise and swear, that I will not give the Grand Omnific Royal Arch word, which I shall hereafter receive, neither in the Chapter nor out of it, except there be present two companions, Royal Arch Masons, who, with myself, make three, and then by three times three, under a living arch, not above my breath. Furthermore, that I will not reveal the ineffable characters belonging to this degree, or retain the key to them in my possession, but destroy it whenever it comes to my sight. Furthermore, do I promise and swear, that I will not wrong this Chapter, nor a companion of this degree, to the value of anything, knowingly, myself, nor suffer it to be done by others, if in my power to prevent it. Furthermore, do I promise and swear, that I will not be at the [Pg 92]exaltation of a candidate to this degree, at a clandestine Chapter, I knowing it to be such. Furthermore, do I promise and swear, that I will not assist, or be present at the exaltation of a candidate to this degree, who has not regularly received the degrees of Entered Apprentice, Fellow Craft, Master Mason, Mark Master, Past Master, Most Excellent Master, to the best of my knowledge and belief. Furthermore, that I will not assist or see more or less than three candidates exalted at one and the same time. Furthermore, that I will not assist, or be present at the forming or opening of a Royal Arch Chapter, unless there be present nine regular Royal Arch Masons. Furthermore, do I promise and swear, that I will not speak evil of a companion Royal Arch Mason, neither behind his back nor before his face, but will apprise him of approaching danger, if in my power. Furthermore, do I promise and swear, that I will not strike a companion Royal Arch Mason in anger, so as to draw his blood. Furthermore, do I promise and swear, that I will support the constitution of the General Grand Royal Arch Chapter of the United States of America, also the constitution of the Grand Royal Arch Chapter of the State under which this Chapter is held, and conform to all the by-laws, rules and regulations of this or any other Chapter of which I may hereafter become a member. Furthermore, do I promise and swear, that I will obey all regular signs, summons, or tokens given, handed, sent, or thrown to me from the hand of a companion Royal Arch Mason, or from the body of a just and lawfully constituted Chapter of such, provided it be within the length of my cable-tow. Furthermore, do I promise and swear, that I will aid and assist a companion Royal Arch Mason when engaged in any difficulty; and espouse his cause, so far as to extricate him from the same, if in my power, whether he be right or wrong. Also that I will promote a companion Royal Arch Mason's political preferment in preference to another of equal qualifications.[13] Furthermore, do I promise and swear, that a companion Royal Arch Mason's secrets, given to me in charge as such, and I knowing them to be such, shall remain as secure and inviolable in my breast as in his own, MURDER AND TREASON NOT EXCEPTED.[14] Furthermore, do I promise and swear, that I will be aiding and assisting all poor and indigent Royal Arch Masons, their widows and orphans, wherever dispersed around the globe, so far as in my power, without material injury to myself or family. All which, I do most solemnly and sincerely promise and swear, with a firm and steadfast resolution to perform the same, without any equivocation, mental reservation, or self-evasion of mind in me whatever; binding myself under no less penalty than that of having my skull smote off, and my brains exposed to the scorching rays of the sun, should I ever knowingly or wilfully violate or transgress any part of this my solemn oath or obligation of a Royal Arch Mason. So help me God, and keep me steadfast in the performance of the same."

Q. After receiving the obligation, what was said to you? A. We were told that we were now obligated and received as Royal Arch Masons, but as this degree was infinitely more important than any of the preceding, it was necessary for us to pass through many trials, and to travel in rough and rugged ways to prove our fidelity, before we could be entrusted with the more important secrets of this degree. We were further told that, though we could not discover the path we were to travel, we were under the direction of a faithful guide, who would "bring the blind by a way they knew not, and lead them in paths they had not known; who would make darkness light before them, and crooked [Pg 93]things straight; who would do these things, and not forsake them." (See Isa. xlii. 16.)

Q. What followed? A. We were caused to travel three times around the room, when we were again conducted to the altar, caused to kneel, and attend to the following prayer:

Supreme Architect of universal nature, who, by Thine Almighty Word, didst speak into being the stupendous arch of heaven! And for the instruction and pleasure of Thy rational creatures, didst adorn us with greater and lesser lights, thereby magnifying Thy power, and endearing Thy goodness unto the sons of men. We humbly adore and worship Thine unspeakable perfection! We bless Thee, that when man had fallen from his innocence and happiness, Thou didst leave him the powers of reasoning, and capacity of improvement and of pleasure. We thank Thee, that amidst the pains and calamities of our present state, so many means of refreshment and satisfaction are reserved to us while traveling the RUGGED PATH of life: especially would we, at this time, render Thee our thanksgiving and praise for the institution, as members of which we are, at this time, assembled, and for all the pleasures we have derived from it. We thank Thee, that the few here assembled before Thee, have been favored with new inducements, and been laid under new and stronger obligations of virtue and holiness. May these obligations, O Blessed Father! have their full effect upon us. Teach us, we pray Thee, the true reverence of Thy great, mighty, and terrible name. Inspire us with a firm and unshaken resolution in our virtuous pursuits. Give us grace diligently to search Thy word in the book of nature, wherein the duties of our high vocation are inculcated with divine authority. May the solemnity of the ceremonies of our institution be duly impressed on our minds, and have a happy and lasting effect on our lives! O Thou, who didst aforetime appear unto Thy servant Moses IN A FLAME OF FIRE OUT OF THE MIDST OF A BUSH, enkindle, we beseech Thee, in each of our hearts, a flame of devotion to Thee, of love to each other, and of charity to all mankind. May all Thy miracles and mighty works fill us with Thy dread, and Thy goodness impress us with the love of Thy holy name. May holiness to the Lord be engraven upon all our thoughts, words, and actions. May the incense of piety ascend continually unto Thee from the altar of our hearts, and burn day and night, as a sacrifice of sweet-smelling savor, well pleasing unto Thee. And since sin has destroyed within us the first temple of purity and innocence, may Thy heavenly grace guide and assist us in rebuilding a SECOND TEMPLE of reformation, and may the glory of this latter house be greater than the glory of the former! Amen. So mote it be.

Q. After the prayer what followed? A. We were again caused to travel three times around the room, during which the following passage of Scripture was read, and we were shown a representation of the bush that burned and was not consumed:

Exodus iii. 1-6. "Now Moses kept the flock of Jethro, his father-in-law, the priest of Midian; and he led the flock to the back side of the desert, and came to the mountain of God, even to Horeb. And the angel of the Lord appeared unto him in a flame of fire out of the midst of a bush, and he looked, and behold, the bush burned with fire, and the bush was not consumed. And Moses said, I will now turn aside and see this great sight, why the bush is not burned. And when the Lord saw that he turned aside to see, God called unto him out of the midst of the bush and said, Moses, Moses. And he said, Here am I. And He said Draw not nigh hither; put off thy shoes from off thy feet; for the place whereon thou standest is holy ground. Moreover he said, I am the God of thy father, the God of Abraham, the God of Isaac, and the God of Jacob. And Moses hid his face; for he was afraid to look upon God."

Q. What followed? A. We again traveled, while the following passage was read:

2 Chron xxxvi. 11-20. "Zedekiah was one and twenty years old when[Pg 94] he began to reign, and reigned eleven years in Jerusalem. And he did THAT WHICH WAS evil in the sight of the Lord, his God, AND humbled not himself before Jeremiah, the prophet, SPEAKING from the mouth of the Lord. And he also rebelled against King Nebuchadnezzar, and he stiffened his neck and hardened his heart from turning unto the Lord God of Israel. Moreover, all the chiefs of the priests and the people transgressed very much after all the abominations of the heathen: and polluted the house of the Lord which He had hallowed in Jerusalem. And the Lord God of their fathers sent to them by His messengers, rising up betimes and sending; because He had compassion on His people, and on His dwelling place. But they mocked the messengers of God, and despised His words, and misused His prophets, until the wrath of the Lord arose against His people, till THERE WAS no remedy. Therefore he brought upon him the King of the Chaldees, who slew their young men with the sword in the house of their sanctuary, and had no compassion on young men or maidens, old men, or him that stooped for age; he gave them all unto his hand. And all the vessels of the house of God, great and small, and the treasures of the house of the Lord, and treasures of the king, and of his princes; all THESE he brought to Babylon. And they burnt the house of God, and broke down the wall of Jerusalem, and burnt all the palaces thereof with fire, and destroyed all the goodly vessels thereof. And them that had escaped from the sword carried he away to Babylon; where they were servants to him and his sons, until the reign of the kingdom of Persia."

At the close of this there was a representation of the destruction of Jerusalem by Nebuchadnezzar, and the carrying captive of the children of Israel to Babylon. We were seized, bound in chains, and confined in a dungeon.

Q. What followed? A. We heard rejoicing, as of good news; the proclamation of Cyrus, King of Persia, was read in our hearing.

Ezra i. 1-3. "Now in the first year of Cyrus, King of Persia, the Lord stirred up the spirit of Cyrus, King of Persia, that he made a proclamation throughout all his kingdom, and put it also in writing, saying, Thus saith Cyrus, King of Persia, the Lord God of heaven hath given me all the kingdoms of the earth, and He hath charged me to build Him an house at Jerusalem, which is in Judah. Who is there among you of all his people? His God be with him, and let him go up to Jerusalem, which is in Judah, and build the house of the Lord God of Israel, which is in Jerusalem."

Q. What was then said to you? A. We were unbound and requested to go up to Jerusalem to assist in rebuilding the Temple, but objected, as we had no pass by which to make ourselves known to our brethren.

Q. What followed? A. The third chapter of Exodus, 13th and 14th verses, were read to us:

"And Moses said unto God, Behold! when I come unto the children of Israel, and shall say unto them, the God of your fathers hath sent me unto you, and they shall say to me, what is his name? What shall I say to them? And God said unto Moses, I am, that I am. And thus thou shalt say unto the children of Israel, I am hath sent me unto you."

We were directed to use the words, "I am, that I am" as a pass-word.

Q. What followed? A. We arose to go up to Jerusalem, and traveled over hills and valleys, rough and rugged ways, for many days; during which time, as we stopped occasionally, to rest and refresh ourselves, the following passages from the Psalms were read in our hearing for our consolation and encouragement [Psalms cxli, cxlii, cxliii]:

Psalm cxli. "Lord, I cry unto Thee; Make haste unto me; give ear[Pg 95] unto my voice. Let my prayer be set forth before Thee as incense, and the lifting up of hands as the evening sacrifice. Set a watch, O Lord, before my mouth; keep the door of my lips. Incline not my heart to any evil thing, to practice wicked works with men that work iniquity. Let the righteous smite me, it shall be a kindness: and let Him reprove me, it shall be an excellent oil. Mine eyes are unto Thee, O God the Lord; in Thee is my trust; leave not my soul destitute. Keep me from the snare which they have laid for me, and the gins of the workers of iniquity. Let the wicked fall into their own nets, while that I withal escape.

Psalm cxlii. I cried unto the Lord with my voice; with my voice unto the Lord did I make my supplication. I poured out my complaint before him; I showed before him my trouble. When my spirit was overwhelmed within me, then thou knewest my path. In the way wherein I walked, have they privily laid a snare for me. I looked on my right hand, and beheld, but there was no man that would know me; refuge failed me; no man cared for my soul. I cried unto Thee, O Lord; I said, Thou art my refuge and my portion in the land of the living. Attend unto my cry, for I am brought very low: deliver me from my persecutors; for they are stronger than I. Bring my soul out of prison, that I may praise Thy name.

Psalm cxliii. Hear my prayer, O Lord; give ear to my supplications; in Thy faithfulness answer me, and in Thy righteousness. And enter not into judgment with Thy servant; for in Thy sight shall no man living be justified. For the enemy hath persecuted my soul; he hath made me to dwell in darkness. Therefore is my spirit overwhelmed within me; my heart within me is desolate. Hear me speedily, O Lord; my spirit faileth; hide not Thy face from me, lest I be like unto them that go down into the pit. Cause me to hear Thy loving kindness in the morning; for in Thee do I trust; cause me to know the way wherein I should walk, for I lift up my soul unto Thee. Bring my soul out of trouble, and of Thy mercy cut off mine enemies; for I am Thy servant."

At length we arrived at Jerusalem, and presented ourselves at the first Veil of the Tabernacle.

Q. What was there said to you? A. The Master of the first Veil demanded of us, "Who comes there? Who dares approach this outer Veil of our sacred Tabernacle? Who comes here?"

Q. Your answer? A. Three weary travelers from Babylon. They then demanded of us who we were, and what were our intentions.

Q. Your answer? A. We are your own brethren and kindred of the tribe of Benjamin; we are the descendants of those noble families of Giblemites, who wrought so hard at the building of the first temple, were present at its destruction by Nebuchadnezzar, by him carried away captive to Babylon, where we remained servants to him and his sons till the first year of Cyrus, King of Persia, by whose order we were liberated, and are now returned to assist in rebuilding the house of the Lord, without expectation of fee or reward.

Q. What further was demanded, of you? A. The pass-word, "I am, that I am." After giving which, the Master of the Veil, assured of his full confidence in us as worthy brethren, commended us for our zeal and gave us the token and words to enable us to pass the second Veil.

Q. What are they? A. The token is an imitation of that which Moses was commanded to exhibit to the children of Israel, casting his rod upon the ground it became a serpent, and putting forth his hand and taking it again by the tail, it became a rod in his hand. The words are these, "Shem, Ham, and Japheth."

[Pg 96]Q. What followed? A. We were conducted to the second Veil, where the same questions were asked, and answers returned as before, with the addition of the pass-words and token given at the first Veil.

Q. What followed? A. The Master of the second Veil told us that we must be true and lawful brethren to pass thus far, but further we could not go without his pass and token, which he accordingly gave to us.

Q. What are they? A. The words are Shem, Japheth, and Adoniram; the token is putting the hand in the bosom, plucking it out again, in imitation of the second sign which Moses was directed to make to the Israelites, when putting his hand into his bosom and taking it out again, it became leprous as snow.

Q. How were you then disposed of? A. We were conducted onwards to the third Veil, when the same questions were asked, and answers returned as before, with the addition of the token and words last received.

Q. What followed? A. The Master of the third Veil then gave us the sign, words, and signet, to enable us to pass the fourth Veil, to the presence of the Grand Council.

Q. What are the words, sign, and signet? A. The words are Japheth, Shem, Noah; the sign, pouring water upon the ground, in imitation of Moses, who poured water upon the ground and it became blood; the signet is called the signet of truth, and is Zerrubbabel. It alludes to this passage, "In that day I will take thee, O Zerrubbabel, my servant, the son of Shealtiel, and will make thee as a signet; for I have chosen thee." [See Haggai, chap. ii. ver. 23.]

Q. What followed? A. We then passed to the fourth Veil, where, after answering the same questions, and giving the sign, words, and signet last received, we were admitted to the presence of the Grand Council, where the High Priest made the same demands as were made at the Veils, and received the same answers.

Q. What did the High Priest further demand of you? A. The signs from Entered Apprentice to Most Excellent Master in succession.

Q. What did he then say to you? A. He said we were truly three worthy Most Excellent Masters, commended us for our zeal and disinterestedness, and asked what part of the work we were willing to undertake.

Q. Your answer? A. That we were willing to undertake any service, however servile or dangerous, for the sake of forwarding so great and noble an undertaking.

Q. What followed? A. We were then furnished with a pick-axe, spade and crow, and were directed to repair to the northwest corner of the ruins of the old temple and commence removing the rubbish, to lay the foundation of the new, and to observe and preserve everything of importance and report to the Grand Council. We accordingly repaired to the place, and after laboring several days, we discovered what seemed a rock, but on striking it with the crow, it gave a hollow sound, and upon closer examination, we discovered in it an iron ring, by help of which we succeeded in removing it from its place, when we found it [Pg 97]to be the keystone of an arch, and through the aperture there appeared to be an immense vault curiously arched. We then took the stone and repaired to the Grand Council, and presented it for their inspection.

Q. What did the Grand Council then say to you? A. They told us that the stone contained the mark of our ancient Grand Master, Hiram Abiff; that it was truly a fortunate discovery, and that without doubt the vault contained things of the utmost consequence to the craft. They then directed us to repair again to the place and continue our researches.

Q. What followed? A. We returned again to the place and agreed that one of our number should descend by means of a rope, the middle of which was fixed firmly around his body, and if he wished to descend, he was to pull the rope in his right hand, if to ascend, that in his left. He accordingly descended, and in groping about, he found what appeared to be some ancient jewels, but the air becoming offensive, he pulled the rope in his left hand, and was immediately drawn out. We then repaired to the Grand Council, made our report, and presented the articles found, which they pronounced the jewels of our three ancient Grand Masters, Solomon, Hiram, and Hiram Abiff. They commended us highly for our zeal and fidelity, assured us that it was a fortunate discovery, that it would probably lead to still more important ones, and that our disinterested perseverance should not go unrewarded. They directed us to repair again to the place, and make what further discoveries lay in our power.

Q. What followed? A. We again returned to the place, and let down one of our companions as before. The sun having now reached its meridian height, darted its rays to the inmost recesses of the vault, and enabled him to discover a small chest or box, curiously wrought; but the air becoming exceedingly offensive, he gave the sign, and was immediately drawn out. We immediately repaired to the Grand Council and presented our discovery. On examination, the Grand Council pronounced it to be the ARK OF THE COVENANT, which was deposited in the vault by our ancient Grand Master for safe keeping. On inspecting it more closely, they found a key with which they opened it. The High Priest then took from it a book, which he opened, and read as follows:

Gen. i. 1-3. "In the beginning God created the heavens and the earth. And the earth was without form, and void; and darkness was upon the face of the deep; and the Spirit of God moved upon the face of the waters. And God said, Let there be light, and there was light."

Deut. xxxi. 24-26. "And it came to pass when Moses had made an end of writing the words of this law in a book, until they were finished, that Moses commanded the Levites, which bare the ark of the covenant of the Lord, saying, Take this book of the law and put it in the side of the ark of the covenant of the Lord your God, that it may be there for a witness against thee."

Ex. xxv. 21. "And thou shalt put the mercy-seat above, upon the ark, and in the ark thou shalt put the testimony that I shall give thee."

He then declared it to be the book of the law upon which the Grand Council, in an ecstasy of joy, exclaimed three times, "Long lost, now found, holiness to the Lord;" at the same time drawing their hands across their foreheads.

[Pg 98]Q. What further was found in the ark? A. A small vessel containing a substance, which, after the Council had examined, and the High Priest again read from the book of the law, Ex. xvi. 32-34, he pronounced to be manna:

"And Moses said, This is the thing which the Lord commanded; fill an omer of the manna to be kept for your generations, that they may see the bread wherewith I have fed you in the wilderness, when I brought you forth from the land of Egypt. And Moses said unto Aaron, Take a pot and put an omer full of manna therein, and lay it up before the Lord to be kept for your generations. As the Lord commanded Moses, so Aaron laid it up before the testimony, to be kept for a token."

The High Priest then took a rod from the ark, which, after he had read the following passage,

Numb. xvii. 10. "And the Lord said unto Moses, Bring Aaron's rod again before the testimony to be kept for a token."

He pronounced to be Aaron's rod, which budded and blossomed as the rose.

Q. Was there anything further found in the ark? A. There was a key to the ineffable characters belonging to

this degree, as follows   beginning at top of this diagram at the left hand angle. The upper left angle without a dot is A, the same with a dot is B, etc.

Q. What further was said to you? A. The High Priest read the following passage:

Exodus vi. 2, 3. "And God spake unto Moses, and said unto him, I am the Lord, and I appealed unto Abraham, unto Isaac, and unto Jacob, by the name of God Almighty, but by my name Jehovah was I not known to them."

He then informed us that the name of Deity, the divine Logos, or word, to which reference is made in John i. 1-5.

"In the beginning was the word, and the word was with God, and the word was God, the same was in the beginning with God, all things were made by Him, and without Him was not anything made that was made. In Him was life, and the life was the light of men. And the light shineth in darkness, and the darkness comprehendeth it not."

That this Logos or word was anciently written only in these sacred characters, and thus preserved from one generation to another. That this was the true Masonic word, which was lost in the death of Hiram Abiff, and was restored at the rebuilding of the temple, in the manner we had at that time assisted to represent.

Q. What followed? A. We were reminded of the manner in which we were sworn to give the Royal Arch word, were instructed in the manner, and finally invested with the all important word in due form.

Q. What is the Grand Royal Arch word? A. JAH BUH LUN.

Q. How is it to be given? A. Under a living arch by three times three, in low breath (see description of opening a Chapter).

[Pg 99]Q. What followed? A. We were presented with the signs belonging to this degree.

Q. Will you give me those signs? Answered by giving the signs thus: Raise the right hand to the forehead, the hand and arm horizontal; thumb towards the forehead, draw it briskly across the forehead, and drop it perpendicularly by the side. This constitutes the due-guard of this degree, and refers to the penalty of the obligation. The grand sign is made by locking the fingers of both hands together, and carrying them to the top of the head, the palms upward, alluding to the manner in which the brother who descended into the vault and found the ark, found his hands involuntarily placed to protect his head from the potent rays of the meridian sun.

Q. What followed. A. The High Priest then placed crowns upon our heads, and told us that we were now invested with all the important secrets of this degree, and crowned and received as worthy companions, Royal Arch Masons. He then gives the charge.

The second section of the Lecture on this degree states minutely the ceremonies and forms of exaltation (as the conferring of this degree is styled), but there seems to be some parts which require explanation. The Principal Sojourner conducts the candidate, and is considered as representing Moses conducting the children of Israel through the wilderness. He is usually dressed to represent an old man, bowed with age, with a mask on his face, and long beard hanging down upon his breast; is introduced to the candidate in the preparation room by the name of Moses. On entering the Chapter, the candidates are received under a "living arch;" that is, the companions arrange themselves in a line on each side of the door, and each joins hands with the one opposite to himself. The candidates entering, the conductor says, "Stoop low, brothers! we are about to enter the arches; remember that he that humbleth himself shall be exalted; stoop low, brothers, stoop low!" The candidates seldom pass the first pair of hands, or, in other words, the first arch, without being so far humbled as to be very glad to support themselves on all fours. Their progress may be imagined to be very slow; for, in addition to their humble posture, they are obliged to support on their backs the whole weight of the living arches above. The conductor, to encourage them, calls out occasionally, "Stoop low, brothers, stoop low!" If they go too slow to suit the companions, it is not unusual for some one to apply a sharp point to their bodies to urge them on; the points of the pasteboard crown answer quite well for this purpose. After they have endured this humiliating exercise as long as suits the convenience of the companions, they pass from under the living arches. The candidates next receive the obligation, travel the room, attend the prayer, travel again, and are shown a representation of the Lord appearing to Moses from the burning bush. This last is done in various ways. Sometimes an earthen pot is filled with earth, and green bushes set around the edge of it, and a candle in the centre; and sometimes a stool is provided with holes about the edge, in which bushes are placed, and a bundle of rags or tow, saturated with oil of turpentine, placed in the centre, to which fire is communicated. Sometimes a [Pg 100]large bush is suspended from the ceiling, around the stem of which tow is wound wet with oil of turpentine. In whatever way the bush is prepared, when the words are read, "He looked, and behold, the bush burned with fire," etc., the bandage is removed from the eyes of the candidates, and they see the fire in the bush,[15] and, at the words, "Draw not nigh hither; put off thy shoes," etc., the shoes of the candidates are taken off, and they remain in the same situation while the rest of the passage is read to the words, "And Moses hid his face; for he was afraid to look upon God." The bandage is then replaced, and the candidates again travel about the room, while the next passage of Scripture is read. [See Lecture.] At the words, "And break down the walls of Jerusalem," the companions make a tremendous crashing and noise, by firing pistols, overturning chairs, benches, and whatever is at hand; rolling cannon balls across the floor, stamping, etc., etc., and in the midst of the uproar the candidates are seized, a chain thrown about them, and they are hurried away to the preparation room. This is the representation of the destruction of Jerusalem, and carrying captive the children of Israel to Babylon. After a short time the proclamation of Cyrus is read, the candidates are unbound, and start to go to Jerusalem, to assist in rebuilding the temple. The candidates, still hoodwinked, are brought into the Chapter, and commence their journey over the rugged and rough paths. They are literally rough paths, sticks of timber framed across the path the candidate must travel, some inches from the floor, make no comfortable traveling for a person blindfolded. But this is not always the way it is prepared; billets of wood singly, or in heaps, ladders, nets of cord, etc., etc., are all put in requisition to form the rough and rugged paths, which are intended as a trial of the FIDELITY of the candidates. If they escape with nothing more than bruised shins they do well. They have been known to faint away under the severity of the discipline, and occasion the WORTHY companions much alarm. After traveling the rugged paths till all are satisfied, they arrive at the first Veil of the Tabernacle, give the pass-word, and pass on to the second, give the pass-words, and present the sign. This, it will be recollected, is in imitation of the sign which Moses was directed to make to the children of Israel. He threw his rod upon the ground and it became a serpent; he put forth his hand and took it by the tail, and it became a rod in his hand. The conductor is provided with a rod, made in the form of a snake, and painted to resemble one. This he drops upon the floor, and takes it up again. They then pass on to the next Veil, give the pass-word and make the sign (put the right hand in the bosom and pluck it out again); pass on to the next, give the pass-words and make the sign (pour water upon the ground), and are [Pg 101]ushered into the presence of the Grand Council. The Veils are four in number, and of the same color as the banners of the three Grand Masters of the Veils, and that of the Royal Arch Captain, blue, purple, scarlet and white, and have the same references and explanations. [See Lecture.] The Grand Council consists of the Most Excellent High Priest, King and Scribe. The High Priest is dressed in a white robe, with a breastplate of cut-glass, consisting of twelve pieces, to represent the twelve tribes of Israel; an apron, and a mitre. The King wears a scarlet robe, apron, and crown. The mitre and crown are generally made of pasteboard: sometimes they have them of the most splendid materials, gold and silk velvet; but these are kept for public occasions. The mitre has the words, "Holiness to the Lord" in gold letters across the forehead. The Scribe wears a purple robe, apron, and turban. After having satisfied the Grand Council that they are true brethren, and stated their object in coming to Jerusalem, the candidates are directed to commence the labor of removing the rubbish of the old temple preparatory to laying the foundation of the new. For the purpose of performing this part of the ceremony, there is in or near the Chapter a narrow kind of closet, the only entrance to which is through a scuttle at the top; there is placed over this scuttle whatever rubbish is at hand, bits of board, brick bats, etc., and among them the keystone. After the candidates are furnished with the tools (pick-axe, spade, and crow), they are directed to this place, and remove the rubbish till they discover the keystone. This they convey to the Grand Council, as stated in the Lecture. After the Grand Council have examined it, they pronounce it to be the work of the Grand Master, Hiram Abiff, and direct them to return and prosecute their researches, not doubting that they will make many important discoveries. The candidates return and let down one of their number by a rope; he finds three squares, is drawn out, and all proceed with them to the Grand Council. The Grand Council inspect them, and pronounce them to be the three ancient jewels that belonged to the three ancient Grand Masters, Solomon, Hiram and Hiram Abiff. The candidates then return to the vault and let down another of their number. Here, let it be remarked, some Chapters, for the purpose of lightening the labor of the candidates, call in the aid of machinery. A pulley is suspended over the vault, and the candidate is EXALTED from the bottom at the tail of a snatch block; the one last let down find at the bottom a small chest or box, upon which he gives the signal to be drawn out; he no sooner discovers the box than the air in the vault, in the language of the Lecture, "becomes exceedingly offensive." This is strictly true; for at the moment he takes up the box and is preparing to ascend, fire is communicated to a quantity of gunpowder at his feet, so that by the time he arrives at the top, he is so completely suffocated with the fumes of the powder, that he is almost deprived of the power of respiration or motion. The box is carried to the Grand Council and pronounced to be the ark of the covenant. It is opened, and a Bible taken out, and some passages read from it. [See Lecture.] One word respecting the representation of the ark. It ought to be a splendid box covered with gold, and some of them are really elegant; but the Chapter must [Pg 102]have such as it can afford; if it is too poor to procure splendid furniture, cheap articles are made to answer; for an ark, if the funds are low, a plain cherry or pine box will answer, and sometimes a cigar box is made the humble representation of the splendid ark, made by divine command, of shittim wood, and overlaid with pure gold. The High Priest takes then from the ark a vessel containing something to represent manna. This vessel is of various forms and materials, from an elegant silver urn to a broken earthen mug; and the substance contained is as various as the vessels in which it is deposited; such as a bit of sugar, a piece of cracker, or a few kernels of wheat. Whichever is used, the High Priest takes it out and gravely asks the King and Scribe their opinion of it; they say they think it is manna. The High Priest then looks at it intently and says, "It looks like manna;" smells it and says, "It smells like manna;" and then tastes it and says, "It is manna." The High Priest then takes from the ark a bit of an apple tree sprout, a few inches long, with some withered buds upon it, or a stick of a similar length, with some artificial buds upon it, which, after consulting with the King and Scribe, he pronounces Aaron's rod. He then takes out the key to the ineffable characters and explains it. This key is kept in the ark on four distinct pieces of paper. The key is marked on a square piece of paper, and the paper is then divided into four equal parts, thus: The outside lines represent the dimensions of the paper; the inside ones are the key, and the dotted ones, the section that is made of the whole for the purpose of keeping it secret, should any GRACELESS COWAN ever get possession of the sacred ark, and attempt to rummage its contents. The other part of the key x is made on the back of the same piece of paper, so that on putting them together, it shows equally plain. It is said that these characters were used by Aaron Burr, in carrying on his treasonable practices, and by that means made public; since which time they have been written and read from left to right. After the ceremonies are ended, the High Priest informs the candidates, in many or few words, according to his ability, that this degree owes its origin to Zerrubbabel and his associates, who rebuilt the temple by order of Cyrus, King of Persia. He informs them that the discovery of the secret vault and the inestimable treasures, with the long lost WORD, actually took place in the manner represented in conferring this degree, and that it is the circumstance upon which the degree is principally founded. The ceremony of closing a Chapter is precisely the same as at opening, to the raising of the living arch. The companions join hands by threes, in the same manner, and say in concert, "As we three did agree the sacred word to keep, as we three did agree the sacred word to search, so we three do agree to close this royal arch." They then break without giving the word, as the High Priest reads the following prayer:

"By the wisdom of the Supreme High Priest may we be directed, by His strength may we be enabled, and by the beauty of virtue may we be incited to perform the obligations here enjoined upon us; to keep inviolable the mysteries here unfolded to us, and invariably to practice all [Pg 103]those duties out of the Chapter, which are inculcated in it. (Response.) So mote it be. Amen."

The High Priest then declares the Chapter closed in due form.

KNIGHTS OF THE RED CROSS.

At the sound of the trumpet the line is formed. Master of Calvary to the Sir Knight Warden, "When a Council of Knights of the Red Cross is about to be formed and opened, what is the first care?" Warden— "To see the Council chamber duly guarded." M. C.—"Please to attend to that part of your duty, see that the sentinels are at their respective posts, and inform the Captain of the Guards that we are about to open a Council of Knights of the Red Cross for the dispatch of business." W.—"The sentinels are at their respective posts, and the Council chamber duly guarded." M. C.—"Are all present Knights of the Red Cross?" W.—"They are." M. C.—"Attention, Sir Knights, count yourselves from right to left—right files handle sword—draw sword—carry sword—right files to the left double—second division forward, march, halt—right about face!" Sir Knight Master of Infantry, accompanied by the sword-bearer and Warden— "Please inform the Sovereign Master that the lines are formed waiting his pleasure." At the approach of the Council the trumpet sounds. M. C.—"Form avenue (the Council pass); the Sovereign Master passes uncovered; recover arms, poise arms!" Sovereign Master—"Attention, Sir Knights; give your attention to the several signs of Masonry; as I do, so do you." [The Sir Knights give the signs from the first to the seventh degree.] S. M.—"Draw swords, and take care to advance and give the Jewish countersign—recover arms; take care to advance and give the Persian countersign—recover arms." S.M. to Sir Knight Master of the Palace—"Advance and give me the word of a Knight of the Red Cross; the word is right—receive it on your left." The word is then passed around; when it arrives at the Chancellor he says, "Sovereign Master of the Red Cross, word has arrived." S. M.—"Pass it on to me [he gives it to the Sovereign Master]. Sir Knight, the word is right." S. M. to Sir Knight Chancellor—"Advance and give me the grand sign, grip, and word of a Knight of the Red Cross; it is right—receive it on your left." The word passes around as before, as will hereafter be explained, and when arrived at the Master of the Palace, he says, "Sovereign Master, the grand sign, grip and word have arrived." S. M.—"Pass them on to me; Sir Knight, they are right. Left face—deposit helmets—centre face—reverse arms—to your devotions [the Sir Knights all kneel and repeat the Lord's prayer]—recover arms—left face—recover helmets—centre face—right about face—to your posts—march!"

First Section.

Question—Are you a Knight of the Red Cross? Answer—That is my profession.

Q. By what test will you be tried? A. By the test of truth.

[Pg 104]Q. Why by the test of truth? A. Because none but the good and true are entitled to the honors and privileges of this illustrious order.

Q. Where did you receive the honors of this illustrious order? A. In a just and regular Council of Knights of the Red Cross.

Q. What number compose a Council? A. There is an indispensable number and a constitutional number.

Q. What is the indispensable number? A. Three.

Q. Under what circumstances are they authorized to form and open a Council of Knights of the Red Cross? A. Three Knights of the Red Cross, being also Knight Templars, and hailing from three different

196

commanderies, may, under the sanction of a legal warrant from some regular Grand Encampment, form and open a Council of Knights of the Red Cross for the dispatch of business.

Q. What is a constitutional number? A. Five, seven, nine, eleven, or more.

Q. When composed of five, seven, nine, eleven, of whom does it consist? A. Sovereign Master, Chancellor, Master of the Palace, Prelate, Master of Cavalry, Master of Infantry, Master of Finance, Master of Dispatches, Standard-Bearer, Sword-Bearer, and Warder.

Q. Warder's station in the Council? A. On the left of the Standard-Bearer in the West.

Q. His duty? A. To announce the approach of the Sovereign Master; to see that the sentinels are at their respective posts, and the Council chambers duly guarded.

Q. Sword-Bearer's station in the Council? A. On the right of the Standard-Bearer in the West.

Q. His duty? A. To assist in the protection of the banner of our Order; to watch all signals from the Sovereign Master, and see his orders duly executed.

Q. Standard-Bearer's station? A. In the West.

Q. His duty? A. To display, support, and protect the banners of our Order.

Q. Why is the Standard-Bearer's station in the West? A. That the brilliant rays of the rising sun, shedding their lustre upon the banners of our Order, may encourage and animate all true and courteous Knights, and dismay and confound their enemies.

Q. Station of Master of Dispatches? A. In front of the Master of the Palace.

Q. His duty? A. To observe with attention the transactions of the Council; to keep a just and regular record thereof, collect the revenue, and pay the same over to the Master of Finance.

Q. Station of the Master of Finance? A. In front of the Chancellor.

Q. His duty? A. To receive in charge the funds and property of the Council, pay all orders drawn upon the Treasurer, and render a just and regular account when called for.

Q. Station of the Master of Infantry? A. On the right of the second division when separately formed: on the left of the whole when formed in line.

[Pg 105]Q. His duty? A. To command the second division or line of infantry, teach them their duty and exercise; also to prepare all candidates, attend them on their journey, answer all questions for them, and finally introduce them into the Council chamber.

Q. Station of the Master of Cavalry? A. On the right of the first division when separately formed, and on the right of the whole when formed in line.

Q. His duty? A. To command the first division or line of cavalry, teach them their duty and exercise; to form the avenue at the approach of the Sovereign Master, and prepare the lines for inspection and review.

Q. Prelate's station? A. On the right of the Chancellor.

Q. His duty? A. To preside in the Royal Arch Council; administer at the altar; to offer up prayers and adoration to Deity.

Q. Station of Master of the Palace? A. On the left of the Sovereign Master in the East.

Q. His duty? A. To see that the proper officers make all due preparations for the several meetings of the Council; to take special care that the Council chamber is in suitable array for the reception of candidates and the dispatch of business; to receive and communicate all orders issued by the Sovereign Master through the officers of the line.

Q. Chancellor's station? A. On the right of the Sovereign Master.

Q. His duty? A. To receive and communicate all orders and petitions; to assist the Sovereign Master in the discharge of his various duties, and in his absence to preside in the Council.

Q. Sovereign Master's station? A. In the East.

Q. His duty? A. To preside in the Council; confer this order of knighthood upon those whom his Council may approve; to preserve inviolable the laws and constitution of our Order; to dispense justice, reward merit, encourage truth, and diffuse the sublime principles of universal benevolence.

S. M.—"Sir Knight Chancellor, it is my will and pleasure that a Council of Knights of the Red Cross be now opened, and to stand open for the dispatch of such business as may regularly come before it at this time, requiring all Sir Knights now assembled, or who may come at this time, to govern themselves according to the sublime principles of our Order. You will communicate this to the Sir Knight Master of the Palace, that the Sir Knights present may have due notice thereof, and govern themselves accordingly." [The Sir Knight Chancellor communicates it to the Sir Knight Master of the Palace, and he to the Knights.] S. M.—"Return arms—right about face—to your posts—march—center face—Sir Knights, this Council is now open for the dispatch of business."

Second Section.

Question—What were the preparatory circumstances attending your reception to this illustrious Order? Answer—A Council of Royal Arch Masons being assembled in a room adjacent to the Council chamber, I was conducted to the door, where a regular demand was made by two, three, and two.

[Pg 106]Q. What was said to you from within? A. Who comes there?

Q. Your answer? A. Companion A. B., who has regularly received the several degrees of Entered Apprentice, Fellow Craft, Master Mason, Mark Master, Past Master, Most Excellent Master, and Royal Arch, and now solicits the honor of being regularly constituted a Knight of the Red Cross.

Q. What was then said to you? A. I was asked if it was of my own free will and accord that I made this request; if I was worthy and well qualified; if I had made suitable proficiency in the foregoing degrees, and was properly vouched for; all of which being answered in the affirmative, I was asked by what further right or benefit I expected to gain admittance.

Q. Your answer? A. By the benefit of a pass-word.

Q. Did you give that pass-word? A. I did, with the assistance of my companions. [Here the Royal Arch word is given as described in the Royal Arch degree.]

Q. What was then said to you? A. I was then directed to wait with patience till the Most Excellent Prelate should be informed of my request, and his answer returned.

Q. What was his answer? A. Let him be admitted.

Q. What was you then informed? A. The Most Excellent Prelate observed that the Council there assembled represented the Grand Council convened at Jerusalem, in the second year of the reign of Darius, King of Persia, to deliberate on the unhappy state of the fraternity during the reigns of Artaxerxes and Ahasuerus, and to devise some means to obtain favor of the new Sovereign, and to gain his consent to proceed in rebuilding their new city and temple.

Q. What followed? A. The Most Excellent Prelate then informed me if I was desirous of attending the deliberations of the Council at this time, it was necessary that I should assume the name and character of Zerrubbabel, a prince of the house of Judah, whose hands laid the foundation of the second temple, and whose hands the Lord has promised should complete it.

Q. What followed? A. The Most Excellent Prelate then read a lesson from the records of the Fathers, stating the impediments with which they were troubled by their adversaries on the other side of the river, and the grievous accusations which were brought against them before the King.

Q. What followed? A. My conductor then addressed the Most Excellent Prelate thus: Most Excellent Prelate, our Sovereign Lord, Darius the King, having now ascended the throne of Persia, new hopes are inspired of protection and support in the noble and glorious undertaking which has been so long and so often interrupted by our adversaries on the other side of the river; for while yet a private man, he made a vow to God that should he ever ascend the throne of Persia, he would send all the holy vessels remaining at Babylon back to Jerusalem. Our Most Excellent and faithful companion, Zerrubbabel, who was formerly honored with the favorable notice and friendship of the Sovereign, now offers his services to encounter the hazardous enterprise of traversing [Pg 107]the Persian dominions, and seeking admission to the presence of the Sovereign, where the first favorable moment will be seized to remind the King of his vow, and impress on his mind the almighty force and importance of truth; and from his known piety no doubt can be entertained of gaining his consent, that our enemies be removed far hence, and that we be no longer hindered or impeded in our noble and glorious undertaking.

Q. What was the Most Excellent Prelate's reply? A. Excellent Zerrubbabel, the Council accept with gratification and joy your noble and generous offer, and will invest you with the necessary passports, by means of which you will be enabled to make yourself known to the favor of one Council wherever you may meet them; but in an undertaking of so much importance, it is necessary that you enter into a solemn obligation to be faithful to the trust reposed in you.

Q. What followed? A. The Most Excellent Prelate then invested me with a sword, to enable me to defend myself against my enemies, and said he was ready to administer the obligation.

Q. Did you consent to that obligation? A. I did, in due form.

Q. What was that due form? A. Kneeling on my left knee, my right foot forming a square, my body erect, my right hand grasping the hilt of my sword, my left hand covering the Holy Bible, Square, and Compass, with two cross-swords thereon, in which due form I took upon me the solemn oath and obligation of Knight of the Red Cross.

Q. Repeat the obligation.

"I, A. B., of my own free will and accord, in the presence of the Supreme Architect of the Universe, and these witnesses, do hereby and hereon most solemnly and sincerely promise and swear, that I will always hail, forever conceal, and never reveal, any of the secret arts, parts, or points of the mysteries appertaining to this Order of Knight of the Red Cross, unless it be to a true and lawful companion Sir Knight of the Order, or within the body of a just and lawful Council of such; and not unto him or them, until by due trial, strict examination, or lawful information, I find him or them lawfully entitled to receive the same. I furthermore promise and swear, that I will answer and obey all due signs and regular summons, which shall be sent to me from a regular Council of Knights of the Red Cross, or given to me from the hands of a companion Sir Knight of the Red Cross, if within the distance of forty miles; natural infirmities and unavoidable accidents only excusing me. I furthermore promise and swear, that I will not be present at the conferring of this Order of Knighthood upon any person, unless he shall have previously regularly received the several degrees of Entered Apprentice, Fellow Craft, Master Mason, Mark Master, Past Master, Most Excellent Master, and Royal Arch degree, to the best of my knowledge and belief. I furthermore promise and swear, that I will not assist or be present at the forming and opening of a Council of Knights of the Red Cross, unless there be present at least five regular Knights of the Order, or the representatives of three different Encampments, acting under the sanction of a legal warrant. I furthermore promise and swear, that I will vindicate the character of a courteous Sir Knight of the Red Cross when wrongfully traduced; that I will help him on a lawful occasion in preference to any brother of an inferior degree, and so far as truth, honor, and justice may warrant. I furthermore promise and swear, that I will support and maintain the by-laws of the Council, of which I may hereafter become a member, the laws and regulations of the Grand Encampment, under which the same may be holden, together with the constitution and ordinances of the General Grand Encampment of the United States of America, so far as the same shall come to my [Pg 108]knowledge. To all which I do most solemnly promise and swear, binding myself under no less penalty than of having my house torn down, the timbers thereof set up, and I hanged thereon; and when the last trump shall blow, that I be forever excluded from the society of all true and courteous Knights, should I ever wilfully or knowingly violate any part of this solemn obligation of Knight of the Red Cross; so help me God, and keep me steadfast to keep and perform the same."[16]

Q. What followed? A. The Most Excellent Prelate then directed me to rise and be invested with a countersign, which he informed me would enable me to make myself known to the friends of our cause wherever I should meet them, and would insure me from them succor, aid, and protection. [Here the Master of Infantry, who is the conductor, gives the candidate the Jewish countersign; it is given under the arch of steel; that is, their swords elevated above their heads, forming a cross, each placing his left hand upon the other's right shoulder, and whispering alternately in each other's ear the names of Judah and Benjamin.]

Q. What followed? A. The Most Excellent Prelate then invested me with a green sash, as a mark of our particular friendship and esteem; you will wear it as a constant memorial to stimulate you to the faithful performance of every duty, being assured that the memory of him, who falls in a just and virtuous cause, shall forever flourish like the green bay tree.

Q. What followed? A. I then commenced my journey, and was frequently accosted by guards, all of which, by means of the countersign I had received, I was enabled to pass in friendship, until I arrived at the bridge, which was represented to be in the Persian dominions; on attempting to pass this bridge, which I found strongly guarded, the Persian countersign was demanded, and being unable to give it, I was attacked, overpowered, and made prisoner.

Q. What followed? A. After remonstrating in vain against their violations, I told them I was a prince of the house of Judah, and demanded an audience with their sovereign.

Q. What was the answer? A. You are a prisoner, and can obtain an audience with the sovereign only in the garb of a captive and slave.

Q. Did you consent to this? A. I did; being firmly persuaded that could I by any means gain access to the presence of the sovereign, I should be able to accomplish the object of my mission.

Q. What followed? A. They then deprived me of my outward apparel, sash and sword, and having confined my hands and feet in chains, the links thereof were of a triangular form, they put sackcloth and ashes on my head.

Q. Why were the links of the captive's chain of a triangular form? A. The Assyrians having learned that among the Jews the triangle was an emblem of the Eternal, caused the links of their chain to be made of a triangular form, thinking thereby to add to the miseries of their captives.

[Pg 109]Q. What followed? A. I was conducted to the door of the Council chamber, where the alarm being given by 4 × 2, the Warder appeared and demanded, "Who comes there?"

Q. What answer was returned? A. A detachment of his majesty's guards, having made prisoner of one, who reports himself to be prince of the house of Judah.

Q. What was then said to you? A. I was asked from whence I came.

Q. Your answer? A. From Jerusalem.

Q. What was then demanded of you? A. Who are you?

Q. Your answer? A. The first among my equals, a Mason, and free by rank, but a captive and slave by misfortune.

Q. What was you then asked? A. My name.

Q. Your answer? A. Zerrubbabel.

Q. What were you then asked? A. What are your demands?

Q. Your answer? A. To see the sovereign, if possible.

Q. What was then said to you? A. I was then directed to wait with patience until the Sovereign Master should be informed of my request, and his answer returned.

Q. What was that answer? A. That the necessary caution should be taken that I was not armed with any hostile weapons, and that I should then be admitted.

Q. How were you then received? A. The guard being drawn up on the right and left of the throne, swords drawn, two of them placed at the door with swords crossed, under which I was permitted to enter, my face covered with my hands.

Q. How were you then disposed of? A. I was conducted in front of the Sovereign Master, who received me with kindness and attention, and listened with patience to my request.

Q. What did the Sovereign Master then observe to the Council? A. That this Zerrubbabel was the friend of his youth, that he could neither be an enemy nor a spy.

Q. What followed? A. The Sovereign Master thus addressed me: "Zerrubbabel, having now gained admittance into our presence, we demand that you immediately declare the particular motives which induced you, without our permission, and with force and arms, to pass the lines of our dominions?"

Q. Your answer? A. Sovereign Master, the tears and complaints of my companions at Jerusalem, who have been so long and so often impeded in the noble and glorious undertaking in which they were permitted to engage by our late sovereign, Lord Cyrus, the King; but our enemies having made that great work to cease by force and power, I have now come up to implore your majesty's clemency, that you would be pleased to restore me to favor, and grant me employment among the servants of your household.

Q. What was the Sovereign's reply? A. Zerrubbabel, I have often reflected with much pleasure upon our early intimacy and friendship, and I have frequently heard, with great satisfaction, of your fame as a wise and accomplished Mason, and having myself a profound veneration for that ancient and honorable institution, and having a sincere desire to [Pg 110]become a member of the same, I will this moment grant your request, on condition that you will reveal to me the secrets of Freemasonry.

Q. Did you consent to that? A. I did not.

Q. What was your reply? A. Sovereign Master, when our Grand Master Solomon, King of Israel, first instituted the fraternity of Free and Accepted Masons, he taught us that truth was a divine attribute, and the foundation of every virtue; to be good and true is the first lesson we are taught in Masonry. My engagements are sacred and inviolable: I cannot reveal our secrets. If I can obtain your majesty's favor only at the expense of my integrity, I humbly beg leave to decline your royal protection, and will cheerfully submit to any honorable exile.

Q. What was the Sovereign's reply? A. Zerrubbabel, your virtue and integrity are truly commendable, and your fidelity to your engagements is worthy of imitation; from this moment you are free—my guards will divest you of those chains and that garb of slavery, and clothe you in suitable habiliments to attend me at the banquet hall. Zerrubbabel, you are free; guards, strike off those chains; and may those emblems of slavery never again disgrace the hands of a Mason, more particularly a prince of the house of Judah; Zerrubbabel, we assign you a seat of rank and honor among the princes and rulers of our assembly.

Q. What followed? A. The guards being drawn up in the court yard, the Warder informed the Sovereign Master that the guards were in readiness, waiting his pleasure.

Q. What followed? A. He then ordered the guards to attend him to the banquet hall.

Q. What occurred there? A. After having participated in a liberal entertainment, the Sovereign Master not being inclined to sleep, and many of the guard having retired, he amused himself by entering into conversation with some of his principal officers and friends, proposing certain questions to them, and offering a princely reward to such as should give the most reasonable and satisfactory answer.

Q. What questions were proposed? A. Among others, "Which was the strongest, wine, the King, or woman?"[17]

Q. What answers were returned? A. The Chancellor said wine was the strongest; the Master of the Palace said the King was the strongest; but I, being firmly persuaded that the time had arrived in which I could remind the King of his vow, and request the fulfilment of it, replied that women were stronger than either of the former, but, above all things, truth beareth the victory.

Q. What followed? A. The King being deeply struck with the addition I made to the question, ordered us to be prepared with proper arguments in support of our respective propositions on the day following.

Q. What followed? A. On the day following, the Council being convened at the sound of the trumpet, the Chancellor was called upon for his answer, and thus replied: (See Templar's Chart of Freemasonry.)

Q. What followed? A. The Master of the Palace thus replied: (See Templar's Chart of Freemasonry.)

[Pg 111]Q. What followed? A. I then being called upon for my defence, answered as follows: (See Templar's Chart of Freemasonry.)

Q. What followed? A. The King being deeply struck with the force of the arguments I had used, involuntarily exclaimed, "Great is truth, and mighty above all things; ask what thou wilt, Zerrubbabel, and it shall be granted thee, for thou art found wisest among thy companions."

Q. Your answer? (See Templar's Chart of Freemasonry.)

Q. What followed? A. The Sovereign Master then addressed me: "Zerrubbabel, I will punctually fulfil my vow; letters and passports shall be immediately issued to my officers throughout the realm, and they shall give you, and those who accompany you, safe conveyance to Jerusalem, and you shall be no longer hindered or impeded in rebuilding your city and temple, until they shall be completed."

Q. What followed? A. The Sovereign Master then invested me with a green sash, and thus addressed me, "This green sash, of which you were deprived by my guards, I now with pleasure restore to you, and will make it one of the insignia of a new Order, calculated to perpetuate the remembrance of the event which caused the renewal of our friendship; its color will remind you that truth is a divine attribute and shall prevail, and shall forever flourish in immortal green. I will now confer on you the highest honor in our power at this time to bestow, and will create you the first Knight of an Order, instituted for the express purpose of inculcating the almighty force and importance of truth.

Q. What followed? A. The Sovereign Master then directed me to kneel, and said, By virtue of the high power in me vested, as the successor and representative of Darius, King of Persia, I now constitute you a Knight of the illustrious Order of the Red Cross (at the same time laying the blade of his sword first upon the right shoulder, then upon the head, and then upon the left shoulder of the candidate).

Q. What followed? A. The Sovereign Master then directed me to arise, and presenting me with a sword, thus addressed me: "This sword, of which you were deprived by my guards, I now restore in your hands, as a true and courteous Knight; it will be endowed with three most excellent properties—its hilt be faith, its blade be hope, its point be charity; it should teach us this important lesson, that when we draw our swords in a just and virtuous cause, having faith in God, we may reasonably hope for victory, ever remembering to extend the hand of charity to the fallen foe; sheathe it, and sooner may it rust in its scabbard than be drawn in the cause of injustice or oppression."

Q. What followed? A. The Sovereign Master then invested me with the Persian countersign.

Q. Give it? A. This countersign is given like the Jewish, excepting this variation, it is given over instead of under the arch of steel. The words are Tatnai Shethar-boznai, Enavdai.

Q. Who were they? A. They were governors of Persian provinces, and enemies of the Jews.

Q. What followed? A. The Sovereign Master then invested me with the Red Cross word.

[Pg 112]Q. Give it? A. (Each placing his left hand upon the other's right shoulder, at the same time bringing the point of the swords to each other's left side, in which position the word Libertas is given.)

Q. What followed? A. The Sovereign Master then invested me with the grand sign, grip, and word of Knight of the Red Cross.

Q. Give them. A. The grand sign is given by bringing the thumb and finger of the left hand to the mouth, and carrying it off in an oblique direction; the grip is given by interlacing the fingers of the left hand; the word is Veritas. The sign, grip, and word are given under the arch of steel.

Q. How do you translate the word? A. Truth.

Q. To what does the sign allude? A. To the blowing of the trumpet upon the walls and watch towers of the Council, but more particularly to the obligation, "that when the last trump shall sound, I shall be forever excluded from the society of all true and faithful Sir Knights."

Q. What is the motto of our Order? A. "Magna est veritas et prevalebit." [Great is truth, and will prevail.]

KNIGHT TEMPLAR, AND KNIGHT OF MALTA.

First Section.

Question—Are you a Knight Templar? Answer—That is my title.

Q. Where were you created a Knight Templar? A. In a just and lawful Encampment of Knight Templars.

Q. What number composes a just and lawful Encampment of Knight Templars? A. There is an indispensable number and a constitutional number.

Q. What is an indispensable number? A. Three.

Q. Under what circumstances are they authorized to form and open an Encampment of Knight Templars? A. Three Knight Templars, hailing from three different commanderies, may, under the sanction of a charter or warrant from some regular Grand Encampment, form and open an Encampment for the dispatch of business.

Q. What is a constitutional number? A. Seven, nine, eleven, or more.

Q. When composed of eleven, of whom does it consist? A. Warden, Sword-Bearer, Standard-Bearer, Recorder, Treasurer, Junior Warden, Senior Warden, Prelate, Captain-General, Generalissimo, and Grand Commander.

Q. Warden's station? A. On the left of the Standard-Bearer in the West, and on the left of the third division.

Q. His duty? A. To observe the orders and directions of the Grand Commander; to see that the sentinels are at their respective posts, and that the Encampment is duly guarded.

Q. Sword-Bearer's station? A. On the right of the Standard-Bearer in the West, and on the right of the third division.

Q. His duty? A. To assist in the protection of the banners of our Order; to watch all signals from the Grand Commander, and see his orders duly executed.

[Pg 113]Q. Standard-Bearer's station in the Encampment? A. In the West, and in the centre of the third division.

Q. His duty? A. To display, support, and protect the banners of our Order.

204

Q. Why is the Standard-Bearer's station in the West? A. That the brilliant rays of the rising sun, shedding their lustre upon the banners of our Order, may encourage and animate all true and courteous Knights, and dismay and confound their enemies.

Q. Recorder's station in the Encampment? A. In front of the Captain-General.

Q. His duty? A. To observe with attention the order of the Encampment; keep a just and regular record of the same; collect the revenue, and pay the same over to the Treasurer.

Q. Treasurer's station in the Encampment? A. In front of the Generalissimo.

Q. His duty? A. To receive in charge all funds and property of the Encampment; pay all orders drawn upon him, and render a just and faithful account when required.

Q. Station of the Junior Warden in the Encampment? A. At the southwest angle of the triangle, and on the left of the first division.

Q. His duty? A. To attend to all poor and weary pilgrims traveling from afar; to accompany them on the journey; answer all questions for them, and finally introduce them into the asylum.

Q. Senior Warden's station in the Encampment? A. At the northwest angle of the triangle, and on the right of the second division.

Q. His duty there? A. To attend on pilgrim warriors traveling from afar; to comfort and support pilgrims penitent, and after due trial, to recommend them to the hospitality of the Generalissimo.

Q. Prelate's station in the Encampment? A. On the right of the Generalissimo.

Q. His duty there? A. To administer at the altar, and offer up prayers and adorations to the Deity.

Q. Captain-General's station? A. On the left of the Grand Commander.

Q. His duty? A. To see that the proper officers make all suitable preparations for the several meetings of the Encampment, and take special care that the asylum is in a suitable array for the introduction of candidates and dispatch of business; also to receive and communicate all orders from the Grand Commander to officers of the line.

Q. Generalissimo's station? A. On the right of the Grand Commander.

Q. His duty? A. To receive and communicate all orders, signals, and petitions, and assist the Grand Commander in the discharge of his various duties, and in his absence to govern the Encampment.

Q. Grand Commander's station? A. In the East.

Q. His duty? A. To distribute alms, and protect weary pilgrims traveling from afar; to encourage pilgrim warriors; to sustain pilgrims penitent; feed the hungry, clothe the naked, bind up the wounds of the afflicted; to inculcate hospitality, and govern his Encampment with justice and moderation.

Second Section.

Question—What were the preparatory circumstances attending your reception into this illustrious Order? Answer—I was conducted to the chamber of reflection, where I was left in silence and solitude, to reflect upon three questions, which were left with me in writing.

Q. What were your answers? A. They were satisfactory to the Grand Commander; but as a trial of my patience and perseverance, he enjoined upon me the performance of seven years' pilgrimage, clothed in pilgrim's weeds.

Q. What followed? A. I was then invested with sandals, staff, and scrip, and commenced my tour of pilgrimage, but was soon accosted by the guard, who demanded of me, "Who comes there?"

Q. Your answer? A. A poor and weary pilgrim, traveling from afar, to join with those who oft have gone before, and offer his devotions at the holy shrine.

Q. What said the guard? A. Pilgrim, I greet thee; gold and silver have I none, but such as I have give I unto thee.

Q. What followed? A. After having participated in the refreshments (which is a glass of water and a cracker), the guard took me by the hand and thus addressed me, "Pilgrim, harken to a lesson to cheer thee on thy way, and insure thee of success."

Q. What followed? Lesson read. (See Templar's chart.) The guard then took me by the hand and said, "Fare thee well! God speed thee on thy way."

Q. What followed? A. I still pursued my pilgrimage, but was often accosted by guards, from whom I received the same friendly treatment as from the first.

Q. Where did your term of pilgrimage end? A. At the door of the asylum, where after giving the alarm by 3 × 3, the Warder appeared and demanded, "Who comes there?"

Q. Your answer? A. A poor and weary pilgrim, traveling from afar, who, having passed full three long years of pilgrimage, now craves permission, if it shall please the Grand Commander, forthwith to dedicate the remaining four years to deeds of more exalted usefulness, and if found worthy, his strong desire is now to be admitted to those valiant Knights, whose well-earned fame has spread both far and near for deeds of charity and pure beneficence.

Q. What were you then asked? A. What surety can you offer that you are no impostor?

Q. Your answer? A. The commendations of a true and courteous Knight, the Junior Warden, who recommends to the Grand Commander the remission of four remaining years of pilgrimage.

Q. What followed? A. The Grand Commander then addressed the Most Excellent Prelate: "This being true, Sir Knight, our Prelate, you will conduct this weary pilgrim to the altar, where having taken an obligation always to be faithful to his vow, cause him forthwith to be invested with a sword and buckler, that as a pilgrim warrior he may perform seven years' warfare as a trial of his courage and constancy."

[Pg 115]Q. What followed? A. The Senior Warden then detached a party of Knights to escort me to the altar, where, in due form, I took upon me the obligation of a Knight Templar.

Q. What was that due form? A. Kneeling on both knees upon two cross swords, my body erect, my naked hands covering the Holy Bible, Square, and Compass, with two cross swords lying thereon, in which due form I received the solemn obligation of Knight Templar.

Q. Repeat the obligation.

"I, A. B., of my own free will and accord, in the presence of Almighty God and this Encampment of Knight Templars, do hereby and hereon most solemnly promise and swear, that I will always hail, forever conceal, and never reveal, any of the secret arts, parts, or points appertaining to the mysteries of this Order of Knight Templars, unless it be to a true and lawful companion Knight Templar, or within the body of a just and lawful Encampment of such; and not unto him or them, until by due trial, strict examination, or lawful information, I find him or them lawfully entitled to receive the same. Furthermore do I promise and swear, that I will answer and obey all due signs and regular summons, which shall be given or sent to me from regular Encampments of Knight Templars, if within the distance of forty miles, natural infirmities and unavoidable accidents only excusing me. Furthermore do I promise and swear, that I will help, aid, and assist with my council, my purse, and my sword, all poor and indigent Knight Templars, their widows and orphans, they making application to me as such, and I finding them worthy, so far as I can do it without material injury to myself, and so far as truth, honor, and justice may warrant. Furthermore do I promise and swear, that I will not assist or be present at the forming and opening of an Encampment of Knight Templars, unless there be present seven Knights of the Order, or the representatives of three different Encampments, acting under the sanction of a legal warrant. Furthermore do I promise and swear, that I will go the distance of forty miles, even barefoot and on frosty ground, to save the life and relieve the distresses of a worthy Knight, should I know that his distresses required it, and my abilities permit. Furthermore do I promise and swear, that I will wield my sword in defence of innocent virgins, destitute widows, helpless orphans, and the Christian religion. Furthermore do I promise and swear, that I will support and maintain the by-laws of the Encampment, of which I may hereafter become a member, the edicts and regulations of the Grand Encampment, under which the same may be holden, together with the laws and constitution of the General Grand Encampment of the United States of America, so far as the same shall come to my knowledge. To all this I most solemnly and sincerely promise and swear, with a firm and steady resolution to perform and keep the same, without any hesitation, equivocation, mental reservation, or self-evasion of mind in me whatever, binding myself under no less penalty than to have my head struck off and placed on the highest spire in Christendom, should I knowingly or wilfully violate any part of this my solemn obligation of a Knight Templar; so help me God, and keep me steadfast to perform and keep the same."

Q. What followed? A. The Most Excellent Prelate directed me to arise, and thus addressed me: "Pilgrim, thou hast craved permission to pass through our solemn ceremonies, and enter the asylum of our Encampment; by thy sandals, scrip, and staff, I judge thee to be a child of humility; charity and hospitality are the grand characteristics of this magnanimous Order; in the characters of Knight Templars, you are bound to give alms to poor and weary pilgrims, traveling from afar; to succor the needy, feed the hungry, clothe the naked, and bind up the wounds of the afflicted. We here wage war against the enemies of innocent virgins, destitute widows, helpless [Pg 116]orphans, and the Christian religion. If thou art desirous of enlisting in this noble and glorious warfare, lay aside thy staff and take up the sword, fighting manfully thy way, and with valor running thy course; and may the Almighty, who is a strong tower and defence to all those who put their trust and confidence in him, be now and ever thy defence and thy salvation."

Q. What followed? A. Having laid aside my staff and taken up the sword, the Most Excellent Prelate continued: "Having now taken up the sword, we expect you will make a public declaration of the cause in which you will wield it."

Q. Your answer? A. I wield my sword in defence of innocent virgins, destitute widows, helpless orphans, and the Christian religion.

Q. What was the Prelate's reply? A. With confidence in this profession, our Senior Warden will invest you with the warrior's pass, and under his direction, as a trial of your courage and constancy, we must now assign you seven years of warfare—success and victory attend you. (The pass-word is Mahershalal-hashbaz, and is given under the arch of steel, as has been described.)

Q. What followed? A. I then commenced my tour of warfare, and made professions of the cause in which I would wield my sword.

Q. Where did your tour of warfare end? A. At the door of the asylum, where, on giving the alarm by 3 × 4, the Warder appeared and demanded, "Who comes there?"

Q. Your reply? A. A pilgrim warrior, traveling from afar, who, having passed full three long years of warfare, is most desirous now, if it should please the Grand Commander, to be admitted to the honors and rewards that await a valiant Templar.

Q. What was then demanded of you? A. What surety can you give that you are no impostor?

Q. Your answer? A. The commendation of a true and courteous Knight, the Senior Warden, who recommends to the Grand Commander the remission of the four remaining years of warfare.

Q. What was then demanded? A. By what further right or benefit do you expect to gain admittance to the asylum?

Q. Your answer? A. By the benefit of a pass-word.

Q. Give it. (Here the warrior's pass is given, as before described.)

Q. What was then said to you? A. I was directed to wait with courage and constancy, and soon an answer would be returned to my request.

Q. What answer was returned? A. Let him be admitted.

Q. What did the Grand Commander then observe? A. Pilgrim, having gained admittance to our asylum, what profession have you now to make in testimony of your fitness to be received a Knight among our number.

Q. Your answer? A. Most Eminent, I now declare, in truth and soberness, that I hold no enmity or hatred against a being on earth, that I would not freely reconcile, should I find him in a corresponding disposition.

Q. What was the Grand Commander's reply? A. Pilgrim, the sentiments you utter are worthy of the cause in which you are engaged; but [Pg 117]still we must require some stronger proofs of your faithfulness; the proofs we demand are, that you participate with us in five libations; this being accomplished, we will receive you a Knight among our number.

Q. What were the ingredients of the libations? A. Four of them were taken in wine and water, and the fifth in pure wine.

Q. What was the first libation? A. To the memory of Solomon, King of Israel.

Q. What was the second libation? A. To the memory of Hiram, King of Tyre.

Q. What was the third? A. To the memory of Hiram, the widow's son, who lost his life in defence of his integrity.

Q. What followed? A. The Grand Commander then addressed me: "Pilgrim, the Order to which you seek to unite yourself is founded on the Christian religion; let us, then, attend to a lesson from the holy evangelist."

Q. What followed? A. The Most Excellent Prelate then read a lesson relative to the apostasy of Judas Iscariot. (See Templar's Chart.)

Q. What followed? A. The Grand Commander then addressed me: "Pilgrim, the twelve tapers you see around the triangle, correspond in number with the disciples of our Saviour while on earth, one of whom fell by transgression, and betrayed his Lord and Master; and as a constant admonition to you always to persevere in the paths of honor, integrity, and truth, and as a perpetual memorial of the apostasy of Judas Iscariot, you are required by the rules of our Order to extinguish one of those tapers; and let it ever remind you that he who can basely violate his vow and betray his secret, is worthy of no better fate than Judas Iscariot." (The candidate extinguishes one of the tapers; the triangle is placed in the centre of the room, on which are twelve burning candles; between each candle stick a glass of wine; in the centre of the triangle is placed a coffin, on which are the Bible, skull and cross-bones.)

Q. What followed? A. The relics were then uncovered, and the Grand Commander thus addressed me: "Pilgrim, you here behold an emblem of mortality resting on divinity—a human skull resting on the Holy Scriptures; it is to teach us that among all the trials and vicissitudes which we are destined to endure while passing through the pilgrimage of this life, a firm reliance on divine protection can alone afford us the consolation and satisfaction which the world can neither give nor take away."

Q. What followed? A. The Most Excellent Prelate then read a lesson to me with respect to the bitter cup.

Q. What followed? A. The Grand Commander took the skull in his hand, and pronounced the following soliloquy: "How striking is this emblem of mortality, once animated, like us, but now it ceases to act or think; its vital energies are extinct, and all the powers of life have ceased their operations; and such, my brethren, is the state to which we are all hastening; let us, therefore, gratefully improve the remaining space of life, that when our weak and frail bodies, like this memento, shall become cold and inanimate and [Pg 118]mouldering in sepulchral dust and ruins, our disembodied spirits may soar aloft to the blessed regions, where dwell light and life eternal."

Q. What followed? A. The Most Excellent Prelate then read a lesson relative to the crucifixion. (See Templar's Chart.)

Q. What was the fourth libation? A. To the memory of Simon of Cyrene, the early friend and disciple of our Saviour, who was compelled to bear his cross, and fell a martyr to his fate.

Q. What followed? A. The Grand Commander then addressed me: "Pilgrim, before you can be permitted to participate in the fifth libation, we must enjoin on you one year's penance as a trial of your faith and humility, which you will perform under the direction of the Junior and Senior Wardens, with the skull in one hand, and a lighted taper in the other; which is to teach you that with faith and humility you should cause your light so to shine before men, that they, seeing your good works, may glorify our Father, which is in heaven."

Q. What followed? A. I then commenced my tour of penance, and passed in an humble posture through the sepulchre, where the fifth lesson was read by the Senior Warden relative to the resurrection. (Here the ascension of the Saviour is represented on canvas, which the candidate is directed to look at: at the same time the Sir Knights sing a hymn.) After the hymn, the Prelate speaks as follows:

"I am the resurrection and the life, saith the Lord; he that believeth on me, though he were dead, yet shall he be made alive; and whosoever liveth and believeth on me shall never die. Pilgrim, the scene before you represents the splendid conclusion of the hallowed sacrifice offered by the Redeemer of the world, to propitiate the anger of an offended Deity. This sacred volume informs us that our Saviour, after having suffered the pains of death, descended into the place of departed spirits, and that on the third day he burst the bands of death, triumphed over the grave, and, in due time, ascended with transcendent majesty to heaven, where he now sits on the right hand of our Heavenly Father, a mediator and intercessor for all those who have faith in Him. I now invest you with an emblem of that faith (at the same time suspends from his neck a black cross): it is also an emblem of our Order, which you will wear as a constant memorial, for you to imitate the virtues of the immaculate Jesus, who died that you might live. Pilgrim, the ceremonies in which you are now engaged are calculated deeply to impress your mind, and I trust will have a happy and lasting effect upon your character. You were first, as a trial of your faith and humility, enjoined to perform seven years of pilgrimage; it represents the great pilgrimage of life, through which we are all passing; we are all weary pilgrims, anxiously looking forward to that asylum, where we shall rest from our labors, and be at rest forever. You were then directed, as a trial of your courage and constancy, to perform seven years' warfare; it represents to you the constant warfare with the lying vanities and deceits of this world, in which it is necessary for us always to be engaged. You are now performing a penance as a trial of your humility. Of this our Lord and Saviour has left us a bright example. For though he was the Eternal Son of God, he humbled himself to be born of a woman, to endure the pains and afflictions incident to human nature, and finally to suffer a cruel and ignominious death upon the cross; it is also a trial of that faith which will conduct you safely over the dark gulf of everlasting death, and land your enfranchised spirit in the peaceful abodes of the blessed. Pilgrim, keep ever in your memory this awful truth; you know not how soon you may be called upon to render an account to that Supreme Judge, from whom not even the most minute action of your life is hidden; for although you now stand erect in all the strength [Pg 119]of manhood and pride of beauty, in a few short moments you may become a pale and lifeless corpse. This moment, even while I yet speak, the angel of death may receive the fatal mandate to strike you from the role of existence; and the friends who now surround you may be called upon to perform the last sad duty of laying you in the earth, a banquet for worms, and this fair body become as the relic you now hold in your hand. Man that is born of a woman is of few days and full of sorrow; he cometh up and is cut down like a flower; he fleeth as a shadow and continueth not; in the midst of life we are in death; of whom may we seek for succor but of Thee, O Lord, who for our sins are justly displeased. Yet, O God most holy, thou God most mighty, O holy and most merciful Saviour, deliver us from the pains of eternal death. I heard a voice from heaven saying unto me, write from henceforth, blessed are the dead that die in the Lord; even so, saith the spirit, for they rest from their labors; be ye also ready, and rest assured that a firm faith in the truths here revealed will afford you consolation in the gloomy hour of dissolution, and insure you ineffable and eternal happiness in the world to come. Amen and amen."

Q. Where did your tour of penance end? A. It has not yet ended; neither can it end until this mortal shall put on immortality; for all men err, and all error need repentance.

Q. Were you then permitted to participate in the fifth libation? A. I was.

Q. Where? A. Within the asylum.

Q. How gained you admittance there? A. After having passed my year of penance, I returned to the door of the asylum, where, on giving the alarm, the Warden appeared and demanded, "Who comes there?"

Q. Your answer? A. Pilgrim penitent, traveling from afar, who begs your permission here to rest, and at the shrine of our departed Lord to offer up his prayers and meditations.

Q. What was then demanded of you? A. What surety can he offer that he is no impostor?

Q. Your answer? A. The commendation of two true and courteous Knights, the Junior and Senior Wardens.

Q. What was then demanded of you? A. By what further right or benefit I expected to gain admittance.

Q. Your answer? A. By the benefit of a pass-word.

Q. Did you give that pass-word? A. I did not; my conductor gave it for me.

Q. Give it? A. Golgotha. (It is given as before described.)

Q. What was then said to you? A. Wait with faith and humility, and soon an answer shall be returned to your request.

Q. What was the answer of the Grand Commander? A. That I should be admitted.

Q. What did the Grand Commander then demand? A. Who have you there in charge, Sir Knight?

Q. What answer was returned? A. A pilgrim penitent, traveling from afar, who, having passed his term of penance, seeks now to participate in the fifth libation, thereby to seal his fate.

Q. What did the Grand Commander then observe? A. Pilgrim, in granting your request and receiving you a Knight among our number, I can only offer you a rough habit, coarse diet, and severe duties; if, on [Pg 120]these conditions, you are still desirous of enlisting under our banners, you will advance and kneel at the base of the triangle.

Q. What did the Grand Commander then observe? A. Pilgrim, the fifth libation is taken in the most solemn and impressive manner; we cannot be too often reminded that we are born to die; and the fifth libation is an emblem of that bitter cup of death, of which we must all sooner or later partake, and from which even the Saviour of the world, notwithstanding his ardent prayers and solicitations, was not exempt.

Q. What was then said to you? A. The Grand Commander asked me if I had any repugnance to participate in the fifth libation.

Q. Your answer? A. I am willing to conform to the requirements of the Order.

Q. What followed? A. I then took the cup (the upper part of the human skull) in my hand, and repeated after the Grand Commander the following obligation:

"This pure wine I now take in testimony of my belief in the mortality of the body and the immortality of the soul, and may this libation appear as a witness against me, both here and hereafter, and as the sins of the world were laid upon the head of the Saviour, so may all the sins committed by the person whose scull this was be heaped upon my head, in addition to my own, should I ever knowingly or wilfully violate or transgress any obligation that I have heretofore taken, take at this time, or shall at any future period take, in relation to any degree of Masonry, or Order of Knighthood. So help me God."

Q. What was this obligation called? A. The sealed obligation.

Q. Why so? A. Because any obligation entered into, or promise made in reference to this obligation, is considered by Knight Templars as more binding and serious than any other special obligation could be.

Q. What followed? A. The Most Excellent Prelate then read the sixth lesson, relative to the election of Matthias. (See Chart.)

Q. What followed? A. The Generalissimo thus addressed the Grand Commander: "Most Eminent, by the extinguished taper on the triangle, I perceive there is a vacancy in our Encampment, which I propose should be filled by a choice from among those valiant Knights who have sustained the trials and performed the ceremonies required by our Order."[18]

Q. What followed? A. The Grand Commander then ordered the lots to be given forth, which being done, I was elected, and the Grand Commander thus addressed me: "In testimony of your election as a companion among us, and of your acceptance of that honor, you will relight that extinguished taper; and may the Almighty lift upon you the light of His countenance, and preserve you from falling."

Q. What followed? A. The Grand Commander then directed me to kneel, and said by virtue of the high power in me vested, as the successor and representative of Hugh De Paganis, and Geoffrey, of St. Omers, I now dub and create you Knight Templar, Knight of Malta, of the Holy Order of St. John of Jerusalem. [This is repeated three times, at the same time laying the blade of the sword first upon the right shoulder, [Pg 121]then upon the head, and then upon the left shoulder of the candidate.]

Q. What followed? A. The Grand Commander then presented me a sword, and thus addressed me: "This sword in your hand, as a true and courteous Knight, will be endowed with three most excellent qualities; its hilt be justice impartial, its blade be fortitude undaunted, and its point be mercy; and let it teach us this important lesson, that we should ever be assured of the justice of the cause in which we draw our swords, and being thus assured, we should persevere with the most undaunted fortitude, and finally, having subdued our enemies, we should consider them no longer such, but extend to them the most glorious attribute of God's mercy."

Q. What followed? A. The Grand Commander then communicated to me the due-guard, the penitent's pass, and the grand sign, grip and word of Knight Templars.

Q. Give the due-guard? [The sign is given by placing the end of the right thumb under the chin.]

Q. To what does it allude? A. To the penalty of my obligation; to have my head struck off and placed upon the highest spire in Christendom.

Q. Give the penitent's pass? A. It is given as before described; the word is Golgotha.

Q. Give the grand sign. [This sign is given by placing yourself in a situation representing the crucifixion of Christ.]

Q. To what does this sign allude? A. To the manner in which the Saviour expired upon the cross, and expiated the sins of the world.

Q. Give the grip and word. [This grip is given by interlacing the fingers of the right and left hands of the candidate, which forms a cross.]

Q. What is the word? A. Immanuel. [The word is given at the time of giving the grip, and is the name of the grip.]

Q. What does the grip teach us? A. That as our fingers are thus strongly interlaced, so should the hearts of Knight Templars be firmly interlaced in friendship and brotherly love.

Q. What is the motto of our Order? A. Rex regum, et Dominus dominorum.

Q. How do you translate it? A. King of kings, and Lord of Lords.

KNIGHTS OF THE CHRISTIAN MARK, AND GUARDS OF THE CONCLAVE.

This Conclave is governed by an Invincible Knight of the Order of St. John of Jerusalem, a Senior and Junior Knight, six Grand Ministers, Recorder, Treasurer, Conductor, and Guard.

Opening.—"Sir Junior Knight, are all convened in a secret place, and secured from the prying eye of the profane?"

"We are, Invincible."

"Sir Senior Knight, instruct the Sir Knights to assemble in form for the purpose of opening this Invincible Order."

The members kneel on both knees in a circle, each with his right hand on his heart, his left on his forehead.

Prayer.—"Eternal source of life, of light, and[Pg 122] perfection, Supreme God and Governor of all things, liberal dispenser of every blessing! We adore and magnify Thy holy name for the many blessings we have received from Thy hands, and acknowledge our unworthiness to appear before Thee; but for the sake, and in the name of Thy atoning Son, we approach Thee as lost and undone children of wrath; but through the blood of sprinkling, and the sanctification of the Holy Ghost, we come imploring a continuation of Thy favors, for thou hast said, that he who cometh to Thee through faith in the Son of Thy love, Thou wilt in no wise cast out; therefore, at the foot of the cross we come, supplicating pardon for our past offences, that they may be blotted out from the book of Thy remembrance and be seen no more, and that the remainder of our days may be spent as becometh the followers of the Holy One of Israel; and graciously grant that love, harmony, peace, and unity may reign in this Council; that one spirit may animate us—one God reign over us—and one heaven receive us, there to dwell in Thine adorable presence forever and ever. Amen."

The Invincible Knight takes the Bible and waves it four times over his head, saying, "Rex regnantium, et Dominus dominantium;" [that is, King of kings, and Lord of Lords;] kisses it and passes it on his right; it goes around until it comes again to the Invincible Knight, who opens and reads, Matthew v. 3-12, 16.

Always interlace the fingers of the left hand, draw your sword and present it to the heart, and say, "Tammuz Touliumeth, I pronounce this Convention opened in ample form. Let us repair to our several stations, and strictly observe silence."

Preparation.—The candidate is shown into the anti-chamber by the conductor, who clothes him in a gown of brown stuff, and leads him to the door of the Council chamber, where he knocks twice, six, and two—2, 6, and 2.

Junior Knight—"Some one knocks for admission, Invincible Knight." Invincible—"See who it is and make report." J. K. (goes to the door and reports)—"One that is faithful in good works wishes admission here." Inv.—"What good works hath he performed?" J. K.—"He hath given food to the hungry, drink to the thirsty, and clothed the naked with a garment." Inv.—"Thus far he hath done well; but there is still much for him to do. To be faithful in my house, saith the Lord, he should be filled with love for my people. If so, let him enter under the penalties of his symbolic obligation." He enters, makes signs until he arrives at the altar, there kneels.

Vow.—"I, A. B., do promise and vow, with this same volume clasped in my hands, that I will keep secret the words, signs, tokens, and grips of this Order of Knighthood from all but those Knights of St. John of Jerusalem, who have shown a Christian disposition to their fellow-men, are professors of the Christian faith, and have passed through the degrees of symbolic Masonry; and that I will protect and support, as far as in me lies, the followers of the Lord Jesus Christ; feed them, if hungry; give them drink, if thirsty; if naked, clothe them with garments; teach them, if ignorant; and advise them for their good and their advantage. All this I promise in the name of the Father, of the Son, and of the Holy Ghost; and if I perform it not, LET ME BE ANATHEMA MARANATHA! ANATHEMA MARANATHA!" [i.e., accursed at the coming of the Lord.]

The Invincible Knight interlaces the fingers of his left hand with those of the candidate, who lays his right hand on his heart. The Invincible Knight draws his sword; the Senior Knight does the same; they cross [Pg 123]them on the back of the candidate's neck, and the Invincible Knight says, "By virtue of the high power in me vested, by a bull of His Holiness, Pope Sylvester, I dub you a Knight of the Christian Mark, member of the Grand Council, and Guard of the Grand Conclave." The Invincible Knight then whispers in his ear, "Tammuz Touliumeth." The Knights come to order; the Senior Knight takes his seat; the candidate continues standing; the conductor brings a white robe; the Senior Knight says:

"Thus saith the Lord, he that believeth and endureth to the end shall overcome, and I will cause his iniquities to pass from him, and he shall dwell in my presence forever and ever. Take away his filthy garments from him, and clothe him with a change of raiment. For he that overcometh the same shall be clothed in white raiment, and his name shall be written in the Book of Life, and I will confess his name before my Father and his holy angels. He that hath an ear to hear, let him hear what the Spirit saith unto the true believer. Set ye a fair mitre upon his head, place a palm in his hand, for he shall go in and out and minister before me, saith the Lord of hosts; and he shall be a disciple of that rod taken from a branch of the stem of Jesse. For a branch has grown out of his root, and the spirit of the Lord hath rested upon it; the spirit of his wisdom, and might, and righteousness is the girdle of his loins and faithfulness the girdle of his vine, and he stands as an insignia to the people, and him shall the Gentiles seek, and his rest shall be glorious. Cause them that have charge over the city to draw near, every one with the destroying weapon in his hand."

The six Grand Ministers came forward from the north with swords and shields. The first is clothed in white, and has an ink-horn by his side, and stands before the Invincible Knight, who says:

"Go through the city: run in the midst thereof and smite: let not thine eye spare, neither have pity; for they have not executed my judgments with clean hands, saith the Lord or Hosts."

The candidate is instructed to exclaim:

"Woe is me, for I am a man of unclean lips, and my dwelling has been In the tents of Kedar, and among the children of Meshec."

Then he that has the ink-horn by his side, takes a live branch with the tongs from the altar, and touches the lips of the candidate, and says:

"If ye believe, thine iniquities shall be taken away, thy sins shall be purged. I will that these be clean with the branch that shall be given up before me. All thy sins are removed, and thine iniquities blotted out. For I have trodden the wine-press alone, and with me was none of my people. For behold, I come with dyed garments from Bozrah, mighty to save. Refuse not, therefore, to hearken; draw not away thy shoulders; shut not thine ear, that thou shouldest not hear."

The six Ministers now proceed as if they were about to commence the slaughter, when the Senior Knight says to him with the ink-horn:

"Stay thine hand; proceed no further until thou hast set a mark on those that are faithful in the house of the Lord, and trust in the power of his might. Take ye the signet, and set a mark on the forehead of my people that have passed through great tribulation, and have washed their robes, and have made them white in the blood of the Lamb, which was slain from the foundation of the world."

The Minister takes the signet and presses it on the candidate's forehead. He leaves the mark in red letters, "King of Kings, and Lord of Lords." The Minister opens the scroll and says, "Sir Invincible Knight, the number of the sealed are one hundred and forty and four thousand." [Pg 124]The Invincible Knight strikes four, and all the Knights stand before him. He says, "Salvation belongeth to our God, which sitteth upon the throne, and unto the Lamb." All the members fall on their faces, and say "Amen. Blessing, honor, glory, wisdom, thanksgiving, and power, might, majesty, and dominion, be unto our God forever and ever. Amen." They all cast down crowns and palm branches, and rise up and say, "Great and numberless are thy works, thou King of saints. Behold the star which I laid before Joshua, on which is engraved seven eyes, as the engraving of a signet, shall be set as a seal on thine arm—as a seal on thine heart; for love is stronger than death: many waters cannot quench it. If a man would give all the treasures of his house for love, he cannot obtain it; it is the gift of God through Jesus Christ, our Lord."

Charge.—"Invincible Knight, I congratulate you on your having been found worthy to be promoted to this honorable Order of Knighthood. It is highly honorable to all those worthy Knights, who with good faith and diligence, perform its many important duties. The honorable situation to which you are now advanced, and the illustrious office which you now fill is one that was much desired by the first noblemen of Italy, but ambition and jealousy caused his highness, Pope Alexander, to call on his ancient friend, the Grand Master of the Knights of St. John of Jerusalem, to guard his person and the Holy See, as those Knights were known to be well grounded in the faith, and zealous followers of the Lord. The members of the guard were chosen BY THEIR COUNTENANCES, for it is believed that a plain countenance is an indication of the heart; and that no stranger should gain admission and discover the secrets of this august assembly, this Order of the Christian Mark was conferred on those who went about doing good, and following the example of their illustrious Master, Jesus Christ. Go thou and do likewise.

Motto.— "Christus regnat, vincit, triumphat;" [i.e., Christ rules, conquers, triumphs.] Rex regnantium, et Dominus dominantium.

Israel on the left breast, a triangular plate of gold, seven eyes engraved on one side, on the other the letter G in the five points.

KNIGHTS OF THE HOLY SEPULCHRE.

History.—St. Helena, daughter of Caylus, King of Britain, consort of Constantine, and mother of Constantine the Great, in the year 296, made a journey to the Holy Land in search of the cross of Jesus Christ. After leveling the hillocks and destroying the temple of Venus, three crosses were discovered. It was now difficult to discover which of the three was the one sought for by her. By order of his Holiness, Pope Marcellinus, they were borne to the bed of a woman who had long been visited by sickness, and lay at the point of death; she placed her hands upon the second cross first, which rendered her no service; but when she laid her hand upon the third, she was restored to her former health. She instantly arose, giving glory to God, saying, He was wounded for our transgressions, he was bruised for our iniquities, the chastisement of sin was upon him, and with his stripes we are healed. On the spot where the crosses were found, St. Helena erected a stately church, one hundred paces long and sixty wide; the east end takes in the place where the crosses stood, and the west of the sepulchre. By leveling the hills, the sepulchre is above the floor of the church, like a grotto, which is twenty feet from the floor to the top of the rock. There is a superb cupola over the sepulchre, and in the aisles are the tombs of Godfrey and Baldwin, kings of Jerusalem. In 302, St. Helena instituted the Order of Knights of the Holy Sepulchre of our Lord and Saviour, Jesus Christ. This Order was confirmed in 304 by his Holiness, Pope Marcellinus; they were bound by a sacred vow to guard the Holy Sepulchre, protect pilgrims, and fight infidels and enemies of the cross of [Pg 125]Christ. The city of Jerusalem was rebuilt and ornamented by Ælius Adrian, Emperor of Rome, and given to the Christians in 120. The Persians took it from them in 637, and in 1008 it fell into the hands of the Turks, under whose oppressions it long groaned, until Peter the Holy steered the western princes to release the distressed church, and in 1096 Godfrey and Baldwin unfurled the banner of the cross and expelled the Turks. He was invested with a crown of laurel, and suffered himself to be called the King of Palestine.

Description, Etc.—The Council must represent a Cathedral Church, the altar covered with black, upon which must be placed three large candles, a cross, and in the centre a skull and cross-bones. The Principal stands on the right side of the altar, with a Bible in one hand, and a staff in the other; soft music plays, and the veil is drawn up, and discovers the altar; the choir say:

Hush, hush, the heavenly choir, They cleave the air in bright attire; See, see, the lute each angel brings, And hark divinely thus they sing.
To the power divine, All glory be given, By man upon earth, And angels in heaven.

The priest steps before the altar and says, "Kyrie Elieson; Christe Elieson; Kyrie Elieson; [that is, O Lord, have mercy; O Christ, have mercy; O Lord, have mercy.] Amen. Gloria Sibi Domino! [i.e., Glory to the Lord himself.] I declare this Grand Council opened and ready to proceed to business." The Priests and Ministers take their several stations and observe order. The candidates being prepared, he alarms at the door by seven raps, and the Prelate says to Verger, "See the cause of that alarm and report." Verger goes to the door and reports, "Right Reverend Prelate, there are seven brethren who solicit admission to this Grand Council." Prelate says, "On what is their desire founded?" Verger—"On a true Christian principle, to serve the church and its members by performing the seven corporeal works of mercy, and to protect and guard the Holy Sepulchre from the destroying hands of our enemies." Prelate—"Admit them, that we may know them, if you please." They are then admitted. Prelate says to them, "Are you followers of the Captain of our salvation?" Verger says, "We are, Right Reverend Prelate." P.—"Attend, then, to the sayings of our Master, Jesus Christ." Thou shalt love the Lord thy God with all thy heart, with all thy mind, with all thy soul, and with all thy might. This is the first great commandment, and the second is like unto it; thou shalt love thy neighbor as thyself; on these two commandments hang all the law and the prophets. The Verger and Beadle hold the Bible, on which the candidates place their right hands.

Vow.—"I, A. B., in the name of the high and undivided Trinity, do promise and vow to keep and conceal the high mysteries of this noble and Invincible Order of Knights of the Holy Sepulchre, from all but such as are ready and willing to serve the church of Christ by acts of valor and charity, and its members by performing all the corporeal works of mercy, and that, as far as in me lies, I will defend the church of the Holy Sepulchre from pillage and violence, and guard and protect pilgrims on their way to and from the Holy Land; and if I perform not this, my vow, to the best of my abilities, let me become INANIMATUS [dead].

Interlace your fingers with the candidate, cross your arms, and say, "De mortuis, nil nisi bonum; [i.e., concerning the dead, say nothing but [Pg 126]good.] Prelate says, "Take the sword and travel onward—guard the Holy Sepulchre—defeat our enemies—unfurl the banner of our cross—protect the Roman Eagle—return to us with victory and safety." The candidates depart, go to the south, where they meet a band of Turks—a desperate conflict ensues—the Knights are victorious; they seize the crescent, and return to the cathedral in triumph, and place the banner, eagle, and crescent before the altar, and take their seats. (22d chapter St. John read by Prelate.) Then the choir sing:

"Creator of the radiant light, Dividing day from sable night; Who with the light bright origin, The world's creation didst begin."

Prelate then says, "Let our prayer come before Thee, and let our exercise be acceptable in thy sight." The seven candidates kneel at the foot of the altar. The Prelate takes the bread, and says, "Brethren, eat ye all of this bread in love, that ye may learn to support each other." He then takes the cup, and says, "Drink ye all of this cup to ratify the vow that ye have made, and learn to sustain one another." The Prelate then raises them up by the grip (interlace the fingers), and says, "1st, Sir, I greet thee a Knight of the Holy Sepulchre; go feed the hungry; 2d, Give drink to the thirsty; 3d, Clothe the naked with a garment; 4th, Visit and ransom the captives; 5th, Harbor the harborless, give the orphan and widow where to lay their heads; 6th, Visit and relieve the sick; 7th, Go and bury the dead." All make crosses and say, "In nomini patria filio et spiritus sancto. Amen." Prelate says, "Brethren, let us recommend to each other the practice of the four cardinal virtues—prudence, justice, temperance, fortitude."

Closing.—The Knights all rise, stand in circle, interlace their fingers, and say, "Sepulchrum." Prelate then says, "Gloria patri, et filio, et spiritus sancto;" [i.e., Glory to the Father, Son, and Holy Spirit.] Brethren answer, "Sicut erat in principio, et nunc, et semper et in secula seculorum; [i.e., As it was in the beginning, is now, and shall be, world without end.] Amen."

Benediction.—"Blessed be thou, O Lord, our God! Great first cause and Governor of all things; thou createst the world with thy bountiful hand, and sustained it by thy wisdom, by thy goodness, and by thy mercy! It cometh to pass that seed time and harvest never fall! It is Thou that givest every good and perfect gift! Blessed be thy name forever and ever!"

To examine a Knight of the Holy Sepulchre; he holds up the first finger of the right hand, Knight holds up the second; you then hold up the third, and he shuts up his first; this signifies three persons in one God.

THE HOLY AND THRICE ILLUSTRIOUS ORDER OF THE CROSS, CALLED A COUNCIL.

Diploma of a Comp. of the Ancient Council of the Trinity, Anno Cr. seu Covt. 896.—The Ancient Council of the Trinity, by Their Successors in the United States of America.

St. Albert, to every Knight Companion of the Holy and Thrice Illustrious Order of the Cross: Be it known unto you, that with regard [Pg 127]to unquestionable vouchers, we have confirmed the Induction of the Knight Templar Mason into the Councils of the said Order of Knighthood, and herein do warrant him as a worthy and Illustrious Companion, thereof; and hoping and confiding that he will ever so demean himself as to conduct to the glory of I. H. S., the Most Holy and Almighty God, and to the honor of his Mark, we do recommend and submit him to the confidence of all those throughout the world, who can truly and deservedly say, "I am a Christian;" and that no unwarrantable benefits shall arise from this Diploma, and we charge all concerned cautiously and prudently to mark the bearer on the mystic letters therein contained, and to regard only the result, in its application and privileges.

Done out of Council, at — —, in the county of — —, and State of — —, on this — — day of — —.

217

Sir — — —
Sovereign Prefect.

Sir — — —
Acting Pref.

      Commendations,
      Sir Knights Comp'ns.

The officers and council all in their places. The Most Illustrious Prefect addresses the Most Worthy Provost thus: "Most Worshipful Provost, what is the o'clock?" Most Worshipful Provost says, rising and facing the east, at the same time raising his mark in his right hand, "Most Illustrious Prefect, it is now the first hour of the day, the time when our Lord suffered and the veil of the temple was rent asunder, when darkness and consternation was spread over the earth, when the confusion of the old covenant was made light in the new in the temple of the cross. It is, Most Illustrious Prefect, the third watch, when the implements of Masonry were broken—when the flame, which led the wise men of the east, reappeared—when the cubic stone was broken, and the word was given." Most Illustrious Prefect says to Worthy Herald, "It is my will that this house of God be closed, and the remembrance of those solemn and sacred events, be here commemorated: make this; Worthy Herald, known to the Most Worshipful Provost, in due and ancient form." The Worthy Herald bows and approaches the Most Worshipful Provost, where he bows thrice, faces about and gives a blast with his horn, and after the Knights have filed out by threes without the door, except the worthy Senior Inductor, he does his errand, viz.:—"Most Worshipful Provost, it is the sovereign will of Count Albertus, of Pergamus, that this house of God be closed, and that those solemn and sacred events in the new covenant be here commemorated: you will observe this." The Worthy Herald bows, and the Most Worshipful Provost rises and addresses the Worthy Senior Inductor thus: "It is the will of the Most Illustrious Prefect that here now be opened a Council of Knights of the Cross: what therein becomes your duty?" Worthy Senior Inductor says, "To receive the commands of my superiors in the order, and pay obedience thereto—to conduct and instruct my ignorant pass-brethren; and to revere, and inculcate reverence in others, for the Most Holy and Almighty God." The Most Worshipful Provost rises fiercely and says, "By what right do you claim this duty?" Worthy S. Inductor says, "By the right of a sign, and the mark of a sign." Most Worshipful Provost says, "Will you give me a sign?" Worthy Sen. "I could if I should." [Pg 128]The Most Worshipful Provost then partly extends both arms, pointing downwards to an angle of 39°, with the palms open, and upwards, to show they are not sullied with iniquity and oppression, and says, "Worthy Sen. Inductor, you may give it." The Worthy Sen. Inductor then looks him full in the face, and with his forefinger touches his right temple, and lets fall his hand, and says, "This is a sign." Most Worshipful Provost says, "A sign of what?" Worthy Senior Inductor says, "Aye, a sign of what?" Most Worshipful Provost says, "A penal sign." Worthy Senior Inductor says, "Your sign is — —." Most Worshipf. Pro. says, "The last sign of my induction. But you have the mark of a sign." Worthy S. Inductor says, "The sign whereof my mark is a mark, I hope is in the Council above." Most Worshipf. Pro. says, "But the mark — —." Worthy S. Inductor says, "Is in my bosom." Thereupon he produces his mark in his left hand, and with the forefinger of his right on the letter S, on the cross, asks, "What's that?" Most Wor. Pro. says, "Lisha." Wor. Pro. puts his finger on the letter H, and asks, "What is this?" Worthy S. Inductor says, "Sha." Worthy S. Inductor then puts his finger on the letter I, and asks, "What is this?" Most Worshipf. Pro. says, "Baal." "What, then, is your mark?" Worthy S. Inductor says, "Baal, Sha-Lisha; ['Lord of the three'] I am the Lord." The Most Worshipful Provost then says, "You are my brother, and the duty is yours of ancient right; please announce the Council open." The Worthy Senior Inductor steps to the door and gives three raps, and is answered by some Knight from without, who is then admitted, and the Worthy S. Inductor gives the CONDITIONAL sign (which is by partly extending both arms, as before described), the Knight answering by putting his finger to his right temple, as before. The Worthy S. Inductor then addresses the chair, thus:—"Most Illustrious Prefect, a professing brother is within the Council by virtue of a sign." Most Illustrious Prefect says to Worthy Herald, "Go to this professing brother, and see him marked before the chair of the Most Worshipful Provost; conduct him thither, Worthy Herald." The Worthy Herald says to the Knight, "Worthy Sir, know you the sacred cross of our Council?" Knight says, "I am a

Christian." The Worthy Herald then says, "Follow me." When arrived before the Most Wor. Pro. the Worthy Herald says, "Most Worthy Provost, by order of the Most Illustrious Prefect, I here bring you to be marked a professing brother of the cross." The Most Worthy Provost says, "Worthy Sir, know you the cross of our Council; and can you, without fear or favor, support and bear that cross?" Knight says, "I am a Christian." The Most Worthy Provost says. "Worthy Sir, know you the cross of our Council; and can you, without fear or favor, support and bear that cross?" Knight says, "I am a Christian." The Most Worthy Provost says, "No more."

THE OBLIGATIONS OF THRICE ILLUSTRIOUS KNIGHTS OF THE CROSS.

First Obligation.—You, Mr. — —, do now, by your honor, and in view of the power and union of the Thrice Illustrious Order of the Cross, now first made known to you, and in the dread presence of the Most Holy and [Pg 129]Almighty God, solemnly and sincerely swear and declare, that, to the end of your life, you will not, either in consideration of gain, interest, or honor, nor with good or bad design, ever take any, the least, step or measure, or be instrumental in any such object, to betray or communicate to any person, or being, or number of the same, in the known world, not thereto of cross and craft entitled, any secret or secrets, or ceremony or ceremonies, or any part thereof appertaining to the order and degree known among Masons as the Thrice Illustrious Order of the Cross. That you will not, at any time or times whatever, either now or hereafter, directly or indirectly, by letter, figure, or character, however or by whoever made, ever communicate any of the information and secret mysteries heretofore alluded to. That you will never speak on or upon, or breathe high or low, any ceremony or secret appertaining thereto, out of Council, where there shall not be two or more Knights companions of the order present, besides yourself, and that in a safe and sure place, whereby any opinion, even of the nature and general principles of the institution, can be formed by any other person, be he Mason or otherwise, than a true Knight companion of the cross; nothing herein going to interfere with the prudent practice of the duties enjoined by the order, or arrangement for their enforcement.

2.—You further swear, that, should you know another to violate any essential part of this obligation, you will use your most decided endeavors, by the blessing of God, to bring such person to the strictest and most condign punishment, agreeably to the rules and usages of our ancient fraternity; and this by pointing him out to the world as an unworthy vagabond; by opposing his interest, by deranging his business, by transferring his character after him wherever he may go, and by exposing him to the contempt of the whole fraternity and the world, but of our illustrious order more especially, during his whole natural life: nothing herein going to prevent yourself, or any other, when elected to the dignity of Thrice Illustrious, from retaining the ritual of the order, if prudence and caution appear to be the governing principle in so retaining it, such dignity authorizing the elected to be governed by no rule but the dictates of his own judgment, in regard to what will best conduce to the interest of the order; but that he be responsible for the character of those whom he may induct, and for the concealment of the said ritual.

3.—Should any Thrice Illustrious Knight or acting officer of any council which may have them in hand, ever require your aid in any emergency in defence of the recovery of his said charge, you swear cheerfully to exercise all assistance in his favor, which the nature of the time and place will admit, even to the sacrifice of life, liberty, and property. To all, and every part thereof, we then bind you, and by ancient usage you bind yourself, under the no less infamous penalty than dying the death of a traitor, by having a spear, or other sharp instrument, like as our divine Master, thrust in your left side, bearing testimony, even in death, of the power and justice of the mark of the holy cross.

219

Second Obligation.—Mr. — —, before you can be admitted to the light and benefit of this Thrice Illustrious order, it becomes my duty, by ancient usage, to propose to you certain questions, not a thing vainly ceremonial; but the companions will expect true answers: they will concern your past life, and resolutions for the future. Have you given me without evasion or addition, your baptismal and family names, and those of your parents, your true age as far as within your knowledge; where you were educated; where you were born, and also where was your last place of residence? or have you not? "I have." It is well.

2d.—Were your parents free and not slaves? had they right and title in the soil of the earth? were they devoted to the religion of the cross, and did they so educate their family? have you searched the spiritual claims of that religion on your gratitude and your affections? and have you continued steadfast in that faith from choice and a conviction of your duty to heaven, or from education? "From duty and choice." This also is right.

3d.—Have you ever up to this time lived according to the principles of that religion, by acting upon the square of virtue with all men, nor [Pg 130]defrauding any, nor defamed the good name of any, nor indulged sensual appetites unreasonably, but more especially to the dishonor of the matrimonial tie, nor extorted on, or oppressed the poor. "I have not been guilty of these things." You have then entitled yourself to our highest confidence, by obeying the injunctions of our Thrice Illustrious Prefect in Heaven, "of doing to all men even as you would that they should do unto you." Mr. — —, can you so continue to act, that yearly on the anniversary of St. Albert, you can solemnly swear for the past season you have not been guilty of the crimes enumerated in these questions? "By the help of God I can." Be it so, then, that annually, on the anniversary of St. Albert you swear to these great questions; and the confidence of the Knights Companions of the order in you, rests on your being able so to do.

4th.—For the future, then, you promise to be a good man, and to be governed by the moral laws of God and the rules of the order, in always dealing openly, honorably, and above deceit, especially with the Knights companions of the order? "I do."

5th.—You promise so to act with all mankind, but especially with the fraternity, as that you shall never be justly called a bad paymaster, ungrateful, a liar, a rake, or a libertine, a man careless in the business of your vocation, a drunkard, or a tyrant? "I do."

6th.—You promise to lead a life so upright and just in relation to all mankind as you are capable of, but in matters of difference to preserve the interest of a companion of the order; of a companion's friend for whom he pleads, to any mere man of the word? "I do."

7th.—You promise never to engage in mean party strife, nor conspiracies against the government or religion of your country, whereby your reputation may suffer, nor ever to associate with dishonorable men even for a moment, except it be to secure the interest of such person, his family or friends, to a companion, whose necessities require this degradation at your hands? "I do."

8th.—You promise to act honorably in all matters of office or vocation, even to the value of the one-third part of a Roman penny, and never to take any advantage therein unworthy the best countenance of your companions, and this, that they shall not, by your unworthiness, be brought into disrepute? "I do."

Third Obligation.—I do now, by the hopes and power of the mark of the Holy and Illustrious Order of the Cross, which I do now hold to Heaven in my right hand as the earnest of my faith, and in the dread presence of the most holy and Almighty God, solemnly swear and declare that I do hereby accept of, and forever will consider the cross and mark of this order as my only hope: that I will make it the test of faith and fellowship; and that I will effect its objects and defend its mysteries to the end of my days, with my life and with my property—and first, that in the state of collision and misunderstanding impiously existing among the princes and pilgrims, defenders and champions of the Holy Cross of Jesus our Lord, now assembled in the land and city of their peace, and considering that the glory of the Most High requires the greatest and strictest unanimity of measures and arms, the most sacred union of sentiment and brotherly love in the soldiers who there thus devote themselves to his cause and banner, I swear strictly to dedicate myself, my life, and my property forever hereafter to his holy name and the purposes of our mark, and to the best interest of all those who thus with me become Knights of the Cross: I swear forever to give myself to this holy and illustrious order, confiding fully and unreservedly in the purity of their morals and the ardor of their pious enthusiasm, for the recovery of the land of their fathers, and the blessed clime of our Lord's sufferings, and never to renounce the mark of the order nor the claims and welfare of my brethren.

2d.—And that the holy and pious enthusiasm of my brethren may not have slander or disgrace at my hands, or the order be injured by my unworthiness, I swear forever to renounce tyranny and oppression in my own person and place, whatever it may be, and to stand forth against it in others, whether public or private; to become the champion of the [Pg 131]cross, to observe the common good; be the protector of the poor and unfortunate; and ever to observe the common rights of human nature without encroachment, or permitting encroachment thereon, if in my power to prevent or lessen it. I will, moreover, act in subordination to the laws of my country, and never countenance any change in the government under which I live, without good and answerable reasons for so doing, that ancient usages and immemorial customs be not overturned.

3d.—I swear to venerate the mark as the wisdom and decree of Heaven, to unite our hands and hearts in the work of the holy crusade, and as an encouragement to act with zeal and efficacy; and I swear to consider its testimonies as the true and only proper test of an illustrious brother of the cross.

4th.—I swear to wear the mark of this order, without any the least addition, except what I shall be legally entitled to by INDUCTION, forever, if not without the physical means of doing so, or it being contrary to propriety; and even then, if possible, to wear the holy cross; and I swear to put a chief dependence for the said worthy and pious objects therein.

5th.—I swear to put confidence unlimited in every illustrious brother of the cross, as a true and worthy follower of the blessed Jesus, who has sought this land, not for private good, but pity, and the glory of the religion of the Most High and Holy God.

6th.—I swear never to permit my political principles nor personal interest to come counter to his, if forbearance and brotherly kindness can operate to prevent it; and never to meet him if I know it, in war or in peace, under such circumstances that I may not, in justice to myself, my cross, and my country wish him unqualified success; and if perchance it should happen without my knowledge, on being informed thereof, that I will use my best endeavors to satisfy him, even to the relinquishing my arms and purpose. I will never shed a brother's blood nor thwart his good fortune, knowing him to be such, nor see it done by others if in my power to prevent it.

7th.—I swear to advance my brother's best interest, by always supporting his military fame and political preferment in opposition to another; and by employing his arms or his aid in his vocation, under all circumstances where I shall not suffer more by so doing, than he, by my neglecting to do so, but this never to the sacrifice of any vital interest in our holy religion, or in the welfare of my country.

8th.—I swear to look on his enemies as my enemies, his friends as my friends, and stand forth to mete out tender kindness or vengeance accordingly; but never to intrude on his social or domestic relations to his hurt or dishonor, by claiming his privileges, or by debauching or defaming his female relations or friends.

9th.—I swear never to see calmly nor without earnest desires and decided measures to prevent the ill-treatment, slander, or defamation, of any brother knight, nor ever to view danger or the least shadow of injury about to fall on his head, without well and truly informing him thereof; and, if in my power to prevent it, never to fail, by my sword or counsel, to defend his welfare and good name.

221

10th.—I do swear never to prosecute a brother before those who know not our order, till the remonstrance of a council shall be inadequate to do me justice.

11th.—I swear to keep sacred my brother's secrets, both when delivered to me as such, and when the nature of the information is such as to require secrecy for his welfare.

12th.—I swear to hold myself bound to him, especially in affliction and adversity, to contribute to his necessities my prayers, my influence, and my purse.

13th.—I swear to be under the control of my council, or, if belonging to none, to that which is nearest to me, and never to demur to, or complain at, any decree concerning me, which my brethren, as a council, shall conceive me to deserve, and enforce on my head, to my hurt and dishonor.

14th.—I swear to obey all summons sent from any council to me, or from any Most Illustrious Knight, whether Illustrious Counsellor for the time being, or by INDUCTION, and to be governed by the constitution, usages, and customs of the order without variation or change.

[Pg 132]15th.—I swear never to see nor permit more than two candidates, who, with the Senior Inductor, will make three, to be advanced, at the same time, in any council where I shall be; nor shall any candidate, by suffrage, be inducted without a unanimous vote of the illustrious brethren in council; nor shall any council advance any member, there not being three illustrious Knights, or one Most Illustrious and four Illustrious Knights of the Cross present, which latter may be substituted by Most Illustrious Induction; nor yet where there shall not be a full and proper mark of the order, such as usage has adopted to our altar, of metal, or other durable and worthy material, contained within the apartment of council, as also the Holy Bible; nor will I ever see a council opened for business, without the ceremony of testing the mark, exercised on the character of every brother, prayers, and the reading of the 35th Psalm of David; nor will I ever see, consent to, or countenance, more than two persons of the same business or calling in life, to belong to, or be inducted and advanced in any one council of which I am a member, at the same time; nothing therein going to exclude members from other parts of the country, or from foreign parts, from joining us, if they consent formally and truly to stand in deference and defence, first, of their special BAR-BRETHREN in the council, nor to prevent advancements to fill vacancies, occasioned by death or removal. To all this, and every part thereof, I do now, as before, by the honor and power of the mark, as by an honorable and awful oath, which confirmeth all things in the dread presence of the Most Holy and Almighty God, solemnly and in truth, bind and obligate my soul; and in the earthly penalties, to wit, that, for the violation of the least matter or particle of any of the here taken obligations, I become the silent and mute subject of the displeasure of the Illustrious Order, and have their power and wrath turned on my head, to my destruction and dishonor, which, like the nail of Jael, may be the sure end of an unworthy wretch, by piercing my temples with a true sense of my ingratitude—and for a breach of silence in case of such an unhappy event, that I shall die the infamous death of a traitor, by having a spear, or other sharp weapon, like as my Lord, thrust in my left side—bearing testimony, even in death, of the power of the mark of the Holy and Illustrious Cross, before I. H. S., our thrice Illustrious Counsellor in Heaven, the Grand Council of the good. To this I swear.

THE LODGE OF PERFECTION: COMPRISING THE ELEVEN INEFFABLE DEGREES OF MASONRY.

In these several degrees some name of God is used, as the distinguishing word. Each name, however, is only a mode of pronouncing the Hebrew word Jehovah. The later Jews have a superstitious fear of pronouncing that name. Whenever it occurs in the Hebrew Text, they substitute the word Adonai in its place. To those who read the original language of the Old Testament, it is known, that while the consonants of the Hebrew word remain, the vowel points may be so changed as to afford several different pronunciations. In the different degrees of Ineffable Masonry, the four consonants (Jod, He, Vau, He) of the name Jehovah are differently pointed, so as to furnish a word for each degree. In the degree of Perfection, the candidate is sworn not to pronounce the word but once during his life, hence it is termed INEFFABLE, or unutterable. The ordinary mode of giving it in that degree consists in simply repeating the names of its letters, "Jod, He, Vau, He." On receiving that degree, the candidate is told that he is to become acquainted with the true pronunciation of the ineffable name of God, as it was revealed to Enoch. He is then taught to pronounce the word "Ya-ho"—sounding the *a* like *a* in wall. When written in Masonic manuscripts, this word is spelled "Ja-hoh."

SECRET MASTER.

Opening.—The Master strikes five. At this signal the Grand Marshal rises, and the Master addresses him: Master. Your place in the Lodge? Answer: In the North, Most Powerful.

[Pg 133]M. Your business there? A. To see that the Sanctum Sanctorum is duly guarded.

M. Please to attend to your duty, and inform the guards that we are about to open a Lodge of Secret Masters by the MYSTERIOUS NUMBER. A. It is done.

M. How are we guarded? A. By seven Secret Masters stationed before the veil of the Sanctum Sanctorum.

The Master strikes six. The Inspector rises. Master. Brother Adoniram, are you a Secret Master? Inspector. I have passed from the square to the compass.

M. What is the hour? I. The dawn of day has driven away darkness, and the great light begins to shine in this Lodge.

The Master strikes seven. The brethren rise. Master. If the great light is the token of the dawn of day, and we are all Secret Masters, it is time to begin our labors; give notice that I am about to open a Lodge of Secret Masters by the mysterious number. The Inspector obeys. The signs of the degrees from Entered Apprentice to Royal Arch, inclusive, are given with that of silence, which belongs to this degree. The Master places the two forefingers of his right hand on his lips. This is answered by the brethren with the two forefingers of the left. All clap hands seven times.

M. I declare this Lodge of Secret Masters open, and in order for business. Brother Grand Marshal, please to inform the guards.

Second Section.—Question—What did you see in the Sanctum Sanctorum when the thick veil was removed? Answer—I saw the great circle, in which was enclosed the blazing star, which filled me with awe and reverence.

Q. What do the Hebrew characters in the triangle signify? A. Something above my knowledge, which I cannot pronounce.

Q. What word did those Hebrew characters compose? A. The ineffable name of the Great Architect of the Universe.

Q. To whom was that name revealed? A. To Moses; he received the pronunciation thereof from the Almighty on the mount, when he appeared to him, and by a law of Moses it was forbidden ever to be pronounced unless in a certain manner, so that in process of time the true pronunciation was lost.

Q. What more did you perceive? A. Nine other words.

Q. Where were they placed? A. In the nine beams of the blazing luminary.

Q. What did they signify? A. The nine names which God gave himself when speaking to Moses on Mount Sinai, and the promise that his posterity should one day discover his real name.

Q. Give them to me, with their significations? A. "Eloah," The Strong. "Hayah," He is. "Shaddai," The Almighty. "Elyon," The Most High. "Adonai," The Lord. "Ahad Kodesh," The Holy One. "Riba," The Mighty. "Mahar," Merciful. "Eloham," Merciful God.

Q. What doth the circle which surrounds the delta signify? A. The eternity of the power of God, which hath neither beginning nor end.

[Pg 134]Q. What doth the blazing star denote? A. That light which should guide us to the Divine Providence.

Q. What is signified by the letter G in the centre of the blazing star? A. Glory, Grandeur and Gomez, or Gibber Hodihu.

Q. What is meant by these? A. By Glory is meant God, by Grandeur, man who may be great by perfection; and Gibber Hodihu, is a Hebrew word signifying thanks to God. It is said to have been the first word spoken by the first man.

Q. What else did you see in the Sanctum Sanctorum? A. The ark of alliance or covenant.

Q. Where was the ark of alliance placed? A. In the west end of the Sanctum Sanctorum, under the blazing star.

Q. What did the ark with the blazing star represent? A. As the ark was the emblem of the alliance which God had made with his people, so is the circle which surrounds the delta in the blazing star, the emblem of the alliance of Brother Masons.

Q. Of what form was the ark? A. A solid oblong square.

Q. Of what was it made? A. Of shittim wood covered within and without with pure gold, surmounted with a golden crown and two cherubims of gold.

Q. What was the covering of the ark called? A. Propitiatory.

Q. Why so? A. Because God's anger was there appeased.

Q. What did the ark contain? A. The tables of the law which God gave to Moses.

Q. Of what were they made? A. Of white marble.

Q. Who constructed the ark? A. Bezeleel of the Tribe of Judah, and Aholiab of the Tribe of Dan, who were filled with the spirit of God in wisdom and understanding, and in knowledge and in all manner of workmanship.

Q. What was the name of the Sanctum Sanctorum in Hebrew? A. "Dabir."

Q. What does the word signify? A. Speech.

Q. Why was it so called? A. Because the Divinity resided there in a peculiar manner, and delivered his oracles.

Q. How many doors were there in the Sanctum Sanctorum? A. Only one on the east side called "Zizon," or Balustrade. It was covered with hangings of purple, scarlet, blue, and fine twined linen of cunning work, embroidered with cherubims, and suspended from four columns.

Q. What did these columns represent? A. The four cardinal points.

Q. Your duty as a Secret Mason? A. To guard the Sanctum Sanctorum, and sacred furniture of the holy place.

Q. What was that furniture? A. The altar of incense, the two tables of shew-bread, and the golden candlesticks.

Q. How were they placed? A. The altar of incense stood nearest the Sanctum Sanctorum, and the tables and candlesticks were placed five on the north and five on the south side of the holy place.

Q. What is meant by the EYE in our Lodge? A. That Secret Masters should keep a careful watch over the conduct of the craft in general.

Q. What is your age? A. Three times 27, and accomplished 81.

[Pg 135]Closing a Lodge of Secret Masters.—The Master strikes five.—The Grand Marshal rises.

Master. Brother Grand Marshal, what is the last as well as the first care of a Lodge of Secret Masters? Answer. To see that the Sanctum Sanctorum is duly guarded.

Master. Please attend to your duty, and inform the guards that we are about to close this Lodge of Secret Masters by the mysterious number. The Grand Marshal obeys, and repeats, "It is done, Most Powerful." Master strikes six.—Adoniram rises.

Master. Brother Adoniram, what is the hour? Answer. The end of day.

Master. What remains to do? Adoniram—To practice virtue, fly from vice, and remain in silence.

Master. Since there remains nothing to do but to practice virtue and fly vice, let us enter again into silence, that the will of God may be accomplished. The signs are given, and seven blows struck as at opening.

Master. I declare this Lodge duly closed.

DEGREE OF PERFECT MASTER.

Opening.—Right Worshipful and Respectable Master strikes two, upon which Grand Marshal rises, and Master says, "Brother Grand Marshal, are we all Perfect Masters?" Answer—We are, Right Worshipful and Respectable.

Q. Your place in the Lodge? A. In the North, Right Worshipful and Respectable.

Q. Your business there? A. To see that the Lodge is duly tyled.

Q. Please to attend to your duty and inform the Tyler that we are about to open a Lodge of Perfect Masters. (Grand Marshal reports.) Right Worshipful and Respectable Master knocks three, upon which the Warden and the Master of Ceremonies in the South rise. Master says, "Brother Stokin, are you a Perfect Master?" Answer—I have seen the tomb of our respectable Master, Hiram Abiff, and have in company with my brethren shed tears at the same.

Q. What is the hour? A. It is four.

Master then knocks four, upon which all the brethren rise. Master says, "If it is four, it is time to set the workmen to labor. Give notice that I am going to open a Lodge of Perfect Masters by four times four." (Senior Warden reports to brethren.) Signs given of former degrees, together with those of this degree. Master knocks four, Stokin four, Master of Ceremonies four, and Grand Marshal four—then all the brethren strike four times four with their hands. Then Master declares the Lodge open, and orders the Marshal to inform the Tyler.

Reception.—The candidate has a green cord put 'round his neck and is led by the Master of Ceremonies to the door, who knocks four, which is repeated by the Warden and answered by the Master. The Senior Warden says, "While the craft are engaged in lamenting the death of our Grand Master, Hiram Abiff," an alarm is heard at the inner door of the Lodge.

[Pg 136]Lecture.—Question—Are you a Perfect Master? Answer—I have seen the tomb of Hiram Abiff, and have in company with my brethren, shed tears at the same.

Q. How were you prepared to be a Perfect Master? Answer—A sprig of cassia was placed in my left hand, and a green cord about my neck.

Q. Why was the sprig of cassia placed in the left hand? A. That I might deposit it in the grave of Hiram Abiff.

Q. Why was a rope of green color put 'round your neck? A. Because the body of Hiram Abiff was lowered into the grave by the brethren, at his second interment, by a rope of that color. There is another reason, to signify thereby that a Perfect Master by flourishing in virtue, might hope for immortality.

Q. How did you gain admission? A. By four distinct knocks.

Q. What did they denote? A. Life, virtue, death, and immortality.

Q. How were they answered? A. By four from within.

Q. What was then said to you? A. Who comes there?

Q. Your answer? A. A Secret Master who is well qualified, etc.

Q. What was then said to you? A. I was then asked by what further right, etc.

Q. Your answer? A. By the right, etc.

Q. What was then said to you? A. Wait until the Right Worshipful and Respectable Master has been informed of your request and his answer returned.

Q. What was his answer? A. Introduce him in due and ancient form.

Q. What was that form? A. I was conducted to the West by the Master of Ceremonies and interrogated by the Master, "What is your request?"

Q. Your answer? A. To receive the degree of Perfect Master.

Q. What was then said to you by the Master? A. Before you can be admitted to this privilege, it will be necessary for you to join the funeral procession of Hiram Abiff.

Q. What followed? A. I joined in the procession, which moved four times 'round the Lodge, the brethren singing a funeral ode; when we arrived at the grave, the procession moved in an inverted order—the coffin was lowered with a green rope, and the sprigs of cassia thrown into the grave.

Q. What followed? A. The Master resumed his station, and the procession moved to the east.

Q. What followed? A. When he directed the Grand Marshal to inform King Solomon that the tomb of Hiram Abiff was completed, and request him to examine the same.

Q. What followed? A. Solomon entered and proceeded with the procession to the tomb of Hiram Abiff, and having examined the same and read the inscription J. M. B., he made a sign of admiration, and said in the joy of his heart, "It is accomplished and complete;" the brethren all making the same sign.

Q. What followed? A. The brethren resumed their places, and the Master directed the Master of Ceremonies to cause me to approach the east by four times four steps from the compass extended from an angle [Pg 137]of seven to that of sixty degrees, and take the obligation of a Perfect Master.

Q. Repeat that obligation. A. Obligation.— "1st point, Secrecy. 2d. Obey orders and decrees of Council of Princes of Jerusalem, under penalty of all the former degrees; also, under penalty of being smitten on the right temple with a common gavel or setting maul. So help," etc.

Q. What did the Master then communicate to you? A. He said, "It is my desire to draw you," etc., and then gave me the signs, words, tokens and history of this degree.

Q. Give me the signs. A. 1st sign—Place the palm of the right hand on the right temple, at the same time stepping back with the right foot, then bring up the right foot to its first position and let the right arm fall perpendicularly on the right side (alluding to the penalty). Second sign is that of admiration.—Raise the hands and eyes to heaven, let the arms fall crossed upon the belly, looking downwards.

Q. Give me the pass-word. A. (Accassia.)

Q. To what does the word allude, etc. Give me the token and mysterious word. A. Token is that of the Mark Master, given on the five points of fellowship; the mysterious word Jeva (pronounced Je-vau).

Q. What was then done? A. The Master invested me with the jewel and apron of this degree, and informed me that my jewel was designed to remind me, that, as a perfect Master, I should measure my conduct by the exact rule of equity.

Q. Give me the history of this degree. A. After the body of Hiram Abiff had been found, Solomon, pleased with having an opportunity of paying a tribute of respect to the memory of so great and good a man, ordered the noble Adoniram, his Grand Inspector, to make the suitable arrangements for his interment; the brethren were ordered to attend with white aprons and gloves, and he forbade that the marks of blood which had been spilled in the temple, should be effaced until the assassins had been punished. In the meantime, Adoniram furnished a plan for a superb tomb and obelisk of white and black marble, which were finished in nine days. The tomb was entered by passing between two pillars, supporting a square stone surrounded by three circles; on the stone was engraved the letter J. On the tomb, was a device representing a virgin, etc. (as in third degree). The heart of Hiram Abiff was enclosed in a golden urn, which was pierced with a sword to denote the desire of the brethren to punish the assassins. A triangular stone was affixed to the side of the urn, and on it were the letters J. M. B., surrounded by a wreath of cassia. This urn was placed on the top of the obelisk which was erected on the tomb. Three days after the interment, Solomon repaired with his court to the temple, and all the brethren being arranged as at the funeral, he directed his prayer to heaven, examined the tomb and the inscription on the urn: struck with admiration, he raised his hands and eyes to heaven, and said in the joy of his heart, "It is accomplished and complete."

Q. Where was this monument situated? A. Near the west end of the temple.

[Pg 138]Q. What is meant by the letter J. on the square stone? A. Jeva. The ineffable name as known by us.

Q. What is meant by the letters J. M. B. on the triangular stone? A. They are the initials of the three Hebrew words, Joshagn, Mawkoms, Bawheer—signifying "the elect sleeps in his place."

Q. What is signified by the pyramids in the Lodge? A. Pyramids were used by our Egyptian brethren, for Masonic purposes. Being built on rocks, they shadow forth the durability of Masonry. Their bases were four-cornered, their external surfaces equilateral triangles, pointing to the four cardinal points. The pyramidical form is also intended to remind us of our mortality. Its broad base represents the commencement, and its termination in a point, the end of human life.

Closing.—Master strikes two.—Marshal rises. Master says, "The last as well as the first care," etc., as in opening.

INTIMATE SECRETARY.

Opening.—Most Illustrious Master knocks nine.—Marshal rises.

Master says, "Are we all Intimate Secretaries?" Answer—We are, Most Illustrious.

Q. Your place? A. In the anti-chamber at the head of the guards.

Q. Your business there? A. To see that the hall of audience is duly guarded.

Q. How are we guarded? A. By Perfect Masters.

The Most Illustrious says, "I appoint Brother — —, Lieutenant of the Guards, to aid you in the execution of your duty. Repair to your station and see that none approach without permission." The guards then fall on their right knees, cross their hands in such a manner that their thumbs touch their temples, and repeat in a low voice, Jeva (pron. Je-vau), thrice, and then retire. Solomon then strikes twice nine, upon which Hiram rises; they make signs of former degrees with twenty signs of this degree. Most Illustrious strikes three times nine and declares Lodge open. A triple triangle is placed on a Bible.

Lecture.—Question—Are you an intimate Secretary? Answer—I am.

Q. How were you received? A. By curiosity.

Q. Explain that. A. Being placed among the guards in the anti-chamber, a brother, representing the King of Tyre, hastily made his way through the guards, with a countenance expressive of anger, and entered the hall of audience, leaving the door partly open; curiosity led me to the door to observe what passed within.

Q. Was you perceived by them? A. I was. Hiram, King of Tyre, hearing the noise I made, suddenly turned his head and discovered me. He exclaimed to Solomon, "My brother, there is a listener." Solomon replied, "It is impossible, since the guards are without."

Q. What followed? A. Hiram, without replying, rushed to the door, and dragging me into the Lodge, exclaimed, "Here he is." Solomon inquired, "What shall we do with him?" Hiram laid his hand on his sword, and answered, "Let him be delivered into the custody of the guards, that we may determine what punishment we shall inflict upon [Pg 139]him, for this offence." Solomon then struck on the table which stood before him, whereupon the guards entered, and saluting the Lodge, received this order from him: "Take this prisoner, secure him, and let him be forthcoming when called for."

Q. Were those Guards Intimate Secretaries or Perfect Masters? A. Of that I was then ignorant, but I am now convinced that I was the first that was made an Intimate Secretary.

Q. What followed? A. I was conducted out of the hall of audience, and detained in the custody of the guards, until a second alarm from within caused them to return with me into the hall; when, the guards taking their seats around me, I was thus addressed by Solomon: "I have, by my entreaties, prevailed upon my worthy ally, Hiram, King of Tyre, whom your vain curiosity had offended, to pardon you, and receive you into favor, etc.; are you willing to take an obligation to that effect?" which question I answered in the affirmative, and then received at the altar the obligation of this degree.

Q. Repeat the obligation (same as Perfect Master). A. Under penalty of having my body quartered. So help me, etc.

Q. What did the Master then communicate to you? A. He addressed me thus: "My brother, I receive you an Intimate Secretary, on your having promised to be faithful," etc., and then gave me the signs, words, and tokens of this degree.

Q. Give me the signs? A. The first alludes to the penalty made by clenching the right hand, and drawing it from the left shoulder to the right hip. The second is the one made at opening by guards.

Q. Give me the token? A. Made by joining right hands, and turning them downwards thrice, saying, the first time, Berith—the second time, Nedir—and the third time, Shelemoth.

Q. Give me the pass-words? A. Joabert, response Terbel. The first is the name of the listener; the second, of the captain of the guards.

Q. Give me the mysterious word? A. Jeva (pronounced Je-vau).

Q. What was then done to you? A. I was invested with the jewel and apron of this degree, and was thus addressed by the Master: "The color of your ribbon is intended to remind you of the blood of Hiram Abiff, the last drop of which he chose to spill, rather than betray his trust; may you be equally faithful. The triple triangle is emblematical of the three theological virtues, faith, hope and charity; it is also emblematical of the three masons who were present at the opening of the first lodge of Intimate Secretaries, to wit: Solomon, King of Israel; Hiram, King of Tyre, and Joabert, a favorite of King Solomon."

Q. What then followed? A. I was ordered to salute the King of Tyre as an Intimate Secretary, and attend to the instruction of this degree.

Q. To what does the three times nine allude in this degree? A. To the twenty-seven lamps with which the hall of audience was enlightened.

Q. What is signified by the letter J which you perceive in the clouds? A. It is the initial of the ineffable name as known by us.

Q. What is represented by the door? A. The door by which they entered from the palace.

Q. Why was the hall of audience furnished with black hangings [Pg 140]strewed with tears? A. To represent the grief of Solomon, for the unhappy fate of Hiram Abiff.

Q. What is meant by the A and the two P's in the triangle? A. Alliance, promise and perfection.

Q. Give me the history of this degree. A. Hiram gave Solomon cedar trees, and fir trees, etc.

Closing.—Master knocks nine (Marshal rises) and says, "Brother Grand Marshal, the last as well as the first care of an Intimate Secretary? To see that the hall of audience is duly guarded. Your place, etc. How are we guarded, etc. Brother Captain of the guards, we are about to close this Lodge of Intimate Secretaries, repair to your station," etc. (Upon this, guards all make sign as at opening, and leave the room.) Then Solomon strikes twice nine, and Hiram rises—signs reversed. Solomon knocks three times nine, and declares Lodge closed.

PROVOST AND JUDGE.

Opening.—Thrice Illustrious knocks three. Marshal rises. Thrice Illustrious says, "Brother Grand Marshal, are we all Provosts and Judges?" Marshal. We are.

Thrice Illustrious. Your place? M. In the North.

T. I. Your business there? M. To see that the middle chamber is duly tyled.

Thrice Illustrious says, "Attend to your duty, and inform the Tyler that we are about to open this Lodge of Provost and Judge." (Grand Marshal obeys.) Thrice Illustrious strikes four. Wardens rise. "Brother Junior Warden, where is the Master placed?" Answer.—Everywhere.

Q. Why so? A. To superintend the workmen, direct the work, and render justice to every man.

Q. What is the hour? A. Break of day, eight, two and seven. Thrice Illustrious strikes five.—Brethren rise. Thrice Illustrious says, "It is then time to begin our labors; give notice that I am going to open a Lodge of Provost and Judge, by four and one." (Signs given, Master strikes four and one—Senior Warden, four and one—Junior Warden, four and one, and Marshal, four and one; the brethren all strike four and one, with their hands, and the Master declares the Lodge open.)

Reception.—Master of Ceremonies conducts candidate to the door, and knocks four and one, which is answered from within by Senior Warden, and Thrice Illustrious and Senior Warden says, "While the Provosts and Judges are engaged in right, an alarm is heard at the inner door of the Lodge," etc. A golden key is placed on the Bible.

Lecture.—Question—Are you a Provost and Judge? A. I am, and render justice to all men without distinction.

Q. Where were you received? A. In the middle chamber.

Q. How did you gain admission there? A. By four and one distinct knocks.

Q. To what do they allude? A. To the qualifications of a Provost and Judge, to wit: impartiality, justice, prudence, discretion and mercy; of which the five lights in the middle chamber are also emblematical.

[Pg 141]Q. How were these knocks answered? A. By four and one from within.

Q. What was then said to you? A. I was asked by what further right, etc.

Q. Your answer? A. By the right of a pass.

Q. What was then said to you? A. Wait until the Thrice Illustrious is informed of your request, and his answer returned.

Q. What was his answer? A. Introduce him in due and ancient form.

Q. What was that form? A. I was conducted by the Master of Ceremonies to the south-west corner of the middle chamber, between the Wardens, and caused to kneel on my right knee and say Beroke.

Q. What answer was given to that? A. The Thrice Illustrious said Kumi.

Q. What do these words signify? A. The first signifies to kneel, the last, to rise.

Q. What followed? A. I was conducted three times 'round the Lodge, giving the signs of the ineffable degrees, and led to the altar, and caused to kneel and take the obligation of this degree.

Q. Repeat that obligation. A. Same as Perfect Master, with the addition, that I will justly and impartially decide all matters of difference between brethren of this degree, if in my power so to do, under penalty of being punished as an unjust Judge, by having my nose severed from my face. So help me, etc.

Q. What followed? A. The Thrice Illustrious gave me the signs, tokens and words of this degree.

Q. Give me the signs? A. (Put the two first fingers of your right hand to the right side of your nose, the thumb under the chin, forming a square.)

Q. Give me the token? A. (Clench the three first fingers of the right hand over the thumb, and join hands by interlacing the little fingers.)

Q. Give me the pass-word? A. Jev (pronounced Jo).

Q. What was then done to you? A. I was invested with the jewel, apron and gloves of this degree, and was thus addressed:—"Respectable Brother, it gives me joy that I am now about to recompense, etc. This key opens a small ebony box, in which are contained the plans for the building of the temple, and this key opens a small ivory box containing all the keys of the temple. I clothe you with a white apron, lined with red, having a pocket in its centre, and in which you are intended to carry the plans for the building of the temple, that they may be laid out on the tressel board for the use of the workmen when wanted. I also give you a balance in equilibrio, as a badge of your office. Let it remind you of that equity of judgment which should characterize your decisions."

Q. What was next done? A. He made me a Provost and Judge.

Q. In what manner? A. He gave me a blow on each shoulder, and said, "By the power with which I am invested, I constitute you Provost and Judge over all the works and workmen of the temple. Be impartial, just, prudent, discreet and merciful. Go salute the Junior and Senior Wardens as a Provost and Judge, and return to the Lodge for further instruction.

[Pg 142]Second Section.—Question—What did you perceive in the middle chamber? Answer—A curtain, behind which was suspended a small ebony box containing the plans for the construction of the temple.

Q. What else did you see? A. A triangle enclosing the letters G. A.

Q. What is their meaning and use? A. Grand Architect, and are designed to make us remember him in all our decisions and actions.

Q. Did you perceive anything more? A. I saw the letters I. H. S. with the sprig of cassia.

Q. What is meant thereby? A. Imitate Hiram's Silence, and Justice, Humanity and Secrecy, which are designed to teach Provost and Judge, that while their decisions are just, they should be tempered with humanity, or mercy, and that all differences which may arise among the craft, should be kept secret from the world.

Q. What was the intention of Solomon in instituting this degree? A. To strengthen the means of preserving order among such a vast number of workmen; the duty of Provosts and Judges being, to decide all differences that might arise among the brethren.

Q. Who was the first that was made Provost and Judge? A. Joabert being honored with the intimate confidence of King Solomon, received this new mark of distinction. Solomon first created Tito, Adoniram, and Abda, his father, Provosts and Judges, and gave them orders to initiate Joabert into the mysteries of this degree, and to give him all the keys of the temple, which were inclosed in a small ivory box suspended in the Sanctum Sanctorum, under a rich canopy. When Joabert was first admitted into this sacred place, he was struck with awe, and involuntarily found himself in a kneeling posture, and said, Beroke; Solomon observing him, said Kumi, which signifies to rise.

Q. Whence came you as a Provost and Judge? A. I came and am going everywhere.

Closing.—Thrice Illustrious Master knocks three (Marshal rises) and says, "Brother Grand Marshal, the last as well as the first care of Provost and Judge?" Answer—To see that the middle chamber is duly tyled.— "Attend to your duty, and inform the Tyler that we are about to close this Lodge of Provosts and Judges by four and one." Marshal reports. Thrice Illustrious strikes four. Wardens rise, and Master says, "Brother Senior Warden, what is the hour?" Ans.—Break of day, 8, 2 and 7.

Q. Brother Junior Warden, how so? A. Because Provosts and Judges should be ready at all times to render Justice. Thrice Illustrious knocks four and one, and brethren all rise. Signs reversed given. Thrice Illustrious strikes four and one, Marshal four and one, Junior Warden four and one, and Senior Warden four and one, and then all the brethren strike four & one with their hands, and Thrice Illustrious declares Lodge duly closed.

INTENDANT OF THE BUILDINGS (OR I. B.).

Opening.—Most Puissant knocks three (Marshal rises) and says, "Brother Grand Marshal, are we all I. B.?" Answer—We are, Most Puissant.

[Pg 143]Q. Your place? A. In the north.

Q. Your business there? A. To see that the Lodge is duly tyled.— "Attend to your duty, and inform the Lodge that we are about to open a Lodge of I. B. by the number five." Marshal obeys. Most Puissant knocks four, and Wardens rise.—Q. Brother Senior Warden, what is the hour? A. Break of day.—Most Puissant knocks five, and brethren all rise. Most Puissant says, "If it is break of day, it is time to begin our labors; give notice that I am going to open a Lodge of I. B." Senior Warden obeys. All make signs. Most Puissant knocks five, Senior Warden five, Junior Warden five, and brethren five, with their hands; and Most Puissant declares the Lodge open.

Reception.—Most Puissant knocks seven, and Senior Warden rises. Most Puissant says, "My excellent brother, how shall we repair the loss of our worthy Hiram Abiff, he is now removed from us, and we are thereby deprived of his counsel and services; can you give me any advice in this important matter?" Senior Warden answers, "The method I would propose, would be to select a chief from the five orders of architecture upon whom we may confer the degree of I. B., and by his assistance fill the secret chamber of the third story." Most Puissant says, "I approve of your advice, and to convince you of my readiness to follow it, I appoint you and brothers Adoniram and Abda to carry the same into execution. Excellent Brothers, let Adoniram go into the middle chamber and see if he can find a chief of the five orders of architecture." Junior Warden goes out of the Lodge into the ante-chamber, and finding the candidate, addresses him as in the Lecture.

Note.—When the alarm of five is given Senior Warden rises and says, "Most Puissant, we are disturbed in our deliberations by an alarm at the inner door of the secret chamber." Most Puissant says, "Brother Senior Warden, see the cause of that alarm."

Lecture.—Question—Are you an Intendant of the Buildings? A. I have made the five steps of exactness; I have penetrated the inmost parts of the temple, and have seen the great light, in which were three mysterious characters, J. J. J.

Q. How were you received? A. Being in the middle chamber, in company with the Master of Ceremonies, Adoniram entered and inquired, "Is there here a chief of the five orders of architecture?"

Q. Your answer? A. I am one.

Q. What followed? A. I was then asked, "My dear brother, have you zeal to apply yourself with attention to that which the Most Puissant shall request of you?"

Q. Your answer? A. I have, and will comply with the request of the Most Puissant, and raise this edifice to his honor and glory.

Q. What followed? Ans. Adoniram demanded of me the signs, words, and tokens of my former degrees, which being given, the Master of Ceremonies conducted me to the door of the Lodge, where he gave me five distinct knocks.

Q. To what did they allude? A. To the five orders of architecture.

Q. How were they answered? A. By five from within.

Q. What was then said to you. A. I was asked, "Who comes there?"

[Pg 144]Q. Your answer? A. A chief of the five orders of architecture, who is to be employed in the works of the secret chamber.

Q. What was then said to you? A. I was then asked by what further right, etc.

Q. Your answer? A. By the right of a pass-word.

Q. Give me that pass-word? A. Bonahim (pronounced Bo-nau-heem).

Q. What was then said to you? A. Wait until the Most Puissant is informed, etc.

Q. What was his answer? A. Let him be introduced in due form.

Q. What followed? A. I was conducted to the altar and caused to recede five steps, and then to advance to the altar by five steps of regular exactness.

Q. What is meant thereby? A. That I should recede from vice, and advance to virtue, before I was qualified to supply the place of so good a man as the lamented Hiram Abiff.

Q. What followed? A. I was laid prostrate before the altar, with a sprig of cassia in my right hand, and my left upon the first great light of Masonry, in which posture I took the obligation of this degree.

Q. Repeat that obligation. A. (Same as Perfect Master) under penalty of being deprived of my sight. So help, etc.

Q. What followed? A. I was thus addressed by the Most Puissant: "Your present posture is that of a dead man, and is designed to remind you of the fate of our worthy Hiram Abiff. I shall now raise you in the same manner he was raised, under the sprig of cassia." I was then raised by the Master's grip, and further addressed, "By your being raised, our hope is signified, that in some measure you will repair his loss, by imitating his bright example."

Q. What followed? A. I received the signs, tokens and words of this degree.

Q. Give me the signs. A. (Interlace the fingers, and place the hands over the eyes, alluding to penalty; second sign is that of grief, made like Fellow Craft's, with left hand on the left hip.)

Q. Give me the token? A. (Take hold of each other by the right wrists with the right hand.)

Q. Give me the pass-word. A. Bonahim.

Q. What does that word signify? A. Builders.

Q. Give me the words. A. Achard, jenok (pronounced yo-kayn).

Q. Give me the mysterious word. A. Jah (pronounced yaw).

Q. What was next done? A. I was invested with the apron, gloves and jewels of this degree, and was thus addressed: "I decorate you with a red ribbon, to be worn crossing the breast from the right shoulder to the left hip, to which is suspended a triangle fastened with a green ribbon. I also present you with a white apron, lined with red, and bordered with green. The red is emblematical of that zeal which should characterize you as an I. of B., and the green, of the hope we entertain that you will supply the place of our lamented Hiram Abiff.

Q. What is meant by the letters B. A. J. in the triangle which you wear? A. They are the initials of the pass-word and words of this degree.

Q. What followed? A. I was directed to salute the Senior Warden as [Pg 145]an Intendant of the Buildings, and return to the east for further instruction.

Second Section.—Question—What did you see in the Lodge? Answer—A triangle enclosing a circle, having on its circumference the letters J. A. I. N., and in its centre the letters J. J. J.

Q. What is signified by the circle in the triangle? A. The eternity of the powers of God, which hath neither beginning nor end.

Q. What is signified by the letters J. A. I. N.? A. They are the initials of the four Hebrew words, Jad, Ail, Jotsare, and Nogah, which are expressive of four attributes of the Deity; power, omnipresence, creation and splendor.

Q. What is signified by the letters J. J. J? A. Jah, Jokayn and Jireh, signifying "The Lord, the Creator seeth."

Q. What else did you see? A. A blazing star with five beams, in the centre of which appeared the letter J.

Q. What is signified by the five beams? A. The five equal lights of Masonry, the Bible, the square, the compass, the key, and the triangle.

Q. What is signified by the letter J.? A. It is the initial of the ineffable name, as known by us.

Q. Are you in darkness? A. No, the blazing star is my guide.

Q. What is your age? A. 27, or 5, 7 and 15.

Q. To what do those three numbers allude? A. To the five chiefs of the five orders of architecture, to seven cubits, which was the breadth of the golden candlestick with seven branches, and the fifteen Fellow Crafts, who conspired against the life of our Grand Master, Hiram Abiff.

Closing.—Most Puissant knocks three (Grand Marshal rises) and says, "Brother Grand Marshal, the last as well as the first care of I. of B.?" Answer. To see that the Lodge is duly tyled. "Attend to your duty," etc. Most Puissant knocks four, and Warden rises; "Brother Senior Warden, what is the hour?" A. Seven at night. Most Puissant strikes five—all brethren rise. Most Puissant says, "As it is seven at night, it is time to retire: Brother Junior Warden, give notice that I am going to close this Lodge of Intendants of the Building." Signs reversed, Most Puissant knocks five, Junior Warden seven, and Senior Warden fifteen, then the brethren five, seven and fifteen, with their hands, and the Most Puissant declares the Lodge closed.

ELECTED KNIGHTS OF NINE.

Opening.—The brethren sit cross-legged, and lean their heads on their right hands. Most Potent knocks seven (Grand Marshal rises), "Brother Grand Marshal, are we all Elected Knights of Nine?" Ans. We are.

Q. Your place? A. In the north, Most Potent.

Q. Your business there? A. To see that the Chapter is duly guarded.—"Please attend to your duty, and inform the Sentinel that we are about to open this Chapter of E. K. and charge him," etc. Marshal obeys. Most Potent knocks eight, and Warden rises, and Master says, "Brother Stokin, are you an E. K.?" A. One cavern received me, one lamp gave [Pg 146]me light, and one fountain refreshed me. Q. What is the hour? A. Break of day. Most Potent knocks eight quick and one slow strokes, and companies all arise. Most Potent says, "If it is break of day, it is time to open a Chapter of E. K's. Inform the companies," etc. Warden obeys. Signs given. Most Potent knocks eight and one, and Warden eight and one, and companies eight and one, with their hands; and Most Potent declares the Chapter open.

Lecture.—Question—Are you an E. K.? A. One cavern received me, one lamp gave me light, and one fountain refreshed me.

Q. Where were you received? A. In the audience chamber of Solomon.

Q. How were you received? A. I was hoodwinked and conducted by the Master of Ceremonies to the door of the Chapter, where he gave eight and one distinct knocks.

Q. To what do those knocks allude? A. To the number of the nine elect.

Q. How were those knocks answered? A. By eight and one from within.

236

Q. What followed? A. I was asked, "Who comes there?"

Q. Your answer? A. A companion, to whose lot it has fallen to accompany the stranger in search of the assassins of Hiram Abiff.

Q. What followed? A. I was conducted by the hand to the west, and asked by the Most Potent, what I wanted.

Q. Your answer? A. To be made an Elected Knight.

Q. What then followed? A. I was asked if I had courage to go in pursuit of the assassins of Hiram Abiff, which question I answered in the affirmative, and was addressed by the Most Potent in the following manner: — "If you have, you shall be shown the place where one of his murderers lies concealed; a stranger has discovered it to me, and if you have resolution, follow this stranger."

Q. What was then done to you? A. The Master of Ceremonies led me out of the Chapter, by intricate roads, and at last seated me on a stone, and thus addressed me: — "I am going to leave you, but be of good cheer, I shall not be long absent; when I am gone, you must take the bandage off your eyes, and drink some water from the fountain beside you, that you may be refreshed after so fatiguing a journey."

Q. What followed? A. I removed the bandage and found myself alone in a cavern, in which was a lamp, a fountain, and a head just severed from the body. In a short time the Master of Ceremonies returned, and directed me to take a poniard in my right hand, and the head in my left, and then conducted me to the door of the Chapter, where I knocked eight and one with my foot, which was answered from within, and I was asked, "What do you want?"

Q. Your answer? A. To enter this Chapter of Elected Knights.

Q. What followed? A. I was asked by what right I claimed this privilege.

Q. Your answer? A. I Have performed a feat for the honor of the craft, which I hope will entitle me to this degree.

Q. What followed? A. I was admitted, and directed to approach the altar by eight quick and one slow steps, still holding the head in my left hand, and the poniard in my right, as if in the act of striking; the ninth step brought me to the altar, where the Most Potent addressed me in an [Pg 147]angry tone: "Wretch, what have you done, do you not know that by this rash act you have deprived me of an opportunity of inflicting condign punishment on the assassin?"

Q. What followed? A. The companies made earnest intercession for me, observing that my offence had doubtless arisen from the wrath of my zeal, and not from any bad intention. Upon this the Most Potent was reconciled, and he administered to me the obligation of this degree, the companies all standing 'round me with their poniards as if going to stab me.

Q. Repeat that obligation? A. (Same as in Perfect Master.) Under penalty of being stabbed in my head and in my heart. So help, etc.

Q. What followed? A. The Most Potent gave me the sign, token and words of this degree.

Q. Give me the sign? A. (Clap your right hand first to your head and then to your heart.)

Q. Give me the token? A. (Grasp the thumb of your brother's right hand, both clenching the fingers and extending the thumb of the hand that is uppermost.)

Q. To what does that token allude? A. The eight fingers and extended thumb allude to the eight and one elect; the one to Joabert, who left his eight companions, and went alone in search of, etc.

Q. Give me the pass-words? A. Rawkam and Akirop.

Q. What is the word? A. Bugelkal, who was chief of the tabernacle.

Q. Give me the mysterious word? A. Jeva (pronounced Je-vau).

Q. What was then done to you? A. I was invested with the apron, gloves and jewels of this degree, and ordered to salute the Warden, and to return to the east for further instructions.

Second Section.—Question—Give me the history of this degree? Ans. After the death of Hiram Abiff, the three ruffians who had been apprehended having made their escape, a great assembly of Masters had sat, etc., he had only time to pronounce Naukam, which signifies, "vengeance is taken," and expired. Joabert being extremely fatigued, refreshed himself at the spring which he found in the cavern, and then slept until he was awakened by the other eight, who arrived shortly after. On beholding what Joabert had done, they all exclaimed Naukam. Joabert then severed the head from the body, divided the body into 4 quarters, which were burnt to ashes, and the ashes scattered to the four winds of heaven. Joabert then taking the head, etc., again reconciled. Solomon then ordered the head to be placed on the east pinnacle of the temple.

Q. What was the name of the assassin? A. Jubelum Akirop.

Q. From what number were the nine elect chosen? A. Ninety-nine.

Q. Where was the assassin found? A. In a cavern, near the coast of Joppa.

Q. How did the nine elect travel? A. By dark and intricate roads, which often obliged them to cross their legs, and this is the reason why the nine elect sit in this manner in the Chapter.

Q. What is meant by the dog you saw on the carpet, in the Lodge? A. [Pg 148]The dog of the stranger, through whose sagacity Akirop was discovered.

Q. What does the color, black, denote in this degree? A. Grief.

Q. What is your age? A. Eight and one, accomplished.

Closing.—Most Potent knocks seven (Grand Marshal rises) and says, "The last as well as the first care of a Chapter of E. K.?" Ans. To see that the Chapter is duly guarded.—Please attend to your duty and inform the Sentinel, etc. Most Potent knocks eight, and Warden rises. Q. What is the hour? A. Evening. Most Potent knocks eight and one. Companies all rise. Companion Stokin gives notice, etc. Most Potent knocks eight and one, Warden eight and one, Companions eight and one, and the Chapter is declared duly closed.

MASTERS ELECTED OF FIFTEEN.

Opening.—Most Potent knocks five (Grand Marshal rises) and says, "Brother Grand Marshal, are we all Masters Elected of Fifteen?" A. We are, Most Potent. Q. Your place, etc.? Your business, etc.? Please inform the Tyler that we are about to open a Lodge of Masters Elected of Fifteen. Most Potent knocks twice five—Senior Warden rises. Most Potent knocks three times five. Brethren rise. Most Potent says, "Brother Inspector, give notice that I am going to open a Lodge of Masters Elected of Fifteen, by three times five." Inspector obeys. Most Potent knocks three times five, Senior Warden three times five, Junior Warden three times five, and the brethren the same, and the lodge is declared open.

Lecture.—Question—Are you a Master Elected of Fifteen? Answer—My zeal and works have prepared me that honor.

Q. How were you prepared? A. A head was placed in my hand, and I was conducted to the door of the Lodge by the Master of Ceremonies who knocked three times five.

Q. How were those knocks answered? A. By three times five from within.

Q. To what do they allude? A. The fifteen elected Masters.

Q. What followed? A. I was asked, "Who comes there?"

Q. Your answer? A. An Elected Knight who is desirous of joining the other Knights, for the purpose of discovering the other assassins.

Q. What was then said to you? A. I was told to wait until the Most Potent had been informed of my request, and his answer returned.

Q. What was his answer? A. Let him be introduced in due form.

Q. What was that due form? A. I was conducted to the altar, and caused to make fifteen steps in a triangular form, which brought me again to the altar, when the Most Potent ordered me to kneel, and thus addressed me: "My brother, the Elected Masters here present, wish me to admit you to this degree; will you take the obligation appertaining to the same?" which being answered in the affirmative, I took the obligation.

Q. Repeat that obligation? A. (Same as Perfect Master.) Under penalty of having my body cut open perpendicularly, and my head cut off and placed on the highest pinnacle in the world. So help me, etc.

[Pg 149]Q. What did the Most Potent then communicate to you? A. He gave me the signs, words, and token of this degree.

Q. Give me the signs? A. (Hold the thumb of the right hand at the bottom of the belly, and move it perpendicularly upwards.) The second sign (that of the Entered Apprentice, with the fingers clenched.)

Q. Give me the token? A. (Join left hands.)

Q. Give me the pass-word? A. Eleham.

Q. Give me the mysterious word? A. Jevah (pronounced Je-vau).

Q. What then followed? A. I was invested with the apron, gloves and jewels of this degree, and directed to salute the Senior Warden as a Master Elected of Fifteen, and return to the east for further instruction.

Second Section.—Question—Give me the history of this degree? A. Not long after the execution, they were discovered cutting stone, in a quarry. They were immediately seized and carried to Jerusalem, and imprisoned in the tower of Achizer, and at ten o'clock on the ensuing morning, they were brought forth for execution. They were bound neck and middle, to posts, with their arms extended, and their bellies were cut open by the executioner, lengthways and across, and thus they remained until six in the evening, their entrails exposed to flies and other insects; their tongues and entrails were afterwards taken out for the beasts of the field and the birds of the air to prey upon, and their heads were cut off and placed upon spikes, like that of Akirop, on the west and south pinnacles of the temple. Thus we see that although corruption, perjury and treason assisted our ancient Knights, their quarters were discovered by the unerring eye of justice, and they were doomed to suffer penalty tantamount to their crimes.

Q. What were the names of the two assassins? A. Jubela Kurmavel, and Jubelo Gravolet.

Q. At what hour did the assassins expire? A. At six in the evening.

Closing.—Most Potent knocks five. Grand Marshal rises. Most Potent says, "Brother Grand Marshal, the last as well as the first care of a Lodge of Masters Elected of Fifteen?" A. To see that the Lodge is duly tyled.—"Please attend," etc. Most Potent knocks twice five.—Senior Warden rises. Signs reversed. Most Potent knocks three times five, which is repeated by Wardens, and then by brothers with their hands, etc.

ILLUSTRIOUS KNIGHTS ELECTED.

Opening.—Most Potent knocks ten. Grand Marshal rises. Most Potent says, "Are we all Illustrious Knights Elected?" A. We are, Most Potent. "Your place? etc. Your duty?" A. To see that the Chapter is duly guarded. "Please attend," etc. Most Potent knocks eleven. Grand Inspector rises. "Companion Inspector, what is the hour?" A. It is twelve. Most Potent knocks twelve. Companions rise. "If it is twelve, it is time to labor by the greatest of lights." Signs given. Most Potent knocks twelve, Inspector twelve, and Companion twelve, with their hands, etc.

[Pg 150]Lecture.—Question—Are you an Illustrious Knight Elected? Answer. My name will inform you.

Q. What is that name? A. Payrawsh Bawheer, or Illustrious Knight elected.

Q. How were you admitted? A. I was hoodwinked and conducted by the Master of Ceremonies to the door of the Chapter, where he gave twelve distinct knocks.

Q. To what did they allude? A. To the twelve tribes of Israel.

Q. How were they answered? A. By twelve from within.

Q. What was then said to you? A. "Who comes there?"

Q. Your answer? A. A Master Elected of Fifteen wishes to receive the degree of Illustrious Knight.

Q. What was then said to you? A. I was asked by what further right, etc., and I was told to wait until the Most Potent was informed of my request, and his answer returned.

Q. What was that answer? A. Let him be introduced in due form.

Q. What then followed? A. I was conducted to the west, and the Most Potent inquired what I wanted.

Q. Your answer? A. To receive the degree of Illustrious Knight, as a reward for my zeal and labor.

Q. What did the Most Potent say to you then? A. My brother, you cannot receive this degree until you have given us satisfactory proof that you have not been an accomplice in the death of our Grand Master, Hiram Abiff; to assure us of this, we require you to participate in a symbolic offering, of a portion of the heart of our Respectable Master, Hiram Abiff, which we have preserved since his assassination. You are to swallow the portion we present to you. Every faithful Mason may receive it without injury, but it cannot remain in the body of one who is perjured. Are you disposed to submit to this trial?

Q. What was your answer? A. I am.

Q. What followed? A. The Most Potent directed the Master of Ceremonies to cause me to advance to the altar, by twelve upright regular steps, where the Most Potent, with the trowel, presented to me the symbolic offering which I swallowed, and was thus addressed by the Most Potent: "This mystic oblation, which, like you, we have received forms a tie so strong that nothing can oppress it; woe to him who attempts to disunite us. I then received the obligation of this degree.

Q. Repeat that obligation. A. (Same as Perfect Master.) Under penalty of having my hands nailed to my breast. So help, etc.

Q. What was then communicated to you? A. The Most Potent removed the bandage, and gave me the sign. (Cross hands on breast) it alludes to penalty.

Q. Give me the token? A. (Token of Intimate Secretary, with left hand on brother's heart.)

Q. Give me the pass-word? A. Emun.

Q. What does that word signify? A. Truth.

Q. Give me the mysterious word? A. Joha (pronounced Yo-hay).

Q. What followed? A. I was invested with the apron, gloves and jewels of this degree, and was told the device on my sash and apron, and [Pg 151]also the color of the latter, was an emblem of a heart inflamed with gratitude for the honors and rewards conferred on me, and the sword of that justice which overtook and punished the assassins, and was designed to admonish me that perjury and treason will never escape the sword of justice, and I was directed to go and salute the Inspector, and return to the east for further instruction.

Second Section.—Of what was the symbolic offering presented to you at your initiation composed? A. Of flour, milk, wine and oil.

Q. What did they represent? A. Flour represents goodness, the milk, gentleness, the wine, strength or fortitude, and the oil, light and wisdom, qualities which distinguished Hiram Abiff, and should distinguish every illustrious Knight.

Q. How were the Illustrious Knights employed at the erection of the temple? A. They had command over the twelve tribes, and by their strict attention, promoted peace and harmony, and animated the laborers with cheerfulness.

Q. What was the intention of Solomon in instituting this degree? A. To reward the zeal, etc., and also by their preferment to make more.

Closing.—Most Potent knocks ten (Grand Marshal rises). "The last as well as the first care of a Chapter of Illustrious Knights?" A. To see that the Chapter is duly guarded. "Attend to your duty, and inform the Sentinel," etc. Most Potent knocks eleven (Senior Warden rises). "Brother Inspector, what is the hour?" A. Low six. Most Potent knocks twelve (brethren rise). "Brother Inspector, give notice," etc. Signs. Most Potent knocks twelve, Inspector twelve, brethren twelve, with their hands, and Most Potent declares the Chapter duly closed.

GRAND MASTER ARCHITECTS.

Opening.—Most Potent knocks one (Grand Marshal rises). "Are we all," etc. Your place? etc. Your duty? A. To see that the Chapter is duly guarded. "Attend," etc. Most Potent knocks two.—Warden rises. Most Potent says, "What is the hour?" A. A star indicates the first instant, the first hour, and the first day, in which the Grand Architect commenced the creation of the universe. Most Potent knocks one and two.— Companions rise. Most Potent says, "Companions, it is the first instant, the first hour, the first day, the first year, when Solomon commenced the temple; the first day, the first hour, the first instant for opening this Chapter. It is time to commence our labors. Give notice," etc. Signs. Most Potent knocks one and two, Senior Warden one and two, Companions one and two, and Most Potent declares Chapter open, etc.

Lecture.—Question—Are you a Grand Master Architect? Answer—I know the use of every mathematical instrument.

Q. What are they? A. A square, a single compass, a compass with four points, a rule, a line, a compass of perfection, a quadrant, a level and plumb.

Q. Where were you received? A. In a white place, painted with flames.

[Pg 152]Q. What does that signify? A. That purity of heart and that zeal which should characterize every Grand Master Architect.

Q. How were you admitted? A. I was conducted by the Master of Ceremonies to the door of the Chapter, where he gave one and two distinct knocks.

Q. How were those knocks answered? A. One and two from within.

Q. What followed? A. I was asked, "Who comes there?"

Q. Your answer? A. An Illustrious Knight who wishes to receive the degree of Grand Architect.

Q. What then followed? A. I was conducted by the Master of Ceremonies to the west, and thus addressed: "It has become necessary to form a school of Architecture for the instruction of the brethren employed in the temple, as none but skilful Architects can bring the same to perfection. In order to prevent some brethren from receiving the honors and rewards due only to brethren of talents, we have deemed it expedient to prove and test all those who present themselves as candidates for this degree. We, therefore, require you to make the tour of the temple, for the purpose of examining the work, and to produce a plan drawn with exactness which you must present for inspection, that we may judge whether you are entitled to this degree."

Q. What followed? A. I was conducted through the anti-chamber and 'round the Lodge, when the Master of Ceremonies again stationed me in the west, and where I drew a plan according to my direction. When the same was finished, the Master of Ceremonies informed the Most Potent that I had obeyed his directions. Most Potent inquired, "My brother, what are the fruits of your travels?"

Q. Your answer? A. "Most Potent, I have brought a plan of the works of the temple, which I am ready to present for inspection."

Q. What followed? A. I was directed to approach the east, and present the plan to the Most Potent, which I accordingly did, and the Most Potent examined the same, and then passed it on to the other companions, who, after examining, returned it with expressions of approbation, and then the Most Potent addressed me thus: "It is with pleasure we witness the skill you have manifested in fulfilling the conditions prescribed to you, but we require further proof before you can be admitted among us. We again require you to travel."

Q. What followed? A. I was conducted once 'round the Lodge, to the north, where I stopped to view the north star, and was told, that as the north star was a guide to mariners, so ought virtue to be a guide to every Grand Master Architect, and was again conducted to the west, and directed to approach the east by one and two steps, which brought me to the altar, when the Most Potent inquired, "What have you learned in your travels?"

Q. Your answer? A. That virtue as well as talents should be possessed by every one who is admitted to this degree.

Q. What followed? A. I received the obligation of a Grand Master Architect.

Q. Repeat the obligation? A. (Same as Perfect Master.) Under the penalty of having my left hand cut in twain. So help, etc.

[Pg 153]Q. What then followed? A. I was then addressed by the Most Potent.

Q. What then followed? A. The Most Potent gave me the signs, words, and tokens of this degree.

Q. Give me the sign? A. (Make the motion of writing in the left hand), also alluding to penalty.

Q. Give me the token? A. (Interlace the last finger of the right hand, so as to form a square, and place the left hand on each other's right shoulder.)

Q. Give me the pass-word? A. Rab-kuam.

Q. What does it signify? A. Grand Master Architect.

Q. Give me the mysterious word? A. Jehovah (pronounced Ye-ho-wah).

Q. What was then done to you? A. The Most Potent invested me with the jewel, apron and gloves of this degree, and thus addressed me: "I have elevated," etc.

Q. What then followed? A. I was directed to salute the Senior Warden, as a Grand Architect, and return to the east for further instruction.

Q. Give me the history? A. Solomon established this degree for the purpose, etc.

Q. What do the seven small rays 'round the north star signify? A. Seven liberal arts and sciences.

Closing.—Most Potent knocks one. (Grand Marshal rises.) Most Potent says, "The last as well as the first care," etc. Most Potent knocks two. Senior Warden rises. Most Potent says, "What is the hour?" Ans. The last instant, the last hour, the last day, in which the Grand Architect completed the creation of the universe. Most Potent knocks one and two.—Companions rise. Most Potent says, "It is the last instant, etc.; it is the last hour, the last day, the last year, in which Solomon completed the temple, the last instant for closing this Chapter. Give notice," etc. Signs. Most Potent knocks one and two, Senior Warden one and two, and Companions one and two, with their hands.

KNIGHTS OF THE NINTH ARCH.

Opening.—Most Potent knocks seven. (Grand Marshal rises.) Most Potent says, "Are we all Knights of the Ninth Arch?" Ans. We are, Most Potent.—Q. Your place? etc., etc. Most Potent Knocks eight. Junior Warden rises. Q. What is the hour? A. The rising of the sun. Most Potent knocks three times three.—Companions rise. Most Potent says, "If it is the rising of the sun, it is time to commence our labors. Give notice," etc. Signs of former degrees. Then two kings kneel at the pedestal, as in the first sign, and raise each other by the token. Companions do the same. Most Potent knocks three times three, Senior Warden same, Junior Warden same, and Companions same, and Most Potent says, "I declare this Chapter open."

Lecture.—Question—Are you a Knight of the Ninth Arch? Answer—I have penetrated the bowels of the earth, through nine arches, and have seen the brilliant triangle.

Q. In what place were you admitted? A. In the audience chamber of King Solomon.

[Pg 154]Q. How did you gain admittance there? A. In company with some Intendants of the Building, Illustrious Knights, and Grand Master Architects. I was conducted by the Master of Ceremonies to the door of the audience chamber, where he gave three times three distinct knocks.

Q. To what did they allude? A. To the nine arches which led from the palace of Solomon to the secret vault, and the nine arches of the temple of Enoch.

Q.—How were they answered? A. By three times three from within.

Q.—What followed? A. I was asked, "Who comes there?"

Q.—Your answer? A. Several I. of B.'s, I. K.'s, and Grand Master Architects solicit the honor of being admitted into the secret vault under the Sanctum Sanctorum.

Q. What was then said to you? A. I was told to wait until the Most Potent had been informed of my request, and his answer returned.

Q. What was his answer? A. My brethren, your request cannot now be granted.

Q. What followed? A. We were conducted back to the anti-chamber, when the nine masters entered and thus addressed us: "My brethren, our Most Potent Master requests Grand Master Architects, Joabert, Stokin, and Gibulum to attend in the audience chamber," whereupon we were introduced into the presence of Solomon, who thus addressed us: "My brethren, you know that in digging for a foundation for the temple, we found the ruins of an ancient edifice. Among the ruins, we have already discovered much treasure which has been deposited in the secret vault. Are you willing to make further researches among the ancient ruins, and report to us your discoveries?"

Q. What was your answer. A. We are.

Q. What followed? A. We were conducted to the ruins, and commenced our labors. Among the rubbish we discovered a large iron ring, fixed in a cubic stone, which we raised with much difficulty. Upon examining the same, we discovered an inscription, of the meaning of which we were ignorant. Beneath the stone, a deep and dismal cavern appeared.

Q. Did you enter that cavern? A. I did.

Q. In what manner? A. A rope was fastened 'round my body, and descending, I found myself in an arched vault, in the floor of which was a secret opening, through which I also descended, and in like manner through a third; being in third vault, I found there was an opening for descending still further, but being afraid of pursuing my search, I gave a signal and was hoisted by my two companions. I then recounted to them what I had seen, and proposed to them to descend by turns, which they refused; upon this I determined to descend again, and told them that through every arch I passed, I would gently shake the rope. In this manner I descended from arch to arch, until I was lowered into the sixth arch, when, finding there was still another opening, my heart failed me, and giving the signal, I was again pulled up. I acquainted my two companions with the particulars of my second descent, and now earnestly urged that one of them should go down, as I was very much fatigued; but, terrified at my relation, they both refused. I then received fresh [Pg 155]courage, went down a third time, taking a lighted flambeau in my hand. When I had descended into the ninth arch, a parcel of stone and mortar suddenly fell in and extinguished my light, and I immediately saw a triangular plate of gold, richly adorned with precious stones, the brilliancy of which struck me with admiration and astonishment. Again I gave the signal, and was assisted in reascending. Having related to my two companions the scene which I had witnessed, they expressed a desire to witness the same; they also concluded to go down together, by means of a ladder of ropes, which they did, and shortly after returned with the golden plate, upon which we saw certain characters, of the meaning of which we were then ignorant.

Q. What followed? A. We repaired to the apartment of King Solomon, the King of Tyre, with him, and said, "Most Potent, we obeyed your commands and present you with the fruits of our labors, and solicit the honor of being made acquainted with the inscription on this cubic stone and this golden triangle." Upon beholding it, the two Kings raised their hands, and exclaimed "Gibulum ishtov." The Kings then examined the sacred characters with attention, and Solomon thus addressed us: "My brethren, your request cannot now be granted. God has bestowed upon you a particular favor, in permitting you to discover the most precious jewel of masonry. The promise which God made to some of the ancient patriarchs, that in fulness of time his name should be discovered, is now accomplished. As a reward for your zeal, constancy, and fidelity, I should now constitute you Knights of the Ninth Arch, and I promise you an explanation of the mysterious characters on the golden plate, when it is fixed in the place designed for it, and I will then confer on you the most sublime and mysterious degree of Perfection."

Q. What followed? A. The Most Potent directed the Master of Ceremonies to conduct us to the south-west, and from thence to approach the altar, by three times three steps, and there to take upon ourselves the obligation of this degree.

Q. Repeat that obligation? A. (Same as Perfect Master.) I further promise never to be concerned in the initiation of any brother in this degree, unless he manifests a charitable disposition for Masonry, and a zeal for the brethren, and also obtains permission, under the hands and seal of the first regular officers of a Lodge of Perfection. I further promise that I will not debauch any female related to a companion of this degree, either by blood or marriage, knowing her to be such, under penalty of being crushed under the ruins of a subterraneous temple. So help, etc.

Q. What followed? A. The Most Potent gave me the signs, token and words of this degree.

Q. Give me the sign? A. (Made by kneeling on the left knee, the right hand on the back, the left raised above the head, the palm upward, the body leaning forward, alluding to the penalty.)

Q. Give me the token? A. (Being in the last mentioned position token is made by raising each other from the same, by interlacing the fingers of the left hand.)

Q. How many pass-words are there? A. One for each arch.

[Pg 156]Q. Give them to me? A. 1st, Jov; 2d, Jeho; 3d, Juha; 4th, Havah; 5th, Elgibbor; 6th, Adonai; 7th, Joken; 8th, Eloah; 9th, Elzeboath.

Q. Give me the grand word? A. Gibulum ishtov.

Q. What does that signify? A. Gibulum is a good man.

Q. What was then done to you? A. I was invested with the jewel, apron and gloves of this degree, and directed to salute the Senior Warden as a Knight of the Ninth Arch, and return to the east for further instruction.

Second Section.—Question—Give me the history and charge of this degree? Ans. My worthy brother, it is my intention, at this time, to give you a clearer account of certain historical traditions, etc. (to the words "favored with a mystical vision"), when the Almighty thus designed to speak to him, as thou art desirous to know my name, attend, and it shall be revealed unto thee. Upon this, a mountain seemed to rise to the heavens, and Enoch was transferred to the top thereof, where he beheld a triangular plate of gold most brilliantly enlightened, and upon which were some characters which he received a strict injunction never to pronounce. Presently he seemed to be lowered perpendicularly into the bowels of the earth through nine arches, in the ninth or deepest of which he saw the same brilliant plate which was shown to him in the mountain. In digging for a foundation they discovered an ancient edifice, among which they found a considerable quantity of treasure, such as vases of gold and silver, urns, marble, jasper, and agate columns, and precious stones. All these treasures were collected and carried to Solomon, who upon deliberation concluded that they were the ruins of some ancient temple, erected before the flood, and possibly to the service of Idolatry. He, therefore, determined to build the temple in another place, lest it should be polluted. Solomon caused a cavern to be constructed under the temple, to which he gave the name of secret vault. He erected in this vault a large pillar of white marble, to support the Sanctum Sanctorum, and which, by inspiration, he called the pillar of beauty, from the beauty of the ark which it sustained. There was a long, narrow descent through nine arches from the palace of Solomon to this vault. To this place he was accustomed to retire with Hiram of Tyre, and Hiram Abiff, when he had occasion to enter upon important business. There were none else, then living, qualified to enter this vault. One of their number being removed, disordered their business for a time. As the two kings were on one occasion consulting on business of the craft, application was made to them by several I's of B., I. K.'s and Grand Master Architects, soliciting the honor of being admitted to the secret vault, to whom Solomon replied, "My brethren, your request cannot now be granted." Some days afterwards Solomon sent for the three Grand Master Architects, Gibulum, Joabert and Stokin, and directed them to go and search among the ancient ruins, in hopes of discovering more treasure. They departed, and one of them, viz., Gibulum, in working with a pickaxe among the rubbish, discovered a large iron ring fixed in a cubic stone. On removing this stone, a cavern was discovered. Gibulum offered to descend. A rope being fastened 'round his body, and [Pg 157]in this manner he descended thrice, and discovered the golden triangle of Enoch, as was represented in the ceremony of your initiation. They then carried the stone and triangle to King Solomon, when the same circumstances occurred, which took place when you presented the same to us. The two Kings then informed the three Knights that they were ignorant of the true pronunciation of the mysterious word until that time, and that this word being handed down through a succession of ages, had been much corrupted. The two Kings, accompanied by the three Knights, descended with the sacred treasure into the secret vault. They encrusted the golden plate upon the pedestal of the pillar of beauty, and the brilliancy of the plate was sufficient to enlighten the place. The secret vault was afterwards called the sacred vault. Whenever the Lodge of Perfection was holden, nine Knights of the Ninth Arch tiled the nine arches which led to the sacred vault; the most ancient stood in the arch next to the anti-chamber of the vault, and so on in regular progression, the youngest taking his station in the first arch, which was near the apartment of Solomon. We were suffered to pass without giving the pass-words of the different arches. There were living at that time several ancient masters, who, excited by jealousy at the honors conferred upon the twenty-five brethren, deputed some of their number to wait upon Solomon, and request that they might participate in those honors. The King answered that the twenty-five masters were justly entitled to the honors conferred on them, for their zeal and fidelity. Go, said he, in peace, you may one day be rewarded according to your merits. Upon this, one of the deputies with an unbecoming warmth, observed to his companions, "What occasion have we for a higher degree? We know the word has been changed, we can travel as masters, and receive pay as such." Solomon mildly replied, "Those whom I have advanced to the degree of perfection, have wrought in the ancient ruins, and though the undertaking was difficult and dangerous, they penetrated the bowels of the earth, and brought thence treasures to enrich and adorn the Temple of God. Go in peace, wait with patience, and aspire to perfection by good works." The deputies returned and reported their reception to the masters. These masters, vexed at the refusal, unanimously determined to go to the ancient ruins, and search under ground, with a view of arrogating the merit necessary for the accomplishment of their desires. They departed the next morning, and raising the cubic stone descended into the cavern with a ladder of ropes, by the light of torches, where no sooner had the last descended, than the nine arches fell in upon them. Solomon hearing of this accident, sent Gibulum, Joabert and Stokin to inform themselves more particularly of the matter. They departed at break of day, and upon their arrival at the place, could discover no remains of the arches, nor could they learn that one single one of all those who had descended escaped the destruction. They examined the place with diligence, but found nothing except a few pieces of marble, on which were inscribed certain hieroglyphics; these they carried to Solomon, and related what they had seen. King Solomon examining these hieroglyphics, discovered that these pieces of marble were part of one of the pillars of Enoch. Solomon ordered these pieces of marble to be carefully put together and deposited in the sacred vault.

[Pg 158]Q. What followed? A. The Most Potent gave me the mysterious characters of this degree, which were engraved on the triangle of Enoch.

Closing.—Most Potent knocks seven (Grand Marshal rising), "the last as well as the first care," etc. Most Potent knocks eight, and Junior Warden rises. "Brother Junior Warden, what is the hour?" A. "The setting of the sun." Most Potent knocks three times three, and companions all rise. "Brother Junior Warden, give notice," etc. Signs.

Most Potent knocks three times three, Junior Warden three times three, and Companions three times three, with their hands, and Most Potent declares Chapter closed.

GRAND ELECT, PERFECT, AND SUBLIME MASON.

Opening.—Most Perfect knocks three (Grand Marshal rises), "Are we all," etc. Most Perfect knocks five, and Junior Warden rises. Most Perfect says, "Brother Junior Warden, what is the hour?" Ans. "High twelve."

Q. What do you understand by high twelve? A. That the sun has gained its meridian height, and darts its rays with greatest force on this Lodge. Most Perfect says, "It is then time that we should profit by its light." Most Perfect knocks seven, and Senior Warden rises, and Most Perfect says, "Venerable Brother Senior Warden, what brings you here?" A. My love of Masonry, my obligation, and a desire for perfection.

Q. What are the proper qualities for acquiring it? A. Frequent innocence and benevolence.

Q. How are you to conduct in this place? A. With the most profound respect.

Q. Why is it that men of all conditions assembled in this place are called brethren, and are all equal? A. Because the ineffable name puts us in mind that there is one being superior to us all.

Q. Why is respect paid to the triangle? A. Because it contains the name of the Grand Architect of the universe. Most Perfect knocks nine, and brethren all rise. Most Perfect says, "Brother Senior Warden, give notice that I am going to open a Lodge of Perfect Grand Elect and Sublime Masons, by the mysterious number 3, 5, 7 and 9. Senior Warden obeys. Signs of former degrees given, then the Most Perfect knocks three, and all the brethren give the first sign of this degree. Most Perfect knocks three, and then third sign. Most Perfect knocks three, five, seven and nine, Senior Warden the same, Junior Warden the same, and then all the brethren with their hands, & Most Perfect declares Lodge open.

Note.—Behind the Master is the burning bush, in which is a transparent triangle, with five Hebrew letters signifying "God" placed therein. In the west is the pillar of beauty. The pedestal appearing to be broken is a part of the pillar of Enoch, the pieces of which were found among the ruins, and carefully put together. The Lodge is adorned with vases of gold and silver, urns, etc., which were found among the ruins. The lights are thus arranged: three in the west, behind the Junior Warden; five in the East, behind the Senior Warden; seven in the south, and nine behind the Master. The brethren are seated in a triangular form around the altar.

[Pg 159]Lecture.—Question—What are you? Ans. I am three times three, the Perfect's number of eighty-one, according to our mysterious numbers.

Q. Explain that? A. I am a Perfect Grand Elect and Sublime Mason; my trials are finished, and it is now time I should reap the fruits of my labor.

Q. Where were you made a Grand Elect Mason? A. In a place not enlightened by the sun nor moon.

Q. Where was that place situated? A. Under the Sanctum Sanctorum.

Q. How did you gain admission? A. By the nine pass-words of Knights of the Ninth Arch, which brought me to the door of the ante-chamber leading to the sacred vaults, where I gave three distinct knocks.

Q. How were they answered? A. By three from within.

Q. What was said to you? A. Who comes there?

Q. Your answer? A. A Knight of the Ninth Arch, who wishes to be admitted into the sacred vault.

Q. What was then said to you? A. I was directed to give the pass; when I did I was permitted to pass to the second door of the ante-chamber, where I gave three and five knocks, which were answered by three and five and seven from within, and the pass-word demanded as before, which I gave, and was permitted to pass to the door of the sacred vault, where I gave three, five and seven and nine distinct knocks. (Note.— These knocks are answered from within by the Junior and Senior Wardens, and Most Perfect; and Most Perfect says, "Brother Junior Warden, see who knocks there in the manner of a Perfect Grand Elect and Sublime Mason.")

Q. To what do these knocks allude? A. The three knocks signify the age of the Entered Apprentice, and the number of the Grand Marshal Architects who penetrated the bowels of the earth. The five allude to the age of the Fellow Craft and the number of the Grand Elect Perfect and Sublime Masters who placed the sacred treasure upon the pedestal of beauty.

Q. What are their names? A. Solomon, Hiram, King of Tyre, Gibulum, Joabert, and Stokin. The seven allude to the age of the Master Mason, and to Enoch who was the seventh from Adam. The nine represent the age of the Perfect Grand Elect and Sublime Mason, and the nine guards of the arches.

Q. How were these knocks answered? A. By three, five, seven and nine from within.

Q. What followed? A. I was asked, "Who comes there?"

Q. Your answer? A. A Knight of the Ninth Arch, who is desirous of being admitted into the sacred vault and arriving at perfection.

Q. What followed? A. The pass was demanded, which I gave and was ordered to wait until the Most Perfect in the East had been informed of my request and his answer returned.

Q. What was his answer? A. Let him be introduced in ancient form.

Q. What was that form? A. I was conducted to the west and placed between the Wardens, and having made the sign of admiration, was thus interrogated by the Most Perfect: "My Brother, what is your desire? A. To be made a Perfect Grand Elect and Sublime Mason."

[Pg 160]Q. What followed? A. The Most Perfect said, "Before I can initiate you, you must satisfy us that you are well skilled in Masonry, otherwise you must be sent back until you are better qualified," whereupon I was thus examined:

Q. Are you a Mason? A. My brethren all know me as such.

Q. Give me the sign, token and word? A. (Given.)

Q. Are you a Fellow Craft? A. I have seen the letter G and know the pass.

Q. Give me the sign, token and word? A. (Given.)

Q. Are you a Master Mason? A. I have seen the sprig of cassia, and know what it means.

Q. Give me the sign, token and words? A. (Given.)

Q. Are you a Secret Master? A. I have passed from the square to the compass opened to seven degrees.

Q. Give me the sign, token and words? A. (Given.)

Q. Are you a Perfect Master? A. I have seen the tomb of our respectable Master, Hiram Abiff, and have, in company with my brethren, shed tears at the same.

Q. Give me the sign, token and words? A. (Given.)

Q. Are you an Intimate Secretary? A. My curiosity is satisfied, but it nearly cost me my life.

Q. Give me the sign, token and words? A. (Given.)

Q. Are you a Provost and Judge? A. I am, and render justice to all men, without distinction.

Q. Give me the sign, token and words? A. (Given.)

Q. Are you an Intendant of the Buildings? A. I have made the five steps of exactness, I penetrated the inmost part of the temple, and have seen the great light in which were three mysterious characters, J. J. J.

Q. Give me the sign, token and words? A. (Given.)

Q. Are you an Elected Knight? A. One cavern received me, one lamp gave me light, and one fountain refreshed me.

Q. Give me the sign, token and words? A. (Given.)

Q. Are you a Master Elected of Fifteen? A. My zeal and works have procured me that honor.

Q. Give me, etc.? Are you an Illustrious Knight? A. My name will inform you.

Q. Give me, etc. Are you a Grand Master Architect? A. I know the use of the mathematical instruments.

Q. Give me, etc. Are you a Knight of the Ninth Arch? A. I have penetrated through the bowels of the earth, through nine arches, and have seen the brilliant triangle.

Q. Give me, etc. What then followed? A. The Most Perfect inquired of the brethren whether they consented that I should be exalted to the sublime and mysterious degree of Perfection, whereupon one of the brethren rose and said, "I have objections to this candidate." The Most Perfect inquired what these objections were, to which this brother answered, "I will communicate them if the candidate retires." I was then ordered to retire, which I did.

Q. What then followed? A. Shortly after, the Master of Ceremonies [Pg 161]conducted me again into the Lodge, and placing me in the west, I was asked the following questions, viz.:— 1st, Have you never wilfully revealed any of the secrets of Masonry? 2d, Have you always been charitable towards your brethren? 3d, Have you never defrauded a brother? 4th, Are you in the habit of using the name of God profanely? 5th, Does your conscience accuse you of having committed any offence against your brethren, which ought to debar you from receiving this degree? Be sincere, and answer me. Which questions being answered, the Most Perfect said, "Brethren, do you consent that this candidate be admitted among us? If you do, raise your right hands." Which being done, I was directed to approach the altar, by three, five, seven and nine steps, which I did, and took upon me the obligation of a Perfect Grand Elect and Sublime Mason.

Q. Repeat that obligation? A. (Same as Perfect Master.) I further promise that I will aid all my worthy brethren in distress and sickness, as far, etc., with my counsel as well as my purse. I further promise, etc. that I will not be concerned in conferring this degree upon any Mason whose character and knowledge I disapprove, nor unless he has been elected and installed as an officer in some regular Lodge, Chapter, Encampment, or Council. I further promise that I will never fully pronounce more than once in my life the mysterious word of this degree, under penalty of having my body cut in twain. So help, etc. Amen, Amen, Amen.

Q. What followed? A. While I was still in a kneeling posture, the Most Most Perfect said, "Let us pray," which was done, and the Master of Ceremonies then presented the hod and trowel to the Most Perfect, who said, "My brother, I shall now proceed to anoint you with the holy oil wherewith Aaron, David, and the wise Solomon were anointed." And then anointing my head, lips and heart, at the same time said, "Behold how good and pleasant," etc., and then placing his hand upon me, said, "I impress you," etc.

Q. What followed? A. The Most Perfect presented me with the bread and wine, and rising, said, "Eat of this bread," etc. When this part of the ceremony was ended the brethren made a libation according to ancient usage.

Q. What followed? A. The Most Perfect raised me and said, "That which I shall now communicate to you, will make you accomplished in Masonry." He then gave me three signs, three tokens, the three pass-words, and the three grand words of this degree.

Q. Give me the signs? [First sign made like Master Mason's, with hands clenched.]

Q. To what does this sign allude? A. To the penalty of the obligation. [Second sign: bring your right hand upright, the palm outwards to guard your left cheek, your left hand supporting your elbow, then guard your right cheek with left hand, etc.]

Q. To what does that sign allude? A. To the manner in which Moses guarded his eyes from the light of the burning bush, from which the Almighty revealed to him his true name. [Third sign is that of surprise: [Pg 162]raise both hands as high as the shoulders, and step back with the right foot.]

Q. To what does this sign allude? A. To the attitude of Solomon and Hiram, when the sacred treasure was first produced.

Q. Give me the first token? [First token same as Intimate Secretary, giving the words Berith, Neder, Shelemoth]

Q. What do those signify? A. Alliance, Promise and Protection.

Q. To what do they allude? A. To the alliance of Moses and Aaron, of Solomon and Hiram, King of Tyre. The promise made by the Almighty to the ancient patriarchs that the true pronunciation of his name should be revealed to their posterity, and the perfection attained when this promise was fulfilled.

Q. Give me the second token? [Pass from Master's grip, and seize his right arm above the elbow, and place your left hand on his right shoulder.]

Q. Give me the third token? [With your left hand seize your brother's right elbow, and with your right hand, his right shoulder.]

Q. Give me the three pass-words? A. First, Master Mason's; second, Elhanon; third, Fellow Craft's, repeated thrice.

Q. Give me the three grand words? A. First, Gibulum; second, Eh-yeh-asher-eh-yeh.

Q. What does that word signify? A. I am what I am. Third, El-hod-dihu kaw-lu.

Q. What does that word signify? A. God be praised, we have finished it.

Q. What followed? A. The Most Perfect caused me to pronounce the mysterious word of this degree.

Q. Pronounce it? A. I cannot but once in my life.

Q. How will you then give it? A. * * * * [A Hebrew pronunciation of God.]

Q. What followed? A. The Most Perfect thus addressed me: "You are already acquainted with the fact, that the true pronunciation of the name of God was revealed to Enoch, and that he engraved the letters composing that name on a triangular plate of gold. The name was represented by the four Hebrew consonants, Jod, He, Vau, and He. The vowel sounds of this language being represented by points placed above the consonants, and being frequently omitted in writing, the consonants composing the mysterious word, at different ages, received different pronunciations. Hence, though the method of writing this word remained uniform, its pronunciation underwent many changes. These changes constitute what are termed the different ages of Masonry. These are 3, 5, 7 and 9. These are the three ages of Masonry, and are thus estimated:

After the death of Enoch, the ineffable name was pronounced by

3 { Methuselah, Lamech, and Noah, } Juha (Yu-haw.)

7 { Reu, Serug, Nahor, Terah, Abraham, {[163] Isaac, Judah, } Jova (Yo-waw). { 7 ages.

5	Shem, Arphaxed, Salah, Eber, and Peleg,	} Jeva (Ye-waw).		5 ages.

9	Hezron, Ram,	} (Yay-wo) Jevo.		
	Aminadab, Nasshou,	} Jevah (Ye-way).		9 ages.
	Salmon, Boaz, Obed,	} Johe (Yo-hay).		
	Jesse, David,	} Jehovah (Ye-ho-waw).		

The true pronunciation of the name was revealed to Enoch, Jacob, and Moses, and on that account are not named in this enumeration. The perfect number is thus formed:—The number of corrupted words is 9. The ages of Masonry, 3, 5, 7, 9—24, multiplied by 3, the number gotten who discovered Tunsune (noticed in the degree of the Knight of the Ninth Arch), gives the product 72; to this add 9, the number of corrupted words, the amount is 81. The mysterious words which you received in the preceding degrees, are all so many corruptions of the true name (of God) which was engraved on the triangle of Enoch. In this engraving the vowel points are so arranged as to give the pronunciation which you have just received (Yow-ho). This word, when thus pronounced, is called the ineffable word, which cannot be altered as other words are, and the degrees which you have received, are called, on this account, INEFFABLE DEGREES. This word you will recollect was not found until after the death of Hiram Abiff, consequently the word engraved by him on the ark is not the true name of God."

Q. What then followed? A. The Most Perfect gave me the secret characters of this degree, and then invested me with the jewels, apron, and girdle of this degree, and I was again addressed:—"I now with the greatest pleasure salute you," etc.

Closing.—Most Perfect knocks three (Grand Marshal rises), "The last," etc., etc. Most Perfect knocks five, and Junior Warden rises. "Brother Junior Warden, what is the hour?" Most Perfect knocks seven, and Senior Warden rises. Most Perfect says, "Venerable Brother Senior Warden, how should the Grand Elect, Perfect and Sublime Mason part?" A. "They should part in peace, love, and unity." Most Perfect knocks nine, all brethren rise. Signs. Most Perfect knocks three, five, seven and nine, Junior Warden the same, Senior Warden the same, and brethren the same, with their hands, etc.

The Philosophical Lodge; or, the Key of Masonry: being the Degree of Knights Adepts of the Eagle or Sun.

This Council must be illuminated by one single light, and is enlightened by one divine light: because there is one single light that shines among men, who have the happiness of going from the darkness of ignorance and of the vulgar prejudices, to follow the only light that leads to the celestial truth. The light that is in our Lodge, is composed of a glass globe filled with water, and a light placed behind it, which renders the light more clear. The glass of reflection, the globe, when it is lighted, is placed in the south.

Robe and Sceptre.—The Grand Master or Thrice Puissant, is named "Father Adam," who is placed in the East, vested in a robe of pale yellow, like the morning. He has his hat on, and in his right hand a sceptre, on the top of which is a globe of gold. The handle or extremity of the sceptre is gilt. The reason that Father Adam carries the globe above the sceptre in this Council is, because he was constituted Sovereign Master of the world, and created Sovereign Father of all men. He carries a Sun suspended by a chain of gold around his neck; and on the reverse of this jewel of gold is a globe. When this degree is given, no jewel or apron is worn.

There is only one Warden, who sits opposite Father Adam in the west, and is called Brother Truth. He is entitled to the same ornaments as Father Adam; and the order that belongs to this degree is a broad white watered ribbon worn as a collar, with an eye of gold embroidered thereon, above the gold chain and jewel of the sun. The number of other officers is seven, and are called by the name of the cherubim, as follows: Zaphriel, Zabriel, Camiel, Uriel, Michael, Zaphael, and Gabriel. These ought to be decorated in the same manner as the Thrice Puissant Father Adam. If there are more than that number of the Knights of the Sun, they go by the name of Sylphs, and are the preparers of the Council, and assistants in all the ceremonies or operations of the Lodge. They are entitled to the same jewel, but have a ribbon of a fiery color tied to the third button-hole of their coat.

To Open the Grand Council.—Father Adam says:—"Brother Truth, what time is it on earth?" Brother Truth: "Mighty Father, it is midnight among the profane, or cowans, but the sun is in its meridian in this Lodge." Father Adam: "My dear children, profit by the favor of this austere luminary, at present showing its light to us, which will conduct us in the path of virtue, and to follow that law which is eternally to be engraved on our hearts, and the only law by which we cannot fail to come to the knowledge of pure truth." He then makes a sign, by putting his right hand on his left breast; on which all the brethren put up the first finger of the right hand above their heads, the other fingers clenched, showing by that, that there is but one God, who is the beginning of all truth; then Father Adam says, "This Lodge is opened."

Form of Reception.—After the Council is opened, the candidate is introduced into an ante-chamber, where there are a number of Sylphs, each with a bellows, blowing a large pot of fire, which the candidate [Pg 165]sees, but they take no notice of him. After he is left in that situation two or three minutes, the most ancient of the Sylphs goes to the candidate and covers his face with black crape. He must be without a sword, and is told that he must find the door of the Sanctuary, and when found, to knock on it six times with an open hand. After he finds the door and knocks, Brother Truth goes to the door, and having opened it a little, asks the candidate the following questions, which he answers by the help of the Sylphs. "Q. What do you desire? A. I desire to go out of darkness to see the true light, and to know the true light in all its purity. Q. What do you desire more? A. To divest myself of original sin, and destroy the juvenile prejudices of error, which all men are liable to, namely, the desire of all worldly attachments and pride." On which Brother Truth comes to Father Adam, and relates what the candidate has told him; when Father Adam gives orders to introduce the candidate to the true happiness. Then Brother Truth opens the door, and takes the candidate by the hand, and conducts him to the middle of the Lodge or Sanctuary, which is also covered by a black cloth, when Father Adam addresses him thus: "My son, seeing by your labor in the royal art, you are now come to the desire of knowledge of the pure and holy truth, we shall lay it open to you without any disguise or covering. But, before we do this, consult your heart, and see in this moment if you feel yourself disposed to obey her (namely truth) in all things which she commands. If you are disposed, I am sure she is ready in your heart, and you must feel an emotion that was unknown to you before. This being the case,

254

you must hope that she will not be long to manifest herself to you. But have a care not to defile the sanctuary by a spirit of curiosity; and take care not to increase the number of the vulgar and profane, that have for so long a time ill-treated her, until Truth was obliged to depart the earth, and now can hardly trace any of her footsteps. But she always appears in her greatest glory, without disguise, to the true, good, and honest Free Masons; that is to say, to the zealous extirpators of superstition and lies. I hope, my dear brother, you will be one of her intimate favorites. The proofs that you have given, assure me of everything I have to expect of your zeal; for as nothing now can be more a secret among us, I shall order brother Truth, that he will instruct you what you are to do in order to come to true happiness." After this discourse of Father Adam, the candidate is unveiled and shown the form of the Lodge or Council, without explaining any part thereof. Brother Truth then proceeds thus: "My dear brother, by my mouth, holy truth speaketh to you, but before she can manifest herself to you, she requires of you proofs in which she is satisfied in your entrance into the Masonic order. She has appeared to you in many things which you could not have apprehended or comprehended without her assistance; but now you have the happiness to arrive at the brilliant day, nothing can be a secret to you. Learn, then, the moral use that is made of the three first parts of the furniture, which you knew after you was received an Entered Apprentice Mason, viz.: Bible, Compass and Square. By the Bible you are to understand that it is the only law you ought to follow. It is that which Adam [Pg 166]received at his creation, and which the Almighty engraved in his heart. This law is called natural law, and shows positively that there is but one God, and to adore him only without any subdivision or interpolation. The Compass gives you the faculty of judging for yourself, that whatever God has created, is well, and he is the sovereign author of every thing. Existing in himself, nothing is either good or evil; because we understand by this expression, an action done which is excellent in itself, is relative, and submits to the human understanding, or judgment, to know the value and price of such action; and that God, with whom every thing is possible, communicates nothing of his will, but such as his great goodness pleases; and every thing in the universe is governed as he has decreed it, with justice, being able to compare it with the attributes of the Divinity. I equally say, that in himself there is no evil; because he has made every thing with exactness, and that every thing exists according to his will; consequently, as it ought to be. This distance between good and evil with the Divinity, cannot be more justly and clearly compared than by a circle formed with a compass. From the points being reunited there is formed an entire circumference; and when any point in particular equally approaches or equally separates from its point, it is only a faint resemblance of the distance between good and evil, which we compare by the points of a compass forming a circle, which circle when completed is God.

Square.—By the Square we discover that God, who has made every thing equal, in the same manner that you are not able to dig a body in a quarry complete, or perfect; thus, the wish of the Eternal in creating the world by a liberal act of his own, well foresaw every matter that could possibly happen in consequence thereof; that is to say, that every thing therein contained at the same time of the creation was good.

Level.—You have also seen a level, a plumb, and a rough stone. By the level you are to learn to be upright and sincere, and not to suffer yourself to be drawn away by the multitude of the blind and ignorant people; to be always firm and steady to sustain the right of the natural law, and the pure and real knowledge of that truth which it teacheth.

Perpendicular and Rough Stone.—By these you ought to understand that the perpendicular man is polished by reason, and put censure away by the excellence of our Master.

Tressle-board.—You have seen the tressle-board, to draw plans on. This represents the man whose whole occupation is the art of thinking, and who employs his reason in that which is just and reasonable.

Cubic Stone.—You have seen the cubic stone, the moral of which, and the sense you ought to draw from it, is, to rule your actions, that they might be equally brought to the sovereign good.

Pillars.—The two pillars teacheth you that all Masons ought to attach themselves firmly to become an ornament to the order, as well as to its support; as the pillars of Hercules formerly determined the end of the ancient world.

Blazing Star.—You have seen the blazing star, the moral sense of which is, "a true Mason perfecting himself in the way of truth," that he [Pg 167]may become like a blazing star which shineth equally during the thickest darkness; and it is useful to those that it shineth upon, and who are ready and desirous of profiting by its light.

The first instructions have conducted you to the knowledge of Hiram Abiff, and the inquiries that were made in finding him out. You have been informed of the words, signs and tokens which were substituted for those we feared would have been surprised, but of which they afterwards learnt that the treacherous villains had not been able to receive any knowledge of; and this ought to be an example and salutary advice to you, to be always on your guard, and well persuaded that it is difficult to escape the snares that ignorance, joined to conceited opinion, lay every day against us, and thereby to overcome us; and the most virtuous men are liable to fall, because their candor renders them unsuspecting. But, in this case, you ought to be firm as our Respectable Father Hiram, who chose rather to be massacred than to give up what he had obtained.

This will teach you that as soon as truth shall be fixed in your heart, you ought never to consider the resolution you should take; you must live and die to sustain the light, by which we acquire the sovereign good. We must never expose ourselves to the conversation of cowans, and must be circumspect even with those with whom we are the most intimate; and not deliver up ourselves to any, excepting those whose character and behavior have proved them brothers, who are worthy to come and appear in the sacred sanctuary where holy Truth delivers her oracles.

You have passed the Secret and Perfect Master; you have been decorated with an ivory key, a symbol of your distinction; you have received the pronunciation of the ineffable name of the Great Architect of the universe, and have been placed at the first balustrade of the sanctuary; you have had rank among the Levites, after which you knew the word "Zizon," which signifies "a balustrade of the Levites;" where all those are placed, as well as yourself, to expect the knowledge of the most sublime mysteries.

Coffin and Rope.—In the degree of Perfect Master they have shown you a grave, a coffin, and a "withe rope," to raise and deposit the body in a sepulchre, made in the form of a pyramid, in the top of which was a triangle, within which was the sacred name of the Eternal, and on the pavement were the two columns of Jachin and Boaz laid across.

Ivory Key.—By the "ivory key" you are to understand that you cannot open your heart with safety, but at proper times. By the corpse and grave is represented the state of man, before he had known the happiness of our order.

Rope.—The rope to which the coffin is tied, in order to raise it, is the symbol of raising one, as you have been raised from the grave of ignorance to the celestial place where truth resides.

Pyramid.—The pyramid represents the true Mason who raises himself by degrees, till he reaches heaven, to adore the sacred and unalterable name of the Eternal Supreme.

[Pg 168]Intimate Secretary.—This new degree leads you near to Solomon and honor; and after you redoubled your zeal, you gained new honors and favors, having nearly lost your life by curiosity; which attachment to Masonry gave you the good qualities of your heart, and which obtained your pardon and let you to the "Intendant of the Buildings," where you saw a "blazing star," a large candlestick with seven branches, with altars, vases, and purification, and a great brazen sea.

Blazing Star.—By the expression of PURIFICATION you are to understand that you are to be cleansed from impiety and prejudice before you can acquire more of the sublime knowledge in passing the other degrees, to be able to support the brilliant light of reason, enlightened by truth, of which the blazing star is the figure.

Candlestick with Seven Branches.—By the candlestick with seven branches you are to remember the mysterious number of the seven Masters who were named to succeed one; and from that time it was resolved that seven Knights of Masonry, united together, were able to initiate into Masonry, and show them the seven gifts of the Eternal, which we shall give you a perfect knowledge of, when you have been purified in the Brazen Sea.

Brazen Sea.—You have passed from the Secret and Perfect Master to the Intimate Secretary, Provost and Judge, and Intendant of the Buildings. In these degrees they have shown you an ebony box, a key suspended, a balance, and an inflamed urn.

Ebony Box.—The ebony box shows you with what scrupulous attention you are to keep the secrets that have been confided to you, and which you are to reserve in the closet of your heart, of which the box is an emblem. And were you to reflect on the black color of said box, it would teach you to cover your secrets with a thick veil, in such a manner that the profane cowans cannot possibly have any knowledge thereof.

Key.—The key demonstrates that you have already obtained a key to our knowledge, and part of our mysteries; and if you behave with equity, fervor, and zeal to your brothers, you will arrive shortly to the knowledge and meaning of our society, and this indicates the reason of the balance.

Inflamed Urn.—By the inflamed urn you are to understand, that as far as you come to the knowledge of the Royal and Sublime Art, you must, by your behavior, leave behind you, in the minds of your brethren and the vulgar, a high idea of your virtue, equal to the perfume of the burning urn.

Two Kings.—In the degree of Intimate Secretary, you have seen and heard two kings who were entering into their new alliance and reciprocal promise, and of the perfection of their grand enterprise. They spoke of the death of Hiram Abiff, our Excellent Master. You saw guards, as a man who was overseen, very near of being put to death for his curiosity of peeping. You also heard of the prospect of a place called the vault, to deposit the precious treasure of Masonry, when the time should be fulfilled, and you afterwards became a brother. The conversation of the two kings is the figure of the coincidence of our laws and the natural [Pg 169]law, which forms a perfect agreement with what is expedient, and promises to those who shall have the happiness to be connected to you in the same manner and perfect alliance that they will afterwards come to the centre of true knowledge.

Tears.—The tears and regret of the two kings are the emblem of the regret you ought to have when you perceive a brother depart from the road of virtue.

The Man Peeping.—By the man you saw peeping, and who was discovered and seized, and conducted to death, is an emblem of those who come to be initiated into our sacred mysteries through a motive of curiosity; and, if so indiscreet as to divulge their obligations, we are bound to take vengeance on the treason by the destruction of the traitor. Let us pray the Eternal to preserve our order from such an evil you have hereof seen an example, in that degree to which you came, by your zeal, fervor and constancy. In that degree you have remarked, that from all the favorites that were at that time in the apartment of Solomon, only nine were elected to avenge the death of Hiram Abiff; this makes good, that a great many are often called, but few chosen. To explain this enigma, a great many of the profane have the happiness to divest themselves of that name, to see and obtain the entrance in our sanctuary; but very few are constant, zealous and fervent, to merit the happiness of coming to the height and knowledge of the sublime truth.

Requisitions To Make a Good Mason.—If you ask me what are the requisite qualities that a Mason must be possessed of, to come to the centre of truth, I answer you, that you must crush the head of the serpent of ignorance. You must shake off the yoke of infant prejudice concerning the mysteries of the reigning religion, which worship has been imaginary, and only founded on the spirit of pride, which envies to command and be distinguished, and to be at the head of the vulgar; in affecting an exterior purity, which characterizes a false piety, joined to a desire of acquiring that which is not its own, and is always the subject of this exterior pride, and unalterable source of many disorders, which being joined to gluttonness, is the daughter of hypocrisy, and employs every matter to satisfy carnal desires, and raises to these predominant passions, altars, upon which she maintains, without ceasing, the light of iniquity, and sacrifices continually offerings to luxury, voluptuousness, hatred, envy, and perjury. Behold, my dear brother, what you must fight against and destroy before you can come to the knowledge of the true good and sovereign happiness! Behold this monster which you must conquer—a serpent which we detest as an idol, that is adored by the idiot and vulgar under the name of religion.

Solomon, King Hiram, and St. John the Baptist.—In the degrees of Elected of Fifteen, Illustrious Knights, Grand Master Architects, and Knights of the Ninth Arch, you have seen many things which are only a repetition of what you have already examined. You will always find in those degrees initial letters enclosed in different triangles, or Deltas. You have also seen the planet Mercury, the chamber called "Gabaon," or the "Third Heaven;" the "winding staircase," the "Ark of Alliance," the "tomb of Hiram Abiff," facing the ark and the urn—the precious [Pg 170]treasure found by the assiduous travels—the three zealous brethren Masons—the punishment of the haughty Master Mason, in being buried under the ancient ruins of Enoch's temple—and finally, you have seen the figures of Solomon, and Hiram, King of Tyre, and St. John the Baptist.

3. I. I. I.—By the 3. I. I. I. you know the three sacred names of the Eternal and "Mount Gabaon" (Third Heaven) which you came to by seven degrees that compose the winding staircase.

The seven stars represent the seven principal and different degrees to which you must come to attain the height of glory represented by the mount, where they formerly sacrificed to the Most High! When you arrive to that, you are to subdue your passions, in not doing anything that is not prescribed in our laws.

By the planet Mercury, you are taught continually to mistrust, shun, and run away from those who, by a false practice, maintain commerce with people of a vicious life, who seem to despise the most sacred mysteries—that is, to depart from those who by the vulgar fear, or a bad understanding, are ready to deny the solemn obligations that they have contracted among us.—When you come to the foot of our arch you are to apprehend that you come to the "Sanctum Sanctorum." You are not to return; but rather to persist in sustaining the glory of our order, and the truth of our laws, principles, and mysteries, in like manner as our Respectable Father Hiram Abiff, who deserved to have been buried there for his constancy and fidelity. We have also another example in the firmness of "Galaad," the son of "Sophonia," chief of the Levites, under Surnam, the High Priest, as mentioned in the history of perfection. Learn in this moment, my dear brother, what you are to understand by the figures of Solomon, Hiram, King of Tyre, and St. John the Baptist. The two first exert you, by their zeal in the royal art, to follow the sublime road of which Solomon was the institutor, and Hiram of Tyre, the "supporter;" a title legitimately due to that king, who not only protected the order, but contributed with all his might to the construction of the temple (furnishing stone from Tyre, and the cedars of Lebanus) which Solomon built to the honor of the Almighty.

The third, or St. John the Baptist, teaches you to preach marvellous to this order, which is as much as to say, you are to make secret missions among men, which you believe to be in a state of entering the road of truth, that they may be able one day to see her virtues and visage uncovered.

Hiram Abiff was the symbol of truth on earth. Jubelum Akirop was accused by the serpent of ignorance, which to this day raises altars in the hearts of the profane and fearful. This profaneness, backened by a fanatic zeal, becomes an instrument to the religious power, which struck the first stroke in the heart of our dear Father, Hiram Abiff; which is as much as to say, undermined the foundation of the celestial temple, which the Eternal himself had ordered to be raised to the sublime truth and his glory.

The first age of the world has been witness to what I have advanced. The simple, natural law rendered to our first fathers the most [Pg 171]uninterrupted happiness. They were in those times more virtuous; but as soon as the "monster of pride" started up in the air and disclosed herself to those unhappy mortals, she promised to them every seat of happiness, and seduced them by her soft and bewitching speeches, viz.: That "they must render to the Eternal Creator of all things an adoration with more testimony, and more extensive, than they had hitherto done," etc. This Hydra with a hundred heads, at that time misled, and continues to this day to mislead men who are so weak as to submit to her empire; and it will subsist, until the moment that the true elected shall appear and destroy her entirely.

The degree of Sublime Elected, that you have passed, gives you the knowledge of those things which conducts you to the true and solid good. The grand circle represents the immensity of the Eternal Supreme, who has neither beginning nor end.

The triangle, or Delta, is the mysterious figure of the Eternal. The three letters which you see, signify as follows:—G, at the top of the triangle, "the grand cause of the Masons": the S, at the left hand, the "submission to the same order": and the U, at the right hand, the "union that ought to reign among the brethren: which, altogether make but one body, or equal figure in all its parts." This is the triangle called "equilateral." The great letter G, placed in the centre of the triangle, signifies "Great Architect of the Universe," who is God; and in this ineffable name is found all the divine attributes. This letter being placed in the centre of the triangle, is for us to understand that every true Mason must have it profoundly in his heart.

There is another triangle, on which is engraved S. B. and N., of which you have had an explanation in a preceding degree. This triangle designs the connection of the brethren in virtue. The solemn promise they have made to love each other; to help, succor, and keep inviolably secret, their mysteries of the perfection proposed, in all their enterprises. It is said in that degree, that "You have entered the Third Heaven, that means you have entered the place where pure truth resides, since she abandoned the earth to monsters who persecuted her."

The end of the degree of Perfection is a preparation to come more clearly to the knowledge of true happiness, in becoming a true Mason, enlightened by the celestial luminary of truth, in renouncing, voluntarily, all adorations but those that are made to one God, the Creator of heaven and earth, great, good, and merciful. End of Brother Truth's harangue.

Father Adam then says to the candidate, "My dear son, what you have heard from the mouth of Truth is an abridgment of all the consequences of all the degrees you have gone through, in order to come to the knowledge of the holy truth, contracted in your last engagements. Do you persist in your demand of coming to the holy brother, and is that what you desire, with a clear heart?—answer me." The candidate [Pg 172]answers, "I persist." Then Father Adam says, "Brother Truth, as the candidate persists, approach with him to the sanctuary, in order that he may take a solemn obligation to follow our laws, principles, and morals, and to attach himself to us forever." Then the candidate falls on his knees, and Father Adam takes his hands between his own, and the candidate repeats the following obligation three times:

Obligation.—I, A. B., promise, in the face of God, and between the hands of my Sovereign, and in presence of all the brethren now present, never to take arms against my country, directly or indirectly, in any conspiracy against the Government thereof. I promise never to reveal any of the degrees of the Knight of the Sun, which is now on the point of being intrusted to me, to any person or persons whatsoever, without being duly qualified to receive the same; and never to give my consent to any one to be admitted into our mysteries, only after the most scrupulous circumspection, and full knowledge of his life and conversation; and who has given at all times full proof of his zeal and fervent attachment for the order, and a submission at all times to the tribunal of the Sovereign Princes of the Royal Secret. I promise never to confer the degree of the Knights of the Sun without having a permission in writing from the Grand Council of Princes of the Royal Secret, or from the Grand Inspector or his deputy, known by their titles and authority. I promise also and swear, that I will not assist any, through my means, to form or raise a Lodge of the Sublime Orders, in this country, "without proper authority." I promise and swear to redouble my zeal for all my brethren, Knights, and Princes, that are present or absent; and if I fail in this my obligation, I consent for all my brethren, when they are convinced of my infidelity, to seize me, and thrust my tongue through with a red-hot iron; to pluck out both my eyes, and to deprive me of smelling and hearing; to cut off both my hands, and to expose me in that condition in the field, to be devoured by the voracious animals; and if none can be found, I wish the lightning of heaven might execute on me the same vengeance. O God, maintain me in right and equity. Amen. Amen. Amen.

After the obligation is three times repeated, Father Adam raises the candidate, and gives him one kiss on his forehead, being the seat of the soul. He then decorates him with the collar and jewel of the order, and gives him the following sign, token and word:—Sign: Place the right hand flat upon the heart, the thumb forming a square. The answer, raise the hand, and with the index point to heaven. This is to show that there is but one God, the source of all truth. Token: Take in your hands those of your brother, and press them gently. Some Knights, in addition to this, kiss the forehead of the brother, saying "Alpha," to which he answers, "Omega." Sacred Word: "Adonai." This word is answered by "Albra," or "Abbraak," which is rendered "a king without reproach." Some contend that this word should be written "Abrah." Pass-word:— "Stibium" (antimony). By this is intended as among the Hermetic Philosophers, "the primitive matter whence all things are formed." To this pass-word some add the following: "Helios," "Mene," "Tetragrammaton."

After these are given, the candidate goes 'round and gives them to every one, which brings him back to Father Adam. He then sits down with the rest of the brethren, and then Brother Truth gives the following explanation of the Philosophical Lodge:

Sun.—The sun represents the unity of the Eternal Supreme, the only grand work of philosophy.

[Pg 173]3. S. S. S.—The 3 S. S. S. signify the "Stiletto, Sidech, Solo," or the residence of the Sovereign Master of all things.

Three Candlesticks.—The three candlesticks show us the three degrees of fire.

Four Triangles.—The four triangles represent the four elements.

Seven Planets.—The seven planets design the seven colors that appear in their original state, from whence we have so many different artificial ones.

Seven Cherubims.—The seven cherubims represent the seven metals, viz., gold, silver, copper, iron, lead, tin and quicksilver.

Conception in the Moon.—The conception, or woman, rising in the moon, demonstrates the purity that matter subsists of, in order to remain in its pure state unmixed with any other body, from which must come a new king, and a revolution or fulness of time filled with glory whose name is Albra.

Holy Spirit.—The Holy Spirit, under the symbol of a dove, is the image of the Universal Spirit, that gives light to all in the three states of nature; and on the animal, vegetable and mineral.

Entrance of the Temple.—The entrance of the temple is represented to you by a body, because the grand work of nature is complete as gold, potable and fixed.

Globe.—The globe represents the matter in the primeval state; that is to say, complete.

Caduceus.—The caduceus represents the double mercury that you must extract from the matter; that is to say, the mercury fixed, and from thence is extracted gold and silver.

Stibium.—The word stibium signifies the antimony, from whence, by the philosophical fire, is taken an alkali which we empty in our grand work. End of the philosophical explanation. Then Father Adam explains the

MORAL LODGE.

Sun.—The sun represents the divinity of the Eternal; for as there is but one Sun to light and invigorate the earth, so there is but one God, to whom we ought to pay our greatest adoration.

3 S. S. S.—The 3 S. S. S. are initials of the words Scienta, Sapientia, Sanctitas, and teach you that science, adorned with wisdom, creates a holy man.

Three Candlesticks.—The three candlesticks are the image of the life of man, considered in youth, manhood, and old age, and happy are those that have been enlightened in these ages, by the light of truth.

Four Triangles.—The four triangles show us the four principal duties that create our tranquil life, viz.: Fraternal love among men in general, and particularly among brethren, and in the same degree with us. Secondly. In not having anything but for the use and advantage of a brother. Thirdly. Doubting of every matter that cannot be demonstrated to you clearly, by which an attempt might be made to insinuate mysteries in matters of religion, and hereby lead you away from the holy truth. Fourthly. Never do anything to another that you would not [Pg 174]have done unto you. The last precept, well understood and followed on all occasions, is the true happiness of philosophy.

Seven Planets.—The seven planets represent the seven principal passions of man.

Seven Cherubims.—The seven cherubims are the images of the delights of life: namely, by seeing, hearing, tasting, smelling, feeling, tranquility, and health.

Conception.—The conception in the moon shows the purity of matter, and that nothing can be impure to the eyes of the Supreme.

Holy Spirit.—The Spirit is the figure of our soul, which is only the breath of the Eternal, and which cannot be soiled by the works of the body.

Temple.—The temple represents our body, which we are obliged to preserve by our natural feelings.

Figure of a Man.—The figure is in the entrance of the temple, which bears a lamb in his arms, and teaches us to be attentive to our wants, as a shepherd takes care of his sheep; to be charitable, and never let slip the present opportunity of doing good, to labor honestly, and to live in this day as if it were our last.

Columns of Jachin and Boaz.—The columns of J. and B. are the symbols of the strength of our souls in bearing equally misfortunes, as well as success in life.

Seven Steps of the Temple.—The seven steps of the temple are the figures of the seven degrees which we must pass before we arrive to the knowledge of the true God.

Globe.—The globe represents the world which we inhabit.

Lux ex Tenebris.—The device of "Lux ex tenebris" teacheth, that when man is enlightened by reason, he is able to penetrate the darkness and obscurity which ignorance and superstition spread abroad.

River.—The river across the globe represents the utility of the passions that are necessary to man in the course of his life, as water is requisite to the earth in order to replenish the plants thereof.

Cross Surrounded.—The cross surrounded by two serpents signifies that we must watch the vulgar prejudices, to be very prudent in giving any of our knowledge and secrets in matters, especially in religion. End of the moral explanation.

Lecture.—Question—Are you a Knight of the Sun? Answer—I have mounted the seven principal steps of Masonry; I have penetrated into the bowels of the earth, and among the ancient ruins of Enoch found the most grand and precious treasures of the Masons. I have seen, contemplated, and admired the great, mysterious, and formidable name engraved on the triangle; I have broken the pillar of beauty, and thrown down the two columns that supported it.

Q. Pray tell me what is that mysterious and formidable name? A. I cannot unfold the sacred characters in this manner, but substitute in its place the grand word of [represented by the Hebrew consonants Jod, He, Vau, He.]

Q. What do you understand by throwing down the columns that sustained the pillar of beauty. A. Two reasons.—First. When the temple [Pg 175]was destroyed by Nebuzaradan, general of the army of Nebuchadnezzar, I was one that helped to defend the Delta on which was engraved the ineffable name; and I broke down the columns of beauty, in order that it should not be profaned by the infidels. Second. As I have deserved, by my travel and labor, the beauty of the great "Adonai" (Lord), the mysteries of Masonry, in passing the seven principal degrees.

Q. What signifies the seven planets? A. The lights of the celestial globe and also their influence, by which every matter exists on the surface of the earth or globe.

Q. From what is the terrestrial globe formed? A. From the matter which is formed by the concord of the four elements, designed by the four triangles, that are in regard to them as the four greater planets.

Q. What are the names of the seven planets? A. Sun, Moon, Mars, Jupiter, Venus, Mercury, and Saturn.

Q. Which are the four elements? A. Air, fire, earth, and water.

Q. What influence have the seven planets on the four elements? A. Three general matters of which all bodies are composed—life, spirit, and body; otherwise, salt, sulphur and mercury.

Q. What is life or salt? A. The life given by the Eternal Supreme, or the planets, the agents of nature.

Q. What is the spirit or sulphur? A. A fixed matter, subject to several productions.

Q. What is the body or mercury? A. Matter conducted or refined to its form by the union of salt and sulphur, or the agreement of the three governors of nature.

Q. What are those three governors of nature? A. Animal, vegetable and mineral.

Q. What is animal? A. We understand in this, life—all that is divine and amiable.

Q. Which of the elements serve for his productions? A. All the four are necessary, among which, nevertheless, air and fire are predominant; and it is those that render the animal the perfection of the three governments, which man is elevated to by one-fourth of the breath of the Divine Spirit, when he receives his soul.

Q. What is the vegetable? A. All that seems attached to the earth reigns on the surface.

Q. Of what is it composed? A. Of a generative fire, formed into a body whilst it remains in the earth, and is purified by its moisture and becomes vegetable, and receives life by air and water; whereby the four elements, though different, co-operate jointly and separately.

Q. What is the mineral? A. All that is generated and secreted in the earth.

Q. What do we understand by this name? A. That which we call metals and demi-metals and minerals.

Q. What is it that composes the minerals? A. The air penetrating by the celestial influence into the earth, meets with a body, which, by its softness, fixes, congeals, and renders the mineral matter more or less perfect.

Q. Which are the perfect metals? A. Gold and silver.

[Pg 176]Q. Which are the imperfect metals? A. Brass, lead, tin, iron and quicksilver.

Q. How come we by the knowledge of these things? A. By frequent observations and the experiments made in natural philosophy, which have decided to a certainty that nature gives a perfection to all things, if she has time to complete her operations.

Q. Can art bring metal to perfection so fully as nature? A. Yes; but in order to do this, you must have an exact knowledge of nature.

Q. What will assist you to bring forth this knowledge? A. A matter brought to perfection, this has been sought for under the name of the philosopher's stone.

Q. What does the globe represent? A. An information of philosophers, for the benefit of the art in this work.

Q. What signify the words, "Lux ex tenebris?" A. That is the depth of darkness you ought to retire from, in order to gain the true light.

Q. What signifies the cross on the globe? A. The cross is the emblem of the true elected.

Q. What represent the three candlesticks? A. The three degrees of fire, which the artist must have knowledge to give, in order to procure the matters from which it proceeds.

Q. What signifies the word Stibium? A. It signifies antimony, or the first matter of all things.

Q. What signify the seven degrees? A. The different effectual degrees of Masonry which you must pass to come to the Sublime Degree of Knights of the Sun.

Q. What signify the divers attributes in those degrees? A. First. The Bible, or God's law, which we ought to follow. Second. The compass teaches us to do nothing unjust. Third. The square conducts us equal to the same end. 4th. The level demonstrates to us, all that is just and equitable. Fifth. The perpendicular, to be upright and subdue the veil of prejudice. Sixth. The tressle-board is the image of our reason, where the functions are combined to effect, compare and think. Seventh. The rough-stone is the resemblance of our vices, which we ought to reform. Eighth. The cubic stone is our passions, which we ought to surmount. Ninth. The columns signify strength in all things. Tenth. The blazing star teaches that our hearts ought to be as a clear sun, among those that are troubled with the things of this life. Eleventh. The key teaches to have a watchful eye over those who are contrary to reason. Twelfth. The box teaches to keep our secrets inviolably. Thirteenth. The urn learns us that we ought to be as delicious perfumes. Fourteenth. The brazen sea, that we ought to purify ourselves, and destroy vice. Fifteenth. The circles on the triangles demonstrate the immensity of the divinity under the symbol of truth. Sixteenth. The poniard teacheth the step of the elected, many are called, but few are chosen to the sublime knowledge of pure truth. Seventeenth. The word albra signifies a king full of glory and without blot. Eighteenth. The word Adonai signifies Sovereign Creator of all things. Nineteenth. The seven cherubims are the symbols of the delights of life, known by seeing, hearing, tasting, feeling, smelling, tranquility, and thought.

[Pg 177]Q. What represents the sun? A. It is an emblem of Divinity, which we ought to regard as the image of God. This immense body represents the infinity of God's wonderful will, as the only source of light and good. The heat of the sun produces the rule of the seasons, recruits nature, takes darkness from the winter, in order that the deliciousness of spring might succeed. End of the physical lecture.

GENERAL LECTURE IN THIS DEGREE.

Question—From whence came you? Answer—From the centre of the earth.

Q. How have you come from thence? A. By reflection, and the study of nature.

Q. Who has taught you this? A. Men in general who are blind, and lead others in their blindness.

Q. What do you understand by this blindness? A. I do not understand it to be privy to their mysteries; but I understand under the name of blindness, those who cease to be ardent, after they have been privy to the light of the spirit of reason.

Q. Who are those? A. Those who, through the prejudices of superstition and fanaticism, render their services to ignorance.

Q. What do you understand by fanaticism? A. The zeal of all particular sects which are spread over the earth, who commit crimes by making offerings to fraud and falsehood.

Q. And do you desire to rise from this darkness? A. My desire is to come to the celestial truth, and to travel by the light of the sun.

Q. What represents that body? A. It is the figure of an only God, to whom we ought to pay our adoration. The sun being the emblem of God, we ought to regard it as the image of the Divinity; for that immense body represents wonderfully the infinity of God. He invigorates and produces the seasons, and replenishes nature, by taking the horrors from winter, and produces the delights of spring.

Q. What does the triangle, with the sun in the centre, represent? A. It represents the immensity of the Supreme.

Q. What signifies the three S. S. S.? A. Sanctitas, Scientia, and Syrentia, which signify the science accompanied with wisdom, and make men holy.

Q. What signifies the three candlesticks? A. It represents the course of life, considered in youth, manhood, and old age.

Q. Has it any other meaning? A. Yes, the triple light that shines among us, in order to take men out of darkness and ignorance into which they are plunged, and to bring them to virtue, truth, and happiness, a symbol of our perfection.

Q. What signifies the four triangles that are in the great circles? A. They are the emblems of the four principal views of the life of tranquility, etc. First. Fraternal love to all mankind in general, more particularly for our brethren, who are more attached to us, and who with honor have seen the wretchedness of the vulgar. Second. To be cautious among us of things, and not to demonstrate them clearly to any who are [Pg 178]not proper to receive them; and to be likewise cautious in giving credit to any matter, however artfully it may be disguised, without a self-conviction in the heart. Third. To cast from us every matter which we perceive we may ever repent of doing, taking care of this moral precept, "To do to every one of your fellow creatures no more than you would choose to be done to." Fourth. We ought always to confide in our Creator's bounty, and to pray without ceasing, that all our necessities might be relieved as it seems best to him for our advantage; to wait for his blessings patiently in this life; to be persuaded of his sublime decrees, that whatever might fall, contrary to our wishes, will be attended with good consequences; to take his chastisements patiently, and be assured that the end of everything has been done by him for the best, and will certainly lead us to eternal happiness hereafter.

Q. Explain the signification of the seven planets which are enclosed in a triangle, that forms the rays of the exterior circles, and are enclosed in the grand triangle. A. The seven planets, according to philosophy, represent the seven principal passions of the life of man; those passions are very useful when they are used in moderation, for which the Almighty gave them to us, but grow fatal and destroy the body when let loose: and, therefore, it is our particular duty to subdue them.

Q. Explain the seven passions to us. A. 1st. The propagation of species. 2d. Ambition of acquiring riches. 3d. Ambition to acquire glory in the arts and sciences among men in general. 4th. Superiority in civil life. 5th. Joys and pleasures of society. 6th. Amusements and gaieties of life. 7th. Religion.

Q. Which is the greatest sin of all that man can commit, and render him odious to God and man? A. Suicide and homicide.

Q. What signifies the seven cherubims whose names are written in the circle called the "First Heaven?" A. They represent the corporeal delights of this life, which the Eternal gave to man when he created him, and are, seeing, hearing, smelling, tasting, feeling, tranquility, and thought.

Q. What signifies the figure in the moon, which we regard as the figure or image of conception? A. The purity of nature, which procures the holiness of the body; and that there is nothing imperfect in the eyes of the Supreme.

Q. What signifies the figure of the columns? A. They are the emblems of our souls, which is the breath of life proceeding from the All Puissant, and ought not to be soiled by the works of the body, but to be firm as columns.

Q. What does the figure in the porch, which carries a lamb in his arms represent? Ans.—The porch ornamented with the columns of Jachin and Boaz, and surmounted with the grand I, represents our body, over which we ought to have a particular care, in watching our conversation, and also to watch our needs, as the shepherd his flock.

Q. What signify the two letters, I and B, at the porch? A. They signify our entrance in the order of Masonry; also the firmness of the soul, which we ought to possess from hour of our initiation; these we ought to merit, before we can come to the sublime degrees of knowing holy [Pg 179]truth, and we ought to preserve them, and be firm in whatever situation we may be in, not knowing whether it may return to our good or evil in the passage of this life.

Q. What signifies the large I in the triangle on the crown of the portico? A. That large I, being the initial of the mysterious name of the Great Architect of the Universe, whose greatness we should always have in our minds, and that our labors ought to be employed to please Him; which we should always have in our view as the sure and only source of our actions.

Q. What signify the seven steps that lead to the entry of the porch? A. They mark the seven degrees in Masonry, which are the principal which we ought to arrive to, in order to come to the knowledge of holy truth.

Q. What does the terrestrial globe represent? A. The world which we inhabit, and wherein Masonry is its principal ornament.

Q. What is the explanation of the great word, Adonai? A. It is the word which God gave to Adam, for him to pray by; a word which our common father never pronounced without trembling.

Q. What signifies "Lux ex tenebris?" A. A man made clear by the light of reason, penetrating this obscurity of ignorance and superstition.

Q. What signifies the river across the globe? A. It represents the utility of our passions, which are necessary to man in the course of his life, as water is necessary to render the earth fertile; as the sun draws up the water, which being purified, falls on the earth and gives verdure.

Q. What signifies the cross, surrounded by two serpents, on the top of the globe? A. It represents to us not to repeat the vulgar prejudices; to be prudent, and to know the bottom of the heart. In matters of religion to be always prepared; not to be of the sentiments with sots, idiots, and the lovers of the mysteries of religion; to avoid such, and not in the least to hold any conversation with them.

Q. What signifies the book, with the word Bible written in it? A. As the Bible is differently interpreted by the different sects who divide the different parts of the earth: Thus the true sons of light, or children of truth, ought to doubt of everything at present, as mysterious or metaphysics: Thus all the decisions of theology and philosophy, teach not to admit that which is not demonstrated as clearly as that 2 and 2 are equal to 4; and on the whole to adore God, and him only; to love him better than yourself; and always to have a confidence on the bounties and promises of our Creator. Amen. Amen. Amen.

To Close the Council.—Question (by Father Adam): Brother Truth, what progress have men made on earth to come to true happiness? Answer (by Brother Truth): Men have always fallen on the vulgar prejudices, which are nothing but falsehood; very few have struggled, and less have knocked at the door of this holy place, to attain the full light of real truth, which we all ought to acquire.

Then says Father Adam, "My dear children, depart and go among men, endeavor to inspire them with the desire of knowing holy truth, the pure source of all perfection." Father Adam then puts his right hand on his left breast; when all the brethren raise the first finger of the right [Pg 180]hand, and then the Council of the Knights of the Sun is closed by seven knocks.

PRINCES OF JERUSALEM.

Prerogatives of the Princes.—Princes of Jerusalem have a right to inspect all Lodges or Councils of an inferior degree, and can revoke and annul all the work done in such Councils or Lodges, if the same shall be inconsistent with the regulations of Masonry.

In countries where there are no Grand Lodges, they have power to confer the blue degrees. They are the supreme judges of all transactions in the lower degrees; and no appeal can be made to the Supreme Councils of the upper degrees, until an opinion has been given by the Grand Council of Princes of Jerusalem, and the result of their opinion has been made known.

A Prince of Jerusalem who visits an inferior Lodge or Council, ought to present himself in the dress and ornaments of this degree. When his approach is announced, the presiding officer must send a Prince of Jerusalem to examine him, and if he reports in his favor, the arch of steel is to be formed, and he is conducted beneath it to his seat on the left of the presiding officer. An entry of his name and rank is made on the records, that he may henceforward receive our honors without any examination.

Five Princes are necessary to form a Grand Council.

Duties of Princes.—They are carefully to observe the rules of justice and good order, and to maintain irreproachable lives. If guilty of unmasonic conduct, they are to be punished at the discretion of the Grand Council. Expulsions are to be notified to the Grand Councils of the upper degrees, and to all inferior Masonic bodies within the district.

If a Prince solicits a vote at an election, he is to be punished with perpetual exclusion.

The annual election is to take place on the twenty third day of the Jewish month Adar. The meetings of the Councils are termed Conventions.

Apartments Used in This Degree.—There are two apartments, connected by a long, narrow passage. The western represents the court of Zerubbabel, at Jerusalem. The hangings are yellow. Over the throne is a yellow canopy. On a triangular pedestal, before the throne, are placed a naked sword, an arrow of justice, a balance, and a shield on which is an equilateral triangle, a sceptre, a chandelier of five branches, which are all lighted in the latter part of the ceremony of reception. The eastern apartment represents the cabinet of Darius. It is hung with red; the canopy is red. Before the throne is a small square pedestal, and in it a drawn sword, a sceptre, paper, pens, etc. The chief Minister of State sits near Darius.

Officers of the Grand Council.—The first officer is styled "Most Equitable Prince," and is on the throne. The Senior Warden and Junior Warden are styled "Most Enlightened;" seated in the West. The other officers and the members are styled "Valiant Princes."

Dress.—The "Most Equitable" wears a yellow robe and turban. The apron is red; on it are painted the temple, a square, a buckler, a triangle, [Pg 181]and a hand; the flap is yellow; on it a balance, and the letters D. Z. [Darius and Zerubbabel.] Gloves are red. Sash is yellow, edged with gold, embroidered by a balance, a hand, a poniard, five stars, and two crowns, it is worn from right to left.

Jewel.—A golden medal; on one side a hand holding a balance in equilibris; on the other a two-edged sword, with five stars around the point, and the letters D. Z.

Alarm.—The alarm is three and two (!!! !!).

Opening.—The "Most Equitable" strikes one, and says, "Valiant Grand Master of Ceremonies, what is the first business of a Grand Council of the Princes of Jerusalem?" Grand Master of Ceremonies. "To see that the guards are at their proper stations." M. E. "Attend to that duty, and inform," etc. G. M. C.—"It is done, Most Equitable." Most Equitable strikes two; the Junior Warden rises. M. E.—"Valiant Junior Warden, what is our next business?" J. W.—"To see that all present are Princes of Jerusalem." M. E.—"Attend to that duty." J. W.—"We are all Princes of Jerusalem." Most Equitable (striking thrice).—"Valiant Senior Warden, what is the hour?" Senior Warden.—"The rising of the sun." M. E.—"What duty remains to be done?" S. W.—"To arrange the Princes in two columns, for the proper discharge of their duties." M. E.— "Attend to that duty." S. W.—"Most Equitable, it is done." M. E.—"Valiant Junior and Senior Wardens, inform your respective columns that I am about to open this Grand Council of Princes of Jerusalem, by three and two." (That is done.) M. E.—"Attention, Valiant Princes! (The signs are given; the Most Equitable strikes three and two; this is repeated by the Wardens.) I declare this Grand Council duly opened and in order for business."

Reception.—The candidate, being hoodwinked, is led by the Master of Ceremonies to the door—the alarm is given—the door is opened without any ceremony, and the candidate is led to the east, and thus addressed: Most Equitable.—"What is your desire?" Candidate.—"I come to prefer the complaints of the people of Israel against the Samaritans, who have refused to pay the tribute imposed on them for defraying the expense of the sacrifices offered to God in the temple." M. E. (who represents Zerubbabel).—"I have no power over the Samaritans; they are subject to King Darius, who is at Babylon; it is to him that such complaints must be preferred; but as we are all interested in this thing, I will arm you, and cause you to be accompanied by four Knights, that you may more easily surmount any difficulty which may present itself in your journey to the court of the King of Persia." The bandage is now removed from the eyes of the candidate; he is armed with a sword and buckler, and decorated as a Knight of the East. The four Knights who accompany him are armed in a similar manner. They commence their journey, and are attacked by some armed ruffians, whom they repulse. They arrive at the door of the cabinet of Darius. The candidate enters with one of the Knights, and thus addresses the King:—"Mighty King! the Samaritans refuse to pay the tribute imposed on them by Cyrus, King of Persia, for defraying the expenses of the sacrifices which are offered in the temple which we have rebuilt; the people of Israel entreat [Pg 182]that you will compel the Samaritans to perform their duty." Darius.—"Your request is just and equitable; I order that the Samaritans shall immediately pay the tribute imposed on them. My Chief Minister shall deliver to you my decree for this purpose. Go in Peace!" The candidate retires; the Chief Minister follows, and delivers the decree to him. After surmounting various obstacles, candidate is met on his return by the Knights with lighted torches, and is thus conducted with triumph into the presence of Zerubbabel, and says:—"I deliver to you the decree of Darius, King of Persia, which we have obtained after defeating our enemies, and encountering many dangers in our journey." Most Equitable reads the decree as follows:—"We, Darius, 'King of Kings!' willing to favor and protect our people at Jerusalem, after the example of our illustrious predecessor, King Cyrus, do will and ordain that the Samaritans, against whom complaints have been made, shall punctually pay the tribute money which they owe for the sacrifices of the temple—otherwise they shall receive the punishment due to their disobedience. Given at Shushan, the palace, this fourth day of the second month, in the year 3534, and of our reign the third, under the seal of our faithful Darius. [L. S.]" M. E.—"The people of Jerusalem are under the greatest obligations to you for the zeal and courage displayed by you in surmounting the obstacles which you encountered in your journey; as a reward we shall confer on you the mysteries of the degree of Prince of Jerusalem. Are you willing to take an obligation, binding you to an exact observance of our laws, and a careful concealment of our mysteries?" Candidate.— "I am." M. E.—"Kneel before the altar for that purpose."

Obligation.—I, A. B., do solemnly promise and swear, in the presence of Almighty God, the Great Architect of heaven and earth, and of these Valiant Princes of Jerusalem, that I will never reveal the mysteries of the degree of Prince of Jerusalem to any one of an inferior degree, or to any other person whatever. I promise and swear, as a Prince of Jerusalem, to do justice to my brethren, and not to rule them tyranically, but in love. I promise and swear that I will never, by word or deed, attack the honor of any Prince of Jerusalem; and that I will not assist in conferring this degree except in a lawful Grand Council of Princes of Jerusalem. All this I promise and swear, under the penalty of being stripped naked, and having my heart pierced with a poniard. So help me God. Amen! Amen! Amen!

The Most Equitable raises the candidate, and gives him the following signs, tokens, and words:—First Sign—Extend the right arm horizontally at the height of the shoulder. This is termed the sign of command. First Token.—Each places his left hand on his left hip, and the right hand on his brother's left shoulder. Second Token.—Join left hands, placing the thumb on the second joint of the little finger; with the thumb strike five times on that joint. Pass-word.—"Tebeth." The name of the Jewish month in which the Ambassadors entered Jerusalem. Sacred Word.—"Adar." The name of the month in which thanks were given to God for the completion of the temple. In some Councils the following sign is given, viz.:—Present yourself before your brother with your sword advanced, and your left hand resting on your hip, as if to commence a [Pg 183]combat. He will answer the sign by extending his arm at the height of the shoulder, the right foot forming a square with the toe of the left. The March.—Five steps on the diagonal of the square towards the throne. Age.—The age of a Prince of Jerusalem, is 5 times 15.

Most Equitable.—"I now appoint and constitute you, with your four companions, Princes and Governors of Jerusalem, that you may render justice to all the people. I decorate you with a yellow sash, to which is attached a gold medal. The 'balance' on it is to admonish you to make equity and justice your guides. The 'hand of justice' is a mark of your authority over the people. The 'emblems' of the 'apron' with which I now invest you, have reference to the works and virtues of Masons, and to your duty in the high office with which you are invested. As Princes of Jerusalem, you will assemble in two chambers of the temple. Be just, merciful, and wise."

Lecture.—Question—Are you a Prince of Jerusalem? Answer—I know the road to Babylon.

Q. What were you formerly? A. A Knight of the East.

Q. How did you arrive at the dignity of a Prince of Jerusalem? A. By the favor of Zerubbabel, and the courage which I manifested in many conflicts.

Q. Where did the Prince of Jerusalem travel? A. From Jerusalem to Babylon.

Q. Why? A. The Samaritans having refused to pay the tribute imposed on them for defraying the expense of the sacrifices offered to God in the temple, an embassy was dispatched to Babylon, to obtain justice of King Darius.

Q. How many Knights constituted this embassy? A. Five.

Q. Did they encounter any difficulty in their journey? A. They did. The Samaritans, against whom they were to prefer a complaint, armed themselves and attacked the ambassadors, but were defeated.

Q. What did they obtain from Darius? A. A decree ordering the Samaritans to pay the tribute, or suffer punishment.

Q. How were the ambassadors received on their return to Jerusalem? A. At some distance from the city they were met by the people, who accompanied them to the temple singing songs of joy. On reaching the temple and making their report, and presenting the decree of Darius, they were constituted Princes of Jerusalem.

Q. How were they habited as Princes of Jerusalem? A. In cloth of gold.

Q. What were their decorations? A. A yellow sash trimmed with gold from right to left; to which was attached a golden medal, on which was engraved a balance, a sword, five stars, and the letters D. Z.

Q. What is signified by the five stars on the sash? A. They are emblematic of the five Knights who journeyed from Jerusalem to Babylon.

Q. What is the age of a Prince of Jerusalem? A. Five times fifteen.

Close.—Most Equitable. "Most Enlightened Junior and Senior Wardens, announce to your respective columns that I am about to close this Grand Council by five times fifteen." Each Warden strikes five; all rise and the notice is given. M. E. "Attention, Princes of Jerusalem? (The [Pg 184]signs are given. The Most Equitable strikes five times fifteen, which is repeated by the Wardens.) Be just, merciful and wise! I declare this Grand Council duly closed."

KNIGHTS OF THE EAST AND WEST.

Form of the Grand Council.—The Grand Council of Knights of the East and West, must be hung with red and sprinkled with gold stars. In the east of the Council Chamber must be a canopy, elevated by seven steps, supported by four lions and four eagles, and between them an angel, or seraphim, with six wings. On one side of the throne there must be a transparent painting of the sun, and, on the other side, one of the moon; below them is stretched a rainbow. In the east there must be a basin with perfume, and a basin of water, and a human skull. On the south side there must be six small canopies, and on the north side five, elevated by three steps, for the Venerable Ancients, and opposite the throne, in the west, are two canopies, elevated by five steps, for the two Venerable Wardens, who act in this Council as Grand Officers, or Wardens. A full Grand Council must be composed of twenty-four Knights. On the pedestal there must be a large Bible, with seven seals suspended therefrom.

The Venerable Master is called "Most Puissant;" the Wardens, and the twenty-one other brethren, are called "Respectable Ancients." If there are more brethren present, they are styled "Respectable Knights," and are placed north and south, behind the small canopies.

The first canopy, at the right side of the Puissant, is always vacant for the candidate. All the brethren are clothed in white, with a zone of gold 'round the waist, long white beards and golden crowns on their heads. The Knights, in their ordinary habits, wear a broad, white ribbon from the right shoulder to the left hip, with the jewel suspended thereto. They also wear a cross of the order, suspended by a black ribbon, 'round their necks. The Most Puissant has his right hand on the large Bible on the pedestal with seven seals. The draft (or carpet) of the Council, is an heptagon in a circle—over the angles are these letters, B. D. S. P. H. F. In the centre, a man clothed in a white robe, with a girdle of gold 'round his waist—his right hand extended and surrounded with seven stars—he has a long white beard, his head surrounded with a glory, and a two-edged sword in his mouth—with seven candlesticks 'round him, and over them the following letters: H. D. P. I. P. R. C.

The jewel is an heptagon of silver—at each angle, a star of gold and one of these letters B. D. S. P. H. G. S. in the centre. A lamb on a book with seven seals—on the reverse, the same letters in the angles, and in the centre, a two-edged sword between a balance.

The apron is white, lined with red, bordered with yellow, or gold; on the flap is painted a two-edged sword, surrounded with the seven holy letters—or the apron may have the plan of the draft painted on it.

To Open the Council.—The Most Puissant, with his right hand on the Bible sealed with seven seals, demands, "Venerable Knights Princes, what is your duty?" A. "To know if we are secure." Most Puissant. "See that we are so." A. "Most Puissant, we are in perfect security." [Pg 185]The Most Puissant strikes seven times, and says, "Respectable Knights Princes, the Grand Council of Knights of the East and West is open; I claim your attention to the business thereof." A. "We promise obedience to the Most Puissant's commands." They rise and salute him, when he returns the compliment, and requests them to be seated.

Reception.—The candidate must be in an antechamber, which must be hung with red, and lighted with seven lights, where he is clothed with a white robe, as an emblem of the purity of his life and manners. The Master of Ceremonies brings him barefooted to the Council Chamber door, on which he knocks seven times, which is answered by the Most Puissant, who desires the youngest Knight to go to the door, and demand who knocks. The master of Ceremonies answers, "It is a valiant brother and Most Excellent Prince of Jerusalem, who requests to be admitted to the Venerable and Most Puissant." The Knight reports the same answer to the Most Puissant, who desires the candidate to be introduced. The Most Ancient Respectable Senior Grand Warden then goes to the door, and takes the candidate by the hand, and says, "Come, my dear brother, I will show you mysteries worthy the contemplation of a sensible man. Give me the sign, token, and word of a prince of Jerusalem;" after which the candidate kneels on both knees, about six feet from the throne, when the Most Ancient Respectable Senior Grand Warden says to him, "Brother, you, no doubt, have always borne in memory the obligations of your former degrees, and that you have, as far as in the power of human nature, lived agreeably to them?" Candidate. "I have ever made it my study, and, I trust, my actions and life will prove it." Q. "Have you particularly regarded your obligations as a 'Sublime Knight of Perfection,' 'Knight of the East and Prince of Jerusalem?' Do you recollect having injured a brother in any respect whatsoever? or have you seen or known of his being injured by others, without giving him timely notice, as far as was in your power? I pray you answer me with candor." Candidate. "I have in all respects done my duty, and acted with integrity to the best of my abilities." The Most Puissant says, "You will be pleased to recollect, my brother, that the questions which have now been put to you, are absolutely necessary for us to demand, in order that the purity of our Most Respectable Council may not be sullied; and it behooves you to be particular in your recollection, as the indispensable ties which we are going to lay you under, will, in case of your default, only increase your sins, and serve to hurl you sooner to destruction, should you have deviated from your duty: answer me, my dear brother." Candidate. "I never have." The Most Puissant says, "We are happy, my brother, that your declaration coincides with our opinion, and are rejoiced to have it into our power to introduce you into our society. Increase our joy by complying with our rules, and declare if you are willing to be united to us by taking a most solemn obligation." Candidate. "I ardently wish to receive it, and to have the honor of being united to so respectable and virtuous a society." The Most Puissant orders one of the Knights to bring an ewer containing some perfume, a basin of water, and a clean white napkin to the candidate, who washes his hands. The Most Puissant repeats the six first verses of the 24th [Pg 186]Psalm. Then the candidate is brought close to the foot of the throne, where he kneels on both knees, and placing his right hand on the Bible, his left hand between the hands of the Most Puissant, in which position he takes the following

Obligation.—I, — — , do promise and solemnly swear, and declare, in the awful presence of the only One Most Holy Puissant Almighty and Most Merciful Grand Architect of heaven and earth, who created the universe and myself through his infinite goodness, and conducts it with wisdom and justice—and in the presence of the Most Excellent and upright Princes and Knights of the East and West, here present in convocation and Grand Council, on my sacred word of honor and under every tie, both moral and religious, that I never will reveal to any person whomsoever below me, or to whom the same may not belong, by being legally and lawfully initiated, the secrets of this degree which is now about to be communicated to me, under the penalty of not only being dishonored, but to consider my life as the immediate forfeiture, and that to be taken from me with all the tortures and pains to be inflicted in manner as I have consented to in my preceding degrees. I further promise and solemnly swear, that I never will fight or combat with my brother Knights, but will, at all times, when he has justice on his side, be ready to draw my sword in his defence, or against such of his enemies who seek the destruction of his person, his honor, peace, or prosperity; that I never will revile a brother, or suffer others to reflect on his character in his absence, without informing him thereof, or noticing it myself, at my option; that I will remember, on all occasions, to observe my former obligations, and be just, upright, and benevolent to all my fellow creatures, as far as in my power. I further solemnly promise and swear, that I will pay due obedience and submission to all the degrees of Masonry; and that I will do all in my power to support them in all justifiable measures for the good of the craft, and advantage thereof, agreeably to the Grand Constitutions.—All this I solemnly swear and sincerely promise, upon my sacred word of honor, under the penalty of the severe wrath of the Almighty Creator of heaven and earth, and may He have mercy on my soul, on the great and awful day of judgment, agreeably to my conformity thereto. Amen. Amen. Amen.

271

The Most Puissant then takes the ewer filled with perfumed ointment, and anoints his head, eyes, mouth, heart, the tip of his right ear, hand, and foot, and says, "You are now, my dear brother, received a member of our society; you will recollect to live up to the precepts of it, and also remember that those parts of your body which have the greatest power of assisting you in good or evil, have this day been made holy!" The Master of Ceremonies then places the candidate between the two Wardens, with the craft before him. The Senior Warden says to him, "Examine with deliberation and attention everything which the Most Puissant is going to show you." After a short pause, he, the Senior Warden, says—"Is there mortal here worthy to open the book with the seven seals?" All the brethren cast their eyes down and sigh. The Senior Warden, hearing their sighs, says to them, "Venerable and respectable brethren, be not afflicted; here is a victim (pointing to the candidate), whose courage will give you content." Senior Warden to the candidate, "Do you know the reason why the ancients have a long white beard?" Candidate. "I do not, but I presume you do." S. W. "They are those who came here, after passing through great tribulation, and having washed their robes in their own blood; will you purchase such robes at so great a price?" Candidate. "Yes; I am willing." The Wardens then conduct him to the basin, and bare both his arms—they place a ligature [Pg 187]on each, the same as in performing the operation of blood-letting. Each Warden being armed with a lancet, makes an incision in each of his arms, just deep enough to draw a drop of blood, which is wiped on a napkin, and shown to the brethren. The Senior Warden then says, "See, my brethren, a man who has spilled his blood to acquire a knowledge of our mysteries, and shrunk not from the trial!" Then the Most Puissant opens the first Seal of the great book, and takes from thence a bone quiver, filled with arrows, and a crown, and gives them to one of the Ancients, and says to him, "Depart and continue the conquest." He opens the second Seal, and takes out a sword, and gives it to the next aged, and says, "Go, and destroy peace among the profane and wicked brethren, that they may never appear in our Council." He opens the third Seal, and takes a balance, and gives it to the next aged, and says, "Dispense rigid justice to the profane and wicked brethren." He opens the fourth Seal, and takes out a scull, and gives it to the next aged, and says, "Go, and endeavor to convince the wicked that death is the reward of their guilt." He opens the fifth Seal, and takes out a cloth, stained with blood, and gives it to the next aged, and says, "When is the time (or, the time will arrive,) that we shall revenge and punish the profane and wicked, who have destroyed so many of their brethren by false accusations." He opens the sixth Seal, and that moment the sun is darkened and the moon stained with blood! He opens the seventh Seal, and takes out incense, which he gives to a brother; and also a vase, with seven trumpets, and gives one to each of the seven aged brethren. After this, the four old men, in the four corners, show their inflated bladders (beeves' bladders, filled with wind under their arms), representing the four winds: when the Most Puissant says "Here is seen the fulfilment of a prophecy;" (Rev. vii. 3). Strike not, nor punish the profane and wicked of our order, until I have selected the true and worthy Masons! Then the four winds raise their bladders, and one of the trumpets sound, when the two Wardens cover the candidate's arms, and take from him his apron and jewel of the last degree. The second trumpet sounds, when the Junior Warden gives the candidate the apron and jewel of this degree. The third trumpet sounds, when the Senior Warden gives him a long white beard. The fourth trumpet sounds, and the Junior Warden gives him a crown of gold. The fifth trumpet sounds, and the Senior Warden gives him a girdle of gold. The sixth trumpet sounds, and the Junior Warden gives him the sign, token and words, as follows:— Sign.—Look at your right shoulder, it will be answered by looking at the left shoulder. One says, "Abaddon," the other "Jubulum." First Token.—Place your left hand in the right hand of your brother, who will cover it with his left; both at the same time look over their right shoulder. Second Token.—Touch your brother's left shoulder with your left hand; he replies by touching your right shoulder with his right hand. Sign for entering the Lodge.—Place your right hand on the brother's forehead (i.e., the Tyler's), he will do the same. Pass-word.—"Jubulum," or, according to some, "Perignan" and "Gadaon." Sacred Word.— "Abaddon." This name will be found in Rev. ix. 11. The seventh trumpet sounds, on which they all sound together, when the Senior Warden conducts the candidate to the vacant canopy.

[Pg 188]Origin of this Degree.—When the Knights and Princes were embodied to conquer the Holy Land, they took a cross to distinguish them, as a mark of being under its banners; they also took an oath to spend the last drop of their blood to establish the true religion of the Most High God. Peace being made, they could not fulfil their vows, and, therefore, returning home to their respective countries, they resolved to do in theory what they could not do by practice, and determined never to admit, or initiate, any into their mystic ceremonies, but those who had given proofs of friendship, zeal, and discretion. They took the name of Knights of the East and West, in memory of their homes and the place where the order began; and they have ever since strictly adhered to their ancient customs and forms. In the year 1118, the first Knights, to the number of eleven, took their vows between the hands of Garimont, Patriarch and Prince of Jerusalem, from whence the custom is derived of taking the obligation in the same position.

Lecture.—Question—Are you a Knight of the East and West? A. I am.

Q. What did you see when you were received? A. Things that were marvellous.

Q. How were you received? A. By water and the effusion of blood.

Q. Explain this to me? A. A Mason should not hesitate to spill his blood for the support of Masonry.

Q. What are the ornaments of the Grand Council? A. Superb thrones, sun, more perfumed ointment, and a basin of water.

Q. What is the figure of the draft? A. An heptagon within a circle.

Q. What is the representation of it? A. A man vested in a white robe, with a golden girdle 'round his waist—'round his right hand seven stars—his head surrounded with a glory, a long, white beard—a two-edged sword across his mouth, surrounded by seven candlesticks, with these letters: H. D. P. I. P. R.

Q. What signifies the circle? A. As the circle is finished by a point, so should a Lodge be united by brotherly love and affection.

Q. What signifies the heptagon? A. Our mystic number which is enclosed in seven letters.

Q. What are the seven letters? A. B. D. W. P. H. G. S.; which signifies Beauty, Divinity, Wisdom, Power, Honor, Glory, and Strength.

Q. Give me the explanation of these words? A. Beauty to adorn; Divinity, that Masonry is of divine origin; Wisdom, a quality to invent; Power, to destroy the profane and unworthy brethren; Honor, is an indispensable quality in a Mason, that he may support himself in his engagements with respectability; Glory, that a good Mason is on an equality with the greatest prince; and Strength, is necessary to sustain us.

Q. What signifies the seven stars? A. The seven qualities which Masons should be possessed of: Friendship, Union, Submission, Discretion, Fidelity, Prudence and Temperance.

Q. Why should a Mason be possessed of these qualities? A. Friendship, is a virtue that should reign among brothers; Union, is the foundation of society; Submission, to the laws, regulations, and decrees of the Lodge, without murmuring; Discretion, that a Mason should always be on his guard, and never suffer himself to be surprised; Fidelity, in [Pg 189]observing strictly our obligations; Prudence, to conduct ourselves in such a manner that the profane, though jealous, may never be able to censure our conduct; and Temperance, to avoid all excesses that may injure either body or soul.

Q. What signifies the seven candlesticks, with their seven letters? A. seven crimes, which Masons should always avoid, viz.: Hatred, Discord, Pride, Indiscretion, Perfidy, Rashness, and Calumny.

Q. What are the reasons that Masons should particularly avoid these crimes? A. Because they are incompatible with the principles and qualities of a good Mason, who should avoid doing an injury to a brother, even should he be ill-treated by him, and to unite in himself all the qualities of a good and upright man. Discord, is contrary to the very principles of society; Pride, prevents the exercise of humanity; Indiscretion, is fatal to Masonry; Perfidy, should be execrated by every honest man; Rashness, may lead us into unpleasant and disagreeable dilemmas; and Calumny, the worst of all, should be shunned as a vice which saps the very foundation of friendship and society.

Q. What signifies the two-edged sword? A. It expresses the superiority of this degree over all others that precede it.

Q. Are there any higher degrees than this? A. Yes; there are several.

Q. What signifies the book with seven seals, which none but one can open? A. A Lodge, or Council, of Masons, which the Most Puissant alone has a right to convene and open.

Q. What is enclosed in the first seal? A. One bow, one arrow, and one crown.

Q. What in the second? A. A two-edged sword.

Q. What in the third? A. A balance.

Q. What in the fourth? A. Death's head.

Q. What in the fifth? A. A cloth stained with blood.

Q. What in the sixth? A. The power to darken the sun, and tinge the moon with blood.

Q. What in the seventh? A. Seven trumpets and perfumes.

Q. Explain these things to me? A. The bow, arrow, and crown, signifies that the orders of this respectable council should be executed with as much quickness as the arrow flies from the bow, and be received with as much submission as if it came from a crowned head, or the chief of a nation. The sword, that the Council is always armed to punish the guilty. The balance is a symbol of justice. The skull is the image of a brother who is excluded from a Lodge or Council. This idea must make all tremble when they recollect the penalties they have imposed on themselves under the most solemn obligations! The cloth stained with blood, that we should not hesitate to spill ours for the good of Masonry. The power of obscuring the sun and tinging the moon with blood, is the representation of the power of the Superior Councils—in interdicting their works, if they are irregular, until they have acknowledged their error, and submitted to the rules and regulations of the craft established by the Grand Constitutions. The seven trumpets, signify that Masonry is extended over the surface of the earth, on the wings of fame, and supports itself with honor. The perfumes denote that the life of a good [Pg 190]Mason should be, and is free from all reproach, and is perfumed by means of good report.

Q. What age are you? A. Very ancient.

Q. Who are you? A. I am a Patmian: (i.e., of Patmos.)

Q. Whence came you? A. From Patmos. End of the lecture.

To Close.—Q. What is the o'clock? Ans. There is no more time. The Most Puissant strikes seven, and says, "Venerable Knights Princes, the Council is closed." The two Wardens repeat the same, and the Council is closed.

SOVEREIGN PRINCES, MASTERS ADVITIAM, OR VENERABLE GRAND MASTERS OF ALL SYMBOLIC LODGES.

Decorations, etc.—This Lodge must be decorated with blue and yellow. The Grand Master sits on a throne elevated by nine steps, under a canopy before it is an altar, on which is a sword, bible, compass, square, mallet, etc., as in the Symbolic Lodges. Between the altar and the south is a candlestick with nine branches, which is always lighted in this Lodge. There are two Wardens in the west. The Grand Master represents Cyrus Artaxerxes (the Masonic name of Cambyses), wearing his royal ornaments, and a large blue and yellow ribbon crossing each other.

To Open.—Grand Master: "I desire to open the Lodge." He then descends to the lowest step of the throne, and when he is assured that the Lodge is tyled, he knocks one and two with his mallet. Each Warden repeats the same, which makes nine. G. M.—"Where is your Master placed?" Warden: "In the East." G. M.—"Why in the East?" W. "Because the glorious sun rises in the East to illumine the world." G. M. "As I sit in the East, I open this Lodge," which is repeated by the Wardens. Then all the brethren clap their hands one and two.

Reception.—The candidate represents Zerubbabel, who enters the Lodge by himself, without being introduced, decorated with the jewels and badges of the highest degrees he has taken. The Wardens take him by the hand, and place him in a blue elbow chair, opposite to the Grand Master, who demands from him all the words, from an Entered Apprentice upwards; and after he has satisfied the Grand Master, and is found worthy to hold a sceptre, they make him travel nine times 'round the Lodge, beginning in the South, and then by nine square steps he advances to the throne, and walks over two drawn swords, laid across. There must be a pot with burning charcoal close by the throne, that the candidate may feel the heat of the fire while taking the obligation; in doing which, he lays his right hand on the Bible, which is covered by the Grand Master's right hand, and then takes the following obligation:

Obligation.—I, A. B., do solemnly and sincerely swear and promise, under the penalties of all my former obligations, to protect the craft and my brethren with all my might, and not to acknowledge any one for a true Mason who was not made in a regularly constituted and lawful Lodge. I furthermore do swear, that I will strictly observe and obey all the statutes and regulations of the Lodge; and that I never will disclose [Pg 191]or discover the secrets of this degree, either directly or indirectly, except by virtue of a full power in writing, given me for that purpose by the Grand Inspector or his deputy, and then to such only as have been Masters of a regular Lodge. All this I swear under the penalties of being forever despised and dishonored by the Craft in general. He then kisses the Bible.

Here follow the signs, token, and word, viz.:—First Sign.—Form four squares, thus: with the fingers joined, and the thumb elevated, place your right hand on your heart (this forms two squares). Place the left hand on the lips, the thumb elevated so as to form a third square; place the heels so as to form a square with the feet. Second Sign.—Place yourself on your knees, elbows on the ground, the head inclined towards the left. Third Sign.—Cross the hands on the breast, the right over the left, fingers extended, thumbs elevated, and the feet forming a square. Token.—Take reciprocally the right elbow with the right hand, the thumb on the outside, the fingers joined, and on the inside; press the elbow thus four times, slip the hands down to the wrists, raising the three last fingers, and press the index on the wrist. Sacred Word.—"Razabassi," or "Razahaz Betzi-Yah." Pass-Words.—"Jechson," "Jubellum," "Zanabosan." Some, however, give Jehovah as the sacred word, and "Belshazzar" as the pass-word.

Lecture.—Question—Are you a Grand Master of all Symbolic Lodges? Answer.—They know me at Jerusalem to be such.

Q. How shall I know that you are a Grand Master of all Symbolic Lodges? A. By observing my zeal in rebuilding the temple.

Q. Which way did you travel? A. From the South to the East.

275

Q. How often? A. Nine.

Q. Why so many? A. In memory of the Grand Masters who traveled to Jerusalem.

Q. Can you give me their names? A. Their names are Esdras, Zerubbabel, Phachi, Joshua, Elial, Toyada, Homen, Nehemias, and Malchias.

Q. What are the pass-words? A. "Jechson," "Jubellum," and "Zanabosan."

Q. What object engaged your attention most, when you first entered the Lodge of Grand Masters? A. The candlestick with nine branches.

Q. Why are the nine candles therein always kept burning in this Lodge? A. To remind us that there cannot be less than nine Masters to form a Grand Master's Lodge.

Q. What were your reasons for wishing to be admitted and received in this Lodge of Grand Masters? A. That I might receive the benefit of the two lights I was unacquainted with.

Q. Have you received those lights, and in what manner? A. In receiving first the small light.

Q. Explain this? A. When I was received by steel and fire.

Q. What signifies the steel? A. To remind us of the steel by which our Most Respectable Chief, Hiram Abiff, lost his life, and which I am sworn to make use of whenever I can revenge that horrible murder of the traitors of Masonry.

[Pg 192]Q. What means the fire? A. To put us in mind that our forefathers were purified by fire.

Q. By whom were you received? A. By Cyrus.

Q. Why by Cyrus? A. Because it was he who ordered Zerubbabel to rebuild the temple.

Q. What did you promise and swear to perform when you received this degree? A. I swore that I would see the laws, statutes, and regulations strictly observed in our Lodge.

Q. What was your name before you received this degree? A. Zerubbabel.

Q. What is your name now? A. Cyrus.

Q. What means the word Animani? A. "I am that, I am;" and it is also the name of him who found the lion's den.

Q. Why is the Lodge decorated with blue and yellow? A. To remind us that the Eternal appeared to Moses on Mount Sinai, in clouds of gold and azure, when he gave to his people the laws of infinite wisdom.

Q. Where do you find the records of our order? A. In the archives of Kilwinning, in the north of Scotland.

Q. Why did you travel from the South 'round to the East? A. In allusion to the power of the Grand Architect of the universe, which extends throughout all the world.

Q. Why did you wash your hands in the taking of one or the previous degrees? A. To show my innocence.

Q. Why is the history of Hiram Abiff so much spoken of? A. To put us always in mind that he chose rather to sacrifice his life than reveal the secrets of Masonry.

Q. Why is the triangle, with the word secret on it, considered as the most precious jewel in Masonry? A. Because by its justness, equality, and proportion, it represents our redemption.

Q. By what mark was the place discovered where Hiram Abiff was buried by his assassins? A. By a sprig of cassia (say granate).

Q. For what reason do the Master Masons in the Symbolic Lodges speak of a sprig of cassia? A. Because the Sublime Grand Elected descendants of the ancient Patriarchs did not think proper to give the real name or truth of Masonry; therefore, they agreed to say that it was a sprig of cassia, because it had a strong smell.

Q. What are the reasons for the different knocks at the door to gain admittance? A. To know and be assured that they have passed the different degrees, which number we must understand.

Q. For what reasons do we keep our mysteries with such circumspection and secrecy? A. For fear there might be found amongst us some traitorous villains similar to the three Fellow Crafts who murdered our chief, Hiram Abiff.

Q. What is the reason that the Grand Masters of all Lodges are received with so much honor in the Symbolic Lodges? A. Those homages are due to their virtues as Princes of Masons, whose firmness has been shown on so many occasions, by spilling their blood in support of Masonry and the fraternity.

[Pg 193]Q. Why do we applaud with our hands? A. In that manner we express our happiness and satisfaction at having done a good action, and rendered justice.

Q. What reflections occur, when contemplating the conduct of Solomon? A. That a wise man may err, and when he is sensible of his fault, correct himself by acknowledging that fault, whereby he claims the indulgence of his brethren.

Q. Why do the Symbolic Lodges take the name of St. John of Jerusalem? A. Because in the time of the Crusades, the Perfect Masons, Knights, and Princes, communicated their mysteries to the Knights of that order; whereupon it was determined to celebrate their festival annually, on St. John's day, being under the same law.

Q. Who was the first architect that conducted the works of Solomon's temple? A. Hiram Abiff; which signifies the inspired man.

Q. Who laid the first stone? A. Solomon cut and laid the first stone, which afterwards supported the temple.

Q. Was there anything enclosed in that stone? A. Yes; some characters, which were, like the name of the Grand Architect of the Universe, only known to Solomon.

Q. What stone was it? A. An agate of a foot square.

Q. What was the form of it? A. Cubical.

Q. At what time of the day was the stone laid? A. Before sunrise.

Q. For what reason? A. To show that we must begin early and work with vigilance and assiduity.

Q. What cement did he make use of? A. A cement which was composed of the finest and purest flour, milk, oil, and wine.

Q. Is there any meaning in this composition? A. Yes; when the Grand Architect of the Universe determined to create the world, he employed his sweetness, bounty, wisdom and power.

Q. What is the reason why the number eighty-one is held in such esteem among Princes of Masons? A. Because that number explains the triple alliance which the Eternal operates by the triple triangle, which was seen at the time Solomon consecrated the temple to God; and also that Hiram Abiff was eighty-one years of age when he was murdered.

Q. Was anything else perceived at the consecration? A. A perfume which not only filled the temple, but all Jerusalem.

Q. Who destroyed the temple? A. Nebuchadnezzar.

Q. How many years after it was built? A. Four hundred and seventy years, six months, and ten days, after its foundation.

Q. Who built the second temple? A. Zerubbabel, by the grant and aid of Cyrus, King of Persia. It was finished in the reign of Darius, when he was known to be a Prince of Jerusalem. Cyrus not only gave Zerubbabel and the captive Masons their liberty, but ordered all the treasures of the old temple to be restored to them, that they might embellish the second temple, which he had ordered Zerubbabel to build.

Q. What signifies the jewel of the Right Worshipful Grand Master of all Lodges being a triangle? A. He wears it in remembrance of the [Pg 194]presents given by monarchs and the protectors of the order, in recompense for their zeal, fervor, and constancy.

Q. What way have you traveled to become a Right Worshipful Grand Master of all Lodges, and Grand Patriarch? A. By the four elements.

Q. Why by the four elements? A. To put us in mind of this world, and the troubles in which we live; to cleanse ourselves from all impurities, and thereby render ourselves worthy of perfect virtue.

Q. Where was the Lodge of Grand Masters first held? A. In the sacred vault, east of the temple.

Q. Where is that lodge held at present? A. All over the world, agreeably to the orders of Solomon, when he told us to travel and to spread over the universe, to teach Masonry to those whom we should find worthy of it, but especially to those who should receive us kindly, and who were virtuous men.

Q. What did Solomon give you to remember him at your departure? A. He rewarded the merits of all the workmen, and showed to the Chief Master the cubic stone of agate, on which was engraved, on a gold plate, the sacred name of God.

Q. How was the agate stone supported? A. On a pedestal of a triangular form, surrounded with three cross pillars, which were also surrounded by a circle of brass.

Q. What signifies the three pillars? A. Strength, wisdom and beauty.

Q. What was in the middle of the circle? A. The point of exactness, which teaches us the point of perfection.

Q. What else did Solomon give you? A. The great sign of admiration and consternation, by which I am known by a brother. He also put a ring on my finger, in remembrance of my alliance with virtue, and loaded us with kindness.

Q. Why have you a sun on the jewel of perfection? A. To show that we have received the full light, and know Masonry in its perfection.

Q. Who destroyed the second temple which was finished by the Princes of Jerusalem? A. Pompey began its destruction, and King Herodes the Great finished it.

Q. Who rebuilt it again? A. King Herodes repenting the action he had unjustly done, recalled all the Masons to Jerusalem who had fled, and directed them to rebuild the temple.

Q. Who destroyed the third temple? A. Tito, the son of the Emperor Vespasian. The Masons, who with sorrow saw the temple again destroyed, departed from Rome, after having embraced the Catholic religion, and determined never to assist in constructing another.

Q. What became of those Masons afterwards? A. They divided themselves into several companies, and went into different parts of Europe, but the greatest part of them went to Scotland, and built a town which they called Kilwinning; at this time there is a Lodge there, bearing the same name.

Q. What happened to them afterwards? A. Twenty-seven thousand of the Masons in Scotland determined to assist the Christian Princes and Knights, who were at that time at Jerusalem, in a crusade for the [Pg 195]purpose of taking the Holy Land and city from the infidels, who were then in possession of it; and they accordingly obtained leave of the Scottish monarch.

Q. What happened most remarkable to them? A. Their bravery and good conduct gained them the esteem and respect of all the Knights of St. John of Jerusalem. The general of that order, and the principal officers, took the resolution of being admitted into the secrets of Masonry, which they accordingly received; and in return they admitted them into their order.

Q. What became of those Masons afterwards? A. After the crusade they returned and spread Masonry throughout all Europe, which flourished for a long time in France and England; but the Scotch, to their great praise be it spoken, were the only people who kept up the practice of it.

Q. How came it again in vogue in France? A. A Scotch nobleman went to France and became a resident at Bordeaux, where he establishes a Lodge of Perfection, from the members of the Lodge in 1744; in which he was assisted by a French gentleman, who took great pleasure in all the Masonic degrees. This still exists in a most splendid manner.

Q. What means the fire in our Lodge? A. Submission, purification of morals, and equality among brethren.

Q. What signifies the air? A. The purity, virtue, and truth of this degree.

Q. What does the sign of the sun mean? A. It signifies that some of us are more enlightened than others in the Mysteries of Masonry; and for that reason we are often called Knights of the Sun.

Q. How many signs have you in this degree of Grand Pontiff, which is Grand Master of all Lodges? A. 1st, The sign of the earth, or Apprentice; 2d, of water—Fellow Craft; 3d, of terror—the Master; 4th, of fire; 5th, of air; 6th, of the point in view; 7th, of the sun; 8th, of astonishment; 9th, of honor; 10th, of stench, or strong smell; 11th, of admiration; 12th, of consternation. End of the Lecture.

To Close.—The Grand Master says, "My brother, enter into the cave of Silol—work with Grand Rofadam—measure your steps to the sun, and then the great black eagle will cover you with his wings, to the end of what you desire, by the help of the Most Sublime Princes Grand Commanders." He then strikes four and two, makes the sign of four squares, which is repeated by the Wardens, and the Lodge is closed.

The examination of a brother in the foregoing degree is as follows:

Q. From whence came you? A. From the sacred vault at Jerusalem.

Q. What are you come to do here? A. I am come to see and visit your works and show you mine, that we may work together and rectify our morals, and, if possible, sanctify the profane—but only by permission of a Prince Adept, or Prince of the Royal Secret (if one is present).

Q. What have you brought? A. Glory, grandeur and beauty.

Q. Why do you give the name of St. John to our Lodge? A. Formerly all the Lodges were under the name of Solomon's Lodge, as the founder of Masonry; but since the crusades we have agreed with the Knights [Pg 196]Templars, or Hospitallers, to dedicate them to St. John, as he was the support of the Christians and the new laws.

Q. What do you ask more? A. Your will and pleasure as you may find me worthy, obedient, and virtuous.

PRINCE OF THE ROYAL SECRET.

The Assembly of Princes is termed a "Consistory."

Officers.—The first officer represents Frederick II., King of Prussia; he is styled "Sovereign of Sovereigns," "Grand Prince," "Illustrious Commander in Chief." The two next officers are styled "Lieutenant Commanders." The fourth officer is the "Minister of State," who acts as the orator. The fifth officer is the "Grand Chancellor." Then the "Grand Secretary;" the "Grand Treasurer;" the "Grand Captain of the Guards;" a "Standard Bearer;" a "Grand Master Architect;" and two "Tylers."

Place of Meeting.—This is to be a building at least two stories in height, situated on elevated ground, in the open country. Three apartments on the second floor are necessary in this degree. In the first of these the guards are stationed. The second is used as a preparation room. The third is occupied by the members of the Consistory. This last apartment is hung with black, sprinkled with tears, "death's heads," "cross bones," and "skeletons." The throne is in the East, elevated by seven steps. On the throne is the chair of state, lined with black satin, flamed with red. Before the chair is a table covered with black satin, strewed with tears. On this cloth, in front, is a "death's head" and "cross bones;" over the "death's head" is the letter I; and under the "cross bones" is the letter M. On the table is placed a naked sword, a buckler, a sceptre, a balance, and a book containing the statutes of the order. In the West is placed another table covered with crimson, bordered with black, and strewed with tears; on the front of this cloth are the letters N. K. M. K. in gold.

Dress and Stations of Officers.—The "Sovereign of Sovereigns" is dressed in royal robes, and seated in the chair of state. The Lieutenant Commanders dressed like the modern princes of Europe, and seated at the table in the West; their swords are crossed on the table. The Minister of State is placed at the Sovereign's right hand. The Grand Chancellor stands on the left hand of the Sovereign. Next to the Minister of State is placed the Grand Secretary. Next to the Grand Chancellor is placed the Grand Treasurer. Below the last named officers are placed on one side the Standard Bearer, the Grand Master Architect, and the Captain of the Guards. Below these officers are placed six members dressed in red, without aprons, wearing the jewel of the order, suspended on the breast by a black ribbon.

Collar of the Order.—The collar is black, and edged with silver. On its point is embroidered in red a Teutonic cross. On the middle of the cross is a double headed eagle in silver. The collar is lined with scarlet, on which is embroidered a black Teutonic cross. Around the waist is girded a black sash, embroidered with silver. The cross is embroidered on that part of the girdle which is in front.

[Pg 197]Jewel.—The jewel is a golden Teutonic cross.

Qualifications of Candidate.—The candidate who receives this degree must be faithfully examined in the previous degree prior to admission. The Master of Ceremonies will acquaint him with the pass-word, which he is to give to the Lieutenant Commander. The Master of Ceremonies will then lead him to the Sovereign of Sovereigns.

Opening and Closing.—The Sovereign of Sovereigns says, "Sal ix." The Lieutenants reply, "Noni." They then together say, "Tengu." All give the sign. The Sovereign of Sovereigns says: Let us imitate our Grand Master Jacques De Molay, Hiram Abiff, who to the last placed all his hopes in the Great Architect of the Universe; and pronounced the following words just as he passed from this transient life into eternal bliss:— "Spes mea in Deo est" (My hope is in God).

Description of the Carpet representing the Camp.—On the carpet is drawn an "enneagen," in which is inscribed a pentagon; within this is an equilateral triangle, and in the triangle a circle. Between the heptagon and pentagon, upon the sides of the latter, are placed the standards of the five Standard Bearers, and the pavilions inscribed by the letters T. E. N. G. U. The emblems on the standard T. are the "ark of the covenant," an "olive tree," and a "lighted candlestick," on each side. The ground color of this standard is purple. On the ark is written the motto "Laus Deo." The standard E. bears a golden lion, holding in his mouth a "golden key;" wearing around his neck a golden collar, on which is engraved "515." The ground is azure; the motto "Admajorem Dei glorium." On the standard N. is an "inflamed heart," in red, with two wings, surrounded by a laurel crown. The ground is white. The flag G. bears a double-headed eagle, crowned, holding a sword in his right claw, and in his left a bloody heart. Ground is sea green. The flag U. has an ox, sable (black), on a golden ground. On the sides of the enneagen are nine tents, and on its angles nine pendants, each belonging to its appropriate tent. The pendants are distinguished by numerals, and the tents by the letters I. N. O. N. X. I. L. A. S. disposed from right to left. These tents signify the different grades of Masonry. Thus:

Tent S. is Malachi—pendant, white, spotted with red; represents Knights of the East and West, and Princes of Jerusalem. Tent A. is Zerubbabel—pendant, light green; represents Knights of the East. Tent L. is Neamiah—pendant, red; represents Grand Elect, Perfect, and Sublime Masons. Tent I. is Hobben or Johaben—pendant, black and red; represents Sublime Elect, and Elect of Fifteen. Tent X. is Peleg— pendant, black; represents Elect of Nine, or Grand Master Architect. Tent N. is Joiada—pendant, red and black in lozenges; represents Provost and Judges. Tent O. is Aholiab—pendant, red and green; represents Intendant of the Buildings and Intimate Secretary. Tent N. is Joshua—pendant, green; represents Perfect Master. Tent I. is Ezra—pendant, blue; represents Master, Fellow Craft, and Entered Apprentice.

The equilateral triangle in the middle represents the centre of the army, and shows where the Knights of Malta are to be placed who have been admitted to our mysteries, and have proved themselves faithful guardians. They are to be joined with the Knights of Kadosh. The [Pg 198]corps in the centre is to be commanded by five princes, who command jointly, or in rotation, according to their degrees, and receive their orders immediately from the Sovereign of Sovereigns. These five Princes must place their standards in the five angles of the pentagon, as above described. These Princes, who are Standard Bearers, have the following name, viz.:—

Standard.
{
T. ...
Bezaleel
E. ...
Aholiab
N. ...
Mahuzen
G. ...
Garimont
U. ...
Amariah
}
Names.

The heptagon points out the Encampment destined for the Princes of Libanus, Jerusalem, etc.; and these are to receive their orders from the five Princes. The enneagen shows the general order of Masons of all degrees.

Instructions for the reunion of the brethren, Knights, Princes, and Commanders of the Royal Secret or Kadosh, which really signifies Holy brethren of all degrees separated.

Frederick III., King of Prussia, Grand Master and Commander in Chief, Sovereign of Sovereigns, with an army composed of the Knights, Princes of the White and Black Eagle, including Prussian, English, and French; likewise joined by the Knights Adepts of the Sun, Princes of Libanus or the Royal Axe, the Knights of the Rose Croix or St. Andrew, Knights of the East and West, the Princes of Jerusalem, Knights of the East or Sword, the Grand Elect Perfect and Sublime Masons, the Knights of the Royal Arch (ninth Arch), Sublime Knights Elected, etc.

The hour for the departure or march of the army is the fifth after the setting of the sun; and is to be made known by the firing of five great guns in the following order (0)—(0 0 0 0)—that is, with an interval between the first and second. The first rendezvous is to be the port of Naples—from Naples to the port of Rhodes—from Rhodes to Cyprus and Malta, whence the whole naval force of all nations is to assemble. The second rendezvous is to be at Cyprus, etc. The third rendezvous is to be at Jerusalem, where they will be joined by our faithful guardians. The watchwords of every day of the week are as follows and they are not to be changed but by express order from the King of Prussia:

	Protectors of Masonry.		Prophets.
Sunday,	Cyrus,		Ezekiel,
Monday,	Darius,		Daniel,
Tuesday,	Xerxes,		Habakkuk,
Wednes.,	Alexander,	Answer.	Zephaniah,
Thurs.,	Philadelphus,		Haggai,
Friday,	Herod,		Zechariah,
Saturday,	Hezekiah,		Malachi.

Sign.—Place the right hand on the heart; extend it forward, the palm downward; let it fall by the right side. Sacred words.—Those of the Carpet, which are to be read backward 'round the circle from right to left, thus:—One says "Salix," to which the other replies "Noni;" both then repeat (by letters) the word "Tengu."

Pass words.—"Phual Kol," which signifies "separated;" "Pharas Kol," which signifies "reunited;" [Pg 199]"Nekam Makah," which signifies "to avenge;" each then letters the word "Shaddai," which signifies "Omnipotent."

Charge Addressed to the Candidate.—My dear brother:—The Saracens having taken possession of the Holy Land, those who were engaged in the Crusades not being able to expel them, agreed with Godfrey de Bouillon, the conductor and chief of the Crusaders, to veil the mysteries of religion under emblems, by which they would be able to maintain the devotion of the soldier, and protect themselves from the incursion of those who were their enemies, after the example of the Scriptures, the style of which is figurative. Those zealous brethren chose Solomon's temple for their model. This building has strong allusions to the Christian church. Since that period they (Masons) have been known by the name of Master Architect; and they have employed themselves in improving the law of that admirable Master. From hence it appears that the mysteries of the craft are the mysteries of religion. Those brethren were careful not to entrust this important secret to any whose discretion they had not proved. For this reason they invented different degrees to try those who entered among them; and only gave them symbolical secrets, without explanation, to prevent treachery, and to make themselves known only to each other. For this purpose it was resolved to use different signs, words, and tokens, in every degree, by which they would be secured against cowans and Saracens. The different degrees were fixed first to the number of seven by the example of the Grand Architect of the Universe, who built all things in six days and rested on the seventh. This is distinguished by seven points of reception in the Master's degrees. Enoch employed six days to construct the arches, and on the seventh, having deposited the secret treasure in the lowest arch, was translated to the abodes of the blessed. Solomon employed six years in constructing his temple; and celebrated its dedication on the seventh, with all the solemnity worthy of the divinity himself. This sacred edifice we choose to make the basis of figurative Masonry. In the first degree are three symbols to be applied. First, the first of the creation, which was only chaos, is figured by the candidate's coming out of the black chamber, neither naked nor clothed, deprived, etc.; and his suffering the painful trial at his reception, etc. The candidate sees nothing before he is brought to light; and his powers of imagination relative to what he has to go through are suspended, which alludes to the figure of the creation of that vast luminous body confused among the other parts of creation before it was extracted from darkness and fixed by the Almighty fiat. Secondly, the candidate approaches the footstool of the Master, and there renounces all cowans; he promises to subdue his passions, by which means he is united to virtue, and by his regularity of life, demonstrates what he proposes. This is figured to him by the steps that he takes in approaching the altar; the symbolic meaning of which is the separation of the firmament from the earth and water on the second day of creation. (The charge proceeds by giving a figurative interpretation of the ceremonies, etc., of the first and second part of the third degree, which I pass over as uninteresting to my readers, and [Pg 200]commence with an interpretation which will be as novel to the Craft of the lower grades as to the cowans, or non-initiated.)

In the Master's degree is represented the assassination of Hiram by false brethren. This ought to put us in mind of the fate of Adam, occasioned by perverseness in his disobeying his great and awful Creator. The symbolic mystery of the death of Hiram Abiff represents to us that of the Messiah; for the three blows which were given to Hiram Abiff, at the three gates of the temple, allude to the three points of condemnation against Christ, at the High Priest's Caiphas, Herod, and Pilate. It was from the last that he was led to that most violent and excruciating death. The said three blows with the square, gauge, and gavel are symbols of the blow on the cheek, the flagellation, and the crown of thorns. The brethren assembled around the tomb of Hiram, is a representation of the disciples lamenting the death of Christ on the cross. The Master's word, which is said to be lost, since the death of Hiram Abiff, is the same that Christ pronounced on the cross, and which the Jews did not comprehend, "Eli, Eli, lama sabacthani," "my God, my God, why hast thou forsaken me! have pity on and forgive my enemies."—Instead of which words were substituted, M. B. N. (Mac-be-nac), which, in Arabian, signifies, "The son of the widow is dead." The false brethren represent Judas Iscariot, who sold Christ. The red collar worn by the Grand Elect Perfect and

Sublime Masons, calls to remembrance the blood of Christ. The sprig of cassia is the figure of the cross, because of this wood was the cross made. The captivity of the Grand Elect and Sublime Masons (i.e., by the Chaldeans), shows us the persecution of the Christian religion under the Roman emperors, and its liberty under Constantine the Great. It also calls to our remembrance the persecution of the Templars, and the situation of Jacques De Molay, who, lying in irons nearly seven years, at the end of which our worthy Grand Master was burnt alive with his four companions, on the eleventh of March, 1314, creating pity and tears in the people, who saw him die with firmness and heroic constancy, sealing his innocence with his blood. My dear brother, in passing to the degree of Perfect Master, in which you shed tears at the tomb of Hiram Abiff, and in some other degrees, has not your heart been led to revenge? Has not the crime of Jubelum Akirop been represented in the most hideous light?—Would it be unjust to compare the conduct of Philip the Fair to his, and the infamous accusers of the Templars, to the two ruffians who were accomplices with Akirop? Do they not kindle in your heart an equal aversion? The different stages you have traveled, and the time you have taken in learning these historical events, no doubt, will lead you to make the proper applications; and by the degree of Master Elect and Kadosh, you are properly disposed to fulfil all your engagements, and to bear an implacable hatred to the Knights of Malta, and to avenge the death of Jacques De Molay. Your extensive acquaintance with symbolic Masonry, which you have attained by your discretion, leaves you nothing more to desire here. You see, my dear brother, how, and by whom, Masonry has come to us. You are to endeavor by every just means to regain our rights, and to remember that we are joined by a society of men, whose courage, merit, and [Pg 201]good conduct, hold out to us that rank that birth alone gave to our ancestors. You are now on the same level with them. Avoid every evil by keeping your obligations, and carefully conceal from the vulgar what you are, and wait that happy moment when we all shall be reunited under the same Sovereign in the mansions of eternal bliss. Let us imitate the example of our Grand Master, Jaques De Molay, who to the end put his hope in God, and at his last dying moments ended his life saying, "Spes mea in Deo est!"

Obligation.—I do, of my own free will and accord, in the presence of the Grand Architect of the Universe, and this consistory of Sovereign Princes of the Royal Secret, or Knights of St. Andrew, faithful guardians of the faithful treasure; most solemnly vow and swear, under all the different penalties of my former obligations, that I will never directly or indirectly reveal or make known to any person or persons whatsoever, any or the least part of this Royal degree, unless to one duly qualified in the body of a regularly constituted Consistory of the same, or to him or them whom I shall find such after strict and due trial. I furthermore vow and swear, under the above penalties, to always abide and regulate myself agreeably to the statutes and regulations now before me; and when in a Consistory to behave and demean myself as one worthy of being honored with so high a degree, that no part of my conduct may in the least reflect discredit on the Royal Consistory, or disgrace myself. So may God maintain me in equity and justice! Amen! Amen! Amen! Amen!

SOVEREIGN GRAND INSPECTOR GENERAL.

The number of Inspectors of a Kingdom or Republic is not to exceed nine. They claim jurisdiction over all the ineffable and sublime degrees, and in reality form an aristocratic body, with power to appoint their own successors, and act as "Sovereigns of Masonry."

Decorations of the Place of Meeting.—The hangings are purple, embroidered with skeletons, death's-heads, and cross-bones. Before the canopy is a transparent delta (equilateral triangle). In the middle of the room is a grand triangular pedestal, near which is seen a skeleton holding in his left hand the standard of the order, and in his right hand a poniard in the attitude of striking. Above the door, or place of entrance, is the motto of the order, "Deus meumque jus." In the East is a chandelier of five branches; in the South is one of two branches; in the West is one of three; and in the North a single one.

Officers and Titles.—The assembly is termed "Supreme Council." The first officer, "Thrice Puissant Sovereign Grand Master." He represents Frederick II. The second officer is termed "Sovereign Lieutenant Commander." Besides these there is a "Treasurer of the Holy Empire;" an "Illustrious Grand Secretary of the Holy Empire;" an "Illustrious Master of Ceremonies;" and an "Illustrious Captain of the Guards"—in all, seven officers.

Dress.—The Thrice Puissant Sovereign wears a crimson robe, bordered with white—a crown on his head, and a sword in his hand. The Lieutenant Commander wears a ducal crown.

[Pg 202]Sash.—The sash is black, edged with gold, from left to right; at the bottom a rose of red, white and green. On the part crossing the breast is a delta, with rays traversed by a poniard, and in the midst the figure "33."

Jewel.—A black double-headed eagle holding a sword. His beak, claws, and sword are of gold. [Pass-words, signs, etc., as may from time to time be agreed upon.]

[THE END.]

FOOTNOTES:

[1] A person wishing to become a Mason must get some one who is a Mason to present his petition to a Lodge, when, if there are no serious objections, it will be entered on the minutes, and a committee of two or three appointed to inquire into his character, and report to the next regular communication. The following is the form of a petition used by a candidate; but a worthy candidate will not be rejected for the want of formality in his petition.

To the Worshipful Master, Wardens, and Brethren of Lodge No. — —, of Free and Accepted Masons.

The subscriber, residing in — —, of lawful age, and by occupation a — —, begs leave to state that, unbiassed by friends, and uninfluenced by mercenary motives, he freely and voluntarily offers himself a candidate for the mysteries of Masonry, and that he is prompt to solicit this privilege by a favorable opinion conceived of the institution, a desire of knowledge, and a sincere wish of being serviceable to his fellow-creatures. Should his petition be granted, he will cheerfully conform to all the ancient established usages and customs of the Fraternity.

(Signed) A. B.

[2] In many Lodges this is put in the form of a question, thus: "Are you willing to take an obligation upon you that does not affect your politics or religion?" The promise "to conform," made before entering the Lodge, the "assurance that the oath is not to interfere with their political or religious principles" and the manner the obligation is administered, only two or three words being repeated at a time, consequently not

fully understood, are among the reasons which have led many great and good men to take oaths incompatible with the laws of God and our country.

[3] Literally a rope several yards in length, but mystically three miles; so that a Master Mason must go on a brother Master Mason's errand whenever required, the distance of three miles, should he have to go barefoot and bareheaded. In the degrees of knighthood the distance is forty miles.

[4] In some Lodges the Master takes the candidate by the Master's grip and says, "Brother, you will please rise," assisting him.

[5] There is much diversity of opinion among Masons respecting this word; some insist that Giblem is the right word; others, that Gibelum is the right word; the latter word was rejected, because it was used by "Jachin and Boaz."

[6] This charge is frequently omitted when conferring the degree on a candidate, but never when really installing a Master of a Lodge.

[7] Here the brethren divest themselves of their jewels, sashes, aprons, etc.

[8] The ark, which had been carried by two brethren in the procession, is here placed on the altar.

[9] At these words the candidate is received into the procession.

[10] Here all kneel in a circle around the altar.

[11] At the words, "For He is good," the Most Excellent Master, who is High Priest of the Chapter, kneels and joins hands with the rest; they all then repeat in concert the words, "For He is good, for His mercy endureth forever" six times, each time bowing their heads low towards the floor.

[12] There is a great difference in the manner of giving the Royal Arch word in the different Chapters. Sometimes it is given at the opening, as above stated; sometimes they commence with the word God, each one pronouncing a letter of it in succession, until they have each pronounced every letter of the word, then the word Jehovah, a syllable at a time, and then the word Jahbuhlun as described. There are also Chapters in which the latter word is not known, and there are others in which the word is not given at all at opening.

[13] This clause is sometimes made a distinct point in the obligation in the following form, viz.: Furthermore, do I promise and swear, that I will vote for a companion Royal Arch Mason before any other of equal qualifications; and in some Chapters both are left out of the obligation.

[14] In some Chapters this is administered: All the secrets of a companion without exception.

[15] This is frequently represented in this manner: When the person reading comes to that part where it says, "God called to him out of the midst of the bush and said," etc., he stops reading, and a person behind the bushes calls out, "Moses, Moses." The conductor answers, "Here am I." The person behind the bush then says, "Draw not nigh hither; put off thy shoes from off thy feet; for the place whereon thou standeth is holy ground (his shoes are then slipped off). Moreover, I am the God of Abraham, the God of Isaac, and the God of Jacob." The person first reading then says, "And Moses hid his face; for he was afraid to look upon God." At these words the bandage is placed over the candidate's eyes.

[16] By this tremendous imprecation, the candidate, of his "own free will and accord," volunteers (in case of a violation) to come forth to the resurrection of damnation and receive the sentence, "Depart thou accursed into everlasting fire prepared for the devil and his angels."

[17] See the Apocryphal books, 1 Esdras, chapters iii. and iv.

[18] Diplomas of this degree, "In the name of the Holy and Undivided Trinity," recommend the bearer as a true and faithful soldier of Jesus Christ.

HISTORICAL SKETCH OF THE KIDNAPPING OF WILLIAM MORGAN.

Captain Morgan was born in Virginia, and was a mason by trade. He commenced the business of a brewer at York, Upper Canada, in 1821, but having lost all his property by fire, he removed to New York State, and worked at his trade both in Rochester and Batavia. In the year 1826 rumors were heard that Morgan, in connection with other persons, was preparing and intended to publish a book which would reveal the secrets of Freemasonry, and an excitement of some kind existed in relation to the publication of the book. In the month of September he was seized under feigned process of the law, in the day time, in the village of Batavia, and forcibly carried to Canandaigua. Captain Morgan was at this time getting ready his book, which purported to reveal the secrets of Freemasonry. This contemplated publication excited the alarm of the fraternity, and numbers of its members were heard to say that it should be suppressed at all events. Meetings of delegates from the different Lodges in the Western counties has been held to devise means for most effectually preventing the publication. The zealous members of the fraternity were angry, excited, and alarmed, and occasionally individuals threw out dark and desperate threats. About this time an incendiary attempt was made to fire the office of Col. Miller, the publisher of the book. The gang who seized Morgan at Batavia were Masons. They took him to Canandaigua; after a mock trial he was discharged, but was immediately arrested and committed to prison on a debt. The next night, in the absence of the jailer, he was released from prison by the pretended friendship of a false and hollow-hearted brother Mason. Upon leaving the prison door he was seized in the streets of Canandaigua, and notwithstanding his cries of murder, he was thrust with ruffian violence into a carriage prepared for that purpose. At Batavia he had been torn from his home—from his wife and infant children. At Canandaigua he was falsely beguiled from the safe custody of the law, and was forcibly carried, by relays of horses, through a thickly populated country, in the space of little more than twenty-four hours, to the distance of one hundred and fifteen miles, and secured as a prisoner in the magazine of Fort Niagara. This was clearly proved on the trial of persons concerned in the outrage, and who were found guilty and [Pg 203]sentenced to various terms of imprisonment. The fate of Captain Morgan was never known, but it is supposed he was taken out into the lake, where his throat was cut, and his body sunken fifty fathoms in water. About the same time, Col. David C. Miller, the publisher of the book, was also seized, in Batavia, under the color of legal process, and taken to Le Roy. The avowed intention of Col. Miller's seizure was to take him where Morgan was—and where that was may be best gathered from the impious declaration of one of the conspirators, James Ganson, for several years a member of our Legislature—that "he was put where he would stay put until God should call for him." Miller was, however, set at liberty, as the inhabitants of Le Roy interfered with the schemes of his kidnappers. He soon after put to press the first part of the volume which is here presented to the public. Additions have been made to Captain Morgan's revelations, from time to time, until we are now able to make public all the Masonic degrees of any note or interest, entered into by modern Freemasons.

Typographical errors corrected in text:

Page 8:   Futhermore replaced with Furthermore
Page 23:   appetities replaced with appetites
Page 23:   tessel replaced with tressel
Page 32:   synonomous replaced with synonymous
Page 57:   emblematicol replaced with emblematical
Page 58:   "a gentlemen" replaced with "a gentleman"
Page 61:   decend replaced with descend
Page 65:   "never against attempt" replaced with "never again attempt"
Page 78:   repution replaced with reputation
Page 85:   Th replaced with To
Page 90:   sanctum sanctortum replaced with sanctum sanctorium
Page 90:   wood replaced with word
Page 104:   Corrected one of the questions which was incorrectly ended with an exclamation mark
Page 113:   Inserted the missing "A." on three of the Questions
Page 128:   Mot replaced with Most
Page 128:   replaced "support and bear that that cross?" with "support and bear that cross?"
Page 135:   "repeated by then Warden" replaced with "repeated by the Warden"
Page 150:   Inserted the missing "A." in one of the Questions
Page 158:   Removed duplicate "the" from "among the the ruins"
Page 177:   Replaced "A." with "Q." at beginning of paragraph
Page 183:   Inserted the missing "A." in one of the Questions
Page 188-9:   oberving replaced with observing

Index of Abbreviations added by the Complier:

Masonic abbreviations include:

- A.Dep. – *Anno Depositionis*. "In the Year of the Deposite", The date used by Royal and Select Masters
- A.&A. – Ancient and Accepted
- A.F.M. – Ancient Freemasons
- A.F.&A.M. – Ancient Free and Accepted Masons
- A.Inv. – *Anno Inventionis*. "In the Year of the Discovery", the date used by Royal Arch Masons
- A.L. – *Anno Lucis*, "In the Year of light" the date used by Ancient Craft Masons
- A∴ L∴ G∴ D∴ G∴ A∴ D∴ L'U∴ – *À la Gloire du Grand Architecte de L'Univers*. "To the Glory of the Grand Architect of the Universe" (French) The usual caption of French Masonic documents.
- A∴ L'O∴ – *À L'Orient*, "At the East" (French) The seat of the Lodge
- A.M. – *Anno Mundi*, "In The Year of the World". The date used in the Ancient and Accepted Scottish Rite

- A.O. – *Anno Ordinis*, "In the Year of the Order" . The date used by <u>Knights Templars</u>
- A.Y.M. – Ancient York Mason
- B∴ – Bruder. German, meaning Brother.
- B∴ A∴ – Buisson Ardent. French, meaning Burning Bush.
- B∴ B∴ – Burning Bush.
- Bn∴ – Brudern. German, meaning Brethren.
- Comp∴ – Companion. Used by Brethren of the Royal Arch.
- C.C. – Celestial Canopy.
- C∴ H∴ – Captain of the Host.
- D∴ – Deputy.
- D. and A.F.– Due and Ancient Form.
- D∴ D∴ G∴ H∴ P∴ – District Deputy Grand High Priest.
- D∴ D∴ G∴ M∴ – <u>District Deputy Grand Master</u>
- D∴ G∴ M∴ – Deputy Grand Master.
- D∴ G∴ B∴ A∴ W∴ – *Der Grosse Baumeister aller Welten*, "The Grand Architect of All Worlds" (German)
- D∴ G∴ G∴ H∴ P∴ – Deputy General Grand High Priest.
- D∴ G∴ H∴ P∴ – Deputy Grand High Priest.
- D∴ G∴ M∴ – Deputy Grand Master.
- D∴ M∴ J∴ – *Deus Meumque Jus*, "God and My Right" (Latin)
- D∴ Prov∴ G∴ M∴ – Deputy Provincial Grand Master.
- Deg. – Degree or Degrees. Another way is as in 33, meaning Thirty-Third Degree. (Although this is more commonly denoted with a degree sign)
- Dist. – District.
- E∴ – Eminent; Excellent; also East.
- EA – Entered Apprentice. Sometimes abbreviated E∴ A∴ P∴
- E∴ C∴ – Excellent Companion.
- Ec∴ – *Écossais*, "Scottish", or belonging to the <u>Scottish Rite</u> (French)
- E∴ G∴ C∴ – Eminent <u>Grand Commander</u>.
- E∴ G∴ M∴ – Early Grand Master.
- E∴ O∴ L∴ – *Ex Oriente Lux*, "Out of the East comes Light" (Latin).
- F∴ – *Frère*, "Brother" (French)
- F.&A.M. – Free and Accepted Masons.
- FC – Fellowcraft.
- FM – Freemason.
- G. – Grand; sometimes read as Great. Also has another meaning well known to the Craft.
- G.A.O.T.U. – Grand Architect of the Universe.
- G∴ A∴ S∴ – Grand Annual Sojourn.
- G.C.– Grand Chapter; Grand Council; Grand Cross; Grand Commander; Grand Chaplain; Grand Conclave; Grand Conductor; Grand Chancellor.
- G∴ C∴ G∴ – Grand Captain General; Grand Captain of the Guard.
- G ∴ C∴ H∴ – Grand Captain of the Host; Grand Chapter of Heredom.
- G∴ Com∴ – Grand Commandery; Grand Commander.
- G∴ D∴ – Grand Deacon.
- G∴ D∴ C∴ – Grand Director of Ceremonies.
- G∴ E∴ – Grand Encampment; Grand Bast; Grand Ezra.
- G∴ J∴ W∴ – Grand Junior Warden.
- G∴ G∴ C∴ – General Grand Chapter
- G∴ G∴ H∴ P∴ – General Grand High Priest.

- G∴ G∴ K∴ – General Grand King.
- G∴ G∴ M∴ F∴ V∴ – General Grand Master of the First Veil.
- G∴ G∴ S∴ – General Grand Scribe.
- G∴ G∴ T∴ – General Grand Treasurer.
- G∴ H∴ P∴ – Grand High Priest.
- G∴ K∴ – Grand King.
- G∴ L∴ – Grand Lodge. *Grande Loge* (French). *Grosse Loge* (German).
- G∴ M∴ – <u>Grand Master</u>; Grand Marshal; Grand Monarch.
- G∴ N∴ – Grand Nehemiah.
- G∴ O∴ – Grand Orient; Grand Organist.
- G∴ P∴ – Grand Pursuivant; Grand Prior; Grand Prelate; Grand Preceptor; Grand Preceptory; Grand Patron; Grand Priory; Grand Patriarch; Grand Principal.
- G∴ P∴ S∴ – Grand Principal Sojourner
- G∴ R∴ – Grand Registrar; Grand Recorder.
- G∴ R∴ A∴ C∴ – Grand Royal Arch Chapter.
- G∴ S∴ – Grand Scribe; Grand Secretory; Grand Steward.
- G∴ S∴ B∴ – Grand Sword Bearer; Grand Sword Bearer.
- G∴ S∴ E∴ – Grand Scribe Ezra.
- G∴ S∴ N∴ – Grand Scribe Nehemiah.
- G∴ S∴ W∴ – Grand Senior Warden.
- G∴ T∴ – Grand Treasurer; Grand Tyler.H∴ A∴ B∴ Hiram Abif.
- H∴ E∴ – Holy Empire.
- H∴ J∴ – *Heilige Johannes*, "Holy Saint John" (German)
- H∴ K∴ T∴ – Hiram, King of Tyre.
- H∴ R∴ D∴ M∴ – Heredom.
- Ill∴ – Illustrious.
- I∴ N∴ R∴ I∴ – Jesus Nazarenus, Rex Iudoeorum. Latin, meaning Jesus of Nazareth, King of the Jews. The Letters are also the initials of a significant sentence in Latin, namely, Igne Natura Renovatur Integra, meaning by fire nature is perfectly renewed.
- I∴ P∴ M∴ – Immediate Past Master. English title of an official last promoted from the chair.
- I∴ T∴ N∴ O∴ T∴ G∴ A∴ O∴ T∴ U∴ – In the Name of the Grand Architect of the Universe. Often forming the caption of Masonic documents.
- J∴ W∴ – Junior Warden.
- K∴ – King.
- K∴ E∴ P∴ – Knight of the Eagle and Pelican
- K∴ H∴ – Kadash, Knight of Kadosh.
- K∴ H∴ S∴ – Knight of the Holy Sepulcher
- K∴ M∴ – Knight of Malta
- K∴ S∴ – King Salomon (Suleiman)
- K∴ T∴ – Knights Templar; Knight Templar.
- L∴ – Lodge. Also *Lehrling* meaning "Apprentice" (German).
- L∴ R∴ – Lonon Rank. A distinction introduced in England in 1908.
- L∴ V∴ X∴ – Lux Latin, meaning Light.
- M∴ – Mason; Masonry; Marshal; Mark; Minister; Master. Meister, in German. Maître, in French.
- M∴ C∴ – Middle Chamber.
- M∴ E∴ – Most Eminent; Most Excellent.
- M∴ E∴ G∴ H∴ P∴ – Most Excellent Grand High Priest.
- M∴ E∴ G∴ M∴ – Most Eminent Grand Master (of Knights Templar).
- M∴ E∴ M∴ – Most Excellent Master.

- M∴ E∴ Z∴ – Most Excellent Zerubbabel.
- M∴ K∴ G∴ – Maurer Kunst Geselle. German, meaning Fellow Craft.
- M∴ L∴ – Maurer Lehrling. German, meaning Entered Apprentice.
- M∴ L∴ – Mère Loge. French, meaning Mother Lodge.
- M∴ M∴ – Master Mason. *Mois Maçonnique*, "Masonic Month" (French): March 18 the first Masonic month among French Freemasons. Also *Meister Maurer*, "Master Mason" (German)
- M∴ P∴ S∴ – Most Puissant Sovereign.
- M∴ W∴ – Most Worshipful.
- M∴ W∴ G∴ M∴ – <u>Most Worshipful Grand Master</u>; Most Worthy Grand Matron.
- M∴ W∴ G∴ P∴ – Most Worthy Grand Patron.
- M∴ W∴ M∴ – Most Wise Master
- M∴ W∴ S∴ – Most Wise Sovereign
- N∴ E∴ C∴ – North-east Corner.
- N'o∴ P∴ V∴ D∴ M∴ – *N'oubliez pas vos décorations Maçonniques*, "Do not forget your Masonic regalia" (French), a phrase used in France on the corner of a summons.
- O∴ – Orient.
- O∴ A∴ C∴ – *Ordo ab Chao*, "Out of Order, Chaos" (Latin)
- OB∴ – Obligation.
- P∴ – Past; Prelate; Prefect; Prior.
- P∴ C∴ W∴ – Principal Conductor of the Work.
- P∴ G∴ M∴ – Past <u>Grand Master</u>; Past Grand Matron.
- P∴ J∴ – Prince of Jerusalem.
- P∴ K∴ – Past King.
- P∴ M∴ – Past <u>Master</u>.
- P∴ S∴ – Principal Sojourner.
- Pro∴ G∴ M∴ – Pro-Grand Master.
- Prov∴ – Provincial.
- Prov∴ G∴ M∴ – Provincial Grand Master.
- R∴ A∴ – Royal Arch; Royal Art.
- R∴ A∴ C∴ – Royal Arch Captain; Royal Arch Chapter.
- R∴ A∴ M∴ – Royal Arch Mason; Royal Arch Masonry; Royal Ark Mariner. R∴ C∴ or R∴ t∴ <u>Rose Croix</u>. Appended to the signature of one having that degree
- R∴ E∴ – Right Eminent.
- R∴ E∴ A∴ et A∴ – *Rite Écossais Ancien et Accepté*, "<u>Ancient and Accepted Scottish Rite</u>" (French).
- R∴ L∴ or R∴ []∴ – *Respectable Loge*, "Worshipful Lodge" (French)
- R∴ S∴ Y∴ C∴ S∴ – Rosy Cross (in the Royal order of Scotland).
- R∴ W∴ – Right Worshipful.
- R∴ W∴ M∴ – Right Worshipful Master.
- S∴ – Scribe, Sentinel, Seneschal, Sponsor.
- S∴ C∴ – Supreme Council.
- S∴ G∴ D∴ – Senior Grand Deacon.
- S∴ G∴ I∴ G∴ – Sovereign Grand Inspector General
- S∴ G∴ W∴ – Senior Grand Warden.
- S∴ M∴ – Secret Master; Substitute Master
- S∴ O∴ – Senior Overseer.
- S∴ P∴ R∴ S∴ – Sublime Prince of the Royal Secret.
- S∴ S∴ – *Sanctum Sanctorum*, "Holy of Holies" (Latin)
- S∴ S∴ M∴ – Senior Substitute Magus.

- S∴ S∴ S∴ – The initials of the Latin word *Salutem*, meaning Greeting, repeated thrice and also found similarly in the French, *Trois Fois Salut*, meaning "Thrice Greeting". A common caption to French Masonic circulars or letters
- S∴ W∴ – Senior Warden.
- Sec∴ – Secretary.
- Soc∴ Ros∴ – Societas Rosicruciana
- Sur∴ – Surveillant. French, meaning Warden.
- T∴ C∴ F∴ – Très Cher Frère. French, meaning Very Dear Brother.
- T∴ G∴ A∴ O∴ T∴ U∴ – The Grand Architect of the Universe.
- T∴ S∴ – Tres Sage. Meaning Very Wise, addressed to the presiding officer of <u>French Rite</u>.
- U∴ D∴ – Under Dispensation.
- V∴ or Vén∴ – Vénérable. French, meaning Worshipful.
- V∴ D∴ B∴ – Very Dear Brother.
- V∴ D∴ S∴ A∴ – *Veut Dieu Saint Amour*, or *Vult Dei Sanctus* Animus. A formula used by Knights Templar. The expression *Veut Dieu Saint Amour* means "Wishes God Holy Love". *Vult Dei Sanctus Animus* is the Latin Version of the same phrase.
- V∴ E∴ – Viceroy Eusebius; Very Eminent.
- V∴ F∴ – *Vénérable Frère*, "Worshipful Brother" (French)
- V∴ L∴ – *Vraie Lumière*, "True Light" (French)
- V∴ S∴ L∴ – Volume of the sacred Law.
- V∴ W∴ – Very Worshipful
- W∴ – Worshipful
- W∴ M∴ – <u>Worshipful Master</u> or *Wurdiger Meister* (German)

The Symbolism of Freemasonry:

Illustrating and Explaining
Its Science and Philosophy, its Legends,
Myths and Symbols.

By

Albert G. Mackey, M.D.,

"*Ea enim quae scribuntur tria habere decent, utilitatem praesentem, certum finem, inexpugnabile fundamentum.*"

Cardanus.

1882.

Entered, according to Act of Congress, in the year 1869, by
ALBERT G. MACKEY,
In the Clerk's Office of the District Court of the District of South Carolina.

To General John C. Fremont.

My Dear Sir:

While any American might be proud of associating his name with that of one who has done so much to increase the renown of his country, and to enlarge the sum of human knowledge, this book is dedicated to you as a slight testimonial of regard for your personal character, and in grateful recollection of acts of friendship.

Yours very truly,

A. G. Mackey.

Preface.

Of the various modes of communicating instruction to the uninformed, the masonic student is particularly interested in two; namely, the instruction by legends and that by symbols. It is to these two, almost exclusively, that he is indebted for all that he knows, and for all that he can know, of the philosophic system which is taught in the institution. All its mysteries and its dogmas, which constitute its philosophy, are intrusted for communication to the neophyte, sometimes to one, sometimes to the other of these two methods of instruction, and sometimes to both of them combined. The Freemason has no way of reaching any of the esoteric teachings of the Order except through the medium of a legend or a symbol.

A legend differs from an historical narrative only in this—that it is without documentary evidence of authenticity. It is the offspring solely of tradition. Its details may be true in part or in whole. There may be no internal evidence to the contrary, or there may be internal evidence that they are altogether false. But neither the possibility of truth in the one case, nor the certainty of falsehood in the other, can remove the traditional narrative from the class of legends. It is a legend simply because it rests on no written foundation. It is oral, and therefore legendary.

In grave problems of history, such as the establishment of empires, the discovery and settlement of countries, or the rise and fall of dynasties, the knowledge of the truth or falsity of the legendary narrative will be of importance, because the value of history is impaired by the imputation of doubt. But it is not so in Freemasonry. Here there need be no absolute question of the truth or falsity of the legend. The object of the masonic legends is not to establish historical facts, but to convey philosophical doctrines. They are a method by which esoteric instruction is communicated, and the student accepts them with reference to nothing else except their positive use and meaning as developing masonic dogmas. Take, for instance, the Hiramic legend of the third degree. Of what importance is it to the disciple of Masonry whether it be true or false? All that he wants to know is its internal signification; and when he learns that it is intended to illustrate the doctrine of the immortality of the soul, he is content with that interpretation, and he does not deem it necessary, except as a matter of curious or antiquarian inquiry, to investigate its historical accuracy, or to reconcile any of its apparent contradictions. So of the lost keystone; so of the second temple; so of the hidden ark: these are to him legendary narratives, which, like the casket, would be of no value were it not for the precious jewel contained within. Each of these legends is the expression of a philosophical idea.

But there is another method of masonic instruction, and that is by symbols. No science is more ancient than that of symbolism. At one time, nearly all the learning of the world was conveyed in symbols. And although modern philosophy now deals only in abstract propositions, Freemasonry still cleaves to the ancient method, and has preserved it in its primitive importance as a means of communicating knowledge.

According to the derivation of the word from the Greek, "to symbolize" signifies "to compare one thing with another." Hence a symbol is the expression of an idea that has been derived from the comparison or contrast of some object with a moral conception or attribute. Thus we say that the plumb is a symbol of rectitude of conduct. The physical qualities of the plumb are here compared or contrasted with the moral conception of virtue, or rectitude. Then to the Speculative Mason it becomes, after he has been taught its symbolic meaning, the visible expression of the idea of moral uprightness.

But although there are these two modes of instruction in Freemasonry,—by legends and by symbols,—there really is no radical difference between the two methods. The symbol is a visible, and the legend an audible representation of some contrasted idea—of some moral conception produced from a comparison. Both the legend and the symbol relate to dogmas of a deep religious character; both of them convey moral sentiments in the same peculiar method, and both of them are designed by this method to illustrate the philosophy of Speculative Masonry.

To investigate the recondite meaning of these legends and symbols, and to elicit from them the moral and philosophical lessons which they were intended to teach, is to withdraw the veil with which ignorance and indifference seek to conceal the true philosophy of Freemasonry.

To study the symbolism of Masonry is the only way to investigate its philosophy. This is the portal of its temple, through which alone we can gain access to the sacellum where its aporrheta are concealed.

Its philosophy is engaged in the consideration of propositions relating to God and man, to the present and the future life. Its science is the symbolism by which these propositions are presented to the mind.

The work now offered to the public is an effort to develop and explain this philosophy and science. It will show that there are in Freemasonry the germs of profound speculation. If it does not interest the learned, it may instruct the ignorant. If so, I shall not regret the labor and research that have been bestowed upon its composition.

Albert G. Mackey, M.D.

Charleston, S.C., Feb. 22, 1869.

Contents.

I.

Preliminary.

The Origin and Progress of Freemasonry.

Any inquiry into the symbolism and philosophy of Freemasonry must necessarily be preceded by a brief investigation of the origin and history of the institution. Ancient and universal as it is, whence did it arise? What were the accidents connected with its birth? From what kindred or similar association did it spring? Or was it original and autochthonic, independent, in its inception, of any external influences, and unconnected with any other institution? These are questions which an intelligent investigator will be disposed to propound in the very commencement of the inquiry; and they are questions which must be distinctly answered before he can be expected to comprehend its true character as a symbolic institution. He must know something of its antecedents, before he can appreciate its character.

But he who expects to arrive at a satisfactory solution of this inquiry must first—as a preliminary absolutely necessary to success—release himself from the influence of an error into which novices in Masonic philosophy are too apt to fall. He must not confound the doctrine of Freemasonry with its outward and extrinsic form. He must not suppose that certain usages and ceremonies, which exist at this day, but which, even now, are subject to extensive variations in different countries, constitute the sum and substance of Freemasonry. "Prudent antiquity," says Lord Coke, "did for more solemnity and better memory and observation of that which is to be done, express substances under ceremonies." But it must be always remembered that the ceremony is not the substance. It is but the outer garment which covers and perhaps adorns it, as clothing does the human figure. But divest man of that outward apparel, and you still have the microcosm, the wondrous creation, with all his nerves, and bones, and muscles, and, above all, with his brain, and thoughts, and feelings. And so take from Masonry these external ceremonies, and you still have remaining its philosophy and science. These have, of course, always continued the same, while the ceremonies have varied in different ages, and still vary in different countries.

The definition of Freemasonry that it is "a science of morality, veiled in allegory, and illustrated by symbols," has been so often quoted, that, were it not for its beauty, it would become wearisome. But this definition contains the exact principle that has just been enunciated. Freemasonry is a science—a philosophy—a system of doctrines which is taught, in a manner peculiar to itself, by allegories and symbols. This is its internal character. Its ceremonies are external additions, which affect not its substance.

Now, when we are about to institute an inquiry into the origin of Freemasonry, it is of this peculiar system of philosophy that we are to inquire, and not of the ceremonies which have been foisted on it. If we pursue any other course we shall assuredly fall into error.

Thus, if we seek the origin and first beginning of the Masonic philosophy, we must go away back into the ages of remote antiquity, when we shall find this beginning in the bosom of kindred associations, where the same philosophy was maintained and taught. But if we confound the ceremonies of Masonry with the philosophy of Masonry, and seek the origin of the institution, moulded into outward form as it is to-day, we can scarcely be required to look farther back than the beginning of the eighteenth century, and, indeed, not quite so far. For many important modifications have been made in its rituals since that period.

Having, then, arrived at the conclusion that it is not the Masonic ritual, but the Masonic philosophy, whose origin we are to investigate, the next question naturally relates to the peculiar nature of that philosophy.

Now, then, I contend that the philosophy of Freemasonry is engaged in the contemplation of the divine and human character; of GOD as one eternal, self-existent being, in contradiction to the mythology of the ancient peoples, which was burdened with a multitude of gods and goddesses, of demigods and heroes; of MAN as an immortal being, preparing in the present life for an eternal future, in like contradiction to the ancient philosophy, which circumscribed the existence of man to the present life.

These two doctrines, then, of the unity of God and the immortality of the soul, constitute the philosophy of Freemasonry. When we wish to define it succinctly, we say that it is an ancient system of philosophy which teaches these two dogmas. And hence, if, amid the intellectual darkness and debasement of the old polytheistic religions, we find interspersed here and there, in all ages, certain institutions or associations which taught these truths, and that, in a particular way, allegorically and symbolically, then we have a right to say that such institutions or associations were the incunabula—the predecessors—of the Masonic institution as it now exists.

With these preliminary remarks the reader will be enabled to enter upon the consideration of that theory of the origin of Freemasonry which I advance in the following propositions:—

1. In the first place, I contend that in the very earliest ages of the world there were existent certain truths of vast importance to the welfare and happiness of humanity, which had been communicated,—no matter how, but,—most probably, by direct inspiration from God to man.

2. These truths principally consisted in the abstract propositions of the unity of God and the immortality of the soul. Of the truth of these two propositions there cannot be a reasonable doubt. The belief in these truths is a necessary consequence of that religious sentiment which has always formed an essential feature of human nature. Man is, emphatically, and in distinction from all other creatures, a religious animal. Gross commences his interesting work on "The Heathen Religion in its Popular and Symbolical Development" by the statement that "one of the most remarkable phenomena of the human race is the universal existence of religious ideas—a belief in something supernatural and divine, and a worship corresponding to it." As nature had implanted the religious sentiment, the same nature must have directed it in a proper channel. The belief and the worship must at first have been as pure as the fountain whence they flowed, although, in subsequent times, and before the advent of Christian light, they may both have been corrupted by the

influence of the priests and the poets over an ignorant and superstitious people. The first and second propositions of my theory refer only to that primeval period which was antecedent to these corruptions, of which I shall hereafter speak.

3. These truths of God and immortality were most probably handed down through the line of patriarchs of the race of Seth, but were, at all events, known to Noah, and were by him communicated to his immediate descendants.

4. In consequence of this communication, the true worship of God continued, for some time after the subsidence of the deluge, to be cultivated by the Noachidae, the Noachites, or the descendants of Noah.

5. At a subsequent period (no matter when, but the biblical record places it at the attempted building of the tower of Babel), there was a secession of a large number of the human race from the Noachites.

6. These seceders rapidly lost sight of the divine truths which had been communicated to them from their common ancestor, and fell into the most grievous theological errors, corrupting the purity of the worship and the orthodoxy of the religious faith which they had primarily received.

7. These truths were preserved in their integrity by but a very few in the patriarchal line, while still fewer were enabled to retain only dim and glimmering portions of the true light.

8. The first class was confined to the direct descendants of Noah, and the second was to be found among the priests and philosophers, and, perhaps, still later, among the poets of the heathen nations, and among those whom they initiated into the secrets of these truths. Of the prevalence of these religious truths among the patriarchal descendants of Noah, we have ample evidence in the sacred records. As to their existence among a body of learned heathens, we have the testimony of many intelligent writers who have devoted their energies to this subject. Thus the learned Grote, in his "History of Greece," says, "The allegorical interpretation of the myths has been, by several learned investigators, especially by Creuzer, connected with the hypothesis of *an ancient and highly instructed body of priests*, having their origin either in Egypt or in the East, and communicating to the rude and barbarous Greeks religious, physical, and historical knowledge, *under the veil of symbols*." What is here said only of the Greeks is equally applicable to every other intellectual nation of antiquity.

9. The system or doctrine of the former class has been called by Masonic writers the "Pure or Primitive Freemasonry" of antiquity, and that of the latter class the "Spurious Freemasonry" of the same period. These terms were first used, if I mistake not, by Dr. Oliver, and are intended to refer—the word *pure* to the doctrines taught by the descendants of Noah in the Jewish line and the word *spurious* to his descendants in the heathen or Gentile line.

10. The masses of the people, among the Gentiles especially, were totally unacquainted with this divine truth, which was the foundation stone of both species of Freemasonry, the pure and the spurious, and were deeply immersed in the errors and falsities of heathen belief and worship.

11. These errors of the heathen religions were not the voluntary inventions of the peoples who cultivated them, but were gradual and almost unavoidable corruptions of the truths which had been at first taught by Noah; and, indeed, so palpable are these corruptions, that they can be readily detected and traced to the original form from which, however much they might vary among different peoples, they had, at one time or another, deviated. Thus, in the life and achievements of Bacchus or Dionysus, we find the travestied counterpart of the career of Moses, and in the name of Vulcan, the blacksmith god, we evidently see an etymological corruption of the appellation of Tubal Cain, the first artificer in metals. For *Vul-can* is but a modified form of *Baal-Cain*, the god Cain.

12. But those among the masses—and there were some—who were made acquainted with the truth, received their knowledge by means of an initiation into certain sacred Mysteries, in the bosom of which it was concealed from the public gaze.

13. These Mysteries existed in every country of heathendom, in each under a different name, and to some extent under a different form, but always and everywhere with the same design of inculcating, by allegorical and symbolic teachings, the great Masonic doctrines of the unity of God and the immortality of the soul. This is an important proposition, and the fact which it enunciates must never be lost sight of in any inquiry into the origin of Freemasonry; for the pagan Mysteries were to the spurious Freemasonry of antiquity precisely what the Masters' lodges are to the Freemasonry of the present day. It is needless to offer any proof of their existence, since this is admitted and continually referred to by all historians, ancient and modern; and to discuss minutely their character and organization would occupy a distinct treatise. The Baron de Sainte Croix has written two large volumes on the subject, and yet left it unexhausted.

14. These two divisions of the Masonic Institution which were defined in the 9th proposition, namely, the pure or primitive Freemasonry among the Jewish descendants of the patriarchs, who are called, by way of distinction, the Noachites, or descendants of Noah, because they had not forgotten nor abandoned the teachings of their great ancestor, and the spurious Freemasonry practised among the pagan nations, flowed down the stream of time in parallel currents, often near together, but never commingling.

15. But these two currents were not always to be kept apart, for, springing, in the long anterior ages, from one common fountain,—that ancient priesthood of whom I have already spoken in the 8th proposition,—and then dividing into the pure and spurious Freemasonry of antiquity, and remaining separated for centuries upon centuries, they at length met at the building of the great temple of Jerusalem, and were united, in the instance of the Israelites under King Solomon, and the Tyrians under Hiram, King of Tyre, and Hiram Abif. The spurious Freemasonry, it is true, did not then and there cease to exist. On the contrary, it lasted for centuries subsequent to this period; for it was not until long after, and in the reign of the Emperor Theodosius, that the pagan Mysteries were finally and totally abolished. But by the union of the Jewish or pure Freemasons and the Tyrian or spurious Freemasons at Jerusalem, there was a mutual infusion of their respective doctrines and ceremonies, which eventually terminated in the abolition of the two distinctive systems and the establishment of a new one, that may be considered as the immediate prototype of the present institution. Hence many Masonic students, going no farther back in their investigations than the facts announced in this 15th proposition, are content to find the origin of Freemasonry at the temple of Solomon. But if my theory be correct, the truth is, that it there received, not its birth, but only a new modification of its character. The legend of the third degree—the golden legend, the *legenda aurea*—of Masonry was there adopted by pure Freemasonry, which before had no such legend, from spurious Freemasonry. But the legend had existed under other names and forms, in all the Mysteries, for ages before. The doctrine of immortality, which had hitherto been taught by the Noachites simply as an abstract proposition, was thenceforth to be inculcated by a symbolic lesson—the symbol of Hiram the Builder was to become forever after the distinctive feature of Freemasonry.

16. But another important modification was effected in the Masonic system at the building of the temple. Previous to the union which then took place, the pure Freemasonry of the Noachites had always been speculative, but resembled the present organization in no other way than in the cultivation of the same abstract principles of divine truth.

17. The Tyrians, on the contrary, were architects by profession, and, as their leaders were disciples of the school of the spurious Freemasonry, they, for the first time, at the temple of Solomon, when they united with their Jewish contemporaries, infused into the speculative science, which was practised by the latter, the elements of an operative art.

18. Therefore the system continued thenceforward, for ages, to present the commingled elements of operative and speculative Masonry. We see this in the *Collegia Fabrorum*, or Colleges of Artificers, first established at Rome by Numa, and which were certainly of a Masonic form in their organization; in the

Jewish sect of the Essenes, who wrought as well as prayed, and who are claimed to have been the descendants of the temple builders, and also, and still more prominently, in the Travelling Freemasons of the middle ages, who identify themselves by their very name with their modern successors, and whose societies were composed of learned men who thought and wrote, and of workmen who labored and built. And so for a long time Freemasonry continued to be both operative and speculative.

19. But another change was to be effected in the institution to make it precisely what it now is, and, therefore, at a very recent period (comparatively speaking), the operative feature was abandoned, and Freemasonry became wholly speculative. The exact time of this change is not left to conjecture. It took place in the reign of Queen Anne, of England, in the beginning of the eighteenth century. Preston gives us the very words of the decree which established this change, for he says that at that time it was agreed to "that the privileges of Masonry should no longer be restricted to operative Masons, but extend to men of various professions, provided they were regularly approved and initiated into the order."

The nineteen propositions here announced contain a brief but succinct view of the progress of Freemasonry from its origin in the early ages of the world, simply as a system of religious philosophy, through all the modifications to which it was submitted in the Jewish and Gentile races, until at length it was developed in its present perfected form. During all this time it preserved unchangeably certain features that may hence be considered as its specific characteristics, by which it has always been distinguished from every other contemporaneous association, however such association may have simulated it in outward form. These characteristics are, first, the doctrines which it has constantly taught, namely, that of the unity of God and that of the immortality of the soul; and, secondly, the manner in which these doctrines have been taught, namely, by symbols and allegories.

Taking these characteristics as the exponents of what Freemasonry is, we cannot help arriving at the conclusion that the speculative Masonry of the present day exhibits abundant evidence of the identity of its origin with the spurious Freemasonry of the ante-Solomonic period, both systems coming from the same pure source, but the one always preserving, and the other continually corrupting, the purity of the common fountain. This is also the necessary conclusion as a corollary from the propositions advanced in this essay.

There is also abundant evidence in the history, of which these propositions are but a meagre outline, that a manifest influence was exerted on the pure or primitive Freemasonry of the Noachites by the Tyrian branch of the spurious system, in the symbols, myths, and legends which the former received from the latter, but which it so modified and interpreted as to make them consistent with its own religious system. One thing, at least, is incapable of refutation; and that is, that we are indebted to the Tyrian Masons for the introduction of the symbol of Hiram Abif. The idea of the symbol, although modified by the Jewish Masons, is not Jewish in its inception. It was evidently borrowed from the pagan mysteries, where Bacchus, Adonis, Proserpine, and a host of other apotheosized beings play the same rôle that Hiram does in the Masonic mysteries.

And lastly, we find in the technical terms of Masonry, in its working tools, in the names of its grades, and in a large majority of its symbols, ample testimony of the strong infusion into its religious philosophy of the elements of an operative art. And history again explains this fact by referring to the connection of the institution with the Dionysiac Fraternity of Artificers, who were engaged in building the temple of Solomon, with the Workmen's Colleges of Numa, and with the Travelling Freemasons of the middle ages, who constructed all the great buildings of that period.

These nineteen propositions, which have been submitted in the present essay, constitute a brief summary or outline of a theory of the true origin of Freemasonry, which long and patient investigation has led me to adopt. To attempt to prove the truth of each of these propositions in its order by logical demonstration, or by historical evidence, would involve the writing of an elaborate treatise. They are now offered simply as suggestions on which the Masonic student may ponder. They are but intended as guide-posts, which may direct him in his journey should he undertake the pleasant although difficult task of instituting an inquiry into the origin and progress of Freemasonry from its birth to its present state of full-grown manhood.

But even in this abridged form they are absolutely necessary as preliminary to any true understanding of the symbolism of Freemasonry.

II.

The Noachidæ.

I proceed, then, to inquire into the historical origin of Freemasonry, as a necessary introduction to any inquiry into the character of its symbolism. To do this, with any expectation of rendering justice to the subject, it is evident that I shall have to take my point of departure at a very remote era. I shall, however, review the early and antecedent history of the institution with as much brevity as a distinct understanding of the subject will admit.

Passing over all that is within the antediluvian history of the world, as something that exerted, so far as our subject is concerned, no influence on the new world which sprang forth from the ruins of the old, we find, soon after the cataclysm, the immediate descendants of Noah in the possession of at least two religious truths, which they received from their common father, and which he must have derived from the line of patriarchs who preceded him. These truths were the doctrine of the existence of a Supreme Intelligence, the Creator, Preserver, and Ruler of the Universe, and, as a necessary corollary, the belief in the immortality of the soul[1], which, as an emanation from that primal cause, was to be distinguished, by a future and eternal life, from the vile and perishable dust which forms its earthly tabernacle.

The assertion that these doctrines were known to and recognized by Noah will not appear as an assumption to the believer in divine revelation. But any philosophic mind must, I conceive, come to the same conclusion, independently of any other authority than that of reason.

The religious sentiment, so far, at least, as it relates to the belief in the existence of God, appears to be in some sense innate, or instinctive, and consequently universal in the human mind[2]. There is no record of any nation, however intellectually and morally debased, that has not given some evidence of a tendency to such belief. The sentiment may be perverted, the idea may be grossly corrupted, but it is nevertheless there, and shows the source whence it sprang[3].

Even in the most debased forms of fetichism, where the negro kneels in reverential awe before the shrine of some uncouth and misshapen idol, which his own hands, perhaps, have made, the act of adoration, degrading as the object may be, is nevertheless an acknowledgment of the longing need of the worshipper to throw himself upon the support of some unknown power higher than his own sphere. And this unknown power, be it what it may, is to him a God.[4]

But just as universal has been the belief in the immortality of the soul. This arises from the same longing in man for the infinite; and although, like the former doctrine, it has been perverted and corrupted, there exists among all nations a tendency to its acknowledgment. Every people, from the remotest times, have wandered involuntarily into the ideal of another world, and sought to find a place for their departed spirits. The deification of the dead, man-worship, or hero-worship, the next development of the religious idea after fetichism, was simply an acknowledgment of the belief in a future life; for the dead could not have been deified unless after death they had continued to live. The adoration of a putrid carcass would have been a form of fetichism lower and more degrading than any that has been discovered.

But man-worship came after fetichism. It was a higher development of the religious sentiment, and included a possible hope for, if not a positive belief in, a future life.

Reason, then, as well as revelation, leads us irresistibly to the conclusion that these two doctrines prevailed among the descendants of Noah, immediately after the deluge. They were believed, too, in all their purity and integrity, because they were derived from the highest and purest source.

These are the doctrines which still constitute the creed of Freemasonry; and hence one of the names bestowed upon the Freemasons from the earliest times was that of the "*Noachidae*" or "*Noachites*" that is to say, the descendants of Noah, and the transmitters of his religious dogmas.

III.

The Primitive Freemasonry of Antiquity.

The next important historical epoch which demands our attention is that connected with what, in sacred history, is known as the dispersion at Babel. The brightness of truth, as it had been communicated by Noah, became covered, as it were, with a cloud. The dogmas of the unity of God and the immortality of the soul were lost sight of, and the first deviation from the true worship occurred in the establishment of Sabianism, or the worship of the sun, moon, and stars, among some peoples, and the deification of men among others. Of these two deviations, Sabianism, or sun-worship, was both the earlier and the more generally diffused.[5] "It seems," says the learned Owen, "to have had its rise from some broken traditions conveyed by the patriarchs touching the dominion of the sun by day and of the moon by night." The mode in which this old system has been modified and spiritually symbolized by Freemasonry will be the subject of future consideration.

But Sabianism, while it was the most ancient of the religious corruptions, was, I have said, also the most generally diffused; and hence, even among nations which afterwards adopted the polytheistic creed of deified men and factitious gods, this ancient sun-worship is seen to be continually exerting its influences. Thus, among the Greeks, the most refined people that cultivated hero-worship, Hercules was the sun, and the mythologic fable of his destroying with his arrows the many-headed hydra of the Lernaean marshes was but an allegory to denote the dissipation of paludal malaria by the purifying rays of the orb of day. Among the Egyptians, too, the chief deity, Osiris, was but another name for the sun, while his arch-enemy and destroyer, Typhon, was the typification of night, or darkness. And lastly, among the Hindus, the three manifestations of their supreme deity, Brahma, Siva, and Vishnu, were symbols of the rising, meridian, and setting sun.

This early and very general prevalence of the sentiment of sun-worship is worthy of especial attention on account of the influence that it exercised over the spurious Freemasonry of antiquity, of which I am soon to speak, and which is still felt, although modified and Christianized in our modern system. Many, indeed nearly all, of the masonic symbols of the present day can only be thoroughly comprehended and properly appreciated by this reference to sun-worship.

This divine truth, then, of the existence of one Supreme God, the Grand Architect of the Universe, symbolized in Freemasonry as the TRUE WORD, was lost to the Sabians and to the polytheists who arose after the dispersion at Babel, and with it also disappeared the doctrine of a future life; and hence, in one portion of the masonic ritual, in allusion to this historic fact, we speak of "the lofty tower of Babel, where language was confounded and Masonry lost."

There were, however, some of the builders on the plain of Shinar who preserved these great religious and masonic doctrines of the unity of God and the immortality of the soul in their pristine purity. These were the patriarchs, in whose venerable line they continued to be taught. Hence, years after the dispersion of the nations at Babel, the world presented two great religious sects, passing onward down the stream of time, side by side, yet as diverse from each other as light from darkness, and truth from falsehood.

One of these lines of religious thought and sentiment was the idolatrous and pagan world. With it all masonic doctrine, at least in its purity, was extinct, although there mingled with it, and at times to some extent influenced it, an offshoot from the other line, to which attention will be soon directed.

The second of these lines consisted, as has already been said, of the patriarchs and priests, who preserved in all their purity the two great masonic doctrines of the unity of God and the immortality of the soul.

This line embraced, then, what, in the language of recent masonic writers, has been designated as the *Primitive Freemasonry of Antiquity*.

Now, it is by no means intended to advance any such gratuitous and untenable theory as that proposed by some imaginative writers, that the Freemasonry of the patriarchs was in its organization, its ritual, or its symbolism, like the system which now exists. We know not indeed, that it had a ritual, or even a symbolism. I am inclined to think that it was made up of abstract propositions, derived from antediluvian traditions. Dr. Oliver thinks it probable that there were a few symbols among these Primitive and Pure Freemasons, and he enumerates among them the serpent, the triangle, and the point within a circle; but I can find no authority for the supposition, nor do I think it fair to claim for the order more than it is fairly entitled to, nor more than it can be fairly proved to possess. When Anderson calls Moses a Grand Master, Joshua his Deputy, and Aholiab and Bezaleel Grand Wardens, the expression is to be looked upon simply as a *façon de parler*, a mode of speech entirely figurative in its character, and by no means intended to convey the idea which is entertained in respect to officers of that character in the present system. It would, undoubtedly, however, have been better that such language should not have been used.

All that can be claimed for the system of Primitive Freemasonry, as practised by the patriarchs, is, that it embraced and taught the two great dogmas of Freemasonry, namely, the unity of God, and the immortality of the soul. It may be, and indeed it is highly probable, that there was a secret doctrine, and that this doctrine was not indiscriminately communicated. We know that Moses, who was necessarily the recipient of the knowledge of his predecessors, did not publicly teach the doctrine of the immortality of the soul. But there was among the Jews an oral or secret law which was never committed to writing until after the captivity; and this law, I suppose, may have contained the recognition of those dogmas of the Primitive Freemasonry.

Briefly, then, this system of Primitive Freemasonry,—without ritual or symbolism, that has come down to us, at least,—consisting solely of traditionary legends, teaching only the two great truths already alluded to, and being wholly speculative in its character, without the slightest infusion of an operative element, was regularly transmitted through the Jewish line of patriarchs, priests, and kings, without alteration, increase, or diminution, to the time of Solomon, and the building of the temple at Jerusalem.

Leaving it, then, to pursue this even course of descent, let us refer once more to that other line of religious history, the one passing through the idolatrous and polytheistic nations of antiquity, and trace from it the regular rise and progress of another division of the masonic institution, which, by way of distinction, has been called the *Spurious Freemasonry of Antiquity*.

IV.

The Spurious Freemasonry of Antiquity.

In the vast but barren desert of polytheism—dark and dreary as were its gloomy domains—there were still, however, to be found some few oases of truth. The philosophers and sages of antiquity had, in the course of their learned researches, aided by the light of nature, discovered something of those inestimable truths in relation to God and a future state which their patriarchal contemporaries had received as a revelation made to their common ancestry before the flood, and which had been retained and promulgated after that event by Noah.

They were, with these dim but still purifying perceptions, unwilling to degrade the majesty of the First Great Cause by sharing his attributes with a Zeus and a Hera in Greece, a Jupiter and a Juno in Rome, an Osiris and an Isis in Egypt; and they did not believe that the thinking, feeling, reasoning soul, the guest and companion of the body, would, at the hour of that body's dissolution, be consigned, with it, to total annihilation.

Hence, in the earliest ages after the era of the dispersion, there were some among the heathen who believed in the unity of God and the immortality of the soul. But these doctrines they durst not publicly teach. The minds of the people, grovelling in superstition, and devoted, as St. Paul testifies of the Athenians, to the worship of unknown gods, were not prepared for the philosophic teachings of a pure theology. It was, indeed, an axiom unhesitatingly enunciated and frequently repeated by their writers, that "there are many truths with which it is useless for the people to be made acquainted, and many fables which it is not expedient that they should know to be false." [6] Such is the language of Varro, as preserved by St. Augustine; and Strabo, another of their writers, exclaims, "It is not possible for a philosopher to conduct a multitude of women and ignorant people by a method of reasoning, and thus to invite them to piety, holiness, and faith; but the philosopher must also make use of superstition, and not omit the invention of fables and the performance of wonders." [7]

While, therefore, in those early ages of the world, we find the masses grovelling in the intellectual debasement of a polytheistic and idolatrous religion, with no support for the present, no hope for the future,—living without the knowledge of a supreme and superintending Providence, and dying without the expectation of a blissful immortality,—we shall at the same time find ample testimony that these consoling doctrines were secretly believed by the philosophers and their disciples.

But though believed, they were not publicly taught. They were heresies which it would have been impolitic and dangerous to have broached to the public ear; they were truths which might have led to a contempt of the established system and to the overthrow of the popular superstition. Socrates, the Athenian sage, is an illustrious instance of the punishment that was meted out to the bold innovator who attempted to insult the gods and to poison the minds of youth with the heresies of a philosophic religion. "They permitted, therefore," says a learned writer on this subject[8], "the multitude to remain plunged as they were in the depth of a gross and complicated idolatry; but for those philosophic few who could bear the light of truth without being confounded by the blaze, they removed the mysterious veil, and displayed to them the Deity in the radiant glory of his unity. From the vulgar eye, however, these doctrines were kept inviolably sacred, and wrapped in the veil of impenetrable mystery."

The consequence of all this was, that no one was permitted to be invested with the knowledge of these sublime truths, until by a course of severe and arduous trials, by a long and painful initiation, and by a formal series of gradual preparations, he had proved himself worthy and capable of receiving the full light of wisdom. For this purpose, therefore, those peculiar religious institutions were organized which the ancients designated as the MYSTERIES, and which, from the resemblance of their organization, their objects, and their doctrines, have by masonic writers been called the "Spurious Freemasonry of Antiquity."

Warburton,[9] in giving a definition of what these Mysteries were, says, "Each of the pagan gods had (besides the public and open) a secret worship paid unto him, to which none were admitted but those who had been selected by preparatory ceremonies, called initiation. This secret worship was termed the Mysteries." I shall now endeavor briefly to trace the connection between these Mysteries and the institution of Freemasonry; and to do so, it will be necessary to enter upon some details of the constitution of those mystic assemblies.

Almost every country of the ancient world had its peculiar Mysteries, dedicated to the occult worship of some especial and favorite god, and to the inculcation of a secret doctrine, very different from that which was taught in the public ceremonial of devotion. Thus in Persia the Mysteries were dedicated to Mithras, or the Sun; in Egypt, to Isis and Osiris; in Greece, to Demeter; in Samothracia, to the gods Cabiri, the Mighty Ones; in Syria, to Dionysus; while in the more northern nations of Europe, such as Gaul and Britain, the initiations were dedicated to their peculiar deities, and were celebrated under the general name of the Druidical rites. But no matter where or how instituted, whether ostensibly in honor of the effeminate Adonis, the favorite of Venus, or of the implacable Odin, the Scandinavian god of war and carnage; whether dedicated to Demeter, the type of the earth, or to Mithras, the symbol of all that fructifies that earth,—the great object and design of the secret instruction were identical in all places, and the Mysteries constituted a school of religion in which the errors and absurdities of polytheism were revealed to the initiated. The candidate was taught that the multitudinous deities of the popular theology were but hidden symbols of the various attributes of the supreme god,—a spirit invisible and indivisible,—and that the soul, as an emanation from his essence, could "never see corruption," but must, after the death of the body, be raised to an eternal life.[10]

That this was the doctrine and the object of the Mysteries is evident from the concurrent testimony both of those ancient writers who flourished contemporaneously with the practice of them, and of those modern scholars who have devoted themselves to their investigation.

Thus Isocrates, speaking of them in his Panegyric, says, "Those who have been initiated in the Mysteries of Ceres entertain better hopes both as to the end of life and the whole of futurity." [11]

Epictetus[12] declares that everything in these Mysteries was instituted by the ancients for the instruction and amendment of life.

And Plato[13] says that the design of initiation was to restore the soul to that state of perfection from which it had originally fallen.

Thomas Taylor, the celebrated Platonist, who possessed an unusual acquaintance with the character of these ancient rites, asserts that they "obscurely intimated, by mystic and splendid visions, the felicity of the soul, both here and hereafter, when purified from the defilements of a material nature, and constantly elevated to the realities of intellectual vision." [14]

Creuzer,[15] a distinguished German writer, who has examined the subject of the ancient Mysteries with great judgment and elaboration, gives a theory on their nature and design which is well worth consideration.

This theory is, that when there had been placed under the eyes of the initiated symbolical representations of the creation of the universe, and the origin of things, the migrations and purifications of the soul, the beginning and progress of civilization and agriculture, there was drawn from these symbols and these scenes in the Mysteries an instruction destined only for the more perfect, or the epopts, to whom were communicated the doctrines of the existence of a single and eternal God, and the destination of the universe and of man.

Creuzer here, however, refers rather to the general object of the instructions, than to the character of the rites and ceremonies by which they were impressed upon the mind; for in the Mysteries, as in Freemasonry, the Hierophant, whom we would now call the Master of the Lodge, often, as Lobeck observes, delivered a mystical lecture, or discourse, on some moral subject.

Faber, who, notwithstanding the predominance in his mind of a theory which referred every rite and symbol of the ancient world to the traditions of Noah, the ark, and the deluge, has given a generally correct view of the systems of ancient religion, describes the initiation into the Mysteries as a scenic representation of the mythic descent into Hades, or the grave, and the return from thence to the light of day.

In a few words, then, the object of instruction in all these Mysteries was the unity of God, and the intention of the ceremonies of initiation into them was, by a scenic representation of death, and subsequent restoration to life,[16] to impress the great truths of the resurrection of the dead and the immortality of the soul.

I need scarcely here advert to the great similarity in design and conformation which existed between these ancient rites and the third or Master's degree of Masonry. Like it they were all funereal in their character: they began in sorrow and lamentation, they ended in joy; there was an aphanism, or burial; a pastos, or grave; an euresis, or discovery of what had been lost; and a legend, or mythical relation,—all of which were entirely and profoundly symbolical in their character.

And hence, looking to this strange identity of design and form, between the initiations of the ancients and those of the modern Masons, writers have been disposed to designate these mysteries as the SPURIOUS FREEMASONRY OF ANTIQUITY.

V.

The Ancient Mysteries.

I now propose, for the purpose of illustrating these views, and of familiarizing the reader with the coincidences between Freemasonry and the ancient Mysteries, so that he may be better enabled to appreciate the mutual influences of each on the other as they are hereafter to be developed, to present a more detailed relation of one or more of these ancient systems of initiation.

As the first illustration, let us select the Mysteries of Osiris, as they were practised in Egypt, the birthplace of all that is wonderful in the arts or sciences, or mysterious in the religion, of the ancient world.

It was on the Lake of Sais that the solemn ceremonies of the Osirian initiation were performed. "On this lake," says Herodotus, "it is that the Egyptians represent by night his sufferings whose name I refrain from mentioning; and this representation they call their Mysteries." [17]

Osiris, the husband of Isis, was an ancient king of the Egyptians. Having been slain by Typhon, his body was cut into pieces[18] by his murderer, and the mangled remains cast upon the waters of the Nile, to be dispersed to the four winds of heaven. His wife, Isis, mourning for the death and the mutilation of her husband, for many days searched diligently with her companions for the portions of the body, and having at length found them, united them together, and bestowed upon them decent interment,—while Osiris, thus restored, became the chief deity of his subjects, and his worship was united with that of Isis, as the fecundating and fertilizing powers of nature. The candidate in these initiations was made to pass through a mimic repetition of the conflict and destruction of Osiris, and his eventual recovery; and the explanations made to him, after he had received the full share of light to which the painful and solemn ceremonies through which he had passed had entitled him, constituted the secret doctrine of which I have already spoken, as the object of all the Mysteries. Osiris,—a real and personal god to the people,—to be worshipped with fear and with trembling, and to be propitiated with sacrifices and burnt offerings, became to the initiate but a symbol of the

"Great first cause, least understood,"

while his death, and the wailing of Isis, with the recovery of the body, his translation to the rank of a celestial being, and the consequent rejoicing of his spouse, were but a tropical mode of teaching that after death comes life eternal, and that though the body be destroyed, the soul shall still live.

"Can we doubt," says the Baron Sainte Croix, "that such ceremonies as those practised in the Mysteries of Osiris had been originally instituted to impress more profoundly on the mind the dogma of future rewards and punishments?" [19]

"The sufferings and death of Osiris," says Mr. Wilkinson,[20] "were the great Mystery of the Egyptian religion; and some traces of it are perceptible among other people of antiquity. His being the divine goodness and the abstract idea of 'good,' his manifestation upon earth (like an Indian god), his death and resurrection, and his office as judge of the dead in a future state, look like the early revelation of a future manifestation of the deity converted into a mythological fable."

A similar legend and similar ceremonies, varied only as to time, and place, and unimportant details, were to be found in all the initiations of the ancient Mysteries. The dogma was the same,—future life,—and the method of inculcating it was the same. The coincidences between the design of these rites and that of Freemasonry, which must already begin to appear, will enable us to give its full value to the expression of Hutchinson, when he says that "the Master Mason represents a man under the Christian doctrine saved from the grave of iniquity and raised to the faith of salvation." [21]

In Phoenicia similar Mysteries were celebrated in honor of Adonis, the favorite lover of Venus, who, having, while hunting, been slain by a wild boar on Mount Lebanon, was restored to life by Proserpine. The mythological story is familiar to every classical scholar. In the popular theology, Adonis was the son of Cinyras, king of Cyrus, whose untimely death was wept by Venus and her attendant nymphs: in the physical theology of the philosophers,[22] he was a symbol of the sun, alternately present to and absent from the earth; but in the initiation into the Mysteries of his worship, his resurrection and return from Hades were adopted as a type of the immortality of the soul. The ceremonies of initiation in the Adonia began with lamentation for his loss,—or, as the prophet Ezekiel expresses it, "Behold, there sat women weeping for Thammuz,"—for such was the name under which his worship was introduced among the Jews; and they ended with the most extravagant demonstrations of joy at the representation of his return to life,[23] while the hierophant exclaimed, in a congratulatory strain,—

"Trust, ye initiates; the god is safe,
And from our grief salvation shall arise."

Before proceeding to an examination of those Mysteries which are the most closely connected with the masonic institution, it will be as well to take a brief view of their general organization.

The secret worship, or Mysteries, of the ancients were always divided into the lesser and the greater; the former being intended only to awaken curiosity, to test the capacity and disposition of the candidate, and by symbolical purifications to prepare him for his introduction into the greater Mysteries.

The candidate was at first called an aspirant, or seeker of the truth, and the initial ceremony which he underwent was a lustration or purification by water. In this condition he may be compared to the Entered Apprentice of the masonic rites, and it is here worth adverting to the fact (which will be hereafter more fully developed) that all the ceremonies in the first degree of masonry are symbolic of an internal purification.

In the lesser Mysteries[24] the candidate took an oath of secrecy, which was administered to him by the mystagogue, and then received a preparatory instruction,[25] which enabled him afterwards to understand the developments of the higher and subsequent division. He was now called a *Mystes*, or initiate, and may be compared to the Fellow Craft of Freemasonry.

In the greater Mysteries the whole knowledge of the divine truths, which was the object of initiation, was communicated. Here we find, among the various ceremonies which assimilated these rites to Freemasonry, the *aphanism*, which was the disappearance or death; the *pastos*, the couch, coffin, or grave; the *euresis*, or the discovery of the body; and the *autopsy*, or full sight of everything, that is, the complete communication

308

of the secrets. The candidate was here called an *epopt*, or eye-witness, because nothing was now hidden from him; and hence he may be compared to the Master Mason, of whom Hutchinson says that "he has discovered the knowledge of God and his salvation, and been redeemed from the death of sin and the sepulchre of pollution and unrighteousness."

VI.

The Dionysiac Artificers.

After this general view of the religious Mysteries of the ancient world, let us now proceed to a closer examination of those which are more intimately connected with the history of Freemasonry, and whose influence is, to this day, most evidently felt in its organization.

Of all the pagan Mysteries instituted by the ancients none were more extensively diffused than those of the Grecian god Dionysus. They were established in Greece, Rome, Syria, and all Asia Minor. Among the Greeks, and still more among the Romans, the rites celebrated on the Dionysiac festival were, it must be confessed, of a dissolute and licentious character.[26] But in Asia they assumed a different form. There, as elsewhere, the legend (for it has already been said that each Mystery had its legend) recounted, and the ceremonies represented, the murder of Dionysus by the Titans. The secret doctrine, too, among the Asiatics, was not different from that among the western nations, but there was something peculiar in the organization of the system. The Mysteries of Dionysus in Syria, more especially, were not simply of a theological character. There the disciples joined to the indulgence in their speculative and secret opinions as to the unity of God and the immortality of the soul, which were common to all the Mysteries, the practice of an operative and architectural art, and occupied themselves as well in the construction of temples and public buildings as in the pursuit of divine truth.

I can account for the greater purity of these Syrian rites only by adopting the ingenious theory of Thirwall,[27] that all the Mysteries "were the remains of a worship which preceded the rise of the Hellenic mythology, and its attendant rites, grounded on a view of nature less fanciful, more earnest, and better fitted to awaken both philosophical thought and religious feeling," and by supposing that the Asiatics, not being, from their geographical position, so early imbued with the errors of Hellenism, had been better able to preserve the purity and philosophy of the old Pelasgic faith, which, itself, was undoubtedly a direct emanation from the patriarchal religion, or, as it has been called, the Pure Freemasonry of the antediluvian world.

Be this, however, as it may, we know that "the Dionysiacs of Asia Minor were undoubtedly an association of architects and engineers, who had the exclusive privilege of building temples, stadia, and theatres, under the mysterious tutelage of Bacchus, and were distinguished from the uninitiated or profane inhabitants by the science which they possessed, and by many private signs and tokens by which they recognized each other." [28]

This speculative and operative society[29]—speculative in the esoteric, theologic lessons which were taught in its initiations, and operative in the labors of its members as architects—was distinguished by many peculiarities that closely assimilate it to the institution of Freemasonry. In the practice of charity, the more opulent were bound to relieve the wants and contribute to the support of the poorer brethren. They were divided, for the conveniences of labor and the advantages of government, into smaller bodies, which, like our lodges, were directed by superintending officers. They employed, in their ceremonial observances, many of the implements of operative Masonry, and used, like the Masons, a universal language; and conventional modes of recognition, by which *one brother might know another in the dark as well as the light*, and which served to unite the whole body, wheresoever they might be dispersed, in one common brotherhood.[30]

I have said that in the mysteries of Dionysus the legend recounted the death of that hero-god, and the subsequent discovery of his body. Some further details of the nature of the Dionysiac ritual are, therefore, necessary for a thorough appreciation of the points to which I propose directly to invite attention.

In these mystic rites, the aspirant was made to represent, symbolically and in a dramatic form, the events connected with the slaying of the god from whom the Mysteries derived their name. After a variety of preparatory ceremonies, intended to call forth all his courage and fortitude, the aphanism or mystical death of Dionysus was figured out in the ceremonies, and the shrieks and lamentations of the initiates, with the confinement or burial of the candidate on the pastos, couch, or coffin, constituted the first part of the ceremony of initiation. Then began the search of Rhea for the remains of Dionysus, which was continued amid scenes of the greatest confusion and tumult, until, at last, the search having been successful, the mourning was turned into joy, light succeeded to darkness, and the candidate was invested with the knowledge of the secret doctrine of the Mysteries—the belief in the existence of one God, and a future state of rewards and punishments.[31]

Such were the mysteries that were practised by the architect,—the Freemasons, so to speak—of Asia Minor. At Tyre, the richest and most important city of that region, a city memorable for the splendor and magnificence of the buildings with which it was decorated, there were colonies or lodges of these mystic architects; and this fact I request that you will bear in mind, as it forms an important link in the chain that connects the Dionysiacs with the Freemasons.

But to make every link in this chain of connection complete, it is necessary that the mystic artists of Tyre should be proved to be at least contemporaneous with the building of King Solomon's temple; and the evidence of that fact I shall now attempt to produce.

Lawrie, whose elaborate researches into this subject leave us nothing further to discover, places the arrival of the Dionysiacs in Asia Minor at the time of the Ionic migration, when "the inhabitants of Attica, complaining of the narrowness of their territory and the unfruitfulness of its soil, went in quest of more extensive and fertile settlements. Being joined by a number of the inhabitants of surrounding provinces, they sailed to Asia Minor, drove out the original inhabitants, and seized upon the most eligible situations, and united them under the name of Ionia, because the greatest number of the refugees were natives of that Grecian province." [32] With their knowledge of the arts of sculpture and architecture, in which the Greeks had already made some progress, the emigrants brought over to their new settlements their religious customs also, and introduced into Asia the mysteries of Athene and Dionysus long before they had been corrupted by the licentiousness of the mother country.

Now, Playfair places the Ionic migration in the year 1044 B.C., Gillies in 1055, and the Abbé Barthelemy in 1076. But the latest of these periods will extend as far back as forty-four years before the commencement of the temple of Solomon at Jerusalem, and will give ample time for the establishment of the Dionysiac fraternity at the city of Tyre, and the initiation of "Hiram the Builder" into its mysteries.

Let us now pursue the chain of historical events which finally united this purest branch of the Spurious Freemasonry of the pagan nations with the Primitive Freemasonry of the Jews at Jerusalem.

When Solomon, king of Israel, was about to build, in accordance with the purposes of his father, David, "a house unto the name of Jehovah, his God," he made his intention known to Hiram, king of Tyre, his friend and ally; and because he was well aware of the architectural skill of the Tyrian Dionysiacs, he besought that monarch's assistance to enable him to carry his pious design into execution. Scripture informs us that Hiram complied with the request of Solomon, and sent him the necessary workmen to assist him in the glorious undertaking. Among others, he sent an architect, who is briefly described, in the First Book of Kings, as "a widow's son, of the tribe of Naphtali, and his father a man of Tyre, a worker in brass, a man filled with wisdom and understanding and cunning to work all works in brass;" and more fully, in the Second Book of Chronicles, as "a cunning man, endued with understanding of Hiram my father's, the son of a woman of the daughters of Dan, and his father, a man of Tyre, skilful to work in gold, and in silver, in brass, in iron, in stone, and in timber, in purple, in blue, and in fine linen and in crimson, also to grave any manner of graving, and to find out any device which shall be put to him."

To this man—this widow's son (as Scripture history, as well as masonic tradition informs us)—was intrusted by King Solomon an important position among the workmen at the sacred edifice, which was constructed on Mount Moriah. His knowledge and experience as an artificer, and his eminent skill in every kind of "curious and cunning workmanship," readily placed him at the head of both the Jewish and Tyrian craftsmen, as the chief builder and principal conductor of the works; and it is to him, by means of the large authority which this position gave him, that we attribute the union of two people, so antagonistical in race, so dissimilar in manners, and so opposed in religion, as the Jews and Tyrians, in one common brotherhood, which resulted in the organization of the institution of Freemasonry. This Hiram, as a Tyrian and an artificer, must have been connected with the Dionysiac fraternity; nor could he have been a very humble or inconspicuous member, if we may judge of his rank in the society, from the amount of talent which he is said to have possessed, and from the elevated position that he held in the affections, and at the court, of the king of Tyre. He must, therefore, have been well acquainted with all the ceremonial usages of the Dionysiac artificers, and must have enjoyed a long experience of the advantages of the government and discipline which they practised in the erection of the many sacred edifices in which they were engaged. A portion of these ceremonial usages and of this discipline he would naturally be inclined to introduce among the workmen at Jerusalem. He therefore united them in a society, similar in many respects to that of the Dionysiac artificers. He inculcated lessons of charity and brotherly love; he established a ceremony of initiation, to test experimentally the fortitude and worth of the candidate; adopted modes of recognition; and impressed the obligations of duty and principles of morality by means of symbols and allegories.

To the laborers and men of burden, the Ish Sabal, and to the craftsmen, corresponding with the first and second degrees of more modern Masonry, but little secret knowledge was confided. Like the aspirants in the lesser Mysteries of paganism, their instructions were simply to purify and prepare them for a more solemn ordeal, and for the knowledge of the sublimest truths. These were to be found only in the Master's degree, which it was intended should be in imitation of the greater Mysteries; and in it were to be unfolded, explained, and enforced the great doctrines of the unity of God and the immortality of the soul. But here there must have at once arisen an apparently insurmountable obstacle to the further continuation of the resemblance of Masonry to the Mysteries of Dionysus. In the pagan Mysteries, I have already said that these lessons were allegorically taught by means of a legend. Now, in the Mysteries of Dionysus, the legend was that of the death and subsequent resuscitation of the god Dionysus. But it would have been utterly impossible to introduce such a legend as the basis of any instructions to be communicated to Jewish candidates. Any allusion to the mythological fables of their Gentile neighbors, any celebration of the myths of pagan theology, would have been equally offensive to the taste and repugnant to the religious prejudices of a nation educated, from generation to generation, in the worship of a divine being jealous of his prerogatives, and who had made himself known to his people as the JEHOVAH, the God of time present, past, and future. How this obstacle would have been surmounted by the Israelitish founder of the order I am unable to say: a substitute would, no doubt, have been invented, which would have met all the symbolic requirements of the legend of the Mysteries, or Spurious Freemasonry, without violating the religious principles of the Primitive Freemasonry of the Jews; but the necessity for such invention never existed, and before the completion of the temple a melancholy event is said to have occurred, which served to cut the Gordian knot, and the death of its chief architect has supplied Freemasonry with its appropriate legend—a legend which, like the legends of all the Mysteries, is used to testify our faith in the resurrection of the body and the immortality of the soul.

Before concluding this part of the subject, it is proper that something should be said of the authenticity of the legend of the third degree. Some distinguished Masons are disposed to give it full credence as an historical fact, while others look upon it only as a beautiful allegory. So far as the question has any bearing upon the symbolism of Freemasonry it is not of importance; but those who contend for its historical character assert that they do so on the following grounds:—

First. Because the character of the legend is such as to meet all the requirements of the well-known axiom of Vincentius Lirinensis, as to what we are to believe in traditionary matters.[33]

"Quod semper, quod ubique, quod ab omnibus traditum est."

That is, we are to believe whatever tradition has been at all times, in all places, and by all persons handed down.

With this rule the legend of Hiram Abif, they say, agrees in every respect. It has been universally received, and almost universally credited, among Freemasons from the earliest times. We have no record of any Masonry having ever existed since the time of the temple without it; and, indeed, it is so closely interwoven into the whole system, forming the most essential part of it, and giving it its most determinative character, that it is evident that the institution could no more exist without the legend, than the legend could have been retained without the institution. This, therefore, the advocates of the historical character of the legend think, gives probability at least to its truth.

Secondly. It is not contradicted by the scriptural history of the transactions at the temple, and therefore, in the absence of the only existing written authority on the subject, we are at liberty to depend on traditional information, provided the tradition be, as it is contended that in this instance it is, reasonable, probable, and supported by uninterrupted succession.

Thirdly. It is contended that the very silence of Scripture in relation to the death of Hiram, the Builder, is an argument in favor of the mysterious nature of that death. A man so important in his position as to have been called the favorite of two kings,—sent by one and received by the other as a gift of surpassing value, and the donation thought worthy of a special record, would hardly have passed into oblivion, when his labor was finished, without the memento of a single line, unless his death had taken place in such a way as to render a public account of it improper. And this is supposed to have been the fact. It had become the legend of the new Mysteries, and, like those of the old ones, was only to be divulged when accompanied with the symbolic instructions which it was intended to impress upon the minds of the aspirants.

But if, on the other hand, it be admitted that the legend of the third degree is a fiction,—that the whole masonic and extra-scriptural account of Hiram Abif is simply a myth,—it could not, in the slightest degree, affect the theory which it is my object to establish. For since, in a mythic relation, as the learned Müller[34] has observed, fact and imagination, the real and the ideal, are very closely united, and since the myth itself always arises, according to the same author, out of a necessity and unconsciousness on the part of its framers, and by impulses which act alike on all, we must go back to the Spurious Freemasonry of the Dionysiacs for the principle which led to the involuntary formation of this Hiramic myth; and then we arrive at the same result, which has been already indicated, namely, that the necessity of the religious sentiment in the Jewish mind, to which the introduction of the legend of Dionysus would have been abhorrent, led to the substitution for it of that of Hiram, in which the ideal parts of the narrative have been intimately blended with real transactions. Thus, that there was such a man as Hiram Abif; that he was the chief builder at the temple of Jerusalem; that he was the confidential friend of the kings of Israel and Tyre, which is indicated by his title of *Ab*, or father; and that he is not heard of after the completion of the temple,—are all historical facts. That he died by violence, and in the way described in the masonic legend, may be also true, or may be merely mythical elements incorporated into the historical narrative.

But whether this be so or not,—whether the legend be a fact or a fiction, a history or a myth,—this, at least, is certain: that it was adopted by the Solomonic Masons of the temple as a substitute for the idolatrous legend of the death of Dionysus which belonged to the Dionysiac Mysteries of the Tyrian workmen.

VII.

The Union of Speculative and Operative Masonry at the Temple of Solomon.

Thus, then, we arrive at another important epoch in the history of the origin of Freemasonry.

I have shown how the Primitive Freemasonry, originating in this new world; with Noah, was handed down to his descendants as a purely speculative institution, embracing certain traditions of the nature of God and of the soul.

I have shown how, soon after the deluge, the descendants of Noah separated, one portion, losing their traditions, and substituting in their place idolatrous and polytheistic religions, while the other and smaller portion retained and communicated those original traditions under the name of the Primitive Freemasonry of antiquity.

I have shown how, among the polytheistic nations, there were a few persons who still had a dim and clouded understanding of these traditions, and that they taught them in certain secret institutions, known as the "Mysteries," thus establishing another branch of the speculative science which is known under the name of the Spurious Freemasonry of antiquity.

Again, I have shown how one sect or division of these Spurious Freemasons existed at Tyre about the time of the building of King Solomon's temple, and added to their speculative science, which was much purer than that of their contemporary Gentile mystics, the practice of the arts of architecture and sculpture, under the name of the Dionysiac Fraternity of Artificers.

And, lastly, I have shown how, at the building of the Solomonic temple, on the invitation of the king of Israel, a large body of these architects repaired from Tyre to Jerusalem, organized a new institution, or, rather, a modification of the two old ones, the Primitive Freemasons among the Israelites yielding something, and the Spurious Freemasons among the Tyrians yielding more; the former purifying the speculative science, and the latter introducing the operative art, together with the mystical ceremonies with which they accompanied its administration.

It is at this epoch, then, that I place the first union of speculative and operative Masonry,—a union which continued uninterruptedly to exist until a comparatively recent period, to which I shall have occasion hereafter briefly to advert.

The other branches of the Spurious Freemasonry were not, however, altogether and at once abolished by this union, but continued also to exist and teach their half-truthful dogmas, for ages after, with interrupted success and diminished influence, until, in the fifth century of the Christian era, the whole of them were proscribed by the Emperor Theodosius. From time to time, however, other partial unions took place, as in the instance of Pythagoras, who, originally a member of the school of Spurious Freemasonry, was, during his visit to Babylon, about four hundred and fifty years after the union at the temple of Jerusalem, initiated by the captive Israelites into the rites of Temple Masonry, whence the instructions of that sage approximate much more nearly to the principles of Freemasonry, both in spirit and in letter, than those of any other of the philosophers of antiquity; for which reason he is familiarly called, in the modern masonic lectures, "an ancient friend and brother," and an important symbol of the order, the forty-seventh problem of Euclid, has been consecrated to his memory.

I do not now propose to enter upon so extensive a task as to trace the history of the institution from the completion of the first temple to its destruction by Nebuchadnezzar; through the seventy-two years of Babylonish captivity to the rebuilding of the second temple by Zerubbabel; thence to the devastation of Jerusalem by Titus, when it was first introduced into Europe; through all its struggles in the middle ages, sometimes protected and sometimes persecuted by the church, sometimes forbidden by the law and oftener encouraged by the monarch; until, in the beginning of the sixteenth century, it assumed its present organization. The details would require more time for their recapitulation than the limits of the present work will permit.

But my object is not so much to give a connected history of the progress of Freemasonry as to present a rational view of its origin and an examination of those important modifications which, from time to time, were impressed upon it by external influences, so as to enable us the more readily to appreciate the true character and design of its symbolism.

Two salient points, at least, in its subsequent history, especially invite attention, because they have an important bearing on its organization, as a combined speculative and operative institution.

VIII.

The Travelling Freemasons of the Middle Ages.

The first of these points to which I refer is the establishment of a body of architects, widely disseminated throughout Europe during the middle ages under the avowed name of *Travelling Freemasons*. This association of workmen, said to have been the descendants of the Temple Masons, may be traced by the massive monuments of their skill at as early a period as the ninth or tenth century; although, according to the authority of Mr. Hope, who has written elaborately on the subject, some historians have found the evidence of their existence in the seventh century, and have traced a peculiar masonic language in the reigns of Charlemagne of France and Alfred of England.

It is to these men, to their preeminent skill in architecture, and to their well-organized system as a class of workmen, that the world is indebted for those magnificent edifices which sprang up in such undeviating principles of architectural form during the middle ages.

"Wherever they came," says Mr. Hope, "in the suite of missionaries, or were called by the natives, or arrived of their own accord, to seek employment, they appeared headed by a chief surveyor, who governed the whole troop, and named one man out of every ten, under the name of warden, to overlook the nine others, set themselves to building temporary huts[35] for their habitation around the spot where the work was to be carried on, regularly organized their different departments, fell to work, sent for fresh supplies of their brethren as the object demanded, and, when all was finished, again raised their encampment, and went elsewhere to undertake other jobs." [36]

This society continued to preserve the commingled features of operative and speculative masonry, as they had been practised at the temple of Solomon. Admission to the community was not restricted to professional artisans, but men of eminence, and particularly ecclesiastics, were numbered among its members. "These latter," says Mr. Hope, "were especially anxious, themselves, to direct the improvement and erection of their churches and monasteries, and to manage the expenses of their buildings, and became members of an establishment which had so high and sacred a destination, was so entirely exempt from all local, civil jurisdiction, acknowledged the pope alone as its direct chief, and only worked under his immediate authority; and thence we read of so many ecclesiastics of the highest rank—abbots, prelates, bishops—conferring additional weight and respectability on the order of Freemasonry by becoming its members—themselves giving the designs and superintending the construction of their churches, and employing the manual labor of their own monks in the edification of them."

Thus in England, in the tenth century, the Masons are said to have received the special protection of King Athelstan; in the eleventh century, Edward the Confessor declared himself their patron; and in the twelfth, Henry I. gave them his protection.

Into Scotland the Freemasons penetrated as early as the beginning of the twelfth century, and erected the Abbey of Kilwinning, which afterwards became the cradle of Scottish Masonry under the government of King Robert Bruce.

Of the magnificent edifices which they erected, and of their exalted condition under both ecclesiastical and lay patronage in other countries, it is not necessary to give a minute detail. It is sufficient to say that in every part of Europe evidences are to be found of the existence of Freemasonry, practised by an organized body of workmen, and with whom men of learning were united; or, in other words, of a combined operative and speculative institution.

What the nature of this speculative science continued to be, we may learn from that very curious, if authentic, document, dated at Cologne, in the year 1535, and hence designated as the "Charter of Cologne." In that instrument, which purports to have been issued by the heads of the order in nineteen different and important cities of Europe, and is addressed to their brethren as a defence against the calumnies of their enemies, it is announced that the order took its origin at a time "when a few adepts, distinguished by their life, their moral doctrine, and their sacred interpretation of the arcanic truths, withdrew themselves from the multitude in order more effectually to preserve uncontaminated the moral precepts of that religion which is implanted in the mind of man."

We thus, then, have before us an aspect of Freemasonry as it existed in the middle ages, when it presents itself to our view as both operative and speculative in its character. The operative element that had been infused into it by the Dionysiac artificers of Tyre, at the building of the Solomonic temple, was not yet dissevered from the pure speculative element which had prevailed in it anterior to that period.

IX.

Disseverance of the Operative Element.

The next point to which our attention is to be directed is when, a few centuries later, the operative character of the institution began to be less prominent, and the speculative to assume a pre-eminence which eventually ended in the total separation of the two.

At what precise period the speculative began to predominate over the operative element of the society, it is impossible to say. The change was undoubtedly gradual, and is to be attributed, in all probability, to the increased number of literary and scientific men who were admitted into the ranks of the fraternity.

The Charter of Cologne, to which I have just alluded, speaks of "learned and enlightened men" as constituting the society long before the date of that document, which was 1535; but the authenticity of this work has, it must be confessed, been impugned, and I will not, therefore, press the argument on its doubtful

315

authority. But the diary of that celebrated antiquary, Elias Ashmole, which is admitted to be authentic, describes his admission in the year 1646 into the order, when there is no doubt that the operative character was fast giving way to the speculative. Preston tells us that about thirty years before, when the Earl of Pembroke assumed the Grand Mastership of England, "many eminent, wealthy, and learned men were admitted."

In the year 1663 an assembly of the Freemasons of England was held at London, and the Earl of St. Albans was elected Grand Master. At this assembly certain regulations were adopted, in which the qualifications prescribed for candidates clearly allude to the speculative character of the institution.

And, finally, at the commencement of the eighteenth century, and during the reign of Queen Anne, who died, it will be remembered, in 1714, a proposition was agreed to by the society "that the privileges of Masonry should no longer be restricted to operative masons, but extend to men of various professions, provided that they were regularly approved and initiated into the order."

Accordingly the records of the society show that from the year 1717, at least, the era commonly, but improperly, distinguished as the restoration of Masonry, the operative element of the institution has been completely discarded, except so far as its influence is exhibited in the choice and arrangement of symbols, and the typical use of its technical language.

The history of the origin of the order is here concluded; and in briefly recapitulating, I may say that in its first inception, from the time of Noah to the building of the temple of Solomon, it was entirely speculative in its character; that at the construction of that edifice, an operative element was infused into it by the Tyrian builders; that it continued to retain this compound operative and speculative organization until about the middle of the seventeenth century, when the latter element began to predominate; and finally, that at the commencement of the eighteenth century, the operative element wholly disappeared, and the society has ever since presented itself in the character of a simply speculative association.

The history that I have thus briefly sketched, will elicit from every reflecting mind at least two deductions of some importance to the intelligent Mason.

In the first place, we may observe, that ascending, as the institution does, away up the stream of time, almost to the very fountains of history, for its source, it comes down to us, at this day, with so venerable an appearance of antiquity, that for that cause and on that claim alone it demands the respect of the world. It is no recent invention of human genius, whose vitality has yet to be tested by the wear and tear of time and opposition, and no sudden growth of short-lived enthusiasm, whose existence may be as ephemeral as its birth was recent. One of the oldest of these modern institutions, the Carbonarism of Italy, boasts an age that scarcely amounts to the half of a century, and has not been able to extend its progress beyond the countries of Southern Europe, immediately adjacent to the place of its birth; while it and every other society of our own times that have sought to simulate the outward appearance of Freemasonry, seem to him who has examined the history of this ancient institution to have sprung around it, like mushrooms bursting from between the roots and vegetating under the shade of some mighty and venerable oak, the patriarch of the forest, whose huge trunk and wide-extended branches have protected them from the sun and the gale, and whose fruit, thrown off in autumn, has enriched and fattened the soil that gives these humbler plants their power of life and growth.

But there is a more important deduction to be drawn from this narrative. In tracing the progress of Freemasonry, we shall find it so intimately connected with the history of philosophy, of religion, and of art in all ages of the world, that it is evident that no Mason can expect thoroughly to understand the nature of the institution, or to appreciate its character, unless he shall carefully study its annals, and make himself conversant with the facts of history, to which and from which it gives and receives a mutual influence. The brother who unfortunately supposes that the only requisites of a skilful Mason consist in repeating with fluency the ordinary lectures, or in correctly opening and closing the lodge, or in giving with sufficient accuracy the modes of recognition, will hardly credit the assertion, that he whose knowledge of the "royal art" extends no farther than these preliminaries has scarcely advanced beyond the rudiments of our science. There is a far nobler series of doctrines with which Freemasonry is connected, and which no student ever began to investigate who did not find himself insensibly led on, from step to step in his researches, his love and admiration of the order increasing with the augmentation of his acquaintance with its character. It is this which constitutes the science and the philosophy of Freemasonry, and it is this alone which will return the scholar who devotes himself to the task a sevenfold reward for his labor.

With this view I propose, in the next place, to enter upon an examination of that science and philosophy as they are developed in the system of symbolism, which owes its existence to this peculiar origin and organization of the order, and without a knowledge of which, such as I have attempted to portray it in this preliminary inquiry, the science itself could never be understood.

X.

The System of Symbolic Instuction.

The lectures of the English lodges, which are far more philosophical than our own,—although I do not believe that the system itself is in general as philosophically studied by our English brethren as by ourselves,—have beautifully defined Freemasonry to be "a science of morality veiled in allegory and illustrated by symbols." But allegory itself is nothing else but verbal symbolism; it is the symbol of an idea, or of a series of ideas, not presented to the mind in an objective and visible form, but clothed in language, and exhibited in the form of a narrative. And therefore the English definition amounts, in fact, to this: that *Freemasonry is a science of morality, developed and inculcated by the ancient method of symbolism*. It is this peculiar character as a symbolic institution, this entire adoption of the method of instruction by symbolism, which gives its whole identity to Freemasonry, and has caused it to differ from every other association that the ingenuity of man has devised. It is this that has bestowed upon it that attractive form which has always secured the attachment of its disciples and its own perpetuity.

The Roman Catholic church[37] is, perhaps, the only contemporaneous institution which continues to cultivate, in any degree, the beautiful system of symbolism. But that which, in the Catholic church, is, in a great measure, incidental, and the fruit of development, is, in Freemasonry, the very life-blood and soul of the institution, born with it at its birth, or, rather, the germ from which the tree has sprung, and still giving it support, nourishment, and even existence. Withdraw from Freemasonry its symbolism, and you take from the body its soul, leaving behind nothing but a lifeless mass of effete matter, fitted only for a rapid decay.

Since, then, the science of symbolism forms so important a part of the system of Freemasonry, it will be well to commence any discussion of that subject by an investigation of the nature of symbols in general.

There is no science so ancient as that of symbolism,[38] and no mode of instruction has ever been so general as was the symbolic in former ages. "The first learning in the world," says the great antiquary, Dr. Stukely, "consisted chiefly of symbols. The wisdom of the Chaldeans, Phoenicians, Egyptians, Jews, of Zoroaster, Sanchoniathon, Pherecydes, Syrus, Pythagoras, Socrates, Plato, of all the ancients that is come to our hand, is symbolic." And the learned Faber remarks, that "allegory and personification were peculiarly agreeable to the genius of antiquity, and the simplicity of truth was continually sacrificed at the shrine of poetical decoration."

In fact, man's earliest instruction was by symbols.[39] The objective character of a symbol is best calculated to be grasped by the infant mind, whether the infancy of that mind be considered *nationally* or *individually*. And hence, in the first ages of the world, in its infancy, all propositions, theological, political, or scientific, were expressed in the form of symbols. Thus the first religions were eminently symbolical, because, as that great philosophical historian, Grote, has remarked, "At a time when language was yet in its infancy, visible symbols were the most vivid means of acting upon the minds of ignorant hearers."

Again: children receive their elementary teaching in symbols. "A was an Archer;" what is this but symbolism? The archer becomes to the infant mind the symbol of the letter A, just as, in after life, the letter becomes, to the more advanced mind, the symbol of a certain sound of the human voice.[40] The first lesson received by a child in acquiring his alphabet is thus conveyed by symbolism. Even in the very formation of language, the medium of communication between man and man, and which must hence have been an elementary step in the progress of human improvement, it was found necessary to have recourse to symbols, for words are only and truly certain arbitrary symbols by which and through which we give an utterance to our ideas. The construction of language was, therefore, one of the first products of the science of symbolism.

We must constantly bear in mind this fact, of the primary existence and predominance of symbolism in the earliest times.[41] when we are investigating the nature of the ancient religions, with which the history of Freemasonry is so intimately connected. The older the religion, the more the symbolism abounds. Modern religions may convey their dogmas in abstract propositions; ancient religions always conveyed them in symbols. Thus there is more symbolism in the Egyptian religion than in the Jewish, more in the Jewish than in the Christian, more in the Christian than in the Mohammedan, and, lastly, more in the Roman than in the Protestant.

But symbolism is not only the most ancient and general, but it is also the most practically useful, of sciences. We have already seen how actively it operates in the early stages of life and of society. We have seen how the first ideas of men and of nations are impressed upon their minds by means of symbols. It was thus that the ancient peoples were almost wholly educated.

"In the simpler stages of society," says one writer on this subject, "mankind can be instructed in the abstract knowledge of truths only by symbols and parables. Hence we find most heathen religions becoming mythic, or explaining their mysteries by allegories, or instructive incidents. Nay, God himself, knowing the nature of the creatures formed by him, has condescended, in the earlier revelations that he made of himself, to teach by symbols; and the greatest of all teachers instructed the multitudes by parables.[42] The great exemplar of the ancient philosophy and the grand archetype of modern philosophy were alike distinguished by their possessing this faculty in a high degree, and have told us that man was best instructed by similitudes." [43]

Such is the system adopted in Freemasonry for the development and inculcation of the great religious and philosophical truths, of which it was, for so many years, the sole conservator. And it is for this reason that I have already remarked, that any inquiry into the symbolic character of Freemasonry, must be preceded by an investigation of the nature of symbolism in general, if we would properly appreciate its particular use in the organization of the masonic institution.

XI.

The Speculative Science and the Operative Art.

And now, let us apply this doctrine of symbolism to an investigation of the nature of a speculative science, as derived from an operative art; for the fact is familiar to every one that Freemasonry is of two kinds. We work, it is true, in speculative Masonry only, but our ancient brethren wrought in both operative and speculative; and it is now well understood that the two branches are widely apart in design and in character—the one a mere useful art, intended for the protection and convenience of man and the gratification of his physical wants, the other a profound science, entering into abstruse investigations of the soul and a future existence, and originating in the craving need of humanity to know something that is above and beyond the mere outward life that surrounds us with its gross atmosphere here below.[44] Indeed, the only bond or link that unites speculative and operative Masonry is the symbolism that belongs altogether to the former, but which, throughout its whole extent, is derived from the latter.

Our first inquiry, then, will be into the nature of the symbolism which operative gives to speculative Masonry; and thoroughly to understand this—to know its origin, and its necessity, and its mode of application—we must begin with a reference to the condition of a long past period of time.

Thousands of years ago, this science of symbolism was adopted by the sagacious priesthood of Egypt to convey the lessons of worldly wisdom and religious knowledge, which they thus communicated to their disciples.[45] Their science, their history, and their philosophy were thus concealed beneath an impenetrable veil from all the profane, and only the few who had passed through the severe ordeal of initiation were put in possession of the key which enabled them to decipher and read with ease those mystic lessons which we still see engraved upon the obelisks, the tombs, and the sarcophagi, which lie scattered, at this day, in endless profusion along the banks of the Nile.

From the Egyptians the same method of symbolic instruction was diffused among all the pagan nations of antiquity, and was used in all the ancient Mysteries[46] as the medium of communicating to the initiated the esoteric and secret doctrines for whose preservation and promulgation these singular associations were formed.

Moses, who, as Holy Writ informs us, was skilled in all the learning of Egypt, brought with him, from that cradle of the sciences, a perfect knowledge of the science of symbolism, as it was taught by the priests of Isis and Osiris, and applied it to the ceremonies with which he invested the purer religion of the people for whom he had been appointed to legislate.[47]

Hence we learn, from the great Jewish historian, that, in the construction of the tabernacle, which gave the first model for the temple at Jerusalem, and afterwards for every masonic lodge, this principle of symbolism was applied to every part of it. Thus it was divided into three parts, to represent the three great elementary divisions of the universe—the land, the sea, and the air. The first two, or exterior portions, which were accessible to the priests and the people, were symbolic of the land and the sea, which all men might inhabit; while the third, or interior division,—the holy of holies,—whose threshold no mortal dared to cross, and which was peculiarly consecrated to GOD, was emblematic of heaven, his dwelling-place. The veils, too, according to Josephus, were intended for symbolic instruction in their color and their materials. Collectively, they represented the four elements of the universe; and, in passing, it may be observed that this notion of symbolizing the universe characterized all the ancient systems, both the true and the false, and that the remains of the principle are to be found everywhere, even at this day, pervading Masonry, which is but a development of these systems. In the four veils of the tabernacle, the white or fine linen signified the earth, from which flax was produced; the scarlet signified fire, appropriately represented by its flaming color; the purple typified the sea, in allusion to the shell-fish murex, from which the tint was obtained; and the blue, the color of the firmament, was emblematic of air.[48]

It is not necessary to enter into a detail of the whole system of religious symbolism, as developed in the Mosaic ritual. It was but an application of the same principles of instruction, that pervaded all the surrounding Gentile nations, to the inculcation of truth. The very idea of the ark itself[49] was borrowed, as the discoveries of the modern Egyptologists have shown us, from the banks of the Nile; and the breastplate of the high priest, with its Urim and Thummim,[50] was indebted for its origin to a similar ornament worn by the Egyptian judge. The system was the same; in its application, only, did it differ.

With the tabernacle of Moses the temple of King Solomon is closely connected: the one was the archetype of the other. Now, it is at the building of that temple that we must place the origin of Freemasonry in its present organization: not that the system did not exist before, but that the union of its operative and speculative character, and the mutual dependence of one upon the other, were there first established.

At the construction of this stupendous edifice—stupendous, not in magnitude, for many a parish church has since excelled it in size,[51] but stupendous in the wealth and magnificence of its ornaments—the wise king of Israel, with all that sagacity for which he was so eminently distinguished, and aided and counselled by the Gentile experience of the king of Tyre, and that immortal architect who superintended his workmen, saw at once the excellence and beauty of this method of inculcating moral and religious truth, and gave, therefore, the impulse to that symbolic reference of material things to a spiritual sense, which has ever since distinguished the institution of which he was the founder.

If I deemed it necessary to substantiate the truth of the assertion that the mind of King Solomon was eminently symbolic in its propensities, I might easily refer to his writings, filled as they are to profusion with tropes and figures. Passing over the Book of Canticles,—that great lyrical drama, whose abstruse symbolism has not yet been fully evolved or explained, notwithstanding the vast number of commentators who have labored at the task,—I might simply refer to that beautiful passage in the twelfth chapter of Ecclesiastes, so familiar to every Mason as being appropriated, in the ritual, to the ceremonies of the third degree, and in which a dilapidated building is metaphorically made to represent the decays and infirmities of old age in the human body. This brief but eloquent description is itself an embodiment of much of our masonic symbolism, both as to the mode and the subject matter.

In attempting any investigation into the symbolism of Freemasonry, the first thing that should engage our attention is the general purport of the institution, and the mode in which its symbolism is developed. Let us first examine it as a whole, before we investigate its parts, just as we would first view, as critics, the general effect of a building, before we began to inquire into its architectural details.

Looking, then, in this way, at the institution—coming down to us, as it has, from a remote age—having passed unaltered and unscathed through a thousand revolutions of nations—and engaging, as disciples in its school of mental labor, the intellectual of all times—the first thing that must naturally arrest the attention is the singular combination that it presents of an operative with a speculative organization—an art with a science—the technical terms and language of a mechanical profession with the abstruse teachings of a profound philosophy.

Here it is before us—a venerable school, discoursing of the deepest subjects of wisdom, in which sages might alone find themselves appropriately employed, and yet having its birth and deriving its first life from a society of artisans, whose only object was, apparently, the construction of material edifices of stone and mortar.

The nature, then, of this operative and speculative combination, is the first problem to be solved, and the symbolism which depends upon it is the first feature of the institution which is to be developed.

Freemasonry, in its character as an operative art, is familiar to every one. As such, it is engaged in the application of the rules and principles of architecture to the construction of edifices for private and public use—houses for the dwelling-place of man, and temples for the worship of Deity. It abounds, like every other art, in the use of technical terms, and employs, in practice, an abundance of implements and materials which are peculiar to itself.

Now, if the ends of operative Masonry had here ceased,—if this technical dialect and these technical implements had never been used for any other purpose, nor appropriated to any other object, than that of enabling its disciples to pursue their artistic labors with greater convenience to themselves,—Freemasonry would never have existed. The same principles might, and in all probability would, have been developed in some other way; but the organization, the name, the mode of instruction, would all have most materially differed.

But the operative Masons, who founded the order, were not content with the mere material and manual part of their profession: they adjoined to it, under the wise instructions of their leaders, a correlative branch of study.

And hence, to the Freemason, this operative art has been symbolized in that intellectual deduction from it, which has been correctly called Speculative Masonry. At one time, each was an integrant part of one undivided system. Not that the period ever existed when every operative mason was acquainted with, or initiated into, the speculative science. Even now, there are thousands of skilful artisans who know as little of that as they do of the Hebrew language which was spoken by its founder. But operative Masonry was, in the inception of our history, and is, in some measure, even now, the skeleton upon which was strung the living muscles, and tendons, and nerves of the speculative system. It was the block of marble—rude and unpolished it may have been—from which was sculptured the life-breathing statue.[52]

Speculative Masonry (which is but another name for Freemasonary in its modern acceptation) may be briefly defined as the scientific application and the religious consecration of the rules and principles, the language, the implements and materials of operative Masonry to the veneration of God, the purification of the heart, and the inculcation of the dogmas of a religious philosophy.

XII.

He Symbolism of Solomon'S Temple.

I have said that the operative art is symbolized—that is to say, used as a symbol—in the speculative science. Let us now inquire, as the subject of the present essay, how this is done in reference to a system of symbolism dependent for its construction on types and figures derived from the temple of Solomon, and which we hence call the "Temple Symbolism of Freemasonry."

Bearing in mind that speculative Masonry dates its origin from the building of King Solomon's temple by Jewish and Tyrian artisans,[53] the first important fact that attracts the attention is, that the operative masons at Jerusalem were engaged in the construction of an earthly and material temple, to be dedicated to the service and worship of God—a house in which Jehovah was to dwell visibly by his Shekinah, and whence he was, by the Urim and Thummim, to send forth his oracles for the government and direction of his chosen people.

Now, the operative art having, *for us*, ceased, we, as speculative Masons, symbolize the labors of our predecessors by engaging in the construction of a spiritual temple in our hearts, pure and spotless, fit for the dwelling-place of Him who is the author of purity—where God is to be worshipped in spirit and in truth, and whence every evil thought and unruly passion is to be banished, as the sinner and the Gentile were excluded from the sanctuary of the Jewish temple.

This spiritualizing of the temple of Solomon is the first, the most prominent and most pervading of all the symbolic instructions of Freemasonry. It is the link that binds the operative and speculative divisions of the order. It is this which gives it its religious character. Take from Freemasonry its dependence on the temple, leave out of its ritual all reference to that sacred edifice, and to the legends connected with it, and the system itself must at once decay and die, or at best remain only as some fossilized bone, imperfectly to show the nature of the living body to which it once belonged.

Temple worship is in itself an ancient type of the religious sentiment in its progress towards spiritual elevation. As soon as a nation emerged, in the world's progress, out of Fetichism, or the worship of visible objects,—the most degraded form of idolatry,—its people began to establish a priesthood and to erect temples.[54] The Scandinavians, the Celts, the Egyptians, and the Greeks, however much they may have differed in the ritual and the objects of their polytheistic worship, all were possessed of priests and temples. The Jews first constructed their tabernacle, or portable temple, and then, when time and opportunity permitted, transferred their monotheistic worship to that more permanent edifice which is now the subject of our contemplation. The mosque of the Mohammedan and the church or the chapel of the Christian are but embodiments of the same idea of temple worship in a simpler form.

The adaptation, therefore, of the material temple to a science of symbolism would be an easy, and by no means a novel task, to both the Jewish and the Tyrian mind. Doubtless, at its original conception, the idea was rude and unembellished, to be perfected and polished only by future aggregations of succeeding intellects. And yet no biblical scholar will venture to deny that there was, in the mode of building, and in all the circumstances connected with the construction of King Solomon's temple, an apparent design to establish a foundation for symbolism.[55]

I propose now to illustrate, by a few examples, the method in which the speculative Masons have appropriated this design of King Solomon to their own use.

To construct his earthly temple, the operative mason followed the architectural designs laid down on the *trestle-board*, or tracing-board, or book of plans of the architect. By these he hewed and squared his materials; by these he raised his walls; by these he constructed his arches; and by these strength and durability, combined with grace and beauty, were bestowed upon the edifice which he was constructing.

The trestle-board becomes, therefore, one of our elementary symbols. For in the masonic ritual the speculative Mason is reminded that, as the operative artist erects his temporal building, in accordance with the rules and designs laid down on the trestle-board of the master-workman, so should he erect that spiritual building, of which the material is a type, in obedience to the rules and designs, the precepts and commands, laid down by the grand Architect of the universe, in those great books of nature and revelation, which constitute the spiritual trestle-board of every Freemason.

The trestle-board is, then, the symbol of the natural and moral law. Like every other symbol of the order, it is universal and tolerant in its application; and while, as Christian Masons, we cling with unfaltering integrity to that explanation which makes the Scriptures of both dispensations our trestle-board, we permit our Jewish and Mohammedan brethren to content themselves with the books of the Old Testament, or the Koran. Masonry does not interfere with the peculiar form or development of any one's religious faith. All that it asks is, that the interpretation of the symbol shall be according to what each one supposes to be the revealed will of his Creator. But so rigidly exacting is it that the symbol shall be preserved, and, in some rational way, interpreted, that it peremptorily excludes the Atheist from its communion, because, believing in no Supreme Being, no divine Architect, he must necessarily be without a spiritual trestle-board on which the designs of that Being may be inscribed for his direction.

But the operative mason required materials wherewith to construct his temple. There was, for instance, the *rough ashlar*—the stone in its rude and natural state—unformed and unpolished, as it had been lying in the quarries of Tyre from the foundation of the earth. This stone was to be hewed and squared, to be fitted and adjusted, by simple, but appropriate implements, until it became a *perfect ashlar*, or well-finished stone, ready to take its destined place in the building.

Here, then, again, in these materials do we find other elementary symbols. The rough and unpolished stone is a symbol of man's natural state—ignorant, uncultivated, and, as the Roman historian expresses it, "grovelling to the earth, like the beasts of the field, and obedient to every sordid appetite;" [56] but when education has exerted its salutary influences in expanding his intellect, in restraining his hitherto unruly passions, and purifying his life, he is then represented by the perfect ashlar, or finished stone, which, under the skilful hands of the workman, has been smoothed, and squared, and fitted for its appropriate place in the building.

Here an interesting circumstance in the history of the preparation of these materials has been seized and beautifully appropriated by our symbolic science. We learn from the account of the temple, contained in the First Book of Kings, that "The house, when it was in building, was built of stone, made ready before it was brought thither, so that there was neither hammer nor axe, nor any tool of iron, heard in the house while it was in building." [57]

Now, this mode of construction, undoubtedly adopted to avoid confusion and discord among so many thousand workmen,[58] has been selected as an elementary symbol of concord and harmony—virtues which are not more essential to the preservation and perpetuity of our own society than they are to that of every human association.

The perfect ashlar, therefore,—the stone thus fitted for its appropriate position in the temple,—becomes not only a symbol of human perfection (in itself, of course, only a comparative term), but also, when we refer to the mode in which it was prepared, of that species of perfection which results from the concord and union of men in society. It is, in fact, a symbol of the social character of the institution.

There are other elementary symbols, to which I may hereafter have occasion to revert; the three, however, already described,—the rough ashlar, the perfect ashlar, and the trestle-board,—and which, from their importance, have received the name of "jewels," will be sufficient to give some idea of the nature of what may be called the "symbolic alphabet" of Masonry. Let us now proceed to a brief consideration of the method in which this alphabet of the science is applied to the more elevated and abstruser portions of the system, and which, as the temple constitutes its most important type, I have chosen to call the "Temple Symbolism of Masonry."

Both Scripture and tradition inform us that, at the building of King Solomon's temple, the masons were divided into different classes, each engaged in different tasks. We learn, from the Second Book of Chronicles, that these classes were the bearers of burdens, the hewers of stones, and the overseers, called by the old masonic writers the *Ish sabal*, the *Ish chotzeb*, and the *Menatzchim*. Now, without pretending to say that the modern institution has preserved precisely the same system of regulations as that which was observed at the temple, we shall certainly find a similarity in these divisions to the Apprentices, Fellow Crafts and Master Masons of our own day. At all events, the three divisions made by King Solomon, in the workmen at Jerusalem, have been adopted as the types of the three degrees now practised in speculative Masonry; and as such we are, therefore, to consider them. The mode in which these three divisions of workmen labored in constructing the temple, has been beautifully symbolized in speculative Masonry, and constitutes an important and interesting part of temple symbolism.

Thus we know, from our own experience among modern workmen, who still pursue the same method, as well as from the traditions of the order, that the implements used in the quarries were few and simple, the work there requiring necessarily, indeed, but two tools, namely, the *twenty-four inch gauge*, or two foot rule, and the *common gavel*, or stone-cutter's hammer. With the former implement, the operative mason took the necessary dimensions of the stone he was about to prepare, and with the latter, by repeated blows, skilfully applied, he broke off every unnecessary protuberance, and rendered it smooth and square, and fit to take its place in the building.

And thus, in the first degree of speculative Masonry, the Entered Apprentice receives these simple implements, as the emblematic working tools of his profession, with their appropriate symbolical instruction. To the operative mason their mechanical and practical use alone is signified, and nothing more of value does their presence convey to his mind. To the speculative Mason the sight of them is suggestive of far nobler and sublimer thoughts; they teach him to measure, not stones, but time; not to smooth and polish the marble for the builder's use, but to purify and cleanse his heart from every vice and imperfection that would render it unfit for a place in the spiritual temple of his body.

In the symbolic alphabet of Freemasonry, therefore, the twenty-four inch gauge is a symbol of time well employed; the common gavel, of the purification of the heart.

Here we may pause for a moment to refer to one of the coincidences between Freemasonry and those *Mysteries*[59] which formed so important a part of the ancient religions, and which coincidences have led the writers on this subject to the formation of a well-supported theory that there was a common connection between them. The coincidence to which I at present allude is this: in all these Mysteries—the incipient ceremony of initiation—the first step taken by the candidate was a lustration or purification. The aspirant was not permitted to enter the sacred vestibule, or take any part in the secret formula of initiation, until, by water or by fire, he was emblematically purified from the corruptions of the world which he was about to leave behind. I need not, after this, do more than suggest the similarity of this formula, in principle, to a corresponding one in Freemasonry, where the first symbols presented to the apprentice are those which inculcate a purification of the heart, of which the purification of the body in the ancient Mysteries was symbolic.

We no longer use the bath or the fountain, because in our philosophical system the symbolization is more abstract, if I may use the term; but we present the aspirant with the *lamb-skin apron*, the *gauge*, and the *gavel*, as symbols of a spiritual purification. The design is the same, but the mode in which it is accomplished is different.

Let us now resume the connected series of temple symbolism.

At the building of the temple, the stones having been thus prepared by the workmen of the lowest degree (the Apprentices, as we now call them, the aspirants of the ancient Mysteries), we are informed that they were transported to the site of the edifice on Mount Moriah, and were there placed in the hands of another class of workmen, who are now technically called the Fellow Crafts, and who correspond to the Mystes, or those who had received the second degree of the ancient Mysteries. At this stage of the operative work more extensive and important labors were to be performed, and accordingly a greater amount of skill and knowledge was required of those to whom these labors were intrusted. The stones, having been prepared by the Apprentices[60] (for hereafter, in speaking of the workmen of the temple, I shall use the equivalent appellations of the more modern Masons), were now to be deposited in their destined places in the building, and the massive walls were to be erected. For these purposes implements of a higher and more complicated character than the gauge and gavel were necessary. The *square* was required to fit the joints with sufficient accuracy, the *level* to run the courses in a horizontal line, and the *plumb* to erect the whole with due regard to perfect perpendicularity. This portion of the labor finds its symbolism in the second degree of the speculative science, and in applying this symbolism we still continue to refer to the idea of erecting a spiritual temple in the heart.

The necessary preparations, then, having been made in the first degree, the lessons having been received by which the aspirant is taught to commence the labor of life with the purification of the heart, as a Fellow Craft he continues the task by cultivating those virtues which give form and impression to the character, as well adapted stones give shape and stability to the building. And hence the "working tools" of the Fellow Craft are referred, in their symbolic application, to those virtues. In the alphabet of symbolism, we find the square, the level, and the plumb appropriated to this second degree. The square is a symbol denoting morality. It teaches us to apply the unerring principles of moral science to every action of our lives, to see that all the motives and results of our conduct shall coincide with the dictates of divine justice, and that all our thoughts, words, and deeds shall harmoniously conspire, like the well-adjusted and rightly-squared joints of an edifice, to produce a smooth, unbroken life of virtue.

The plumb is a symbol of rectitude of conduct, and inculcates that integrity of life and undeviating course of moral uprightness which can alone distinguish the good and just man. As the operative workman erects his temporal building with strict observance of that plumb-line, which will not permit him to deviate a hair's breadth to the right or to the left, so the speculative Mason, guided by the unerring principles of right and truth inculcated in the symbolic teachings of the same implement, is steadfast in the pursuit of truth, neither bending beneath the frowns of adversity nor yielding to the seductions of prosperity.[61]

The level, the last of the three working tools of the operative craftsman, is a symbol of equality of station. Not that equality of civil or social position which is to be found only in the vain dreams of the anarchist or the Utopian, but that great moral and physical equality which affects the whole human race as the children of one common Father, who causes his sun to shine and his rain to fall on all alike, and who has so appointed the universal lot of humanity, that death, the leveller of all human greatness, is made to visit with equal pace the prince's palace and the peasant's hut.[62]

Here, then, we have three more signs or hieroglyphics added to our alphabet of symbolism. Others there are in this degree, but they belong to a higher grade of interpretation, and cannot be appropriately discussed in an essay on temple symbolism only.

We now reach the third degree, the Master Masons of the modern science, and the Epopts, or beholders of the sacred things in the ancient Mysteries.

In the third degree the symbolic allusions to the temple of Solomon, and the implements of Masonry employed in its construction, are extended and fully completed. At the building of that edifice, we have already seen that one class of the workmen was employed in the preparation of the materials, while another was engaged in placing those materials in their proper position. But there was a third and higher class,—the master workmen,—whose duty it was to superintend the two other classes, and to see that the stones were not only duly prepared, but that the most exact accuracy had been observed in giving to them their true juxtaposition in the edifice. It was then only that the last and finishing labor[63] was performed, and the cement was applied by these skilful workmen, to secure the materials in their appropriate places, and to unite the building in one enduring and connected mass. Hence the *trowel*, we are informed, was the most important, though of course not the only, implement in use among the master builders. They did not permit this last, indelible operation to be performed by any hands less skilful than their own. They required that the craftsmen should prove the correctness of their work by the square, level, and plumb, and test, by these unerring instruments, the accuracy of their joints; and, when satisfied of the just arrangement of every part, the cement, which was to give an unchangeable union to the whole, was then applied by themselves.

Hence, in speculative Masonry, the trowel has been assigned to the third degree as its proper implement, and the symbolic meaning which accompanies it has a strict and beautiful reference to the purposes for which it was used in the ancient temple; for as it was there employed "to spread the cement which united the building in one common mass," so is it selected as the symbol of brotherly love—that cement whose object is to unite our mystic association in one sacred and harmonious band of brethren.

Here, then, we perceive the first, or, as I have already called it, the elementary form of our symbolism—the adaptation of the terms, and implements, and processes of an operative art to a speculative science. The temple is now completed. The stones having been hewed, squared, and numbered in the quarries by the apprentices,—having been properly adjusted by the craftsmen, and finally secured in their appropriate places, with the strongest and purest cement, by the master builders,—the temple of King Solomon presented, in its finished condition, so noble an appearance of sublimity and grandeur as to well deserve to be selected, as it has been, for the type or symbol of that immortal temple of the body, to which Christ significantly and symbolically alluded when he said, "Destroy this temple, and in three days I will raise it up."

This idea of representing the interior and spiritual man by a material temple is so apposite in all its parts as to have occurred on more than one occasion to the first teachers of Christianity. Christ himself repeatedly alludes to it in other passages, and the eloquent and figurative St. Paul beautifully extends the idea in one of his Epistles to the Corinthians, in the following language: "Know ye not that ye are the temple of God, and that the spirit of God dwelleth in you?" And again, in a subsequent passage of the same Epistle, he reiterates the idea in a more positive form: "What, know ye not that your body is the temple of the Holy Ghost which is in you, which ye have of God, and ye are not your own?" And Dr. Adam Clarke, while commenting on this latter passage, makes the very allusions which have been the topic of discussion in the present essay. "As truly," says he, "as the living God dwelt in the Mosaic tabernacle and in the temple of

Solomon, so truly does the Holy Ghost dwell in the souls of genuine Christians; and as the temple and all its *utensils* were holy, separated from all common and profane uses, and dedicated alone to the service of God, so the bodies of genuine Christians are holy, and should be employed in the service of God alone."

The idea, therefore, of making the temple a symbol of the body, is not exclusively masonic; but the mode of treating the symbolism by a reference to the particular temple of Solomon, and to the operative art engaged in its construction, is peculiar to Freemasonry. It is this which isolates it from all other similar associations. Having many things in common with the secret societies and religious Mysteries of antiquity, in this "temple symbolism" it differs from them all.

XIII.

The Form of the Lodge.

In the last essay, I treated of that symbolism of the masonic system which makes the temple of Jerusalem the archetype of a lodge, and in which, in consequence, all the symbols are referred to the connection of a speculative science with an operative art. I propose in the present to discourse of a higher and abstruser mode of symbolism; and it may be observed that, in coming to this topic, we arrive, for the first time, at that chain of resemblances which unites Freemasonry with the ancient systems of religion, and which has given rise, among masonic writers, to the names of Pure and Spurious Freemasonry—the pure Freemasonry being that system of philosophical religion which, coming through the line of the patriarchs, was eventually modified by influences exerted at the building of King Solomon's temple, and the spurious being the same system as it was altered and corrupted by the polytheism of the nations of heathendom.[64]

As this abstruser mode of symbolism, if less peculiar to the masonic system, is, however, far more interesting than the one which was treated in the previous essay,—because it is more philosophical,—I propose to give an extended investigation of its character. And, in the first place, there is what may be called an elementary view of this abstruser symbolism, which seems almost to be a corollary from what has already been described in the preceding article.

As each individual mason has been supposed to be the symbol of a spiritual temple,—"a temple not made with hands, eternal in the heavens,"—the lodge or collected assemblage of these masons, is adopted as a symbol of the world.[65]

It is in the first degree of Masonry, more particularly, that this species of symbolism is developed. In its detail it derives the characteristics of resemblance upon which it is founded, from the form, the supports, the ornaments, and general construction and internal organization of a lodge, in all of which the symbolic reference to the world is beautifully and consistently sustained.

The form of a masonic lodge is said to be a parallelogram, or oblong square; its greatest length being from east to west, its breadth from north to south. A square, a circle, a triangle, or any other form but that of an *oblong square*, would be eminently incorrect and unmasonic, because such a figure would not be an expression of the symbolic idea which is intended to be conveyed.

Now, as the world is a globe, or, to speak more accurately, an oblate spheroid, the attempt to make an oblong square its symbol would seem, at first view, to present insuperable difficulties. But the system of masonic symbolism has stood the test of too long an experience to be easily found at fault; and therefore this very symbol furnishes a striking evidence of the antiquity of the order. At the Solomonic era—the era of the building of the temple at Jerusalem—the world, it must be remembered, was supposed to have that very oblong form,[66] which has been here symbolized. If, for instance, on a map of the world we should inscribe an oblong figure whose boundary lines would circumscribe and include just that portion which was known to be inhabited in the clays of Solomon, these lines, running a short distance north and south of the Mediterranean Sea, and extending from Spain in the west to Asia Minor in the east, would form an oblong square, including the southern shore of Europe, the northern shore of Africa, and the western district of Asia, the length of the parallelogram being about sixty degrees from east to west, and its breadth being about twenty degrees from north to south. This oblong square, thus enclosing the whole of what was then supposed to be the habitable globe,[67] would precisely represent what is symbolically said to be *the form of the lodge*, while the Pillars of Hercules in the west, on each side of the straits of Gades or Gibraltar, might appropriately be referred to the two pillars that stood at the porch of the temple.

A masonic lodge is, therefore, a symbol of the world.

This symbol is sometimes, by a very usual figure of speech, extended, in its application, and the world and the universe are made synonymous, when the lodge becomes, of course, a symbol of the universe. But in this case the definition of the symbol is extended, and to the ideas of length and breadth are added those of height and depth, and the lodge is said to assume the form of a double cube.[68] The solid contents of the earth below and the expanse of the heavens above will then give the outlines of the cube, and the whole created universe[69] will be included within the symbolic limits of a mason's lodge.

By always remembering that the lodge is the symbol, in its form and extent, of the world, we are enabled, readily and rationally, to explain many other symbols, attached principally to the first degree; and we are enabled to collate and compare them with similar symbols of other kindred institutions of antiquity, for it should be observed that this symbolism of the world, represented by a place of initiation, widely pervaded all the ancient rites and mysteries.

It will, no doubt, be interesting to extend our investigations on this subject, with a particular view to the method in which this symbolism of the world or the universe was developed, in some of its most prominent details; and for this purpose I shall select the mystical explanation of the *officers* of a lodge, its *covering*, and a portion of its *ornaments*.

XIV.

The Officers of a Lodge.

The Three Principal Officers of a lodge are, it is needless to say, situated in the east, the west, and the south. Now, bearing in mind that the lodge is a symbol of the world, or the universe, the reference of these three officers to the sun at its rising, its setting, and its meridian height, must at once suggest itself.

This is the first development of the symbol, and a very brief inquiry will furnish ample evidence of its antiquity and its universality.

In the Brahminical initiations of Hindostan, which are among the earliest that have been transmitted to us, and may almost be considered as the cradle of all the others of subsequent ages and various countries, the ceremonies were performed in vast caverns, the remains of some of which, at Salsette, Elephanta, and a few other places, will give the spectator but a very inadequate idea of the extent and splendor of these ancient Indian lodges.[70] More imperfect remains than these are still to be found in great numbers throughout Hindostan and Cashmere. Their form was sometimes that of a cross, emblematic of the four elements of which the earth is composed,—fire, water, air, and earth,—but more generally an oval, as a representation of the mundane egg, which, in the ancient systems, was a symbol of the world.[71]

The interior of the cavern of initiation was lighted by innumerable lamps, and there sat in the east, the west, and the south the principal Hierophants, or explainers of the Mysteries, as the representatives of Brahma, Vishnu, and Siva. Now, Brahma was the supreme deity of the Hindoos, borrowed or derived from the Sun-god of their Sabean ancestors, and Vishnu and Siva were but manifestations of his attributes. We learn from the Indian Pantheon that "when the sun rises in the east, he is Brahma; when he gains his meridian in the south, he is Siva; and when he sets in the west, he is Vishnu."

Again, in the Zoroasteric mysteries of Persia, the temple of initiation was circular, being made so to represent the universe; and the sun in the east, with the surrounding zodiac, formed an indispensable part of the ceremony of reception.[72]

In the Egyptian mysteries of Osiris, the same reference to the sun is contained, and Herodotus, who was himself an initiate, intimates that the ceremonies consisted in the representation of a Sun-god, who had been incarnate, that is, had appeared upon earth, or rose, and who was at length put to death by Typhon, the symbol of darkness, typical of the sun's setting.

In the great mysteries of Eleusis,[73] which were celebrated at Athens, we learn from St. Chrysostom, as well as other authorities, that the temple of initiation was symbolic of the universe, and we know that one of the officers represented the sun.[74]

In the Celtic mysteries of the Druids, the temple of initiation was either oval, to represent the mundane egg—a symbol, as has already been said, of the world; or circular, because the circle was a symbol of the universe; or cruciform, in allusion to the four elements, or constituents of the universe. In the Island of Lewis, in Scotland, there is one combining the cruciform and circular form. There is a circle, consisting of twelve stones, while three more are placed in the east, and as many in the west and south, and thirty-eight, in two parallel lines, in the north, forming an avenue to the circular temple. In the centre of the circle is the image of the god. In the initiations into these rites, the solar deity performed an important part, and the celebrations commenced at daybreak, when the sun was hailed on his appearance above the horizon as "the god of victory, the king who rises in light and ascends the sky."

But I need not multiply these instances of sun-worship. Every country and religion of the ancient world would afford one.[75] Sufficient has been cited to show the complete coincidence, in reference to the sun, between the symbolism of Freemasonry and that of the ancient rites and Mysteries, and to suggest for them a common origin, the sun being always in the former system, from the earliest times of the primitive or patriarchal Masonry, considered simply as a manifestation of the Wisdom, Strength, and Beauty of the Divine Architect, visibly represented by the position of the three principal officers of a lodge, while by the latter, in their degeneration from, and corruption of the true Noachic faith, it was adopted as the special object of adoration.

XV.

The Point Within a Circle.

The point within a Circle is another symbol of great importance in Freemasonry, and commands peculiar attention in this connection with the ancient symbolism of the universe and the solar orb. Everybody who has read a masonic "Monitor" is well acquainted with the usual explanation of this symbol. We are told that the point represents an individual brother, the circle the boundary line of his duty to God and man, and the two perpendicular parallel lines the patron saints of the order—St. John the Baptist and St. John the Evangelist.

Now, this explanation, trite and meagre as it is, may do very well for the exoteric teaching of the order; but the question at this time is, not how it has been explained by modern lecturers and masonic system-makers, but what was the ancient interpretation of the symbol, and how should it be read as a sacred hieroglyphic in reference to the true philosophic system which constitutes the real essence and character of Freemasonry?

Perfectly to understand this symbol, I must refer, as a preliminary matter, to the worship of the *Phallus*, a peculiar modification of sun-worship, which prevailed to a great extent among the nations of antiquity.

The Phallus was a sculptured representation of the *membrum virile*, or male organ of generation,[76] and the worship of it is said to have originated in Egypt, where, after the murder of Osiris by Typhon, which is symbolically to be explained as the destruction or deprivation of the sun's light by night, Isis, his wife, or the symbol of nature, in the search for his mutilated body, is said to have found all the parts except the organs of generation, which myth is simply symbolic of the fact, that the sun having set, its fecundating and invigorating power had ceased. The Phallus, therefore, as the symbol of the male generative principle, was very universally venerated among the ancients,[77] and that too as a religious rite, without the slightest reference to any impure or lascivious application.[78] He is supposed, by some commentators, to be the god mentioned under the name of Baal-peor, in the Book of Numbers,[79] as having been worshipped by the idolatrous Moabites. Among the eastern nations of India the same symbol was prevalent, under the name of "Lingam." But the Phallus or Lingam was a representation of the male principle only. To perfect the circle of generation it is necessary to advance one step farther. Accordingly we find in the *Cteis* of the Greeks, and the *Yoni* of the Indians, a symbol of the female generative principle, of co-extensive prevalence with the Phallus. The *Cteis* was a circular and concave pedestal, or receptacle, on which the Phallus or column rested, and from the centre of which it sprang.

The union of the Phallus and Cteis, or the Lingam and Yoni, in one compound figure, as an object of adoration, was the most usual mode of representation. This was in strict accordance with the whole system of ancient mythology, which was founded upon a worship of the prolific powers of nature. All the deities of pagan antiquity, however numerous they may be, can always be reduced to the two different forms of the generative principle—the active, or male, and the passive, or female. Hence the gods were always arranged in pairs, as Jupiter and Juno, Bacchus and Venus, Osiris and Isis. But the ancients went farther. Believing that the procreative and productive powers of nature might be conceived to exist in the same individual, they made the older of their deities hermaphrodite, and used the term ἀῤῥενοθέλυς, or *man-virgin*, to denote the union of the two sexes in the same divine person.[80]

Thus, in one of the Orphic Hymns, we find this line:—

"Ζεὺς ἄρσην γένετο, Ζεὺς ἄμβροτος ἔπλετο νύμφη."

Jove was created a male and an unspotted virgin.

And Plutarch, in his tract "On Isis and Osiris," says, "God, who is a male and female intelligence, being both life and light, brought forth another intelligence, the Creator of the World."

Now, this hermaphrodism of the Supreme Divinity was again supposed to be represented by the sun, which was the male generative energy, and by nature, or the universe, which was the female prolific principle.[81] And this union was symbolized in different ways, but principally by *the point within the circle*, the point indicating the sun, and the circle the universe, invigorated and fertilized by his generative rays. And in some of the Indian cave-temples, this allusion was made more manifest by the inscription of the signs of the zodiac on the circle.

So far, then, we arrive at the true interpretation of the masonic symbolism of the point within the circle. It is the same thing, but under a different form, as the Master and Wardens of a lodge. The Master and Wardens are symbols of the sun, the lodge of the universe, or world, just as the point is the symbol of the same sun, and the surrounding circle of the universe.

But the two perpendicular parallel lines remain to be explained. Every one is familiar with the very recent interpretation, that they represent the two Saints John, the Baptist and the Evangelist. But this modern exposition must be abandoned, if we desire to obtain the true ancient signification.

In the first place, we must call to mind the fact that, at two particular points of his course, the sun is found in the zodiacal signs of Cancer and Capricorn. These points are astronomically distinguished as the summer and winter solstice. When the sun is in these points, he has reached his greatest northern and southern declination, and produces the most evident effects on the temperature of the seasons, and on the length of the days and nights. These points, if we suppose the circle to represent the sun's apparent course, will be indicated by the points where the parallel lines touch the circle, or, in other words, the parallels will indicate the limits of the sun's extreme northern and southern declination, when he arrives at the solstitial points of Cancer and Capricorn.

But the days when the sun reaches these points are, respectively, the 21st of June and the 22d of December, and this will account for their subsequent application to the two Saints John, whose anniversaries have been placed by the church near those days.

XVI.

The Covering of the Lodge.

The Covering of the lodge is another, and must be our last reference to this symbolism of the world or the universe. The mere mention of the fact that this covering is figuratively supposed to be "a clouded canopy," or the firmament, on which the host of stars is represented, will be enough to indicate the continued allusion to the symbolism of the world. The lodge, as a representative of the world, is of course supposed to have no other roof than the heavens;[82] and it would scarcely be necessary to enter into any discussion on the subject, were it not that another symbol—the theological ladder—is so intimately connected with it, that the one naturally suggests the other. Now, this mystic ladder, which connects the ground floor of the lodge with its roof or covering, is another important and interesting link, which binds, with one common chain, the symbolism and ceremonies of Freemasonry, and the symbolism and rites of the ancient initiations.

This mystical ladder, which in Masonry is referred to "the theological ladder, which Jacob in his vision saw, reaching from earth to heaven," was widely dispersed among the religions of antiquity, where it was always supposed to consist of seven rounds or steps.

For instance, in the Mysteries of Mithras, in Persia, where there were seven stages or degrees of initiation, there was erected in the temples, or rather caves,—for it was in them that the initiation was conducted,—a high ladder, of seven steps or gates, each of which was dedicated to one of the planets, which was typified by one of the metals, the topmost step representing the sun, so that, beginning at the bottom, we have Saturn represented by lead, Venus by tin, Jupiter by brass, Mercury by iron, Mars by a mixed metal, the Moon by silver, and the Sun by gold, the whole being a symbol of the sidereal progress of the solar orb through the universe.

In the Mysteries of Brahma we find the same reference to the ladder of seven steps; but here the names were different, although there was the same allusion to the symbol of the universe. The seven steps were emblematical of the seven worlds which constituted the Indian universe. The lowest was the Earth; the second, the World of Reexistence; the third, Heaven; the fourth, the Middle World, or intermediate region between the lower and upper worlds; the fifth, the World of Births, in which souls are again born; the sixth, the Mansion of the Blessed; and the seventh, or topmost round, the Sphere of Truth, the abode of Brahma, he himself being but a symbol of the sun, and hence we arrive once more at the masonic symbolism of the universe and the solar orb.

Dr. Oliver thinks that in the Scandinavian Mysteries he has found the mystic ladder in the sacred tree *Ydrasil*;[83] but here the reference to the septenary division is so imperfect, or at least abstruse, that I am unwilling to press it into our catalogue of coincidences, although there is no doubt that we shall find in this sacred tree the same allusion as in the ladder of Jacob, to an ascent from earth, where its roots were planted, to heaven, where its branches expanded, which ascent being but a change from mortality to immortality, from time to eternity, was the doctrine taught in all the initiations. The ascent of the ladder or of the tree was the ascent from life here to life hereafter—from earth to heaven.

It is unnecessary to carry these parallelisms any farther. Any one can, however, see in them an undoubted reference to that septenary division which so universally prevailed throughout the ancient world, and the influence of which is still felt even in the common day life and observances of our time. Seven was, among the Hebrews, their perfect number; and hence we see it continually recurring in all their sacred rites. The creation was perfected in seven days; seven priests, with seven trumpets, encompassed the walls of Jericho for seven days; Noah received seven days' notice of the commencement of the deluge, and seven persons accompanied him into the ark, which rested on Mount Ararat on the seventh month; Solomon was seven years in building the temple: and there are hundreds of other instances of the prominence of this talismanic number, if there were either time or necessity to cite them.

Among the Gentiles the same number was equally sacred. Pythagoras called it a "venerable number." The septenary division of time into weeks of seven days, although not universal, as has been generally supposed, was sufficiently so to indicate the influence of the number. And it is remarkable, as perhaps in some way referring to the seven-stepped ladder which we have been considering, that in the ancient Mysteries, as Apuleius informs us, the candidate was seven times washed in the consecrated waters of ablution.

There is, then, an anomaly in giving to the mystical ladder of Masonry only *three* rounds. It is an anomaly, however, with which Masonry has had nothing to do. The error arose from the ignorance of those inventors who first engraved the masonic symbols for our monitors. The ladder of Masonry, like the equipollent ladders of its kindred institutions, always had seven steps, although in modern times the three principal or upper ones are alone alluded to. These rounds, beginning at the lowest, are *Temperance, Fortitude, Prudence, Justice, Faith, Hope,* and *Charity*. Charity, therefore, takes the same place in the ladder of masonic virtues as the sun does in the ladder of planets. In the ladder of metals we find gold, and in that of colors yellow, occupying the same elevated position. Now, St. Paul explains Charity as signifying, not alms-giving, which is the modern popular meaning, but love—that love which "suffereth long and is kind;" and when, in our lectures on this subject, we speak of it as the greatest of virtues, because, when Faith is lost and Hope has ceased, it extends "beyond the grave to realms of endless bliss," we there refer it to the Divine Love of our Creator. But Portal, in his Essay on Symbolic Colors, informs us that the sun represents Divine Love, and gold indicates the goodness of God.

So that if Charity is equivalent to Divine Love, and Divine Love is represented by the sun, and lastly, if Charity be the topmost round of the masonic ladder, then again we arrive, as the result of our researches, at the symbol so often already repeated of the solar orb. The natural sun or the spiritual sun—the sun, either as the vivifying principle of animated nature, and therefore the special object of adoration, or as the most prominent instrument of the Creator's benevolence—was ever a leading idea in the symbolism of antiquity.

Its prevalence, therefore, in the masonic institution, is a pregnant evidence of the close analogy existing between it and all these systems. How that analogy was first introduced, and how it is to be explained, without detriment to the purity and truthfulness of our own religious character, would involve a long inquiry into the origin of Freemasonry, and the history of its connection with the ancient systems.

These researches might have been extended still farther; enough, however, has been said to establish the following leading principles:—

1. That Freemasonry is, strictly speaking, a science of symbolism.

2. That in this symbolism it bears a striking analogy to the same science, as seen in the mystic rites of the ancient religions.

3. That as in these ancient religions the universe was symbolized to the candidate, and the sun, as its vivifying principle, made the object of his adoration, or at least of his veneration, so, in Masonry, the lodge is made the representative of the world or the universe, and the sun is presented as its most prominent symbol.

4. That this identity of symbolism proves an identity of origin, which identity of origin can be shown to be strictly compatible with the true religious sentiment of Masonry.

5. And fifthly and lastly, that the whole symbolism of Freemasonry has an exclusive reference to what the Kabalists have called the ALGABIL—the *Master Builder*—him whom Freemasons have designated as the Grand Architect of the Universe.

XVII.

Ritualistic Symbolism.

We have hitherto been engaged in the consideration of these simple symbols, which appear to express one single and independent idea. They have sometimes been called the "alphabet of Freemasonry," but improperly, I think, since the letters of the alphabet have, in themselves, unlike these masonic symbols, no significance, but are simply the component parts of words, themselves the representatives of ideas.

These masonic symbols rather may be compared to the elementary characters of the Chinese language, each of which denotes an idea; or, still better, to the hieroglyphics of the ancient Egyptians, in which one object was represented in full by another which bore some subjective relation to it, as the wind was represented by the wings of a bird, or courage by the head and shoulders of a lion.

It is in the same way that in Masonry the plumb represents rectitude, the level, human equality, and the trowel, concord or harmony. Each is, in itself, independent, each expresses a single elementary idea.

But we now arrive at a higher division of masonic symbolism, which, passing beyond these tangible symbols, brings us to those which are of a more abstruse nature, and which, as being developed in a ceremonial form, controlled and directed by the ritual of the order, may be designated as the *ritualistic symbolism* of Freemasonry.

It is to this higher division that I now invite attention; and for the purpose of exemplifying the definition that I have given, I shall select a few of the most prominent and interesting ceremonies of the ritual.

Our first researches were into the symbolism of objects; our next will be into the symbolism of ceremonies.

In the explanations which I shall venture to give of this ritualistic symbolism, or the symbolism of ceremonies, a reference will constantly be made to what has so often already been alluded to, namely, to the analogy existing between the system of Freemasonry and the ancient rites and Mysteries, and hence we will again develop the identity of their origin.

Each of the degrees of Ancient Craft Masonry contains some of these ritualistic symbols: the lessons of the whole order are, indeed, veiled in their allegoric clothing; but it is only to the most important that I can find opportunity to refer. Such, among others, are the rites of discalceation, of investiture, of circumambulation, and of intrusting. Each of these will furnish an appropriate subject for consideration.

XVIII.

The Rite of Discalceation.

The *rite of discalceation*, or uncovering the feet on approaching holy ground, is derived from the Latin word *discalceare*, to pluck off one's shoes. The usage has the prestige of antiquity and universality in its favor.

That it not only very generally prevailed, but that its symbolic signification was well understood in the days of Moses, we learn from that passage of Exodus where the angel of the Lord, at the burning bush, exclaims to the patriarch, "Draw not nigh hither; put off thy shoes from off thy feet, for the place whereon thou standest is holy ground." [84] Clarke[85] thinks it is from this command that the Eastern nations have derived the custom of performing all their acts of religious worship with bare feet. But it is much more probable that the ceremony was in use long anterior to the circumstance of the burning bush, and that the Jewish lawgiver at once recognized it as a well-known sign of reverence.

Bishop Patrick[86] entertains this opinion, and thinks that the custom was derived from the ancient patriarchs, and was transmitted by a general tradition to succeeding times.

Abundant evidence might be furnished from ancient authors of the existence of the custom among all nations, both Jewish and Gentile. A few of them, principally collected by Dr. Mede, must be curious and interesting.

The direction of Pythagoras to his disciples was in these words: "Ανυπόδητος θύε χαι πρόσχυνει;" that is, Offer sacrifice and worship with thy shoes off.[87]

Justin Martyr says that those who came to worship in the sanctuaries and temples of the Gentiles were commanded by their priests to put off their shoes.

Drusius, in his Notes on the Book of Joshua, says that among most of the Eastern nations it was a pious duty to tread the pavement of the temple with unshod feet.[88]

Maimonides, the great expounder of the Jewish law, asserts that "it was not lawful for a man to come into the mountain of God's house with his shoes on his feet, or with his staff, or in his working garments, or with dust on his feet." [89]

Rabbi Solomon, commenting on the command in Leviticus xix. 30, "Ye shall reverence my sanctuary," makes the same remark in relation to this custom. On this subject Dr. Oliver observes, "Now, the act of going with naked feet was always considered a token of humility and reverence; and the priests, in the temple worship, always officiated with feet uncovered, although it was frequently injurious to their health." [90]

Mede quotes Zago Zaba, an Ethiopian bishop, who was ambassador from David, King of Abyssinia, to John III., of Portugal, as saying, "We are not permitted to enter the church, except barefooted." [91]

The Mohammedans, when about to perform their devotions, always leave their slippers at the door of the mosque. The Druids practised the same custom whenever they celebrated their sacred rites; and the ancient Peruvians are said always to have left their shoes at the porch when they entered the magnificent temple consecrated to the worship of the sun.

Adam Clarke thinks that the custom of worshipping the Deity barefooted was so general among all nations of antiquity, that he assigns it as one of his thirteen proofs that the whole human race have been derived from one family. [92]

A theory might be advanced as follows: The shoes, or sandals, were worn on ordinary occasions as a protection from the defilement of the ground. To continue to wear them, then, in a consecrated place, would be a tacit insinuation that the ground there was equally polluted and capable of producing defilement. But, as the very character of a holy and consecrated spot precludes the idea of any sort of defilement or impurity, the acknowledgment that such was the case was conveyed, symbolically, by divesting the feet of all that protection from pollution and uncleanness which would be necessary in unconsecrated places.

So, in modern times, we uncover the head to express the sentiment of esteem and respect. Now, in former days, when there was more violence to be apprehended than now, the casque, or helmet, afforded an ample protection from any sudden blow of an unexpected adversary. But we can fear no violence from one whom we esteem and respect; and, therefore, to deprive the head of its accustomed protection, is to give an evidence of our unlimited confidence in the person to whom the gesture is made.

The rite of discalceation is, therefore, a symbol of reverence. It signifies, in the language of symbolism, that the spot which is about to be approached in this humble and reverential manner is consecrated to some holy purpose.

Now, as to all that has been said, the intelligent mason will at once see its application to the third degree. Of all the degrees of Masonry, this is by far the most important and sublime. The solemn lessons which it teaches, the sacred scene which it represents, and the impressive ceremonies with which it is conducted, are all calculated to inspire the mind with feelings of awe and reverence. Into the holy of holies of the temple, when the ark of the covenant had been deposited in its appropriate place, and the Shekinah was hovering over it, the high priest alone, and on one day only in the whole year, was permitted, after the most careful purification, to enter with bare feet, and to pronounce, with fearful veneration, the tetragrammaton or omnific word.

And into the Master Mason's lodge—this holy of holies of the masonic temple, where the solemn truths of death and immortality are inculcated—the aspirant, on entering, should purify his heart from every contamination, and remember, with a due sense of their symbolic application, those words that once broke upon the astonished ears of the old patriarch, "Put off thy shoes from off thy feet, for the place whereon thou standest is holy ground."

XIX.

The Rite of Investiture.

Another ritualistic symbolism, of still more importance and interest, is the *rite of investiture*.

The rite of investiture, called, in the colloquially technical language of the order, the *ceremony of clothing*, brings us at once to the consideration of that well-known symbol of Freemasonry, the LAMB-SKIN APRON.

This rite of investiture, or the placing upon the aspirant some garment, as an indication of his appropriate preparation for the ceremonies in which he was about to engage, prevailed in all the ancient initiations. A few of them only it will be requisite to consider.

Thus in the Levitical economy of the Israelites the priests always wore the abnet, or linen apron, or girdle, as a part of the investiture of the priesthood. This, with the other garments, was to be worn, as the text expresses it, "for glory and for beauty," or, as it has been explained by a learned commentator, "as emblematical of that holiness and purity which ever characterize the divine nature, and the worship which is worthy of him."

In the Persian Mysteries of Mithras, the candidate, having first received light, was invested with a girdle, a crown or mitre, a purple tunic, and, lastly, a white apron.

In the initiations practised in Hindostan, in the ceremony of investiture was substituted the sash, or sacred zennaar, consisting of a cord, composed of nine threads twisted into a knot at the end, and hanging from the left shoulder to the right hip. This was, perhaps, the type of the masonic scarf, which is, or ought to be, always worn in the same position.

The Jewish sect of the Essenes, who approached nearer than any other secret institution of antiquity to Freemasonry in their organization, always invested their novices with a white robe.

And, lastly, in the Scandinavian rites, where the military genius of the people had introduced a warlike species of initiation, instead of the apron we find the candidate receiving a white shield, which was, however, always presented with the accompaniment of some symbolic instruction, not very dissimilar to that which is connected with the masonic apron.

In all these modes of investiture, no matter what was the material or the form, the symbolic signification intended to be conveyed was that of purity.

And hence, in Freemasonry, the same symbolism is communicated by the apron, which, because it is the first gift which the aspirant receives,—the first symbol in which he is instructed,—has been called the "badge of a mason." And most appropriately has it been so called; for, whatever may be the future advancement of the candidate in the "Royal Art," into whatever deeper arcana his devotion to the mystic institution or his thirst for knowledge may carry him, with the apron—his first investiture—he never parts. Changing, perhaps, its form and its decorations, and conveying at each step some new and beautiful allusion, its substance is still there, and it continues to claim the honorable title by which it was first made known to him on the night of his initiation.

The apron derives its significance, as the symbol of purity, from two sources—from its color and from its material. In each of these points of view it is, then, to be considered, before its symbolism can be properly appreciated.

And, first, the color of the apron must be an unspotted white. This color has, in all ages, been esteemed an emblem of innocence and purity. It was with reference to this symbolism that a portion of the vestments of the Jewish priesthood was directed to be made white. And hence Aaron was commanded, when he entered into the holy of holies to make an expiation for the sins of the people, to appear clothed in white linen, with his linen apron, or girdle, about his loins. It is worthy of remark that the Hebrew word LABAN, which signifies *to make white*, denotes also *to purify*; and hence we find, throughout the Scriptures, many allusions to that color as an emblem of purity. "Though thy sins be as scarlet," says Isaiah, "they shall be *white* as snow;" and Jeremiah, in describing the once innocent condition of Zion, says, "Her Nazarites were purer than snow; they were *whiter* than milk."

In the Apocalypse a *white stone* was the reward promised by the Spirit to those who overcame; and in the same mystical book the apostle is instructed to say, that fine linen, clean and *white*, is the righteousness of the saints.

In the early ages of the Christian church a *white garment* was always placed upon the catechumen who had been recently baptized, to denote that he had been cleansed from his former sins, and was thenceforth to lead a life of innocence and purity. Hence it was presented to him with this appropriate charge: "Receive the white and undefiled garment, and produce it unspotted before the tribunal of our Lord Jesus Christ, that you may obtain immortal life."

The *white alb* still constitutes a part of the vestments of the Roman church, and its color is said by Bishop England "to excite to piety by teaching us the purity of heart and body which we should possess in being present at the holy mysteries."

The heathens paid the same attention to the symbolic signification of this color. The Egyptians, for instance, decorated the head of their principal deity, Osiris, with a white tiara, and the priests wore robes of the whitest linen.

In the school of Pythagoras, the sacred hymns were chanted by the disciples clothed in garments of white. The Druids gave white vestments to those of their initiates who had arrived at the ultimate degree, or that of perfection. And this was intended, according to their ritual, to teach the aspirant that none were admitted to that honor but such as were cleansed from all impurities, both of body and mind.

In all the Mysteries and religions rites of the other nations of antiquity the same use of white garments was observed.

Portal, in his "Treatise on Symbolic Colors," says that "white, the symbol of the divinity and of the priesthood, represents divine wisdom; applied to a young girl, it denotes virginity; to an accused person, innocence; to a judge, justice;" and he adds—what in reference to its use in Masonry will be peculiarly appropriate—that, "as a characteristic sign of purity, it exhibits a promise of hope after death." We see, therefore, the propriety of adopting this color in the masonic system as a symbol of purity. This symbolism pervades the whole of the ritual, from the lowest to the highest degree, wherever white vestments or white decorations are used.

As to the material of the apron, this is imperatively required to be of lamb-skin. No other substance, such as linen, silk, or satin, could be substituted without entirely destroying the symbolism of the vestment. Now, the lamb has, as the ritual expresses it, "been, in all ages, deemed an emblem of innocence;" but more particularly in the Jewish and Christian churches has this symbolism been observed. Instances of this need hardly be cited. They abound throughout the Old Testament, where we learn that a lamb was selected by the Israelites for their sin and burnt offerings, and in the New, where the word *lamb* is almost constantly employed as synonymous with innocence. "The paschal lamb," says Didron, "which was eaten by the Israelites on the night preceding their departure, is the type of that other divine Lamb, of whom Christians are to partake at Easter, in order thereby to free themselves from the bondage in which they are held by vice." The paschal lamb, a lamb bearing a cross, was, therefore, from an early period, depicted by the Christians as referring to Christ crucified, "that spotless Lamb of God, who was slain from the foundation of the world."

The material, then, of the apron, unites with its color to give to the investiture of a mason the symbolic signification of purity. This, then, together with the fact which I have already shown, that the ceremony of investiture was common to all the ancient religious rites, will form another proof of the identity of origin between these and the masonic institution.

This symbolism also indicates the sacred and religious character which its founders sought to impose upon Freemasonry, and to which both the moral and physical qualifications of our candidates undoubtedly have a reference, since it is with the masonic lodge as it was with the Jewish church, where it was declared that "no man that had a blemish should come nigh unto the altar;" and with the heathen priesthood, among whom we are told that it was thought to be a dishonor to the gods to be served by any one that was maimed, lame, or in any other way imperfect; and with both, also, in requiring that no one should approach the sacred things who was not pure and uncorrupt.

The pure, unspotted lamb-skin apron is, then, in Masonry, symbolic of that perfection of body and purity of mind which are essential qualifications in all who would participate in its sacred mysteries.

XX.

The Symbolism of the Gloves.

The investiture with the gloves is very closely connected with the investiture with the apron, and the consideration of the symbolism of the one naturally follows the consideration of the symbolism of the other.

In the continental rites of Masonry, as practised in France, in Germany, and in other countries of Europe, it is an invariable custom to present the newly-initiated candidate not only, as we do, with a white leather apron, but also with two pairs of white kid gloves, one a man's pair for himself, and the other a woman's, to be presented by him in turn to his wife or his betrothed, according to the custom of the German masons, or, according to the French, to the female whom he most esteems, which, indeed, amounts, or should amount, to the same thing.

There is in this, of course, as there is in everything else which pertains to Freemasonry, a symbolism. The gloves given to the candidate for himself are intended to teach him that the acts of a mason should be as pure and spotless as the gloves now given to him. In the German lodges, the word used for *acts* is of course *handlungen*, or *handlings*, "the works of his hands," which makes the symbolic idea more impressive.

Dr. Robert Plott—no friend of Masonry, but still an historian of much research—says, in his "Natural History of Staffordshire," that the Society of Freemasons, in his time (and he wrote in 1660), presented their candidates with gloves for themselves and their wives. This shows that the custom still preserved on the continent of Europe was formerly practised in England, although there as well as in America, it is discontinued, which is, perhaps, to be regretted.

But although the presentation of the gloves to the candidate is no longer practised as a ceremony in England or America, yet the use of them as a part of the proper professional clothing of a mason in the duties of the lodge, or in processions, is still retained, and in many well-regulated lodges the members are almost as regularly clothed in their white gloves as in their white aprons.

The symbolism of the gloves, it will be admitted, is, in fact, but a modification of that of the apron. They both signify the same thing; both are allusive to a purification of life. "Who shall ascend," says the Psalmist, "into the hill of the Lord? or who shall stand in his holy place? He that hath clean hands and a pure heart." The apron may be said to refer to the "pure heart," the gloves to the "clean hands." Both are significant of purification—of that purification which was always symbolized by the ablution which preceded the ancient initiations into the sacred Mysteries. But while our American and English masons have adhered only to the apron, and rejected the gloves as a Masonic symbol, the latter appear to be far more important in symbolic science, because the allusions to pure or clean hands are abundant in all the ancient writers.

"Hands," says Wemyss, in his "Clavis Symbolica," "are the symbols of human actions; pure hands are pure actions; unjust hands are deeds of injustice." There are numerous references in sacred and profane writers to this symbolism. The washing of the hands has the outward sign of an internal purification. Hence the Psalmist says, "I will wash my hands in innocence, and I will encompass thine altar, Jehovah."

In the ancient Mysteries the washing of the hands was always an introductory ceremony to the initiation, and, of course, it was used symbolically to indicate the necessity of purity from crime as a qualification of those who sought admission into the sacred rites; and hence on a temple in the Island of Crete this inscription was placed: "Cleanse your feet, wash your hands, and then enter."

Indeed, the washing of hands, as symbolic of purity, was among the ancients a peculiarly religious rite. No one dared to pray to the gods until he had cleansed his hands. Thus Homer makes Hector say,—

"Χερσὶ δ' ἀνίπτοισιν Διϊλείβειν Ἄζομαι."—*Iliad*, vi. 266.

"I dread with unwashed hands to bring
My incensed wine to Jove an offering."

In a similar spirit of religion, Æneas, when leaving burning Troy, refuses to enter the temple of Ceres until his hands, polluted by recent strife, had been washed in the living stream.

"Me bello e tanto digressum et cæde recenti,
Attrectare nefas, donec me flumine vivo
Abluero."—*Æn*. ii. 718.

"In me, now fresh from war and recent strife,
'Tis impious the sacred things to touch
Till in the living stream myself I bathe."

The same practice prevailed among the Jews, and a striking instance of the symbolism is exhibited in that well-known action of Pilate, who, when the Jews clamored for Jesus, that they might crucify him, appeared before the people, and, having taken water, washed his hands, saying at the same time, "I am innocent of the blood of this just man. See ye to it." In the Christian church of the middle ages, gloves were always worn by bishops or priests when in the performance of ecclesiastical functions. They were made of linen, and were white; and Durandus, a celebrated ritualist, says that "by the white gloves were denoted chastity and purity, because the hands were thus kept clean and free from all impurity."

There is no necessity to extend examples any further. There is no doubt that the use of the gloves in Masonry is a symbolic idea borrowed from the ancient and universal language of symbolism, and was intended, like the apron, to denote the necessity of purity of life.

We have thus traced the gloves and the apron to the same symbolic source. Let us see if we cannot also derive them from the same historic origin.

The apron evidently owes its adoption in Freemasonry to the use of that necessary garment by the operative masons of the middle ages. It is one of the most positive evidences—indeed we may say, absolutely, the most tangible evidence—of the derivation of our speculative science from an operative art. The builders, who associated in companies, who traversed Europe, and were engaged in the construction of palaces and cathedrals, have left to us, as their descendants, their name, their technical language, and that distinctive piece of clothing by which they protected their garments from the pollutions of their laborious employment. Did they also bequeath to us their gloves? This is a question which some modern discoveries will at last enable us to solve.

M. Didron, in his "Annales Archeologiques," presents us with an engraving, copied from the painted glass of a window in the cathedral of Chartres, in France. The painting was executed in the thirteenth century, and represents a number of operative masons at work. *Three* of them are adorned with laurel crowns. May not these be intended to represent the three officers of a lodge? All of the Masons wear gloves. M. Didron remarks that in the old documents which he has examined, mention is often made of gloves which are intended to be presented to masons and stone-cutters. In a subsequent number of the "Annales," he gives the following three examples of this fact:—

In the year 1331, the Chatelan of Villaines, in Duemois, bought a considerable quantity of gloves, to be given to the workmen, in order, as it is said, "to shield their hands from the stone and lime."

In October, 1383, as he learns from a document of that period, three dozen pairs of gloves were bought and distributed to the masons when they commenced the buildings at the Chartreuse of Dijon.

And, lastly, in 1486 or 1487, twenty-two pair of gloves were given to the masons and stone-cutters who were engaged in work at the city of Amiens.

It is thus evident that the builders—the operative masons—of the middle ages wore gloves to protect their hands from the effects of their work. It is equally evident that the speculative masons have received from their operative predecessors the gloves as well as the apron, both of which, being used by the latter for practical uses, have been, in the spirit of symbolism, appropriated by the former to "a more noble and glorious purpose."

XXI.

The Rite of Circumambulation.

The *rite of circumambulation* will supply us with another ritualistic symbol, in which we may again trace the identity of the origin of Freemasonry with that of the religious and mystical ceremonies of the ancients.

"Circumambulation" is the name given by sacred archaeologists to that religious rite in the ancient initiations which consisted in a formal procession around the altar, or other holy and consecrated object.

The prevalence of this rite among the ancients appears to have been universal, and it originally (as I shall have occasion to show) alluded to the apparent course of the sun in the firmament, which is from east to west by the way of the south.

In ancient Greece, when the priests were engaged in the rites of sacrifice, they and the people always walked three times around the altar while chanting a sacred hymn or ode. Sometimes, while the people stood around the altar, the rite of circumambulation was performed by the priest alone, who, turning towards the right hand, went around it, and sprinkled it with meal and holy water. In making this circumambulation, it was considered absolutely necessary that the right side should always be next to the altar, and consequently, that the procession should move from the east to the south, then to the west, next to the north, and afterwards to the east again. It was in this way that the apparent revolution was represented.

This ceremony the Greeks called moving εχ δεξια εν δεξια, *from the right to the right*, which was the direction of the motion, and the Romans applied to it the term *dextrovorsum*, or *dextrorsum*, which signifies the same thing. Thus Plautus makes Palinurus, a character in his comedy of "Curculio," say, "If you would do reverence to the gods, you must turn to the right hand." Gronovius, in commenting on this passage of Plautus, says, "In worshipping and praying to the gods they were accustomed to *turn to the right hand*."

A hymn of Callimachus has been preserved, which is said to have been chanted by the priests of Apollo at Delos, while performing this ceremony of circumambulation, the substance of which is, "We imitate the example of the sun, and follow his benevolent course."

It will be observed that this circumambulation around the altar was accompanied by the singing or chanting of a sacred ode. Of the three parts of the ode, the *strophe*, the *antistrophe*, and the *epode*, each was to be sung at a particular part of the procession. The analogy between this chanting of an ode by the ancients and the recitation of a passage of Scripture in the masonic circumambulation, will be at once apparent.

Among the Romans, the ceremony of circumambulation was always used in the rites of sacrifice, of expiation or purification. Thus Virgil describes Corynasus as purifying his companions, at the funeral of Misenus, by passing three times around them while aspersing them with the lustral waters; and to do so conveniently, it was necessary that he should have moved with his right hand towards them.

"Idem ter socios pura circumtulit unda,
Spargens rore levi et ramo felicis olivæ."
Æn. vi. 229.

"Thrice with pure water compassed he the crew,
Sprinkling, with olive branch, the gentle dew."

In fact, so common was it to unite the ceremony of circumambulation with that of expiation or purification, or, in other words, to make a circuitous procession, in performing the latter rite, that the term *lustrare*, whose primitive meaning is "to purify," came at last to be synonymous with *circuire*, to walk round anything; and hence a purification and a circumambulation were often expressed by the same word.

Among the Hindoos, the same rite of circumambulation has always been practised. As an instance, we may cite the ceremonies which are to be performed by a Brahmin upon first rising from bed in the morning, an accurate account of which has been given by Mr. Colebrooke in the "Asiatic Researches." The priest, having first adored the sun while directing his face to the east, then walks towards the west by the way of the south, saying, at the same time, "I follow the course of the sun," which he thus explains: "As the sun in his course moves round the world by the way of the south, so do I follow that luminary, to obtain the benefit arising from a journey round the earth by the way of the south." [93]

Lastly, I may refer to the preservation of this rite among the Druids, whose "mystical dance" around the *cairn*, or sacred stones, was nothing more nor less than the rite of circumambulation. On these occasions the priest always made three circuits, from east to west, by the right hand, around the altar or cairn, accompanied by all the worshippers. And so sacred was the rite once considered, that we learn from Toland[94] that in the Scottish Isles, once a principal seat of the Druidical religion, the people "never come to the ancient sacrificing and fire-hallowing *cairns*, but they walk three times around them, from east to west, according to the course of the sun." This sanctified tour, or round by the south, he observes, is called *Deiseal*, as the contrary, or unhallowed one by the north, is called *Tuapholl*. And he further remarks, that this word *Deiseal* was derived "from *Deas*, the *right* (understanding *hand*) and *soil*, one of the ancient names of the sun, the right hand in this round being ever next the heap."

I might pursue these researches still further, and trace this rite of circumambulation to other nations of antiquity; but I conceive that enough has been said to show its universality, as well as the tenacity with which the essential ceremony of performing the motion a mystical number of times, and always by the right hand, from the east, through the south, to the west, was preserved. And I think that this singular analogy to the same rite in Freemasonry must lead us to the legitimate conclusion, that the common source of all these rites is to be found in the identical origin of the Spurious Freemasonry or pagan mysteries, and the pure, Primitive Freemasonry, from which the former seceded only to be deteriorated.

In reviewing what has been said on this subject, it will at once be perceived that the essence of the ancient rite consisted in making the circumambulation around the altar, from the east to the south, from the south to the west, thence to the north, and to the east again.

Now, in this the masonic rite of circumambulation strictly agrees with the ancient one.

But this circuit by the right hand, it is admitted, was done as a representation of the sun's motion. It was a symbol of the sun's apparent course around the earth.

And so, then, here again we have in Masonry that old and often-repeated allusion to sun-worship, which has already been seen in the officers of a lodge, and in the point within a circle. And as the circumambulation is made around the lodge, just as the sun was supposed to move around the earth, we are brought back to the original symbolism with which we commenced—that the lodge is a symbol of the world.

XXII.

The Rite of Intrusting, and the Symbolism of Light.

The *rite of intrusting*, to which we are now to direct our attention, will supply us with many important and interesting symbols.

There is an important period in the ceremony of masonic initiation, when the candidate is about to receive a full communication of the mysteries through which he has passed, and to which the trials and labors which he has undergone can only entitle him. This ceremony is technically called the "*rite of intrusting*," because it is then that the aspirant begins to be intrusted with that for the possession of which he was seeking.[95] It is equivalent to what, in the ancient Mysteries, was called the "autopsy," [96] or the seeing of what only the initiated were permitted to behold.

This *rite of intrusting* is, of course, divided into several parts or periods; for the *aporreta*, or secret things of Masonry, are not to be given at once, but in gradual progression. It begins, however, with the communication of LIGHT, which, although but a preparation for the development of the mysteries which are to follow, must be considered as one of the most important symbols in the whole science of masonic symbolism. So important, indeed, is it, and so much does it pervade with its influence and its relations the whole masonic system, that Freemasonry itself anciently received, among other appellations, that of Lux, or Light, to signify that it is to be regarded as that sublime doctrine of Divine Truth by which the path of him who has attained it is to be illuminated in his pilgrimage of life.

The Hebrew cosmogonist commences his description of the creation by the declaration that "God said, Let there be light, and there was light"—a phrase which, in the more emphatic form that it has received in the original language of "Be light, and light was," [97] is said to have won the praise, for its sublimity, of the greatest of Grecian critics. "The singularly emphatic summons," says a profound modern writer,[98] "by which light is called into existence, is probably owing to the preëminent utility and glory of that element, together with its mysterious nature, which made it seem as

'The God of this new world,'

and won for it the earliest adoration of mankind."

Light was, in accordance with this old religious sentiment, the great object of attainment in all the ancient religious Mysteries. It was there, as it is now, in Masonry, made the symbol of *truth* and *knowledge*. This was always its ancient symbolism, and we must never lose sight of this emblematic meaning, when we are considering the nature and signification of masonic light. When the candidate makes a demand for light, it is not merely for that material light which is to remove a physical darkness; that is only the outward form, which conceals the inward symbolism. He craves an intellectual illumination which will dispel the darkness of mental and moral ignorance, and bring to his view, as an eye-witness, the sublime truths of religion, philosophy, and science, which it is the great design of Freemasonry to teach.

In all the ancient systems this reverence for light, as the symbol of truth, was predominant. In the Mysteries of every nation, the candidate was made to pass, during his initiation, through scenes of utter darkness, and at length terminated his trials by an admission to the splendidly-illuminated sacellum, or sanctuary, where he was said to have attained pure and perfect light, and where he received the necessary instructions which were to invest him with that knowledge of the divine truth which it had been the object of all his labors to gain, and the design of the institution, into which he had been initiated, to bestow.

Light, therefore, became synonymous with truth and knowledge, and *darkness* with falsehood and ignorance. We shall find this symbolism pervading not only the institutions, but the very languages, of antiquity.

Thus, among the Hebrews, the word AUR, in the singular, signified *light*, but in the plural, AURIM, it denoted the revelation of the divine will; and the *aurim* and *thummim*, literally the *lights* and *truths*, constituted a part of the breastplate whence the high priest obtained oracular responses to the questions which he proposed.[99]

There is a peculiarity about the word "light," in the old Egyptian language, which is well worth consideration in this connection. Among the Egyptians, the *hare* was the hieroglyphic of *eyes that are open*; and it was adopted because that timid animal was supposed never to close his organs of vision, being always on the watch for his enemies. The hare was afterwards adopted by the priests as a symbol of the mental illumination or mystic light which was revealed to the neophytes, in the contemplation of divine truth, during the progress of their initiation; and hence, according to Champollion, the hare was also the symbol of Osiris, their chief god; thus showing the intimate connection which they believed to exist between the process of initiation into their sacred rites and the contemplation of the divine nature. But the Hebrew word for hare is ARNaBeT. Now, this is compounded of the two words AUR, *light*, and NaBaT, *to behold*, and therefore the word which in the Egyptian denoted *initiation*, in the Hebrew signified *to behold the light*. In two nations so intimately connected in history as the Hebrew and the Egyptian, such a

342

coincidence could not have been accidental. It shows the prevalence of the sentiment, at that period, that the communication of light was the prominent design of the Mysteries—so prominent that the one was made the synonyme of the other.[100]

The worship of light, either in its pure essence or in the forms of sun-worship and fire-worship, because the sun and the fire were causes of light, was among the earliest and most universal superstitions of the world. Light was considered as the primordial source of all that was holy and intelligent; and darkness, as its opposite, was viewed as but another name for evil and ignorance. Dr. Beard, in an article on this subject, in Kitto's Cyclopaedia of Biblical Literature, attributes this view of the divine nature of light, which was entertained by the nations of the East, to the fact that, in that part of the world, light "has a clearness and brilliancy, is accompanied by an intensity of heat, and is followed in its influence by a largeness of good, of which the inhabitants of less genial climates have no conception. Light easily and naturally became, in consequence, with Orientals, a representative of the highest human good. All the more joyous emotions of the mind, all the pleasing sensations of the frame, all the happy hours of domestic intercourse, were described under imagery derived from light. The transition was natural—from earthly to heavenly, from corporeal to spiritual things; and so light came to typify true religion and the felicity which it imparts. But as light not only came from God, but also makes man's way clear before him, so it was employed to signify moral truth, and preëminently that divine system of truth which is set forth in the Bible, from its earliest gleamings onward to the perfect day of the Great Sun of Righteousness."

I am inclined to believe that in this passage the learned author has erred, not in the definition of the symbol, but in his deduction of its origin. Light became the object of religious veneration, not because of the brilliancy and clearness of a particular sky, nor the warmth and genial influence of a particular climate,— for the worship was universal, in Scandinavia as in India,—but because it was the natural and inevitable result of the worship of the sun, the chief deity of Sabianism—a faith which pervaded to an extraordinary extent the whole religious sentiment of antiquity.[101]

Light was venerated because it was an emanation from the sun, and, in the materialism of the ancient faith, *light* and *darkness* were both personified as positive existences, the one being the enemy of the other. Two principles were thus supposed to reign over the world, antagonistic to each other, and each alternately presiding over the destinies of mankind.[102]

The contests between the good and evil principle, symbolized by light and darkness, composed a very large part of the ancient mythology in all countries.

Among the Egyptians, Osiris was light, or the sun; and his arch-enemy, Typhon, who ultimately destroyed him, was the representative of darkness.

Zoroaster, the father of the ancient Persian religion, taught the same doctrine, and called the principle of light, or good, Ormuzd, and the principle of darkness, or evil, Ahriman. The former, born of the purest light, and the latter, sprung from utter darkness, are, in this mythology, continually making war on each other.

Manes, or Manichaeus, the founder of the sect of Manichees, in the third century, taught that there are two principles from which all things proceed; the one is a pure and subtile matter, called Light, and the other a gross and corrupt substance, called Darkness. Each of these is subject to the dominion of a superintending being, whose existence is from all eternity. The being who presides over the light is called *God*; he that rules over the darkness is called *Hyle*, or *Demon*. The ruler of the light is supremely happy, good, and benevolent, while the ruler over darkness is unhappy, evil, and malignant.

Pythagoras also maintained this doctrine of two antagonistic principles. He called the one, unity, *light*, the right hand, equality, stability, and a straight line; the other he named binary, *darkness*, the left hand, inequality, instability, and a curved line. Of the colors, he attributed white to the good principle, and black to the evil one.

343

The Cabalists gave a prominent place to light in their system of cosmogony. They taught that, before the creation of the world, all space was filled with what they called *Aur en soph*, or the *Eternal Light*, and that when the Divine Mind determined or willed the production of Nature, the Eternal Light withdrew to a central point, leaving around it an empty space, in which the process of creation went on by means of emanations from the central mass of light. It is unnecessary to enter into the Cabalistic account of creation; it is sufficient here to remark that all was done through the mediate influence of the *Aur en soph*, or eternal light, which produces coarse matter, but one degree above nonentity, only when it becomes so attenuated as to be lost in darkness.

The Brahminical doctrine was, that "light and darkness are esteemed the world's eternal ways; he who walketh in the former returneth not; that is to say, he goeth to eternal bliss; whilst he who walketh in the latter cometh back again upon earth," and is thus destined to pass through further transmigrations, until his soul is perfectly purified by light.[103]

In all the ancient systems of initiation the candidate was shrouded in darkness, as a preparation for the reception of light. The duration varied in the different rites. In the Celtic Mysteries of Druidism, the period in which the aspirant was immersed in darkness was nine days and nights; among the Greeks, at Eleusis, it was three times as long; and in the still severer rites of Mithras, in Persia, fifty days of darkness, solitude, and fasting were imposed upon the adventurous neophyte, who, by these excessive trials, was at length entitled to the full communication of the light of knowledge.

Thus it will be perceived that the religious sentiment of a good and an evil principle gave to darkness, in the ancient symbolism, a place equally as prominent as that of light.

The same religious sentiment of the ancients, modified, however, in its details, by our better knowledge of divine things, has supplied Freemasonry with a double symbolism—that of *Light* and *Darkness*.

Darkness is the symbol of initiation. It is intended to remind the candidate of his ignorance, which Masonry is to enlighten; of his evil nature, which Masonry is to purify; of the world, in whose obscurity he has been wandering, and from which Masonry is to rescue him.

Light, on the other hand, is the symbol of the autopsy, the sight of the mysteries, the intrusting, the full fruition of masonic truth and knowledge.

Initiation precedes the communication of knowledge in Masonry, as darkness preceded light in the old cosmogonies. Thus, in Genesis, we see that in the beginning "the world was without form, and void, and darkness was on the face of the deep." The Chaldean cosmogony taught that in the beginning "all was darkness and water." The Phoenicians supposed that "the beginning of all things was a wind of black air, and a chaos dark as Erebus." [104]

But out of all this darkness sprang forth light, at the divine command, and the sublime phrase, "Let there be light," is repeated, in some substantially identical form, in all the ancient histories of creation.

So, too, out of the mysterious darkness of Masonry comes the full blaze of masonic light. One must precede the other, as the evening preceded the morning. "So the evening and the morning were the first day."

This thought is preserved in the great motto of the Order, "*Lux e tenebris*"—Light out of darkness. It is equivalent to this other sentence: Truth out of initiation. *Lux*, or light, is truth; *tenebrae*, or darkness, is initiation.

It is a beautiful and instructive portion of our symbolism, this connection of darkness and light, and well deserves a further investigation.

"Genesis and the cosmogonies," says Portal, "mention the antagonism of light and darkness. The form of this fable varies according to each nation, but the foundation is everywhere the same. Under the symbol of the creation of the world it presents the picture of regeneration and initiation." [105]

Plutarch says that to die is to be initiated into the greater Mysteries; and the Greek word τελευτᾷν, which signifies *to die*, means also *to be initiated*. But black, which is the symbolic color of darkness, is also the symbol of death. And hence, again, darkness, like death, is the symbol of initiation. It was for this reason that all the ancient initiations were performed at night. The celebration of the Mysteries was always nocturnal. The same custom prevails in Freemasonry, and the explanation is the same. Death and the resurrection were taught in the Mysteries, as they are in Freemasonry. The initiation was the lesson of death. The full fruition or autopsy, the reception of light, was the lesson of regeneration or resurrection.

Light is, therefore, a fundamental symbol in Freemasonry. It is, in fact, the first important symbol that is presented to the neophyte in his instructions, and contains within itself the very essence of Speculative Masonry, which is nothing more than the contemplation of intellectual light or truth.[106]

XXIII.

Symbolism of the Corner-Stone.

We come next, in a due order of precedence, to the consideration of the symbolism connected with an important ceremony in the ritual of the first degree of Masonry, which refers to the north-east corner of the lodge. In this ceremony the candidate becomes the representative of a spiritual corner-stone. And hence, to thoroughly comprehend the true meaning of the emblematic ceremony, it is essential that we should investigate the symbolism of the *corner-stone*.

The corner-stone,[107] as the foundation on which the entire building is supposed to rest, is, of course, the most important stone in the whole edifice. It is, at least, so considered by operative masons. It is laid with impressive ceremonies; the assistance of speculative masons is often, and always ought to be, invited, to give dignity to the occasion; and the event is viewed by the workmen as an important era in the construction of the edifice.[108]

In the rich imagery of Orientalism, the corner-stone is frequently referred to as the appropriate symbol of a chief or prince who is the defence and bulwark of his people, and more particularly in Scripture, as denoting that promised Messiah who was to be the sure prop and support of all who should put their trust in his divine mission.[109]

To the various properties that are necessary to constitute a true corner-stone,—its firmness and durability, its perfect form, and its peculiar position as the connecting link between the walls,—we must attribute the important character that it has assumed in the language of symbolism. Freemasonry, which alone, of all existing institutions, has preserved this ancient and universal language, could not, as it may well be supposed, have neglected to adopt the corner-stone among its most cherished and impressive symbols; and hence it has referred to it many of its most significant lessons of morality and truth.

I have already alluded to that peculiar mode of masonic symbolism by which the speculative mason is supposed to be engaged in the construction of a spiritual temple, in imitation of, or, rather, in reference to, that material one which was erected by his operative predecessors at Jerusalem. Let us again, for a few moments, direct our attention to this important fact, and revert to the connection which originally existed between the operative and speculative divisions of Freemasonry. This is an essential introduction to any inquiry into the symbolism of the corner-stone.

The difference between operative and speculative Masonry is simply this—that while the former was engaged in the construction of a material temple, formed, it is true, of the most magnificent materials which the quarries of Palestine, the mountains of Lebanon, and the golden shores of Ophir could contribute, the latter occupies itself in the erection of a spiritual house,—a house not made with hands,—in which, for stones and cedar, and gold and precious stones, are substituted the virtues of the heart, the pure emotions of the soul, the warm affections gushing forth from the hidden fountains of the spirit, so that the very presence of Jehovah, our Father and our God, shall be enshrined within us as his Shekinah was in the holy of holies of the material temple at Jerusalem.

The Speculative Mason, then, if he rightly comprehends the scope and design of his profession, is occupied, from his very first admission into the order until the close of his labors and his life,—and the true mason's labor ends only with his life,—in the construction, the adornment, and the completion of this spiritual temple of his body. He lays its foundation in a firm belief and an unshaken confidence in the wisdom, power, and goodness of God. This is his first step. Unless his trust is in God, and in him only, he can advance no further than the threshold of initiation. And then he prepares his materials with the gauge and gavel of Truth, raises the walls by the plumb-line of Rectitude, squares his work with the square of Virtue, connects the whole with the cement of Brotherly Love, and thus skilfully erects the living edifice of thoughts, and words, and deeds, in accordance with the designs laid down by the Master Architect of the universe in the great Book of Revelation.

The aspirant for masonic light—the Neophyte—on his first entrance within our sacred porch, prepares himself for this consecrated labor of erecting within his own bosom a fit dwelling-place for the Divine Spirit, and thus commences the noble work by becoming himself the corner-stone on which this spiritual edifice is to be erected.

Here, then, is the beginning of the symbolism of the corner-stone; and it is singularly curious to observe how every portion of the archetype has been made to perform its appropriate duty in thoroughly carrying out the emblematic allusions.

As, for example, this symbolic reference of the corner-stone of a material edifice to a mason, when, at his first initiation, he commences the intellectual task of erecting a spiritual temple in his heart, is beautifully sustained in the allusions to all the various parts and qualities which are to be found in a "well-formed, true and trusty" corner-stone.[110] Its form and substance are both seized by the comprehensive grasp of the symbolic science.

Let us trace this symbolism in its minute details. And, first, as to the form of the corner-stone.

The corner-stone of an edifice must be perfectly square on its surfaces, lest, by a violation of this true geometric figure, the walls to be erected upon it should deviate from the required line of perpendicularity which can alone give strength and proportion to the building.

Perfectly square on its surfaces, it is, in its form and solid contents, a cube. Now, the square and the cube are both important and significant symbols.

The square is an emblem of morality, or the strict performance of every duty.[111] Among the Greeks, who were a highly poetical and imaginative people, the square was deemed a figure of perfection, and the ἀνὴρ τετράγωνος—"the square or cubical man," as the words may be translated—was a term used to designate a man of unsullied integrity. Hence one of their most eminent metaphysicians[112] has said that "he who valiantly sustains the shocks of adverse fortune, demeaning himself uprightly, is truly good and of a square posture, without reproof; and he who would assume such a square posture should often subject himself to the perfectly square test of justice and integrity."

The cube, in the language of symbolism, denotes truth.[113] Among the pagan mythologists, Mercury, or Hermes, was always represented by a cubical stone, because he was the type of truth,[114] and the same form was adopted by the Israelites in the construction of the tabernacle, which was to be the dwelling-place of divine truth.

And, then, as to its material: This, too, is an essential element of all symbolism. Constructed of a material finer and more polished than that which constitutes the remainder of the edifice, often carved with appropriate devices and fitted for its distinguished purpose by the utmost skill of the sculptor's art, it becomes the symbol of that beauty of holiness with which the Hebrew Psalmist has said that we are to worship Jehovah.[115]

The ceremony, then, of the north-east corner of the lodge, since it derives all its typical value from this symbolism of the corner-stone, was undoubtedly intended to portray, in this consecrated language, the necessity of integrity and stability of conduct, of truthfulness and uprightness of character, and of purity and holiness of life, which, just at that time and in that place, the candidate is most impressively charged to maintain.

But there is also a symbolism about the position of the corner-stone, which is well worthy of attention. It is familiar to every one,—even to those who are without the pale of initiation,—that the custom of laying the corner-stones of public buildings has always been performed by the masonic order with peculiar and impressive ceremonies, and that this stone is invariably deposited in the north-east corner of the foundation of the intended structure. Now, the question naturally suggests itself, Whence does this ancient and invariable usage derive its origin? Why may not the stone be deposited in any other corner or portion of the edifice, as convenience or necessity may dictate? The custom of placing the foundation-stone in the north-east corner must have been originally adopted for some good and sufficient reason; for we have a right to suppose that it was not an arbitrary selection.[116] Was it in reference to the ceremony which takes place in the lodge? Or is that in reference to the position of the material stone? No matter which has the precedence in point of time, the principle is the same. The position of the stone in the north-east corner of the building is altogether symbolic, and the symbolism exclusively alludes to certain doctrines which are taught in the speculative science of Masonry.

The interpretation, I conceive, is briefly this: Every Speculative Mason is familiar with the fact that the east, as the source of material light, is a symbol of his own order, which professes to contain within its bosom the pure light of truth. As, in the physical world, the morning of each day is ushered into existence by the reddening dawn of the eastern sky, whence the rising sun dispenses his illuminating and prolific rays to every portion of the visible horizon, warming the whole earth with his embrace of light, and giving new-born life and energy to flower and tree, and beast and man, who, at the magic touch, awake from the sleep of darkness, so in the moral world, when intellectual night was, in the earliest days, brooding over the world, it was from the ancient priesthood living in the east that those lessons of God, of nature, and of humanity first emanated, which, travelling westward, revealed to man his future destiny, and his dependence on a superior power. Thus every new and true doctrine, coming from these "wise men of the east," was, as it were, a new day arising, and dissipating the clouds of intellectual darkness and error. It was a universal opinion among the ancients that the first learning came from the east; and the often-quoted line of Bishop Berkeley, that—

"Westward the course of empire takes its way"—

is but the modern utterance of an ancient thought, for it was always believed that the empire of truth and knowledge was advancing from the east to the west.

Again: the north, as the point in the horizon which is most remote from the vivifying rays of the sun when at his meridian height, has, with equal metaphorical propriety, been called the place of darkness, and is, therefore, symbolic of the profane world, which has not yet been penetrated and illumined by the intellectual rays of masonic light. All history concurs in recording the fact that, in the early ages of the world, its northern portion was enveloped in the most profound moral and mental darkness. It was from the remotest regions of Northern Europe that those barbarian hordes "came down like the wolf on the fold," and devastated the fair plains of the south, bringing with them a dark curtain of ignorance, beneath whose heavy folds the nations of the world lay for centuries overwhelmed. The extreme north has ever been, physically and intellectually, cold, and dark, and dreary. Hence, in Masonry, the north has ever been esteemed the place of darkness; and, in obedience to this principle, no symbolic light is allowed to illumine the northern part of the lodge.

The east, then, is, in Masonry, the symbol of the order, and the north the symbol of the profane world.

Now, the spiritual corner-stone is deposited in the north-east corner of the lodge, because it is symbolic of the position of the neophyte, or candidate, who represents it in his relation to the order and to the world. From the profane world he has just emerged. Some of its imperfections are still upon him; some of its darkness is still about him; he as yet belongs in part to the north. But he is striving for light and truth; the pathway upon which he has entered is directed towards the east. His allegiance, if I may use the word, is divided. He is not altogether a profane, nor altogether a mason. If he were wholly in the world, the north would be the place to find him—the north, which is the reign of darkness. If he were wholly in the order,—a Master Mason,—the east would have received him—the east, which is the place of light. But he is neither; he is an Apprentice, with some of the ignorance of the world cleaving to him, and some of the light of the order beaming upon him. And hence this divided allegiance—this double character—this mingling of the departing darkness of the north with the approaching brightness of the east—is well expressed, in our symbolism, by the appropriate position of the spiritual corner-stone in the north-east corner of the lodge. One surface of the stone faces the north, and the other surface faces the east. It is neither wholly in the one part nor wholly in the other, and in so far it is a symbol of initiation not fully developed—that which is incomplete and imperfect, and is, therefore, fitly represented by the recipient of the first degree, at the very moment of his initiation.[117]

But the strength and durability of the corner-stone are also eminently suggestive of symbolic ideas. To fulfil its design as the foundation and support of the massive building whose erection it precedes, it should be constructed of a material which may outlast all other parts of the edifice, so that when that "eternal ocean whose waves are years" shall have ingulfed all who were present at the construction of the building in the vast vortex of its ever-flowing current; and when generation after generation shall have passed away, and the crumbling stones of the ruined edifice shall begin to attest the power of time and the evanescent nature of all human undertakings, the corner-stone will still remain to tell, by its inscriptions, and its form, and its beauty, to every passer-by, that there once existed in that, perhaps then desolate, spot, a building consecrated to some noble or some sacred purpose by the zeal and liberality of men who now no longer live.

So, too, do this permanence and durability of the corner-stone, in contrast with the decay and ruin of the building in whose foundations it was placed, remind the mason that when this earthly house of his tabernacle shall have passed away, he has within him a sure foundation of eternal life—a corner-stone of immortality—an emanation from that Divine Spirit which pervades all nature, and which, therefore, must survive the tomb, and rise, triumphant and eternal, above the decaying dust of death and the grave.[118]

It is in this way that the student of masonic symbolism is reminded by the corner-stone—by its form, its position, and its permanence—of significant doctrines of duty, and virtue, and religious truth, which it is the great object of Masonry to teach.

But I have said that the material corner-stone is deposited in its appropriate place with solemn rites and ceremonies, for which the order has established a peculiar ritual. These, too, have a beautiful and significant symbolism, the investigation of which will next attract our attention.

And here it may be observed, in passing, that the accompaniment of such act of consecration to a particular purpose, with solemn rites and ceremonies, claims our respect, from the prestige that it has of all antiquity. A learned writer on symbolism makes, on this subject, the following judicious remarks, which may be quoted as a sufficient defence of our masonic ceremonies:—

"It has been an opinion, entertained in all past ages, that by the performance of certain acts, things, places, and persons acquire a character which they would not have had without such performances. The reason is plain: certain acts signify firmness of purpose, which, by consigning the object to the intended use, gives it, in the public opinion, an accordant character. This is most especially true of things, places, and persons connected with religion and religious worship. After the performance of certain acts or rites, they are held to be altogether different from what they were before; they acquire a sacred character, and in some instances a character absolutely divine. Such are the effects imagined to be produced by religious dedication." [119]

The stone, therefore, thus properly constructed, is, when it is to be deposited by the constituted authorities of our order, carefully examined with the necessary implements of operative masonry,—the square, the level, and the plumb,—and declared to be "well-formed, true, and trusty." This is not a vain nor unmeaning ceremony. It teaches the mason that his virtues are to be tested by temptation and trial, by suffering and adversity, before they can be pronounced by the Master Builder of souls to be materials worthy of the spiritual building of eternal life, fitted "as living stones, for that house not made with hands, eternal in the heavens." But if he be faithful, and withstand these trials,—if he shall come forth from these temptations and sufferings like pure gold from the refiner's fire,—then, indeed, shall he be deemed "well-formed, true, and trusty," and worthy to offer "unto the Lord an offering in righteousness."

In the ceremony of depositing the corner-stone, the sacred elements of masonic consecration are then produced, and the stone is solemnly set apart by pouring corn, wine, and oil upon its surface. Each of these elements has a beautiful significance in our symbolism.

Collectively, they allude to the Corn of Nourishment, the Wine of Refreshment, and the Oil of Joy, which are the promised rewards of a faithful and diligent performance of duty, and often specifically refer to the anticipated success of the undertaking whose incipiency they have consecrated. They are, in fact, types and symbols of all those abundant gifts of Divine Providence for which we are daily called upon to make an offering of our thanks, and which are enumerated by King David, in his catalogue of blessings, as "wine that maketh glad the heart of man, and oil to make his face to shine, and bread which strengtheneth man's heart."

"Wherefore, my brethren," says Harris, "do you carry *corn, wine, and oil* in your processions, but to remind you that in the pilgrimage of human life you are to impart a portion of your bread to feed the hungry, to send a cup of your wine to cheer the sorrowful, and to pour the healing oil of your consolation into the wounds which sickness hath made in the bodies, or affliction rent in the hearts, of your fellow-travellers?" [120]

But, individually, each of these elements of consecration has also an appropriate significance, which is well worth investigation.

Corn, in the language of Scripture, is an emblem of the resurrection, and St. Paul, in that eloquent discourse which is so familiar to all, as a beautiful argument for the great Christian doctrine of a future life, adduces the seed of grain, which, being sown, first dieth, and then quickeneth, as the appropriate type of that corruptible which must put on incorruption, and of that mortal which must assume immortality. But, in Masonry, the sprig of acacia, for reasons purely masonic, has been always adopted as the symbol of immortality, and the ear of corn is appropriated as the symbol of plenty. This is in accordance with the Hebrew derivation of the word, as well as with the usage of all ancient nations. The word *dagan*, דגן which signifies *corn*, is derived from the verb *dagah*, דגה, *to increase, to multiply*, and in all the ancient religions the horn or vase, filled with fruits and with grain, was the recognized symbol of plenty. Hence, as an element of consecration, corn is intended to remind us of those temporal blessings of life and health, and comfortable support, which we derive from the Giver of all good, and to merit which we should strive, with "clean hands and a pure heart," to erect on the corner-stone of our initiation a spiritual temple, which shall be adorned with the "beauty of holiness."

Wine is a symbol of that inward and abiding comfort with which the heart of the man who faithfully performs his part on the great stage of life is to be refreshed; and as, in the figurative language of the East, Jacob prophetically promises to Judah, as his reward, that he shall wash his garments in wine, and his clothes in the blood of the grape, it seems intended, morally, to remind us of those immortal refreshments which, when the labors of this earthly lodge are forever closed, we shall receive in the celestial lodge above, where the G.A.O.T.U. forever presides.

Oil is a symbol of prosperity, and happiness, and joy. The custom of anointing every thing or person destined for a sacred purpose is of venerable antiquity.[121] The statues of the heathen deities, as well as the altars on which the sacrifices were offered to them, and the priests who presided over the sacred rites, were always anointed with perfumed ointment, as a consecration of them to the objects of religious worship.

When Jacob set up the stone on which he had slept in his journey to Padan-aram, and where he was blessed with the vision of ascending and descending angels, he anointed it with oil, and thus consecrated it as an altar to God. Such an inunction was, in ancient times, as it still continues to be in many modern countries and contemporary religions, a symbol of the setting apart of the thing or person so anointed and consecrated to a holy purpose.

Hence, then, we are reminded by this last impressive ceremony, that the cultivation of virtue, the practice of duty, the resistance of temptation, the submission to suffering, the devotion to truth, the maintenance of integrity, and all those other graces by which we strive to fit our bodies, as living stones, for the spiritual building of eternal life, must, after all, to make the object effectual and the labor successful, be consecrated by a holy obedience to God's will and a firm reliance on God's providence, which alone constitute the chief corner-stone and sure foundation, on which any man can build with the reasonable hope of a prosperous issue to his work.

It may be noticed, in concluding this topic, that the corner-stone seems to be peculiarly a Jewish symbol. I can find no reference to it in any of the ancient pagan rites, and the EBEN PINAH, the *corner-stone*, which is so frequently mentioned in Scripture as the emblem of an important personage, and most usually, in the Old Testament, of the expected Messiah, appears, in its use in Masonry, to have had, unlike almost every other symbol of the order, an exclusively temple origin.

XXIV.

The Ineffable Name.

Another important symbol is the Ineffable Name, with which the series of ritualistic symbols will be concluded.

The Tetragrammaton,[122] or Ineffable Word,—the Incommunicable Name,—is a symbol—for rightly-considered it is nothing more than a symbol—that has more than any other (except, perhaps, the symbols connected with sun-worship), pervaded the rites of antiquity. I know, indeed, of no system of ancient initiation in which it has not some prominent form and place.

But as it was, perhaps, the earliest symbol which was corrupted by the spurious Freemasonry of the pagans, in their secession from the primitive system of the patriarchs and ancient priesthood, it will be most expedient for the thorough discussion of the subject which is proposed in the present paper, that we should begin the investigation with an inquiry into the nature of the symbol among the Israelites.

That name of God, which we, at a venture, pronounce Jehovah,—although whether this is, or is not, the true pronunciation can now never be authoritatively settled,—was ever held by the Jews in the most profound veneration. They derived its origin from the immediate inspiration of the Almighty, who communicated it to Moses as his especial appellation, to be used only by his chosen people; and this communication was made at the Burning Bush, when he said to him, "Thus shalt thou say unto the children of Israel: Jehovah, the God of your fathers, the God of Abraham, the God of Isaac, and the God of Jacob, hath sent me unto you: this [Jehovah] is my name forever, and this is my memorial unto all generations." [123] And at a subsequent period he still more emphatically declared this to be his peculiar name: "I am *Jehovah*; and I appeared unto Abraham, unto Isaac, and unto Jacob, by the name of *El Shaddai*; but by my name *Jehovah* was I not known unto them." [124]

It will be perceived that I have not here followed precisely the somewhat unsatisfactory version of King James's Bible, which, by translating or anglicizing one name, and not the other, leaves the whole passage less intelligible and impressive than it should be. I have retained the original Hebrew for both names. El Shaddai, "the Almighty One," was the name by which he had been heretofore known to the preceding patriarchs; in its meaning it was analogous to Elohim, who is described in the first chapter of Genesis as creating the world. But his name of Jehovah was now for the first time to be communicated to his people.

Ushered to their notice with all the solemnity and religious consecration of these scenes and events, this name of God became invested among the Israelites with the profoundest veneration and awe. To add to this mysticism, the Cabalists, by the change of a single letter, read the passage, "This is my name forever," or, as it is in the original, *Zeh shemi l'olam*, זה שמי לעלם as if written *Zeh shemi l'alam*, זה שמי לאלם that is to say, "This is my name to be concealed."

This interpretation, although founded on a blunder, and in all probability an intentional one, soon became a precept, and has been strictly obeyed to this day.[125] The word *Jehovah* is never pronounced by a pious Jew, who, whenever he meets with it in Scripture, substitutes for it the word *Adonai* or *Lord*—a practice which has been followed by the translators of the common English version of the Bible with almost Jewish scrupulosity, the word "Jehovah" in the original being invariably translated by the word "Lord." [126] The pronunciation of the word, being thus abandoned, became ultimately lost, as, by the peculiar construction of the Hebrew language, which is entirely without vowels, the letters, being all consonants, can give no possible indication, to one who has not heard it before, of the true pronunciation of any given word.

To make this subject plainer to the reader who is unacquainted with the Hebrew, I will venture to furnish an explanation which will, perhaps, be intelligible.

The Hebrew alphabet consists entirely of consonants, the vowel sounds having always been inserted orally, and never marked in writing until the "vowel points," as they are called, were invented by the Masorites, some six centuries after the Christian era. As the vowel sounds were originally supplied by the reader, while reading, from a knowledge which he had previously received, by means of oral instruction, of the proper pronunciation of the word, he was necessarily unable to pronounce any word which had never before been uttered in his presence. As we know that *Dr.* is to be pronounced *Doctor*, and *Mr. Mister*, because we have always heard those peculiar combinations of letters thus enunciated, and not because the letters themselves give any such sound; so the Jew knew from instruction and constant practice, and not from the power of the letters, how the consonants in the different words in daily use were to be vocalized. But as the four letters which compose the word *Jehovah*, as we now call it, were never pronounced in his presence, but were made to represent another word, *Adonai*, which was substituted for it, and as the combination of these four consonants would give no more indication for any sort of enunciation than the combinations *Dr.* or *Mr.* give in our language, the Jew, being ignorant of what vocal sounds were to be supplied, was unable to pronounce the word, so that its true pronunciation was in time lost to the masses of the people.

There was one person, however, who, it is said, was in possession of the proper sound of the letters and the true pronunciation of the word. This was the high priest, who, receiving it from his predecessor, preserved the recollection of the sound by pronouncing it three times, once a year, on the day of the atonement, when he entered the holy of holies of the tabernacle or the temple.

If the traditions of Masonry on this subject are correct, the kings, after the establishment of the monarchy, must have participated in this privilege; for Solomon is said to have been in possession of the word, and to have communicated it to his two colleagues at the building of the temple.

This is the word which, from the number of its letters, was called the "tetragrammaton," or four-lettered name, and, from its sacred inviolability, the "ineffable" or unutterable name.

The Cabalists and Talmudists have enveloped it in a host of mystical superstitions, most of which are as absurd as they are incredible, but all of them tending to show the great veneration that has always been paid to it.[127] Thus they say that it is possessed of unlimited powers, and that he who pronounces it shakes heaven and earth, and inspires the very angels with terror and astonishment.

The Rabbins called it "shem hamphorash," that is to say, "the name that is declaratory," and they say that David found it engraved on a stone while digging into the earth.

From the sacredness with which the name was venerated, it was seldom, if ever, written in full, and, consequently, a great many symbols, or hieroglyphics, were invented to express it. One of these was the letter ' or *Yod*, equivalent nearly to the English I, or J, or Y, which was the initial of the word, and it was often inscribed within an equilateral triangle, thus, the triangle itself being a symbol of Deity.

This symbol of the name of God is peculiarly worthy of our attention, since not only is the triangle to be found in many of the ancient religions occupying the same position, but the whole symbol itself is undoubtedly the origin of that hieroglyphic exhibited in the second degree of Masonry, where, the explanation of the symbolism being the same, the form of it, as far as it respects the letter, has only been anglicized by modern innovators. In my own opinion, the letter *G*, which is used in the Fellow Craft's degree, should never have been permitted to intrude into Masonry; it presents an instance of absurd anachronism, which would never have occurred if the original Hebrew symbol had been retained. But being there now, without the possibility of removal, we have only to remember that it is in fact but the symbol of a symbol.[128]

Widely spread, as I have already said, was this reverence for the name of God; and, consequently, its symbolism, in some peculiar form, is to be found in all the ancient rites.

Thus the Ineffable Name itself, of which we have been discoursing, is said to have been preserved in its true pronunciation by the Essenes, who, in their secret rites, communicated it to each other only in a whisper, and in such form, that while its component parts were known, they were so separated as to make the whole word a mystery.

Among the Egyptians, whose connection with the Hebrews was more immediate than that of any other people, and where, consequently, there was a greater similarity of rites, the same sacred name is said to have been used as a password, for the purpose of gaining admission to their Mysteries.

In the Brahminic Mysteries of Hindostan the ceremony of initiation was terminated by intrusting the aspirant with the sacred, triliteral name, which was AUM, the three letters of which were symbolic of the creative, preservative, and destructive principles of the Supreme Deity, personified in the three manifestations of Bramah, Siva, and Vishnu. This word was forbidden to be pronounced aloud. It was to be the subject of silent meditation to the pious Hindoo.

In the rites of Persia an ineffable name was also communicated to the candidate after his initiation.[129] Mithras, the principal divinity in these rites, who took the place of the Hebrew Jehovah, and represented the sun, had this peculiarity in his name—that the numeral value of the letters of which it was composed amounted to precisely 365, the number of days which constitute a revolution of the earth around the sun, or, as they then supposed, of the sun around the earth.

In the Mysteries introduced by Pythagoras into Greece we again find the ineffable name of the Hebrews, obtained doubtless by the Samian Sage during his visit to Babylon.[130] The symbol adopted by him to express it was, however, somewhat different, being ten points distributed in the form of a triangle, each side containing four points, as in the annexed figure.

The apex of the triangle was consequently a single point then followed below two others, then three; and lastly, the base consisted of four. These points were, by the number in each rank, intended, according to the Pythagorean system, to denote respectively the *monad*, or active principle of nature; the *duad*, or passive principle; the *triad*, or world emanating from their union; and the *quaterniad*, or intellectual science; the whole number of points amounting to ten, the symbol of perfection and consummation. This figure was called by Pythagoras the *tetractys*—a word equivalent in signification to the *tetragrammaton*; and it was deemed so sacred that on it the oath of secrecy and fidelity was administered to the aspirants in the Pythagorean rites.[131]

Among the Scandinavians, as among the Jewish Cabalists, the Supreme God who was made known in their mysteries had twelve names, of which the principal and most sacred one was *Alfader*, the Universal Father.

Among the Druids, the sacred name of God was *Hu*[132]—a name which, although it is supposed, by Bryant, to have been intended by them for Noah, will be recognized as one of the modifications of the Hebrew tetragrammaton. It is, in fact, the masculine pronoun in Hebrew, and may be considered as the symbolization of the male or generative principle in nature—a sort of modification of the system of Phallic worship.

This sacred name among the Druids reminds me of what is the latest, and undoubtedly the most philosophical, speculation on the true meaning, as well as pronunciation, of the ineffable tetragrammaton. It is from the ingenious mind of the celebrated Lanci; and I have already, in another work, given it to the public as I received it from his pupil, and my friend, Mr. Gliddon, the distinguished archaeologist. But the results are too curious to be omitted whenever the tetragrammaton is discussed.

Elsewhere I have very fully alluded to the prevailing sentiment among the ancients, that the Supreme Deity was bisexual, or hermaphrodite, including in the essence of his being the male and female principles, the generative and prolific powers of nature. This was the universal doctrine in all the ancient religions, and was very naturally developed in the symbol of the *phallus* and *cteis* among the Greeks, and in the corresponding one of the *lingam* and *yoni* among the Orientalists; from which symbols the masonic *point within a circle* is a legitimate derivation. They all taught that God, the Creator, was both male and female.

Now, this theory is undoubtedly unobjectionable on the score of orthodoxy, if we view it in the spiritual sense, in which its first propounders must necessarily have intended it to be presented to the mind, and not in the gross, sensual meaning in which it was subsequently received. For, taking the word *sex*, not in its ordinary and colloquial signification, as denoting the indication of a particular physical organization, but in that purely philosophical one which alone can be used in such a connection, and which simply signifies the mere manifestation of a power, it is not to be denied that the Supreme Being must possess in himself, and in himself alone, both a generative and a prolific power. This idea, which was so extensively prevalent among all the nations of antiquity,[133] has also been traced in the tetragrammaton, or name of Jehovah, with singular ingenuity, by Lanci; and, what is almost equally as interesting, he has, by this discovery, been enabled to demonstrate what was, in all probability, the true pronunciation of the word.

In giving the details of this philological discovery, I will endeavor to make it as comprehensible as it can be made to those who are not critically acquainted with the construction of the Hebrew language; those who are will at once appreciate its peculiar character, and will excuse the explanatory details, of course unnecessary to them.

The ineffable name, the tetragrammaton, the shem hamphorash,—for it is known by all these appellations,—consists of four letters, *yod*, *heh*, *vau*, and *heh*, forming the word יהוה. This word, of course, in accordance with the genius of the Hebrew language, is read, as we would say, backward, or from right to left, beginning with *yod* [י], and ending with *heh* [ה].

Of these letters, the first, *yod* [י], is equivalent to the English *i* pronounced as *e* in the word *machine*.

The second and fourth letter, *heh* [ה], is an aspirate, and has here the sound of the English *h*.

And the third letter, *vau* [ו], has the sound of open *o*.

Now, reading these four letters, י, or I, ה, or H, ו, or O, and ה, or H, as the Hebrew requires, from right to left, we have the word יהוה, יהוה, which is really as near to the pronunciation as we can well come, notwithstanding it forms neither of the seven ways in which the word is said to have been pronounced, at different times, by the patriarchs.[134]

But, thus pronounced, the word gives us no meaning, for there is no such word in Hebrew as *ihoh*; and, as all the Hebrew names were significative of something, it is but fair to conclude that this was not the original pronunciation, and that we must look for another which will give a meaning to the word. Now, Lanci proceeds to the discovery of this true pronunciation, as follows:—

In the Cabala, a hidden meaning is often deduced from a word by transposing or reversing its letters, and it was in this way that the Cabalists concealed many of their mysteries.

Now, to reverse a word in English is to read its letters from *right to left*, because our normal mode of reading is from *left to right*. But in Hebrew the contrary rule takes place, for there the normal mode of reading is from *right to left*; and therefore, to reverse the reading of a word, is to read it from *left to right*.

Lanci applied this cabalistic mode to the tetragrammaton, when he found that IH-OH, being read reversely, makes the word HO-HI.[135]

But in Hebrew, *ho* is the masculine pronoun, equivalent to the English *he*; and *hi* is the feminine pronoun, equivalent to *she*; and therefore the word HO-HI, literally translated, is equivalent to the English compound HE-SHE; that is to say, the Ineffable Name of God in Hebrew, being read cabalistically, includes within itself the male and female principle, the generative and prolific energy of creation; and here we have, again, the widely-spread symbolism of the phallus and the cteis, the lingam and the yoni, or their equivalent, the point within a circle, and another pregnant proof of the connection between Freemasonry and the ancient Mysteries.

And here, perhaps, we may begin to find some meaning for the hitherto incomprehensible passage in Genesis (i. 27): "So God created man *in his own image; in the image of God* created he him; *male and female* created he them." They could not have been "in the image" of IHOH, if they had not been "male and female."

The Cabalists have exhausted their ingenuity and imagination in speculations on this sacred name, and some of their fancies are really sufficiently interesting to repay an investigation. Sufficient, however, has been here said to account for the important position that it occupies in the masonic system, and to enable us to appreciate the symbols by which it has been represented.

The great reverence, or indeed the superstitious veneration, entertained by the ancients for the name of the Supreme Being, led them to express it rather in symbols or hieroglyphics than in any word at length.

We know, for instance, from the recent researches of the archaeologists, that in all the documents of the ancient Egyptians, written in the demotic or common character of the country, the names of the gods were invariably denoted by symbols; and I have already alluded to the different modes by which the Jews expressed the tetragrammaton. A similar practice prevailed among the other nations of antiquity. Freemasonry has adopted the same expedient, and the Grand Architect of the Universe, whom it is the usage, even in ordinary writing, to designate by the initials G.A.O.T.U., is accordingly presented to us in a variety of symbols, three of which particularly require attention. These are the letter *G*, the equilateral triangle, and the All-Seeing Eye.

Of the letter *G* I have already spoken. A letter of the English alphabet can scarcely be considered an appropriate symbol of an institution which dates its organization and refers its primitive history to a period long anterior to the origin of that language. Such a symbol is deficient in the two elements of antiquity and universality which should characterize every masonic symbol. There can, therefore, be no doubt that, in its present form, it is a corruption of the old Hebrew symbol, the letter *yod*, by which the sacred name was often expressed. This letter is the initial of the word *Jehovah*, or *Ihoh*, as I have already stated, and is constantly to be met with in Hebrew writings as the symbol or abbreviature of *Jehovah*, which word, it will be remembered, is never written at length. But because *G* is, in like manner, the initial of *God*, the equivalent of *Jehovah*, this letter has been incorrectly, and, I cannot refrain from again saying, most injudiciously, selected to supply, in modern lodges, the place of the Hebrew symbol.

Having, then, the same meaning and force as the Hebrew *yod*, the letter *G* must be considered, like its prototype, as the symbol of the life-giving and life-sustaining power of God, as manifested in the meaning of the word Jehovah, or Ihoh, the generative and prolific energy of the Creator.

The *All-Seeing Eye* is another, and a still more important, symbol of the same great Being. Both the Hebrews and the Egyptians appear to have derived its use from that natural inclination of figurative minds to select an organ as the symbol of the function which it is intended peculiarly to discharge. Thus the foot was often adopted as the symbol of swiftness, the arm of strength, and the hand of fidelity. On the same principle, the open eye was selected as the symbol of watchfulness, and the eye of God as the symbol of divine watchfulness and care of the universe. The use of the symbol in this sense is repeatedly to be found in the Hebrew writers. Thus the Psalmist says (Ps. xxxiv. 15), "The eyes of the Lord are upon the righteous, and his ears are open to their cry," which explains a subsequent passage (Ps. cxxi. 4), in which it is said, "Behold, he that keepeth Israel shall neither slumber nor sleep." [136]

On the same principle, the Egyptians represented Osiris, their chief deity, by the symbol of an open eye, and placed this hieroglyphic of him in all their temples. His symbolic name, on the monuments, was represented by the eye accompanying a throne, to which was sometimes added an abbreviated figure of the god, and sometimes what has been called a hatchet, but which, I consider, may as correctly be supposed to be a representation of a square.

The All-Seeing Eye may, then, be considered as a symbol of God manifested in his omnipresence — his guardian and preserving character — to which Solomon alludes in the Book of Proverbs (xv. 3), when he says, "The eyes of Jehovah are in every place, beholding (or as it might be more faithfully translated, watching) the evil and the good." It is a symbol of the Omnipresent Deity.

The *triangle* is another symbol which is entitled to our consideration. There is, in fact, no other symbol which is more various in its application or more generally diffused throughout the whole system of both the Spurious and the Pure Freemasonry.

The equilateral triangle appears to have been adopted by nearly all the nations of antiquity as a symbol of the Deity.

Among the Hebrews, it has already been stated that this figure, with a *yod* in the centre, was used to represent the tetragrammaton, or ineffable name of God.

The Egyptians considered the equilateral triangle as the most perfect of figures, and a representative of the great principle of animated existence, each of its sides referring to one of the three departments of creation—the animal, the vegetable, and the mineral.

The symbol of universal nature among the Egyptians was the right-angled triangle, of which the perpendicular side represented Osiris, or the male principle; the base, Isis, or the female principle; and the hypothenuse, their offspring, Horus, or the world emanating from the union of both principles.

All this, of course, is nothing more nor less than the phallus and cteis, or lingam and yoni, under a different form.

The symbol of the right-angled triangle was afterwards adopted by Pythagoras when he visited the banks of the Nile; and the discovery which he is said to have made in relation to the properties of this figure, but which he really learned from the Egyptian priests, is commemorated in Masonry by the introduction of the forty-seventh problem of Euclid's First Book among the symbols of the third degree. Here the same mystical application is supplied as in the Egyptian figure, namely, that the union of the male and female, or active and passive principles of nature, has produced the world. For the geometrical proposition being that the squares of the perpendicular and base are equal to the square of the hypothenuse, they may be said to produce it in the same way as Osiris and Isis are equal to, or produce, the world.

Thus the perpendicular—Osiris, or the active, male principle—being represented by a line whose measurement is 3; and the base—Isis, or the passive, female principle—by a line whose measurement is 4; then their union, or the addition of the squares of these numbers, will produce a square whose root will be the hypothenuse, or a line whose measurement must be 5. For the square of 3 is 9, and the square of 4 is 16, and the square of 5 is 25; but 9 added to 16 is equal to 25; and thus, out of the addition, or coming together, of the squares of the perpendicular and base, arises the square of the hypothenuse, just as, out of the coming together, in the Egyptian system, of the active and passive principles, arises, or is generated, the world.

In the mediaeval history of the Christian church, the great ignorance of the people, and their inclination to a sort of materialism, led them to abandon the symbolic representations of the Deity, and to depict the Father with the form and lineaments of an aged man, many of which irreverent paintings, as far back as the twelfth century, are to be found in the religious books and edifices of Europe.[137] But, after the period of the renaissance, a better spirit and a purer taste began to pervade the artists of the church, and thenceforth the Supreme Being was represented only by his name—the tetragrammaton—inscribed within an equilateral triangle, and placed within a circle of rays. Didron, in his invaluable work on Christian Iconography, gives one of these symbols, which was carved on wood in the seventeenth century, of which I annex a copy.

But even in the earliest ages, when the Deity was painted or sculptured as a personage, the nimbus, or glory, which surrounded the head of the Father, was often made to assume a triangular form. Didron says on this subject, "A nimbus, of a triangular form, is thus seen to be the exclusive attribute of the Deity, and most frequently restricted to the Father Eternal. The other persons of the trinity sometimes wear the triangle, but only in representations of the trinity, and because the Father is with them. Still, even then, beside the Father, who has a triangle, the Son and the Holy Ghost are often drawn with a circular nimbus only." [138]

The triangle has, in all ages and in all religions, been deemed a symbol of Deity.

The Egyptians, the Greeks, and the other nations of antiquity, considered this figure, with its three sides, as a symbol of the creative energy displayed in the active and passive, or male and female, principles, and their product, the world; the Christians referred it to their dogma of the trinity as a manifestation of the Supreme God; and the Jews and the primitive masons to the three periods of existence included in the signification of the tetragrammaton—the past, the present, and the future.

In the higher degrees of Masonry, the triangle is the most important of all symbols, and most generally assumes the name of the *Delta*, in allusion to the fourth letter of the Greek alphabet, which is of the same form and bears that appellation.

The Delta, or mystical triangle, is generally surrounded by a circle of rays, called a "glory." When this glory is distinct from the figure, and surrounds it in the form of a circle (as in the example just given from Didron), it is then an emblem of God's eternal glory. When, as is most usual in the masonic symbol, the rays emanate from the centre of the triangle, and, as it were, enshroud it in their brilliancy, it is symbolic of the Divine Light. The perverted ideas of the pagans referred these rays of light to their Sun-god and their Sabian worship.

But the true masonic idea of this glory is, that it symbolizes that Eternal Light of Wisdom which surrounds the Supreme Architect as with a sea of glory, and from him, as a common centre, emanates to the universe of his creation, and to which the prophet Ezekiel alludes in his eloquent description of Jehovah: "And I saw as the color of amber, as the appearance of fire round about within it, from the appearance of his loins even upward, and from his loins even downward, I saw, as it were, the appearance of fire, and it had brightness round about." (Chap. 1, ver. 27.)

Dante has also beautifully described this circumfused light of Deity:—

"There is in heaven a light whose goodly shine
Makes the Creator visible to all
Created, that in seeing him, alone
Have peace; and in a circle spreads so far,
That the circumference were too loose a zone
To girdle in the sun."

On a recapitulation, then, of the views that have been advanced in relation to these three symbols of the Deity which are to be found in the masonic system, we may say that each one expresses a different attribute.

The letter *G* is the symbol of the self-existent Jehovah.

The *All-Seeing Eye* is the symbol of the omnipresent God.

The *triangle*[139] is the symbol of the Supreme Architect of the Universe—the Creator; and when surrounded by rays of glory, it becomes a symbol of the Architect and Bestower of Light.

And now, after all, is there not in this whole prevalence of the name of God, in so many different symbols, throughout the masonic system, something more than a mere evidence of the religious proclivities of the institution? Is there not behind this a more profound symbolism, which constitutes, in fact, the very essence of Freemasonry? "The names of God," said a learned theologian at the beginning of this century, "were intended to communicate the knowledge of God himself. By these, men were enabled to receive some scanty ideas of his essential majesty, goodness, and power, and to know both whom we are to believe, and what we are to believe of him."

And this train of thought is eminently applicable to the admission of the name into the system of Masonry. With us, the name of God, however expressed, is a symbol of DIVINE TRUTH, which it should be the incessant labor of a Mason to seek.

XXV.

The Legends of Freemasonry.

The compound character of a speculative science and an operative art, which the masonic institution assumed at the building of King Solomon's temple, in consequence of the union, at that era, of the Pure Freemasonry of the Noachidae[140] with the Spurious Freemasonry of the Tyrian workmen, has supplied it with two distinct kinds of symbols—the *mythical*, or *legendary*, and the *material*; but these are so thoroughly united in object and design, that it is impossible to appreciate the one without an investigation of the other.

Thus, by way of illustration, it may be observed, that the temple itself has been adopted as a material symbol of the world (as I have already shown in former articles), while the legendary history of the fate of its builder is a mythical symbol of man's destiny in the world. Whatever is visible or tangible to the senses in our types and emblems—such as the implements of operative masonry, the furniture and ornaments of a lodge, or the ladder of seven steps—is a *material symbol*; while whatever derives its existence from tradition, and presents itself in the form of an allegory or legend, is a *mythical symbol*. Hiram the Builder, therefore, and all that refers to the legend of his connection with the temple, and his fate,—such as the sprig of acacia, the hill near Mount Moriah, and the lost word,—are to be considered as belonging to the class of mythical or legendary symbols.

And this division is not arbitrary, but depends on the nature of the types and the aspect in which they present themselves to our view.

Thus the sprig of acacia, although it is material, visible, and tangible, is, nevertheless, not to be treated as a material symbol; for, as it derives all its significance from its intimate connection with the legend of Hiram Abif, which is a mythical symbol, it cannot, without a violent and inexpedient disruption, be separated from the same class. For the same reason, the small hill near Mount Moriah, the search of the twelve Fellow Crafts, and the whole train of circumstances connected with the lost word, are to be viewed simply as mythical or legendary, and not as material symbols.

These legends of Freemasonry constitute a considerable and a very important part of its ritual. Without them, the most valuable portions of the masonic as a scientific system would cease to exist. It is, in fact, in the traditions and legends of Freemasonry, more, even, than in its material symbols, that we are to find the deep religious instruction which the institution is intended to inculcate. It must be remembered that Freemasonry has been defined to be "a system of morality, veiled in allegory and illustrated by symbols." Symbols, then, alone, do not constitute the whole of the system: allegory comes in for its share; and this allegory, which veils the divine truths of masonry, is presented to the neophyte in the various legends which have been traditionally preserved in the order.

The close connection, at least in design and method of execution, between the institution of Freemasonry and the ancient Mysteries, which were largely imbued with the mythical character of the ancient religions, led, undoubtedly, to the introduction of the same mythical character into the masonic system.

So general, indeed, was the diffusion of the myth or legend among the philosophical, historical, and religious systems of antiquity, that Heyne remarks, on this subject, that all the history and philosophy of the ancients proceeded from myths.[141]

The word *myth*, from the Greek μῦθος, *a story*, in its original acceptation, signified simply a statement or narrative of an event, without any necessary implication of truth or falsehood; but, as the word is now used, it conveys the idea of a personal narrative of remote date, which, although not necessarily untrue, is certified only by the internal evidence of the tradition itself.[142]

Creuzer, in his "Symbolik," says that myths and symbols were derived, on the one hand, from the helpless condition and the poor and scanty beginnings of religious knowledge among the ancient peoples, and on the other, from the benevolent designs of the priests educated in the East, or of Eastern origin, to form them to a purer and higher knowledge.

But the observations of that profoundly philosophical historian, Mr. Grote, give so correct a view of the probable origin of this universality of the mythical element in all the ancient religions, and are, withal, so appropriate to the subject of masonic legends which I am now about to discuss, that I cannot justly refrain from a liberal quotation of his remarks.

"The allegorical interpretation of the myths," he says, "has been, by several learned investigators, especially by Creuzer, connected with the hypothesis of an ancient and highly-instructed body of priests, having their origin either in Egypt or the East, and communicating to the rude and barbarous Greeks religious, physical, and historical knowledge, under the veil of symbols. At a time (we are told) when language was yet in its infancy, visible symbols were the most vivid means of acting upon the minds of ignorant hearers. The next step was to pass to symbolical language and expressions; for a plain and literal exposition, even if understood at all, would at least have been listened to with indifference, as not corresponding with any mental demand. In such allegorizing way, then, the early priests set forth their doctrines respecting God, nature, and humanity,—a refined monotheism and theological philosophy,—and to this purpose the earliest myths were turned. But another class of myths, more popular and more captivating, grew up under the hands of the poets—myths purely epical, and descriptive of real or supposed past events. The allegorical myths, being taken up by the poets, insensibly became confounded in the same category with the purely narrative myths; the matter symbolized was no longer thought of, while the symbolizing words came to be construed in their own literal meaning, and the basis of the early allegory, thus lost among the general public, was only preserved as a secret among various religious fraternities, composed of members allied together by initiation in certain mystical ceremonies, and administered by hereditary families of presiding priests.

"In the Orphic and Bacchic sects, in the Eleusinian and Samothracian Mysteries, was thus treasured up the secret doctrine of the old theological and philosophical myths, which had once constituted the primitive legendary stock of Greece in the hands of the original priesthood and in the ages anterior to Homer. Persons who had gone through the preliminary ceremonies of initiation were permitted at length to hear, though under strict obligation of secrecy, this ancient religion and cosmogonic doctrine, revealing the destination of man and the certainty of posthumous rewards and punishments, all disengaged from the corruptions of poets, as well as from the symbols and allegories under which they still remained buried in the eyes of the vulgar. The Mysteries of Greece were thus traced up to the earliest ages, and represented as the only faithful depositaries of that purer theology and physics which had been originally communicated, though under the unavoidable inconvenience of a symbolical expression, by an enlightened priesthood, coming from abroad, to the then rude barbarians of the country." [143]

In this long but interesting extract we find not only a philosophical account of the origin and design of the ancient myths, but a fair synopsis of all that can be taught in relation to the symbolical construction of Freemasonry, as one of the depositaries of a mythical theology.

The myths of Masonry, at first perhaps nothing more than the simple traditions of the Pure Freemasonry of the antediluvian system, having been corrupted and misunderstood in the separation of the races, were again purified, and adapted to the inculcation of truth, at first by the disciples of the Spurious Freemasonry, and then, more fully and perfectly, in the development of that system which we now practise. And if there be any leaven of error still remaining in the interpretation of our masonic myths, we must seek to disengage them from the corruptions with which they have been invested by ignorance and by misinterpretation. We must give to them their true significance, and trace them back to those ancient doctrines and faith whence the ideas which they are intended to embody were derived.

The myths or legends which present themselves to our attention in the course of a complete study of the symbolic system of Freemasonry may be considered as divided into three classes:—

1. The historical myth.
2. The philosophical myth.
3. The mythical history.

And these three classes may be defined as follows:—

1. The myth may be engaged in the transmission of a narrative of early deeds and events, having a foundation in truth, which truth, however, has been greatly distorted and perverted by the omission or introduction of circumstances and personages, and then it constitutes the *historical myth*.

2. Or it may have been invented and adopted as the medium of enunciating a particular thought, or of inculcating a certain doctrine, when it becomes a *philosophical myth*.

3. Or, lastly, the truthful elements of actual history may greatly predominate over the fictitious and invented materials of the myth, and the narrative may be, in the main, made up of facts, with a slight coloring of imagination, when it forms a *mythical history*.[144]

These form the three divisions of the legend or myth (for I am not disposed, on the present occasion, like some of the German mythological writers, to make a distinction between the two words[145]); and to one of these three divisions we must appropriate every legend which belongs to the mythical symbolism of Freemasonry.

These masonic myths partake, in their general character, of the nature of the myths which constituted the foundation of the ancient religions, as they have just been described in the language of Mr. Grote. Of these latter myths, Müller[146] says that "their source is to be found, for the most part, in oral tradition," and that the real and the ideal—that is to say, the facts of history and the inventions of imagination—concurred, by their union and reciprocal fusion, in producing the myth.

Those are the very principles that govern the construction of the masonic myths or legends. These, too, owe their existence entirely to oral tradition, and are made up, as I have just observed, of a due admixture of the real and the ideal—the true and the false—the facts of history and the inventions of allegory.

Dr. Oliver remarks that "the first series of historical facts, after the fall of man, must necessarily have been traditional, and transmitted from father to son by oral communication." [147] The same system, adopted in all the Mysteries, has been continued in the masonic institution; and all the esoteric instructions contained in the legends of Freemasonry are forbidden to be written, and can be communicated only in the oral intercourse of Freemasons with each other.[148]

De Wette, in his Criticism on the Mosaic History, lays down the test by which a myth is to be distinguished from a strictly historical narrative, as follows, namely: that the myth must owe its origin to the intention of the inventor not to satisfy the natural thirst for historical truth by a simple narration of facts, but rather to delight or touch the feelings, or to illustrate some philosophical or religious truth.

This definition precisely fits the character of the myths of Masonry. Take, for instance, the legend of the master's degree, or the myth of Hiram Abif. As "a simple narration of facts," it is of no great value—certainly not of value commensurate with the labor that has been engaged in its transmission. Its invention—by which is meant, not the invention or imagination of all the incidents of which it is composed, for there are abundant materials of the true and real in its details, but its invention or composition in the form of a myth by the addition of some features, the suppression of others, and the general arrangement of the whole—was not intended to add a single item to the great mass of history, but altogether, as De Wette says, "to illustrate a philosophical or religious truth," which truth, it is hardly necessary for me to say, is the doctrine of the immortality of the soul.

It must be evident, from all that has been said respecting the analogy in origin and design between the masonic and the ancient religious myths, that no one acquainted with the true science of this subject can, for a moment, contend that all the legends and traditions of the order are, to the very letter, historical facts. All that can be claimed for them is, that in some there is simply a substratum of history, the edifice constructed on this foundation being purely inventive, to serve us a medium for inculcating some religious truth; in others, nothing more than an idea to which the legend or myth is indebted for its existence, and of which it is, as a symbol, the exponent; and in others, again, a great deal of truthful narrative, more or less intermixed with fiction, but the historical always predominating.

Thus there is a legend, contained in some of our old records, which states that Euclid was a distinguished Mason, and that he introduced Masonry among the Egyptians.[149] Now, it is not at all necessary to the orthodoxy of a Mason's creed that he should literally believe that Euclid, the great geometrician, was really a Freemason, and that the ancient Egyptians were indebted to him for the establishment of the institution among them. Indeed, the palpable anachronism in the legend which makes Euclid the contemporary of Abraham necessarily prohibits any such belief, and shows that the whole story is a sheer invention. The intelligent Mason, however, will not wholly reject the legend, as ridiculous or absurd; but, with a due sense of the nature and design of our system of symbolism, will rather accept it as what, in the classification laid down on a preceding page, would be called "a philosophical myth"—an ingenious method of conveying, symbolically, a masonic truth.

Euclid is here very appropriately used as a type of geometry, that science of which he was so eminent a teacher, and the myth or legend then symbolizes the fact that there was in Egypt a close connection between that science and the great moral and religious system, which was among the Egyptians, as well as other ancient nations, what Freemasonry is in the present day—a secret institution, established for the inculcation of the same principles, and inculcating them in the same symbolic manner. So interpreted, this legend corresponds to all the developments of Egyptian history, which teach us how close a connection existed in that country between the religious and scientific systems. Thus Kenrick tells us, that "when we read of foreigners [in Egypt] being obliged to submit to painful and tedious ceremonies of initiation, it was not that they might learn the secret meaning of the rites of Osiris or Isis, but that they might partake of the knowledge of astronomy, physic, geometry, and theology." [150]

Another illustration will be found in the myth or legend of the *Winding Stairs*, by which the Fellow Crafts are said to have ascended to the middle chamber to receive their wages. Now, this myth, taken in its literal sense, is, in all its parts, opposed to history and probability. As a myth, it finds its origin in the fact that there was a place in the temple called the "Middle Chamber," and that there were "winding stairs" by which it was reached; for we read, in the First Book of Kings, that "they went up with winding stairs into the middle chamber." [151] But we have no historical evidence that the stairs were of the construction, or that the chamber was used for the purpose, indicated in the mythical narrative, as it is set forth in the ritual of the second degree. The whole legend is, in fact, an historical myth, in which the mystic number of the steps, the process of passing to the chamber, and the wages there received, are inventions added to or ingrafted on the fundamental history contained in the sixth chapter of Kings, to inculcate important symbolic instruction relative to the principles of the order. These lessons might, it is true, have been inculcated in a dry, didactic form; but the allegorical and mythical method adopted tends to make a stronger and deeper impression on the mind, and at the same time serves more closely to connect the institution of Masonry with the ancient temple.

Again: the myth which traces the origin of the institution of Freemasonry to the beginning of the world, making its commencement coeval with the creation,—a myth which is, even at this day, ignorantly interpreted, by some, as an historical fact, and the reference to which is still preserved in the date of "anno lucis," which is affixed to all masonic documents,—is but a philosophical myth, symbolizing the idea which analogically connects the creation of physical light in the universe with the birth of masonic or spiritual and intellectual light in the candidate. The one is the type of the other. When, therefore, Preston says that "from the commencement of the world we may trace the foundation of Masonry," and when he goes on to assert that "ever since symmetry began, and harmony displayed her charms, our order has had a being," we are not to suppose that Preston intended to teach that a masonic lodge was held in the Garden of Eden. Such a supposition would justly subject us to the ridicule of every intelligent person. The only idea intended to be conveyed is this: that the principles of Freemasonry, which, indeed, are entirely independent of any special organization which it may have as a society, are coeval with the existence of the world; that when God said, "Let there be light," the material light thus produced was an antitype of that spiritual light that must burst upon the mind of every candidate when his intellectual world, theretofore "without form and void," becomes adorned and peopled with the living thoughts and divine principles which constitute the great system of Speculative Masonry, and when the spirit of the institution, brooding over the vast deep of his mental chaos, shall, from intellectual darkness, bring forth intellectual light.[152]

In the legends of the Master's degree and of the Royal Arch there is a commingling of the historical myth and the mythical history, so that profound judgment is often required to discriminate these differing elements. As, for example, the legend of the third degree is, in some of its details, undoubtedly mythical—in others, just as undoubtedly historical. The difficulty, however, of separating the one from the other, and of distinguishing the fact from the fiction, has necessarily produced a difference of opinion on the subject among masonic writers. Hutchinson, and, after him, Oliver, think the whole legend an allegory or philosophical myth. I am inclined, with Anderson and the earlier writers, to suppose it a mythical history. In the Royal Arch degree, the legend of the rebuilding of the temple is clearly historical; but there are so many accompanying circumstances, which are uncertified, except by oral tradition, as to give to the entire narrative the appearance of a mythical history. The particular legend of the *three weary sojourners* is undoubtedly a myth, and perhaps merely a philosophical one, or the enunciation of an idea—namely, the reward of successful perseverance, through all dangers, in the search for divine truth.

"To form symbols and to interpret symbols," says the learned Creuzer, "were the main occupation of the ancient priesthood." Upon the studious Mason the same task of interpretation devolves. He who desires properly to appreciate the profound wisdom of the institution of which he is the disciple, must not be content, with uninquiring credulity, to accept all the traditions that are imparted to him as veritable histories; nor yet, with unphilosophic incredulity, to reject them in a mass, as fabulous inventions. In these extremes there is equal error. "The myth," says Hermann, "is the representation of an idea." It is for that idea that the student must search in the myths of Masonry. Beneath every one of them there is something richer and more spiritual than the mere narrative.[153] This spiritual essence he must learn to extract from the ore in which, like a precious metal, it lies imbedded. It is this that constitutes the true value of Freemasonry. Without its symbols, and its myths or legends, and the ideas and conceptions which lie at the bottom of them, the time, the labor, and the expense incurred in perpetuating the institution, would be thrown away. Without them, it would be a "vain and empty show." Its grips and signs are worth nothing, except for social purposes, as mere means of recognition. So, too, would be its words, were it not that they are, for the most part, symbolic. Its social habits and its charities are but incidental points in its constitution—of themselves good, it is true, but capable of being attained in a simpler way. Its true value, as a science, consists in its symbolism—in the great lessons of divine truth which it teaches, and in the admirable manner in which it accomplishes that teaching. Every one, therefore, who desires to be a skilful Mason, must not suppose that the task is accomplished by a perfect knowledge of the mere phraseology of the ritual, by a readiness in opening and closing a lodge, nor by an off-hand capacity to confer degrees. All these are good in their places, but without the internal meaning they are but mere child's play. He must study the myths, the traditions, and the symbols of the order, and learn their true interpretation; for this alone constitutes the science and the philosophy—the end, aim, and design of Speculative Masonry.

XXVI.

The Legend of the Winding Stairs.

Before proceeding to the examination of those more important mythical legends which appropriately belong to the Master's degree, it will not, I think, be unpleasing or uninstructive to consider the only one which is attached to the Fellow Craft's degree—that, namely, which refers to the allegorical ascent of the Winding Stairs to the Middle Chamber, and the symbolic payment of the workmen's wages.

Although the legend of the Winding Stairs forms an important tradition of Ancient Craft Masonry, the only allusion to it in Scripture is to be found in a single verse in the sixth chapter of the First Book of Kings, and is in these words: "The door for the middle chamber was in the right side of the house; and they went up with winding stairs into the middle chamber, and out of the middle into the third." Out of this slender material has been constructed an allegory, which, if properly considered in its symbolical relations, will be found to be of surpassing beauty. But it is only as a symbol that we can regard this whole tradition; for the historical facts and the architectural details alike forbid us for a moment to suppose that the legend, as it is rehearsed in the second degree of Masonry, is anything more than a magnificent philosophical myth.

Let us inquire into the true design of this legend, and learn the lesson of symbolism which it is intended to teach.

In the investigation of the true meaning of every masonic symbol and allegory, we must be governed by the single principle that the whole design of Freemasonry as a speculative science is the investigation of divine truth. To this great object everything is subsidiary. The Mason is, from the moment of his initiation as an Entered Apprentice, to the time at which he receives the full fruition of masonic light, an investigator—a laborer in the quarry and the temple—whose reward is to be Truth. All the ceremonies and traditions of the order tend to this ultimate design. Is there light to be asked for? It is the intellectual light of wisdom and truth. Is there a word to be sought? That word is the symbol of truth. Is there a loss of something that had been promised? That loss is typical of the failure of man, in the infirmity of his nature, to discover divine truth. Is there a substitute to be appointed for that loss? It is an allegory which teaches us that in this world man can only approximate to the full conception of truth.

Hence there is in Speculative Masonry always a progress, symbolized by its peculiar ceremonies of initiation. There is an advancement from a lower to a higher state—from darkness to light—from death to life—from error to truth. The candidate is always ascending; he is never stationary; he never goes back, but each step he takes brings him to some new mental illumination—to the knowledge of some more elevated doctrine. The teaching of the Divine Master is, in respect to this continual progress, the teaching of Masonry—"No man having put his hand to the plough, and looking back, is fit for the kingdom of heaven." And similar to this is the precept of Pythagoras: "When travelling, turn not back, for if you do the Furies will accompany you."

Now, this principle of masonic symbolism is apparent in many places in each of the degrees. In that of the Entered Apprentice we find it developed in the theological ladder, which, resting on earth, leans its top upon heaven, thus inculcating the idea of an ascent from a lower to a higher sphere, as the object of masonic labor. In the Master's degree we find it exhibited in its most religious form, in the restoration from death to life—in the change from the obscurity of the grave to the holy of holies of the Divine Presence. In all the degrees we find it presented in the ceremony of circumambulation, in which there is a gradual inquisition, and a passage from an inferior to a superior officer. And lastly, the same symbolic idea is conveyed in the Fellow Craft's degree in the legend of the Winding Stairs.

In an investigation of the symbolism of the Winding Stairs we shall be directed to the true explanation by a reference to their origin, their number, the objects which they recall, and their termination, but above all by a consideration of the great design which an ascent upon them was intended to accomplish.

The steps of this Winding Staircase commenced, we are informed, at the porch of the temple; that is to say, at its very entrance. But nothing is more undoubted in the science of masonic symbolism than that the temple was the representative of the world purified by the Shekinah, or the Divine Presence. The world of the profane is without the temple; the world of the initiated is within its sacred walls. Hence to enter the temple, to pass within the porch, to be made a Mason, and to be born into the world of masonic light, are all synonymous and convertible terms. Here, then, the symbolism of the Winding Stairs begins.

The Apprentice, having entered within the porch of the temple, has begun his masonic life. But the first degree in Masonry, like the lesser Mysteries of the ancient systems of initiation, is only a preparation and purification for something higher. The Entered Apprentice is the child in Masonry. The lessons which he receives are simply intended to cleanse the heart and prepare the recipient for that mental illumination which is to be given in the succeeding degrees.

As a Fellow Craft, he has advanced another step, and as the degree is emblematic of youth, so it is here that the intellectual education of the candidate begins. And therefore, here, at the very spot which separates the Porch from the Sanctuary, where childhood ends and manhood begins, he finds stretching out before him a winding stair which invites him, as it were, to ascend, and which, as the symbol of discipline and instruction, teaches him that here must commence his masonic labor—here he must enter upon those glorious though difficult researches, the end of which is to be the possession of divine truth. The Winding Stairs begin after the candidate has passed within the Porch and between the pillars of Strength and Establishment, as a significant symbol to teach him that as soon as he has passed beyond the years of irrational childhood, and commenced his entrance upon manly life, the laborious task of self-improvement is the first duty that is placed before him. He cannot stand still, if he would be worthy of his vocation; his destiny as an immortal being requires him to ascend, step by step, until he has reached the summit, where the treasures of knowledge await him.

The number of these steps in all the systems has been odd. Vitruvius remarks—and the coincidence is at least curious—that the ancient temples were always ascended by an odd number of steps; and he assigns as the reason, that, commencing with the right foot at the bottom, the worshipper would find the same foot foremost when he entered the temple, which was considered as a fortunate omen. But the fact is, that the symbolism of numbers was borrowed by the Masons from Pythagoras, in whose system of philosophy it plays an important part, and in which odd numbers were considered as more perfect than even ones. Hence, throughout the masonic system we find a predominance of odd numbers; and while three, five, seven, nine, fifteen, and twenty-seven, are all-important symbols, we seldom find a reference to two, four, six, eight, or ten. The odd number of the stairs was therefore intended to symbolize the idea of perfection, to which it was the object of the aspirant to attain.

As to the particular number of the stairs, this has varied at different periods. Tracing-boards of the last century have been found, in which only *five* steps are delineated, and others in which they amount to *seven*. The Prestonian lectures, used in England in the beginning of this century, gave the whole number as thirty-eight, dividing them into series of one, three, five, seven, nine, and eleven. The error of making an even number, which was a violation of the Pythagorean principle of odd numbers as the symbol of perfection, was corrected in the Hemming lectures, adopted at the union of the two Grand Lodges of England, by striking out the eleven, which was also objectionable as receiving a sectarian explanation. In this country the number was still further reduced to *fifteen*, divided into three series of *three, five*, and *seven*. I shall adopt this American division in explaining the symbolism, although, after all, the particular number of the steps, or the peculiar method of their division into series, will not in any way affect the general symbolism of the whole legend.

The candidate, then, in the second degree of Masonry, represents a man starting forth on the journey of life, with the great task before him of self-improvement. For the faithful performance of this task, a reward is promised, which reward consists in the development of all his intellectual faculties, the moral and spiritual elevation of his character, and the acquisition of truth and knowledge. Now, the attainment of this moral and intellectual condition supposes an elevation of character, an ascent from a lower to a higher life, and a passage of toil and difficulty, through rudimentary instruction, to the full fruition of wisdom. This is therefore beautifully symbolized by the Winding Stairs; at whose foot the aspirant stands ready to climb the toilsome steep, while at its top is placed "that hieroglyphic bright which none but Craftsmen ever saw," as the emblem of divine truth. And hence a distinguished writer has said that "these steps, like all the masonic symbols, are illustrative of discipline and doctrine, as well as of natural, mathematical, and metaphysical science, and open to us an extensive range of moral and speculative inquiry."

The candidate, incited by the love of virtue and the desire of knowledge, and withal eager for the reward of truth which is set before him, begins at once the toilsome ascent. At each division he pauses to gather instruction from the symbolism which these divisions present to his attention.

At the first pause which he makes he is instructed in the peculiar organization of the order of which he has become a disciple. But the information here given, if taken in its naked, literal sense, is barren, and unworthy of his labor. The rank of the officers who govern, and the names of the degrees which constitute the institution, can give him no knowledge which he has not before possessed. We must look therefore to the symbolic meaning of these allusions for any value which may be attached to this part of the ceremony.

The reference to the organization of the masonic institution is intended to remind the aspirant of the union of men in society, and the development of the social state out of the state of nature. He is thus reminded, in the very outset of his journey, of the blessings which arise from civilization, and of the fruits of virtue and knowledge which are derived from that condition. Masonry itself is the result of civilization; while, in grateful return, it has been one of the most important means of extending that condition of mankind.

All the monuments of antiquity that the ravages of time have left, combine to prove that man had no sooner emerged from the savage into the social state, than he commenced the organization of religious mysteries, and the separation, by a sort of divine instinct, of the sacred from the profane. Then came the invention of architecture as a means of providing convenient dwellings and necessary shelter from the inclemencies and vicissitudes of the seasons, with all the mechanical arts connected with it; and lastly, geometry, as a necessary science to enable the cultivators of land to measure and designate the limits of their possessions. All these are claimed as peculiar characteristics of Speculative Masonry, which may be considered as the type of civilization, the former bearing the same relation to the profane world as the latter does to the savage state. Hence we at once see the fitness of the symbolism which commences the aspirant's upward progress in the cultivation of knowledge and the search after truth, by recalling to his mind the condition of civilization and the social union of mankind as necessary preparations for the attainment of these objects. In the allusions to the officers of a lodge, and the degrees of Masonry as explanatory of the organization of our own society, we clothe in our symbolic language the history of the organization of society.

Advancing in his progress, the candidate is invited to contemplate another series of instructions. The human senses, as the appropriate channels through which we receive all our ideas of perception, and which, therefore, constitute the most important sources of our knowledge, are here referred to as a symbol of intellectual cultivation. Architecture, as the most important of the arts which conduce to the comfort of mankind, is also alluded to here, not simply because it is so closely connected with the operative institution of Masonry, but also as the type of all the other useful arts. In his second pause, in the ascent of the Winding Stairs, the aspirant is therefore reminded of the necessity of cultivating practical knowledge.

So far, then, the instructions he has received relate to his own condition in society as a member of the great social compact, and to his means of becoming, by a knowledge of the arts of practical life, a necessary and useful member of that society.

But his motto will be, "Excelsior." Still must he go onward and forward. The stair is still before him; its summit is not yet reached, and still further treasures of wisdom are to be sought for, or the reward will not be gained, nor the *middle chamber*, the abiding place of truth, be reached.

In his third pause, he therefore arrives at that point in which the whole circle of human science is to be explained. Symbols, we know, are in themselves arbitrary and of conventional signification, and the complete circle of human science might have been as well symbolized by any other sign or series of doctrines as by the seven liberal arts and sciences. But Masonry is an institution of the olden time; and this selection of the liberal arts and sciences as a symbol of the completion of human learning is one of the most pregnant evidences that we have of its antiquity.

In the seventh century, and for a long time afterwards, the circle of instruction to which all the learning of the most eminent schools and most distinguished philosophers was confined, was limited to what were then called the liberal arts and sciences, and consisted of two branches, the *trivium* and the *quadrivium*.[154] The *trivium* included grammar, rhetoric, and logic; the *quadrivium* comprehended arithmetic, geometry, music, and astronomy.

"These seven heads," says Enfield, "were supposed to include universal knowledge. He who was master of these was thought to have no need of a preceptor to explain any books or to solve any questions which lay within the compass of human reason, the knowledge of the *trivium* having furnished him with the key to all language, and that of the *quadrivium* having opened to him the secret laws of nature." [155]

At a period, says the same writer, when few were instructed in the *trivium*, and very few studied the *quadrivium*, to be master of both was sufficient to complete the character of a philosopher. The propriety, therefore, of adopting the seven liberal arts and sciences as a symbol of the completion of human learning is apparent. The candidate, having reached this point, is now supposed to have accomplished the task upon which he had entered—he has reached the last step, and is now ready to receive the full fruition of human learning.

So far, then, we are able to comprehend the true symbolism of the Winding Stairs. They represent the progress of an inquiring mind with the toils and labors of intellectual cultivation and study, and the preparatory acquisition of all human science, as a preliminary step to the attainment of divine truth, which it must be remembered is always symbolized in Masonry by the WORD.

Here let me again allude to the symbolism of numbers, which is for the first time presented to the consideration of the masonic student in the legend of the Winding Stairs. The theory of numbers as the symbols of certain qualities was originally borrowed by the Masons from the school of Pythagoras. It will be impossible, however, to develop this doctrine, in its entire extent, on the present occasion, for the numeral symbolism of Masonry would itself constitute materials for an ample essay. It will be sufficient to advert to the fact that the total number of the steps, amounting in all to *fifteen*, in the American system, is a significant symbol. For *fifteen* was a sacred number among the Orientals, because the letters of the holy name JAH, יה, were, in their numerical value, equivalent to fifteen; and hence a figure in which the nine digits were so disposed as to make fifteen either way when added together perpendicularly, horizontally, or diagonally, constituted one of their most sacred talismans.[156] The fifteen steps in the Winding Stairs are therefore symbolic of the name of God.

But we are not yet done. It will be remembered that a reward was promised for all this toilsome ascent of the Winding Stairs. Now, what are the wages of a Speculative Mason? Not money, nor corn, nor wine, nor oil. All these are but symbols. His wages are TRUTH, or that approximation to it which will be most appropriate to the degree into which he has been initiated. It is one of the most beautiful, but at the same time most abstruse, doctrines of the science of masonic symbolism, that the Mason is ever to be in search of truth, but is never to find it. This divine truth, the object of all his labors, is symbolized by the WORD, for which we all know he can only obtain a *substitute*; and this is intended to teach the humiliating but necessary lesson that the knowledge of the nature of God and of man's relation to him, which knowledge constitutes divine truth, can never be acquired in this life. It is only when the portals of the grave open to us, and give us an entrance into a more perfect life, that this knowledge is to be attained. "Happy is the man," says the father of lyric poetry, "who descends beneath the hollow earth, having beheld these mysteries; he knows the end, he knows the origin of life."

The Middle Chamber is therefore symbolic of this life, where the symbol only of the word can be given, where the truth is to be reached by approximation only, and yet where we are to learn that that truth will consist in a perfect knowledge of the G.A.O.T.U. This is the reward of the inquiring Mason; in this consist the wages of a Fellow Craft; he is directed to the truth, but must travel farther and ascend still higher to attain it.

It is, then, as a symbol, and a symbol only, that we must study this beautiful legend of the Winding Stairs. If we attempt to adopt it as an historical fact, the absurdity of its details stares us in the face, and wise men will wonder at our credulity. Its inventors had no desire thus to impose upon our folly; but offering it to us as a great philosophical myth, they did not for a moment suppose that we would pass over its sublime moral teachings to accept the allegory as an historical narrative, without meaning, and wholly irreconcilable with the records of Scripture, and opposed by all the principles of probability. To suppose that eighty thousand craftsmen were weekly paid in the narrow precincts of the temple chambers, is simply to suppose an absurdity. But to believe that all this pictorial representation of an ascent by a Winding Staircase to the place where the wages of labor were to be received, was an allegory to teach us the ascent of the mind from ignorance, through all the toils of study and the difficulties of obtaining knowledge, receiving here a little and there a little, adding something to the stock of our ideas at each step, until, in the middle chamber of life,—in the full fruition of manhood,—the reward is attained, and the purified and elevated intellect is invested with the reward in the direction how to seek God and God's truth,—to believe this is to believe and to know the true design of Speculative Masonry, the only design which makes it worthy of a good or a wise man's study.

Its historical details are barren, but its symbols and allegories are fertile with instruction.

XXVII.

The Legend of the Third Degree.

The most important and significant of the legendary symbols of Freemasonry is, undoubtedly, that which relates to the fate of Hiram Abif, commonly called, "by way of excellence," the Legend of the Third Degree.

The first written record that I have been able to find of this legend is contained in the second edition of Anderson's Constitutions, published in 1738, and is in these words:—

"It (the temple) was finished in the short space of seven years and six months, to the amazement of all the world; when the cape-stone was celebrated by the fraternity with great joy. But their joy was soon interrupted by the sudden death of their dear master, Hiram Abif, whom they decently interred, in the lodge near the temple, according to ancient dusage." [157]

In the next edition of the same work, published in 1756, a few additional circumstances are related, such as the participation of King Solomon in the general grief, and the fact that the king of Israel "ordered his obsequies to be conducted with great solemnity and decency." [158] With these exceptions, and the citations of the same passages, made by subsequent authors, the narrative has always remained unwritten, and descended, from age to age, through the means of oral tradition.

The legend has been considered of so much importance that it has been preserved in the symbolism of every masonic rite. No matter what modifications or alterations the general system may have undergone,—no matter how much the ingenuity or the imagination of the founders of rites may have perverted or corrupted other symbols, abolishing the old and substituting new ones,—the legend of the Temple Builder has ever been left untouched, to present itself in all the integrity of its ancient mythical form.

What, then, is the signification of this symbol, so important and so extensively diffused? What interpretation can we give to it that will account for its universal adoption? How is it that it has thus become so intimately interwoven with Freemasonry as to make, to all appearances, a part of its very essence, and to have been always deemed inseparable from it?

To answer these questions, satisfactorily, it is necessary to trace, in a brief investigation, the remote origin of the institution of Freemasonry, and its connection with the ancient systems of initiation.

It was, then, the great object of all the rites and mysteries which constituted the "Spurious Freemasonry" of antiquity to teach the consoling doctrine of the immortality of the soul.[159] This dogma, shining as an almost solitary beacon-light in the surrounding gloom of pagan darkness, had undoubtedly been received from that ancient people or priesthood[160] what has been called the system of "Pure Freemasonry," and among whom it probably existed only in the form of an abstract proposition or a simple and unembellished tradition. But in the more sensual minds of the pagan philosophers and mystics, the idea, when presented to the initiates in their Mysteries, was always conveyed in the form of a scenic representation.[161] The influence, too, of the early Sabian worship of the sun and heavenly bodies, in which the solar orb was adored, on its resurrection, each morning, from the apparent death of its evening setting, caused this rising sun to be adopted in the more ancient Mysteries as a symbol of the regeneration of the soul.

Thus in the Egyptian Mysteries we find a representation of the death and subsequent regeneration of Osiris; in the Phœnician, of Adonis; in the Syrian, of Dionysus; in all of which the scenic apparatus of initiation was intended to indoctrinate the candidate into the dogma of a future life.

It will be sufficient here to refer simply to the fact, that through the instrumentality of the Tyrian workmen at the temple of King Solomon, the spurious and pure branches of the masonic system were united at Jerusalem, and that the same method of scenic representation was adopted by the latter from the former, and the narrative of the temple builder substituted for that of Dionysus, which was the myth peculiar to the mysteries practised by the Tyrian workmen.

The idea, therefore, proposed to be communicated in the myth of the ancient Mysteries was the same as that which is now conveyed in the masonic legend of the Third Degree.

Hence, then, Hiram Abif is, in the masonic system, the symbol of human nature, as developed in the life here and the life to come; and so, while the temple was, as I have heretofore shown, the visible symbol of the world, its builder became the mythical symbol of man, the dweller and worker in that world.

Now, is not this symbolism evident to every reflective mind?

Man, setting forth on the voyage of life, with faculties and powers fitting him for the due exercise of the high duties to whose performance he has been called, holds, if he be "a curious and cunning workman," [162] skilled in all moral and intellectual purposes (and it is only of such men that the temple builder can be the symbol), within the grasp of his attainment the knowledge of all that divine truth imparted to him as the heirloom of his race—that race to whom it has been granted to look, with exalted countenance, on high;[163] which divine truth is symbolized by the WORD.

Thus provided with the word of life, he occupies his time in the construction of a spiritual temple, and travels onward in the faithful discharge of all his duties, laying down his designs upon the trestle-board of the future and invoking the assistance and direction of God.

But is his path always over flowery meads and through pleasant groves? Is there no hidden foe to obstruct his progress? Is all before him clear and calm, with joyous sunshine and refreshing zephyrs? Alas! not so. "Man is born to trouble, as the sparks fly upward." At every "gate of life"—as the Orientalists have beautifully called the different ages—he is beset by peril. Temptations allure his youth, misfortunes darken the pathway of his manhood, and his old age is encumbered with infirmity and disease. But clothed in the armor of virtue he may resist the temptation; he may cast misfortunes aside, and rise triumphantly above them; but to the last, the direst, the most inexorable foe of his race, he must eventually yield; and stricken down by death, he sinks prostrate into the grave, *and is buried in the rubbish* of his sin and human frailty.

Here, then, in Masonry, is what was called the *aphanism*[164] in the ancient Mysteries. The bitter but necessary lesson of death has been imparted. The living soul, with the lifeless body which encased it, has disappeared, and *can nowhere be found*. All is darkness—confusion— despair. Divine truth—the WORD—for a time is lost, and the Master Mason may now say, in the language of Hutchinson, "I prepare my sepulchre. I make my grave in the pollution of the earth. I am under the shadow of death."

But if the mythic symbolism ended here, with this lesson of death, then were the lesson incomplete. That teaching would be vain and idle—nay, more, it would be corrupt and pernicious—which should stop short of the conscious and innate instinct for another existence. And hence the succeeding portions of the legend are intended to convey the sublime symbolism of a resurrection from the grave and a new birth into a future life. The discovery of the body, which, in the initiations of the ancient Mysteries, was called the *euresis*,[165] and its removal, from the polluted grave into which it had been cast, to an honored and sacred place within the precincts of the temple, are all profoundly and beautifully symbolic of that great truth, the discovery of which was the object of all the ancient initiations, as it is almost the whole design of Freemasonry, namely, that when man shall have passed the gates of life and have yielded to the inexorable fiat of death, he shall then (not in the pictured ritual of an earthly lodge, but in the realities of that eternal one, of which the former is but an antitype) be raised, at the omnific word of the Grand Master of the Universe, from time to eternity; from the tomb of corruption to the chambers of hope; from the darkness of death to the celestial beams of life; and that his disembodied spirit shall be conveyed as near to the holy of holies of the divine presence as humanity can ever approach to Deity.

Such I conceive to be the true interpretation of the symbolism of the legend of the Third Degree.

I have said that this mythical history of the temple builder was universal in all nations and all rites, and that in no place and at no time had it, by alteration, diminution, or addition, acquired any essentially new or different form: the myth has always remained the same.

But it is not so with its interpretation. That which I have just given, and which I conceive to be the correct one, has been very generally adopted by the Masons of this country. But elsewhere, and by various writers, other interpretations have been made, very different in their character, although always agreeing in retaining the general idea of a resurrection or regeneration, or a restoration of something from an inferior to a higher sphere or function.

Thus some of the earlier continental writers have supposed the myth to have been a symbol of the destruction of the Order of the Templars, looking upon its restoration to its original wealth and dignities as being prophetically symbolized.

In some of the high philosophical degrees it is taught that the whole legend refers to the sufferings and death, with the subsequent resurrection, of Christ.[166]

Hutchinson, who has the honor of being the earliest philosophical writer on Freemasonry in England, supposes it to have been intended to embody the idea of the decadence of the Jewish religion, and the substitution of the Christian in its place and on its ruins.[167]

Dr. Oliver—"clarum et venerabile nomen"—thinks that it is typical of the murder of Abel by Cain, and that it symbolically refers to the universal death of our race through Adam, and its restoration to life in the Redeemer,[168] according to the expression of the apostle, "As in Adam we all died, so in Christ we all live."

Ragon makes Hiram a symbol of the sun shorn of its vivifying rays and fructifying power by the three winter months, and its restoration to generative heat by the season of spring.[169]

And, finally, Des Etangs, adopting, in part, the interpretation of Ragon, adds to it another, which he calls the moral symbolism of the legend, and supposes that Hiram is no other than eternal reason, whose enemies are the vices that deprave and destroy humanity.[170]

To each of these interpretations it seems to me that there are important objections, though perhaps to some less so than to others.

As to those who seek for an astronomical interpretation of the legend, in which the annual changes of the sun are symbolized, while the ingenuity with which they press their argument cannot but be admired, it is evident that, by such an interpretation, they yield all that Masonry has gained of religious development in past ages, and fall back upon that corruption and perversion of Sabaism from which it was the object, even of the Spurious Freemasonry of antiquity, to rescue its disciples.

The Templar interpretation of the myth must at once be discarded if we would avoid the difficulties of anachronism, unless we deny that the legend existed before the abolition of the Order of Knights Templar, and such denial would be fatal to the antiquity of Freemasonry.[171]

And as to the adoption of the Christian reference, Hutchinson, and after him Oliver, profoundly philosophical as are the masonic speculations of both, have, I am constrained to believe, fallen into a great error in calling the Master Mason's degree a Christian institution. It is true that it embraces within its scheme the great truths of Christianity upon the subject of the immortality of the soul and the resurrection of the body; but this was to be presumed, because Freemasonry is truth, and Christianity is truth, and all truth must be identical. But the origin of each is different; their histories are dissimilar. The institution of Freemasonry preceded the advent of Christianity. Its symbols and its legends are derived from the Solomonic temple, and from the people even anterior to that. Its religion comes from the ancient priesthood. Its faith was that primitive one of Noah and his immediate descendants. If Masonry were simply a Christian institution, the Jew and the Moslem, the Brahmin and the Buddhist, could not conscientiously partake of its illumination; but its universality is its boast. In its language citizens of every nation may converse; at its altar men of all religions may kneel; to its creed disciples of every faith may subscribe.

Yet it cannot be denied, that since the advent of Christianity a Christian element has been almost imperceptibly infused into the masonic system, at least among Christian Masons. This has been a necessity; for it is the tendency of every predominant religion to pervade with its influences all that surrounds it, or is about it, whether religious, political, or social. This arises from a need of the human heart. To the man deeply imbued with the spirit of his religion there is an almost unconscious desire to accommodate and adapt all the business and the amusements of life, the labors and the employments of his every-day existence, to the indwelling faith of his soul.

The Christian Mason, therefore, while acknowledging and justly appreciating the great doctrines taught in Masonry, and while grateful that these doctrines were preserved in the bosom of his ancient order at a time when they were unknown to the multitudes of the surrounding nations, is still anxious to give to them a Christian character, to invest them, in some measure, with the peculiarities of his own creed, and to bring the interpretation of their symbolism more nearly home to his own religious sentiments.

The feeling is an instinctive one, belonging to the noblest aspirations of our human nature; and hence we find Christian masonic writers indulging in it almost to an unwarrantable excess, and by the extent of their sectarian interpretations materially affecting the cosmopolitan character of the institution.

This tendency to Christianization has, in some instances, been so universal, and has prevailed for so long a period, that certain symbols and myths have been, in this way, so deeply and thoroughly imbued with the Christian element as to leave those who have not penetrated into the cause of this peculiarity, in doubt whether they should attribute to the symbol an ancient or a modern and Christian origin.

As an illustration of the idea here advanced, and as a remarkable example of the result of a gradually Christianized interpretation of a masonic symbol, I will refer to the subordinate myth (subordinate, I mean, to the great legend of the Builder), which relates the circumstances connected with the grave upon "*the brow of a small hill near Mount Moriah.*"

Now, the myth or legend of a grave is a legitimate deduction from the symbolism of the ancient Spurious Masonry. It is the analogue of the *Pastos, Couch*, or *Coffin*, which was to be found in the ritual of all the pagan Mysteries. In all these initiations, the aspirant was placed in a cell or upon a couch, in darkness, and for a period varying, in the different rites, from the three days of the Grecian Mysteries to the fifty of the Persian. This cell or couch, technically called the "pastos," was adopted as a symbol of the being whose death and resurrection or apotheosis, was represented in the legend.

The learned Faber says that this ceremony was doubtless the same as the descent into Hades,[172] and that, when the aspirant entered into the mystic cell, he was directed to lay himself down upon the bed which shadowed out the tomb of the Great Father, or Noah, to whom, it will be recollected, that Faber refers all the ancient rites. "While stretched upon the holy couch," he continues to remark, "in imitation of his figurative deceased prototype, he was said to be wrapped in the deep sleep of death. His resurrection from the bed was his restoration to life or his regeneration into a new world."

Now, it is easy to see how readily such a symbolism would be seized by the Temple Masons, and appropriated at once to *the grave at the brow of the hill*. At first, the interpretation, like that from which it had been derived, would be cosmopolitan; it would fit exactly to the general dogmas of the resurrection of the body and the immortality of the soul.

But on the advent of Christianity, the spirit of the new religion being infused into the old masonic system, the whole symbolism of the grave was affected by it. The same interpretation of a resurrection or restoration to life, derived from the ancient "pastos," was, it is true, preserved; but the facts that Christ himself had come to promulgate to the multitudes the same consoling dogma, and that Mount Calvary, "the place of a skull," was the spot where the Redeemer, by his own death and resurrection, had testified the truth of the doctrine, at once suggested to the old Christian Masons the idea of Christianizing the ancient symbol.

Let us now examine briefly how that idea has been at length developed.

In the first place, it is necessary to identify the spot where the "newly-made grave" was discovered with Mount Calvary, the place of the sepulchre of Christ. This can easily be done by a very few but striking analogies, which will, I conceive, carry conviction to any thinking mind.

1. Mount Calvary was a *small hill*.[173]

2. It was situated in a *westward direction* from the temple, and *near Mount Moriah*.

3. It was on the direct road from Jerusalem to Joppa, and is thus the very spot where a *weary brother*, travelling on that road, would find it convenient to *sit down to rest and refresh himself*.[174]

4. It was *outside* the gate of the temple.

5. It has at least *one cleft in the rock*, or cave, which was the place which subsequently became the sepulchre of our Lord. But this coincidence need scarcely to be insisted on, since the whole neighborhood abounds in rocky clefts, which meet at once the conditions of the masonic legend.

But to bring this analogical reasoning before the mind in a more expressive mode, it may be observed that if a party of persons were to start forth from the temple at Jerusalem, and travel in a westward direction towards the port of Joppa, Mount Calvary would be the first hill met with; and as it may possibly have been used as a place of sepulture, which its name of Golgotha[175] seems to import, we may suppose it to have been the very spot alluded to in the Third Degree, as the place where the craftsmen, on their way to Joppa, discovered the evergreen acacia.

Having thus traced the analogy, let us look a little to the symbolism.

Mount Calvary has always retained an important place in the legendary history of Freemasonry, and there are many traditions connected with it that are highly interesting in their import.

One of these traditions is, that it was the burial-place of Adam, in order, says the old legend, that where he lay, who effected the ruin of mankind, there also might the Savior of the world suffer, die, and be buried. Sir R. Torkington, who published a pilgrimage to Jerusalem in 1517, says that "under the Mount of Calvary is another chapel of our Blessed Lady and St. John the Evangelist, that was called Golgotha; and there, right under the mortise of the cross, was found the head of our forefather, Adam." [176] Golgotha, it will be remembered, means, in Hebrew, "the place of a skull;" and there may be some connection between this tradition and the name of Golgotha, by which the Evangelists inform us, that in the time of Christ Mount Calvary was known. Calvary, or Calvaria, has the same signification in Latin.

Another tradition states, that it was in the bowels of Mount Calvary that Enoch erected his nine-arched vault, and deposited on the foundation-stone of Masonry that Ineffable Name, whose investigation, as a symbol of divine truth, is the great object of Speculative Masonry.

A third tradition details the subsequent discovery of Enoch's deposit by King Solomon, whilst making excavations in Mount Calvary, during the building of the temple.

On this hallowed spot was Christ the Redeemer slain and buried. It was there that, rising on the third day from his sepulchre, he gave, by that act, the demonstrative evidence of the resurrection of the body and the immortality of the soul.

And it was on this spot that the same great lesson was taught in Masonry—the same sublime truth—the development of which evidently forms the design of the Third or Master Mason's degree.

There is in these analogies a sublime beauty as well as a wonderful coincidence between the two systems of Masonry and Christianity, that must, at an early period, have attracted the attention of the Christian Masons.

Mount Calvary is consecrated to the Christian as the place where his crucified Lord gave the last great proof of the second life, and fully established the doctrine of the resurrection which he had come to teach. It was the sepulchre of him

"Who captive led captivity,
Who robbed the grave of victory,
And took the sting from death."

It is consecrated to the Mason, also, as the scene of the *euresis*, the place of the discovery, where the same consoling doctrines of the resurrection of the body and the immortality of the soul are shadowed forth in profoundly symbolic forms.

These great truths constitute the very essence of Christianity, in which it differs from and excels all religious systems that preceded it; they constitute, also, the end, aim, and object of all Freemasonry, but more especially that of the Third Degree, whose peculiar legend, symbolically considered, teaches nothing more nor less than that there is an immortal and better part within us, which, as an emanation from that divine spirit which pervades all nature, can never die.

The identification of the spot on which this divine truth was promulgated in both systems—the Christian and the Masonic—affords an admirable illustration of the readiness with which the religious spirit of the former may be infused into the symbolism of the latter. And hence Hutchinson, thoroughly imbued with these Christian views of Masonry, has called the Master Mason's order a Christian degree, and thus Christianizes the whole symbolism of its mythical history.

"The Great Father of all, commiserating the miseries of the world, sent his only Son, who was *innocence* itself, to teach the doctrine of salvation—by whom man was raised from the death of sin unto the life of righteousness—from the tomb of corruption unto the chamber of hope—from the darkness of despair to the celestial beams of faith; and not only working for us this redemption, but making with us the covenant of regeneration; whence we are become the children of the Divinity, and inheritors of the realms of heaven.

"We, *Masons*, describing the deplorable estate of religion under the Jewish law, speak in figures: 'Her tomb was in the rubbish and filth cast forth of the temple, and *acacia* wove its branches over her monuments;' *akakia* being the Greek word for innocence, or being free from sin; implying that the sins and corruptions of the old law, and devotees of the Jewish altar, had hid Religion from those who sought her, and she was only to be found where *innocence* survived, and under the banner of the Divine Lamb, and, as to ourselves, professing that we were to be distinguished by our *Acacy*, or as true *Acacians* in our religious faiths and tenets.

"The acquisition of the doctrine of redemption is expressed in the typical character of *Huramen* (I have found it.—*Greek*), and by the applications of that name with Masons, it is implied that we have discovered the knowledge of God and his salvation, and have been redeemed from the death of sin and the sepulchre of pollution and unrighteousness.

"Thus the *Master Mason* represents a man, under the Christian doctrine, saved from the grave of iniquity and raised to the faith of salvation."

It is in this way that Masonry has, by a sort of inevitable process (when we look to the religious sentiment of the interpreters), been Christianized by some of the most illustrious and learned writers on masonic science—by such able men as Hutchinson and Oliver in England, and by Harris, by Scott, by Salem Towne, and by several others in this country.

I do not object to the system when the interpretation is not strained, but is plausible, consistent, and productive of the same results as in the instance of Mount Calvary: all that I contend for is, that such interpretations are modern, and that they do not belong to, although they may often be deduced from, the ancient system.

But the true ancient interpretation of the legend,—the universal masonic one,—for all countries and all ages, undoubtedly was, that the fate of the temple builder is but figurative of the pilgrimage of man on earth, through trials and temptations, through sin and sorrow, until his eventual fall beneath the blow of death and his final and glorious resurrection to another and an eternal life.

XXVIII.

The Sprig of Acacia.

Intimately connected with the legend of the third degree is the mythical history of the Sprig of Acacia, which we are now to consider.

There is no symbol more interesting to the masonic student than the Sprig of Acacia, not only on account of its own peculiar import, but also because it introduces us to an extensive and delightful field of research; that, namely, which embraces the symbolism of sacred plants. In all the ancient systems of religion, and Mysteries of initiation, there was always some one plant consecrated, in the minds of the worshippers and participants, by a peculiar symbolism, and therefore held in extraordinary veneration as a sacred emblem. Thus the ivy was used in the Mysteries of Dionysus, the myrtle in those of Ceres, the erica in the Osirian, and the lettuce in the Adonisian. But to this subject I shall have occasion to refer more fully in a subsequent part of the present investigation.

Before entering upon an examination of the symbolism of the *Acacia*, it will be, perhaps, as well to identify the true plant which occupies so important a place in the ritual of Freemasonry.

And here, in passing, I may be permitted to say that it is a very great error to designate the symbolic plant of Masonry by the name of "Cassia"—an error which undoubtedly arose, originally, from the very common habit among illiterate people of sinking the sound of the letter *a* in the pronunciation of any word of which it constitutes the initial syllable. Just, for instance, as we constantly hear, in the conversation of the uneducated, the words *pothecary* and *prentice* for *apothecary* and *apprentice*, shall we also find *cassia* used for *acacia*.[177] Unfortunately, however, this corruption of *acacia* into *cassia* has not always been confined to the illiterate: but the long employment of the corrupted form has at length introduced it, in some instances, among a few of our writers. Even the venerable Oliver, although well acquainted with the symbolism of the acacia, and having written most learnedly upon it, has, at times, allowed himself to use the objectionable corruption, unwittingly influenced, in all probability, by the too frequent adoption of the latter word in the English lodges. In America, but few Masons fall into the error of speaking of the *Cassia*. The proper teaching of the *Acacia* is here well understood.[178]

The *cassia* of the ancients was, in fact, an ignoble plant having no mystic meaning and no sacred character, and was never elevated to a higher function than that of being united, as Virgil informs us, with other odorous herbs in the formation of a garland:—

"...violets pale,
The poppy's flush, and dill which scents the gale,
Cassia, and hyacinth, and daffodil,
With yellow marigold the chaplet fill." [179]

Alston says that the "Cassia lignea of the ancients was the larger branches of the cinnamon tree, cut off with their bark and sent together to the druggists; their Cassia fistula, or Syrinx, was the same cinnamon in the bark only;" but Ruæus says that it also sometimes denoted the lavender, and sometimes the rosemary.

In Scripture the cassia is only three times mentioned,[180] twice as the translation of the Hebrew word *kiddak*, and once as the rendering of *ketzioth*, but always as referring to an aromatic plant which formed a constituent portion of some perfume. There is, indeed, strong reason for believing that the cassia is only another name for a coarser preparation of cinnamon, and it is also to be remarked that it did not grow in Palestine, but was imported from the East.

The *acacia*, on the contrary, was esteemed a sacred tree. It is the *acacia vera* of Tournefort, and the *mimosa nilotica* of Linnæus. It grew abundantly in the vicinity of Jerusalem,[181] where it is still to be found, and is familiar to us all, in its modern uses at least, as the tree from which the gum arabic of commerce is obtained.

The acacia, which, in Scripture, is always called *shittah*[182] and in the plural *shittim*, was esteemed a sacred wood among the Hebrews. Of it Moses was ordered to make the tabernacle, the ark of the covenant, the table for the showbread, and the rest of the sacred furniture. Isaiah, in recounting the promises of God's mercy to the Israelites on their return from the captivity, tells them, that, among other things, he will plant in the wilderness, for their relief and refreshment, the cedar, the acacia (or, as it is rendered in our common version, the *shittah*), the fir, and other trees.

The first thing, then, that we notice in this symbol of the acacia, is, that it had been always consecrated from among the other trees of the forest by the sacred purposes to which it was devoted. By the Jew the tree from whose wood the sanctuary of the tabernacle and the holy ark had been constructed would ever be viewed as more sacred than ordinary trees. The early Masons, therefore, very naturally appropriated this hallowed plant to the equally sacred purpose of a symbol which was to teach an important divine truth in all ages to come.

Having thus briefly disposed of the natural history of this plant, we may now proceed to examine it in its symbolic relations.

First. The acacia, in the mythic system of Freemasonry, is preeminently the symbol of the IMMORTALITY OF THE SOUL—that important doctrine which it is the great design of the institution to teach. As the evanescent nature of the flower which "cometh forth and is cut down" reminds us of the transitory nature of human life, so the perpetual renovation of the evergreen plant, which uninterruptedly presents the appearance of youth and vigor, is aptly compared to that spiritual life in which the soul, freed from the corruptible companionship of the body, shall enjoy an eternal spring and an immortal youth. Hence, in the impressive funeral service of our order, it is said, "This evergreen is an emblem of our faith in the immortality of the soul. By this we are reminded that we have an immortal part within us, which shall survive the grave, and which shall never, never, never die." And again, in the closing sentences of the monitorial lecture of the Third Degree, the same sentiment is repeated, and we are told that by "the ever green and ever living sprig" the Mason is strengthened "with confidence and composure to look forward to a blessed immortality." Such an interpretation of the symbol is an easy and a natural one; it suggests itself at once to the least reflective mind, and consequently, in some one form or another, is to be found existing in all ages and nations. It was an ancient custom, which is not, even now, altogether disused, for mourners to carry in their hands at funerals a sprig of some evergreen, generally the cedar or the cypress, and to deposit it in the grave of the deceased. According to Dalcho,[183] the Hebrews always planted a sprig of the acacia at the head of the grave of a departed friend. Potter tells us that the ancient Greeks "had a custom of bedecking tombs with herbs and flowers." [184] All sorts of purple and white flowers were acceptable to the dead, but principally the amaranth and the myrtle. The very name of the former of these plants, which signifies "never fading," would seem to indicate the true symbolic meaning of the usage, although archaeologists have generally supposed it to be simply an exhibition of love on the part of the survivors. Ragon says, that the ancients substituted the acacia for all other plants because they believed it to be incorruptible, and not liable to injury from the attacks of any kind of insect or other animal—thus symbolizing the incorruptible nature of the soul.

Hence we see the propriety of placing the sprig of acacia, as an emblem of immortality, among the symbols of that degree, all of whose ceremonies are intended to teach us the great truth, that "the life of man, regulated by morality, faith, and justice, will be rewarded at its closing hour by the prospect of eternal bliss." [185] So, therefore, says Dr. Oliver, when the Master Mason exclaims, "My name is Acacia," it is equivalent to saying, "I have been in the grave,—I have triumphed over it by rising from the dead,—and being regenerated in the process, I have a claim to life everlasting."

The sprig of acacia, then, in its most ordinary signification, presents itself to the Master Mason as a symbol of the immortality of the soul, being intended to remind him, by its evergreen and unchanging nature, of that better and spiritual part within us, which, as an emanation from the Grand Architect of the Universe, can never die. And as this is the most ordinary, the most generally accepted signification, so also is it the most important; for thus, as the peculiar symbol of immortality, it becomes the most appropriate to an order all of whose teachings are intended to inculcate the great lesson that "life rises out of the grave." But incidental to this the acacia has two other interpretations, which are well worthy of investigation.

Secondly, then, the acacia is a symbol of INNOCENCE. The symbolism here is of a peculiar and unusual character, depending not on any real analogy in the form or use of the symbol to the idea symbolized, but simply on a double or compound meaning of the word. For αχαχια, in the Greek language, signifies both the plant in question and the moral quality of innocence or purity of life. In this sense the symbol refers, primarily, to him over whose solitary grave the acacia was planted, and whose virtuous conduct, whose integrity of life and fidelity to his trusts, have ever been presented as patterns to the craft, and consequently to all Master Masons, who, by this interpretation of the symbol, are invited to emulate his example.

Hutchinson, indulging in his favorite theory of Christianizing Masonry, when he comes to this signification of the symbol, thus enlarges on the interpretation: "We Masons, describing the deplorable estate of religion under the Jewish law, speak in figures: 'Her tomb was in the rubbish and filth cast forth of the temple, and *Acacia* wove its branches over her monument;' *akakia* being the Greek word for innocence, or being free from sin; implying that the sins and corruptions of the old law and devotees of the Jewish altar had hid Religion from those who sought her, and she was only to be found where *innocence* survived, and under the banner of the divine Lamb; and as to ourselves, professing that we were to be distinguished by our *Acacy*, or as true *Acacians* in our religious faith and tenets." [186]

Among the nations of antiquity, it was common thus by peculiar plants to symbolize the virtues and other qualities of the mind. In many instances the symbolism has been lost to the moderns, but in others it has been retained, and is well understood, even at the present day. Thus the olive was adopted as the symbol of peace, because, says Lee, "its oil is very useful, in some way or other, in all arts manual which principally flourish in times of peace." [187]

The quince among the Greeks was the symbol of love and happiness;[188] and hence, by the laws of Solon, in Athenian marriages, the bride and bridegroom were required to eat a quince together.

The palm was the symbol of victory;[189] and hence, in the catacombs of Rome, the burial-place of so many of the early Christians, the palm leaf is constantly found as an emblem of the Christian's triumph over sin and death.

The rosemary was a symbol of remembrance, and hence was used both at marriages and at funerals, the memory of the past being equally appropriate in both rites.[190]

The parsley was consecrated to grief; and hence all the Greeks decked their tombs with it; and it was used to crown the conquerors in the Nemean games, which were of a funereal character.[191]

But it is needless to multiply instances of this symbolism. In adopting the acacia as a symbol of innocence, Masonry has but extended the principle of an ancient and universal usage, which thus consecrated particular plants, by a mystical meaning, to the representation of particular virtues.

But lastly, the acacia is to be considered as the symbol of INITIATION. This is by far the most interesting of its interpretations, and was, we have every reason to believe, the primary and original, the others being but incidental. It leads us at once to the investigation of that significant fact to which I have already alluded, that in all the ancient initiations and religious mysteries there was some plant, peculiar to each, which was consecrated by its own esoteric meaning, and which occupied an important position in the celebration of the rites; so that the plant, whatever it might be, from its constant and prominent use in the ceremonies of initiation, came at length to be adopted as the symbol of that initiation.

A reference to some of these *sacred plants*—for such was the character they assumed—and an investigation of their symbolism will not, perhaps, be uninteresting or useless, in connection with the subject of the present article.

In the Mysteries of Adonis, which originated in Phoenicia, and were afterwards transferred to Greece, the death and resurrection of Adonis was represented. A part of the legend accompanying these mysteries was, that when Adonis was slain by a wild boar, Venus laid out the body on a bed of lettuce. In memorial of this supposed fact, on the first day of the celebration, when funeral rites were performed, lettuces were carried in the procession, *newly planted* in shells of earth. Hence the lettuce became the sacred plant of the Adonia, or Adonisian Mysteries.

The lotus was the sacred plant of the Brahminical rites of India, and was considered as the symbol of their elemental trinity,—earth, water, and air,—because, as an aquatic plant, it derived its nutriment from all of these elements combined, its roots being planted in the earth, its stem rising through the water, and its leaves exposed to the air.[192] The Egyptians, who borrowed a large portion of their religious rites from the East, adopted the lotus, which was also indigenous to their country, as a mystical plant, and made it the symbol of their initiation, or the birth into celestial light. Hence, as Champollion observes, they often on their monuments represented the god Phre, or the sun, as borne within the expanded calyx of the lotus. The lotus bears a flower similar to that of the poppy, while its large, tongue-shaped leaves float upon the surface of the water. As the Egyptians had remarked that the plant expands when the sun rises, and closes when it sets, they adopted it as a symbol of the sun; and as that luminary was the principal object of the popular worship, the lotus became in all their sacred rites a consecrated and mystical plant.

The Egyptians also selected the *erica*[193] or heath, as a sacred plant. The origin of the consecration of this plant presents us with a singular coincidence, that will be peculiarly interesting to the masonic student. We are informed that there was a legend in the mysteries of Osiris, which related, that Isis, when in search of the body of her murdered husband, discovered it interred at the brow of a hill, near which an erica, or heath plant, grew; and hence, after the recovery of the body and the resurrection of the god, when she established the mysteries to commemorate her loss and her recovery, she adopted the erica, as a sacred plant,[194] in memory of its having pointed out the spot where the *mangled remains* of Osiris were concealed.[195]

The *mistletoe* was the sacred plant of Druidism. Its consecrated character was derived from a legend of the Scandinavian mythology, and which is thus related in the Edda, or sacred books. The god Balder, the son of Odin, having dreamed that he was in some great danger of life, his mother, Friga, exacted an oath from all the creatures of the animal, the vegetable, and the mineral kingdoms, that they would do no harm to her son. The mistletoe, contemptible from its size and weakness, was alone neglected, and of it no oath of immunity was demanded. Lok, the evil genius, or god of Darkness, becoming acquainted with this fact, placed an arrow made of mistletoe in the hands of Holder, the blind brother of Balder, on a certain day, when the gods were throwing missiles at him in sport, and wondering at their inability to do him injury with any arms with which they could attack him. But, being shot with the mistletoe arrow, it inflicted a fatal wound, and Balder died.

Ever afterwards the mistletoe was revered as a sacred plant, consecrated to the powers of darkness; and annually it became an important rite among the Druids to proceed into the forest in search of the mistletoe, which, being found, was cut down by the Arch Druid, and its parts, after a solemn sacrifice, were distributed among the people. Clavel[196] very ingeniously remarks, that it is evident, in reference to the legend, that as Balder symbolizes the Sun-god, and Lok, Darkness, this search for the mistletoe was intended to deprive the god of Darkness of the power of destroying the god of Light. And the distribution of the fragments of the mistletoe among their pious worshippers, was to assure them that henceforth a similar attempt of Lok would prove abortive, and he was thus deprived of the means of effecting his design.[197]

The *myrtle* performed the same office of symbolism in the Mysteries of Greece as the lotus did in Egypt, or the mistletoe among the Druids. The candidate, in these initiations, was crowned with myrtle, because, according to the popular theology, the myrtle was sacred to Proserpine, the goddess of the future life. Every classical scholar will remember the golden branch with which Aeneas was supplied by the Sibyl, before proceeding on his journey to the infernal regions[198]—a voyage which is now universally admitted to be a mythical representation of the ceremonies of initiation.

In all of these ancient Mysteries, while the sacred plant was a symbol of initiation, the initiation itself was symbolic of the resurrection to a future life, and of the immortality of the soul. In this view, Freemasonry is to us now in the place of the ancient initiations, and the acacia is substituted for the lotus, the erica, the ivy, the mistletoe, and the myrtle. The lesson of wisdom is the same; the medium of imparting it is all that has been changed.

Returning, then, to the acacia, we find that it is capable of three explanations. It is a symbol of immortality, of innocence, and of initiation. But these three significations are closely connected, and that connection must be observed, if we desire to obtain a just interpretation of the symbol. Thus, in this one symbol, we are taught that in the initiation of life, of which the initiation in the third-degree is simply emblematic, innocence must for a time lie in the grave, at length, however, to be called, by the word of the Grand Master of the Universe, to a blissful immortality. Combine with this the recollection of the place where the sprig of acacia was planted, and which I have heretofore shown to be Mount Calvary, the place of sepulture of Him who "brought life and immortality to light," and who, in Christian Masonry, is designated, as he is in Scripture, as "the lion of the tribe of Judah," and remember, too, that in the mystery of his death, the wood of the cross takes the place of the acacia, and in this little and apparently insignificant symbol, but which is really and truly the most important and significant one in masonic science, we have a beautiful suggestion of all the mysteries of life and death, of time and eternity, of the present and of the future. Thus read (and thus all our symbols should be read), Masonry proves something more to its disciples than a mere social society or a charitable association. It becomes a "lamp to our feet," whose spiritual light shines on the darkness of the deathbed, and dissipates the gloomy shadows of the grave.

XXIX.

The Symbolism of Labor.

It is one of the most beautiful features of the Masonic Institution, that it teaches not only the necessity, but the nobility, of labor. Among the earliest of the implements in whose emblematic use it instructs its neophytes is the Trestle Board, the acknowledged symbol of the Divine Law, in accordance with whose decree[199] labor was originally instituted as the common lot of all; and therefore the important lesson that is closely connected with this symbol is, that to labor well and truly, to labor honestly and persistently, is the object and the chief end of all humanity.

To work out well the task that is set before us is our highest duty, and should constitute our greatest happiness. All men, then, must have their trestle boards; for the principles that guide us in the discharge of our duty—the schemes that we devise—the plans that we propose—are but the trestle board, whose designs we follow, for good or for evil, in our labor of life.

Earth works with every coming spring, and within its prolific bosom designs the bursting seed, the tender plant, and the finished tree, upon its trestle board.

Old ocean works forever—restless and murmuring—but still bravely working; and storms and tempests, the purifiers of stagnant nature, are inscribed upon its trestle board.

And God himself, the Grand Architect, the Master Builder of the world, has labored from eternity; and working by his omnipotent will, he inscribes his plans upon illimitable space, for the universe is his trestle board.

There was a saying of the monks of old which is well worth meditation. They taught that "*laborare est orare*"—labor is worship. They did not, it is true, always practise the wise precept. They did not always make labor a part of their religion. Like Onuphrius, who lived threescore years and ten in the desert, without human voice or human sympathy to cheer him, because he had not learned that man was made for man, those old ascetics went into the wilderness, and built cells, and occupied themselves in solitary meditation and profitless thought. They prayed much, but they did no work. And thus they passed their lives, giving no pity, aid, or consolation to their fellow-men, adding no mite to the treasury of human knowledge, and leaving the world, when their selfish pilgrimage was finished, without a single contribution, in labor of mind or body, to its welfare.[200]

And men, seeing the uselessness of these ascetic lives, shrink now from their example, and fall back upon that wiser teaching, that he best does God's will who best does God's work. The world now knows that heaven is not served by man's idleness—that the "*dolce far niente*," though it might suit an Italian lazzaroni, is not fit for a brave Christian man, and that they who would do rightly, and act well their part, must take this distich for their motto:—

"With this hand work, and with the other pray,
And God will bless them both from day to day."

Now, this doctrine, that labor is worship, is the very doctrine that has been advanced and maintained, from time immemorial, as a leading dogma of the Order of Freemasonry. There is no other human institution under the sun which has set forth this great principle in such bold relief. We hear constantly of Freemasonry as an institution that inculcates morality, that fosters the social feeling, that teaches brotherly love; and all this is well, because it is true; but we must never forget that from its foundation-stone to its pinnacle, all over its vast temple, is inscribed, in symbols of living light, the great truth that *labor is worship*.

It has been supposed that, because we speak of Freemasonry as a speculative system, it has nothing to do with the practical. But this is a most grievous error. Freemasonry is, it is true, a speculative science, but it is a speculative science based upon an operative art. All its symbols and allegories refer to this connection. Its very language is borrowed from the art, and it is singularly suggestive that the initiation of a candidate into its mysteries is called, in its peculiar phraseology, *work*.

I repeat that this expression is singularly suggestive. When the lodge is engaged in reading petitions, hearing reports, debating financial matters, it is said to be occupied in *business*; but when it is engaged in the form and ceremony of initiation into any of the degrees, it is said to be at *work*. Initiation is masonic labor. This phraseology at once suggests the connection of our speculative system with an operative art that preceded it, and upon which it has been founded. This operative art must have given it form and features and organization. If the speculative system had been founded solely on philosophical or ethical principles, if it had been derived from some ancient or modern sect of philosophers,—from the Stoics, the Epicureans, or the Platonists of the heathen world, or from any of the many divisions of the scholastics of the middle ages,—this origin would most certainly have affected its interior organization as well as its external form, and we should have seen our modern masonic reunions assuming the style of academies or schools. Its technical language—for, like every institution isolated from the ordinary and general pursuits of mankind, it would have had its own technical dialect—would have been borrowed from, and would be easily traced to, the peculiar phraseology of the philosophic sects which had given it birth. There would have been the *sophists* and the *philosophers*; the *grammatists* and the *grammarians*; the *scholars*, the *masters*, and the *doctors*. It would have had its *trivial* and its *quadrivial* schools; its occupation would have been research, experiment, or investigation; in a word, its whole features would have been colored by a grammatical, a rhetorical, or a mathematical cast, accordingly as it should have been derived from a sect in which any one of these three characteristics was the predominating influence.

But in the organization of Freemasonry, as it now presents itself to us, we see an entirely different appearance. Its degrees are expressive, not of advancement in philosophic attainments, but of progress in a purely mechanical pursuit. Its highest grade is that of *Master of the Work*. Its places of meeting are not schools, but *lodges*, places where the workmen formerly lodged, in the neighborhood of the building on whose construction they were engaged. It does not form theories, but builds temples. It knows nothing of the rules of the dialecticians,—of the syllogism, the dilemma, the enthymeme, or the sorites,—but it recurs to the homely implements of its operative parent for its methods of instruction, and with the plumb-line it inculcates rectitude of conduct, and draws lessons of morality from the workman's square. It sees in the Supreme God that it worships, not a "*numen divinum*," a divine power, nor a "*moderator rerum omnium*," a controller of all things, as the old philosophers designated him, but a *Grand Architect of the Universe*. The masonic idea of God refers to Him as the Mighty Builder of this terrestrial globe, and all the countless worlds that surround it. He is not the *ens entium*, or *to theion*, or any other of the thousand titles with which ancient and modern speculation has invested him, but simply the Architect,—as the Greeks have it, the ἀρχὸς, the chief workman,—under whom we are all workmen also;[201] and hence our labor is his worship.

This idea, then, of masonic labor, is closely connected with the history of the organization of the institution. When we say "the lodge is at work," we recognize that it is in the legitimate practice of that occupation for which it was originally intended. The Masons that are in it are not occupied in thinking, or speculating, or reasoning, but simply and emphatically in working. The duty of a Mason as such, in his lodge, is to work. Thereby he accomplishes the destiny of his Order. Thereby he best fulfils his obligation to the Grand Architect, for with the Mason *laborare est orare*—labor is worship.

The importance of masonic labor being thus demonstrated, the question next arises as to the nature of that labor. What is the work that a Mason is called upon to perform?

Temple building was the original occupation of our ancient brethren. Leaving out of view that system of ethics and of religious philosophy, that search after truth, those doctrines of the unity of God and the immortality of the soul, which alike distinguish the ancient Mysteries and the masonic institution, and which both must have derived from a common origin,—most probably from some priesthood of the olden time,—let our attention be exclusively directed, for the present, to that period, so familiar to every Mason, when, under the supposed Grand Mastership of King Solomon, Freemasonry first assumed "a local habitation and a name" in the holy city of Jerusalem. There the labor of the Israelites and the skill of the Tyrians were occupied in the construction of that noble temple whose splendor and magnificence of decoration made it one of the wonders of the world.

Here, then, we see the two united nations directing their attention, with surprising harmony, to the task of temple building. The Tyrian workmen, coming immediately from the bosom of the mystical society of Dionysian artificers, whose sole employment was the erection of sacred edifices throughout all Asia Minor, indoctrinated the Jews with a part of their architectural skill, and bestowed upon them also a knowledge of those sacred Mysteries which they had practised at Tyre, and from which the present interior form of Freemasonry is said to be derived.

Now, if there be any so incredulous as to refuse their assent to the universally received masonic tradition on this subject, if there be any who would deny all connection of King Solomon with the origin of Freemasonry, except it be in a mythical or symbolical sense, such incredulity will, not at all affect the chain of argument which I am disposed to use. For it will not be denied that the corporations of builders in the middle ages, those men who were known as "Travelling Freemasons," were substantial and corporeal, and that the cathedrals, abbeys, and palaces, whose ruins are still objects of admiration to all observers, bear conclusive testimony that their existence was nothing like a myth, and that their labors were not apocryphal. But these Travelling Freemasons, whether led into the error, if error it be, by a mistaken reading of history, or by a superstitious reverence for tradition, always esteemed King Solomon as the founder of their Order. So that the first absolutely historical details that we have of the masonic institution, connect it with the idea of a temple. And it is only for this idea that I contend, for it proves that the first Freemasons of whom we have authentic record, whether they were at Jerusalem or in Europe, and whether they flourished a thousand years before or a thousand years after the birth of Christ, always supposed that temple building was the peculiar specialty of their craft, and that their labor was to be the erection of temples in ancient times, and cathedrals and churches in the Christian age.

So that we come back at last to the proposition with which I had commenced, namely: that temple building was the original occupation of our ancient brethren. And to this is added the fact, that after a long lapse of centuries, a body of men is found in the middle ages who were universally recognized as Freemasons, and who directed their attention and their skill to the same pursuit, and were engaged in the construction of cathedrals, abbeys, and other sacred edifices, these being the Christian substitute for the heathen or the Jewish temple.

And therefore, when we view the history of the Order as thus developed in its origin and its design, we are justified in saying that, in all times past, its members have been recognized as men of labor, and that their labor has been temple building.

But our ancient brethren wrought in both operative and speculative Masonry, while we work only in speculative. They worked with the hand; we work with the brain. They dealt in the material; we in the spiritual. They used in their labor wood and stones; we use thoughts, and feelings, and affections. We both devote ourselves to labor, but the object of the labor and the mode of the labor are different.

The French rituals have given us the key-note to the explanation of what is masonic labor when they say that "Freemasons erect temples for virtue and dungeons for vice."

The modern Freemasons, like the Masons of old, are engaged in the construction of a temple;—but with this difference: that the temple of the latter was material, that of the former spiritual. When the operative art was the predominant characteristic of the Order, Masons were engaged in the construction of material and earthly temples. But when the operative art ceased, and the speculative science took its place, then the Freemasons symbolized the labors of their predecessors by engaging in the construction of a spiritual temple in their hearts, which was to be made so pure that it might become the dwelling-place of Him who is all purity. It was to be "a house not made with hands," where the hewn stone was to be a purified heart.

This symbolism, which represents man as a temple, a house, a sacred building in which God is to dwell, is not new, nor peculiar to the masonic science. It was known to the Jewish, and is still recognized by the Christian, system. The Talmudists had a saying that the threefold repetition of the words "Temple of Jehovah," in the seventh chapter and fourth verse of the book of Jeremiah, was intended to allude to the existence of three temples; and hence in one of their treatises it is said, "Two temples have been destroyed, but the third will endure forever," in which it is manifest that they referred to the temple of the immortal soul in man.

By a similar allusion, which, however, the Jews chose wilfully to misunderstand, Christ declared, "Destroy this temple, and in three days I will raise it up." And the beloved disciple, who records the conversation, does not allow us to doubt of the Saviour's meaning.

"Then said the Jews, Forty and six years was this temple in building, and wilt thou rear it up in three days?

"But he spake of the temple of his body." [202]

In more than one place the apostle Paul has fondly dwelt upon this metaphor. Thus he tells the Corinthians that they are "God's building," and he calls himself the "wise master builder," who was to lay the foundation in his truthful doctrine, upon which they were to erect the edifice.[203] And he says to them immediately afterwards, "Know ye not that ye are the temple of God, and that the Spirit of God dwelleth in you?"

In consequence of these teachings of the apostles, the idea that the body was a temple has pervaded, from the earliest times to the present day, the system of Christian or theological symbolism. Indeed, it has sometimes been carried to an almost too fanciful excess. Thus Samuel Lee, in that curious and rare old work, "*The Temple of Solomon, pourtrayed by Scripture Light*," thus dilates on this symbolism of the temple:—

"The *foundation* of this temple may be laid in humility and contrition of spirit, wherein the inhabiter of eternity delighteth to dwell; we may refer the *porch* to the mouth of a saint, wherein every holy Jacob erects the *pillars* of God's praise, calling upon and blessing his name for received mercies; when songs of deliverance are uttered from the *doors* of his lips. The *holy place* is the renewed mind, and the *windows* therein may denote divine illumination from above, cautioning a saint lest they be darkened with the smoke of anger, the mist of grief, the dust of vain-glory, or the filthy mire of worldly cares. The *golden candlesticks*, the infused habits of divine knowledge resting within the soul. The *shew-bread*, the word of grace exhibited in the promises for the preservation of a Christian's life and glory. The *golden altar* of odors, the breathings, sufferings, and groanings after God, ready to break forth into Abba, Father. The *veiles*, the righteousness of Christ. The *holy of holies* may relate to the conscience purified from dead works and brought into a heavenly frame." [204] And thus he proceeds, symbolizing every part and utensil of the temple as alluding to some emotion or affection of man, but in language too tedious for quotation.

In a similar vein has the celebrated John Bunyan, the author of the "*Pilgrim's Progress*" proceeded in his "*Temple of Solomon Spiritualized*" to refer every part of that building to a symbolic meaning, selecting, however, the church, or congregation of good men, rather than the individual man, as the object of the symbolism.

In the middle ages the Hermetic philosophers seem to have given the same interpretation of the temple, and Swedenborg, in his mystical writings, adopts the idea.

Hitchcock, who has written an admirable little work on Swedenborg considered as a Hermetic Philosopher, thus alludes to this subject, and his language, as that of a learned and shrewd investigator, is well worthy of quotation:—

"With, perhaps, the majority of readers, the Tabernacle of Moses and the Temple of Solomon were mere buildings; very magnificent indeed, but still mere buildings for the worship of God. But some are struck with many portions of the account of their erection, admitting a moral interpretation; and while the buildings are allowed to stand (or to have stood once) visible objects, these interpreters are delighted to meet with indications that Moses and Solomon, in building the temples, were wise in the knowledge of God and of man; from which point it is not difficult to pass on to the moral meaning altogether, and to affirm that the building which was erected without 'the noise of a hammer or axe, or any tool of iron,' was altogether a moral building—a building of God, not made with hands: in short, many see in the story of Solomon's temple a symbolical representation of MAN as the temple of God, with its *holy of holies* deep-seated in the centre of the human heart." [205]

The French Masons have not been inattentive to this symbolism. Their already quoted expression that the "Freemasons build temples for virtue and dungeons for vice," has very clearly a reference to it, and their most distinguished writers never lose sight of it.

Thus Ragon, one of the most learned of the French historians of Freemasonry, in his lecture to the Apprentice, says that the founders of our Order "called themselves Masons, and proclaimed that they were building a temple to truth and virtue." [206] And subsequently he addresses the candidate who has received the Master's degree in the following language:—

"Profit by all that has been revealed to you. Improve your heart and your mind. Direct your passions to the general good; combat your prejudices; watch over your thoughts and your actions; love, enlighten, and assist your brethren; and you will have perfected that *temple* of which you are at once the *architect*, the *material*, and the *workman*." [207]

Rebold, another French historian of great erudition, says, "If Freemasonry has ceased to erect temples, and by the aid of its architectural designs to elevate all hearts to the Deity, and all eyes and hopes to heaven, it has not therefore desisted from its work of moral and intellectual building;" and he thinks that the success of the institution has justified this change of purpose and the disruption of the speculative from the operative character of the Order. [208]

Eliphas Levi, who has written abstrusely and mystically on Freemasonry and its collateral sciences, sees very clearly an allegorical and a real design in the institution, the former being the rebuilding of the temple of Solomon, and the latter the improvement of the human race by a reconstruction of its social and religious elements. [209]

The Masons of Germany have elaborated this idea with all the exhaustiveness that is peculiar to the German mind, and the masonic literature of that country abounds in essays, lectures, and treatises, in which the prominent topic is this building of the Solomonic temple as referring to the construction of a moral temple.

Thus writes Bro. Rhode, of Berlin:—

"So soon as any one has received the consecration of our Order, we say to him that we are building a mystical temple;" and he adds that "this temple which we Masons are building is nothing else than that which will conduce to the greatest possible happiness of mankind." [210]

And another German brother, Von Wedekind, asserts that "we only labor in our temple when we make man our predominating object, when we unite goodness of heart with polished manners, truth with beauty, virtue with grace." [211]

Again we have Reinhold telling us, in true Teutonic expansiveness of expression, that "by the mystical Solomonic temple we are to understand the high ideal or archetype of humanity in the best possible condition of social improvement, wherein every evil inclination is overcome, every passion is resolved into the spirit of love, and wherein each for all, and all for each, kindly strive to work." [212]

And thus the German Masons call this striving for an almost millennial result *labor in the temple*.

The English Masons, although they have not treated the symbolism of the Order with the same abstruse investigation that has distinguished those of Germany and France, still have not been insensible to this idea that the building of the Solomonic temple is intended to indicate a cultivation of the human character. Thus Hutchinson, one of the earliest of the symbolic writers of England, shows a very competent conception— for the age in which he lived—of the mystical meaning of the temple; and later writers have improved upon his crude views. It must, however, be acknowledged that neither Hutchinson nor Oliver, nor any other of the distinguished masonic writers of England, has dwelt on this peculiar symbolism of a moral temple with that earnest appreciation of the idea that is to be found in the works of the French and German Masons. But although the allusions are rather casual and incidental, yet the symbolic theory is evidently recognized.[213]

Our own country has produced many students of Masonic symbolism, who have thoroughly grasped this noble thought, and treated it with eloquence and erudition.

Fifty years ago Salem Towne wrote thus: "Speculative Masonry, according to present acceptation, has an ultimate reference to that spiritual building erected by virtue in the heart, and summarily implies the arrangement and perfection of those holy and sublime principles by which the soul is fitted for a meet temple of God in a world of immortality." [214]

Charles Scott has devoted one of the lectures in his "Analogy of Ancient Craft Masonry to Natural and Revealed Religion" to a thorough consideration of this subject. The language is too long for quotation, but the symbol has been well interpreted by him.[215]

Still more recently, Bro. John A. Loclor has treated the topic in an essay, which I regret has not had a larger circulation. A single and brief passage may show the spirit of the production, and how completely it sustains the idea of this symbolism.

"We may disguise it as we will," says Bro. Lodor, "we may evade a scrutiny of it; but our character, as it is, with its faults and blemishes, its weaknesses and infirmities, its vices and its stains, together with its redeeming traits, its better parts, is our speculative temple." And he goes on to extend the symbolic idea: "Like the exemplar temple on Mount Moriah, it should be preserved as a hallowed shrine, and guarded with the same vigilant care. It should be our pearl of price set round with walls and enclosures, even as was the Jewish temple, and the impure, the vicious, the guilty, and the profane be banished from even its outer courts. A faithful sentinel should be placed at every gate, a watchman on every wall, and the first approach of a cowan and eavesdropper be promptly met and resisted."

Teachings like this are now so common that every American Mason who has studied the symbolism of his Order believes, with Carlyle, that "there is but one temple in the world, and that is the body of man."

This inquiry into the meaning and object of labor, as a masonic symbol, brings us to these conclusions:—

1. That our ancient brethren worked as long as the operative art predominated in the institution at material temples, the most prominent of these being the temple of King Solomon.

2. That when the speculative science took the place of the operative art, the modern Masons, working no longer at material temples, but holding still to the sacred thought, the reverential idea, of a holy temple, a Lord's house to be built, began to labor at living temples, and to make man, the true house of the Lord, the tabernacle for the indwelling of the Holy Spirit.

And, 3. Therefore to every Freemason who rightly comprehends his art, this construction of a living temple is his labor.

"Labor," says Gadicke, the German masonic lexicographer, "is an important word in Masonry; indeed, we might say the most important. For this, and this alone, does a man become a Freemason. Every other object is secondary or incidental. Labor is the accustomed design of every lodge meeting. But does such meeting always furnish evidence of industry? The labor of an operative mason will be visible, and he will receive his reward for it, even though the building he has constructed may, in the next hour, be overthrown by a tempest. He knows that he has done his labor. And so must the Freemason labor. His labor must be visible to himself and to his brethren, or, at least, it must conduce to his own internal satisfaction. As we build neither a visible Solomonic temple nor an Egyptian pyramid, our industry must become visible in works that are imperishable, so that when we vanish from the eyes of mortals it may be said of us that our labor was well done."

And remembering what the apostle has said, that we are the temple of God, and that the Spirit of God dwelleth in us, we know that our labor is so to build that temple that it shall become worthy of its divine Dweller.

And thus, too, at last, we can understand the saying of the old monks that "labor is worship;" and as Masons we labor in our lodge, labor to make ourselves a perfect building, without blemish, working hopefully for the consummation, when the house of our earthly tabernacle shall be finished, when the LOST WORD of divine truth shall at last be discovered, and when we shall be found by our own efforts at perfection to have done God service. For so truly is the meaning of those noble words—LABOR IS WORSHIP.

XXX.

The Stone of Foundation.[216]

The Stone of Foundation constitutes one of the most important and abstruse of all the symbols of Freemasonry. It is referred to in numerous legends and traditions, not only of the Freemasons, but also of the Jewish Rabbins, the Talmudic writers, and even the Mussulman doctors. Many of these, it must be confessed, are apparently puerile and absurd; but some of them, and especially the masonic ones, are deeply interesting in their allegorical signification.

The Stone of Foundation is, properly speaking, a symbol of the higher degrees. It makes its first appearance in the Royal Arch, and forms, indeed, the most important symbol of that degree. But it is so intimately connected, in its legendary history, with the construction of the Solomonic temple, that it must be considered as a part of Ancient Craft Masonry, although he who confines the range of his investigations to the first three degrees, will have no means, within that narrow limit, of properly appreciating the symbolism of the Stone of Foundation.

As preliminary to the inquiry which is about to be instituted, it is necessary to distinguish the Stone of Foundation, both in its symbolism and in its legendary history, from other stones which play an important part in the masonic ritual, but which are entirely distinct from it. Such are the *corner-stone*, which was always placed in the north-east corner of the building about to be erected, and to which such a beautiful reference is made in the ceremonies of the first degree; or the *keystone*, which constitutes an interesting part of the Mark Master's degree; or, lastly, the *cape-stone*, upon which all the ritual of the Most Excellent Master's degree is founded. These are all, in their proper places, highly interesting and instructive symbols, but have no connection whatever with the Stone of Foundation or its symbolism. Nor, although the Stone of Foundation is said, for peculiar reasons, to have been of a cubical form, must it be confounded with that stone called by the continental Masons the *cubical stone*—the *pierre cubique* of the French, and the *cubik stein* of the German Masons, but which in the English system is known as the *perfect ashlar*.

The Stone of Foundation has a legendary history and a symbolic signification which are peculiar to itself, and which differ from the history and meaning which belong to these other stones.

Let us first define this masonic Stone of Foundation, then collate the legends which refer to it, and afterwards investigate its significance as a symbol. To the Mason who takes a pleasure in the study of the mysteries of his institution, the investigation cannot fail to be interesting, if it is conducted with any ability.

But in the very beginning, as a necessary preliminary to any investigation of this kind, it must be distinctly understood that all that is said of this Stone of Foundation in Masonry is to be strictly taken in a mythical or allegorical sense. Dr. Oliver, the most learned of our masonic writers, while undoubtedly himself knowing that it was simply a symbol, has written loosely of it, as though it were a substantial reality; and hence, if the passages in his "Historical Landmarks," and in his other works which refer to this celebrated stone are accepted by his readers in a literal sense, they will present absurdities and puerilities which would not occur if the Stone of Foundation was received, as it really is, as a philosophical myth, conveying a most profound and beautiful symbolism. Read in this spirit, as all the legends of Masonry should be read, the mythical story of the Stone of Foundation becomes one of the most important and interesting of all the masonic symbols.

The Stone of Foundation is supposed, by the theory which establishes it, to have been a stone placed at one time within the foundations of the temple of Solomon, and afterwards, during the building of the second temple, transported to the Holy of Holies. It was in form a perfect cube, and had inscribed upon its upper face, within a delta or triangle, the sacred tetragrammaton, or ineffable name of God. Oliver, speaking with the solemnity of an historian, says that Solomon thought that he had rendered the house of God worthy, so far as human adornment could effect, for the dwelling of God, "when he had placed the celebrated Stone of Foundation, on which the sacred name was mystically engraven, with solemn ceremonies, in that sacred depository on Mount Moriah, along with the foundations of Dan and Asher, the centre of the Most Holy Place, where the ark was overshadowed by the shekinah of God." [217] The Hebrew Talmudists, who thought as much of this stone, and had as many legends concerning it as the masonic Talmudists, called it *eben shatijah*[218] or "Stone of Foundation," because, as they said, it had been laid by Jehovah as the foundation of the world; and hence the apocryphal book of Enoch speaks of the "stone which supports the corners of the earth."

This idea of a foundation stone of the world was most probably derived from that magnificent passage of the book of Job, in which the Almighty demands of the afflicted patriarch,—

"Where wast thou, when I laid the foundation of the earth?
Declare, since thou hast such knowledge!
Who fixed its dimensions, since thou knowest?
Or who stretched out the line upon it?
Upon what were its foundations fixed?
And who laid its corner-stone,
When the morning stars sang together,
And all the sons of God shouted for joy?" [219]

Noyes, whose beautiful translation I have adopted as not materially differing from the common version, but which is far more poetical and more in the strain of the original, thus explains the allusions to the foundation-stone: "It was the custom to celebrate the laying of the corner-stone of an important building with music, songs, shouting, &c. Hence the morning stars are represented as celebrating the laying of the corner-stone of the earth." [220]

Upon this meagre statement have been accumulated more traditions than appertain to any other masonic symbol. The Rabbins, as has already been intimated, divide the glory of these apocryphal histories with the Masons; indeed, there is good reason for a suspicion that nearly all the masonic legends owe their first existence to the imaginative genius of the writers of the Jewish Talmud. But there is this difference between the Hebrew and the masonic traditions, that the Talmudic scholar recited them as truthful histories, and swallowed, in one gulp of faith, all their impossibilities and anachronisms, while the masonic student has received them as allegories, whose value is not in the facts, but in the sentiments which they convey.

With this understanding of their meaning, let us proceed to a collation of these legends.

In that blasphemous work, the "*Toldoth Jeshu*" or *Life of Jesus*, written, it is supposed, in the thirteenth or fourteenth century, we find the following account of this wonderful stone: —

"At that time [the time of Jesus] there was in the House of the Sanctuary [that is, the temple] a Stone of Foundation, which is the very stone that our father Jacob anointed with oil, as it is described in the twenty-eighth chapter of the book of Genesis. On that stone the letters of the tetragrammaton were inscribed, and whosoever of the Israelites should learn that name would be able to master the world. To prevent, therefore, any one from learning these letters, two iron dogs were placed upon two columns in front of the Sanctuary. If any person, having acquired the knowledge of these letters, desired to depart from the Sanctuary, the barking of the dogs, by magical power, inspired so much fear, that he suddenly forgot what he had acquired."

This passage is cited by the learned Buxtorf, in his "*Lexicon Talmudicum*;" [221] but in the copy of the "*Toldoth Jeshu*" which I have the good fortune to possess (for it is among the rarest of books), I find another passage which gives some additional particulars, in the following words: —

"At that time there was in the temple the ineffable name of God, inscribed upon the Stone of Foundation. For when King David was digging the foundation for the temple, he found in the depths of the excavation a certain stone, on which the name of God was inscribed. This stone he removed, and deposited it in the Holy of Holies." [222]

The same puerile story of the barking dogs is repeated, still more at length. It is not pertinent to the present inquiry, but it may be stated as a mere matter of curious information, that this scandalous book, which is throughout a blasphemous defamation of our Saviour, proceeds to say, that he cunningly obtained a knowledge of the tetragrammaton from the Stone of Foundation, and by its mystical influence was enabled to perform his miracles.

The masonic legends of the Stone of Foundation, based on these and other rabbinical reveries, are of the most extraordinary character, if they are to be viewed as histories, but readily reconcilable with sound sense, if looked at only in the light of allegories. They present an uninterrupted succession of events, in which the Stone of Foundation takes a prominent part, from Adam to Solomon, and from Solomon to Zerubbabel.

Thus the first of these legends, in order of time, relates that the Stone of Foundation was possessed by Adam while in the garden of Eden; that he used it as an altar, and so reverenced it, that, on his expulsion from Paradise, he carried it with him into the world in which he and his descendants were afterwards to earn their bread by the sweat of their brow.

Another legend informs us that from Adam the Stone of Foundation descended to Seth. From Seth it passed by regular succession to Noah, who took it with him into the ark, and after the subsidence of the deluge, made on it his first thank-offering. Noah left it on Mount Ararat, where it was subsequently found by Abraham, who removed it, and consequently used it as an altar of sacrifice. His grandson Jacob took it with him when he fled to his uncle Laban in Mesopotamia, and used it as a pillow when, in the vicinity of Luz, he had his celebrated vision.

Here there is a sudden interruption in the legendary history of the stone, and we have no means of conjecturing how it passed from the possession of Jacob into that of Solomon. Moses, it is true, is said to have taken it with him out of Egypt at the time of the exodus, and thus it may have finally reached Jerusalem. Dr. Adam Clarke[223] repeats what he very properly calls "a foolish tradition," that the stone on which Jacob rested his head was afterwards brought to Jerusalem, thence carried after a long lapse of time to Spain, from Spain to Ireland, and from Ireland to Scotland, where it was used as a seat on which the kings of Scotland sat to be crowned. Edward I., we know, brought a stone, to which this legend is attached, from Scotland to Westminster Abbey, where, under the name of Jacob's Pillow, it still remains, and is always placed under the chair upon which the British sovereign sits to be crowned, because there is an old distich which declares that wherever this stone is found the Scottish kings shall reign.[224]

But this Scottish tradition would take the Stone of Foundation away from all its masonic connections, and therefore it is rejected as a masonic legend.

The legends just related are in many respects contradictory and unsatisfactory, and another series, equally as old, are now very generally adopted by masonic scholars, as much better suited to the symbolism by which all these legends are explained.

This series of legends commences with the patriarch Enoch, who is supposed to have been the first consecrator of the Stone of Foundation. The legend of Enoch is so interesting and important in masonic science as to excuse something more than a brief reference to the incidents which it details.

The legend in full is as follows: Enoch, under the inspiration of the Most High, and in obedience to the instructions which he had received in a vision, built a temple under ground on Mount Moriah, and dedicated it to God. His son, Methuselah, constructed the building, although he was not acquainted with his father's motives for the erection. This temple consisted of nine vaults, situated perpendicularly beneath each other, and communicating by apertures left in each vault.

Enoch then caused a triangular plate of gold to be made, each side of which was a cubit long; he enriched it with the most precious stones, and encrusted the plate upon a stone of agate of the same form. On the plate he engraved the true name of God, or the tetragrammaton, and placing it on a cubical stone, known thereafter as the Stone of Foundation, he deposited the whole within the lowest arch.

When this subterranean building was completed, he made a door of stone, and attaching to it a ring of iron, by which it might be occasionally raised, he placed it over the opening of the uppermost arch, and so covered it that the aperture could not be discovered. Enoch himself was not permitted to enter it but once a year, and after the days of Enoch, Methuselah, and Lamech, and the destruction of the world by the deluge, all knowledge of the vault or subterranean temple, and of the Stone of Foundation, with the sacred and ineffable name inscribed upon it, was lost for ages to the world.

At the building of the first temple of Jerusalem, the Stone of Foundation again makes its appearance. Reference has already been made to the Jewish tradition that David, when digging the foundations of the temple, found in the excavation which he was making a certain stone, on which the ineffable name of God was inscribed, and which stone he is said to have removed and deposited in the Holy of Holies. That King David laid the foundations of the temple upon which the superstructure was subsequently erected by Solomon, is a favorite theory of the legend-mongers of the Talmud.

The masonic tradition is substantially the same as the Jewish, but it substitutes Solomon for David, thereby giving a greater air of probability to the narrative; and it supposes that the stone thus discovered by Solomon was the identical one that had been deposited in his secret vault by Enoch. This Stone of Foundation, the tradition states, was subsequently removed by King Solomon, and, for wise purposes, deposited in a secret and safer place.

In this the masonic tradition again agrees with the Jewish, for we find in the third chapter of the "*Treatise on the Temple*" written by the celebrated Maimonides, the following narrative—

"There was a stone in the Holy of Holies, on its west side, on which was placed the ark of the covenant, and before it the pot of manna and Aaron's rod. But when Solomon had built the temple, and foresaw that it was, at some future time, to be destroyed, he constructed a deep and winding vault under ground, for the purpose of concealing the ark, wherein Josiah afterwards, as we learn in the Second Book of Chronicles, xxxv. 3, deposited it, with the pot of manna, the rod of Aaron, and the oil of anointing."

The Talmudical book "*Yoma*" gives the same tradition, and says that "the ark of the covenant was placed in the centre of the Holy of Holies, upon a stone rising three fingers' breadth above the floor, to be, as it were, a pedestal for it." "This stone," says Prideaux,[225] "the Rabbins call the Stone of Foundation, and give us a great deal of trash about it."

There is much controversy as to the question of the existence of any ark in the second temple. Some of the Jewish writers assert that a new one was made; others, that the old one was found where it had been concealed by Solomon; and others again contend that there was no ark at all in the temple of Zerubbabel, but that its place was supplied by the Stone of Foundation on which it had originally rested.

Royal Arch Masons well know how all these traditions are sought to be reconciled by the masonic legend, in which the substitute ark and the Stone of Foundation play so important a part.

In the thirteenth degree of the Ancient and Accepted Rite, the Stone of Foundation is conspicuous as the resting-place of the sacred delta.

In the Royal Arch and Select Master's degrees of the Americanized York Rite, the Stone of Foundation constitutes the most important part of the ritual. In both of these it is the receptacle of the ark, on which the ineffable name is inscribed.

Lee, in his "*Temple of Solomon*", has devoted a chapter to this Stone of Foundation, and thus recapitulates the Talmudic and Rabbinical traditions on the subject: —

"Vain and futilous are the feverish dreams of the ancient Rabbins concerning the Foundation Stone of the temple. Some assert that God placed this stone in the centre of the world, for a future basis and settled consistency for the earth to rest upon. Others held this stone to be the first matter, out of which all the beautiful visible beings of the world have been hewn forth and produced to light. Others relate that this was the very same stone laid by Jacob for a pillow under his head, in that night when he dreamed of an angelic vision at Bethel, and afterwards anointed and consecrated it to God. Which when Solomon had found (no doubt by forged revelation, or some tedious search, like another Rabbi Selemoh), he durst not but lay it sure, as the principal foundation stone of the temple. Nay, they say further, he caused to be engraved upon it the tetragrammaton, or the ineffable name of Jehovah." [226]

It will be seen that the masonic traditions on the subject of the Stone of Foundation do not differ very materially from these Rabbinical ones, although they give a few additional circumstances.

In the masonic legend, the Foundation Stone first makes its appearance, as I have already said, in the days of Enoch, who placed it in the bowels of Mount Moriah. There it was subsequently discovered by King Solomon, who deposited it in a crypt of the first temple, where it remained concealed until the foundations of the second temple were laid, when it was discovered and removed to the Holy of Holies. But the most important point of the legend of the Stone of Foundation is its intimate and constant connection with the tetragrammaton, or ineffable name. It is this name, inscribed upon it, within the sacred and symbolic delta, that gives to the stone all its masonic value and significance. It is upon this fact, that it was so inscribed, that its whole symbolism depends.

Looking at these traditions in anything like the light of historical narratives, we are compelled to consider them, to use the plain language of Lee, "but as so many idle and absurd conceits." We must go behind the legend, viewing it only as an allegory, and study its symbolism.

The symbolism of the Foundation Stone of Masonry is therefore the next subject of investigation.

In approaching this, the most abstruse, and one of the most important, symbols of the Order, we are at once impressed with its apparent connection with the ancient doctrine of stone worship. Some brief consideration of this species of religious culture is therefore necessary for a proper understanding of the real symbolism of the Stone of Foundation.

The worship of stones is a kind of fetichism, which in the very infancy of religion prevailed, perhaps, more extensively than any other form of religious culture. Lord Kames explains the fact by supposing that stones erected as monuments of the dead became the place where posterity paid their veneration to the memory of the deceased, and that at length the people, losing sight of the emblematical signification, which was not readily understood, these monumental stones became objects of worship.

Others have sought to find the origin of stone-worship in the stone that was set up and anointed by Jacob at Bethel, and the tradition of which had extended into the heathen nations and become corrupted. It is certain that the Phoenicians worshipped sacred stones under the name of *Baetylia*, which word is evidently derived from the Hebrew *Bethel*; and this undoubtedly gives some appearance of plausibility to the theory.

But a third theory supposes that the worship of stones was derived from the unskilfulness of the primitive sculptors, who, unable to frame, by their meagre principles of plastic art, a true image of the God whom they adored, were content to substitute in its place a rude or scarcely polished stone. Hence the Greeks, according to Pausanias, originally used unhewn stones to represent their deities, thirty of which that historian says he saw in the city of Pharas. These stones were of a cubical form, and as the greater number of them were dedicated to the god Hermes, or Mercury, they received the generic name of *Hermaa*. Subsequently, with the improvement of the plastic art, the head was added.[227]

One of these consecrated stones was placed before the door of almost every house in Athens. They were also placed in front of the temples, in the gymnasia or schools, in libraries, and at the corners of streets, and in the roads. When dedicated to the god Terminus they were used as landmarks, and placed as such upon the concurrent lines of neighboring possessions.

The Thebans worshipped Bacchus under the form of a rude, square stone.

Arnobius[228] says that Cybele was represented by a small stone of a black color. Eusebius cites Porphyry as saying that the ancients represented the deity by a black stone, because his nature is obscure and inscrutable. The reader will here be reminded of the black stone *Hadsjar el Aswad*, placed in the south-west corner of the Kaaba at Mecca, which was worshipped by the ancient Arabians, and is still treated with religious veneration by the modern Mohammedans. The Mussulman priests, however, say that it was originally white, and of such surprising splendor that it could be seen at the distance of four days' journey, but that it has been blackened by the tears of pilgrims.

The Druids, it is well known, had no other images of their gods but cubical, or sometimes columnar, stones, of which Toland gives several instances.

The Chaldeans had a sacred stone, which they held in great veneration, under the name of *Mnizuris*, and to which they sacrificed for the purpose of evoking the Good Demon.

Stone-worship existed among the early American races. Squier quotes Skinner as asserting that the Peruvians used to set up rough stones in their fields and plantations, which were worshipped as protectors of their crops. And Gam a says that in Mexico the presiding god of the spring was often represented without a human body, and in place thereof a pilaster or square column, whose pedestal was covered with various sculptures.

Indeed, so universal was this stone-worship, that Higgins, in his "*Celtic Druids*," says that, "throughout the world the first object of idolatry seems to have been a plain, unwrought stone, placed in the ground, as an emblem of the generative or procreative powers of nature." And the learned Bryant, in his "*Analysis of Ancient Mythology*," asserts that "there is in every oracular temple some legend about a stone."

Without further citations of examples from the religious usages of other countries, it will, I think, be conceded that the cubical stone formed an important part of the religious worship of primitive nations. But Cudworth, Bryant, Faber, and all other distinguished writers who have treated the subject, have long since established the theory that the pagan religions were eminently symbolic. Thus, to use the language of Dudley, the pillar or stone "was adopted as a symbol of strength and firmness,—a symbol, also, of the divine power, and, by a ready inference, a symbol or idol of the Deity himself." [229] And this symbolism is confirmed by Cornutus, who says that the god Hermes was represented without hands or feet, being a cubical stone, because the cubical figure betokened his solidity and stability. [230]

Thus, then, the following facts have been established, but not precisely in this order: First, that there was a very general prevalence among the earliest nations of antiquity of the worship of stones as the representatives of Deity; secondly, that in almost every ancient temple there was a legend of a sacred or mystical stone; thirdly, that this legend is found in the masonic system; and lastly, that the mystical stone there has received the name of the "Stone of Foundation."

Now, as in all the other systems the stone is admitted to be symbolic, and the tradition connected with it mystical, we are compelled to assume the same predicates of the masonic stone. It, too, is symbolic, and its legend a myth or an allegory.

Of the fable, myth, or allegory, Bailly has said that, "subordinate to history and philosophy, it only deceives that it may the better instruct us. Faithful in preserving the realities which are confided to it, it covers with its seductive envelope the lessons of the one and the truths of the other." [231] It is from this stand-point that we are to view the allegory of the Stone of Foundation, as developed in one of the most interesting and important symbols of Masonry.

The fact that the mystical stone in all the ancient religions was a symbol of the Deity, leads us necessarily to the conclusion that the Stone of Foundation was also a symbol of Deity. And this symbolic idea is strengthened by the tetragrammaton, or sacred name of God, that was inscribed upon it. This ineffable name sanctifies the stone upon which it is engraved as the symbol of the Grand Architect. It takes from it its heathen signification as an idol, and consecrates it to the worship of the true God.

The predominant idea of the Deity, in the masonic system, connects him with his creative and formative power. God is, to the Freemason, *Al Gabil*, as the Arabians called him, that is, *The Builder*; or, as expressed in his masonic title, the *Grand Architect of the Universe*, by common consent abbreviated in the formula G.A.O.T.U. Now, it is evident that no symbol could so appropriately suit him in this character as the Stone of Foundation, upon which he is allegorically supposed to have erected his world. Such a symbol closely connects the creative work of God, as a pattern and exemplar, with the workman's erection of his temporal building on a similar foundation stone.

But this masonic idea is still further to be extended. The great object of all Masonic labor is *divine truth*. The search for the *lost word* is the search for truth. But divine truth is a term synonymous with God. The ineffable name is a symbol of truth, because God, and God alone, is truth. It is properly a scriptural idea. The Book of Psalms abounds with this sentiment. Thus it is said that the truth of the Lord "reacheth unto the clouds," and that "his truth endureth unto all generations." If, then, God is truth, and the Stone of Foundation is the masonic symbol of God, it follows that it must also be the symbol of divine truth.

When we have arrived at this point in our speculations, we are ready to show how all the myths and legends of the Stone of Foundation may be rationally explained as parts of that beautiful "science of morality, veiled in allegory and illustrated by symbols," which is the acknowledged definition of Freemasonry.

In the masonic system there are two temples; the first temple, in which the degrees of Ancient Craft Masonry are concerned, and the second temple, with which the higher degrees, and especially the Royal Arch, are related. The first temple is symbolic of the present life; the second temple is symbolic of the life to come. The first temple, the present life, must be destroyed; on its foundations the second temple, the life eternal, must be built.

But the mystical stone was placed by King Solomon in the foundations of the first temple. That is to say, the first temple of our present life must be built on the sure foundation of divine truth, "for other foundation can no man lay."

But although the present life is necessarily built upon the foundation of truth, yet we never thoroughly attain it in this sublunary sphere. The Foundation Stone is concealed in the first temple, and the Master Mason knows it not. He has not the true word. He receives only a substitute.

But in the second temple of the future life, we have passed from the grave, which had been the end of our labors in the first. We have removed the rubbish, and have found that Stone of Foundation which had been hitherto concealed from our eyes. We now throw aside the substitute for truth which had contented us in the former temple, and the brilliant effulgence of the tetragrammaton and the Stone of Foundation are discovered, and thenceforth we are the possessors of the true word—of divine truth. And in this way, the Stone of Foundation, or divine truth, concealed in the first temple, but discovered and brought to light in the second, will explain that passage of the apostle, "For now we see through a glass darkly, but then face to face: now I know in part; but then shall I know even as also I am known."

And so, the result of this inquiry is, that the masonic Stone of Foundation is a symbol of divine truth, upon which all Speculative Masonry is built, and the legends and traditions which refer to it are intended to describe, in an allegorical way, the progress of truth in the soul, the search for which is a Mason's labor, and the discovery of which is his reward.

XXXI.

The Lost Word.

The last of the symbols, depending for its existence on its connection with a myth to which I shall invite attention, is *the Lost Word, and the search for it*. Very appropriately may this symbol terminate our investigations, since it includes within its comprehensive scope all the others, being itself the very essence of the science of masonic symbolism. The other symbols require for their just appreciation a knowledge of the origin of the order, because they owe their birth to its relationship with kindred and anterior institutions. But the symbolism of the Lost Word has reference exclusively to the design and the objects of the institution.

First, let us define the symbol, and then investigate its interpretation.

The mythical history of Freemasonry informs us that there once existed a WORD of surpassing value, and claiming a profound veneration; that this Word was known to but few; that it was at length lost; and that a temporary substitute for it was adopted. But as the very philosophy of Masonry teaches us that there can be no death without a resurrection,—no decay without a subsequent restoration,—on the same principle it follows that the loss of the Word must suppose its eventual recovery.

Now, this it is, precisely, that constitutes the myth of the Lost Word and the search for it. No matter what was the word, no matter how it was lost, nor why a substitute was provided, nor when nor where it was recovered. These are all points of subsidiary importance, necessary, it is true, for knowing the legendary history, but not necessary for understanding the symbolism. The only term of the myth that is to be regarded in the study of its interpretation, is the abstract idea of a word lost and afterwards recovered.

This, then, points us to the goal to which we must direct our steps in the pursuit of the investigation.

But the symbolism, referring in this case, as I have already said, solely to the great design of Freemasonry, the nature of that design at once suggests itself as a preliminary subject of inquiry in the investigation.

What, then, is the design of Freemasonry? A very large majority of its disciples, looking only to its practical results, as seen in the every-day business of life,—to the noble charities which it dispenses, to the tears of widows which it has dried, to the cries of orphans which it has hushed, to the wants of the destitute which it has supplied,—arrive with too much rapidity at the conclusion that Charity, and that, too, in its least exalted sense of eleemosynary aid, is the great design of the institution.

Others, with a still more contracted view, remembering the pleasant reunions at their lodge banquets, the unreserved communications which are thus encouraged, and the solemn obligations of mutual trust and confidence that are continually inculcated, believe that it was intended solely to promote the social sentiments and cement the bonds of friendship.

But, although the modern lectures inform us that Brotherly Love and Relief are two of "the principal tenets of a Mason's profession," yet, from the same authority, we learn that Truth is a third and not less important one; and Truth, too, not in its old Anglo-Saxon meaning of fidelity to engagements,[232] but in that more strictly philosophical one in which it is opposed to intellectual and religious error or falsehood.

But I have shown that the Primitive Freemasonry of the ancients was instituted for the purpose of preserving that truth which had been originally communicated to the patriarchs, in all its integrity, and that the Spurious Masonry, or the Mysteries, originated in the earnest need of the sages, and philosophers, and priests, to find again the same truth which had been lost by the surrounding multitudes. I have shown, also, that this same truth continued to be the object of the Temple Masonry, which was formed by a union of the Primitive, or Pure, and the Spurious systems. Lastly, I have endeavored to demonstrate that this truth related to the nature of God and the human soul.

The search, then, after this truth, I suppose to constitute the end and design of Speculative Masonry. From the very commencement of his career, the aspirant is by significant symbols and expressive instructions directed to the acquisition of this divine truth; and the whole lesson, if not completed in its full extent, is at least well developed in the myths and legends of the Master's degree. *God and the soul*—the unity of the one and the immortality of the other—are the great truths, the search for which is to constitute the constant occupation of every Mason, and which, when found, are to become the chief corner-stone, or the stone of foundation, of the spiritual temple—"the house not made with hands"—which he is engaged in erecting.

Now, this idea of a search after truth forms so prominent a part of the whole science of Freemasonry, that I conceive no better or more comprehensive answer could be given to the question, *What is Freemasonry?* than to say that it is a science which is engaged in the search after divine truth.

But Freemasonry is eminently a system of symbolism, and all its instructions are conveyed in symbols. It is, therefore, to be supposed that so prominent and so prevailing an idea as this,—one that constitutes, as I have said, the whole design of the institution, and which may appropriately be adopted as the very definition of its science,—could not with any consistency be left without its particular symbol.

The WORD, therefore, I conceive to be the symbol of *Divine Truth;* and all its modifications—the loss, the substitution, and the recovery—are but component parts of the mythical symbol which represents a search after truth.

How, then, is this symbolism preserved? How is the whole history of this Word to be interpreted, so as to bear, in all its accidents of time, and place, and circumstance, a patent reference to the substantive idea that has been symbolized?

The answers to these questions embrace what is, perhaps, the most intricate as well as most ingenious and interesting portion of the science of masonic symbolism.

This symbolism may be interpreted, either in an application to a general or to a special sense.

The general application will embrace the whole history of Freemasonry, from its inception to its consummation. The search after the Word is an epitome of the intellectual and religious progress of the order, from the period when, by the dispersion at Babel, the multitudes were enshrouded in the profundity of a moral darkness where truth was apparently forever extinguished. The true name of God was lost; his true nature was not understood; the divine lessons imparted by our father Noah were no longer remembered; the ancient traditions were now corrupted; the ancient symbols were perverted. Truth was buried beneath the rubbish of Sabaism, and the idolatrous adoration of the sun and stars had taken the place of the olden worship of the true God. A moral darkness was now spread over the face of the earth, as a dense, impenetrable cloud, which obstructed the rays of the spiritual sun, and covered the people as with a gloomy pall of intellectual night.

But this night was not to last forever. A brighter dawn was to arise, and amidst all this gloom and darkness there were still to be found a few sages in whom the religious sentiment, working in them with powerful throes, sent forth manfully to seek after truth. There were, even in those days of intellectual and religious darkness, craftsmen who were willing to search for the *Lost Word*. And though they were unable to find it, their approximation to truth was so near that the result of their search may well be symbolized by the *Substitute Word*.

It was among the idolatrous multitudes that the *Word* had been lost. It was among them that the Builder had been smitten, and that the works of the spiritual temple had been suspended; and so, losing at each successive stage of their decline, more and more of the true knowledge of God and of the pure religion which had originally been imparted by Noah, they finally arrived at gross materialism and idolatry, losing all sight of the divine existence. Thus it was that the truth—the Word—was said to have been lost; or, to apply the language of Hutchinson, modified in its reference to the time, "in this situation, it might well be said that the guide to heaven was lost, and the master of the works of righteousness was smitten. The nations had given themselves up to the grossest idolatry, and the service of the true God was effaced from the memory of those who had yielded themselves to the dominion of sin."

And now it was among the philosophers and priests in the ancient Mysteries, or the spurious Freemasonry, that an anxiety to discover the truth led to the search for the Lost Word. These were the craftsmen who saw the fatal-blow which had been given, who knew that the Word was now lost, but were willing to go forth, manfully and patiently, to seek its restoration. And there were the craftsmen who, failing to rescue it from the grave of oblivion into which it had fallen, by any efforts of their own incomplete knowledge, fell back upon the dim traditions which had been handed down from primeval times, and through their aid found a substitute for truth in their own philosophical religions.

And hence Schmidtz, speaking of these Mysteries of the pagan world, calls them the remains of the ancient Pelasgian religion, and says that "the associations of persons for the purpose of celebrating them must therefore have been formed at the time when the overwhelming influence of the Hellenic religion began to gain the upper hand in Greece, and when persons who still entertained a reverence for the worship of former times united together, with the intention of preserving and upholding among themselves as much as possible of the religion of their forefathers."

Applying, then, our interpretation in a general sense, the *Word* itself being the symbol of *Divine Truth*, the narrative of its loss and the search for its recovery becomes a mythical symbol of the decay and loss of the true religion among the ancient nations, at and after the dispersion on the plains of Shinar, and of the attempts of the wise men, the philosophers, and priests, to find and retain it in their secret Mysteries and initiations, which have hence been designated as the Spurious Freemasonry of Antiquity.

But I have said that there is a special, or individual, as well as a general interpretation. This compound or double symbolism, if I may so call it, is by no means unusual in Freemasonry. I have already exhibited an illustration of it in the symbolism of Solomon's temple, where, in a general sense, the temple is viewed as a symbol of that spiritual temple formed by the aggregation of the whole order, and in which each mason is considered as a stone; and, in an individual or special sense, the same temple is considered as a type of that spiritual temple which each mason is directed to erect in his heart.

Now, in this special or individual interpretation, the Word, with its accompanying myth of a loss, a substitute, and a recovery, becomes a symbol of the personal progress of a candidate from his first initiation to the completion of his course, when he receives a full development of the Mysteries.

The aspirant enters on this search after truth, as an Entered Apprentice, in darkness, seeking for light—the light of wisdom, the light of truth, the light symbolized by the Word. For this important task, upon which he starts forth gropingly, falteringly, doubtingly, in want and in weakness, he is prepared by a purification of the heart, and is invested with a first substitute for the true Word, which, like the pillar that went before the Israelites in the wilderness, is to guide him onwards in his weary journey. He is directed to take, as a staff and scrip for his journey, all those virtues which expand the heart and dignify the soul. Secrecy, obedience, humility, trust in God, purity of conscience, economy of time, are all inculcated by impressive types and symbols, which connect the first degree with the period of youth.

And then, next in the degree of Fellow Craft, he fairly enters upon his journey. Youth has now passed, and manhood has come on. New duties and increased obligations press upon the individual. The thinking and working stage of life is here symbolized. Science is to be cultivated; wisdom is to be acquired; the lost Word—divine truth—is still to be sought for. But even yet it is not to be found.

And now the Master Mason comes, with all the symbolism around him of old age—trials, sufferings, death. And here, too, the aspirant, pressing onward, *always onward*, still cries aloud for "light, more light." The search is almost over, but the lesson, humiliating to human nature, is to be taught, that in this life—gloomy and dark, earthly and carnal—pure truth has no abiding place; and contented with a substitute, and to that *second temple* of eternal life, for that true Word, that divine Truth, which will teach us all that we shall ever learn of God and his emanation, the human soul.

So, the Master Mason, receiving this substitute for the lost Word, waits with patience for the time when it shall be found, and perfect wisdom shall be attained.

But, work as we will, this symbolic Word—this knowledge of divine Truth—is never thoroughly attained in this life, or in its symbol, the Master Mason's lodge. The corruptions of mortality, which encumber and cloud the human intellect, hide it, as with a thick veil, from mortal eyes. It is only, as I have just said, beyond the tomb, and when released from the earthly burden of life, that man is capable of fully receiving and appreciating the revelation. Hence, then, when we speak of the recovery of the Word, in that higher degree which is a supplement to Ancient Craft Masonry, we intimate that that sublime portion of the masonic system is a symbolic representation of the state after death. For it is only after the decay and fall of this temple of life, which, as masons, we have been building, that from its ruins, deep beneath its foundations, and in the profound abyss of the grave, we find that divine truth, in the search for which life was spent, if not in vain, at least without success, and the mystic key to which death only could supply.

And now we know by this symbolism what is meant by masonic *labor*, which, too, is itself but another form of the same symbol. The search for the Word—to find divine Truth—this, and this only, is a mason's work, and the WORD is his reward.

Labor, said the old monks, is worship—*laborare est orare*; and thus in our lodges do we worship, working for the Word, working for the Truth, ever looking forward, casting no glance behind, but cheerily hoping for the consummation and the reward of our labor in the knowledge which is promised to him who plays no laggard's part.

Goethe, himself a mason and a poet, knew and felt all this symbolism of a mason's life and work, when he wrote that beautiful poem, which Carlyle has thus thrown into his own rough but impulsive language.

"The mason's ways are
A type of existence,—
And to his persistence
Is as the days are
Of men in this world.

"The future hides in it
Gladness and sorrow;
We press still thorow,
Nought that abides in it
Daunting us—onward.

"And solemn before us
Veiled the dark portal,
Goal of all mortal;
Stars silent rest o'er us
Graves under us silent.

"While earnest thou gazest
Come boding of terror,
Comes phantasm and error,
Perplexing the bravest
With doubt and misgiving.

"But heard are the voices,
Heard are the sages,
The worlds and the ages;
'Choose well; your choice is
Brief and yet endless.

"'Here eyes do regard you,
In eternity's stillness;
Here is all fullness,
Ye, brave to reward you;
Work and despair not.'"

And now, in concluding this work, so inadequate to the importance of the subjects that have been discussed, one deduction, at least, may be drawn from all that has been said.

In tracing the progress of Freemasonry, and in detailing its system of symbolism, it has been found to be so intimately connected with the history of philosophy, of religion, and of art, in all ages of the world, that the conviction at once forces itself upon the mind, that no mason can expect thoroughly to comprehend its nature, or to appreciate its character as a science, unless he shall devote himself, with some labor and assiduity, to this study of its system. That skill which consists in repeating, with fluency and precision, the ordinary lectures, in complying with all the ceremonial requisitions of the ritual, or the giving, with sufficient accuracy, the appointed modes of recognition, pertains only to the very rudiments of the masonic science.

But there is a far nobler series of doctrines with which Freemasonry is connected, and which it has been my object, in this work, to present in some imperfect way. It is these which constitute the science and the philosophy of Freemasonry, and it is these alone which will return the student who devotes himself to the task, a sevenfold reward for his labor.

Freemasonry, viewed no longer, as too long it has been, as a merely social institution, has now assumed its original and undoubted position as a speculative science. While the mere ritual is still carefully preserved, as the casket should be which contains so bright a jewel; while its charities are still dispensed as the necessary though incidental result of all its moral teachings; while its social tendencies are still cultivated as the tenacious cement which is to unite so fair a fabric in symmetry and strength, the masonic mind is everywhere beginning to look and ask for something, which, like the manna in the desert, shall feed us, in our pilgrimage, with intellectual food. The universal cry, throughout the masonic world, is for light; our lodges are henceforth to be schools; our labor is to be study; our wages are to be learning; the types and symbols, the myths and allegories, of the institution are beginning to be investigated with reference to their ultimate meaning; our history is now traced by zealous inquiries as to its connection with antiquity; and Freemasons now thoroughly understand that often quoted definition, that "Masonry is a science of morality veiled in allegory and illustrated by symbols."

Thus to learn Masonry is to know our work and to do it well. What true mason would shrink from the task?

Synoptical Index.

A

AB. The Hebrew word בא, AB, signifies "father," and was among the Hebrews a title of honor. From it, by the addition of the possessive pronoun, is compounded the word *Abif*, signifying "his father," and applied to the Temple Builder.

ABIF. See *Hiram Abif*.

ABNET. The band or apron, made of fine linen, variously wrought, and worn by the Jewish priesthood. It seems to have been borrowed directly from the Egyptians, upon the representations of all of whose gods is to be found a similar girdle. Like the zennaar, or sacred cord of the Brahmins, and the white shield of the Scandinavians, it is the analogue of the masonic apron.

ACACIA, SPRIG OF. No symbol is more interesting to the masonic student than the sprig of acacia.

It is the *mimosa nilotica* of Linnæus, the *shittah* of the Hebrew writers, and grows abundantly in Palestine.

It is preeminently the symbol of the immortality of the soul.

It was for this reason planted by the Jews at the head of a grave.

This symbolism is derived from its never-fading character as an evergreen.

It is also a symbol of innocence, and this symbolism is derived from the double meaning of the word αχαχια, which in Greek signifies the plant, and innocence; in this point of view Hutchinson has Christianized the symbol.

It is, lastly, a symbol of initiation.

This symbolism is derived from the fact that it is the sacred plant of Masonry; and in all the ancient rites there were sacred plants, which became in each rite the respective symbol of initiation into its Mysteries; hence the idea was borrowed by Freemasonry.

ADONIA. The Mysteries of Adonis, principally celebrated in Phoenicia and Syria. They lasted for two days, and were commemorative of the death and restoration of Adonis. The ceremonies of the first day were funereal in their character, and consisted in the lamentations of the initiates for the death of Adonis, whose picture or image was carried in procession. The second day was devoted to mirth and joy for the return of Adonis to life. In their spirit and their mystical design, these Mysteries bore a very great resemblance to the third degree of Masonry, and they are quoted to show the striking analogy between the ancient and the modern initiations.

ADONIS. In mythology, the son of Cinyras and Myrrha, who was greatly beloved by Venus, or Aphrodite. He was slain by a wild boar, and having descended into the realm of Pluto, Persephone became enamoured of him. This led to a contest for him between Venus and Persephone, which was finally settled by his restoration to life upon the condition that he should spend six months upon earth, and six months in the inferior regions. In the mythology of the philosophers, Adonis was a symbol of the sun; but his death by violence, and his subsequent restoration to life, make him the analogue of Hiram Abif in the masonic system, and identify the spirit of the initiation in his Mysteries, which was to teach the second life with that of the third degree of Freemasonry.

AHRIMAN, or ARIMANES. In the religious system of Zoroaster, the principle of evil, or darkness, which was perpetually opposing Ormuzd, the principle of good, or light. See *Zoroaster*.

ALFADER. The father of all, or the universal Father. The principal deity of the Scandinavian mythology.

The Edda gives twelve names of God, of which Alfader is the first and most ancient, and is the one most generally used.

ALGABIL. One of the names of the Supreme Being among the Cabalists. It signifies "the Master Builder," and is equivalent to the masonic epithet of "Grand Architect of the Universe."

ALLEGORY. A discourse or narrative, in which there is a literal and a figurative sense, a patent and a concealed meaning; the literal or patent sense being intended by analogy or comparison to indicate the figurative or concealed one. Its derivation from the Greek ἀλλος and ἀγορειν, *to say something different*, that is, to say something where the language is one thing, and the true meaning different, exactly expresses the character of an allegory. It has been said in the text that there is no essential difference between an allegory and a symbol. There is not in design, but there is this in their character: An allegory may be interpreted without any previous conventional agreement, but a symbol cannot. Thus the legend of the third degree is an allegory evidently to be interpreted as teaching a restoration to life; and this we learn from the legend itself, without any previous understanding. The sprig of acacia is a symbol of the immortality of the soul. But this we know only because such meaning had been conventionally determined when the symbol was first established. It is evident, then, that an allegory which is obscure is imperfect. The enigmatical meaning should be easy of interpretation; and hence Lemière, a French poet, has said, "L'allégorie habite un palais diaphane"—*Allegory lives in a transparent palace*. All the legends of Freemasonry are more or less allegorical, and whatever truth there may be in some of them in an historical point of view, it is only as allegories, or legendary symbols, that they are important.

ALL-SEEING EYE. A symbol of the third degree, of great antiquity. See *Eye*.

ANCIENT CRAFT MASONRY. The first three degrees of Freemasonry; viz., Entered Apprentice, Fellow Craft, and Master Mason. They are so called because they alone are supposed to have been practised by the ancient craft. In the agreement between the two grand lodges of England in 1813, the definition was made to include the Royal Arch degree. Now if by the "ancient craft" are meant the workmen at the first temple, the definition will be wrong, because the Royal Arch degree could have had no existence until the time of the building of the second temple. But if by the "ancient craft" is meant the body of workmen who introduced the rites of Masonry into Europe in the early ages of the history of the Order, then it will be correct; because the Royal Arch degree always, from its origin until the middle of the eighteenth century, formed a part of the Master's. "Ancient Craft Masonry," however, in this country, is generally understood to embrace only the first three degrees.

ANDERSON. James Anderson, D.D., is celebrated as the compiler and editor of "The Constitutions of the Freemasons," published by order of the Grand Lodge of England, in 1723. A second edition was published by him in 1738. Shortly after, Anderson died, and the subsequent editions, of which there are several, have been edited by other persons. The edition of 1723 has become exceedingly rare, and copies of it bring fancy prices among the collectors of old masonic books. Its intrinsic value is derived only from the fact that it contains the first printed copy of the "Old Charges," and also the "General Regulations." The history of Masonry which precedes these, and constitutes the body of the work, is fanciful, unreliable, and pretentious to a degree that often leads to absurdity. The craft are greatly indebted to Anderson for his labors in reorganizing the institution, but doubtless it would have been better if he had contented himself with giving the records of the Grand Lodge from 1717 to 1738 which are contained in his second edition, and with preserving for us the charges and regulations, which without his industry might have been lost. No masonic writer would now venture to quote Anderson as authority for the history of the Order anterior to the eighteenth century. It must also be added that in the republication of the old charges in the edition of 1738, he made several important alterations and interpolations, which justly gave some offence to the Grand Lodge, and which render the second edition of no authority in this respect.

ANIMAL WORSHIP. The worship of animals is a species of idolatry that was especially practised by the ancient Egyptians. Temples were erected by this people in their honor, in which they were fed and cared for during life; to kill one of them was a crime punishable with death; and after death, they were embalmed, and interred in the catacombs. This worship was derived first from the earlier adoration of the stars, to certain constellations of which the names of animals had been given; next, from an Egyptian tradition that the gods, being pursued by Typhon, had concealed themselves under the forms of animals; and lastly, from the doctrine of the metempsychosis, according to which there was a continual circulation of the souls of men and animals. But behind the open and popular exercise of this degrading worship the priests concealed a symbolism full of philosophical conceptions. How this symbolism was corrupted and misinterpreted by the uninitiated people, is shown by Gliddon, and quoted in the text.

APHANISM (Greek ἀφανίζω, *to conceal*). In each of the initiations of the ancient Mysteries, there was a scenic representation of the death or disappearance of some god or hero, whose adventures constituted the legend of the Mystery. That part of the ceremony of initiation which related to and represented the death or disappearance was called the *aphanism*.

Freemasonry, which has in its ceremonial form been framed after the model of these ancient Mysteries, has also its aphanism in the third degree.

APORRHETA (Greek απορρέτα). The holy things in the ancient Mysteries which were known only to the initiates, and were not to be disclosed to the profane, were called the *aporrheta*. What are the aporrheta of Freemasonry? what are the arcana of which there can be no disclosure? is a question that for some years past has given rise to much discussion among the disciples of the institution. If the sphere and number of these aporrheta be very considerably extended, it is evident that much valuable investigation by public discussion of the science of Masonry will be prohibited. On the other hand, if the aporrheta are restricted to only a few points, much of the beauty, the permanency, and the efficacy of Freemasonry, which are dependent on its organization as a secret and mystical association, will be lost. We move between Scylla and Charybdis, and it is difficult for a masonic writer to know how to steer so as, in avoiding too frank an exposition of the principles of the Order, not to fall by too much reticence into obscurity. The European Masons are far more liberal in their views of the obligation of secrecy than the English or the American. There are few things, indeed, which a French or German masonic writer will refuse to discuss with the utmost frankness. It is now beginning to be very generally admitted, and English and American writers are acting on the admission, that the only real aporrheta of Freemasonry are the modes of recognition, and the peculiar and distinctive ceremonies of the Order; and to these last it is claimed that reference may be publicly made for the purposes of scientific investigation, provided that the reference be so made as to be obscure to the profane, and intelligible only to the initiated.

APRON. The lambskin, or white leather apron, is the peculiar and distinctive badge of a mason.

Its color must be white, and its material a lambskin.

It is a symbol of purity, and it derives this symbolism from its color, white being symbolic of purity; from its material, the lamb having the same symbolic character; and from its use, which is to preserve the garments clean.

The apron, or abnet, worn by the Egyptian and the Hebrew priests, and which has been considered as the analogue of the masonic apron, is supposed to have been a symbol of authority; but the use of the apron in Freemasonry originally as an implement of labor, is an evidence of the derivation of the speculative science from an operative art.

APULEIUS. Lucius Apuleius, a Latin writer, born at Medaura, in Africa, flourished in the reigns of the emperors Antoninus and Marcus Aurelius. His most celebrated book, entitled "Metamorphoses, or the Golden Ass," was written, Bishop Warburton thinks, for the express purpose of recommending the ancient Mysteries. He had been initiated into many of them, and his descriptions of them, and especially of his own initiation into those of the Egyptian Isis, are highly interesting and instructive, and should be read by every student of the science of masonic symbolism.

ARCHETYPE. The principal type, figure, pattern, or example, whereby and whereon a thing is formed. In the science of symbolism, the archetype is the thing adopted as a symbol, whence the symbolic idea is derived. Thus we say the temple is the archetype of the lodge, because the former is the symbol whence all the temple symbolism of the latter is derived.

ARCHITECTURE. The art which teaches the proper method of constructing public and private edifices. It is to Freemasonry the "ars artium," the art of arts, because to it the institution is indebted for its origin in its present organization. The architecture of Freemasonry is altogether related to the construction of public edifices, and principally sacred or religious ones,—such as temples, cathedrals, churches,—and of these, masonically, the temple of Solomon is the archetype. Much of the symbolism of Freemasonry is drawn from the art of architecture. While the improvements of Greek and Roman architecture are recognized in Freemasonry, the three ancient orders, the Doric, Ionic, and Corinthian are alone symbolized. No symbolism attaches to the Tuscan and Composite.

ARK OF THE COVENANT. One of the most sacred objects among the Israelites. It was a chest made of shittim wood, or acacia, richly decorated, forty-five inches long, and eighteen inches wide, and contained the two tables of stone on which the ten commandments were engraved, the golden pot that held manna, and Aaron's rod. It was placed in the holy of holies, first of the tabernacle, and then of the temple. Such is its masonic and scriptural history. The idea of this ark was evidently borrowed from the Egyptians, in whose religious rites a similar chest or coffer is to be found. Herodotus mentions several instances. Speaking of the festival of Papremis, he says (ii. 63) that the image of the god was kept in a small wooden shrine covered with plates of gold, which shrine was conveyed in a procession of the priests and people from the temple into a second sacred building. Among the sculptures are to be found bass reliefs of the ark of Isis. The greatest of the religious ceremonies of the Egyptians was the procession of the shrines mentioned in the Rosetta stone, and which is often found depicted on the sculptures. These shrines were of two kinds, one a canopy, but the other, called the great shrine, was an ark or sacred boat. It was borne on the shoulders of priests by means of staves passing through rings in its sides, and was taken into the temple and deposited on a stand. Some of these arks contained, says Wilkinson (*Notes to Herod*. II. 58, *n*. 9), the elements of life and stability, and others the sacred beetle of the sun, overshadowed by the wings of two figures of the goddess Thmei. In all this we see the type of the Jewish ark. The introduction of the ark into the ceremonies of Freemasonry evidently is in reference to its loss and recovery; and hence its symbolism is to be interpreted as connected with the masonic idea of loss and recovery, which always alludes to a loss of life and a recovery of immortality. In the first temple of this life the ark is lost; in the second temple of the future life it is recovered. And thus the ark of the covenant is one of the many masonic symbols of the resurrection.

ARTS AND SCIENCES, LIBERAL. In the seventh century, and for many centuries afterwards, all learning was limited to and comprised in what were called the seven liberal arts and sciences; namely, grammar, rhetoric, logic, arithmetic, geometry, music, and astronomy. The epithet "liberal" is a fair translation of the Latin "ingenuus," which means "free-born;" thus Cicero speaks of the "artes ingenuæ," or the arts befitting a free-born man; and Ovid says in the well-known lines,—

"Ingenuas didicisse fideliter artes
Emollit mores nec sinit esse feros,"—

To have studied carefully the liberal arts refines the manners, and prevents us from being brutish. And Phillips, in his "New World of Words" (1706), defines the liberal arts and sciences to be "such as are fit for gentlemen and scholars, as mechanic trades and handicrafts for meaner people." As Freemasons are required by their landmarks to be *free-born*, we see the propriety of incorporating the arts of free-born men among their symbols. As the system of Masonry derived its present form and organization from the times when the study of these arts and sciences constituted the labors of the wisest men, they have very appropriately been adopted as the symbol of the completion of human learning.

ASHLAR. In builders' language, a stone taken from the quarries.

ASHLAR, PERFECT. A stone that has been hewed, squared, and polished, so as to be fit for use in the building. Masonically, it is a symbol of the state of perfection attained by means of education. And as it is the object of Speculative Masonry to produce this state of perfection, it may in that point of view be also considered as a symbol of the social character of the institution of Freemasonry.

ASHLAR, ROUGH. A stone in its rude and natural state. Masonically, it is a symbol of men's natural state of ignorance. But if the perfect ashlar be, in reference to its mode of preparation, considered as a symbol of the social character of Freemasonry, then the rough ashlar must be considered as a symbol of the profane world. In this species of symbolism, the rough and perfect ashlars bear the same relation to each other as ignorance does to knowledge, death to life, and light to darkness. The rough ashlar is the profane, the perfect ashlar is the initiate.

ASHMOLE, ELIAS. A celebrated antiquary of England, who was born in 1617. He has written an autobiography, or rather diary of his life, which extends to within eight years of his death. Under the date of October 16, 1646, he has made the following entry: "I was made a Free-Mason at Warrington, in Lancashire, with Col. Henry Mainwaring, of Carticham, in Cheshire; the names of those that were then at the lodge: Mr. Richard Penket, warden; Mr. James Collier, Mr. Richard Sankey, Henry Littler, John Ellam and Hugh Brewer." Thirty-six years afterwards, under date of March 10, 1682, he makes the following entry: "I received a summons to appear at a lodge to be held the next day at Masons' Hall, in London. 11. Accordingly I went, and about noon was admitted into the fellowship of Freemasons by Sir William Wilson, Knight, Captain Richard Borthwick, Mr. William Woodman, Mr. William Grey, Mr. Samuel Taylour, and Mr. William Wise. I was the senior fellow among them (it being thirty-five years since I was admitted); there was present beside myself the fellows after named: Mr. Thomas Wise, master of the Masons' Company this year; Mr. Thomas Shorthose, Mr. Thomas Shadbolt, ---- Waidsfford, Esq., Mr.

Nicholas Young, Mr. John Shorthose, Mr. William Hamon, Mr. John Thompson, and Mr. William Stanton. We all dined at the Half-Moon Tavern, in Cheapside, at a noble dinner prepared at the charge of the new-accepted Masons." The titles of some of the persons named in these two receptions confirm what is said in the text, that the operative was at that time being superseded by the speculative element. It is deeply to be regretted that Ashmole did not carry out his projected design of writing a history of Freemasonry, for which it is said that he had collected abundant materials. His History of the Order of the Garter shows what we might have expected from his treatment of the masonic institution.

ASPIRANT. One who aspires to or seeks after the truth. The title given to the candidate in the ancient Mysteries.

ATHELSTAN. King of England, who ascended the throne in 924. Anderson cites the old constitutions as saying that he encouraged the Masons, and brought many over from France and elsewhere. In his reign, and in the year 926, the celebrated General Assembly of the Craft was held in the city of York, with prince Edward, the king's brother, for Grand Master, when new constitutions were framed. From this assembly the York Rite dates its origin.

AUTOPSY (Greek αὐτοψία, *a seeing with one's own eyes*). The complete communication of the secrets in the ancient Mysteries, when the aspirant was admitted into the sacellum, or most sacred place, and was invested by the Hierophant with all the aporrheta, or sacred things, which constituted the perfect knowledge of the initiate. A similar ceremony in Freemasonry is called the Rite of Intrusting.

AUM. The triliteral name of God in the Brahminical mysteries, and equivalent among the Hindoos to the tetragrammaton of the Jews. In one of the Puranas, or sacred books of the Hindoos, it is said, "All the rites ordained in the Vedas, the sacrifices to fire, and all other solemn purifications, shall pass away; but that which shall never pass away is the word AUM, for it is the symbol of the Lord of all things."

B

BABEL. The biblical account of the dispersion of mankind in consequence of the confusion of tongues at Babel, has been incorporated into the history of Masonry. The text has shown the probability that the pure and abstract principles of the Primitive Freemasonry had been preserved by Noah and his immediate descendants; and also that, as a consequence of the dispersion, these principles had been lost or greatly corrupted by the Gentiles, who were removed from the influence and teachings of the great patriarch.

Now there was in the old rituals a formula in the third degree, preserved in some places to the present day, which teaches that the candidate has come *from the tower of Babel, where language was confounded and Masonry lost*, and that he is travelling *to the threshing-floor of Ornan the Jebusite, where language was restored and Masonry found*. An attentive perusal of the nineteen propositions set forth in the preliminary chapter of this work will furnish the reader with a key for the interpretation of this formula. The principles of the Primitive Freemasonry of the early priesthood were corrupted or lost at Babel by the defection of a portion of mankind from Noah, the conservator of those principles. Long after, the descendants of this people united with those of Noah at the temple of Solomon, whose site was the threshing-floor of Ornan the Jebusite, from whom it had been bought by David; and here the lost principles were restored by this union of the Spurious Freemasons of Tyre with the Primitive Freemasons of Jerusalem. And this explains the latter clause of the formula.

BABYLONISH CAPTIVITY. When the city and temple of Jerusalem were destroyed by the army of Nebuchadnezzar, and the inhabitants conveyed as captives to Babylon, we have a right to suppose,—that is to say, if there be any truth in masonic history, the deduction is legitimate,—that among these captives were many of the descendants of the workmen at the temple. If so, then they carried with them into captivity the principles of Masonry which they had acquired at home, and the city of Babylon became the great seat of Speculative Masonry for many years. It was during the captivity that the philosopher Pythagoras, who was travelling as a seeker after knowledge, visited Babylon. With his ardent thirst for wisdom, he would naturally hold frequent interviews with the leading Masons among the Jewish captives. As he suffered himself to be initiated into the Mysteries of Egypt during his visit to that country, it is not unlikely that he may have sought a similar initiation into the masonic Mysteries. This would account for the many analogies and resemblances to Masonry that we find in the moral teachings, the symbols, and the peculiar organization of the school of Pythagoras—resemblances so extraordinary as to have justified, or at least excused, the rituals for calling the sage of Samos "our ancient brother."

BACCHUS. One of the appellations of the "many-named" god Dionysus. The son of Jupiter and Semele was to the Greeks Dionysus, to the Romans Bacchus.

BARE FEET. A symbol of reverence when both feet are uncovered. Otherwise the symbolism is modern; and from the ritualistic explanation which is given in the first degree, it would seem to require that the single bare foot should be interpreted as the symbol of a covenant.

BLACK. Pythagoras called this color the symbol of the evil principle in nature. It was equivalent to darkness, which is the antagonist of light. But in masonic symbolism the interpretation is different. There, black is a symbol of grief, and always refers to the fate of the temple-builder.

BRAHMA. In the mythology of the Hindoos there is a trimurti, or trinity, the Supreme Being exhibiting himself in three manifestations; as, Brahma the Creator, Vishnu the Preserver, and Siva the Destroyer,—the united godhead being a symbol of the sun.

Brahma was a symbol of the rising sun, Siva of the sun at meridian, and Vishnu of the setting sun.

BRUCE. The introduction of Freemasonry into Scotland has been attributed by some writers to King Robert Bruce, who is said to have established in 1314 the Order of Herodom, for the reception of those Knights Templars who had taken refuge in his dominions from the persecutions of the Pope and the King of France. Lawrie, who is excellent authority for Scottish Masonry, does not appear, however, to give any credit to the narrative. Whatever Bruce may have done for the higher degrees, there is no doubt that Ancient Craft Masonry was introduced into Scotland at an earlier period. See *Kilwinning*. Yet the text is right in making Bruce one of the patrons and encouragers of Scottish Freemasonry.

BRYANT. Jacob Bryant, frequently quoted in this work, was a distinguished English antiquary, born in the year 1715, and deceased in 1804. His most celebrated work is "A New System of Ancient Mythology," which appeared in 1773-76. Although objectionable on account of its too conjectural character, it contains a fund of details on the subject of symbolism, and may be consulted with advantage by the masonic student.

BUILDER. The chief architect of the temple of Solomon is often called "the Builder." But the word is also applied generally to the craft; for every Speculative Mason is as much a builder as was his operative predecessor. An American writer (F.S. Wood, of Arkansas) thus alludes to this symbolic idea. "Masons are called moral builders. In their rituals, they declare that a more noble and glorious purpose than squaring stones and hewing timbers is theirs, fitting immortal nature for that spiritual building not made with hands, eternal in the heavens." And he adds, "The builder builds for a century; masons for eternity." In this sense, "the builder" is the noblest title that can be bestowed upon a mason.

BUNYAN, JOHN. Familiar to every one as the author of the "Pilgrim's Progress." He lived in the seventeenth century, and was the most celebrated allegorical writer of England. His work entitled "Solomon's Temple Spiritualized" will supply the student of masonic symbolism with many valuable suggestions.

C

CABALA. The mystical philosophy of the Jews. The word which is derived from a Hebrew root, signifying *to receive*, has sometimes been used in an enlarged sense, as comprehending all the explanations, maxims, and ceremonies which have been traditionally handed down to the Jews; but in that more limited acceptation, in which it is intimately connected with the symbolic science of Freemasonry, the cabala may be defined to be a system of philosophy which embraces certain mystical interpretations of Scripture, and metaphysical speculations concerning the Deity, man, and spiritual beings. In these interpretations and speculations, according to the Jewish doctors, were enveloped the most profound truths of religion, which, to be comprehended by finite beings, are obliged to be revealed through the medium of symbols and allegories. Buxtorf (Lex. Talm.) defines the Cabala to be a secret science, which treats in a mystical and enigmatical manner of things divine, angelical, theological, celestial, and metaphysical, the subjects being enveloped in striking symbols and secret modes of teaching.

CABALIST. A Jewish philosopher. One who understands and teaches the doctrines of the Cabala, or the Jewish philosophy.

CABIRI. Certain gods, whose worship was first established in the Island of Samothrace, where the Cabiric Mysteries were practised until the beginning of the Christian era. They were four in number, and by some are supposed to have referred to Noah and his three sons. In the Mysteries there was a legend of the death and restoration to life of Atys, the son of Cybele. The candidate represented Cadmillus, the youngest of the Cabiri, who was slain by his three brethren. The legend of the Cabiric Mysteries, as far as it can be understood from the faint allusions of ancient authors, was in spirit and design very analogous to that of the third degree of Masonry.

CADMILLUS. One of the gods of the Cabiri, who was slain by his brothers, on which circumstance the legend of the Cabiric or Samothracian Mysteries is founded. He is the analogue of the Builder in the Hiramic legend of Freemasonry. 256

CAIRNS. Heaps of stones of a conical form, erected by the Druids. Some suppose them to have been sepulchral monuments, others altars. They were undoubtedly of a religious character, since sacrificial fires were lighted upon them, and processions were made around them. These processions were analogous to the circumambulations in Masonry, and were conducted like them with reference to the apparent course of the sun.

CASSIA. A gross corruption of *Acacia*. The cassia is an aromatic plant, but it has no mystical or symbolic character.

CELTIC MYSTERIES. The religious rites of ancient Gaul and Britain, more familiarly known as *Druidism*, which see.. 109

CEREMONIES. The outer garments which cover and adorn Freemasonry as clothing does the human body.

Although ceremonies give neither life nor truth to doctrines or principles, yet they have an admirable influence, since by their use certain things are made to acquire a sacred character which they would not otherwise have had; and hence Lord Coke has most wisely said that "prudent antiquity did, for more solemnity and better memory and observation of that which is to be done, express substances under ceremonies.".

CERES. Among the Romans the goddess of agriculture; but among the more poetic Greeks she became, as Demeter, the symbol of the prolific earth. See *Demeter*.

CHARTER OF COLOGNE. A masonic document of great celebrity, but not of unquestioned authenticity. It is a declaration or affirmation of the design and principles of Freemasonry, issued in the year 1535, by a convention of masons who had assembled in the city of Cologne. The original is in the Latin language. The assertors of the authenticity of the document claim that it was found in the chest of a lodge at Amsterdam in 1637, and afterwards regularly transmitted from hand to hand until the year 1816, when it was presented to Prince Frederick of Nassau, through whom it was at that time made known to the masonic world. Others assert that it is a forgery, which was perpetrated about the year 1816. Like the Leland manuscript, it is one of those vexed questions of masonic literary history over which so much doubt has been thrown, that it will probably never be satisfactorily solved. For a translation of the charter, and copious explanatory notes, by the author of this work, the reader is referred to the "American Quarterly Review of Freemasonry," vol. ii. p. 52.

CHRISTIANIZATION OF FREEMASONRY. The interpretation of its symbols from a Christian point of view. This is an error into which Hutchinson and Oliver in England, and Scott and one or two others of less celebrity in this country, have fallen. It is impossible to derive Freemasonry from Christianity, because the former, in point of time, preceded the latter. In fact, the symbols of Freemasonry are Solomonic, and its religion was derived from the ancient priesthood.

The infusion of the Christian element was, however, a natural result of surrounding circumstances; yet to sustain it would be fatal to the cosmopolitan character of the institution.

Such interpretation is therefore modern, and does not belong to the ancient system.

CIRCULAR TEMPLES. These were used in the initiations of the religion of Zoroaster. Like the square temples of Masonry, and the other Mysteries, they were symbolic of the world, and the symbol was completed by making the circumference of the circle a representation of the zodiac.

CIRCUMAMBULATION. The ceremony of perambulating the lodge, or going in procession around the altar, which was universally practised in the ancient initiations and other religious ceremonies, and was always performed so that the persons moving should have the altar on their right hand. The rite was symbolic of the apparent daily course of the sun from the east to the west by the way of the south, and was undoubtedly derived from the ancient sun-worship.

CIVILIZATION. Freemasonry is a result of civilization, for it exists in no savage or barbarous state of society; and in return it has proved, by its social and moral principles, a means of extending and elevating the civilization which gave it birth.

Freemasonry is therefore a type of civilization, bearing the same relation to the profane world that civilization does to the savage state.

COLLEGES OF ARTIFICERS. The *Collegia Fabrorum*, or Workmen's Colleges, were established in Rome by Numa, who for this purpose distributed all the artisans of the city into companies, or colleges, according to their arts and trades. They resembled the modern corporations, or *guilds*, which sprang up in the middle ages. The rule established by their founder, that not less than three could constitute a college,— "*tres faciunt collegium*,"—has been retained in the regulations of the third degree of masonry, to a lodge of which these colleges bore other analogies.

COLOGNE, CHARTER OF. See *Charter of Cologne*.

COMMON GAVEL. See *Gavel*.

CONSECRATION. The appropriating or dedicating, with certain ceremonies, anything to sacred purposes or offices, by separating it from common use. Masonic lodges, like ancient temples and modern churches, have always been consecrated. Hobbes, in his *Leviathan* (p. iv. c. 44), gives the best definition of this ceremony. "To consecrate is in Scripture to offer, give, or dedicate, in pious and decent language and gesture, a man, or any other thing, to God, by separating it from common use.".

CONSECRATION, ELEMENTS OF. Those things, the use of which in the ceremony as constituent and elementary parts of it, are necessary to the perfecting and legalizing of the act of consecration. In Freemasonry, these elements of consecration are *corn*, *wine*, and *oil*,—which see.

CORN. One of the three elements of masonic consecration, and as a symbol of plenty it is intended, under the name of the "corn of nourishment," to remind us of those temporal blessings of life, support, and nourishment which we receive from the Giver of all good.

CORNER STONE. The most important stone in the edifice, and in its symbolism referring to an impressive ceremony in the first degree of Masonry.

The ancients laid it with peculiar ceremonies, and among the Oriental nations it was the symbol of a prince, or chief.

It is one of the most impressive symbols of Masonry.

It is a symbol of the candidate on his initiation.

As a symbol it is exclusively masonic, and confined to a temple origin.

COVERING OF THE LODGE. Under the technical name of the "clouded canopy or starry-decked heavens," it is a symbol of the future world,—of the celestial lodge above, where the G.A.O.T.U. forever presides, and which constitutes the "foreign country" which every mason hopes to reach.

CREUZER. George Frederick Creuzer, who was born in Germany in 1771, and was a professor at the University of Heidelberg, devoted himself to the study of the ancient religions, and with profound learning, established a peculiar system on the subject. Many of his views have been adopted in the text of the present work. His theory was, that the religion and mythology of the ancient Greeks were borrowed from a far more ancient people,—a body of priests coming from the East,—who received them as a revelation. The myths and traditions of this ancient people were adopted by Hesiod, Homer, and the later poets, although not without some misunderstanding of them, and they were finally preserved in the Mysteries, and became subjects of investigation for the philosophers. This theory Creuzer has developed in his most important work, entitled "Symbolik und Mythologie der alten Völker, besonders der Greichen," which was published at Leipsic in 1819. There is no translation of this work into English, but Guigniaut published at Paris, in 1824, a paraphrastic translation of it, under the title of "Religions de l'Antiquité considérées principalement dans leur Formes Symboliques et Mythologiques." Creuzer's views throw much light on the symbolic history of Freemasonry.

CROSS. No symbol was so universally diffused at an early period as the cross. It was, says Faber (Cabir. ii. 390), a symbol throughout the pagan world long previous to its becoming an object of veneration to Christians. In ancient symbology it was a symbol of eternal life. M. de Mortillet, who in 1866 published a work entitled "Le Signe de la Croix avant le Christianisme," found in the very earliest epochs three principal symbols of universal occurrences; viz., the *circle*, the *pyramid*, and the *cross*. Leslie (Man's Origin and Destiny, p. 312), quoting from him in reference to the ancient worship of the cross, says "It seems to have been a worship of such a peculiar nature as to exclude the worship of idols." This sacredness of the crucial symbol may be one reason why its form was often adopted, especially by the Celts in the construction of their temples, though I have admitted in the text the commonly received opinion that in cross-shaped temples the four limbs of the cross referred to the four elements. But in a very interesting work lately published—"The Myths of the New World" (N.Y., 1863)—Mr. Brinton assigns another symbolism. "The symbol," says this writer, "that beyond all others has fascinated the human mind, THE CROSS, finds here its source and meaning. Scholars have pointed out its sacredness in many natural religions, and have reverently accepted it as a mystery, or offered scores of conflicting, and often debasing, interpretations. *It is but another symbol of the four cardinal points, the four winds of heaven.* This will luminously appear by a study of its use and meaning in America." (p. 95.) And Mr. Brinton gives many instances of the religious use of the cross by several of the aboriginal tribes of this continent, where the allusion, it must be confessed, seems evidently to be to the four cardinal points, or the four winds, or four spirits, of the earth. If this be so, and if it is probable that a similar reference was adopted by the Celtic and other ancient peoples, then we would have in the cruciform temple as much a symbolism of the world, of which the four cardinal points constitute the boundaries, as we have in the square, the cubical, and the circular.

CTEIS. A representation of the female generative organ. It was, as a symbol, always accompanied by the phallus, and, like that symbol, was extensively venerated by the nations of antiquity. It was a symbol of the prolific powers of nature. See *Phallus*.

CUBE. A geometrical figure, consisting of six equal sides and six equal angles. It is the square solidified, and was among the ancients a symbol of truth. The same symbolism is recognized in Freemasonry.

D

DARKNESS. It denotes falsehood and ignorance, and was a very universal symbol among the nations of antiquity.

In all the ancient initiations, the aspirant was placed in darkness for a period differing in each,—among the Druids for three days, among the Greeks for twenty-seven, and in the Mysteries of Mithras for fifty.

In all of these, as well as in Freemasonry, darkness is the symbol of initiation not complete.

DEATH. Because it was believed to be the entrance to a better and eternal life, which was the dogma of the Mysteries, death became the symbol of initiation; and hence among the Greeks the same word signified *to die*, and *to be initiated*. In the British Mysteries, says Davies (Mythol. of the British Druids), the novitiate passed the river of death in the boat of Garanhir, the Charon of the Greeks; and before he could be admitted to this privilege, it was requisite that he should have been mystically buried, as well as mystically dead.

DEFINITION OF FREEMASONRY. The definition quoted in the text, that it is a science of morality, veiled in allegory and illustrated by symbols, is the one which is given in the English lectures.

But a more comprehensive and exact definition is, that it is a science which is engaged in the search after divine truth.

DELTA. In the higher degrees of Masonry, the triangle is so called because the Greek letter of that name is of a triangular form.

It is a symbol of Deity, because it is the first perfect figure in geometry; it is the first figure in which space is enclosed by lines.

DEMETER. Worshipped by the Greeks as the symbol of the prolific earth. She was the Ceres of the Romans. To her is attributed the institution of the Eleusinian Mysteries in Greece, the most popular of all the ancient initiations.

DESIGN OF FREEMASONRY. It is not charity or alms-giving.

Nor the cultivation of the social sentiment; for both of these are merely incidental to its organization.

But it is the search after truth, and that truth is the unity of God, and the immortality of the soul.

DIESEAL. A term used by the Druids to designate the circumambulation around the sacred cairns, and is derived from two words signifying "on the right of the sun," because the circumambulation was always in imitation of the course of the sun, with the right hand next to the cairn or altar.

DIONYSIAC ARTIFICERS. An association of architects who possessed the exclusive privilege of erecting temples and other public buildings in Asia Minor. The members were distinguished from the uninitiated inhabitants by the possession of peculiar marks of recognition, and by the secret character of their association. They were intimately connected with the Dionysiac Mysteries, and are supposed to have furnished the builders for the construction of the temple of Solomon.

DIONYSIAC MYSTERIES. In addition to what is said in the text, I add the following, slightly condensed, from the pen of that accomplished writer, Albert Pike: "The initiates in these Mysteries had preserved the ritual and ceremonies that accorded with the simplicity of the earliest ages, and the manners of the first men. The rules of Pythagoras were followed there. Like the Egyptians, who held wool unclean, they buried no initiate in woollen garments. They abstained from bloody sacrifices, and lived on fruits or vegetables. They imitated the life of the contemplative sects of the Orient. One of the most precious advantages promised by their initiation was to put man in communion with the gods by purifying his soul of all the passions that interfere with that enjoyment, and dim the rays of divine light that are communicated to every soul capable of receiving them. The sacred gates of the temple, where the ceremonies of initiation were performed, were opened but once in each year, and no stranger was allowed to enter. Night threw her veil over these august Mysteries. There the sufferings of Dionysus were represented, who, like Osiris, died, descended to hell, and rose to life again; and raw flesh was distributed to the initiates, which each ate in memory of the death of the deity torn in pieces by the Titans."

DIONYSUS. Or Bacchus; mythologically said to be the son of Zeus and Semele. In his Mysteries he was identified with Osiris, and regarded as the sun. His Mysteries prevailed in Greece, Rome, and Asia, and were celebrated by the Dionysiac artificers—those builders who united with the Jews in the construction of King Solomon's temple. Hence, of all the ancient Mysteries, they are the most interesting to the masonic student.

DISSEVERANCE. The disseverance of the operative from the speculative element of Freemasonry occurred at the beginning of the eighteenth century.

DISCALCEATION, RITE OF. The ceremony of uncovering the feet, or taking off the shoes; from the Latin *discalceare*. It is a symbol of reverence. See *Bare Feet*.

DRUIDICAL MYSTERIES. The Celtic Mysteries celebrated in Britain and Gaul. They resembled, in all material points, the other mysteries of antiquity, and had the same design. The aspirant was subjected to severe trials, underwent a mystical death and burial in imitation of the death of the god Hu, and was eventually enlightened by the communication to him of the great truths of God and immortality, which it was the object of all the Mysteries to teach.

DUALISM. A mythological and philosophical doctrine, which supposes the world to have been always governed by two antagonistic principles, distinguished as the good and the evil principle. This doctrine pervaded all the Oriental religions, and its influences are to be seen in the system of Speculative Masonry, where it is developed in the symbolism of Light and Darkness.

E

EAST. That part of the heavens where the sun rises; and as the source of material light to which we figuratively apply the idea of intellectual light, it has been adopted as a symbol of the Order of Freemasonry. And this symbolism is strengthened by the fact that the earliest learning and the earliest religion came from the east, and have ever been travelling to the west.

In Freemasonry, the east has always been considered the most sacred of the cardinal points, because it is the place where light issues; and it was originally referred to the primitive religion, or sun-worship. But in Freemasonry it refers especially to that east whence an ancient priesthood first disseminated truth to enlighten the world; wherefore the east is masonically called "the place of light."

EGG. The mundane egg is a well-recognized symbol of the world. "The ancient pagans," says Faber, "in almost every part of the globe, were wont to symbolize the world by an egg. Hence this symbol is introduced into the cosmogony of nearly all nations; and there are few persons, even among those who have not made mythology their study, to whom the *Mundane Egg* is not perfectly familiar. It was employed not only to represent the earth, but also the universe in its largest extent." *Origin of Pag. Idolatry*, i. 175.

EGG AND LUNETTE. The egg, being a symbol not only of the resurrection, but also of the world rescued from destruction by the Noachic ark, and the lunette, or horizontal crescent, being a symbol of the Great Father, represented by Noah, the egg and lunette combined, which was the hieroglyphic of the god Lunus, at Heliopolis, was a symbol of the world proceeding from the Great Father.

EGYPT. Egypt has been considered as the cradle not only of the sciences, but of the religions of the ancient world. Although a monarchy, with a king nominally at the head of the state, the government really was in the hands of the priests, who were the sole depositaries of learning, and were alone acquainted with the religious formularies that in Egypt controlled all the public and private actions of the life of every inhabitant.

ELEPHANTA. An island in the Bay of Bombay, celebrated for the stupendous caverns artificially excavated out of the solid rock, which were appropriated to the initiations in the ancient Indian Mysteries.

ELEUSINIAN MYSTERIES. Of all the Mysteries of the ancients these were the most popular. They were celebrated at the village of Eleusis, near Athens, and were dedicated to Demeter. In them the loss and the restoration of Persephone were scenically represented, and the doctrines of the unity of God and the immortality of the soul were taught. See *Demeter*.

ENTERED APPRENTICE. The first degree of Ancient Craft Masonry, analogous to the aspirant in the Lesser Mysteries.

It is viewed as a symbol of childhood, and is considered as a preparation and purification for something higher.

EPOPT. (From the Greek ἐπόπτης, *an eye witness*.) One who, having been initiated in the Greater Mysteries of paganism, has seen the aporrheta.

ERA OF MASONRY. The legendary statement that the origin of Masonry is coeval with the beginning of the world, is only a philosophical myth to indicate the eternal nature of its principles.

ERICA. The tree heath; a sacred plant among the Egyptians, and used in the Osirian Mysteries as the symbol of immortality, and the analogue of the masonic acacia.

ESSENES. A society or sect of the Jews, who combined labor with religious exercises, whose organization partook of a secret character, and who have been claimed to be the descendants of the builders of the temple of Solomon.

EUCLID. The masonic legend which refers to Euclid is altogether historically untrue. It is really a philosophical myth intended to convey a masonic truth.

EURESIS. (From the Greek εὕρεσις, *a discovery*.) That part of the initiation in the ancient Mysteries which represented the finding of the body of the god or hero whose death was the subject of the initiation.

The euresis has been adopted in Freemasonry, and forms an essential part of the ritual of the third degree.

EVERGREEN. A symbol of the immortality of the soul.

Planted by the Hebrews and other ancient peoples at the heads of graves.

For this purpose the Hebrews preferred the acacia, because its wood was incorruptible, and because, as the material of the ark, it was already considered as a sacred plant.

EYE, ALL-SEEING. A symbol of the omniscient and watchful providence of God. It is a very ancient symbol, and is supposed by some to be a relic of the primitive sun-worship. Volney says (*Les Ruines*, p. 186) that in most of the ancient languages of Asia, the *eye* and the *sun* are expressed by the same word. Among the Egyptians the eye was the symbol of their supreme god, Osiris, or the sun.

F

FABER. The works of the Rev. G.S. Faber, on the Origin of Pagan Idolatry, and on the Cabiri, are valuable contributions to the science of mythology. They abound in matters of interest to the investigator of masonic symbolism and philosophy, but should be read with a careful view of the preconceived theory of the learned author, who refers everything in the ancient religions to the influences of the Noachic cataclysm, and the arkite worship which he supposes to have resulted from it.

FELLOW CRAFT. The second degree of Ancient Craft Masonry, analogous to the mystes in the ancient Mysteries.

The symbol of a youth setting forth on the journey of life.

FETICHISM. The worship of uncouth and misshapen idols, practised only by the most ignorant and debased peoples, and to be found at this day among some of the least civilized of the negro tribes of Africa. "Their fetiches," says Du Chaillu, speaking of some of the African races, "consisted of fingers and tails of monkeys; of human hair, skin, teeth, bones; of clay, old nails, copper chains; shells, feathers, claws, and skulls of birds; pieces of iron, copper, or wood; seeds of plants, ashes of various substances, and I cannot tell what more." *Equatorial Africa*, p. 93.

FIFTEEN. A sacred number, symbolic of the name of God, because the letters of the holy name יה, JAH, are equal, in the Hebrew mode of numeration by the letters of the alphabet, to fifteen; for י is equal to ten, and ה is equal to five. Hence, from veneration for this sacred name, the Hebrews do not, in ordinary computations, when they wish to express the number 15, make use of these two letters, but of two others, which are equivalent to 9 and 6.

FORTY-SEVENTH PROBLEM. The forty-seventh problem of the first book of Euclid is, that in any right-angled triangle the square which is described upon the side subtending the right angle is equal to the squares described upon the sides which contain the right angle. It is said to have been discovered by Pythagoras while in Egypt, but was most probably taught to him by the priests of that country, in whose rites he had been initiated; it is a symbol of the production of the world by the generative and prolific powers of the Creator; hence the Egyptians made the perpendicular and base the representatives of Osiris and Isis, while the hypothenuse represented their child Horus. Dr. Lardner says (*Com. on Euclid*, p. 60) of this problem, "Whether we consider the forty-seventh proposition with reference to the peculiar and beautiful relation established by it, or to its innumerable uses in every department of mathematical science, or to its fertility in the consequences derivable from it, it must certainly be esteemed the most celebrated and important in the whole of the elements, if not in the whole range of mathematical science."

FOURTEEN. Some symbologists have referred the fourteen pieces into which the mutilated body of Osiris was divided, and the fourteen days during which the body of the builder was buried, to the fourteen days of the disappearance of the moon. The Sabian worshippers of "the hosts of heaven" were impressed with the alternate appearance and disappearance of the moon, which at length became a symbol of death and resurrection. Hence fourteen was a sacred number. As such it was viewed in the Osirian Mysteries, and may have been introduced into Freemasonry with other relics of the old worship of the sun and planets.

FREEMASONRY, DEFINITION OF. See *Definition*.

FREEMASONS, TRAVELLING. The travelling Freemasons were a society existing in the middle ages, and consisting of learned men and prelates, under whom were operative masons. The operative masons performed the labors of the craft, and travelling from country to country, were engaged in the construction of cathedrals, monasteries, and castles. "There are few points in the history of the middle ages," says Godwin, "more pleasing to look back upon than the existence of the associated masons; they are the bright spot in the general darkness of that period; the patch of verdure when all around is barren." *The Builder*, ix. 463

G

G. The use of the letter G in the Fellow Craft's degree is an anachronism. It is really a corruption of, or perhaps rather a substitution for, the Hebrew letter ' (yod), which is the initial of the ineffable name. As such, it is a symbol of the life-giving and life-sustaining power of God.

G.A.O.T.U. A masonic abbreviation used as a symbol of the name of God, and signifying the *Grand Architect of the Universe*. It was adopted by the Freemasons in accordance with a similar practice among all the nations of antiquity of noting the Divine Name by a symbol.

GAVEL. What is called in Masonry a common gavel is a stone-cutter's hammer; it is one of the working tools of an Entered Apprentice, and is a symbol of the purification of the heart.

GLOVES. On the continent of Europe they are given to candidates at the same time that they are invested with the apron; the same custom formerly prevailed in England; but although the investiture of the gloves is abandoned as a ceremony both there and in America, they are worn as a part of masonic clothing.

They are a symbol of purification of life.

In the middle ages gloves were worn by operative masons.

GOD, UNITY OF. See *Unity of God*.

GOD, NAME OF. See *Name*.

GOLGOTHA. In Hebrew and Syriac it means *a skull*; a name of Mount Calvary, and so called, probably, because it was the place of public execution. The Latin *Calvaria*, whence Mount Calvary, means also a skull.

GRAVE. In the Master's degree, a symbol which is the analogue of the pastos, or couch, in the ancient Mysteries.

The symbolism has been Christianized by some masonic writers, and the grave has thus been referred to the sepulchre of Christ.

GRIPS AND SIGNS. They are valuable only for social purposes as modes of recognition.

H

HAND. The hand is a symbol of human actions; pure hands symbolize pure actions, and impure or unclean hands symbolize impure actions.

HARE. Among the Egyptians the hare was a hieroglyphic of *eyes that are open*, and was the symbol of initiation into the Mysteries of Osiris. The Hebrew word for *hare* is *arnabet*, and this is compounded of two words that signify *to behold the light*. The connection of ideas is apparent.

HELLENISM. The religion of the Helles, or ancient Greeks who immediately succeeded the Pelasgians in the settlement of that country. It was, in consequence of the introduction of the poetic element, more refined than the old Pelasgic worship for which it was substituted. Its myths were more philosophical and less gross than those of the religion to which it succeeded.

HERMAE. Stones of a cubical form, which were originally unhewn, by which the Greeks at first represented all their deities. They came in the progress of time to be especially dedicated by the Greeks to the god Hermes, whence the name, and by the Romans to the god Terminus, who presided over landmarks.

HERO WORSHIP. The worship of men deified after death. It is a theory of some, both ancient and modern writers, that all the pagan gods were once human beings, and that the legends and traditions of mythology are mere embellishments of the acts of these personages when alive. It was the doctrine taught by Euhemerus among the ancients, and has been maintained among the moderns by such distinguished authorities as Bochart, Bryant, Voss, and Banier.

HERMETIC PHILOSOPHY. The system of the Alchemists, the Adepts, or seekers of the philosopher's stone. No system has been more misunderstood than this. It was secret, esoteric, and highly symbolical. No one has so well revealed its true design as E.A. Hitchcock, who, in his delightful work entitled "Remarks upon Alchemy and the Alchemists," says, "The genuine Alchemists were religious men, who passed their time in legitimate pursuits, earning an honest subsistence, and in religious contemplation, studying how to realize in themselves the union of the divine and human nature, expressed in man by an enlightened submission to God's will; and they thought out and published, after a manner of their own, a method of attaining or entering upon this state, as the only rest of the soul." There is a very great similarity between their doctrines and those of the Freemasons; so much so that the two associations have sometimes been confounded.

HIEROPHANT. (From the Greek ἱερὸς, *holy, sacred*, and φαίνω *to show*.) One who instructs in sacred things; the explainer of the aporrheta, or secret doctrines, to the initiates in the ancient Mysteries. He was the presiding officer, and his rank and duties were analogous to those of the master of a masonic lodge.

HIRAM ABIF. The architect of Solomon's temple. The word "Abif" signifies in Hebrew "his father," and is used by the writer of Second Chronicles (iv. 16) when he says, "These things did *Hiram his father* [in the original *Hiram Abif*] do for King Solomon.".

The legend relating to him is of no value as a mere narrative, but of vast importance in a symbolical point of view, as illustrating a great philosophical and religious truth; namely, the dogma of the immortality of the soul.

Hence, Hiram Abif is the symbol of man in the abstract sense, or human nature, as developed in the life here and in the life to come.

HIRAM OF TYRE. The king of Tyre, the friend and ally of King Solomon, whom he supplied with men and materials for building the temple. In the recent, or what I am inclined to call the grand lecturer's symbolism of Masonry (a sort of symbolism for which I have very little veneration), Hiram of Tyre is styled the symbol of strength, as Hiram Abif is of beauty. But I doubt the antiquity or authenticity of any such symbolism. Hiram of Tyre can only be considered, historically, as being necessary to complete the myth and symbolism of Hiram Abif. The king of Tyre is an historical personage, and there is no necessity for transforming him into a symbol, while his historical character lends credit and validity to the philosophical myth of the third degree of Masonry.

HIRAM THE BUILDER. An epithet of Hiram Abif. For the full significance of the term, see the word *Builder*.

HO-HI. A cabalistic pronunciation of the tetragrammaton, or ineffable name of God; it is most probably the true one; and as it literally means HE-SHE, it is supposed to denote the hermaphroditic essence of Jehovah, as containing within himself the male and the female principle,—the generative and the prolific energy of creation.

HO The sacred name of God among the Druids. Bryant supposes that by it they intended the Great Father Noah; but it is very possible that it was a modification of the Hebrew tetragrammaton, being the last syllable read cabalistically (see *ho-hi*); if so, it signified the great male principle of nature. But HU, in Hebrew הוא, is claimed by Talmudic writers to be one of the names of God; and the passage in Isaiah xlii. 8, in the original *ani Jehovah, Hu shemi*, which is in the common version "I am the LORD; that is my name," they interpret, "I am Jehovah; my name is Hu."

HUTCHINSON, WILLIAM. A distinguished masonic writer of England, who lived in the eighteenth century. He is the author of "The Spirit of Masonry," published in 1775. This was the first English work of any importance that sought to give a scientific interpretation of the symbols of Freemasonry; it is, in fact, the earliest attempt of any kind to treat Freemasonry as a science of symbolism. Hutchinson, however, has to some extent impaired the value of his labors by contending that the institution is exclusively Christian in its character and design.

I

IH-HO. See *Ho-hi*.

IMMORTALITY OF THE SOUL. This is one of the two religious dogmas which have always been taught in Speculative Masonry.

It was also taught in all the Rites and Mysteries of antiquity.

The doctrine was taught as an abstract proposition by the ancient priesthood of the Pure or Primitive Freemasonry of antiquity, but was conveyed to the mind of the initiate, and impressed upon him by a scenic representation in the ancient Mysteries, or the Spurious Freemasonry of the ancients.

INCOMMUNICABLE NAME. The tetragrammaton, so called because it was not common to, and could not be bestowed upon, nor shared by, any other being. It was proper to the true God alone. Thus Drusius (Tetragrammaton, sive de Nomine Dei proprio, p. 108) says, "Nomen quatuor literarum proprie et absolute non tribui nisi Deo vero. Unde doctores catholici dicunt *incommunicabile* [not common] esse creaturae."

INEFFABLE NAME. The tetragrammaton. So called because it is *ineffabile*, or unpronounceable. See *Tetragrammaton*.

INTRUSTING, RITE OF. That part of the ceremony of initiation which consists in communicating to the aspirant or candidate the aporrheta, or secrets of the mystery.

INUNCTION. The act of anointing. This was a religious ceremony practised from the earliest times. By the pouring on of oil, persons and things were consecrated to sacred purposes.

INVESTITURE, RITE OF. That part of the ceremony of initiation which consists of clothing the candidate masonically. It is a symbol of purity.

ISH CHOTZEB. Hebrew איש הצב, *hewers of stones*. The Fellow Crafts at the temple of Solomon. (2 Chron. ii. 2.).

ISH SABAL. Hebrew איש סבל, *bearers of burdens*. The Apprentices at the temple of Solomon. (2 Chron. ii. 2.).

J

JAH. It is in Hebrew יה whence Maimonides calls it "the two-lettered name," and derives it from the tetragrammaton, of which it is an abbreviation. Others have denied this, and assert that *Jah* is a name independent of Jehovah, but expressing the same idea of the divine essenee. See Gataker, *De Nom. Tetrag.*.

JEHOVAH. The incommunicable, ineffable name of God, in Hebrew יהוה, and called, from the four letters of which it consists, the tetragrammaton, or four-lettered name.

L

LABOR. Since the article on the Symbolism of Labor was written, I have met with an address delivered in 1868 by brother Troué, before St. Peter's Lodge in Martinico, which contains sentiments on the relation of Masonry to labor which are well worth a translation from the original French. See *Bulletin du Grand Orient de France*, December, 1868.

"Our name of Mason, and our emblems, distinctly announce that our object is the elevation of labor.

"We do not, as masons, consider labor as a punishment inflicted on man; but on the contrary, we elevate it in our thought to the height of a religious act, which is the most acceptable to God because it is the most useful to man and to society.

"We decorate ourselves with the emblems of labor to affirm that our doctrine is an incessant protest against the stigma branded on the law of labor, and which an error of apprehension, proceeding from the ignorance of men in primitive times has erected into a dogma; an error that has resulted in the production of this anti-social phenomenon which we meet with every day; namely, that the degradation of the workman is the greater as his labor is more severe, and the elevation of the idler is higher as his idleness is more complete. But the study of the laws which maintain order in nature, released from the fetters of preconceived ideas, has led the Freemasons to that doctrine, far more moral than the contrary belief, that labor is not an expiation, but a law of harmony, from the subjection to which man cannot be released without impairing his own happiness, and deranging the order of creation. The design of Freemasons is, then, the rehabilitation of labor, which is indicated by the apron which we wear, and the gavel, the trowel, and the level, which are found among our symbols."

Hence the doctrine of this work is, that Freemasonry teaches not only the necessity, but the nobility, of labor.

And that labor is the proper worship due by man to God.

LADDER. A symbol of progressive advancement from a lower to a higher sphere, which is common to Masonry, and to many, if not all, of the ancient Mysteries.

LADDER, BRAHMINICAL. The symbolic ladder used in the Mysteries of Brahma. It had seven steps, symbolic of the seven worlds of the Indian universe.

LADDER, MITHRAITIC. The symbolic ladder used in the Persian Mysteries of Mithras. It had seven steps, symbolic of the seven planets and the seven metals.

LADDER, SCANDINAVIAN. The symbolic ladder used in the Gothic Mysteries. Dr. Oliver refers it to the Yggrasil, or sacred ash tree. But the symbolism is either very abstruse or very doubtful.

LADDER, THEOLOGICAL. The symbolic ladder of the masonic Mysteries. It refers to the ladder seen by Jacob in his vision, and consists, like all symbolical ladders, of seven rounds, alluding to the four cardinal and the three theological virtues.

LAMB. A symbol of innocence. A very ancient symbol.

LAMB, PASCHAL. See *Paschal Lamb*.

LAMBSKIN APRON. See *Apron*.

LAW, ORAL. See *Oral Law*.

LEGEND. A narrative, whether true or false, that has been traditionally preserved from the time of its first oral communication. Such is the definition of a masonic legend. The authors of the Conversations-Lexicon, referring to the monkish Lives of the Saints which originated in the twelfth and thirteenth centuries, say that the title *legend* was given to all fictions which make pretensions to truth. Such a remark, however correct it may be in reference to these monkish narratives, which were often invented as ecclesiastical exercises, is by no means applicable to the legends of Freemasonry. These are not necessarily fictitious, but are either based on actual and historical facts which have been but slightly modificd, or they are the offspring and expansion of some symbolic idea in which latter respect they differ entirely from the monastic legends, which often have only the fertile imagination of some studious monk for the basis of their construction.

LEGEND OF THE ROYAL ARCH DEGREE. Much of this legend is a mythical history; but some portion of it is undoubtedly a philosophical myth. The destruction and the reëdification of the temple, the captivity and the return of the captives, are matters of history; but many of the details have been invented and introduced for the purpose of giving form to a symbolic idea.

LEGEND OF THE THIRD DEGREE. In all probability this legend is a mythical history, in which truth is very largely and preponderatingly mixed with fiction.

It is the most important and significant of the legendary symbols of Freemasonry.

Has descended from age to age by oral tradition, and has been preserved in every masonic rite.

No essential alteration of it has ever been made in any masonic system, but the interpretations of it have been various; the most general one is, that it is a symbol of the resurrection and the immortality of the soul.

Some continental writers have supposed that it was a symbol of the downfall of the Order of Templars, and its hoped-for restoration. In some of the high philosophical degrees it is supposed to be a symbol of the sufferings, death, and resurrection Christ. Hutchinson thought it a symbol of the decadence of the Jewish religion, and the rise of the Christian on its ruins. Oliver says that it symbolically refers to the murder of Abel, the death of our race through Adam, and its restoration through Christ.

Ragon thinks that it is a symbol of the sun shorn of its vigor by the three winter months, and restored to generative power by the spring. And lastly, Des Etangs says that it is a symbol of eternal reason, whose enemies are the vices that deprave and finally destroy humanity.

But none of these interpretations, except the first, can be sustained.

LETTUCE. The sacred plant of the Mysteries of Adonis; a symbol of immortality, and the analogue of the acacia.

LEVEL. One of the working tools of a Fellow Craft. It is a symbol of the equality of station of all men before God.

LIBERAL ARTS AND SCIENCES. In the seventh century, all learning was limited to the seven liberal arts and sciences; their introduction into Freemasonry, referring to this theory, is a symbol of the completion of human learning.

LIGHT. It denotes truth and knowledge, and is so explained in all the ancient systems; in initiation, it is not material but intellectual light that is sought.

It is predominant as a symbol in all the ancient initiations.

There it was revered because it was an emanation from the sun, the common object of worship; but the theory advanced by some writers, that the veneration of light originally proceeded from its physical qualities, is not correct.

Pythagoras called it the good principle in nature; and the Cabalists taught that eternal light filled all space before the creation, and that after creation it retired to a central spot, and became the instrument of the Divine Mind in creating matter.

It is the symbol of the autopsy, or the full perfection and fruition of initiation.

It is therefore a fundamental symbol in Freemasonry, and contains within itself the very essence of the speculative science.

LINGAM. The phallus was so called by the Indian nations of the East. See *Phallus*.

LODGE. The place where Freemasons meet, and also the congregation of masons so met. The word is derived from the *lodges* occupied by the travelling Freemasons of the middle ages.

It is a symbol of the world, or universe.

Its form, an oblong square, is symbolic of the supposed oblong form of the world as known to the ancients.

LOST WORD. There is a masonic myth that there was a certain word which was lost and afterwards recovered.

It is not material what the word was, nor how lost, nor when recovered: the symbolism refers only to the abstract idea of a loss and a recovery.

It is a symbol of divine truth.

The search for it was also made by the philosophers and priests in the Mysteries of the Spurious Freemasonry.

LOTUS. The sacred plant of the Brahminical Mysteries, and the analogue of the acacia.

It was also a sacred plant among the Egyptians.

LUSTRATION. A purification by washing the hands or body in consecrated water, practised in the ancient Mysteries. See *Purification*.

LUX (*light*). One of the appellations bestowed upon Freemasonry, to indicate that it is that sublime doctrine of truth by which the pathway of him who has attained it is to be illumined in the pilgrimage of life. Among the Rosicrucians, light was the knowledge of the philosopher's stone; and Mosheim says that in chemical language the cross was an emblem of light, because it contains within its figure the forms of the three figures of which LVX, or light, is composed.

LUX E TENEBRIS (*light out of darkness*). A motto of the Masonic Order, which is equivalent to "truth out of initiation;" light being the symbol of truth, and darkness the symbol of initiation commenced.

M

MAN. Repeatedly referred to by Christ and the apostles as the symbol of a temple.

MASTER MASON. The third degree of Ancient Craft Masonry, analogous to the epopt of the ancient Mysteries.

MENATZCHIM. Hebrew מנצהים *superintendents*, or *overseers*. The Master Masons at the temple of Solomon. (2 Chron. ii. 2.)

MENU. In the Indian mythology, Menu is the son of Brahma, and the founder of the Hindoo religion. Thirteen other Menus are said to exist, seven of whom have already reigned on earth. But it is the first one whose instructions constitute the whole civil and religious polity of the Hindoos. The code attributed to him by the Brahmins has been translated by Sir William Jones, with the title of "The Institutes of Menu."

MIDDLE CHAMBER. A part of the Solomonic temple, which was approached by winding stairs, but which was certainly not appropriated to the purpose indicated in the Fellow Craft's degree.

The legend of the Winding Stairs is therefore only a philosophical myth.

It is a symbol of this life and its labors.

MISTLETOE. The sacred plant of Druidism; commemorated also in the Scandinavian rites. It is the analogue of the acacia, and like all the other sacred plants of antiquity, is a symbol of the immortality of the soul. Lest the language of the text should be misunderstood, it may be remarked here that the Druidical and the Scandinavian rites are not identical. The former are Celtic, the latter Gothic. But the fact that in both the mistletoe was a sacred plant affords a violent presumption that there must have been a common point from which both religions started. There was, as I have said, an identity of origin for the same ancient and general symbolic idea.

MITHRAS. He was the god worshipped by the ancient Persians, and celebrated in their Mysteries as the symbol of the sun. In the initiation in these Mysteries, the candidate passed through many terrible trials, and his courage and fortitude were exposed to the most rigorous tests. Among others, after ascending the mystical ladder of seven steps, he passed through a scenic representation of Hades, or the infernal regions; out of this and the surrounding darkness he was admitted into the full light of Elysium, where he was obligated by an oath of secrecy, and invested by the Archimagus, or High Priest, with the secret instructions of the rite, among which was a knowledge of the Ineffable Name.

MOUNT CALVARY. A small hill of Jerusalem, in a westerly direction, and not far from Mount Moriah. In the legends of Freemasonry it is known as "a small hill near Mount Moriah," and is referred to in the third degree. This "small hill" having been determined as the burial-place of Jesus, the symbol has been Christianized by many modern masons.

There are many masonic traditions, principally borrowed from the Talmud, connected with Mount Calvary; such as, that it was the place where Adam was buried, &c.

MOUNT MORIAH. The hill in Jerusalem on which the temple of Solomon was built.

MYRTLE. The sacred plant in the Eleusinian Mysteries, and, as symbolic of a resurrection and immortality, the analogue of the acacia.

MYSTERIES. A secret worship paid by the ancients to several of the pagan gods, to which none were admitted but those who had been solemnly initiated. The object of instruction in these Mysteries was, to teach the unity of God and the immortality of the soul. They were divided into Lesser and Greater Mysteries. The former were merely preparatory. In the latter the whole knowledge was communicated. Speaking of the doctrine that was communicated to the initiates, Philo Judaeus says that "it is an incorruptible treasure, not like gold or silver, but more precious than everything beside; for it is the knowledge of the Great Cause, and of nature, and of that which is born of both." And his subsequent language shows that there was a confraternity existing among the initiates like that of the masonic institution; for he says, with his peculiar mysticism, "If you meet an initiate, besiege him with your prayers that he conceal from you no new mysteries that he may know; and rest not until you have obtained them. For me, although I was initiated into the Great Mysteries by Moses, the friend of God, yet, having seen Jeremiah, I recognized him not only as an Initiate, but as a Hierophant; and I followed his school." So, too, the mason acknowledges every initiate as his brother, and is ever ready and anxious to receive all the light that can be bestowed on the Mysteries in which he has been indoctrinated.

MYSTES. (From the Greek μύω, *to shut the eyes*.) One who had been initiated into the Lesser Mysteries of paganism. He was now blind, but when he was initiated into the Greater Mysteries he was called an Epopt, or one who saw.

MYTH. Grote's definition of the myth, which is cited in the text, may be applied without modification to the myths of Freemasonry, although intended by the author only for the myths of the ancient Greek religion.

The myth, then, is a narrative of remote date, not necessarily true or false, but whose truth can only be certified by internal evidence. The word was first applied to those fables of the pagan gods which have descended from the remotest antiquity, and in all of which there prevails a symbolic idea, not always, however, capable of a positive interpretation. As applied to Freemasonry, the words *myth* and *legend* are synonymous.

From this definition it will appear that the myth is really only the interpretation of an idea. But how we are to read these myths will best appear from these noble words of Max Müller: "Everything is true, natural, significant, if we enter with a reverent spirit into the meaning of ancient art and ancient language. Everything becomes false, miraculous, and unmeaning, if we interpret the deep and mighty words of the seers of old in the shallow and feeble sense of modern chroniclers." (Science of Language, 2d Ser. p. 578.).

MYTH, HISTORICAL. An historical myth is a myth that has a known and recognized foundation in historical truth, but with the admixture of a preponderating amount of fiction in the introduction of personages and circumstances. Between the historical myth and the mythical history, the distinction as laid down in the text cannot always be preserved, because we are not always able to determine whether there is a preponderance of truth or of fiction in the legend or narrative under examination.

MYTHICAL HISTORY. A myth or legend in which the historical and truthful greatly preponderate over the inventions of fiction.

MYTHOLOGY. Literally, the science of myths; and this is a very appropriate definition, for mythology is the science which treats of the religion of the ancient pagans, which was almost altogether founded on myths, or popular traditions and legendary tales; and hence Keightly (Mythol. of Ancient Greece and Italy, p. 2) says that "mythology may be regarded as the repository of the early religion of the people." Its interest to a masonic student arises from the constant antagonism that existed between its doctrines and those of the Primitive Freemasonry of antiquity and the light that the mythological Mysteries throw upon the ancient organization of Speculative Masonry.

MYTH, PHILOSOPHICAL. This is a myth or legend that is almost wholly unhistorical, and which has been invented only for the purpose of enunciating and illustrating a particular thought or dogma.

N

NAME. All Hebrew names are significant, and were originally imposed with reference to some fact or feature in the history or character of the persons receiving them. Camden says that the same custom prevailed among all the nations of antiquity. So important has this subject been considered, that "Onomastica," or treatises on the signification of names have been written by Eusebius and St. Jerome, by Simonis and Hillerus, and by several other scholars, of whom Eusebe Salverte is the most recent and the most satisfactory. Shuckford (Connect. ii. 377) says that the Jewish Rabbins thought that the true knowledge of names was a science preferable to the study of the written law.

NAME OF GOD. The true pronunciation, and consequently the signification, of the name of God can only be obtained through a cabalistical interpretation.

It is a symbol of divine truth. None but those who are familiar with the subject can have any notion of the importance bestowed on this symbol by the Orientalists. The Arabians have a science called *Ism Allah*, or the *science of the name of God*; and the Talmudists and Rabbins have written copiously on the same subject. The Mussulmans, says Salverte (Essai sur les Noms, ii. 7), have one hundred names of God, which they repeat while counting the beads of a rosary.

NEOPHYTE. (From the Greek νέον and φυτὸν, *a new plant*.) One who has been recently initiated in the Mysteries. St. Paul uses the same word (I Tim. iii. 6) to denote one who had been recently converted to the Christian faith.

NOACHIDAE. The descendants of Noah, and the transmitters of his religious dogmas, which were the unity of God and the immortality of the soul. The name has from the earliest times been bestowed upon the Freemasons, who teach the same doctrines. Thus in the "old charges," as quoted by Anderson (Const. edit. 1738, p. 143), it is said, "A mason is obliged by his tenure to observe the moral law as a true Noachidae."

NOACHITES. The same as *Noachidae*, which see.

NORTH. That part of the earth which, being most removed from the influence of the sun at his meridian height, is in Freemasonry called "a place of darkness." Hence it is a symbol of the profane world.

NORTH-EAST CORNER. An important ceremony of the first degree, which refers to the north-east corner of the lodge, is explained by the symbolism of the corner-stone.

The corner-stone of a building is always laid in the north-east corner, for symbolic reasons.

The north-east point of the heavens was especially sacred among the Hindoos.

In the symbolism of Freemasonry, the north refers to the outer or profane world, and the east to the inner world of Masonry; and hence the north-east is symbolic of the double position of the neophyte, partly in the darkness of the former, partly in the light of the latter.

NUMBERS. The symbolism of sacred numbers, which prevails very extensively in Freemasonry, was undoubtedly borrowed from the school of Pythagoras; but it is just as likely that he got it from Egypt or Babylon, or from both. The Pythagorean doctrine was, according to Aristotle (Met. xii. 8), that all things proceed from numbers. M. Dacier, however, in his life of the philosopher, denies that the doctrine of numbers was taught by Pythagoras himself, but attributes it to his later disciples. But his arguments are not conclusive or satisfactory.

O

OATH OF SECRECY. It was always administered to the candidate in the ancient Mysteries.

ODD NUMBERS. In the system of Pythagoras, odd numbers were symbols of perfection. Hence the sacred numbers of Freemasonry are all odd. They are 3, 5, 7, 9, 15, 27, 33, and 81.

OIL. An element of masonic consecration, and, as a symbol of prosperity and happiness, is intended, under the name of the "oil of joy," to indicate the expected propitious results of the consecration of any thing or person to a sacred purpose.

OLIVE. In a secondary sense, the symbol of peace and of victory; but in its primary meaning, like all the other Sacred plants of antiquity, a symbol of immortality; and thus in the Mysteries it was the analogue of the acacia of the Freemasons.

OLIVER. The Rev. George Oliver, D.D., of Lincolnshire, England, who died in 1868, is by far the most distinguished and the most voluminous of the English writers on Freemasonry. Looking to his vast labors and researches in the arcana of the science, no student of masonry can speak of his name or his memory without profound reverence for his learning, and deep gratitude for the services that he has accomplished. To the author of this work the recollection will ever be most grateful that he enjoyed the friendship of so good and so great a man; one of whom we may testify, as Johnson said of Goldsmith, that "nihil quod tetigit non ornavit." In his writings he has traversed the whole field of masonic literature and science, and has treated, always with great ability and wonderful research, of its history, its antiquities, its rites and ceremonies, its ethics, and its symbols. Of all his works, his "Historical Landmarks," in two volumes, is the most important, the most useful, and the one which will perhaps the longest perpetuate his memory. In the study of his works, the student must be careful not to follow too implicitly all his conclusions. These were in his own mind controlled by the theory which he had adopted, and which he continuously maintained, that Freemasonry was a Christian institution, and that the connection between it and the Christian religion was absolute and incontrovertible. He followed in the footsteps of Hutchinson, but with a far more expanded view of the masonic system.

OPERATIVE MASONRY. Masonry considered merely as a useful art, intended for the protection and the convenience of man by the erection of edifices which may supply his intellectual, religious, and physical wants.

In contradistinction to Speculative Masonry, therefore, it is said to be engaged in the construction of a material temple.

ORAL LAW. The oral law among the Jews was the commentary on and the interpretation of the written contained in the Pentateuch; and the tradition is, that it was delivered to Moses at the same time, accompanied by the divine command, "Thou shalt not divulge the words which I have said to thee out of my mouth." The oral law was, therefore, never intrusted to books; but being preserved in the memories of the judges, prophets, priests, and wise men, was handed down from one to the other through a long succession of ages. But after the destruction of Jerusalem by the Romans under Adrian, A.D. 135, and the final dispersion of the Jews, fears being entertained that the oral law would be lost, it was then committed to writing, and now constitutes the text of the Talmud.

ORMUZD. Worshipped by the disciples of Zoroaster as the principle of good, and symbolized by light. See *Ahriman*.

OSIRIS. The chief god of the ancient Egyptians, and worshipped as a symbol of the sun, and more philosophically as the male or generative principle. Isis, his wife, was the female or prolific principle; and Horus, their child, was matter, or the world—the product of the two principles.

OSIRIS, MYSTERIES OF. The Osirian Mysteries consisted in a scenic representation of the murder of Osiris by Typhon, the subsequent recovery of his mutilated body by Isis, and his deification, or restoration to immortal life.

OVAL TEMPLES. Temples of an oval form were representations of the mundane egg, a symbol of the world.

P

PALM TREE. In its secondary sense the palm tree is a symbol of victory; but in its primary signification it is a symbol of the victory over death, that is, immortality.

PARABLE. A narrative in which one thing is compared with another. It is in principle the same as a symbol or an allegory.

PARALLEL LINES. The lines touching the circle in the symbol of the point within a circle. They are said to represent St. John the Baptist and St. John the Evangelist; but they really refer to the solstitial points Cancer and Capricorn, in the zodiac.

PASTOS. (From the Greek παστὸς, *a nuptial couch*.) The coffin or grave which contained the body of the god or hero whose death was scenically represented in the ancient Mysteries.

It is the analogue of the grave in the third degree of Masonry.

PELASGIAN RELIGION. The Pelasgians were the oldest if not the aboriginal inhabitants of Greece. Their religion differed from that of the Hellenes who succeeded them in being less poetical, less mythical, and more abstract. We know little of their religious worship, except by conjecture; but we may suppose it resembled in some respects the doctrines of the Primitive Freemasonry. Creuzer thinks that the Pelasgians were either a nation of priests or a nation ruled by priests.

PHALLUS. A representation of the virile member, which was venerated as a religious symbol very universally, and without the slightest lasciviousness, by the ancients. It was one of the modifications of sun worship, and was a symbol of the fecundating power of that luminary. The masonic point within a circle is undoubtedly of phallic origin.

PHILOSOPHY OF FREEMASONRY. The dogmas taught in the masonic system constitute its philosophy. These consist in the contemplation of God as one and eternal, and of man as immortal. In other words, the philosophy of Freemasonry inculcates the unity of God and the immortality of the soul.

PLUMB. One of the working tools of a Fellow Craft, and a symbol of rectitude of conduct.

POINT WITHIN A CIRCLE. It is derived from the ancient sun worship, and is in reality of phallic origin. It is a symbol of the universe, the sun being represented by the point, while the circumference is the universe.

PORCH OF THE TEMPLE. A symbol of the entrance into life.

PRIMITIVE FREEMASONRY. The Primitive Freemasonry of the antediluvians is a term for which we are indebted to Oliver, although the theory was broached by earlier writers, and among them by the Chevalier Ramsay. The theory is, that the principles and doctrines of Freemasonry existed in the earliest ages of the world, and were believed and practised by a primitive people, or priesthood, under the name of Pure or Primitive Freemasonry. That this Freemasonry, that is to say, the religious doctrine inculcated by it, was, after the flood, corrupted by the pagan philosophers and priests, and, receiving the title of *Spurious Freemasory*, was exhibited in the ancient Mysteries. The Noachidae, however, preserved the principles of the Primitive Freemasonry, and transmitted them to succeeding ages, when at length they assumed the name of *Speculative Masonry*. The Primitive Freemasonry was probably without ritual or symbolism, and consisted only of a series of abstract propositions derived from antediluvian traditions. Its dogmas were the unity of God and the immortality of the soul.

PROFANE. One who has not been initiated as a Freemason. In the technical language of the Order, all who are not Freemasons are profanes. The term is derived from the Latin words *pro fano*, which literally signify "in front of the temple," because those in the ancient religions who were not initiated in the sacred rites or Mysteries of any deity were not permitted to enter the temple, but were compelled to remain outside, or in front of it. They were kept on the outside. The expression a *profane* is not recognized as a noun substantive in the general usage of the language; but it has been adopted as a technical term in the dialect of Freemasonry, in the same relative sense in which the word *layman* is used in the professions of law and divinity.

PURE FREEMASONRY OF ANTIQUITY. The same as Primitive Freemasonry,—which see.

PURIFICATION. A religious rite practised by the ancients, and which was performed before any act of devotion. It consisted in washing the hands, and sometimes the whole body, in lustral or consecrated water. It was intended as a symbol of the internal purification of the heart. It was a ceremony preparatory to initiation in all the ancient Mysteries.

PYTHAGORAS. A Grecian philosopher, supposed to have been born in the island of Samos, about 584 B.C. He travelled extensively for the purpose of acquiring knowledge. In Egypt he was initiated in the Mysteries of that country by the priests. He also repaired to Babylon, where he became acquainted with the mystical learning of the Chaldeans, and had, no doubt, much communication with the Israelitish captives who had been exiled from Jerusalem, and were then dwelling in Babylon. On his return to Europe he established a school, which in its organization, as well as its doctrines, bore considerable resemblance to Speculative Masonry; for which reason he has been claimed as "an ancient friend and brother" by the modern Freemasons.

R

RESURRECTION. This doctrine was taught in the ancient Mysteries, as it is in Freemasonry, by a scenic representation. The initiation was death, the autopsy was resurrection. Freemasonry does not interest itself with the precise mode of the resurrection, or whether the body buried and the body raised are in all their parts identical. Satisfied with the general teaching of St. Paul, concerning the resurrection that "it is sown a natural body, it is raised a spiritual body," Freemasonry inculcates by its doctrine of the resurrection the simple fact of a progressive advancement from a lower to a higher sphere, and the raising of the soul from the bondage of death to its inheritance of eternal life.

RITUAL. The forms and ceremonies used in conferring the degrees, or in conducting the labors, of a lodge are called the ritual. There are many rites of Freemasonry, which differ from each other in the number and division of the degrees, and in their rituals, or forms and ceremonies. But the great principles of Freemasonry, its philosophy and its symbolism, are alike in all. It is evident, then, that in an investigation of the symbolism of Freemasonry, we have no concern with its ritual, which is but an outer covering that is intended to conceal the treasure that is within.

ROSICRUCIANS. A sect of hermetical philosophers, founded in the fifteenth century, who were engaged in the study of abstruse sciences. It was a secret society much resembling the masonic in its organization, and in some of the subjects of its investigation; but it was in no other way connected with Freemasonry. It is, however, well worth the study of the masonic student on account of the light that it throws upon many of the masonic symbols.

ROYAL ART. Freemasonry is so called because it is supposed to have been founded by two kings,—the kings of Israel and Tyre,—and because it has been subsequently encouraged and patronized by monarchs in all countries.

S

SABIANISM, or SABAISM. The worship of the sun, moon, and stars, the השמים צבא TSABA *Hashmaim*, "the host of heaven." It was practised in Persia, Chaldea, India, and other Oriental countries, at an early period of the world's history. Sun-worship has had a powerful influence on subsequent and more rational religions, and relics of it are to be found even in the symbolism of Freemasonry.

SACELLUM. A sacred place consecrated to a god, and containing an altar.

SAINTE CROIX. The work of the Baron de Sainte Croix, in two volumes, entitled, "Recherches Historiques et Critiques sur les Mystères du Paganisme," is one of the most valuable and instructive works that we have in any language on the ancient Mysteries,—those religious associations whose history and design so closely connect them with Freemasonry. To the student of masonic philosophy and symbolism this work of Sainte Croix is absolutely essential.

SALSETTE. An island in the Bay of Bombay, celebrated for stupendous caverns excavated artificially out of the solid rock, and which were appropriated to the initiations in the ancient Mysteries of India.

SENSES, FIVE HUMAN. A symbol of intellectual cultivation.

SETH. It is the masonic theory that the principles of the Pure or Primitive Freemasonry were preserved in the race of Seth, which had always kept separate from that of Cain, but that after the flood they became corrupted, by a secession of a portion of the Sethites, who established the Spurious Freemasonry of the Gentiles.

SEVEN. A sacred number among the Jews and the Gentiles, and called by Pythagoras a "venerable number."

SHEM HAMPHORASH. (המפירש שם *the declaratory name*.) The tetragrammaton is so called, because, of all the names of God, it alone distinctly declares his nature and essence as self-existent and eternal.

SHOE. See *Investiture, Rite of*.

SIGNS. There is abundant evidence that they were used in the ancient Mysteries. They are valuable only as modes of recognition. But while they are absolutely conventional, they have, undoubtedly, in Freemasonry, a symbolic reference.

SIVA. One of the manifestations of the supreme deity of the Hindoos, and a symbol of the sun in its meridian.

SONS OF LIGHT. Freemasons are so called because *Lux*, or *Light*, is one of the names of Speculative Masonry.

SOLOMON. The king of Israel, and the founder of the temple of Jerusalem and of the temple organization of Freemasonry.

That his mind was eminently symbolic in its propensities, is evident from all the writings that are attributed to him.

SPECULATIVE MASONRY. Freemasonry considered as a science which speculates on the character of God and man, and is engaged in philosophical investigations of the soul and a future existence, for which purpose it uses the terms of an operative art.

It is engaged symbolically in the construction of a spiritual temple.

There is in it always a progress—an advancement from a lower to a higher sphere.

SPIRITUAL TEMPLE. The body of man; that temple alluded to by Christ and St. Paul; the temple, in the construction of which the Speculative Mason is engaged, in contradistinction to that material temple which occupies the labors of the Operative Mason.

SPURIOUS FREEMASONRY OF ANTIQUITY. A term applied to the initiations in the Mysteries of the ancient pagan world, and to the doctrines taught in those Mysteries. See *Mysteries*.

SQUARE. A geometric figure consisting of four equal sides and equal angles. In Freemasonry it is a symbol of morality, or the strict performance of every duty. The Greeks deemed it a figure of perfection, and the "square man" was a man of unsullied integrity.

SQUARE, TRYING. One of the working-tools of a Fellow Craft, and a symbol of morality.

STONE OF FOUNDATION. A very important symbol in the masonic system. It is like the *word*, the symbol of divine truth.

STONE WORSHIP. A very early form of fetichism. The Pelasgians are supposed to have given to their statues of the gods the general form of cubical stones, whence in Hellenic times came the Hermae, or images of Hermes.

SUBSTITUTE WORD. A symbol of the unsuccessful search after divine truth, and the discovery in this life of only an approximation to it.

SUN, RISING. In the Sabian worship the rising sun was adored on its resurrection from the apparent death of its evening setting. Hence, in the ancient Mysteries, the rising sun was a symbol of the regeneration of the soul.

SUN-WORSHIP. The most ancient of all superstitions. It prevailed especially in Phoenicia, Chaldea. and Egypt, and traces of it have been discovered in Peru and Mexico. Its influence was felt in the ancient Mysteries, and abundant allusions to it are to be found in the symbolism of Freemasonry.

SWEDENBORG. A Swedish philosopher, and the founder of a religious sect. Clavel, Ragon, and some other writers have sought to make him the founder of a masonic rite also, but without authority. In 1767 Chastanier established the rite of Illuminated Theosophists, whose instructions are derived from the writings of Swedenborg, but the sage himself had nothing to do with it. Yet it cannot be denied that the mind of Swedenborg was eminently symbolic in character, and that the masonic student may derive many valuable ideas from portions of his numerous works, especially from his "Celestial Arcana" and his "Apocalypse Revealed."

SYMBOL. A visible sign with which a spiritual feeling, emotion, or idea is connected.—*Müller*. Every natural thing which is made the sign or representation of a moral idea is a symbol.

SYMBOL, COMPOUND. A species of symbol not unusual in Freemasonry, where the symbol is to be taken in a double sense, meaning in its general application one thing, and then in a special application another.

SYMBOLISM, SCIENCE OF. To what has been said in the text, may be added the following apposite remarks of Squier: "In the absence of a written language or forms of expression capable of conveying abstract ideas, we can readily comprehend the necessity, among a primitive people, of a symbolic system. That symbolism in a great degree resulted from this necessity, is very obvious; and that, associated with man's primitive religious systems, it was afterwards continued, when in the advanced stage of the human mind, the previous necessity no longer existed, is equally undoubted. It thus came to constitute a kind of sacred language, and became invested with an esoteric significance understood only by the few."—*The Serpent Symbol in America*, p. 19.

T

TABERNACLE. Erected by Moses in the wilderness as a temporary place for divine worship. It was the antitype of the temple of Jerusalem, and, like it, was a symbol of the universe.

TALISMAN. A figure either carved in metal or stone, or delineated on parchment or paper, made with superstitious ceremonies under what was supposed to be the special influence of the planetary bodies, and believed to possess occult powers of protecting the maker or possessor from danger. The figure in the text is a talisman, and among the Orientals no talisman was more sacred than this one where the nine digits are so disposed as to make 15 each way. The Arabians called it *zahal*, which was the name of the planet Saturn, because the nine digits added together make 45, and the letters of the word *zahal* are, according to the numerical powers of the Arabic alphabet, equivalent to 45. The cabalists esteem it because 15 was the numerical power of the letters composing the word JAH, which is one of the names of God.

TALMUD. The mystical philosophy of the Jewish Rabbins is contained in the Talmud, which is a collection of books divided into two parts, the *Mishna*, which contains the record of the oral law, first committed to writing in the second or third century, and the *Gemara*, or commentaries on it. In the Talmud much will be found of great interest to the masonic student.

TEMPLE. The importance of the temple in the symbolism of Freemasonry will authorize the following citation from the learned Montfaucon (*Ant*. ii. 1. ii. ch. ii.): "Concerning the origin of *temples*, there is a variety of opinions. According to Herodotus, the Egyptians were the first that made altars, statues, and temples. It does not, however, appear that there were any in Egypt in the time of Moses, for he never mentions them, although he had many opportunities for doing so. Lucian says that the Egyptians were the first people who built temples, and that the Assyrians derived the custom from them, all of which is, however, very uncertain. The first allusion to the subject in Scripture is the Tabernacle, which was, in fact, a portable temple, and contained one place within it more holy and secret than the others, called the *Holy of Holies*, and to which the *adytum* in the pagan temples corresponded. The first heathen temple mentioned in Scripture is that of Dagon, the god of the Philistines. The Greeks, who were indebted to the Phoenicians for many things, may be supposed to have learned from them the art of building temples; and it is certain that the Romans borrowed from the Greeks both the worship of the gods and the construction of temples."

TEMPLE BUILDER. The title by which Hiram Abif is sometimes designated.

TEMPLE OF SOLOMON. The building erected by King Solomon on Mount Moriah, in Jerusalem, has been often called "the cradle of Freemasonry," because it was there that that union took place between the operative and speculative masons, which continued for centuries afterwards to present the true organization of the masonic system.

As to the size of the temple, the dimensions given in the text may be considered as accurate so far as they agree with the description given in the First Book of Kings. Josephus gives a larger measure, and makes the length 105 feet, the breadth 35 feet, and the height 210 feet; but even these will not invalidate the statement in the text, that in size it was surpassed by many a parish church.

TEMPLE SYMBOLISM. That symbolism which is derived from the temple of Solomon. It is the most fertile of all kinds of symbolism in the production of materials for the masonic science.

TERMINUS. One of the most ancient of the Roman deities. He was the god of boundaries and landmarks, and his statue consisted only of a cubical stone, without arms or legs, to show that he was immovable.

TETRACTYS. A figure used by Pythagoras, consisting of ten points, arranged in a triangular form so as to represent the monad, duad, triad, and quarterniad. It was considered as very sacred by the Pythagoreans, and was to them what the tetragrammaton was to the Jews.

TETRAGRAMMATON. (From the Greek τετϱὰς, *four*, and γϱὰμμα, a letter). The four-lettered name of God in the Hebrew language, which consisted of four letters, viz. יהוה commonly, but incorrectly, pronounced *Jehovah*. As a symbol it greatly pervaded the rites of antiquity, and was perhaps the earliest symbol corrupted by the Spurious Freemasonry of the pagan Mysteries.

It was held by the Jews in profound veneration, and its origin supposed to have been by divine revelation at the burning bush.

The word was never pronounced, but wherever met with *Adonai* was substituted for it, which custom was derived from the perverted reading of a, passage in the Pentateuch. The true pronunciation consequently was utterly lost; this is explained by the want of vowels in the Hebrew alphabet, so that the true vocalization of a word cannot be learned from the letters of which it is composed.

The true pronunciation was intrusted to the high priest; but lest the knowledge of it should be lost by his sudden death, it was also communicated to his assistant; it was known also, probably, to the kings of Israel.

The Cabalists and Talmudists enveloped it in a host of superstitions.

It was also used by the Essenes in their sacred rites, and by the Egyptians as a pass-word.

Cabalistically read and pronounced, it means the male and female principle of nature, the generative and prolific energy of creation.

THAMMUZ. A Syrian god, who was worshipped by those women of the Hebrews who had fallen into idolatry. The idol was the same as the Phoenician Adonis, and the Mysteries of the two were identical.

TRAVELLING FREEMASONS. See *Freemasons, Travelling*.

TRESTLE BOARD. The board or tablet on which the designs of the architect are inscribed. It is a symbol of the moral law as set forth in the revealed will of God.

Every man must have his trestle board, because it is the duty of every man to work out the task which God, the chief Architect, has assigned to him.

TRIANGLE. A symbol of Deity.

This symbolism is found in many of the ancient religions.

Among the Egyptians it was a symbol of universal nature, or of the protection of the world by the male and female energies of creation.

TRIANGLE, RADIATED. A triangle placed within a circle of rays. In Christian art it is a symbol of God; then the rays are called a *glory*. When they surround the triangle in the form of a circle, the triangle is a symbol of the glory of God. When the rays emanate from the centre of the triangle, it is a symbol of divine light. This is the true form of the masonic radiated triangle.

TRILITERAL NAME. This is the word AUM, which is the ineffable name of God among the Hindoos, and symbolizes the three manifestations of the Brahminical supreme god, Brahma, Siva, and Vishnu. It was never to be pronounced aloud, and was analogous to the sacred tetragrammaton of the Jews.

TROWEL. One of the working tools of a Master Mason. It is a symbol of brotherly love.

TRUTH. It was not always taught publicly by the ancient philosophers to the people.

The search for it is the object of Freemasonry. It is never found on earth, but a substitute for it is provided.

TUAPHOLL. A term used by the Druids to designate an unhallowed circumambulation around the sacred cairn, or altar, the movement being against the sun, that is, from west to east by the north, the cairn being on the left hand of the circumambulator.

TUBAL CAIN. Of the various etymologies of this name, only one is given in the text; but most of the others in some way identify him with Vulcan. Wellsford (*Mithridates Minor* p. 4) gives a singular etymology, deriving the name of the Hebrew patriarch from the definite article ה converted into ת, or *T* and *Baal*, "Lord," with the Arabic *kayn*, "a blacksmith," so that the word would then signify "the lord of the blacksmiths." Masonic writers have, however, generally adopted the more usual derivation of *Cain*, from a word signifying *possession*; and Oliver descants on Tubal Cain as a symbol of worldly possessions. As to the identity of Vulcan with Tubal Cain, we may learn something from the definition of the offices of the former, as given by Diodorus Siculus: "Vulcan was the first founder of works in iron, brass, gold, silver, and all fusible metals; and he taught the uses to which fire can be applied in the arts." See Genesis: "Tubal Cain, an instructor of every artificer in brass and iron."

TWENTY-FOUR INCH GAUGE. A two-foot rule. One of the working-tools of an Entered Apprentice, and a symbol of time well employed.

TYPHON. The brother and slayer of Osiris in the Egyptian mythology. As Osiris was a type or symbol of the sun, Typhon was the symbol of winter, when the vigor, heat, and, as it were, life of the sun are destroyed, and of darkness as opposed to light.

TYRE. A city of Phoenicia, the residence of King Hiram, the friend and ally of Solomon, whom he supplied with men and materials for the construction of the temple.

TYRIAN FREEMASONS. These were the members of the Society of Dionysiac Artificers, who at the time of the building of Solomon's temple flourished at Tyre. Many of them were sent to Jerusalem by Hiram, King of Tyre, to assist King Solomon in the construction of his temple. There, uniting with the Jews, who had only a knowledge of the speculative principles of Freemasonry, which had been transmitted to them from Noah, through the patriarchs, the Tyrian Freemasons organized that combined system of Operative and Speculative Masonry which continued for many centuries, until the beginning of the eighteenth, to characterize the institution. See *Dionysiac Artificers*.

U

UNION. The union of the operative with the speculative element of Freemasonry took place at the building of King Solomon's temple.

UNITY OF GOD. This, as distinguished from the pagan doctrine of polytheism, or a multitude of gods, is one of the two religious truths taught in Speculative Masonry, the other being the immortality of the soul.

W

WEARY SOJOURNERS. The legend of the "three weary sojourners" in the Royal Arch degree is undoubtedly a philosophical myth, symbolizing the search after truth.

WHITE. A symbol of innocence and purity.

Among the Pythagoreans it was a symbol of the good principle in nature, equivalent to light.

WIDOW'S SON. An epithet bestowed upon the chief architect of the temple, because he was "a widow's son of the tribe of Naphthali." 1 Kings vii. 14.

WINDING STAIRS, LEGEND OF. A legend in the Fellow Craft's degree having no historical truth, but being simply a philosophical myth or legendary symbol intended to communicate a masonic dogma.

It is the symbol of an ascent from a lower to a higher sphere.

It commences at the porch of the temple, which is a symbol of the entrance into life.

The number of steps are always odd, because odd numbers are a symbol of perfection.

But the fifteen steps in the American system are a symbol of the name of God, *Jah*.

WINE. An element of masonic consecration, and, as a symbol of the inward refreshment of a good conscience, is intended under the name of the "wine of refreshment," to remind us of the eternal refreshments which the good are to receive in the future life for the faithful performance of duty in the present.

WORD. In Freemasonry this is a technical and symbolic term, and signifies divine truth. The search after this word constitutes the whole system of speculative masonry.

WORD, LOST. See *Lost Word*.

WORD, SUBSTITUTE. See *Substitute Word*.

WORK. In Freemasonry the initiation of a candidate is called *work*. It is suggestive of the doctrine that labor is a masonic duty.

Y

YGGDRASIL. The sacred ash tree in the Scandinavian Mysteries. Dr. Oliver propounds the theory that it is the analogue of the theological ladder in the Masonic Mysteries. But it is doubtful whether this theory is tenable.

YOD. A Hebrew letter, in form thus ', and about equivalent to the English I or Y. It is the initial letter of the tetragrammaton, and is often used, especially enclosed within a triangle, as a substitute for, or an abridgement of, that sacred word.

It is a symbol of the life-giving and sustaining power of God.

YONI. Among the nations and religions of India the yoni was the representation of the female organ of generation, and was the symbol of the prolific power of nature. It is the same as the *cteis* among the Occidental nations.

Z

ZENNAAR. The sacred girdle of the Hindoos. It is supposed to be the analogue of the masonic apron.

ZOROASTER. A distinguished philosopher and reformer, whose doctrines were professed by the ancient Persians. The religion of Zoroaster was a dualism, in which the two antagonizing principles were Ormuzd and Abriman, symbols of Light and Darkness. It was a modification and purification of the old fire-worship, in which the fire became a symbol of the sun, so that it was really a species of sun-worship. Mithras, representing the sun, becomes the mediator between Ormuzd, or the principle of Darkness, and the world.

Footnotes

1. "The doctrine of the immortality of the soul, if it is a real advantage, follows unavoidably from the idea of God. The *best* Being, he must *will* the best of good things; the *wisest*, he must devise plans for that effect; the *most powerful*, he must bring it about. None can deny this."—THEO. PARKER, *Discourse of Matters pertaining to Religion*, b. ii. ch. viii. p. 205.

2. "This institution of religion, like society, friendship, and marriage, comes out of a principle, deep and permanent in the heart: as humble, and transient, and partial institutions come out of humble, transient, and partial wants, and are to be traced to the senses and the phenomena of life, so this sublime, permanent, and

useful institution came out from sublime, permanent, and universal wants, and must be referred to the soul, and the unchanging realities of life."—PARKER, *Discourse of Religion*, b. i. ch. i. p. 14.

3. "The sages of all nations, ages, and religions had some ideas of these sublime doctrines, though more or less degraded, adulterated and obscured; and these scattered hints and vestiges of the most sacred and exalted truths were originally rays and emanations of ancient and primitive traditions, handed down from, generation to generation, since the beginning of the world, or at least since the fall of man, to all mankind."—CHEV. RAMSAY, *Philos. Princ. of Nat. and Rev. Relig.*, vol ii. p. 8.

4. "In this form, not only the common objects above enumerated, but gems, metals, stones that fell from heaven, images, carved bits of wood, stuffed skins of beasts, like the medicine-bags of the North American Indians, are reckoned as divinities, and so become objects of adoration. But in this case, the visible object, is idealized; not worshipped as the brute thing really is, but as the type and symbol of God."—PARKER, *Disc. of Relig.* b. i. ch. v. p. 50.

5. A recent writer thus eloquently refers to the universality, in ancient times, of sun-worship: "Sabaism, the worship of light, prevailed amongst all the leading nations of the early world. By the rivers of India, on the mountains of Persia, in the plains of Assyria, early mankind thus adored, the higher spirits in each country rising in spiritual thought from the solar orb up to Him whose vicegerent it seems—to the Sun of all being, whose divine light irradiates and purifies the world of soul, as the solar radiance does the world of sense. Egypt, too, though its faith be but dimly known to us, joined in this worship; Syria raised her grand temples to the sun; the joyous Greeks sported with the thought while feeling it, almost hiding it under the mythic individuality which their lively fancy superimposed upon it. Even prosaic China makes offerings to the yellow orb of day; the wandering Celts and Teutons held feasts to it, amidst the primeval forests of Northern Europe; and, with a savagery characteristic of the American aborigines, the sun temples of Mexico streamed with human blood in honor of the beneficent orb."—*The Castes and Creeds of India*, Blackw. Mag., vol. lxxxi. p. 317.—"There is no people whose religion is known to us," says the Abbé Banier, "neither in our own continent nor in that of America, that has not paid the sun a religious worship, if we except some inhabitants of the torrid zone, who are continually cursing the sun for scorching them with his beams."—*Mythology*, lib. iii. ch. iii.—Macrobius, in his *Saturnalia*, undertakes to prove that all the gods of Paganism may be reduced to the sun.

6. "Varro de religionibus loquens, evidenter dicit, multa esse vera, quae vulgo scire non sit utile; multaque, quae tametsi falsa sint, aliter existimare populum expediat."—St. AUGUSTINE, *De Civil. Dei.*—We must regret, with the learned Valloisin, that the sixteen books of Varro, on the religious antiquities of the ancients, have been lost; and the regret is enhanced by the reflection that they existed until the beginning of the fourteenth century, and disappeared only when their preservation for less than two centuries more would, by the discovery of printing, have secured their perpetuity.

7. Strabo, Geog., lib. i.

8. Maurice, Indian Antiquities, vol. ii. p. 297.

9. Div. Leg., vol. i. b. ii. § iv. p. 193, 10th Lond. edit.

10. The hidden doctrines of the unity of the Deity and the immortality of the soul were taught originally in all the Mysteries, even those of Cupid and Bacchus.—WARBURTON, apud Spence's *Anecdotes*, p. 309.

11. Isoc. Paneg., p. 59.

12. Apud Arrian. Dissert., lib. iii. c. xxi.

13. Phaedo.

14. Dissert. on the Eleusinian and Bacchic Mysteries, in the Pamphleteer, vol. viii. p. 53.

15. Symbol. und Mythol. der Alt. Völk.

16. In these Mysteries, after the people had for a long time bewailed the loss of a particular person, he was at last supposed to be restored to life.—BRYANT, *Anal. of Anc. Mythology*, vol. iii. p. 176.

17. Herod. Hist., lib. iii. c. clxxi.

18. The legend says it was cut into *fourteen* pieces. Compare this with the *fourteen* days of burial in the masonic legend of the third degree. Why the particular number in each? It has been thought by some, that in the latter legend there was a reference to the half of the moon's age, or its dark period, symbolic of the darkness of death, followed by the fourteen days of bright moon, or restoration to life.

19. Mystères du Paganisme, tom. i. p. 6.

20. Notes to Rawlinson's Herodotus, b. ii. ch. clxxi. Mr. Bryant expresses the same opinion: "The principal rites in Egypt were confessedly for a person lost and consigned for a time to darkness, who was at last found. This person I have mentioned to have been described under the character of Osiris."—*Analysis of Ancient Mythology*, vol. iii. p. 177.

21. Spirit of Masonry, p. 100.

22. Varro, according to St. Augustine (De Civ. Dei, vi. 5), says that among the ancients there were three kinds of theology—a *mythical*, which was used by the poets; a *physical*, by the philosophers, and a *civil*, by the people.

23. "Tous les ans," says Sainte Croix, "pendant les jours consacrés au souvenir de sa mort, tout étoit plongé dans la tristesse: on ne cessoit de pousser des gémissemens; on alloit même jusqu'à se flageller et se donner des coups. Le dernier jour de ce deuil, on faisoit des sacrifices funèbres en l'honneur de ce dieu. Le jour suivant, on recevoit la nouvelle qu'Adonis venoit d'être rappelé à la vie, qui mettoit fin à leur deuil."— *Recherches sur les Myst. du Paganisme*, tom. ii. p. 105.

24. Clement of Alexandria calls them μυστήρια τὰ πρὸ μυστηρίων, "the mysteries before the mysteries."

25. Les petits mystères ne consistoient qu'en cérémonies préparatoires.—*Sainte Croix*, i. 297.—As to the oath of secrecy, Bryant says, "The first thing at these awful meetings was to offer an oath of secrecy to all who were to be initiated, after which they proceeded to the ceremonies."—*Anal. of Anc. Myth.*, vol. iii. p. 174.—The Orphic Argonautics allude to the oath: μετὰ δ' ὁρϰια Μύσῖαις, ϰ. τ. λ., "after the oath was administered to the mystes," &c.—*Orph. Argon.*, v. 11.

26. The satirical pen of Aristophanes has not spared the Dionysiac festivals. But the raillery and sarcasm of a comic writer must always be received with many grains of allowance. He has, at least, been candid enough to confess that no one could be initiated who had been guilty of any crime against his country or the public security.—*Ranae*, v. 360-365.—Euripides makes the chorus in his Bacchae proclaim that the Mysteries were practised only for virtuous purposes. In Rome, however, there can be little doubt that the initiations partook at length of a licentious character. "On ne peut douter," says Ste. Croix, "que l'introduction des fêtes de Bacchus en Italie n'ait accéleré les progrès du libertinage et de la débauche dans cette contrée."—*Myst. du Pag.*, tom. ii. p. 91.—St. Augustine (De Civ. Dei, lib. vii. c. xxi.) inveighs against the impurity of the ceremonies in Italy of the sacred rites of Bacchus. But even he does not deny that the motive with which they were performed was of a religious, or at least superstitious nature— "Sic videlicet Liber deus placandus fuerat." The propitiation of a deity was certainly a religious act.

27. Hist. Greece, vol. ii. p. 140.

28. This language is quoted from Robison (*Proofs of a Conspiracy*, p. 20, Lond. edit. 1797), whom none will suspect or accuse of an undue veneration for the antiquity or the morality of the masonic order.

29. We must not confound these Asiatic builders with the play-actors, who were subsequently called by the Greeks, as we learn from Aulus Gellius (lib. xx. cap. 4), "artificers of Dionysus"—Διονυσιαχοι τεχνιταὶ.

30. There is abundant evidence, among ancient authors, of the existence of signs and passwords in the Mysteries. Thus Apuleius, in his Apology, says, "Si qui forte adest eorundem Solemnium mihi particeps, signum dato," etc.; that is, "If any one happens to be present who has been initiated into the same rites as myself, if he will give me the sign, he shall then be at liberty to hear what it is that I keep with so much care." Plautus also alludes to this usage, when, in his "Miles Gloriosus," act iv. sc. 2, he makes Milphidippa say to Pyrgopolonices, "Cedo signum, si harunc Baccharum es;" i.e., "Give the sign if you are one of these Bacchae," or initiates into the Mysteries of Bacchus. Clemens Alexandrinus calls these modes of recognition σωθηματα, as if *means of safety*. Apuleius elsewhere uses *memoracula*, I think to denote passwords, when he says, "sanctissimè sacrorum signa et memoracula custodire," which I am inclined to translate, "most scrupulously to preserve the signs and passwords of the sacred rites."

31. The Baron de Sainte Croix gives this brief view of the ceremonies: "Dans ces mystères on employoit, pour remplir l'âme des assistans d'une sainte horreur, les mêmes moyens qu'à Eleusis. L'apparition de fantômes et de divers objets propres à effrayer, sembloit disposer les esprits à la crédulité. Ils en avoient sans doute besoin, pour ajouter foi à toutes les explications des mystagogues: elles rouloient sur le massacre de Bacchus par les Titans," &c.—*Recherches sur les Mystères du Paganisme*, tom. ii. sect. vii. art. iii. p. 89.

32. Lawrie, Hist. of Freemasonry, p. 27.

33. Vincentius Lirinensis or Vincent of Lirens, who lived in the fifth century of the Christian era, wrote a controversial treatise entitled "Commonitorium," remarkable for the blind veneration which it pays to the voice of tradition. The rule which he there lays down, and which is cited in the text, may be considered, in a modified application, as an axiom by which we may test the *probability*, at least, of all sorts of traditions. None out of the pale of Vincent's church will go so far as he did in making it the criterion of positive truth.

34. Prolog. zu einer wissenshaftlich. Mythologie.

35. In German *hutten*, in English *lodges*, whence the masonic term.

36. Historical Essay on Architecture, ch. xxi.

37. Bishop England, in his "Explanation of the Mass," says that in every ceremony we must look for three meanings: "the first, the literal, natural, and, it may be said, the original meaning; the second, the figurative or emblematic signification; and thirdly, the pious or religious meaning: frequently the two last will be found the same; sometimes all three will be found combined." Here lies the true difference between the symbolism of the church and that of Masonry. In the former, the symbolic meaning was an afterthought applied to the original, literal one; in the latter, the symbolic was always the original signification of every ceremony.

38. /P "Was not all the knowledge Of the Egyptians writ in mystic symbols? Speak not the Scriptures oft in parables? Are not the choicest fables of the poets, That were the fountains and first springs of wisdom, Wrapped in perplexed allegories?"

BEN JONSON, *Alchemist*, act ii. sc. i. P/

39. The distinguished German mythologist Müller defines a symbol to be "an eternal, visible sign, with which a spiritual feeling, emotion, or idea is connected." I am not aware of a more comprehensive, and at the same time distinctive, definition.

40. And it may be added, that the word becomes a symbol of an idea; and hence, Harris, in his "Hermes," defines language to be "a system of articulate voices, the symbols of our ideas, but of those principally which are general or universal."—*Hermes*, book iii. ch. 3.

41. "Symbols," says Müller, "are evidently coeval with the human race; they result from the union of the soul with the body in man; nature has implanted the feeling for them in the human heart."—*Introduction to a Scientific System of Mythology*, p. 196, Leitch's translation.—R.W. Mackay says, "The earliest instruments of education were symbols, the most universal symbols of the multitudinously present Deity, being earth or heaven, or some selected object, such as the sun or moon, a tree or a stone, familiarly seen in either of them."—*Progress of the Intellect*, vol. i p. 134.

42. Between the allegory, or parable, and the symbol, there is, as I have said, no essential difference. The Greek verb παραβαλλω, whence comes the word *parable*, and the verb συμβαλλω in the same language, which is the root of the word *symbol*, both have the synonymous meaning "to compare." A parable is only a spoken symbol. The definition of a parable given by Adam Clarke is equally applicable to a symbol, viz.: "A comparison or similitude, in which one thing is compared with another, especially spiritual things with natural, by which means these spiritual things are better understood, and make a deeper impression on the attentive mind."

43. North British Review, August, 1851. Faber passes a similar encomium. "Hence the language of symbolism, being so purely a language of ideas, is, in one respect, more perfect than any ordinary language can be: it possesses the variegated elegance of synonymes without any of the obscurity which arises from the use of ambiguous terms."—*On the Prophecies*, ii. p. 63.

44. "By speculative Masonry we learn to subdue our passions, to act upon the square, to keep a tongue of good report, to maintain secrecy, and practise charity."—*Lect. of Fel. Craft*. But this is a very meagre definition, unworthy of the place it occupies in the lecture of the second degree.

45. "Animal worship among the Egyptians was the natural and unavoidable consequence of the misconception, by the vulgar, of those emblematical figures invented by the priests to record their own philosophical conception of absurd ideas. As the pictures and effigies suspended in early Christian churches, to commemorate a person or an event, became in time objects of worship to the vulgar, so, in Egypt, the esoteric or spiritual meaning of the emblems was lost in the gross materialism of the beholder. This esoteric and allegorical meaning was, however, preserved by the priests, and communicated in the mysteries alone to the initiated, while the uninstructed retained only the grosser conception."—GLIDDON, *Otia Aegyptiaca*, p. 94.

46. "To perpetuate the esoteric signification of these symbols to the initiated, there were established the Mysteries, of which institution we have still a trace in Freemasonry."—GLIDDON, *Otia Aegyp*. p. 95.

47. Philo Judaeus says, that "Moses had been initiated by the Egyptians into the philosophy of symbols and hieroglyphics, as well as into the ritual of the holy animals." And Hengstenberg, in his learned work on "Egypt and the Books of Moses," conclusively shows, by numerous examples, how direct were the Egyptian references of the Pentateuch; in which fact, indeed, he recognizes "one of the most powerful arguments for its credibility and for its composition by Moses."—HENGSTENBERG, p. 239, Robbins's trans.

48. Josephus, *Antiq*. book iii. ch. 7.

49. The ark, or sacred boat, of the Egyptians frequently occurs on the walls of the temples. It was carried in great pomp by the priests on the occasion of the "procession of the shrines," by means of staves passed through metal rings in its side. It was thus conducted into the temple, and deposited on a stand. The representations we have of it bear a striking resemblance to the Jewish ark, of which it is now admitted to have been the prototype.

50. "The Egyptian reference in the Urim and Thummim is especially distinct and incontrovertible."—HENGSTENBERG, p. 158.

51. According to the estimate of Bishop Cumberland, it was only one hundred and nine feet in length, thirty-six in breadth, and fifty-four in height.

52. "Thus did our wise Grand Master contrive a plan, by mechanical and practical allusions, to instruct the craftsmen in principles of the most sublime speculative philosophy, tending to the glory of God, and to secure to them temporal blessings here and eternal life hereafter, as well as to unite the speculative and operative Masons, thereby forming a twofold advantage, from the principles of geometry and architecture on the one part, and the precepts of wisdom and ethics on the other."—CALCOTT, *Candid Disquisition*, p. 31, ed. 1769.

53. This proposition I ask to be conceded; the evidences of its truth are, however, abundant, were it necessary to produce them. The craft, generally, will, I presume, assent to it.

54.

"The groves were God's first temples. Ere man learned
To hew the shaft, and lay the architrave,
And spread the roof above them—ere he framed
The lofty vault, to gather and roll back
The sound of anthems—in the darkling wood,
Amid the cool and silence, he knelt down,
And offered to the Mightiest solemn thanks
And supplication."—BRYANT.

55. Theologians have always given a spiritual application to the temple of Solomon, referring it to the mysteries of the Christian dispensation. For this, consult all the biblical commentators. But I may particularly mention, on this subject, Bunyan's "Solomon's Temple Spiritualized," and a rare work in folio, by Samuel Lee, Fellow of Wadham College, Oxford, published at London in 1659, and entitled "Orbis Miraculum, or the Temple of Solomon portrayed by Scripture Light." A copy of this scarce work, which treats very learnedly of "the spiritual mysteries of the gospel veiled under the temple," I have lately been, by good fortune, enabled to add to my library.

56. Veluti pecora, quae natura finxit prona et obedientia ventri.—SALLUST, *Bell. Catil.* i.

57. I Kings vi. 7.

58. In further illustration of the wisdom of these temple contrivances, it may be mentioned that, by marks placed upon the materials which had been thus prepared at a distance, the individual production of every craftsman was easily ascertained, and the means were provided of rewarding merit and punishing indolence.

59. "Each of the pagan gods had (besides the *public* and *open*) a *secret worship* paid unto him; to which none were admitted but those who had been selected by preparatory ceremonies, called Initiation. This *secret-worship* was termed the Mysteries."—WARBURTON, *Div. Leg. I. i. p. 189.*

60. It must be remarked, however, that many of the Fellow Crafts were also stone-cutters in the mountains, *chotzeb bahor*, and, with their nicer implements, more accurately adjusted the stones which had been imperfectly prepared by the apprentices. This fact does not at all affect the character of the symbolism we are describing. The due preparation of the materials, the symbol of purification, was necessarily continued in all the degrees. The task of purification never ceases.

61. The classical reader will here be reminded of that beautiful passage of Horace, commencing with "Justum et tenacem propositi virum."—Lib. iii. od. 3.

62. "Pallida mors aequo pulsat pede pauperum tabernas Regumque turres."—HOR. lib. i. od. 4.

63. It is worth noticing that the verb *natzach*, from which the title of the *menatzchim* (the overseers or Master Masons in the ancient temple), is derived, signifies also in Hebrew *to be perfected, to be completed*. The third degree is the perfection of the symbolism of the temple, and its lessons lead us to the completion of life. In like manner the Mysteries, says Christie, "were termed τελεταί, *perfections*, because they were supposed to induce a perfectness of life. Those who were purified by them were styled τελουμένοι, and τετελεσμένοι, that is, brought to perfection."—*Observations on Ouvaroff's Essay on the Eleusinian Mysteries*, p. 183.

64. Dr. Oliver, in the first or preliminary lecture of his "Historical Landmarks," very accurately describes the difference between the pure or primitive Freemasonry of the Noachites, and the spurious Freemasonry of the heathens.

65. The idea of the world, as symbolically representing God's temple, has been thus beautifully developed in a hymn by N.P. Willis, written for the dedication of a church:—

"The perfect world by Adam trod
Was the first temple built by God;
His fiat laid the corner stone,
And heaved its pillars, one by one.

"He hung its starry roof on high—
The broad, illimitable sky;
He spread its pavement, green and bright,
And curtained it with morning light.

"The mountains in their places stood,
The sea, the sky, and 'all was good;'
And when its first pure praises rang,
The 'morning stars together sang.'

"Lord, 'tis not ours to make the sea,
And earth, and sky, a house for thee;
But in thy sight our offering stands,
A humbler temple, made with hands."

66. "The idea," says Dudley, "that the earth is a level surface, and of a square form, is so likely to have been entertained by persons of little experience and limited observation, that it may be justly supposed to have prevailed generally in the early ages of the world."—*Naology*, p. 7.

67. The quadrangular form of the earth is preserved in almost all the scriptural allusions that are made to it. Thus Isaiah (xi. 12) says, "The Lord shall gather together the dispersed of Judah from the *four corners* of

the earth;" and we find in the Apocalypse (xx. 9) the prophetic version of "four angels standing on the *four corners* of the earth."

68. "The form of the lodge ought to be a double cube, as an expressive emblem of the powers of darkness and light in the creation."—OLIVER, *Landmarks*, i. p. 135, note 37.

69. Not that whole visible universe, in its modern signification, as including solar systems upon solar systems, rolling in illimitable space, but in the more contracted view of the ancients, where the earth formed the floor, and the sky the ceiling. "To the vulgar and untaught eye," says Dudley, "the heaven or sky above the earth appears to be co-extensive with the earth, and to take the same form, enclosing a cubical space, of which the earth was the base, the heaven or sky the upper surface."—*Naology*, 7.—And it is to this notion of the universe that the masonic symbol of the lodge refers.

70. "These rocky shrines, the formation of which Mr. Grose supposes to have been a labor equal to that of erecting the Pyramids of Egypt, are of various height, extent, and depth. They are partitioned out, by the labor of the hammer and the chisel, into many separate chambers, and the roof, which in the pagoda of Elephanta is flat, but in that of Salsette is arched, is supported by rows of pillars of great thickness, and arranged with much regularity. The walls are crowded with gigantic figures of men and women, engaged in various actions, and portrayed in various whimsical attitudes; and they are adorned with several evident symbols of the religion now prevailing in India. Above, as in a sky, once probably adorned with gold and azure, in the same manner as Mr. Savary lately observed in the ruinous remains of some ancient Egyptian temples, are seen floating the children of imagination, genii and dewtahs, in multitudes, and along the cornice, in high relief, are the figures of elephants, horses, and lions, executed with great accuracy. Two of the principal figures at Salsette are twenty-seven feet in height, and of proportionate magnitude; the very bust only of the triple-headed deity in the grand pagoda of Elephanta measures fifteen feet from the base to the top of the cap, while the face of another, if Mr. Grose, who measured it, may be credited, is above five feet in length, and of corresponding breadth."—MAURICE, *Ind. Ant.* vol. ii. p. 135.

71. According to Faber, the egg was a symbol of the world or megacosm, and also of the ark, or microcosm, as the lunette or crescent was a symbol of the Great Father, the egg and lunette—which was the hieroglyphic of the god Lunus, at Heliopolis—was a symbol of the world proceeding from the Great Father.—*Pagan Idolatry*, vol. i. b. i. ch. iv.

72. Zoroaster taught that the sun was the most perfect fire of God, the throne of his glory, and the residence of his divine presence, and he therefore instructed his disciples "to direct all their worship to God first towards the sun (which they called Mithras), and next towards their sacred fires, as being the things in which God chiefly dwelt; and their ordinary way of worship was to do so towards both. For when they came before these fires to worship, *they always approached them on the west side*, that, having their faces towards them and also towards the rising sun at the same time, they might direct their worship to both. And in this posture they always performed every act of their worship."—PRIDEAUX. *Connection.* i. 216.

73. "The mysteries of Ceres (or Eleusis) are principally distinguished from all others as having been the depositories of certain traditions coeval with the world."—OUVAROFF, *Essay on the Mysteries of Eleusis*, p. 6.

74. The dadouchus, or torch-bearer, carried a symbol of the sun.

75. "Indeed, the most ancient superstition of all nations," says Maurice, "has been the worship of the sun, as the lord of heaven and the governor of the world; and in particular it prevailed in Phoenicia, Chaldaea, Egypt, and from later information we may add, Peru and Mexico, represented in a variety of ways, and concealed under a multitude of fanciful names. Through all the revolutions of time the great luminary of heaven hath exacted from the generations of men the tribute of devotion."—*Indian Antiquities*, vol. ii. p. 91.

76. Facciolatus thus defines the Phallus: "penis ligneus, vel vitreus, vel coriaceus, quem in Bacchi festis plaustro impositum per rura et urbes magno honore circumferebant."—*Lex. in voc.*

77. The exhibition of these images in a colossal form, before the gates of ancient temples, was common. Lucian tells us of two colossal Phalli, each one hundred and eighty feet high, which stood in the fore court of the temple at Hierapolis. Mailer, in his "Ancient Art and its Remains," mentions, on the authority of Leake, the fact that a colossal Phallus, which once stood on the top of the tomb of the Lydian king Halyattes, is now lying near the same spot; it is not an entire Phallus, but only the head of one; it is twelve feet in diameter below and nine feet over the glands. The Phallus has even been found, so universal was this worship, among the savages of America. Dr. Arthaut discovered, in the year 1790, a marble Phallic image in a cave of the island of St. Domingo.—CLAVEL, *Hist. Pittoresq. des Religions*, p. 9.

78. Sonnerat (Voyage aux Indes Orient, i. p. 118) observes, that the professors of this worship were of the purest principles and most unblemished conduct, and it seems never to have entered into the heads of the Indian legislator and people that anything natural could be grossly obscene.—Sir William Jones remarks (Asiatic Researches, i. 254), that from the earliest periods the women of Asia, Greece, and Italy wore this symbol as a jewel, and Clavel tells us that a similar usage prevails at this day among the women in some of the villages of Brittany. Seely tells us that the Lingam, or Indian Phallus, is an emblem as frequently met with in Hindostan as the cross is in Catholic countries.—*Wonders of Elora.* p. 278.

79. Num. xxv. 1-3. See also Psalm cvi. 28: "They joined themselves also unto Baal-peor, and ate the sacrifices of the dead." This last expression, according to Russel, has a distinct reference to the physical qualities of matter, and to the time when death, by the winter absence of the solar heat, gets, as it were, possession of the earth. Baal-peor was, he says, the sun exercising his powers of fecundity.—*Connection of Sacred and Profane History*

80. Is there not a seeming reference to this thought of divine hermaphrodism in the well-known passage of Genesis? "So God created man in his own image, in the image of God created he him: *male and female* created he them." And so being created "male and female," they were "in the image of God."

81. The world being animated by man, says Creuzer, in his learned work on Symbolism, received from him the two sexes, represented by heaven and the earth. Heaven, as the fecundating principle, was male, and the source of fire; the earth, as the fecundated, was female, and the source of humidity. All things issued from the alliance of these two principles. The vivifying powers of the heavens are concentrated in the sun, and the earth, eternally fixed in the place which it occupies, receives the emanations from the sun, through the medium of the moon, which sheds upon the earth the germs which the sun had deposited in its fertile bosom. The Lingam is at once the symbol and the mystery of this religious idea.

82. Such was the opinion of some of the ancient sun-worshippers, whose adorations were always performed in the open air, because they thought no temple was spacious enough to contain the sun; and hence the saying, "Mundus universus est templum solis"—the universe is the temple of the sun. Like our ancient brethren, they worshipped only on *the highest hills.* Another analogy.

83. *Asgard*, the abode of the gods, is shaded by the ash tree, *Ydrasil*, where the gods assemble every day to do justice. The branches of this tree extend themselves over the whole world, and reach above the heavens. It hath three roots, extremely distant from each other: one of them is among the gods; the second is among the giants, where the abyss formerly was; the third covers *Niflheim*, or hell, and under this root is the fountain *Vergelmer*, whence flow the infernal rivers.—*Edda, Fab.* 8.

84. Exod. iii. 5.

85. Commentaries *in loco.*

86. Commentary on Exod. iii. 5.

87. Iamblichi Vita Pythag. c. 105. In another place he says, "Θύειν χρὴ ἀνυπόδετον, χαι πρὸς τα ἱερὰ προστιέναι,"—We must sacrifice and enter temples with the shoes off. Ibid. c. 85.

88. "Quod etiam nunc apud plerasque Orientis nationes piaculum sit, calceato pede templorum pavimenta calcasse."

89. Beth Habbechirah, cap. vii.

90. Histor. Landm. vol. ii. p. 481.

91. "Non datur nobis potestas adeundi templum nisi nudibus pedibus."

92. Commentaries, *ut supra*.

93. See a paper "on the religious ceremonies of the Hindus," by H.T. Colebrooke, Esq. in the Asiatic Researches, vol. vi. p. 357.

94. A Specimen of the Critical History of the Celtic Religion and Learning. Letter ii. § xvii.

95. Dr. Oliver, referring to the "twelve grand points in Masonry," which formed a part of the old English lectures, says, "When the candidate was *intrusted*, he represented Asher, for he was then presented with the glorious fruit of masonic knowledge, as Asher was represented by fatness and royal dainties."—*Hist. Landm.*, vol. i. lect. xi. p. 313.

96. From the Greek αὐτοψία, signifying *a seeing with ones own eyes*. The candidate, who had previously been called a *mystes*, or a *blind man*, from μίω, to *shut the eyes*, began at this point to change his title to that of an *epopt*, or an *eye-witness*.

97. אדך ויהי אדך יהי *Yehi aur va yehi aur*.

98. Robert William Mackay, Progress of the Intellect, vol. i. p. 93.

99. "And thou shalt put in the breastplate of judgment the Urim and the Thummim."—*Exod*. xxviii. 30.—The Egyptian judges also wore breastplates, on which was represented the figure of *Ra*, the sun, and *Thme*, the goddess of Truth, representing, says Gliddon, "*Ra*, or the sun, in a double capacity—physical and intellectual light; and *Thme*, in a double capacity—justice and truth."—*Ancient Egypt*, p. 33.

100. We owe this interesting discovery to F. Portal, who has given it in his elaborate work on Egyptian symbols as compared with those of the Hebrews. To those who cannot consult the original work in French, I can safely recommend the excellent translation by my esteemed friend, Bro. John W. Simons, of New York, and which will be found in the thirtieth volume of the "Universal Masonic Library."

101. "The most early defection to Idolatry," says Bryant, "consisted in the adoration of the sun and the worship of demons, styled Baalim."—*Analysts of Anc. Mythol.* vol. iii. p. 431.

102. The remarks of Mr. Duncan on this subject are well worth perusal. "Light has always formed one of the primary objects of heathen adoration. The glorious spectacle of animated nature would lose all its interest if man were deprived of vision, and light extinguished; for that which is unseen and unknown becomes, for all practical purposes, as valueless as if it were non-existent. Light is a source of positive happiness; without it, man could barely exist; and since all religious opinion is based on the ideas of

pleasure and pain, and the corresponding sensations of hope and fear, it is not to be wondered if the heathen reverenced light. Darkness, on the contrary, by replunging nature, as it were, into a state of nothingness, and depriving man of the pleasurable emotions conveyed through the organ of sight, was ever held in abhorrence, as a source of misery and fear. The two opposite conditions in which man thus found himself placed, occasioned by the enjoyment or the banishment of light, induced him to imagine the existence of two antagonist principles in nature, to whose dominion he was alternately subject. Light multiplied his enjoyments, and darkness diminished them. The former, accordingly, became his friend, and the latter his enemy. The words 'light' and 'good,' and 'darkness' and 'evil,' conveyed similar ideas, and became, in sacred language, synonymous terms. But as good and evil were not supposed to flow from one and the same source, no more than light and darkness were supposed to have a common origin, two distinct and independent principles were established, totally different in their nature, of opposite characters, pursuing a conflicting line of action, and creating antagonistic effects. Such was the origin of this famous dogma, recognized by all the heathens, and incorporated with all the sacred fables, cosmogonies, and mysteries of antiquity." — *The Religions of Profane Antiquity*, p. 186.

103. See the "Bhagvat Geeta," one of the religious books of Brahminism. A writer in Blackwood, in an article on the "Castes and Creeds of India," vol. lxxxi. p. 316, thus accounts for the adoration of light by the early nations of the world: "Can we wonder at the worship of light by those early nations? Carry our thoughts back to their remote times, and our only wonder would be if they did not so adore it. The sun is life as well as light to all that is on the earth—as we of the present day know even better than they of old. Moving in dazzling radiance or brilliant-hued pageantry through the sky, scanning in calm royalty all that passes below, it seems the very god of this fair world, which lives and blooms but in his smile."

104. The *Institutes of Menu*, which are the acknowledged code of the Brahmins, inform us that "the world was all darkness, undiscernible, undistinguishable altogether, as in a profound sleep, till the self-existent, invisible God, making it manifest with five elements and other glorious forms, perfectly dispelled the gloom." — Sir WILLIAM JONES, *On the Gods of Greece. Asiatic Researches*, i. 244.

Among the Rosicrucians, who have, by some, been improperly confounded with the Freemasons, the word *lux* was used to signify a knowledge of the philosopher's stone, or the great desideratum of a universal elixir and a universal menstruum. This was their *truth*.

105. On Symbolic Colors, p. 23, Inman's translation.

106. Freemasonry having received the name of *lux*, or light, its disciples have, very appropriately, been called "the Sons of Light." Thus Burns, in his celebrated Farewell:—

"Oft have I met your social band,
And spent the cheerful, festive night;
Oft, honored with supreme command,
Presided o'er the *sons of light*."

107. Thus defined: "The stone which lies at the corner of two walls, and unites them; the principal stone, and especially the stone which forms the corner of the foundation of an edifice." — Webster.

108. Among the ancients the corner-stone of important edifices was laid with impressive ceremonies. These are well described by Tacitus, in his history of the rebuilding of the Capitol. After detailing the preliminary ceremonies which consisted in a procession of vestals, who with chaplets of flowers encompassed the ground and consecrated it by libations of living water, he adds that, after solemn prayer, Helvidius, to whom the care of rebuilding the Capitol had been committed, "laid his hand upon the fillets that adorned the foundation stone, and also the cords by which it was to be drawn to its place. In that instant the magistrates, the priests, the senators, the Roman knights, and a number of citizens, all acting with one effort and general demonstrations of joy, laid hold of the ropes and dragged the ponderous load to its destined spot. They then threw in ingots of gold and silver, and other metals, which had never been melted in the

furnace, but still retained, untouched by human art, their first formation in the bowels of the earth." — *Tac. Hist.*, 1. iv. c. 53, Murphy's transl.

109. As, for instance, in Psalm cxviii. 22, "The stone which the builders refused is become the head-stone of the corner," which, Clarke says, "seems to have been originally spoken of David, who was at first rejected by the Jewish rulers, but was afterwards chosen by the Lord to be the great ruler of his people in Israel;" and in Isaiah xxviii. 16, "Behold, I lay in Zion, for a foundation, a stone, a tried stone, a precious corner-stone, a sure foundation," which clearly refers to the promised Messiah.

110. In the ritual "observed at laying the foundation-stone of public structures," it is said, "The principal architect then presents the working tools to the Grand Master, who applies the plumb, square, and level to the stone, in their proper positions, and pronounces it to be *well-formed, true, and trusty*." — WEBB'S *Monitor*, p. 120.

111. "The square teaches us to regulate our conduct by the principles of morality and virtue." — *Ritual of the E. A. Degree.* — The old York lectures define the square thus: "The square is the theory of universal duty, and consisteth in two right lines, forming an angle of perfect sincerity, or ninety degrees; the longest side is the sum of the lengths of the several duties which we owe to all men. And every man should be agreeable to this square, when perfectly finished."

112. Aristotle.

113. "The cube is a symbol of truth, of wisdom, and moral perfection. The new Jerusalem, promised in the Apocalypse, is equal in length, breadth, and height. The Mystical city ought to be considered as a new church, where divine wisdom will reign." — OLIVER'S *Landmarks*, ii. p. 357. — And he might have added, where eternal truth will be present.

114. In the most primitive times, all the gods appear to have been represented by cubical blocks of stone; and Pausanias says that he saw thirty of these stones in the city of Pharae, which represented as many deities. The first of the kind, it is probable, were dedicated to Hermes, whence they derived their name of "Hermae."

115. "Give unto Jehovah the glory due unto His name; worship Jehovah in the beauty of holiness." — *Psalm* xxix. 2.

116. It is at least a singular coincidence that in the Brahminical religion great respect was paid to the north-east point of the heavens. Thus it is said in the Institutes of Menu, "If he has any incurable disease, let him advance in a straight path towards *the invincible north-east point*, feeding on water and air till his mortal frame totally decay, and his soul become united with the Supreme."

117. This symbolism of the double position of the corner-stone has not escaped the attention of the religious symbologists. Etsius, an early commentator, in 1682, referring to the passage in Ephesians ii. 20, says, "That is called the corner-stone, or chief corner-stone, which is placed in the extreme angle of a foundation, conjoining and holding together two walls of the pile, meeting from different quarters. And the apostle not only would be understood by this metaphor that Christ is the principal foundation of the whole church, but also that in him, as in a corner-stone, the two peoples, Jews and Gentiles, are conjoined, and so conjoined as to rise together into one edifice, and become one church." And Julius Firmicius, who wrote in the sixteenth century, says that Christ is called the corner-stone, because, being placed in the angle of the two walls, which are the Old and the New Testament, he collects the nations into one fold. "Lapis sanctus, i.e. Christus, aut fidei fundamenta sustentat aut in angulo positus duorum parietum membra aequata moderatione conjungit, i.e., Veteris et Novi Testamenti in unum colligit gentes." — *De Errore profan. Religionum*, chap. xxi.

118. This permanence of position was also attributed to those cubical stones among the Romans which represented the statues of the god Terminus. They could never lawfully be removed from the spot which they occupied. Hence, when Tarquin was about to build the temple of Jupiter, on the Capitoline Hill, all the shrines and statues of the other gods were removed from the eminence to make way for the new edifice, except that of Terminus, represented by a stone. This remained untouched, and was enclosed within the temple, to show, says Dudley, "that the stone, having been a personification of the God Supreme, could not be reasonably required to yield to Jupiter himself in dignity and power."—DUDLEY'S *Naology*, p 145.

119. Dudley's Naology, p. 476.

120. Masonic Discourses, Dis. iv. p. 81.

121. "The act of consecration chiefly consisted in the unction, which was a ceremony derived from the most primitive antiquity. The sacred tabernacle, with all the vessels and utensils, as also the altar and the priests themselves, were consecrated in this manner by Moses, at the divine command. It is well known that the Jewish kings and prophets were admitted to their several offices by unction. The patriarch Jacob, by the same right, consecrated the altars which he made use of; in doing which it is more probable that he followed the tradition of his forefathers, than that he was the author of this custom. The same, or something like it, was also continued down to the times of Christianity."—POTTER'S *Archaeologia Graeca*, b. ii. p. 176.

122. From the Greek τετϱὰς, four, and γϱάμμα, letter, because it is composed of four Hebrew letters. Brande thus defines it: "Among several ancient nations, the name of the mystic number *four*, which was often symbolized to represent the Deity, whose name was expressed by four letters." But this definition is incorrect. The tetragrammaton is not the name of the number *four*, but the word which expresses the name of God in four letters, and is always applied to the Hebrew word only.

123. Exod. iii. 15. In our common version of the Bible, the word "Lord" is substituted for "Jehovah," whence the true import of the original is lost.

124. Exod. vi. 2. 3.

125. "The Jews have many superstitious stories and opinions relative to this name, which, because they were forbidden to mention *in vain*, they would not mention *at all*. They substituted *Adonai*, &c., in its room, whenever it occurred to them in reading or speaking, or else simply and emphatically styled it השם *the Name*. Some of them attributed to a certain repetition of this name the virtue of a charm, and others have had the boldness to assert that our blessed Savior wrought all his miracles (for they do not deny them to be such) by that mystical use of this venerable name. See the *Toldoth Jeschu*, an infamously scurrilous life of Jesus, written by a Jew not later than the thirteenth century. On p. 7, edition of Wagenseilius, 1681, is a succinct detail of the manner in which our Savior is said to have entered the temple and obtained possession of the Holy Name. Leusden says that he had offered to give a sum of money to a very poor Jew at Amsterdam, if he would only once deliberately pronounce the name *Jehovah*; but he refused it by saying that he did not dare."—*Horae Solitariae*, vol. i. p. 3.—"A Brahmin will not pronounce the name of the Almighty, without drawing down his sleeve and placing it on his mouth with fear and trembling."—MURRAY, *Truth of Revelation*, p. 321.

126. The same scrupulous avoidance of a strict translation has been pursued in other versions. For Jehovah, the Septuagint substitutes "Κύϱιος," the Vulgate "Dominus," and the German "der Herr," all equivalent to "the Lord." The French version uses the title "l'Eternel." But, with a better comprehension of the value of the word, Lowth in his "Isaiah," the Swedenborgian version of the Psalms, and some other recent versions, have restored the original name.

127. In the Talmudical treatise, *Majan Hachochima*, quoted by Stephelin (Rabbinical Literature, i. p. 131), we are informed that rightly to understand the shem hamphorash is a key to the unlocking of all mysteries.

"There," says the treatise, "shalt thou understand the words of men, the words of cattle, the singing of birds, the language of beasts, the barking of dogs, the language of devils, the language of ministering angels, the language of date-trees, the motion of the sea, the unity of hearts, and the murmuring of the tongue—nay, even the thoughts of the reins."

128. The gamma, Γ, or Greek letter G, is said to have been sacred among the Pythagoreans as the initial of Γεωμειρία or Geometry.

129. Vide Oliver, *Hist. Init.* p. 68, note.

130. Jamblichus says that Pythagoras passed over from Miletus to Sidon, thinking that he could thence go more easily into Egypt, and that while there he caused himself to be initiated into all the mysteries of Byblos and Tyre, and those which were practised in many parts of Syria, not because he was under the influence of any superstitious motives, but from the fear that if he were not to avail himself of these opportunities, he might neglect to acquire some knowledge in those rites which was worthy of observation. But as these mysteries were originally received by the Phoenicians from Egypt, he passed over into that country, where he remained twenty-two years, occupying himself in the study of geometry, astronomy, and all the initiations of the gods (πάσας θεῶν τελετάς), until he was carried a captive into Babylon by the soldiers of Cambyses, and that twelve years afterwards he returned to Samos at the age of sixty years.—*Vit. Pythag*, cap. iii., iv.

131. "The sacred words were intrusted to him, of which the Ineffable Tetractys, or name of God, was the chief."—OLIVER, *Hist. Init.* p. 109.

132. "Hu, the mighty, whose history as a patriarch is precisely that of Noah, was promoted to the rank of the principal demon-god among the Britons; and, as his chariot was composed of rays of the sun, it may be presumed that he was worshipped in conjunction with that luminary, and to the same superstition we may refer what is said of his light and swift course."—DAVIES, *Mythol. and Rites of the Brit. Druids*, p. 110.

133. "All the male gods (of the ancients) may be reduced to one, the generative energy; and all the female to one, the prolific principle. In fact, they may all be included in the one great Hermaphrodite, the ἀῤῥενοθηλυς who combines in his nature all the elements of production, and who continues to support the vast creation which originally proceeded from his will."—RUSSELL'S *Connection*, i. p. 402.

134. It is a tradition that it was pronounced in the following seven different ways by the patriarchs, from Methuselah to David, viz.: *Juha, Jeva, Jova, Jevo, Jeveh, Johe*, and *Jehovah*. In all these words the *j* is to be pronounced as *y*, the *a* as *ah*, the *e* as a, and the *v* as *w*.

135. The *i* is to be pronounced as *e*, and the whole word as if spelled in English *ho-he*.

136. In the apocryphal "Book of the Conversation of God with Moses on Mount Sinai," translated by the Rev. W. Cureton from an Arabic MS. of the fifteenth century, and published by the Philobiblon Society of London, the idea of the eternal watchfulness of God is thus beautifully allegorized:—

"Then Moses said to the Lord, O Lord, dost thou sleep or not? The Lord said unto Moses, I never sleep: but take a cup and fill it with water. Then Moses took a cup and filled it with water, as the Lord commanded him. Then the Lord cast into the heart of Moses the breath of slumber; so he slept, and the cup fell from his hand, and the water which was therein was spilled. Then Moses awoke from his sleep. Then said God to Moses, I declare by my power, and by my glory, that if I were to withdraw my providence from the heavens and the earth for no longer a space of time than thou hast slept, they would at once fall to ruin and confusion, like as the cup fell from thy hand."

137. I have in my possession a rare copy of the Vulgate Bible, in black letter, printed at Lyons, in 1522. The frontispiece is a coarsely executed wood cut, divided into six compartments, and representing the six days of the creation. The Father is, in each compartment, pictured as an aged man engaged in his creative task.

138. Christian Iconography, Millington's trans., vol. i. p. 59.

139. The triangle, or delta, is the symbol of Deity for this reason. In geometry a single line cannot represent a perfect figure; neither can two lines; three lines, however, constitute the triangle or first perfect and demonstrable figure. Hence this figure symbolizes the Eternal God, infinitely perfect in his nature. But the triangle properly refers to God only in his quality as an Eternal Being, its three sides representing the Past, the Present, and the Future. Some Christian symbologists have made the three sides represent the Father, Son, and Holy Ghost; but they evidently thereby destroy the divine unity, making a trinity of Gods in the unity of a Godhead. The Gnostic trinity of Manes consisted of one God and two principles, one of good and the other of evil. The Indian trinity, symbolized also by the triangle, consisted of Brahma, Siva, and Vishnu, the Creator, Preserver, and Destroyer, represented by Earth, Water, and Air. This symbolism of the Eternal God by the triangle is the reason why a trinitarian scheme has been so prevalent in all religions — the three sides naturally suggesting the three divisions of the Godhead. But in the Pagan and Oriental religions this trinity was nothing else but a tritheism.

140. Noachidae, or Noachites, the descendants of Noah. This patriarch having alone preserved the true name and worship of God amid a race of impious idolaters, the Freemasons claim to be his descendants, because they preserve that pure religion which distinguished this second father of the human race from the rest of the world. (See the author's *Lexicon of Freemasonry*.) The Tyrian workmen at the temple of Solomon were the descendants of that other division of the race who fell off, at Shinar, from the true worship, and repudiated the principles of Noah. The Tyrians, however, like many other ancient mystics, had recovered some portion of the lost light, and the complete repossession was finally achieved by their union with the Jewish masons, who were Noachidae.

141. "A mythis omnis priscorum hominum tum historia tum philosophia procedit." — *Ad Apollod. Athen. Biblioth. not.* f. p. 3. — And Faber says, "Allegory and personification were peculiarly agreeable to the genius of antiquity; and the simplicity of truth was continually sacrificed at the shrine of poetical decoration." — *On the Cabiri.*

142. See Grote, History of Greece, vol. i. ch. xvi. p. 479, whence this definition has been substantially derived. The definitions of Creuzer, Hermann, Buttmann, Heyne, Welcker, Voss, and Müller are none of them Better, and some of them not as good.

143. Hist. of Greece, vol. i. ch. xvi. p. 579. The idea of the existence of an enlightened people, who lived at a remote era, and came from the East, was a very prevalent notion among the ancient traditions. It is corroborative of this that the Hebrew word קֶדֶם, *kedem*, signifies, in respect to place, *the east*, and, in respect to time, *olden time, ancient days*. The phrase in Isaiah xix. 11, which reads, "I am the son of the wise, the son of ancient kings," might just as well have been translated "the son of kings of the East." In a note to the passage Ezek. xliii. 2, "the glory of the God of Israel came from the way of the East," Adam Clarke says, "All knowledge, all religion, and all arts and sciences, have travelled, according to the *course of the sun*, FROM EAST TO WEST!" Bazot tells us (in his Manuel du Franc-maçon, p. 154) that "the veneration which masons entertain for the east confirms an opinion previously announced, that the religious system of Masonry came from the east, and has reference to the *primitive religion*, whose first corruption was the worship of the sun." And lastly, the masonic reader will recollect the answer given in the Leland MS. to the question respecting the origin of Masonry, namely, "It did begin" (I modernize the orthography) "with the first men in the east, which were before the first men of the west; and coming westerly, it hath brought herewith all comforts to the wild and comfortless." Locke's commentary on this answer may conclude this note: "It should seem, by this, that masons believe there were men in the east before Adam, who is called the 'first man of the west,' and that arts and sciences began in the east. Some authors, of great

note for learning, have been of the same opinion; and it is certain that Europe and Africa (which, in respect to Asia, may be called western countries) were wild and savage long after arts and politeness of manners were in great perfection in China and the Indies." The Talmudists make the same allusions to the superiority of the east. Thus, Rabbi Bechai says, "Adam was created with his face towards the east that he might behold the light and the rising sun, whence the east was to him the anterior part of the world."

144. Strauss makes a division of myths into historical, philosophical, and poetical.—*Leben Jesu.*—His poetical myth agrees with my first division, his philosophical with my second, and his historical with my third. But I object to the word *poetical*, as a distinctive term, because all myths have their foundation in the poetic idea.

145. Ulmann, for instance, distinguishes between a myth and a legend—the former containing, to a great degree, fiction combined with history, and the latter having but a few faint echoes of mythical history.

146. In his "Prolegomena zu einer wissenshaftlichen Mythologie," cap. iv. This valuable work was translated in 1844, by Mr. John Leitch.

147. Historical Landmarks, i. 53.

148. See an article, by the author, on "The Unwritten Landmarks of Freemasonry," in the first volume of the Masonic Miscellany, in which this subject is treated at considerable length.

149. As a matter of some interest to the curious reader, I insert the legend as published in the Gentleman's Magazine of June, 1815, from, it is said, a parchment roll supposed to have been written early in the seventeenth century, and which, if so, was in all probability copied from one of an older date:—

"Moreover, when Abraham and Sara his wife went into Egipt, there he taught the Seaven Scyences to the Egiptians; and he had a worthy Scoller that height Ewclyde, and he learned right well, and was a master of all the vij Sciences liberall. And in his dayes it befell that the lord and the estates of the realme had soe many sonns that they had gotten some by their wifes and some by other ladyes of the realme; for that land is a hott land and a plentious of generacion. And they had not competent livehode to find with their children; wherefor they made much care. And then the King of the land made a great counsell and a parliament, to witt, how they might find their children honestly as gentlemen. And they could find no manner of good way. And then they did crye through all the realme, if there were any man that could enforme them, that he should come to them, and he should be soe rewarded for his travail, that he should hold him pleased.

"After that this cry was made, then came this worthy clarke Ewclyde, and said to the King and to all his great lords: 'If yee will, take me your children to governe, and to teach them one of the Seaven Scyences, wherewith they may live honestly as gentlemen should, under a condicion that yee will grant mee and them a commission that I may have power to rule them after the manner that the science ought to be ruled.' And that the Kinge and all his counsell granted to him anone, and sealed their commission. And then this worthy tooke to him these lords' sonns, and taught them the science of Geometric in practice, for to work in stones all manner of worthy worke that belongeth to buildinge churches, temples, castells, towres, and mannors, and all other manner of buildings."

150. Ancient Egypt under the Pharaohs, vol. I p. 393.

151. 1 Kings vi. 8.

152. An allusion to this symbolism is retained in one of the well-known mottoes of the order—"*Lux e tenebris.*"

153. "An allegory is that in which, under borrowed characters and allusions, is shadowed some real action or moral instruction; or, to keep more strictly to its derivation (ἄλλος, *alius*, and ἀγορεύω, *dico*), it is that in which one thing is related and another thing is understood. Hence it is apparent that an allegory must have two senses—the literal and mystical; and for that reason it must convey its instruction under borrowed characters and allusions throughout."—*The Antiquity, Evidence, and Certainty of Christianity canvassed, or Dr. Middleton's Examination of the Bishop of London's Discourses on Prophecy. By Anselm Bayly, LL.B., Minor Canon of St. Paul's.* Lond, 1751.

154. The words themselves are purely classical, but the meanings here given to them are of a mediaeval or corrupt Latinity. Among the old Romans, a *trivium* meant a place where three ways met, and a *quadrivium* where four, or what we now call a *cross-road*. When we speak of the *paths of learning*, we readily discover the origin of the signification given by the scholastic philosophers to these terms.

155. Hist. of Philos. vol. ii. p. 337.

156. Such a talisman was the following figure:—

157. Anderson's Constitutions, 2d ed. 1738, p. 14.

158. Anderson's Constitutions, 3d ed. 1756, p. 24.

159. "The hidden doctrines of the unity of the Deity and the immortality of the soul were originally in all the Mysteries, even those of Cupid and Bacchus."—WARBURTON, *in Spence's Anecdotes*, p. 309.

160. "The allegorical interpretation of the myths has been, by several learned investigators, especially by Creuzer, connected with the hypothesis of an ancient and highly instructed body of priests, having their origin either in Egypt or in the East, and communicating to the rude and barbarous Greeks religious, physical, and historical knowledge, under the veil of symbols."—GROTE, *Hist. of Greece*, vol. i. ch. xvi. p. 579.—And the Chevalier Ramsay corroborates this theory: "Vestiges of the most sublime truths are to be found in the sages of all nations, times, and religions, both sacred and profane, and these vestiges are emanations of the antediluvian and noevian tradition, more or less disguised and adulterated."—*Philosophical Principles of Natural and Revealed Religion unfolded in a Geometrical Order*, vol. 1, p. iv.

161. Of this there is abundant evidence in all the ancient and modern writers on the Mysteries. Apuleius, cautiously describing his initiation into the Mysteries of Isis, says, "I approached the confines of death, and having trod on the threshold of Proserpine, I returned therefrom, being borne through all the elements. At midnight I saw the sun shining with its brilliant light; and I approached the presence of the gods beneath, and the gods of heaven, and stood near and worshipped them."—*Metam.* lib. vi. The context shows that all this was a scenic representation.

162. *Aish hakam iodea binah*, "a cunning man, endued with understanding," is the description given by the king of Tyre of Hiram Abif. See 2 Chron. ii. 13. It is needless to say that "cunning" is a good old Saxon word meaning *skilful*.

163.

"Pronaque cum spectent animalia cætera terram;
Os homini sublime dedit: coelumque tueri
Jussit, et erectos ad sidera tollere vultus."

OVID, *Met.* i. 84.

"Thus, while the mute creation downward bend
Their sight, and to their earthly mother tend,
Man looks aloft, and with erected eyes
Beholds his own hereditary skies."

DRYDEN.

164. "Ἀφανισμὸς, disappearance, destruction, a perishing, death, from ἀφανίζω, to remove from one's view, to conceal," &c.—*Schrevel. Lex.*

165. "Εὕρεσις, a finding, invention, discovery."—*Schrevel. Lex.*

166. A French writer of the last century, speaking of the degree of "Très Parfait Maitre," says, "C'est ici qu'on voit réellement qu'Hiram n'a été que le type de Jésus Christ, que le temple et les autres symboles maçonniques sont des allegories relatives à l'Eglise, à la Foi, et aux bonnes moeurs."—*Origine et Objet de la Franchemaçonnerie, par le F.B.* Paris, 1774.

167. "This our order is a positive contradiction to the Judaic blindness and infidelity, and testifies our faith concerning the resurrection of the body."—HUTCHINSON, *Spirit of Masonry*, lect. ix. p. 101.—The whole lecture is occupied in advancing and supporting his peculiar theory.

168. "Thus, then, it appears that the historical reference of the legend of Speculative Freemasonry, in all ages of the world, was—to our death in Adam and life in Christ. What, then, was the origin of our tradition? Or, in other words, to what particular incident did the legend of initiation refer before the flood? I conceive it to have been the offering and assassination of Abel by his brother Cain; the escape of the murderer; the discovery of the body by his disconsolate parents, and its subsequent interment, under a certain belief of its final resurrection from the dead, and of the detection and punishment of Cain by divine vengeance."—OLIVER, *Historical Landmarks of Freemasonry*, vol. ii. p. 171.

169. "Le grade de Maître va donc nous retracer allegoriquement la mort du *dieu-lumière*—mourant en hiver pour reparaître et ressusciter au printemps."—RAGON, *Cours Philos. et Interp. des Init.* p. 158.

170. "Dans l'ordre moral, Hiram n'est autre chose que la raison éternelle, par qui tout est pondéré, réglé, conservé."—DES ETANGS, *Œuvres Maçonniques*, p. 90.

171. With the same argument would I meet the hypothesis that Hiram was the representative of Charles I. of England—an hypothesis now so generally abandoned, that I have not thought it worth noticing in the text.

172. "The initiation into the Mysteries," he says, "scenically represented the mythic descent into Hades and the return from thence to the light of day; by which was meant the entrance into the Ark and the subsequent liberation from its dark enclosure. Such Mysteries were established in almost every part of the pagan world; and those of Ceres were substantially the same as the Orgies of Adonis, Osiris, Hu, Mithras, and the Cabiri. They all equally related to the allegorical disappearance, or death, or descent of the great father at their commencement, and to his invention, or revival, or return from Hades, at their conclusion."—*Origin of Pagan Idolatry*, vol. iv. b. iv. ch. v. p. 384—But this Arkite theory, as it is called, has not met with the general approbation of subsequent writers.

173. Mount Calvary is a small hill or eminence, situated in a westerly direction from that Mount Moriah on which the temple of Solomon was built. It was originally a hillock of notable eminence, but has, in modern times, been greatly reduced by the excavations made in it for the construction of the Church of the Holy

Sepulchre. Buckingham, in his Palestine, p. 283, says, "The present rock, called Calvary, and enclosed within the Church of the Holy Sepulchre, bears marks, in every part that is naked, of its having been a round nodule of rock standing above the common level of the surface."

174. Dr. Beard, in the art. "Golgotha," in Kitto's Encyc. of Bib. Lit., reasons in a similar method as to the place of the crucifixion, and supposing that the soldiers, from the fear of a popular tumult, would hurry Jesus to the most convenient spot for execution, says, "Then the road to Joppa or Damascus would be most convenient, and no spot in the vicinity would probably be so suitable as the slight rounded elevation which bore the name of Calvary."

175. Some have supposed that it was so called because it was the place of public execution. *Gulgoleth* in Hebrew, or *gogultho* in Syriac, means *a skull*.

176. Quoted in Oliver, *Landmarks*, vol. i. p. 587, note.

177. Oliver's idea (*Landm.*, ii. 149) that *cassia* has, since the year 1730, been corrupted into *acacia*, is contrary to all etymological experience. Words are corrupted, not by lengthening, but by abbreviating them. The uneducated and the careless are always prone to cut off a syllable, not to add a new one.

178. And yet I have been surprised by seeing, once or twice, the word "Cassia" adopted as the name of a lodge. "Cinnamon" or "sandal wood" would have been as appropriate, for any masonic meaning or symbolism.

179. Eclog. ii. 49.

"Pallentes violas et summa papavera carpens,
Narcissum et florem jungit benè olentis anethi:
Tum casia, atque aliis intexens suavibus herbis,
Mollia luteola pingit vaccinia, caltha."

180. Exod. xxx. 24, Ezek. xxvii. 9, and Ps. xlv. 8.

181. Oliver, it is true, says, that "there is not the smallest trace of any tree of the kind growing so far north as Jerusalem" (*Landm.* ii. 136); but this statement is refuted by the authority of Lieutenant Lynch, who saw it growing in great abundance at Jericho, and still farther north.—*Exped. to the Dead Sea*, p. 262.—The Rabbi Joseph Schwarz, who is excellent authority, says, "The Acacia (Shittim) Tree, Al Sunt, is found in Palestine of different varieties; it looks like the Mulberry tree, attains a great height, and has a hard wood. The gum which is obtained from it is the gum Arabic."—*Descriptive Geography and Historical Sketch of Palestine*, p. 308, Leeser's translation. Phila., 1850.—Schwarz was for sixteen years a resident of Palestine, and wrote from personal observation. The testimony of Lynch and Schwarz should, therefore, forever settle the question of the existence of the acacia in Palestine.

182. Calmet, Parkhurst, Gesenius, Clarke, Shaw, and all the best authorities, concur in saying that the *otzi shittim*, or shittim wood of Exodus, was the common acacia or mimosa nilotica of Linnæus.

183. "This custom among the Hebrews arose from this circumstance. Agreeably to their laws, no dead bodies were allowed to be interred within the walls of the city; and as the Cohens, or priests, were prohibited from crossing a grave, it was necessary to place marks thereon, that they might avoid them. For this purpose the acacia was used."—DALCHO, *Oration*, p. 27, note.—I object to the reason assigned by Dalcho; but of the existence of the custom there can be no question, notwithstanding the denial or doubt of Dr. Oliver. Blount (*Travels in the Levant*, p. 197) says, speaking of the Jewish burial customs, "those who bestow a marble stone over any [grave] have a hole a yard long and a foot broad, in which *they plant an evergreen*, which seems to grow from the body, and is carefully watched." Hasselquist (*Travels*, p. 28)

confirms his testimony. I borrow the citations from Brown (*Antiquities of the Jews*, vol. ii. p. 356), but have verified the reference to Hasselquist. The work of Blount I have not been enabled to consult.

184. Antiquities of Greece, p. 569.

185. Dr. Crucefix, MS., quoted by Oliver, *Landmarks*, ii. 2.

186. Spirit of Masonry, lect. ix. p. 99.

187. The Temple of Solomon, ch. ix. p. 233.

188. It is probable that the quince derived this symbolism, like the acacia, from its name; for there seems to be some connection between the Greek word χυδώνιος, which means *a quince*, and the participle χυδίων, which signifies *rejoicing, exulting*. But this must have been an afterthought, for the name is derived from Cydon, in Crete, of which island the quince is a native.

189. Desprez, speaking of the palm as an emblem of victory, says (*Comment. in Horat. Od.* I. i. 5), "Palma verò signum victoriae passim apud omnes statuitur, ex Plutarcho, propterea quod ea est ejus natura ligni, ut urgentibus opprimentibusque minimè cedat. Unde est illud Alciati epigramma,—

'Nititur in pondus palma, et consurgit in altum:
Quoque magis premitur, hoc magè tollit onus.'"

It is in the eighth book of his Symposia that Plutarch states this peculiar property of the palm to resist the oppression of any superincumbent weight, and to rise up against it, whence it was adopted as the symbol of victory. Cowley also alludes to it in his *Davideis*.

"Well did he know how palms by oppression speed
Victorious, and the vctor's sacred meed."

190. "Rosemary was anciently supposed to strengthen the memory, and was not only carried at funerals, but worn at weddings."—STEEVENS, *Notes on Hamlet*, a. iv. s. 5.—Douce (*Illustrations of Shakspeare*, i. 345) gives the following old song in reference to this subject:—

"Rosemarie is for remembrance
   Betweene us daie and night,
Wishing that I might always have
   You present in my sight."

191. Ste. Croix (*Recherches sur les Mystères*, i. 56) says that in the Samothracian Mysteries it was forbidden to put parsley on the table, because, according to the mystagogues, it had been produced by the blood of Cadmillus, slain by his brothers.

192. "The Hindoos," says Faber, "represent their mundane lotus, as having four large leaves and four small leaves placed alternately, while from the centre of the flower rises a protuberance. Now, the circular cup formed by the eight leaves they deem a symbol of the earth, floating on the surface of the ocean, and consisting of four large continents and four intermediate smaller islands; while the centrical protuberance is viewed by them as representing their sacred Mount Menu."—*Communication to Gent. Mag.* vol. lxxxvi. p. 408.

193. The *erica arborea* or tree heath.

194. Ragon thus alludes to this mystical event: "Isis found the body of Osiris in the neighborhood of Biblos, and near a tall plant called the *erica*. Oppressed with grief, she seated herself on the margin of a fountain, whose waters issued from a rock. This rock is the *small hill* mentioned in the ritual; the erica has been replaced by the acacia, and the grief of Isis has been changed for that of the fellow crafts."—*Cours des Initiations*, p. 151.

195. It is singular, and perhaps significant, that the word *eriko*, in Greek, ἐρίχω, whence *erica* is probably derived, means *to break in pieces, to mangle*.

196. Histoire Pittoresque des Religions, t. i. p. 217.

197. According to Toland (*Works*, i. 74), the festival of searching, cutting, and consecrating the mistletoe, took place on the 10th of March, or New Year's day. "This," he says, "is the ceremony to which Virgil alludes, by his *golden branch*, in the Sixth Book of the Æneid." No doubt of it; for all these sacred plants had a common origin in some ancient and general symbolic idea.

198. "Under this branch is figured the wreath of myrtle, with which the initiated were crowned at the celebration of the Mysteries."—WARBURTON, *Divine Legation*, vol. i. p. 299.

199. "In the sweat of thy face shalt thou eat bread." Gen. iii. 19. Bush interprets the decree to mean that "some species of toilsome occupation is the appointed lot of all men."

200. Aristotle says, "He that cannot contract society with others, or who, through his own self-sufficiency αὐτάρχειαν, does not need it, forms no part of the community, but is either a wild beast or a god."

201. "Der Arbeiter," says Lenning, "ist der symbolische Name eines Freimaurers"—the Workman is the symbolic name of a Freemason.—*Encyclop. der Fraumererei.*

202. John iii. 19-21.

203. I Corinth, iii. 9.

204. Orbis Miraculum, or the Temple of Solomon, pourtrayed by Scripture Light, ch. ix. p. 192. London, 1659.

205. Swedenborg a Hermetic Philosopher, &c., p. 210. The object of the author is to show that the Swedish sage was an adept, and that his writings may be interpreted from the point of view of Hermetic philosophy.

206. Cours Philosophique et Interprétatif des Initiations Anciennes et Modernes, p. 99.

207. Ibid., p. 176.

208. Histoire Générale de la Franc-maçonnerie, p. 52.

209. Histoire de la Magie, liv. v. ch. vii. p. 100.

210. Vorlesung über das Symbol des Tempels, in the "Jarbüchern der Gross. Loge Roy. York zur Freundschaft," cited by Lenning, Encyc., voc. *Tempel.*

211. In an Essay on the Masonic Idea of Man's Destination, cited by Lenning, *ut supra*, from the Altenburg *Zeitschift der Freimaurerei.*

212. Cited by Lenning, *ut sup*.

213. Thus Dr. Oliver, while treating of the relation of the temple to the lodge, thus briefly alludes to this important symbol: "As our ancient brethren erected a material temple, without the use of axe, hammer, or metal tool, so is our moral temple constructed."—*Historical Landmarks*, lect. xxxi.

214. System of Speculative Masonry, ch. vi. p. 63.

215. On the Speculative Temple—an essay read in 1861 before the Grand Lodge of Alabama.

216. A portion of this essay, but in a very abridged form, was used by the author in his work on "Cryptic Masonry."

217. Hist. Landmarks, i. 459, note 52.

218. שתייה אבן See the Gemara and Buxtorf Lex. Talm., p. 2541.

219. Job xxxviii. 4-7.

220. A New Translation of the Book of Job, notes, p. 196.

221. In voc. שתייה, where some other curious extracts from the Talmud and Talmudic writers on the subject of the Stone of Foundation are given.

222. Sepher Toldoth Jeshu, p. 6. The abominably scurrilous character of this work aroused the indignation of the Christians, who, in the fifteenth century, were not distinguished for a spirit of tolerance, and the Jews, becoming alarmed, made every effort to suppress it. But, in 1681, it was republished by Wagenselius in his "Tela Ignea Satanae," with a Latin translation.

223. Comment, on Gen. xxviii. 18.

224. "Ni fallit fatum, Scoti quocunque locatum Invenient lapidem, regnare tenentur ibidem."

225. Old and New Testament connected, vol. i. p. 148.

226. The Temple of Solomon, pourtrayed by Scripture Light, ch. ix. p. 194. Of the Mysteries laid up in the Foundation of the Temple.

227. See Pausanias, lib. iv.

228. The "Disputationes adversus Gentes" of Arnobius supplies us with a fund of information on the symbolism of the classic mythology.

229. Naology, ch. iii. p. 119.

230. Cornut. de Nat. Deor. c. 16.

231. Essais sur les Fables, t. i. lett. 2. p. 9.

232. Bosworth (*Aug. Sax. Dict.*) defines *treowth* to signify "troth, truth, treaty, league, pledge, covenant."